Studies in the History of Civil Engineering

Volume 10

Structural Iron and Steel, 1850–1900

STUDIES IN THE HISTORY OF CIVIL ENGINEERING

General Editor: Joyce Brown

with the assistance of M.M. Chrimes, A.W. Skempton,
N.A.F. Smith and R.J.M. Sutherland

Twelve volumes are to appear from the Autumn of 1997:

Studies in the History of Civil Engineering
General Editor: Joyce Brown

Volume 10

Structural Iron and Steel, 1850–1900

edited by
Robert Thorne

VARIORUM

Aldershot • Burlington USA • Singapore • Sydney

Published in the series **Studies in the History of Civil Engineering** by

Ashgate Publishing Limited
Gower House, Croft Road
Aldershot, Hampshire GU11 3HR
Great Britain

Ashgate Publishing Company
131 Main Street
Burlington, Vermont 05401–5600
USA

Ashgate website: http://www.ashgate.com

ISBN 0–86078–759–1

British Library CIP data
Structural Iron and Steel, 1850–1900.
   (Studies in the History of Civil Engineering; CE10).
   1. Building, Iron and Steel–Great Britain–History–19th century.
   2. Iron, structural–Great Britain–History–19th century.
   3. Steel, structural–Great Britain–History–19th century.
   4. Civil engineering–History–19th century.
   I. Thorne, Robert.
   624. 1'821'0941'09034

Library of Congress Card Number: 00–102912

This book is printed on acid free paper.

Printed in Great Britain by St Edmundsbury Press Ltd,
Bury St Edmunds, Suffolk

Contents

Acknowledgements

The chapters in this volume are taken from the sources listed below, for which the editors and publishers wish to thank their authors, original publishers or other copyright holders for permission to use their material as follows:

Chapter 1: Tom F. Peters, 'Some structural problem encountered in the building of the Crystal Palace of 1851', paper presented at The International Association for Bridge and Structural Engineering colloquium on the History of Structures (Cambridge, 13–15 July 1982), pp. 27–41. Copyright © 1986 by T. F. Peters.

Chapter 2: A.W. Skempton, 'The Boat Store, Sheerness (1858–60) and its place in structural history', *Transactions of the Newcomen Society*, 32 (1959–60), pp. 57–78. Copyright © 1959–60 by The Newcomen Society, London.

Chapter 3: Turpin C. Bannister, 'Bogardus revisited. Part I: The iron fronts and Part II: The iron towers', *Journal of the Society of Architectural Historians*, 15, pt. 4 (1956), pp. 12–22; ibid., 16 (1957), pp. 11–19. Copyright © 1956/1957 by The Society of Architectural Historians, Chicago, IL.

Chapter 4: Sarah Wermiel, 'The development of fireproof construction in Great Britain and the United States in the nineteenth century', *Construction History*, 9 (1993), pp. 3–26. Copyright © 1993 by The Construction History Society, c/o The Chartered Institute of Building, Ascot, Berks.

Chapter 5: Stanley Smith, 'The development and use of the tubular beam, 1830–1860', *History of Technology*, 14 (1992), pp. 100–134. Copyright © 1992 by Mansell Information/Publishing Limited and the Contributors. Reproduced by permission of Mansell, an imprint of Cassell, Wellington House, 125 Strand, London, WC2R 0BB.

Chapter 6: Eric Deloney, 'Surviving cast- and wrought-iron bridges in America', *IA: Journal of the Society for Industrial Archaeology*, 19, no. 2 (1993), pp. 17–47. Copyright © 1993 by The Society for Industrial Archaeology, Washington, DC.

Chapter 7: John A. Kouwenhoven, 'The designing of the Eads Bridge', *Technology and Culture*, 23, no. 4 (1982), pp. 535–568. Copyright © 1982 by The Society for the History of Technology, c/o The University of Chicago Press.

Chapter 8: J.S. Shipway, 'Tay Rail Bridge centenary: some notes on its construction, 1882–87', *Proceedings of the Institution of Civil Engineers*, 86, pt. 1 (1989), pp. 1089–1109. Copyright © 1989 by The Institution of Civil Engineers, c/o Thomas Telford Ltd, London.

Chapter 9: J.S. Shipway, 'The Forth Railway Bridge centenary, 1890–1990: some notes on its design', *Proceedings of the Institution of Civil Engineers*, 88, pt. 1 (1990), pp. 1079–1107. Copyright © 1990 by The Institution of Civil Engineers, c/o Thomas Telford Ltd, London.

Chapter 10: Bertrand Lemoine, 'L'entreprise Eiffel', *Historie, Économie et Société*, 14 (1995), pp. 273–285.

Chapter 11: John W. Stamper, 'The Galerie des Machines of the 1889 Paris world's fair', *Technology and Culture*, 30, no. 2 (1989), pp. 330–353. Copyright © 1989 by The Society for the History of Technology c/o The University of Chicago Press.

Chapter 12: Carl W. Condit, 'The two centuries of technical evolution underlying the skyscraper', *Second Century of the Skyscraper*, ed. Lynn S. Beedle (New York, 1988), pp. 11–24. Copyright © 1988 by Van Nostrand Reinhold Company Inc., New York.

Chapter 13: G.R. Larson and R.M. Geraniotis, 'Toward a better understanding of the evolution of the iron skeleton frame in Chicago', *Journal of the Society for Architectural Historians*, 46, pt. 1 (1987), pp. 39–48. Copyright © 1987 by the Society of Architectural Historians, Chicago, IL.

Chapter 14: S. Bylander, 'Steelwork in building: thirty years' progress', *The Structural Engineer*, 15 (1937), pp. 2–25, 128–132. Copyright © 1937 by the Institution of Structural Engineers, London.

Chapter 15: Jeanne C. Lawrence, 'Steel frame architecture versus the London Building Regulations: Selfridges, the Ritz, and America technology', *Construction History*, 6 (1990), pp. 23–46. Copyright © 1990 by the Construction History Society, c/o The Chartered Institute of Building, Ascot, Berks.

Chapter 2 is reproduced from the *Transactions of the Newcomen Society* by permission of the Society's Council. The Newcomen Society promotes, encourages and co-ordinates the study of the history of all types of engineering and technology from the earliest times to the present day. Details from the Executive

Secretary, The Newcomen Society, The Science Museum, London SW7 2DD, Tel-Fax 020–7589–1793.

Every effort has been made to trace all the copyright holders, but if any have been inadvertently overlooked the publishers will be pleased to make the necessary arrangement at the first opportunity.

General Editor's Preface

Joyce Brown

Civil engineering has a long history. Although practitioners did not begin to describe themselves as 'civil engineers' until the eighteenth century, the origins of their work lie in the construction skills of the ancient world and in the works of military engineers. Shortly after British civil engineers had formed themselves into a professional body, the Institution of Civil Engineers in London, their role was described in 1828 by Thomas Tredgold in these words:

> Civil engineering is the art of directing the great sources of power in Nature for the use and convenience of man.[1]

He thus neatly encapsulated what the civil engineer's job is about – the provision of the means to give society what it wants for its survival.

As time has gone by, the civil engineer's skills have had to diffuse over an ever-widening field and at the same time become more specialised. In all periods he has had to be the ingenious 'fixer', but more than a mere artisan – a point observed in the Institution's motto, *scientia et ingenio*.

The history of civil engineering is a fascinating one. Certainly 'the great sources of power in Nature' are not always directed without a certain amount of opposition by them, and the provision of the basic requirements – habitation, water supply, main drainage, harbours, bridges, places of worship, transport systems by land and water – has called for inventiveness and sometimes for daring and courage.

Yet interest in the history of civil engineering is not of long standing, and it seems fair to state that most of the important work has been done in the last forty years. With a few notable exceptions, most of the major books on the subject have appeared in that era; many specialist societies with their own transactions have been founded; and many of the journals in which articles might be published have come into existence. While archaeologists and architectural historians have long made their contribution to this subject, their ranks have been swelled by a large number of serious scholars – including engineers themselves – now interested in recording and evaluating the engineering achievements of earlier times. In particular, there is a lively interest in the study of our industrial past, at least in part because some of the evidences of it are already disappearing from the landscape.

Our intention in creating the series of which this volume forms part is to provide, through the reproduction of important contributions to this subject, an

---

[1] *Minutes of Council, Institution of Civil Engineers*, 4 January 1828.

invaluable reference collection for its study. The series encompasses many different branches of engineering from early times to the beginning of the twentieth century; its perspective is global; and the chosen articles have an international authorship, to the extent that this can be achieved for an essentially English-language series. The introduction to each volume has allowed the volume editor to set the pages selected in the context of the whole history of the subject and its historiography, while the provision of references and a bibliography will enable the reader to go further into the study of the topic.

This series will have succeeded if it gives civil engineers some unexpected insights into their own craft and other readers a new way of looking at engineering structures.

***

The volume editors were chosen for their particular knowledge and expertise in the field. They have worked with enthusiasm and good will to put together collections of articles intended to be both informative and stimulating, and I am grateful to them for their efforts. Where possible, they have incorporated the work of the best scholars, while at the same time giving preference to articles often obscurely published and not readily available. The learned journals are represented, as also are conference proceedings and essay chapters contributed to books.

In all of this, I have been much assisted by my Advisory Panel. Emeritus Professor Sir Alec Skempton (Imperial College) has made himself freely available to me for consultation on many aspects of this venture. Mike Chrimes (Librarian of the Institution of Civil Engineers), Dr. Norman Smith (Emeritus Reader, Imperial College) and James Sutherland (formerly a Senior Partner in Harris and Sutherland, London, consulting engineers) have all contributed valuable advice based on their extensive knowledge of particular fields. The idea for the series was developed in discussion with Dr John Smedley of Ashgate, and Publisher of the Variorum Collected Studies Series, who has given me much personal support and the benefit of his experience.

I am grateful also for the help given by the staff of several libraries, notably Kay Crooks and Susannah Parry in the library of the Department of Civil Engineering, Imperial College, and Mike Chrimes and staff of the library of the Institution of Civil Engineers, London. Many friends have given me encouragement and useful advice; in particular, I want to thank Paula Kahn and Mark Baldwin.

Joyce Brown,
Formerly Department of Civil Engineering,
Imperial College, London

Introduction

Robert Thorne

The most important technological change of the second half of the nineteenth century in civil and structural engineering was the substitution of steel for iron. The transition was neither sudden nor dramatic, because the processes for the manufacture of high quality steel at competitive prices took time to develop, but the ultimate result was momentous. Not only was steel used instead of iron for existing functions; it also transformed what engineering could achieve. As the historian David Landes has said, if we want to give labels to different chronological periods, the obvious title for the late nineteenth century is the 'Age of Steel'.[1]

Whether that title is justified or not, it is natural to compare one age with another. In the previous volume of this series, on the subject of structural iron in the period 1750–1850, R.J.M. Sutherland has charted the equally significant changes that resulted from the introduction of iron in construction, 'The Iron Revolution', as he calls it. Since there was a clear progression from iron to steel, it might seem simple to drop periodization and labelling in favour of treating the whole century and a half, 1750–1900, as a single sequence. However, the use of labels does serve a useful purpose, as does the division of this subject into shorter periods, with a separation around 1850. What happened in civil and structural engineering in the second half of the nineteenth century had a very different flavour from what had happened before, and it is right to treat the two periods differently.

During the period of the 'Iron Revolution', from the mid-eighteenth century onwards, Britain was pre-eminent, both in iron production and the application of iron to engineering structures. The innovations which permitted the mass production of cast and wrought iron were mostly British, enabling manufacturers to dominate world output. Iron production was both a manifestation and cause of industrialization, and an immense stimulus to the design of new types of structure. Though French structural theorists were important, and the Americans made significant contributions to bridge design, it was British engineers and contractors who exploited the potential of iron to its fullest. The results were buildings, bridges and railway structures, not to mention industrial machinery, which astonished the rest of the world and are still today regarded as classics of their kind.

Conventional descriptions of this historical episode reach their climax with the building of the Crystal Palace in 1850–51: not just the extraordinary skills

---

[1] David S. Landes, *The Unbound Prometheus* (Cambridge, 1969), 249–69.

and logistics involved in constructing the building, but also the superiority of the British technology at the Exhibition. Thereafter the story falters, and the tone of progressive optimism gives way to one of doubt and failure. This transition in the historical view of the period echoes how contemporaries themselves observed it. Concern about Britain's industrial performance was confirmed by the Paris Exhibition of 1867, where the products of the United States, France, Germany and other countries challenged her previous leadership. What was asked at the time, and has preoccupied historians ever since, is whether Britain could have avoided that change in status, and if so by what means.

This reversal of fortune was only gradual, but it deserves to be emphasized because it forms the context for many of the issues discussed in this volume. Historians who have debated the causes of Britain's relative economic decline have often focused on the iron and steel industry as symptomatic of what occurred generally.[2] In industrial production Britain led the way in the transition from iron to steel, yet failed to sustain that leadership. By 1914 British production of steel had been overtaken by Germany and the United States, and was even being rivalled by Belgium. There is no satisfactory single explanation for why this happened: partly, it is suggested, because of a failure to exploit the right technical processes, and the retention of small-scale, inefficient plant, but above all because the American and German industries developed behind tariff barriers which drove the British to dependence on more difficult markets. A key secondary explanation is that Britain's technical education system was inferior to those of its rivals, or that its contribution was undervalued by industrial leaders.

Linked to this debate about industrial performance is a parallel discussion, still in its infancy, about engineering design. Compared with the heroic years of the Iron Revolution, it seems that in the late nineteenth century Britain lost the initiative in creative engineering; not totally, as projects such as the Forth Railway Bridge testify, but in comparison with what was being achieved elsewhere. In considering this changing situation it may be useful to draw upon the well-established analysis of Britain's economic position, because the same kinds of explanation may apply to both. It was perhaps inevitable that the creativity of the period before 1850 would not be maintained, particularly once other countries began to reach the same stage of industrial maturity, but there were also cultural factors which had begun to limit the opportunities for British engineering to flourish.

There is more to these issues than simply patriotic pride, and the question of which country led the way in engineering achievement. Historians, such as those whose articles are gathered here, are all concerned to explain the process of change. That must include discussion of why some things did not happen, just

---

[2] Payne, 'Iron and steel manufacturers', and other works cited in the Bibliography.

as much as why other things did occur. In the history of the application of iron and steel to engineering structures the period after 1850 is more complex and tortuous than what had gone before, with more paradoxes to be accounted for. Why, for instance, were the principles of modular construction embodied in the Crystal Palace not widely adopted in the decades that followed; and why were the lessons of skyscraper building not recognised in Britain for fifty years or more following their development in America? More than with the preceding period, what is dealt with in this volume is a shifting story from which there are yet no firm conclusions.

The Transition from Iron to Steel

Before discussing the articles assembled in this volume it is useful to recall how the change from iron to steel production happened, as well as some of the uses of steel that had an influence on developments in civil and structural engineering. Steel was not a new product in the late-nineteenth century, but the mass production of competitively-priced, reliable steel for a multitude of purposes was a fundamental innovation.

Steel is distinguished as a metal in combining strength, hardness and ductility. Because malleable, it can be worked without breaking, yet it can retain its shape in the toughest of uses. These qualities relate to its carbon content, less than cast iron but more than wrought iron. Its virtues had been known long before the nineteenth century but the cost of producing it, because of the fuel and effort involved, meant that it was used only for small, high value objects such as tools and watch parts, and of course for armaments. Crucible steel, produced from the 1740s onwards, could only yield large pieces if a series of crucibles were operated in tandem.

The invention of the Bessemer (1856) and Siemens-Martin (1863–4) processes opened the way to larger scale steel production, resulting in a dramatic reduction in prices. By comparison with crucible steel and wrought iron manufacture the output of a steelworks was prodigious. With wrought iron, productivity was limited by the human muscle-power of the puddler who worked the molten iron in the furnace: 27–38 cwt. in a shift. By contrast, an early Bessemer converter had a capacity of 2–5 tons, and by the end of the century 20–25 tons. And whereas the level of carbon content in wrought iron was a matter of skill or luck, in steel production (particularly using the Siemens-Martin process) it could be closely controlled.

The triumph of steel was not immediate, because of early technical difficulties, especially in using phosphoric ores, and because there was too much existing investment in wrought iron plant. Indeed wrought iron production continued to grow: in Britain it was not overtaken by steel until 1885, and in

Germany not until two years later. By the mid-1880s Germany was annually producing *c*. 1.3 million tons of steel: Britain and America were each producing *c*. 2 million tons. In 1900 America, by then the world leader, was producing 11.4 million tons.[3]

Amongst the first major users of steel made by the new processes were the railways, for whom its qualities of strength and ductility answered a crying need. Steel rails were first laid at Derby in 1857 and at Crewe four years later. The London and North Western Railway established its own steelworks, using first the Bessemer and later the Siemens-Martin process, and by 1868 was producing 130 tons of steel rails a week.[4] In America the first steel rails were rolled in 1865. The weight for strength attributes of steel were also an obvious advantage in shipbuilding, but although it was soon adopted for marine boilers, mistrust of Bessemer steel inhibited its use in ships' hulls until the 1880s. These and similar uses are worth bearing in mind when it comes to considering the transition to steel in civil and structural engineering. Steel manufacturers supplied more than just the market for buildings and structures, and gave a high priority to railways, shipbuilding and armaments; so much so that structures were slow to command attention. But there was also a positive aspect to this interaction, because it allowed the lessons from one sphere of engineering to be taken up and applied in another.

The Selection and Grouping of Articles

None of the articles which follow deals directly with the process of iron and steel manufacture, nor with the firms involved, subjects which have usually been the domain of economic and business historians. Those whose main interest is the development of new structural forms do, of course, acknowledge the metallurgical advances which made more daring or economical structures possible, but without feeling obliged to describe those advances in detail. Likewise the familiar names of industrial giants such as Carnegie and Dorman Long get mentioned in passing, but are not placed at the centre of the story. In many ways this division of labour between historians of the iron and steel industry and historians of engineering is to the disadvantage of both, particularly when it comes to dealing with a period when the manufacturers took an increasingly active interest in structural developments. In the future it would be fruitful to connect the two sides of the story, and the results would form a useful addition to a volume such as this. But in the meantime engineering history has been treated largely as a subject on its own, as shown in the articles reproduced here.

---

[3] Payne, 'Iron and steel manufacturers', Chart II, 74.
[4] Brooke, 'The advent of the steel rail 1857–1914', 22–3.

The way the articles have been grouped follows a three-part sequence in which the first and third parts focus mainly on developments in the structural engineering of buildings, whilst the second part looks at other kinds of structure, especially bridges. Part One is concerned with the use of cast and wrought iron in building construction in the years immediately after 1850, a period almost as innovatory as the preceding decades, yet also, in Britain at least, a period when innovation began to diminish or be stifled. In Part Two the main focus is on bridge construction, where the transition from iron to steel can be traced in both standardized solutions and major, unique projects. The French contribution, particularly of Gustave Eiffel, is included here. Finally, in Part Three the volume returns to the subject of building structures, to pick up the history of framed construction, especially for tall buildings. There steel came into its own in the late 1880s.

Before discussing the contributions which make up each section, a word needs to be said about how they have been selected. In the overall historiography of engineering the late nineteenth century does not yet feature very prominently. This is surprising, not least because so many of the structures of that period still survive, and can be studied at first hand as well as through archival material. However copious the documentation and drawings, there is no substitute for seeing a structure in reality, as a way of understanding how it was built and how it has fared since completion. It is curious, not to say foolish, for historians to deny themselves such opportunities. But also, for practising engineers, there is the further consideration that the structures of this period are approaching, or have reached, the time of their first major overhaul. The question arises whether or how they will survive for the next hundred years, and the answer can only be given by understanding how they were originally constructed. So there are tangible reasons why the history of late nineteenth-century structures deserves attention, quite apart from the inherent interest of the problems it poses. Yet except perhaps for the issue of skyscraper construction (which developed a historiography almost while it was happening) detailed coverage and debate is only just beginning. Some individual structures, such as the Eads Bridge or the Galerie des Machines, have been well accounted for, but others are still outside the pale, and many general themes are still awaiting their first analysis.

The result is that this volume, more than others in this series, offers simply an initial stock-taking, and a foretaste of what is yet to come. Some topics – for instance the design of large-span station trainsheds – do not feature here because, however significant, they have not been the subject of general historical assessment. And the contribution of some countries, notably Germany and Russia, is unrepresented because of the absence of English language articles. Such are the vagaries of assembling a compilation like this. But the fifteen contributors included here give an excellent sense of why the years after 1850 should be brought to the top of the agenda in engineering history. In other spheres of history the same period is familiar and well-charted, so there is a well-prepared context in which this particular subject can be developed.

Iron in Construction: The Crystal Palace and After

In the structural engineering of buildings, iron had already established its importance before 1850: for mills, warehouses and industrial buildings where it was substituted for wood because of its combination of strength and apparent incombustibility; in conservatories and large-span roofs, including slip roofs in naval dockyards; and in the floor structures of large public and commercial buildings. At first it was solely cast iron that was used, but wrought iron was adopted once the relative performance of the two metals became better understood. Beginning in the 1840s, wrought-iron beams, built up from plates and angles, superseded cast-iron beams because of their superior tensile strength and reliability. Wrought-iron joist sections were not so easy to produce, but became increasingly available a decade later.

In discussing the use of iron in buildings, it is helpful to distinguish between two essential types: buildings reliant on rectangular, beam and column construction, and arched or triangulated structures. It is the beam and column (or trabeated) type which has most interested historians, because in its development can be traced the ancestry of multi-storeyed, fully-framed construction. As usually described, this lineage starts with the early textile mills and runs, via early exhibition buildings, factories and railway structures to the first fully-framed tall buildings in New York and Chicago at the end of the nineteenth century. Amongst the buildings most commonly cited as part of this interpretation are the Crystal Palace, the Boat Store at Sheerness in Kent, and the iron-fronted buildings of James Bogardus. All of these feature in the first articles reprinted here. They are unavoidable landmarks, even though their significance may not be quite as obvious as it may first appear.

The problem posed by these major structures concerns their influence rather than their design. Though referred to as significant episodes in the progressive development of framed construction, the historical link between each of them is not always clear: they appear as isolated events, not as part of a conscious, well-orchestrated movement. What is curious is that their initial impact was less far-reaching than their ultimate reputation would suggest. They were highly inventive yet they had few immediate progeny, and it is only in retrospect that their contribution to the overall story can be detected.

The Crystal Palace is by far the most famous of these pioneering iron-framed structures, yet it is also pre-eminently an example of an innovative building whose influence was partially stillborn. The article by Tom F. Peters (chapter 1) is one of the few, amidst a huge literature on the building, which begins to examine why that was so.[5] Despite the colossal overall size of the Crystal Palace, the iron girders which made up its frame were modest in span compared to some earlier iron structures, and were designed according to principles which by then were well known. In those respects Joseph Paxton and the contractors Fox Henderson were not, strictly speaking, pioneers. But in conceiving of a prefabricated, modular system of construction, in which the process of assembly was fundamental to the design, what they achieved was unprecedented. The 8 ft. (2.4m) module, based on the dimensions of the ridge and furrow roof, determined the 24 ft. (7.3m) grid of the bays and thus the sizes of the girders, columns and other components. The precision and speed with which they were erected – Paxton claimed to have seen two columns and three girders put up in just sixteen minutes – astonished onlookers and reporters; so much so that when the Great Exhibition opened it was already renowned for the nature of its construction.

But the Crystal Palace was not without its faults, and therein lie at least some of the clues about why it was not more influential. Tom Peters emphasises that the frame had insufficient stiffening, which in the eyes of at least one contemporary threatened its stability during the hottest days of 1851. And to those engineering doubts should be added the long-term reputation of the building amongst architects and the general public. Jealous that it had been completed with almost no architectural help, the architectural profession closed ranks in its hostility to iron construction on such a systematic scale. Meanwhile the public acclaim which greeted its completion gave way to partial disappointment once it was realized that the repetitive structure could seem tiring and monotonous after more than one visit.[6]

The issue of how to brace an iron-framed structure was critical at the Crystal Palace because it had no masonry walls to rely on. The same was true of the Sheerness Boat Store of 1858–60 where the frame was exposed, with infill cladding of corrugated iron and glass. A.W. Skempton analysed this building following its discovery by the photographer Eric de Maré in 1957 (chapter 2). In his article he demonstrates that its designer, Colonel G.T. Greene, made a fundamental advance in framed construction by devising a rigidly-jointed structure, reliant for its stability on neither masonry walls nor diagonal bracing. This was completed twelve years before the Menier Chocolate Factory at Noisiel outside Paris, which, until Skempton's research, had been claimed as the first fully-framed building of its kind, and almost a quarter of a century before the developments in New York and Chicago which it anticipates. Yet again this raises the question, why was it not more immediately influential? The answer in this case seems to lie, not in the opinion of architects or the general public but in the simple fact

---

[5] The issues raised in his article are dealt with more fully in his *Building the Nineteenth Century* (Cambridge, Mass. and London, 1996), 205–11, 226–54.

[6] Robert Thorne, 'Crystal exemplar', *Architectural Review*, 176 (July 1984), 49–53.

that it lay hidden from view in a naval dockyard where its existence was unappreciated for almost a hundred years.

Skempton concludes his article on the Boat Store with the assertion that 'it led, finally, to the creation of the first masterpieces of modern architecture, in Chicago, in the 1890s'. While it is true that the engineering principle of portal frame construction was applied in both places, that is not to say that the idea was transmitted from one to the other. American historians such as Turpin C. Bannister have preferred to cite their own indigenous tradition of iron construction, centred on the New York designer and contractor James Bogardus (chapter 3). America was not self-sufficient in iron production until the 1840s, but thereafter caught up fast: the first wrought-iron joists were rolled there in 1855. Bogardus saw the advantage of cast iron as a repetitive, incombustible material, which he used in the design of commercial buildings and warehouses, as well as fire watch towers, gun shot towers and a lighthouse, all completed in the short period 1848–62. His multi-storeyed iron fronts, some of which survive, are astonishing, but he was not the only person producing them. What is equally important is how he formed the buildings behind the fronts. Some historians have accepted his claim that his own factory of 1847–9 was fully iron-framed, but Bannister suspects that it was partly reliant on timber components. There is clearer evidence that the Harper Brothers building of 1854–5 was fully-framed, with both composite[7] and wrought-iron beams. But more important than these buildings, insists Bannister, were the two shot towers that he designed, because in those he really did complete a form of curtain wall construction, using a cast-iron frame infilled with brick. These interesting precursors were both demolished in 1907, so we may never know the exact details of how they were constructed and braced.

Discussion of the most spectacular early examples of framed construction draws attention away from the main reason why iron was used in buildings. From the origins of its adoption in early textile mills iron was pressed into service because it was believed to be a fireproof material: used in floors and roofs it could help provide a horizontal firebreak just as impregnable as masonry walls and partitions. Because of that attribute iron was to be found, not just in industrial structures but also in major public buildings, especially when, as at the Houses of Parliament, the reason for their construction was the destruction of their predecessor by fire. Iron also came into its own for floor spans over 20 ft. (6m), where timber floors have a tendency to sag. Architects who joined the chorus which dismissed the idea of an all-embracing iron architecture made no apology for incorporating iron in buildings when the safety of people or goods was paramount.

The great virtue of Sara Wermiel's article (chapter 4), which concludes Part One, is that it highlights this more utilitarian, yet essential application of iron,

---

[7] Cast-iron beams stiffened by wrought-iron tie-rods.

distinguishing between the different approaches favoured in Britain and America. In both countries it came to be realised that iron was far from perfect as a fireproof material: because it was liable to expand or fracture it could be unreliable or dangerous in the event of fire. The solution was to protect it with plaster, cement or clay tiles. The British preference, says Wermiel, was to use one of the proprietary flooring systems which offered some form of protection to the cast- or wrought-iron joists. These proliferated after the 1850s, leading eventually to the typical filler joist floor of the early twentieth century. During the same period the height and cubic capacity of buildings was limited through the Building Acts. In America, by contrast, there was more interest in protecting iron columns as well as floors, a circumstance which prepared the way for tall building construction. Wermiel's argument, that the fire-proofing of the frame was as important as the design of the frame itself, is worth bearing in mind when the subject of the American skyscraper is returned to in Part Three.

Other uses of iron in construction, in particular arched and triangulated roofs, are less fully covered in this collection because they have engendered less debate. There is a broad consensus that after the pioneering slipway roofs in English and Welsh naval dockyards it was in the design of station trainsheds that the most significant roof structures were developed.[8] Triangulated trusses of cast and wrought iron, or entirely wrought iron, were adequate for spans up to 80 ft. (25m), but in station planning longer spans were often called for. The demand for flexibility in platform layouts, and the fear that intermediate supports could be a safety hazard, weighed in favour of arched roofs; either crescent trusses or arched trusses with a high or low level tie. In Britain these were epitomized by the trainsheds built during the 1860s boom in station construction in London: crescent trusses at Cannon Street and Charing Cross, a twin-arched shed with a high level tie at Victoria, and the 240 ft. (73m) arched span of St Pancras, tied beneath the platforms by beams which form part of the basement roof structure. W.H. Barlow, the principal engineer of the St Pancras roof, claimed that a two-span roof would have cost only £6,000 less than his bravura design, a saving of about five per cent on the main station contract.[9] For the publicity it brought to the railway company it was worth it.

After the 1860s the focus of railway-building shifted abroad, particularly to America and to the British colonies. In Britain itself there were few major stations left to build, and those that were completed had more modest, utilitarian roofs. By contrast, in countries where railways were still being developed, the tradition of the long-span shed carried on, into the age of the steel three-pin arch. This part of the story is taken up more fully in the next section.

---

[8] On the slipway roofs, see R.J.M. Sutherland, 'Shipbuilding and the long span roof', *Transactions of the Newcomen Society*, 60 (1988–9), 107–26, reprinted in Volume 9 of this series.

[9] W.H. Barlow, 'Description of the St Pancras Station and roof, Midland Railway', *Minutes of the Proceedings of the Institution of Civil Engineers*, 30 (1869–70), Part II, 81.

Bridges and Exhibition Buildings

Turning to the subject of bridge design, the question of Britain's relative contribution once again comes to the fore. A frequent comment on the country's technological performance is that the inventiveness of her scientists and manufacturers was inadequately matched by the ability to produce general applications of new ideas. Spectacular solutions, tailored to suit particular circumstances, received more attention than designs which could be repeated many times over. In bridge-building this seems to be illustrated by what happened in the thirty years after 1850.

The Britannia Bridge over the Menai Straits, completed in 1850, holds a special place in engineering history because of the way in which theory, model-testing and the knowledge of materials were applied in solving a problem of long-span design. The relative contribution of Stephenson, Fairbairn, Hodgkinson and Edwin Clark is still being debated, but what is not disputed is that the idea of stiffened rectangular tubes through which the trains could run was a brilliant solution; and that structural understanding was advanced in many other ways, including the principle of joining the tubes to form a continuous beam unsupported by cables.[10] Stanley Smith's article (chapter 5), which opens the second part of this collection, is unusual because in addition to discussing these innovations it considers why tubular bridges were not more widely used. Box-girder bridges, a derivative of the Britannia idea which was patented by Fairbairn in 1846, were built quite frequently until the 1860s, but Stephenson only designed five more tubular bridges. The most spectacular of these, the Great Victoria Bridge across the St Lawrence at Montreal (a total length of 1¾ miles), is cited by Smith to explain why the idea was not more widely adopted. It was uneconomical in the use of iron compared with other types, and in the long term the riveted tubes required intensive maintenance. For long-span bridges other forms found favour even before the Great Victoria Bridge had been completed in 1859.

The emergence of standardised bridge types was predominantly an American phenomenon, generated by the demands of road and railway building. Eric DeLony's article (chapter 6), based on the identification and recording of surviving examples, discusses the many variants that were available from the 1840s. Broadly speaking these can be categorized as either bowstring or parallel-chord trusses, and their design follows the transition from timber (or timber plus iron) to all-iron construction. Thus the Howe truss, patented in 1840, was conceived of as a composite structure using diagonal timber compression members and vertical wrought-iron tension members. Four years later, Thomas Pratt patented a truss

---

[10] The most recent discussion of the relationship between those involved in the design of the Britannia Bridge is John Rapley, *The Britannia Bridge 1845–1850* (London, 1999).

that was the reverse of this, with diagonal iron tension rods and vertical timber members. In its subsequent all-iron version this led to a further variant, devised by Squire Whipple in 1847, in which the diagonals stretch across two panels to form a double intersection. Using standard forms and materials, the Pratt and Whipple trusses became the most popular types for railway bridges of up to 400 ft. (120m) span. In Britain, James Warren patented a truss in 1848 with only diagonal members connecting the top and bottom chords: the diagonals alternately take the compressive and tensile forces. This type also became popular in America, as well as for prefabricated bridges exported to India and the colonies.

As Eric DeLony emphasises, American bridge trusses were 'as much a marketing phenomenon as a technological fact'. The first generation of American railway bridges were built by the railway companies, but from the 1850s independent bridge companies gained in importance, promoting variants of the standard types. The merger of twenty-eight companies in 1900 to form the American Bridge Company accelerated the process of standardization, to serve both the home and export markets. One interesting question deserving further research is whether American companies, selling standard types as kits for on-site assembly, were more efficient and entrepreneurial than their British counterparts.

After the mid-1850s the main alternatives to the tubular bridge, apart from lattice trusses of the kind just described, were suspension and arched bridges. Previously suspension bridges had been discounted for railway use because of the oscillations caused by a moving train. However, at the Niagara Suspension Bridge (1851–55), John A. Roebling produced a version sufficiently stiffened (by the truss carrying the deck and by diagonal stay cables) to carry both a railway and road. It was claimed that this bridge used one-sixth of the amount of iron, in proportion to its length, as the Britannia Bridge. The same essential formula was repeated at the Cincinnati Suspension Bridge (1856–67) and above all at the Brooklyn Bridge (1869–83), spanning 1,595 ft. (476m) across the East River. What distinguished the Roebling bridges, apart from their method of stiffening, was the use of parallel wire cables instead of chains: at Brooklyn steel wires were used for the first time.

Arched bridges can best be considered alongside the evolution of arched roofs, whose evolution has previously been traced as far as the St Pancras train shed. The Eads Bridge, dealt with here in an article by John A. Kouwenhoven (chapter 7), represents the epitome in fixed arch (or statically indeterminate) bridge design. Each of the three main spans consists of four parallel-chord arches of tubular construction, bound together by diagonal bracing. The road and rail decks are carried above the arches. Whatever its virtuosity, the Eads Bridge did not solve the general problem of the rigidity of long-span arches. The alternative to the fixed arch was demonstrated by Gustave Eiffel in his two-hinged arched bridges, in particular the Maria Pia Bridge in Portugal (1875–6) and the Garabit Viaduct in the French Massif Central (1880–84). As described in the article by

Bertrand Lemoine (chapter 10), Eiffel's experience as a constructor led him to focus on the most buildable solutions. One advantage of the two-hinged arch was that it could be adjusted during erection. The three-hinged arch, on the other hand, was considered insufficiently rigid for long spans. Its virtues came to the fore in the design of roofs for stations and exhibition halls. John W. Stamper's (chapter 11) contribution discusses the engineering pedigree of the most famous three-hinged roof, the 364 ft. (111m) span Galerie des Machines of the Paris Exhibition of 1889. The design had the double advantage of being statically determinate, and therefore more easy to calculate, and more responsive to temperature changes than earlier iron arched roofs.

With these structures of the 1870s and 1880s the change from iron to steel was reached, and as at any point of transition the choice of material depended on particular circumstances of reliability, price and supply. Eads used a chrome-steel alloy in the tubes of his bridge, yet Eiffel built his bridges in wrought iron. One of the surprising conclusions of John Stamper's article is that the Galerie des Machines was also constructed of wrought iron, not steel as most other historians have assumed. Stamper relies on one particular account of the structure, which stresses the use of iron, whereas most contemporary accounts suggest that steel was the main material.[11] The fact of this uncertainty reflects how delicate the decision was concerning which material to use.

A steel Whipple truss railway bridge was built at Glasgow, Missouri in 1879, but the real triumph of steel in bridge construction is marked by the Forth Railway Bridge, completed in 1890. This extraordinary project is often discussed in conjunction with the Tay Bridge, because Thomas Bouch had designed a bridge across the Firth of Forth on which work had started before the collapse of his Tay Bridge in 1878. It is useful to be able to read J.S. Shipway's articles on the two bridges alongside each other as a comprehensive account of both projects (chapters 8 and 9). Not only does he give a rounded, undogmatic view of the causes for the failure of the first Tay Bridge; he also devotes equal attention to the design of its replacement by W.H. and Crawford Barlow. Of all the lessons from the collapse of the first bridge, the most important concerned the provision for wind pressure, the full importance of which Bouch failed to appreciate. In addition to the height of spans required to cross the Forth, and the issue of how to construct the bridge, it was the question of wind pressure which led Fowler and Baker to the decision to use a balanced cantilever design. William Arrol & Co, who were also the contractors for the second Tay Bridge, demonstrated the advantages of completing the Forth Bridge in steel. The result was a project which, for its innovations in design and the use of materials, was as significant as the Britannia Bridge of forty years before.

---

[11] For instance, *Engineering*, May 3rd 1889, 452.

The Advent of Steel-Framed Construction

Along with the completion of the Forth Bridge, the most obvious indication of the advent of steel in structural engineering was the development of the American skyscraper. As G.R. Larson and R.M. Geraniotis are quick to point out in their article reproduced here (chapter 13), the term 'skyscraper' as originally used in the early 1880s did not automatically mean an iron- or steel-framed building, yet within a decade framed construction was regarded as a characteristic quality of skyscraper development. This question of definition is one way of approaching the more fundamental problem of why high buildings were erected in American cities, and what role the introduction of steel played in that tendency. There is then the related problem of why similar buildings were not sought after in British and European cities at the same time, and whether that can be explained by the state of the steel industry in the countries concerned.

Carl W. Condit's summary of the preconditions for the development of the skyscraper (chapter 12) reaffirms the point made by Skempton, Bannister and others, that the structural forms which were exploited so characteristically in Chicago and New York in the 1880s and 1890s had a pedigree in earlier iron-framed construction, even though the links with European developments are often not directly tangible. As he emphasises, non-structural preconditions were also important: the availability of heating systems, power-operated lifts and forced draught ventilation, as well as, crucially, the development of ways to fireproof the floors and frame. What is not dealt with by Condit here, but was acknowledged in his other contributions to the subject, is the fact that these technologies evolved to help maximize rentable space in the central areas of American cities. Developers, building agents and contractors played as important a role in the emergence of the new building type as architects or engineers. As Cass Gilbert, architect of the New York Woolworth Building, put it, skyscrapers were 'the machine that made the land pay'.[12]

Iron- or steel-framing was a prerequisite for skyscraper construction because masonry walls carried above ten storeys exerted too heavy a load on foundations (a major consideration in Chicago's difficult soil conditions) and limited the natural lighting of the rooms within. In addition, framed construction was quicker to erect, which mattered immensely to building investors. Larson and Geraniotis are contributors to a debate which has been going on for as long as skyscrapers have existed, concerning when the first fully-framed tall building was erected and

---

[12] Quoted in Sarah Bradford Landau and Carl W. Condit, *Rise of the New York Skyscraper, 1865–1913* (New Haven and London, 1996), xiii. See also, Jane Bonshek, 'The skyscraper: a catalyst of change in the Chicago construction industries, 1882–1892', *Construction History*, 4 (1988), 53–74, and Carol Willis, *Form follows Finance: Skyscrapers and Skylines in New York and Chicago* (New York, 1995).

by whom. Since the time of its completion in 1885 the chief claimant for primacy has been the Home Insurance Building in Chicago by William LeBaron Jenny, but there are also New York contenders including the Produce Exchange (1881–4) and the Tower Building (1888–9). What is at issue is not the use of the frame to support the floors, but whether the frame carries the outer walls as well. There is also the question whether the frame alone provides lateral stability. The Home Insurance building had cast-iron columns built into the masonry piers of its two street façades which supported the floor beams, but the exterior wall including the spandrel panels between the windows was not wholly dependent on the iron columns. Even if it had been, the fact that the building had two masonry party walls means that it was not as fully-framed as a more free-standing structure such as the Tower Building.

Because of the claims made for it, the Home Insurance Building has been the subject of more critical analysis than any other building of its time. What this has shown is that it was built at the transition-point from iron to steel. Jenny used cast and wrought iron, except for the top three storeys where he substituted steel beams. Other early Chicago skyscrapers such as the Tacoma Building (1887–9) also had frames which combined iron and steel. However, by the early 1890s the all-steel frame was becoming the norm, as at the Rand McNally Building in Chicago (1889–91) and the famous Wainwright Building in St Louis (1890–91). Although commercial imperatives dictated the design of these buildings, it has been argued that the entrepreneurial zeal of the steel industry (notably the Carnegie Steel Company) also played a part in the urge to build high. Recognizing that the market for steel rails was stagnating, Carnegie's directed their efforts to the supply of structural steel sections. They helped secure their position by acting as engineering advisers to Chicago architects, and thus dominated the first phase of steel-framed skyscraper construction in the early 1890s. Without a steel industry alive to the potential of this new market these architectural developments might not have occurred quite so rapidly.[13]

Until recently it has been customary to attribute the advent of the steel frame in Britain to the import of American knowledge and practice, despite the fact that the country had long experience of iron construction. The argument for an 'American invasion', presented in the article by Jeanne Lawrence (chapter 15), relies on the role of three men: Gordon Selfridge, who brought American department store methods to London and opened the first part of his London shop in 1909; Daniel Burnham of Chicago who acted as his first architect; and above all, the Swedish-born engineer Sven Bylander who arrived in London in 1902 fresh from the experience of working with American contractors. Bylander

[13] Thomas J. Misa, *A Nation of Steel. The Making of Modern America, 1865–1925* (Baltimore, 1995), xvii, 60–88.

designed the steel frame for Selfridges's, and also for the Ritz Hotel (1904–6) and other buildings. Lawrence argues that it was the Bylander projects which helped persuade the London County Council of the need to establish rules for the design of iron- and steel-framed buildings, as it ultimately did in 1909. The evidence is weighted in favour of the importance of his contribution because he was such an energetic promoter of the steel-framed cause, through lectures and articles. Quite understandably he illustrated the design and construction process through the projects he had worked on; but subsequently, as in the article reproduced here (chapter 14), this led to his giving an undue prominence to those projects and a neglect of other contributors.

Bylander did indeed apply American thinking to his projects: the detailed preparation of framing plans, the systematic organization of the construction process, and the use of the Carnegie Handbook in the calculation of working stresses. But the publicity which the Ritz attracted has led to the neglect of earlier steel-framed projects. As Alastair Jackson and others have pointed out, the British steel industry began to produce reliable steel sections in the mid-1880s, and Dorman Long produced their first section book in 1887. A number of buildings can claim precedence over the Ritz in the use of steel-framing, including warehouses in Manchester, the Royal Insurance Building in Liverpool (1895–1903) and the Strand extension to the Ritz's main rival, The Savoy (1903–4).[14] As with the Ritz, these were not permitted to take advantage of the frame to reduce the thickness of the external walls, but in every other respect they showed that the British industry was not far behind its American counterparts.

Yet even though the British and other European countries had the know-how, they chose not to build tall. In Paris new buildings could go no more than fifty per cent higher than the width of the street, while in London the restriction was one of 80 ft., with the addition of two storeys in the roof. To appreciate why the skyscraper was not imported means looking beyond engineering knowledge, or the capacity of the steel industry, to an understanding of the opinions which led to the drafting of the Building Regulations. A combination of factors led to the conclusion that tall buildings were not wanted, even though the expertise to build them existed.

Conclusion

Within the overall compass of engineering history the period discussed in this volume is a comparatively recent one. We are still living in the Age of Steel

---

[14] Alastair Jackson, 'The development of steel-framed buildings in Britain, 1880–1905', *Construction History*, 14 (1998), 21–40.

that was inaugurated in the late nineteenth century. Many of the structures that were completed then are still in use today, and they hold lessons which are relevant to contemporary engineering practice.

However, the more recent past is often the most neglected period of history. The sources of information are usually overwhelmingly abundant and it is difficult to know where to start. The lines of inquiry which are well-defined for earlier periods are still indistinct. The period of engineering history dealt with here is at this tentative stage. Some of the territory has been well-mapped, but there remain some significant gaps: some issues, such as the development of the American skyscraper, have been almost overworked, while others remain untouched. There is still a long way to go before a first synthesis of the subject will have been reached.

In other branches of history – political, economic and social – the late nineteenth century has been thoroughly researched and analysed, and there is much to be learnt from the major themes which have emerged. It was above all a period of internationalization; not just through colonial expansion and the growth of international trade, but through the flow of people, knowledge and ideas between different countries. It also saw more intense international competition than ever before, accompanied by a heightened awareness of different countries' relative performance; in Britain's case, a growing despondence about national decline.

This international theme underlies many of the articles reproduced here, because they refer to the way engineering knowledge and experience was shared between countries, but also the way that different national cultures affected engineering developments. It is probably on these themes that the most fruitful developments in the subject will occur in coming years. What are still most needed are comparative studies of engineering education and professionalization, and a broad analysis of how economic investment induced the development of engineering. The great engineering achievements of the period are well-known, but the context in which they emerged still awaits further exploration.

Select Bibliography

This bibliography includes the most notable works on the subject published in the period 1850–1900, as well as more recent books and articles. In many cases the best analysis of a well-known structure remains the one which was published at the time. For articles and the general development of engineering theory and design see Volume 12 in this series, edited by William Addis.

Articles reproduced in this volume have not been included in this bibliography.

Part 1: The Manufacture of Iron and Steel

Brooke, David, 'The advent of the steel rail, 1857–1914', *Journal of Transport History*, 3rd series, 7 (March 1986), 18–31.

Burn, Duncan, *The Economic History of Steelmaking, 1867–1939*, 2nd edn. (Cambridge, 1961).

Carr, J.C., and W. Taplin, *History of the British Steel Industry* (Oxford, 1962).

Clarke, J.F., and F. Storr, 'The introduction of the use of mild steel into the shipbuilding and marine engineering industries', *Occasional Papers in the History of Science and Technology, no. 1* (Newcastle-upon-Tyne Polytechnic, 1983).

Fairbairn, W., *Iron, its History, Properties and Processes of Manufacture*, 1st edn. (Edinburgh, 1861); 2nd edn. (Edinburgh, 1865).

Gale, W.K.V., *Iron and Steel* (London, 1969).

Hyde, Charles K., *Technological Change and the British Iron Industry, 1700–1870* (Princeton, NJ, 1970).

Jeans, J.S., *Steel: Its History, Manufacture, Properties and Use* (London, 1880).

McCloskey, Donald N., *Economic Maturity and Entrepreneurial Decline: British Iron and Steel, 1870–1913* (Cambridge, Mass., 1973).

Misa, Thomas J., *A Nation of Steel: The Making of Modern America, 1865–1925* (Baltimore, Maryland, 1995).

Payne, Peter L., 'Iron and steel manufacturers', in Derek H. Aldcroft, ed., *The Development of British Industry and Foreign Competition, 1875–1914* (London, 1968).

Schubert, H.R., 'The steel industry', in Charles Singer, ed., *A History of Technology*, 5 (Oxford, 1958).

Wengenroth, Ulrich, *Enterprise and Technology: The German and British Steel Industries, 1865–95* (Cambridge, 1994).

Part 2: Iron in Construction

(See also Volume 9 in this series, edited by R.J.M. Sutherland.)

Barlow, W.H., 'Description of the St Pancras Station and roof, Midland Railway', *Minutes of the Proceedings of the Institution of Civil Engineers*, 30 (1869–70), 78–93.

Barrett, James, 'On the construction of fire-proof buildings', *Minutes of the Proceedings of the Institution of Civil Engineers*, 12 (1852–3), 244–71.

Charlton, T.M., *A History of Theory of Structures in the Nineteenth Century* (Cambridge, 1982).

Downes, Charles, and Charles Cowper, *The Building Erected in Hyde Park for the Great Exhibition of the Works of Industry of All Nations* (London, 1852).

Fairbairn, W., *On the Application of Cast and Wrought Iron to Building Purposes*, 1st edn. (London, 1854); 2nd edn. (London, 1857–8).

Gayle, Margot, and Carol Gayle, *Cast Iron Architecture in America: The Significance of James Bogardus* (New York, 1998).

Herbert, Gilbert, *Pioneers of Prefabrication: The British Contribution in the Nineteenth Century* (Baltimore, Maryland, 1978).

Lemoine, Bertrand, *L'architecture du fer. France: XIXe siècle* (Paris, 1986).

McKean, John, *Crystal Palace: Joseph Paxton and Charles Fox* (London, 1994).

Meeks, Carroll L.V., *The Railroad Station* (New Haven, Conn., 1956).

Peters, Tom F., *Building the Nineteenth Century* (Cambridge, Mass. and London, 1996).

Steiner, Frances H., *French Iron Architecture* (Ann Arbor, Michigan, 1978).

Timoshenko, S.P., *History of the Strength of Materials* (New York, 1953).

Unwin, W.C., *Wrought Iron Bridges and Roofs* (London, 1869).

Walmisley, Arthur T., *Iron Roofs* (London, 1884).

Wyatt, M.D., 'On the construction of the building for the Exhibition of the Works of Industry of all Nations', *Minutes of the Proceedings of the Institution of Civil Engineers*, 10 (1850–51), 127–91.

Part 3: Bridges

Campin, Francis, *A Treatise on the Application of Iron to the Construction of Bridges, Girders, Roofs and Other Works* (London, 1871).

Condit, Carl W., *American Building Art: The Nineteenth Century* (New York, 1960).

DeLony, Eric, *Landmark American Bridges* (New York, 1993).

Fairbairn, William, 'On tubular bridges', *Minutes of the Proceedings of the Institution of Civil Engineers*, 9 (1849–50), 233–87.

Haupt, Herman, *General Theory of Bridge Construction* (New York, 1866).

Humber, William, *A Complete Treatise on Cast and Wrought Iron Bridge Construction* (London, 1861).

James, John G., *The Origins and World Wide Spread of Warren-Truss Bridges in the Mid-Nineteenth Century. Part 2: Overseas Railways and the Spread of Iron Bridges c. 1850–70* (London, privately printed, 1987). Available in the Institution of Civil Engineers Library.

Lemoine, Bertrand, *Gustave Eiffel* (Paris) 1984.

Mehrtens, George G., *A Hundred Years of German Bridge Building* (Berlin, 1900).

Steinman, D.B., *The Builders of the Bridge* (New York, 1950). On John and Washington Roebling.

Westhofen, W., 'The Forth Bridge' *Engineering* (London, 1890).

Whipple, Squire, *A Work on Bridge Building* (New York, 1847).

Woodward, C.M., *A History of the St Louis Bridge* (St Louis, 1881).

Part 4:   The American Skyscraper

Birkmire, William H., *Planning and Construction of High Office Buildings* (New York, 1898).

Condit, Carl W., *The Chicago School of Architecture* (Chicago, 1964).

Freitag, Joseph K., *Architectural Engineering with Special Reference to High Building Construction* (New York, 1895).

Landau, Sarah Bradford, and Carl W. Condit, *Rise of the New York Skyscraper, 1865–1913* (New Haven and London, 1996).

Landau, Sarah Bradford, *P.B. Wright: Architect, Contractor and Critic, 1838–1925* (Chicago, 1981).

Larson, Gerald R., 'The iron skeleton frame: interactions between Europe and the United States', in John Zukowsky, ed., *Chicago Architecture, 1872–1922: Birth of a Metropolis* (Chicago and Munich, 1987), 38–55.

Peck, Ralph B., *History of Building Foundations in Chicago* (Chicago: University of Illinois Engineering Experimental Station, 1948).

Shankland, E.C., 'Steel skeleton construction in Chicago', *Minutes of the Proceedings of the Institution of Civil Engineers*, 127 (1896–7), 1–57.

Wermiel, Sara E., *The Fireproof Building: Technology and Public Safety in the Nineteenth-century American City* (Baltimore and London, 2000).

Part 5:   British Steel-Framed Construction

Bates, W., *Historical Structural Steel Handbook* (London, British Constructional Steelwork Association Ltd., 1984).

Bylander, S., 'Steel frame buildings in London', *Transactions and Notes of the Concrete Institute*, 5 (1913), 55–125.

Dawnay, Archibald D., 'Constructional steelwork as applied to building', *Builder*, April 20th 1901, 385–90.

Hurst, Lawrance, 'An iron lineage', *The Structural Engineer*, 77 (18th May 1999), 17–28.

Jackson, Alastair A., 'The development of steel-framed buildings in Britain, 1880–1905', *Construction History*, 14 (1998), 21–40.

Kent, Lewis E. and G.W. Kirkland, 'Construction of steel-framed buildings', *The Structural Engineer*, Jubilee Issue (1958), 102–10.

Matheson, Ewing, 'Steel for structures', *Minutes of the Proceedings of the Institution of Civil Engineers*, 69 (1881–2), 1–78.

Scott, W. Basil, 'Some historical notes on the application of iron and steel to building construction', *The Structural Engineer*, 7 (January 1929), 4–12.

Stratton, Michael, 'New materials for a new age: Steel and concrete construction in the North of England, 1860–1939', *Industrial Archaeology Review*, 21 (June 1999), 5–24.

Twelvetrees, W.N., *Structural Iron and Steel* (London, 1900).

1

Some structural problems encountered in the building of the Crystal Palace of 1851

Tom F. Peters

For the modern architect, and to a certain extent by association, even for the civil engineer, the Crystal Palace of 1851 has come to represent a structure, futuristic in intent, which the builders of the 19th century had but to follow in order to attain the fully developed modern steel structural system. The truly pioneer structure has been so idealized and its problems reduced to fit historical preconceptions and euphemism, essentially in order to provide an historical rationale for the "modern movement",that the true value of the effort made by the builders and the real structural problems have been long obscured[1].

It is certainly correct to state that this innovative structure was indeed materially responsible for the proliferation of iron as a new structural material and for the widespread use of glass in representational building, officially termed architecture. It was however, not the first to use cast iron structurally.

The first major structure to use cast iron successfully had, of course, been the famous Ironbridge of 1779. Many greenhouses particularly in Britain but also some notable examples in France, had also preceeded the Crystal Palace, and indeed, the structural detailing, if not the actual system itself, had been largely developed and tested in advance several times and in several stages in greenhouses built by Joseph Paxton ranging from his first experiments in 1828, through the Great Conservatory he built at Chatsworth from 1837-1840, to the hastily built Lily House of 1850, also at Chatsworth. These were however, not representational structures, not counting officially as architecture. But here too the Crystal Palace had been presaged by Bunnings' Coal Exchange of 1849 in London which also had a visible cast-iron structure. This in turn leads us back to the elegant use of cast iron in early neo-gothic church building in Liverpool, to Thomas Rickman's St. George's of 1813, St. Michael's of 1814 and St. Philip's of 1816. J ohn Nash had also used undisguised cast-iron columns in the Brighton Pavilion of 1818-1821, not only in the famed palm-frond columns of the kitchens, but also for instance in the Red Drawing Room. And in France, Henri Labrouste had built the interior of the small reading room, called "La Reserve" of the Bibliothèque Sainte-Geneviève in Paris with the same material in 1843. Tredgold had advocated the use of the material especially as a fireproof construction in his book "Practical Essay on the Strength of Cast Iron and other Metals" of 1824. The early mills of Manchester had used post and beam construction in cast iron in conjunction with massive outer walls of masonry for precisely this reason ever since the end of the 18th century, and it has been shown that this idea had been imported from France where wrought-iron roof trusses had not been uncommon, especially for theaters, after 1780. James Bogardus had built a fireproof warehouse of cast iron in New York in 1848. However, these were all individual experiments, and a single great symbolic effort was needed to coalesce these disunited events into a new direction.

It was of course not to be the brittle cast iron, but the more flexible wrought iron in standardized sections from the rolling mills and the various forms of steel which were to make frame construction successful in the field of building. Many historians have been blinded to this fact by a misunderstanding of the structural role played by the many fascinating precast iron structures built in the latter half of the 19th century, and by the many attempts to make these structures work as frames in spite of the very obvious disadvantages inherent in the material they used. It is indeed rare in the history of architecture to hear any reference to the material and structural problems of expansion, stiffness, bending, shear, torsion and buckling which were the main concerns of builders intent on the introduction of the new material into the field of building.

Another misconception is the widespread belief that the Crystal Palace was built only of cast iron and glass. This statement was culled uncritically from the many lay reports of the time which appeared in journals and newspapers all over Britain, Europe and the United States. What fascinated these many reporters was the large-scale use of glass to an extent unknown before, and the thinness of the cast-iron columns. Understandable exaggeration of these novel and surprising features was the result. For instance, the skin of the building was not a curtain wall construction as has since been often presumed, but rather hung between the outermost posts of the structure. It was made of wood, and the cast-iron frame with its characteristic circle in the upper portion of the panel and the arch below was a superimposed decorative element. On the ground floor, no glass was used at all except for that in the panels immediately adjoining the entrances. Indeed the skin of the lowest floor consisted almost entirely of ventilation louvers in the uppermost and lowermost portions of the panels and of boarding between them. On the other hand, however, the two upper storeys were glazed over about 80% of their surface. The ground floor was $1/3$ higher than the upper storeys which were also smaller in area. On an estimation, the glass surface accounted therefore for about 45% of the total outer skin, far less than is usually supposed. The roof, on the other hand, was about 90% glass, built according to Paxton's ridge-and-furrow patent, only a small part of the building adjacent to the barrel vault of the transept being flat and covered with lead sheeting.

In the interior, the partition walls, the flooring of both the gallery and the ground floor levels, the floorbeams, all trusses of the one-storey areas which made up about 30% of the total surface, and the great trussed-arches of the barrel vaulted transept, were made of timber.

The 48 and 72 foot trusses of the double and triple spans were manufactured in a combination of wrought iron, cast iron and timber. However, all trusses of whatever material were painted the same colour throughout the building so that evidently only professionals noted that they were made of varied materials. The famous window mullions and the gutter-cum-joist structure of the ridge-and-furrow patent roofing for which Paxton had developed his famed money saving machinery, were also all of wood.

So the Crystal Palace was in fact not quite as simple and evident a structure as has been claimed. There were also essential structural differences between it and the many Victorian greenhouses from which it had originally evolved and with which it is always compared. Perhaps the most essential of these differences were the complex organisation of the erection process[2] and the use of a modular structural unit of 24 x 24 ft. (7.3 x 7.3 m). This element was made up of several components, the chief of which were four cast iron posts and four trusses of the same material

which interconnected them. This unit was incremental and could be
extended by simple addition both in plan and in height. In fact, and
this too was new, the building was entirely conceived as a structural
system rather than a building in the conventional sense from the very
outset[3].

The concept of the additive, three-dimensional module is in itself one
of the most important aspects of this structure for the history of technology. Therefore we say that the Crystal Palace was basically different
in structural concept from all greenhouses from which it derived, even if
it was similar in detailing.

The degree of innovation in the design of the system and details was
astonishing for such a rapidly conceived structure. It can only be
explained by the long experience which the designer, Joseph Paxton had
gained in his work on the design of greenhouses while in the service of
the Duke of Devonshire. For example, the hollow posts of the system
permitted rain water to be evacuated from the roof every 7.3 m in both
directions. Paxton had originally developed this drainage system for the
Great Conservatory at Chatsworth in 1837, and he adapted it cleverly for
the exhibition building. New was that the hollow posts permitted the
thickness of the sections to be varied according to their required height
of one, two or three storeys or to account for the additional eccentric
loading due to an unusually large span. By adjusting the thickness of
the post on the inside instead of increasing the diameter, the outer
dimensions could be kept constant and the joint geometry consequently be
retained throughout. It appears to be the first time that this type of
consideration, essential for any adaptable system of modular prefabrication, had entered the field of building.

This adaptability in section as opposed to our more modern and far less
subtle overdimensioning of all components to account for unique cases
involving maximum conditions, was of course rational only in a period when
the cost of material was appreciable in relation to manufacturing costs.
Considerations of this kind were obviously a direct consequence of the use
of the new material iron in structural work, as neither masonry nor timber
construction could ever have given rise to such detailing.

As in so many instances, the original idea for the development of modular
elements built up of complex combinations of individual components stems
from an entirely different area, in this case from the planning concepts
of the architects of the French revolutionary period. In particular, the
work of J. N. L. Durand (c.1750-1833) whose repetitive spatial units of
identical size and form corresponded well to the stone construction he
envisaged using while inadvertently pointing the way toward later steel
construction. Structurally Durand's buildings were as traditional as the
classic Greek ashlar architecture from which he derived his formal
expression, but such modular problems gave rise to new structural
possibilities as well. These came to the fore in the first large-scale
construction of cheap and prefabricated speculative terrace-housing in
Britain around 1830.[4] This in turn was based upon the large-scale manufacture of brick and standardized timber sections which were often
expressly imported from the United States for the purpose. Especially
Sir William Cubitt (1785-1861), who was both Chairman of the Building
Committee on the Crystal Palace and who directed a large part of the works
on the site itself, contributed greatly to the spread of cheap modular
construction in housing. The idea gradually spread to other areas as
well, to the building of prefabricated military field hospitals around

mid-century, then to hotel construction, particularly in the United States, and to the first great department stores. In the history of the genealogy of modular construction the Crystal Palace played a major role.

The structural clarity which supposedly emanated from the Crystal Palace, is yet another myth provoked by a superficial retrospective instead of a contemporary viewpoint. This so-called clarity was merely the result of the lack of planning time available for the design of the structure. It would be more correct to term the structure of the Crystal Palace a schematic idea rather than a mature system. In contrast to a normal design procedure, in which a slow process of rationalization is followed, refining, adapting, standardizing and clarifying details and forms in gradual stages, Paxton's first rapid design, the famous so-called "blotting-paper" sketch, was the simplest, and each further design step brought increasing complication rather than increasing clarity. It was the speed with which the building had to be erected and not the search for structural clarification which led to the apparent simplicity.

When the building was later reerected in Sydenham in 1854, and the original pressure of deadlines no longer applied, other criteria came to the fore. Neither the clarity of the system nor the rapidity of erection were important. The Crystal Palace had achieved the status of an international symbol of industrial preeminence and was to be emulated as prototypical in many of the remaining industrial exhibitions through-out the century: 1853 Dublin and New York, 1854 Munich, 1855 Paris, 1864 Amsterdam, 1867 and 1889 again, Paris. When it was rebuilt in Sydenham, however, what was in fact erected was a new building which used the original parts and many more besides. The Sydenham building had a vaulted nave and three vaulted transepts, two more than the original. It was, in parts, five instead of three storeys high and had exedra at both ends, open porticos, a cellar and many further features not present in the original. The simplicity of the original idea was obscured. This had to be the case, as there were many structural problems which had become manifest in the use of the building which had to be solved before it could be expected to stand for any length of time. Condensation plagued the exhibition hall, often dripping from the glass roofs onto the exhibits and the visitors in spite of Paxton's internal gutter system. The whole building had not one useful expansion joint built into its fabric and certain conceptual oversights unnecessarily complicated some of the components, such as for example the base pieces of the posts.

The site on which the original Crystal Palace stood in Hyde Park was slightly inclined over the 560 m length of the building. To compensate for this slope and so as not to have a high plinth at the lower end, the floor was built following the incline, but at a lesser angle. This floor was taken as baseline for setting out the whole building and all levels were measured perpendicularly to the floor. No post was therefore vertical in the entire structure. We can see from this that a certain logic was followed in the construction of the building, but it was certainly not one we would consider following today. The idea was obviously to avoid having to compensate for the angle. But as all the posts were bolted on to concrete blocks cast to a certain height above ground level, this meant that their distance to the floor level or base line varied from one column row to the next[5]. As a consequence, the base pieces of the columns had to be cast in varying lengths which had all to be checked individually on site. This was clearly at odds with the principle of serial prefabrication in large quantities which had been the premise upon which the original design was based although, on the other hand, it did make full use of that particular form of variability

inherent in the use of moulds for casting components. The solution
would of course have been obvious once construction was under way. The
concrete foundations which were that part of the structure that had to
be cast in situ at any rate, should have been cast to within a certain
distance from the base line and thus at varying heights above ground.
Then the prefabricated base pieces could have been all cast the same
length. It was simply not possible to recognise and to solve all novel
problems in advance in the course of the mere six weeks allotted to the
detailing of the building.

In part due to these faults in structural logic and shortcomings in
detailing, the Crystal Palace did not give rise to an immediate widespread prefabrication industry as might have been expected. Eminent
architectural theoreticians such as Lothar Bucher and Gottfried Semper
called for just such a development. The structure of the Crystal Palace
resembled partially that of the American balloon-frame system which was
just beginning to achieve popularity at the time. This system consisted
of precut, standardized timber sections nailed together to form a framework which was then stiffened to form panels by means of either diagonal
or clapboard surfacing.[6]   The balloon-frame in constrast to the cast-
iron system used for the Crystal Palace, achieved immediate widespread
success as it was readily adaptable to many forms of small-span
building structures and of varying grid. The Crystal Palace system was
unable to come up to this level of flexibility and fell short especially
with respect to stiffening and joint structure.

Connections were particularly difficult to design in cast iron, as the
material primarily only withstands compression. In all traditional
structural systems, in timber and stone, there is no clear differentiation between the problems of joints and connections. The joint
essentially defines an interface problem, the formal continuity from one
component to another. The connection on the other hand, defines
continuity of function. The two had always previously been intimately
coupled and their manufacture was a matter of little technical concern.
But in cast iron, the joint was defined by the problems posed by the
construction of the mould for casting whereas the connection was defined
by considerations of statics and strengths, insulation, expansion,
sealing and the like.

The earliest example of cast-iron construction on a large scale in the
building field, the Ironbridge of 1779, had derived its joint geometry
and its connection method from traditional timber construction. The
Crystal Palace on the other hand, drew in part upon experience gained in
the field of machine design. Both connection and stiffening flanges
were used and the modular unit was obviously supposed to be a stiff
frame. However it wasn't one as we understand it today, since the
material used had very little tensile, shear or torsional strength.
Charles Cowper who wrote one of the most detailed professional articles
on the building of the Crystal Palace, recounts the following in 1852:

> "One of the most important features in the construction is the
> form of girder or truss adopted by the contractors, and which
> has two distinct duties to perform. The first and most obvious
> duty of the girders is to support the roof, but their second
> and equally important duty is to give lateral stiffness to the
> whole structure."[7]

We see that the idea of a new structural system, the portal frame, was
beginning to appear. The first known true portal in the form we know it

32

today, has been traced by Skempton to the Navy Boot Store at Sheerness built by Godfrey T. Greene (1807-1886) eight years later[8], but a case could perhaps also be made for the Munich Kristallpalast of 1854. The obvious solution to use for stiffening, as long as only cast iron was to be employed for the purpose however, was obviously knee-bracing, as had been usual in timber construction and as had been first adapted to cast iron in the Hungerford Fish Market built by Charles Fowler in 1835.[9] However, it was clear that for reasons of spatial flexibility, the attempt was to be made to do away with the knee-bracing as soon as possible and to rely on the bolting and the resistance of the material alone in order to achieve the necessary stiffness. But although the connections of the Crystal Palace appeared overdimensioned by our steel-building standards, the brittle cast iron could take only part of the strain. To avoid failure therefore, additional diagonal bracing was provided of wrought iron. In actual fact, however, the structure probably derived the stability it possessed from a combination of a partial frame-effect of the post-and-truss construction, partially from the diagonal bracing and the rest from the wooden floor "plates", the glass surfaces, the internal walls and the effect of the extra longitudinal trusses mentioned by Matthew Digby Wyatt in his report to the Institution of Civil Engineers[10].

Three years later, in 1854, the Munich Kristallpalast managed to do away with diagonal bracing entirely. The trusses were in this case a combination of cast and wrought iron and they were bolted to the posts on flanges. The plans give only this information which would have given us little clue as to the stability of the joint. But a report on the condition of the structure written in 1900 mentions clamps which served as subsidiary connectors between the posts and the trusses and which were obviously part of the original construction. The Munich Kristallpalast was gutted by fire in 1931, just five years before the Crystal Palace suffered the same fate. No photograph or detail sketch of this interesting detail has survived to give us more than the vaguest idea of the solution adopted[11].

The planning commission for the Crystal Palace in 1850 was divided as to whether or not the stiffening provided by the bolted and wedged frames combined perhaps with a few extra diagonal braces was sufficient. Professor George Bidell Airy (1801-1882), the Astronomer Royal, who was to play such a disastrous role in the affair of the Tay Bridge which collapsed in1879, was originally against Paxton's project as he considered it not stiff enough. He cited as examples the many iron-framed factory buildings built in the last years of the 18th century. In these structures, the beams and posts were indeed of cast iron, but the stiffening for the structure was provided by the surrounding masonry walls.

We are informed by Mallet, who wrote a very illuminating article on the structure of the Crystal Palace which has remained largely unknown because it was published only in 1862 in the rare report on the London exhibition of that year, that it was finally decided to build many more diagonal bars into the structure that had originally been planned, and he adds:

> "The building was taken down, and has been reerected at
> Sydenham in a manner greatly to increase its stability, as
> regards the greater part of the structure at least; and
> from 1851 to the present day London has never been visited
> by one of those 'first class' tornadoes that about twice in
> a century sweep over even our temperate regions. Yet,
> nevertheless, a very large wing of the Crystal Palace has

33

been actually blown down in the interval - that
portion of the whole, that probably more accurately
represented the structure of the building as it
stood in 1851, than any other part of it now does.
More than enough was destroyed to prove that
Professor Airy was not so widely wrong after all..."[12]

The structure stood in 1851 in spite of winds and above all in spite of
the thermal stresses in the structure caused by the summer sun. The
joints between the posts and trusses had been wedged tightly by means of
wrought iron keys in the width and iron and oaken keys in the length of
the building. These last were intended to guarantee room for thermal
expansion.[13] However, this was illusory. As the great wooden arches of
the barrel vault transept were totally unstiffened in their plane, a
useful expansion joint was built into the middle of the long side of the
building. Digby Wyatt commented on the possibility of this effect.[14]
Therefore, the two largest continuous roof surfaces were about 260 m long.
This was of course still too much, and how narrowly the building escaped
from collapse is implicit in Mallet's eyewitness account:

"We ourselves, however, had an opportunity, during
the early afternoon of one of the hottest days of the
summer of 1851, of examining with some accuracy the
effects of expansion by solar heat upon the frame of
the building; and we can testify to this as a fact,
that at the extreme western end, and at the fronts of
the nave galleries, where they had been here the
longest and the most heated, the columns were actually
about two inches out of plumb in the first range in
height only. Unaided by measurements, we could not
perceive that any change in the plumbness of the coupled
columns at the corners of the intersection of the nave
and transept had taken place. Their rigidity, and
probably other causes, appeared to have resisted the
whole thrust, and visited it upon the extreme outer
ends of the building.

"As we gazed up at these west-end galleries densely
crowded with people, and over the ample spread of the
nave equally thronged, and thought of the prodigious
cross-strains that were at that moment in unseen play
in the brittle stilting of the cast iron fabric, we
certainly felt that 'ignorance was bliss.' "[15]

The idea for the frame structure was obviously in advance of the technical
knowledge of the time. Detail solutions developed first not in the field
of architecture, but rather in the engineering projects of the time, in
the offices of the engineers who were struggling to understand the new
materials in terms of their technical and material characteristics.

Gradually further experience was gained, but it was a slow process. In
Paris, even greater roofs were attempted for the Palais de l'Industrie
for the exhibition of 1855. This structure which, together with the
single vaulted Galerie des Machines, was to become the prototype for the
later Machine Halls throughout the rest of the 19th century, was a long
hall with a triple barrel vault. The high central aisle of 48 m span,
or more than double that of the transept of the Crystal Palace, was the
largest yet built. Wrought-iron truss griders were used, the first known
instance of their use in such a way.[16]

34

The builder Barrault had had great difficulty with the glazing of these vaults; and Mallet writes:

> "Accordingly, in the Palais de l'Industrie of 1855,
> M. Barrault tells us that [the wedges used to stiffen the
> frames] ... were useless, and that under the bright sun
> of Paris the expansion of the building was sufficient to
> break glass and produce leakage; although structurally
> his building was incomparably better designed to break up
> into short lengths the expandable iron frame, everywhere
> but along the length of the three great parallel roofs ...
>
> "To meet the evil there is but one method - that pointed
> out and recommended by M. Barrault - namely, to subdivide
> all right-lined continuations in iron, cutting them up into
> separate short lengths, without abutting faces, though
> still connected by such ingenious arrangements as shall
> preserve at those points, staunchness or the other
> conditions required of the structures."[17]

The most interesting follow-up of the Crystal Palace was the Museum of Art and Science of 1855-1856 which stood on the site now occupied by part of the Victoria and Albert Museum in South Kensington.[18] Many of the problems inherent in the Crystal Palace structure were here avoided for the first time. The responsible planning commission, obviously influenced by the exhibition building, demanded a demountable iron structure. The startling project came from the architect D. Young of Edinburgh and the works were carried out by none other than Sir William Cubitt, the same who had been on the Building Committee and in charge of the works on the Crystal Palace. The museum was a rectangular building with three 12.8 m wide naves supported by 7.8 m high posts of cast iron. The roof trusses were arched and made of wrought iron. The inner posts were cylindrical and the outer H-shaped. Once again the skin was not conceived as a curtain wall structure (this was only to appear in Peter Ellis' Oriel Chambers of 1864),[19] but it was fixed between the outer posts in much the same manner as that of the Crystal Palace had been. The exterior was covered in corrugated iron, which provoked the editor of "the Builder", presumably George Godwin who had taken over that job in 1859, and who was later to become the chief advocate of reinforced concrete in Britain, to take an immediate dislike to the structure and dub it the "Brompton Boilers', a name which stuck. Today the building still stands, albeit with a brick skin, as the Bethnal Green Museum.

Once again stiffness was sought through portal bracing incorporating the wrought iron roof trusses. But in the longitudinal direction, the traditional knee-bracing was readopted. Joseph Paxton had already resumed this method in his conservatoire project of 1852 for the New York "Crystal Palace" of 1853 which was however not built to his plans. Finally this building was followed by Greene's Boat Store at Sheerness. Skempton showed that this structure derived directly from the "Brompton Boilers" in all essential details. Here, for the first time we encounter true portal bracing and a fully stiffened iron frame structure. Here too, we first encounter rational structural arguments for the adoption of the frame structure: poor foundation conditions requiring piling and consequently lightweight construction, quick erection and large window surfaces to light the large interior volume.

Thus in 1858 the development of frame structure had progressed far enough to support the evolution of the modern forms of warehouse, sky-

35

scraper and office block, essentially to be developed in Chicago in the last quarter of the century. The Crystal Palace, its structural problems and the resolution of these in subsequent projects, gave an impetus and a direction to the genesis of a structural type.

FOOTNOTES:

1. Siegfried Giedion: Time, Space and Architecture, the growth of a new tradition. 1941 Cambridge MA: Harvard University Press, 5th ed. 1974 pp. 249-255.

2. Tom F. Peters: Time is Money. Die Entwicklung des modernen Bauwesens. 1981 Stuttgart: Julius Hoffman, pp.159-183.

3. David M. Usborne: unpublished manuscript on the building process of the Crystal Palace. Communicated by the author.

4. Steen Eiler Rasmussen: London the Unique City. 1937 New York: Macmillan.

5. Charles Fowler, Jr.: The Crystal Palace Building, in The Illustrated Exhibitor. 1851 London, p.80.

6. Daniel Boorstin: The Americans, 2nd end. 1969 Penguin, vol. I, pp.193-196. This construction system became known to architectural historians through the work of Siegfried Giedion op.cit. pp.346-354. In 1942, a most comprehensive paper was published on this subject by Walker Field: A reexamination of the invention of the balloon-frame. Journal of the American Society of Architectural Historians, vol. 2, No.4, October, 1942, pp.3-29.

7. Charles Cowper in Charles Downes: The Building Erected in Hyde Park for the Great Exhibition of the Works of Industry of All Nations 1851 - 1852 London: John Weale, p.ii.

8. A. W. Skempton: The Boat Store 1851-1860 and its place in structural history. Lecture given in London 1960.

9. Matthew Digby Wyatt: On the Construction of the Building for the Exhibition of the Works of All Nations in 1851. Minutes of the Proceedings of the Institution of Civil Engineers, Vol.X, 1850-1851, p.150.

10. Carl W. Condit: The wind bracing of buildings. Scientific American Feb. 1974, pp.92-105.

11. Volker Huetsch: Der Muenchner Glaspalast 1854-1931. Geschichte und Bedeutung. Catalogue. 1981 Munich: Muenchner Stadtmuseum, p.48.

12. Robert Mallet: The Record of the International Exhibition 1862. no date (1862). Glasgow/Edinburgh/London: William Mackenzie, p.60.

13. Charles Cowper: op.cit. p.6 and Digby Wyatt, op.cit. p.151.

14. M. Digby Wyatt: op.cit. p.151.

15. R. Mallet, op.cit. p.59.

36

16.   S. Giedion: op.cit. pp.256-259.

17.   R. Mallet: op.cit. p.59.

18.   Giselher Hartung: Rationalismus und Eklektizismus: zur Rolle des
      Eisens in der zweiten Haelfte des 19. Jahrhunderts in
      Grossbritannien. Paper given at a meeting of the ICOMOS
      (International Committee on Monuments and Sites) 1981, Bad ems,
      Germany.

19.   Ibid.

37

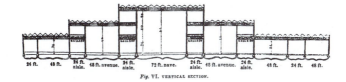

Fig. VI. VERTICAL SECTION.

Section through the modular structure of the Crystal Palace as built

Erection of the unstable, frail framework

38

The lack of stiffening and expansion joints in the
Crystal Palace make it remarkable that the building
stood up in 1851

The barrel-vault
of the transept
had no lateral
stiffening thus
providing an
expansion joint

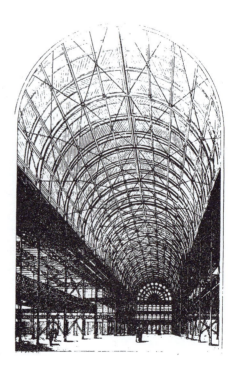

39

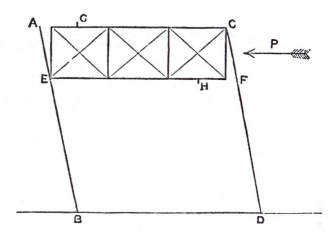

Diagram of the instability of the pseudo-frame structure of the post-and-truss system in cast-iron. Illustration from M. Digby Wyatt 1851. Republished in Mallet 1862.

The insufficient diagonal bracing and the pseudo-frame structure of the post-and-truss system

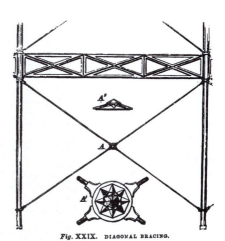

Fig. XXIX. DIAGONAL BRACING.

40

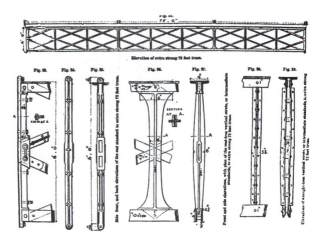

The components of a 72-foot truss consisting of cast-iron, wrought-iron and timber pieces

Outer skin of the building with wooden frame, cast iron decorative frame superimposed upon it and boarding finish between upper and lower ventilation louvers as carried out on the ground floor

41

Fig. 4.

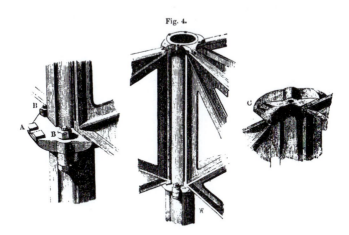

The cast-iron post-and-truss system used details derived
from machine engineering. However it was not capable of
guaranteeing a frame-effect.

Base-piece for
the columns of
the Crystal
Palace

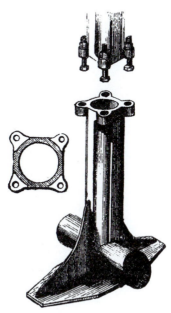

Fig. IX.

2

The Boat Store, Sheerness (1858–60) and its place in structural history

A.W. Skempton

INTRODUCTION

The Boat Store in H.M. Dockyard, Sheerness, stands today almost unchanged since it was erected a century ago. Distinctly modern in appearance, with frame-and-panel construction and windows running from end to end in four identical tiers, the building would be difficult to date from visual or stylistic evidence alone (Plate VI). Fortunately its date is securely established. The structural drawings were prepared in 1858 and work began that year. The iron columns bear plaques of 1859 and the contractor's final account was settled in August 1860 when construction had been completed. The reading of this Paper may, indeed, be considered an unofficial centenary occasion.

The Boat Store was discovered, in effect, by Mr. Eric de Maré during his photographic exploration of early industrial architecture in England; the results of which appear in "The Functional Tradition," a special number of the *Architectural Review*,[1] in July 1957, edited by Mr. J. M. Richards. It was at once apparent that the Boat Store merited further investigation. Accompanied by Mr. de Maré, I therefore made a detailed study of this building. Through the courtesy of Captain P. Chavasse, R.N., and his staff we were able to take measurements and photographs, and our attention was directed to a number of original working drawings, still kept at Sheerness, which proved that the present building was erected in strict accordance with these plans of 1858. The drawings were signed by G. T. Greene; and Mr. L. G. Harris, Civil Engineer in Chief, Admiralty, later told me that Colonel Greene was one of his predecessors, holding the office of Director of Engineering and Architectural Works from 1850 to 1864. With the help of Mr. A. H. Attrill of the Admiralty, and Mr. J. R. Rea of the Public Records Office, my assistant Miss Carlotta Hacker and I thereupon examined various plans and letters which enabled us to prove that Greene had been personally responsible for the design of the Boat Store. From these sources it was also possible to establish the dates of construction with some precision. Moreover, on looking through other drawings in the Admiralty and letters in the Public Records Office, we found that Greene had produced the general scheme for the great iron-framed Smithery at Portsmouth in 1851, although the details were worked out by Fox, Henderson & Co., the contractors (who erected this structure 1851–54), whilst he carried through virtually the whole design for a very large "roof" over No. 7 Slip at Chatham in 1852; 300 ft. long, 90 ft. high to the ridge with a central span of 82 ft., constructed 1852–54 by Messrs. Grissell, who were also contractors for the Boat Store.

Further research would no doubt reveal other works, and already Mrs. Charlotte Baden Powell[2] has obtained prints of the drawings of a number of buildings at Sheerness which show that Greene designed the iron-framed Gun-mounting Store of 1862 as well as several buildings that had load-bearing walls but made considerable use of interior iron-framing. The fine Smithery[3] at Sheerness 1856) is very probably also by him, and is clearly the immediate prototype for the Boat Store.

---

[1] Published in book form, with same title, London 1958.
[2] Thesis on the History of Sheerness Dockyard, Architectural Association School, 1959.
[3] Unfortunately all drawings of the Smithery have been lost.

THE BOAT STORE, SHEERNESS (1858–60)

Sufficient evidence is now available, therefore, to show that Greene must be reckoned a significant figure in the development of iron structure, with the Boat Store as his master work. The external appearance has already been briefly mentioned. But the interior is equally interesting; it includes H-section columns, I-beams and rivetted plate girders of 30 ft. span, with portal bracing. Indeed, but for the incontrovertible evidence of the 1858 drawings, it would be tempting to assume that substantial reconstruction had taken place around the end of the century. In fact, the only changes made during the past hundred years have been (i) re-tiling the roof, (ii) replacement of the original corrugated iron wall panels by their modern equivalent, (iii) substitution of brick panels below the ground-floor windows, (iv) replacement of the windows by a new set having five instead of four frames in each bay and (v) new sliding doors.

To anyone at all conversant with the history of nineteenth-century building construction it will be obvious that the Boat Store provides a challenge. A mere 8 years later than the Crystal Palace, it seems to belong to a different age, in spite of the advanced technique of that work. Moreover, the Boat Store was completed 12 years before the famous Menier factory in France, traditionally though quite incorrectly considered to be the first multi-storey iron-framed building. Also, the Menier factory is far less elegant structurally, whilst architecturally it is altogether typical of the late Victorian period.

PART I

DESCRIPTION OF THE BOAT STORE

The Boat Store consists essentially of two buildings or "aisles" four storeys high flanking a central "nave" (Fig. 1). The entire structure is 210 ft. long by 135 ft. wide with a skylight along the length of the roof over the nave, and windows extending from end to end of the external walls. The total height to the ridge is 53 ft. The nave is spanned by three travelling girders—one at each floor level. Boats are manoeuvred into position on the floor, then hoisted on to a trolley, or "boat truck," on any one of the travellers, which is moved into the required position, and the truck is run off on to the adjacent floor (Plate VII, Fig. 1).

There are four rows of columns in each aisle, spaced at 14 ft. 6 in. centres transversally and at 30 ft. centres longitudinally except in the walls, where they are 15 ft. apart (Plate VIII). Each column is founded on four 12 in. diam. whole-timber piles driven to a depth of about 60 ft. below ground level. The piles are cut off 12 ft. below the surface and capped with four 12 in. by 12 in. timbers set in concrete. A 3 ft. by 3 ft. brick pier is built up, with a 12 in. thick granite block to receive the column base (Fig. 2). The columns (referred to as "standards" in the original drawings) are cast-iron H-section members with 9 in. flanges and different depths in each storey, but typically 14 in. (Plate IX). They were cast in two lengths and bolted together; just below second-floor level, for the internal columns, and just above this floor, for the external columns (Plate X, Fig. 1). The corner columns are 9 in. sq. in section (hollow) with projecting flanges on the two outer faces. They were cast in four lengths (Plate X, Fig. 2). The height of the columns is 40 ft.

The ground floor is a concrete slab, but the upper three floors consist of oak planks 9 in. wide by 3 in. thick. These run longitudinally and are supported on cast-iron transverse I-section beams at 30 ft. centres on plan, and by intermediate timber joists at 7 ft. 6 in. centres (Plate XI). The beams are 12 in. deep with 6 in. flanges but the flange width is increased to 9 in. at the ends to agree with the flanges of the columns (Plate XII). The first-floor joists are 12 in. by 6 in. and those supporting the second and third floors are 12 in. by 4 in. and 12 in. by 3 in. respectively.[1] The beams have a clear span of 13 ft. 6 in. and frame into the columns, but the joists bear on longitudinal wrought-iron plate

---

[1] The safe loadings are now given as 60, 40 and 30 lb. per sq. ft. for the first, second and third floors. The original loadings are not known.

THE BOAT STORE, SHEERNESS (1858–60)

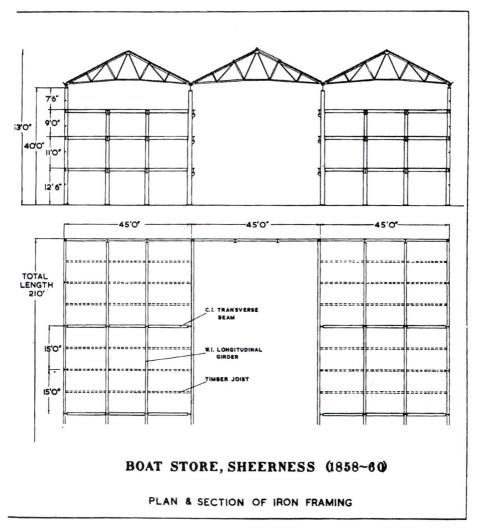

BOAT STORE, SHEERNESS (1858–60)

PLAN & SECTION OF IRON FRAMING

Fig. 1. (Drawn by the Author.)

·ders of 29 ft. 9 in. span (Plate XIII, Fig. 1). These floor girders are 18 in. deep by 12 in. wide, d the roof trusses are supported on similar girders 24 in. deep. The web plates are ½ in. thick in ree lengths, with joint plates, and T-stiffeners every 7 ft. 6 in. The flanges are made up from three 16 in. plates in six lengths (Plate XIV). Rivets 1 in. diam. are used throughout. The wall beams outside girders" on the drawings) are of cast iron 12 in. deep with 9 in. flanges (Plate XII). The :b is stiffened by raised panels which give a pleasant decorative effect, since these beams, like the .ter flanges of the columns, can be seen in the elevations. All the beams and girders are fixed to

THE BOAT STORE, SHEERNESS (1858–60)

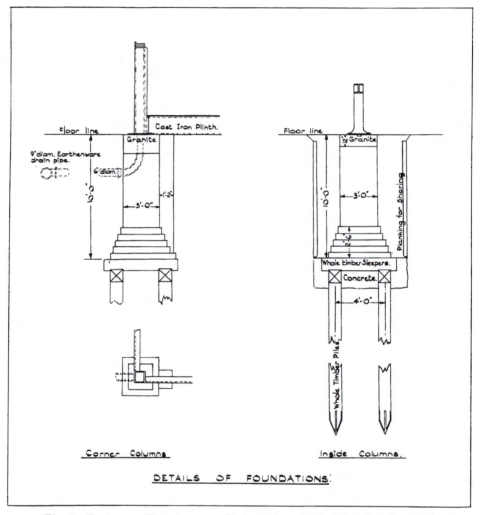

Fig. 2. Details of Foundations. (Redrawn from Original Drawing No. 2810.)

the columns by four ¾ in. bolts at each connection, and the stability of the whole building is entirely dependent on the portal bracing derived from the rigidity of these joints (Plate XIII, Fig. 2). There can be no doubt that the cast-iron beams were regarded by the designer as an essential component of stability. They are called "transverse bracing girders" on the working drawing (Plate XII) and, as we have seen, the timber joists are sufficient merely to support the floor. Vertical reactions at the ends of the beams and girders are transmitted by cantilever brackets on the columns.

The windows rest on a 6 in. by 4 in. angle iron. Originally they were of the sliding-sash type, but recently they have been replaced by casement windows (Plate VII, Fig. 2). The wall panels,

THE BOAT STORE, SHEERNESS (1858–60)

consisting of corrugated iron, nestle in behind the column flanges and are supported by four small wrought-iron angles in each bay (Plate XV). There is a cast-iron plinth 18 in. deep along the base of the walls.

Across the width of the building there are three pitched roofs of 45 ft. span, supported by wrought-iron tension members and cruciform section cast-iron struts displaying a nice entasis. These trusses are pin-jointed at their supports on the longitudinal girders and external capping beams. The slates were originally carried on 3 in. by 2 in. battens at 11 in. centres, spanning 7 ft. 6 in. between the trusses. Rainwater is carried off in iron gutters and down the interior of the corner columns. Expansion joints are provided in the gutters, but I have not been able to find any other expansion joints in the building.

The structural details are admirably thought out and executed. They bear comparison with the best modern work, such as that by Mies van der Rohe and Frank Kornacker in the Lake Shore Apartments, Chicago, 1950–51. The elevations of the Boat Store are also of a high quality; crisp, orderly and well proportioned.

DRAWINGS, LETTERS, AND BUILDING DATES

The working drawings are in Indian ink on Imperial paper, headed *SHEERNESS YARD, New Boat Store*, signed G. T. Greene, with the date and the letters S. H. standing for Somerset House where the Director of Works Department was situated at this time.[1] Each drawing carried a serial number and the initials of one or other of the five draughtsmen employed. There are also three drawings prepared at Sheerness, signed by F. Turner, Clerk of Works, and his assistant, John W. Johnstone. The date on the Somerset House drawings corresponds to the day on which they were sent to the Captain Superintendent at Sheerness. Nine of these still exist. But paper tracings were retained in London for record and what seems to be an almost complete set is in possession of the Civil Engineer in Chief. A second set of tracings must have been sent to the contractor.

It appears that none of the original letters relating to the Boat Store has survived. Yet the essential contents of several are known from the Digest of Letters to the Secretary, Admiralty, now kept in the Public Records Office.[2] We first hear of the Boat Store in a letter from Greene, 1 September 1855, in which he recommends that the Captain Superintendent be instructed as to a number of requirements to be submitted to the Board of Admiralty, on their annual Visitation to Sheerness, for consideration in the Estimates for 1856–57. Included in this list is "A Store Boat House." It seems, however, that as a first step the Board only approved the provision of an additional floor on the old single-storey boat house of 1830; and the contract for this work was let to Fox, Henderson & Co. in July 1856. In the next year, nevertheless, on the occasion of their Lordships' visitation in July, they authorised the construction of a "Boat House Store," submitted by the Captain Superintendent with the note "much required." The site was then occupied by a timber boat shed. A plan by Turner and Johnstone dated 28 April 1858, "shewing in red the site of New Store Boat House and also the proposed site for re-erecting the centre portion of present Wooden Boat Shed" was forwarded by Greene to the Secretary with the suggestion that the lean-to structures on each side of the present

---

[1] I am indebted to Mr. C. F. Armstrong, Superintending Civil Engineer, Admiralty, for "translating" these initials: also to Lt. M. W. Collinson, R.N., at Sheerness, who first deciphered Greene's almost illegible signature.

[2] Almost all Admiralty correspondence dating from the early 1850's seems to have been lost. Some letters in the period 1858–60 still exist, but these include very few relating to buildings and none of any importance on Sheerness.

THE BOAT STORE, SHEERNESS (1858–60)

shed be cleared away, and the contractors be called to take down and re-erect the shed itself, "the expense being charged to the Vote for the New Boat Store." Tenders were received on 14 May, and on 25 May Messrs. Kirk & Parry were engaged for this work.

Meanwhile the design of the Boat Store had evidently been well advanced, for a *General Plan* and *Details of Foundations* had been sent to Sheerness on 28 April, returned to the drawing office on 4 May and re-sent to Sheerness on 9 May. These show the precise location of the columns, and their section, as well as the cast-iron plinth and full details of the foundations. The drainage system for the corner columns is also shown. It is, indeed, certain that a design with at least the leading dimensions had already been produced for there is a note that estimates for the Boat Store and the adjacent Anchor Rack were approved on 6 May. Moreover, the drawing for the foundations, which was sent to Sheerness on 28 April 1858, had the serial number 2810; whilst the working drawings[1] (mentioned in the next paragraph) are numbered consecutively from 2811 to 2823. The very distinct possibility therefore exists that the entire design in all its detail[2] was complete by about this date.

On 17 August Kirk & Parry were reminded of "The time for completion of the necessary works, with a view to expediting same" and on 2 September they were engaged to fit up machinery for the new anchor rack, situated between the Boat Store and the small basin. Thus in all probability the site had been cleared by September 1858, and it is likely that work on the foundations began in this or the following month. Unfortunately the date of the main contract, which was awarded to Messrs. Henry Grissell, is not recorded. But they must have been well under way by 17 November when they applied for an advance of £3,000—paid on 30 November—and the thirteen ironwork drawings were sent from Somerset House to Sheerness on 11 November. Perhaps erection of the super-structure was shortly due to commence. At any rate, Grissells were bound by contract to complete the work by 1 May 1859; and a construction period of much less than five winter months could hardly be envisaged. In the event the structural framework and cladding were completed shortly before 20 July 1859, when Greene submitted the contractor's claim for payment of the balance. The précis of this letter states that "by the *strict* term of the Contract Messrs. Grissell are liable to a penalty of £10 a week for the time the work remained unfinished after May 1st. But as great exertions at great expense were made; and the delay caused no inconvenience, the penalty is not enforced; and payment of £1,491 11s. 4d., the balance of the Contract, minus £6 8s. 8d. for Yard stores supplied, should be allowed." The payment was made on 26 July.

The flooring, however, was to be carried out by direct labour and a plan "shewing the proposed manner of forming the floors" was prepared at Sheerness in May 1859. The proposal involved 11 in. by 3 in. joists at 16 in. centres spanning between the wrought-iron girders, and the wall beams; with a slatted floor. But the scheme actually carried out is shown on a drawing sent from London to Sheerness on 3 November, where joists at 7 ft. 6 in. centres are supported by cast-iron shoes fixed on the girders and carry a floor of 9 in. by 3 in. oak plankings said to be ship's timber.

Earlier in 1859 working drawings of the travellers and the associated machinery had been prepared, together with details of sliding doors at the west end. Messrs. Grissell's tender "to supply Cradles to take boats into store, and one traveller and Boat truck to each of the 3 stages, for £941" was submitted on 5 July, and approved 8 August. The relevant drawings were sent to Sheerness on 9 July. Some modifications to the sliding doors were proposed by Turner in February 1860, and the contractors submitted their final account on 19 July. This was at once recommended to the Treasury, where payment was authorised on 2 August 1860. It is probable that the flooring had also been completed by that date. Apart from a few comparatively modern alterations, previously mentioned ,

---

[1] A list of all surviving drawings is given in Appendix II.
[2] With one exception, namely the joints in the H-columns at second-floor level. These must have been added by Grissell for ease of casting.

THE BOAT STORE, SHEERNESS (1858–60)

the only additional work was the signalman's look-out turret placed on the roof in 1866. A summary of progress is thus as follows:—

July 1857—construction authorised.
April 1858—design well advanced and estimates submitted.
Sept. 1858—site cleared and foundations begun soon afterwards.
Nov. 1858—working drawings of ironwork sent to Sheerness.
July 1859—erection of structural ironwork completed.
Aug. 1859—contract let for travellers, etc.
Nov. 1859—floor construction started.
July 1860—contractor's final payment recommended.

The reasons for adopting an iron-framed structure are not given in the available documents. There are, however, at least three evident advantages over a brick-wall building: (*a*) speed of construction, (*b*) larger windows, giving better light on the floors, (*c*) smaller foundation loads. The last point is perhaps the most important. The older buildings at Sheerness, with load-bearing walls, had massive inverted arch foundations supported by a great number of piles.

GODFREY GREENE (1807–86)

Godfrey Thomas Greene, the designer of the Boat Store, was born in 1807, the son of Major Anthony Greene of the Honourable East India Company Service. At the age of 14 he entered the Military College, Addiscombe, and from 1823 to 1825 was trained as an engineer at Chatham under Colonel (later General Sir Charles) Pasley, F.R.S. Greene then left for Bengal, where he took part, in December 1826, in the gallant siege and capture of Bhurtpore. Later he served for 3 years in the Canal Department, North-West Provinces, and in 1831 married Harriet Cowell, the daughter of William Cowell, Civil and Sessions Judge, India. Afterwards he was successively Executive Engineer at Bareilly, Cawnpore and Dinapore. In May 1849 Greene left the H.E.I.C.S. with the rank of Colonel and early in the following year was appointed Director of Engineering and Architectural Works, Admiralty, a post which he held until 1864. On retirement he was created C.B. in "acknowledgement of the services he had rendered to the Admiralty." During the last 20 years of his life he had a house in Eastbourne, and died there on 27 December 1886.[1]

When Greene went to the Admiralty his Department consisted of the Director and the Chief Assistant, William Scamp, with three draughtsmen (principal, James Trotter) and seven clerks, occupying a suite of rooms in the south-west corner of Somerset House. Additionally, there were "Officers of Royal Engineers in charge of Works" at Portsmouth (Captain Henry James), Chatham (Captain Thomas Mould) and Devonport (Captain Montgomery Williams). A few years earlier, and for some time previously, Captains of the Royal Engineers had also been stationed at Woolwich and Pembroke, but after retirement they were not replaced, and when Mould was transferred to Portsmouth (succeeding James) his post at Chatham was not filled. By 1853 Mould and Williams had both retired and no further appointments were made at any of the yards.[2]

This gradual centralisation caused only a slight expansion of the Department in Somerset House. In August 1853 the establishment was still as in 1850 (and, for that matter, as in 1847 when a survey of the rooms was carried out), but Scamp's salary had been increased from £650 to £800 a year. By 1858, when details are next vailable, the senior staff again consisted of Greene and Scamp (with the

---

[1] The brief outline of Greene's career, in this paragraph, is chiefly taken from his obituary notice in *The Times*, which follows Debrett closely, and from "List of Officers of Corps of the Royal Engineers from 1660–1898."
[2] Until the establishment of Superintendent Civil Engineers at Devonport (1859), Portsmouth (1864) and Chatham (1865).

THE BOAT STORE, SHEERNESS (1858–60)

title Deputy Director of Works, from 1855, but with the same salary—Greene's salary was £1,000). The number of draughtsmen had been doubled, however, in direct proportion to the amount of work carried out (£265,000 in 1852, £586,000 in 1858), and the two principal draughtsmen were now E. J. Woodhead and W. H. Mansbridge. Two rooms only were still allocated to the clerks, so their number cannot have increased appreciably. There were also three "model rooms" and it is possible that the superb model of Sheerness may have been made in Somerset House around this time.[1]

William Scamp was evidently a civil engineer of great ability. He joined the Admiralty about 1838 and entered the Director of Works Department in 1845. In supporting (unsuccessfully) Scamp's application for an increased salary, Greene wrote to the Secretary (9.12.58): "His reputation at home and abroad had been established long before I joined the Department. All the Home Establishments had more or less been indebted to his professional ability and skill, and Gibraltar, Malta and Bermuda had been, so to say, entirely formed under his supervision; and the very Office I hold was made efficient by his energy and ability . . . I have never known him otherwise than devoted to his profession . . . and the whole Department . . . has the impress of his genius and labour." Most of Scamp's work seems to have been in planning and in heavy engineering works, whilst Greene was more concerned with buildings (and administration, of course). Naturally the Director and his Deputy, as the two engineers in the Department, would have worked together on many projects but, in general, they signed individually the drawings for which they were responsible. Thus, to take a few examples, we find Greene's signature on drawings for the Chatham Slip Roof in 1852, but the plans and the report of January 1857 on "Design for Extending and Improving her Majesty's Dockyard at Chatham" are signed by Scamp, as are the drawings for additions to the No. 7 slip in October 1856. Similarly Greene's name is on all the Sheerness Boat Store drawings (except for those by Turner), whilst an important report on Portsmouth Harbour and Dockyard Extension, in February 1863, is by Scamp: although it was Greene who piloted the Report through the Parliamentary Select Committee on Dockyards the following year.

A particularly interesting case is provided by the drawings for the Boiler Shop at Sheerness. These are initialled by Scamp, but on 26 December 1854 we find a sketch by Greene of details concerning the iron ties for a girder, where it bears on a wall. Then comes a pencil drawing setting out the idea more fully, and finally the tracing of the final drawing, dated 28 December, initialled by Scamp and the draughtsman James Trotter. Presumably some problem had suddenly arisen during construction;[2] so Greene came into the office on Boxing Day, discussed the point with his deputy who immediately got the drawing made and sent down to Sheerness. And, at this time, Greene was designing the Saw Mills and Testing House, the contracts for which were awarded in May 1856 to Rigby (general work) and in July to Fox, Henderson & Co. (ironwork).

Another glimpse of the day-to-day work is seen in the drawings for the Gun-mounting Store. This was designed by Greene, and the contract let in November 1861 (to W. R. Spencelayh of Rochester) but the purlins were omitted in the drawing of the timber roof truss. One imagines a troubled Clerk of Works writing to Somerset House, and we find a tracing entitled "Sketch showing the additions of Purlins to Roof" signed by Scamp and endorsed "The original given to Mr. Turner on his visit to this office, 13 Jany. 1862."

These minutiae have been recorded since they show that Greene was no mere official, signing the drawings without having had more than a general control over the work. Moreover his experience as a structural designer in iron can to some extent be studied from the drawings and records. Thus,

---

[1] Kept until recently in the Boat Store but now, I believe, to be moved to Chatham. This vast model shows all the docks and walls, with their pile foundations, and the various buildings, in great detail.
[2] Work had begun in October, with Messrs. Rigby as building contractors and Grissell supplying the ironwork.

THE BOAT STORE, SHEERNESS (1858–60)

n April 1851 he presented an outline design for the new Smithery at Portsmouth to be erected entirely with iron framing, in contrast with the proposals from the officers at the yard for a brick building. In his there can be little doubt he was inspired by the Crystal Palace, then just completed. But his knowledge of detailing was probably limited; and, in fact, the details[1] were worked out by the contractors Fox, Henderson & Co., using some of the ideas they had similarly evolved for Paxton's design. On the other hand, in his next big iron structure, the No. 7 Slip Roof at Chatham, Greene produced a set of eight drawings (16 July 1852) showing a complete design, with H-section iron columns; although from the absence of *working* drawings at the Admiralty it is probable that the contractors in this case were later responsible for the particulars of connections and other technicalities of the ironwork. And this is the more likely since the work was carried out by Grissell who, as will be seen, was renowned for his unsparing attention to detail.

Regarding the Sheerness Boat Store, however, the evidence of the serial numbers on the drawings suggests that the design had been fully worked out by April 1858, and it seems improbable that Grissell had already been awarded the contract. But to pursue this point any further is somewhat academic, for Greene would have had ample opportunity to acquire the necessary knowledge, not only from the jobs at Portsmouth and Chatham but also from a number of buildings at Sheerness, including the Smithery which was erected by Grissell 1855–56. The extent of Greene's responsibility for these buildings has received considerable attention[2] since no mention of his name is known in any previous publication dealing with structural or architectural history in the mid-nineteenth century. Yet as we now see he can be credited with the basic idea of the Portsmouth Smithery, all but the minute details of the Chatham No. 7 Roof, and the entire design of the Sheerness Boat Store: all decidedly notable, and early, iron-frame structures.

HENRY GRISSELL (1817–83)

Each corner column of the Boat Store bears an oval plaque inscribed:—

Henry Grissell 1859

Regents Canal Iron Works
London

Grissell was well-known as an iron founder, machinist and contractor for structural iron. A pupil and then assistant of John Joseph Bramah, he set up a partnership with his brother Martin[3] and started in business at the Regent's Canal Ironworks, Eagle Wharf Road, Hoxton, on the south bank of the canal, in 1841. One of their earliest big contracts was the iron roof over London Bridge Station in 1844 and, at about the same time, they were engaged to supply the iron floors and roofs of the new Houses of Parliament, then being built by their elder brother Thomas and his partner (and cousin) Morton Peto.[4] In 1846 they constructed the 60 ft. span composite wrought- and cast-iron plate girder bridge at Chalk Farm, to Robert Stephenson's design, and in the following year his

---

[1] i.e. details of the ironwork. There are many working drawings by Greene for the foundations, brick chimneys, etc., some of which have technical memoranda added in his own handwriting. It should be noted that Fox Henderson & Co. hardly altered Greene's basic design for the structure.

[2] It is clear that the draughtsmen could have done little apart from the physical task of producing the drawings and tracings. The average output from the office between 1854 and 1859 amounted to nine drawings and probably as many tracings, a week. Moreover, an examination of the Boat Store drawings (see Appendix) shows that M. T. C. drew the external and internal standards, but J. W. C. drew the intermediate and corner standards. Similarly W. H. M. made the drawing for the roof principals but C. D. A. drew the other roof details.

[3] Martin seems to have left the firm around 1856.

[4] Grissell and Peto carried out many important contracts during their partnership 1830–46. Grissell's mother was Ann Peto, aunt to Morton Peto; and the latter, in 1831, married Mary Grissell, the sister of Thomas, Henry and Martin (H. Peto, *Sir Morton Peto: a Memorial Sketch*, London, 1893).

THE BOAT STORE, SHEERNESS (1858–60)

120 ft. span cast-iron girder bridge over the Nene at Wisbech. Stephenson "had a very high opinion of Mr. Henry Grissell, which was reciprocated with the greatest veneration," and several of the great engineer's later bridges were fabricated at the Regent's Canal Ironworks, including three in Egypt at Benha and Berket-el-Saba (both completed 1855) and at Kaffr-Azayat (completed 1860). In the naval dockyards, as we have seen, Grissell erected the No. 7 Slip Roof at Chatham[1] (1852–54), the Boat Store at Sheerness (1858–60) and several other buildings. His technical knowledge was considerable and the Regent's Canal Ironworks soon gained a reputation as a testing laboratory. Thus, in 1843, John Rastrick was making tests there on cast iron,[2] whilst in 1847 compression tests were carried out under the direction of J. M. Rendell on specimens of Portland cement concrete, 9 in. sq. by 18 in. long, in a hydraulic testing machine of 75 tons capacity.[3] In the same year Grissell was chosen, among a most distinguished gathering, to give evidence before the Royal Commission on the Application of Iron to Railway Structures.

Some idea of his character is conveyed by the following paragraph from the obituary notice in the *Proceedings Inst. Civil Engineers*:—[4]

> "No man could be more devoted to his business than was Henry Grissell: his work always possessed charms for him, and the love of his art was carried to such an extent as to make it almost a mania. He scarcely ever had a contract but he must do some-thing, at his own cost, to improve the details: and he would frequently lose his profit by this process of the French-polishing other people's work; in most cases it was unappreciated, sometimes it even led him into trouble. Notwithstanding all this, what he did was honestly meant, he being entirely free from ambitious notions or unjust motives. He was often known amongst engineers as 'Iron Henry,' and was loved and respected by all with whom he was associated."

The workmanship of the Boat Store is first-class, and fully justifies the high opinion of his contemporaries. It is pleasant to recall that Greene advised not enforcing the penalty for delay in completing the contract, "as great exertions at great expense were made, and the delay caused no inconvenience." The castings and the 30 ft. girders would have been shipped from Eagle Wharf Road, along the canal and down the river to Sheerness. No doubt they were proof-loaded before leaving the works.

PART II

HISTORICAL SIGNIFICANCE OF THE BOAT STORE

Our knowledge of structural ironwork in the mid-nineteenth century is far from complete; yet three claims can be made for the Boat Store with some confidence.

(i)   It is a very early example of a multi-storey iron-framed building.

(ii) It is perhaps the first of such buildings to use simple H-section columns and beams, in contrast with the more elaborate and decorated forms typical of the period.[5]

(iii) With well-proportioned elevations and a sensitive use of materials, it has an aesthetic value comparable to its structural interest: and we may be justified in considering this building a prototype of modern architecture.[6]

---

[1] The columns are inscribed "H. & M. D. GRISSELL, London, 1853."
[2] *Report of the Commissioners appointed to enquire into the Application of Iron to Railway Structures*, London, 1849, p. 387.
[3] *Min. Proc. Inst. C.E.*, Vol. 11, 1852, p. 497. The cement was manufactured by J. B. White & Sons.
[4] Vol. 73, 1883, pp. 376–378. Grissell was elected an Associate in 1843.
[5] For a brief historical analysis of the structural elements of the Boat Store, see Appendix I.
[6] Dr. Pevsner tells me that he is including the Boat Store in the new edition of *Pioneers of the Modern Movement*. This book (2nd ed., 1949) and S. Giedion's *Space, Time and Architecture* (1949) are standard works on the topics considered in Part II of the present Paper.

THE BOAT STORE, SHEERNESS (1858–60)

Two main classes of iron-framed structures can be recognised; those depending on the arch, and those in which the rectangular element of the beam and column is dominant. The former, stemming from Ironbridge and including (besides countless bridges) the Kew Palm House, St. Pancras Station and the Galerie des Machines in Paris, are not our present concern.

Iron beams and columns were first used, in conjunction, for the interior framing of the Benyons & Marsnall flax mill at Shrewsbury 1796–97 by Charles Bage, developing the lead given by his friend William Strutt in the Derby cotton mill of 1792–93. This form of construction, with load-bearing external brick walls, rapidly became standard practice in textile mills, warehouses, and other buildings where a fireproof structure was required.[1] The floors were usually carried on segmental brick arches springing from the beams, but in some cases flat stone slabs spanned directly between closely-spaced beams framing into iron girders.[2] The lateral stability of these structures, typically five or six storeys high, was provided by the massive exterior walls. And it was not until many years after the Shrewsbury mill that anyone dared to erect a completely iron-framed building of even moderate height constructed exclusively of beams and columns: and depending, therefore, on portal bracing for lateral stiffness.

Possibly the earliest multi-storey building of this type was the factory erected 1848–49 at the corner of Centre and Duane Street, New York, by James Bogardus.[3] Although quite famous in its day, and mentioned several times in recent publications, detailed information on this structure is curiously lacking. Judging from a contemporary illustration, and from drawings in Bogardus's U.S. Patent of 1850 for "The Construction of the Frame, Roof and Floors of Iron Buildings," it appears that the two street elevations, rising to a height of four storeys, consisted of hollow semi-columns and channel lintels, bolted together with iron wall-panels beneath the windows. It also seems that the floors were supported on composite cast and wrought-iron beams and round columns. However, no specific description of the interior construction has come to light, and the building was demolished when Duane Street was widened in 1859.

More definite information is available for a small flour mill designed and built by Fairbairn in 1840, of which Bogardus was almost certainly aware. This had plate iron walls stiffened by hollow iron pilasters and beams, and internal iron framing carrying two floors, surmounted by an arched roof formed of plates of corrugated sheet iron.[4] When completed this was exhibited in Fairbairn's Millwall works, before being dismantled and shipped to Istanbul. It was the forerunner of a whole series of prefabricated iron houses, churches and warehouses exported to the Colonies and the western States. But the flour mill is hardly an iron-framed building in the strictest sense and, for stability, it depended partially on a transverse brick wall supporting the main shaft of the machinery.

It is difficult to say whether any other multi-storey buildings were constructed, before 1858, similar to the Bogardus factory (presuming this had iron-framed rear and side walls). Iron fronts were commonly used from about 1845 for the next 30 years, owing to the economical way in which they could be used to reproduce architectural detail, but behind these fronts brick partition walls and timber floors were generally employed and, in most cases, brick party walls and rear walls as well.[5] Nevertheless there may have been a few buildings erected in the 'fifties with iron fronts used

---

[1] H. R. Johnson and A. W. Skempton, "William Strutt's cotton mills, 1793–1812," *Trans. Newcomen Soc.*, Vol. XXX, 1956, pp. 179–201.

[2] As in the two-storey saw mill at Chatham (1813–14) designed by Marc Brunel; and on a large scale in the Quadrangular Storehouse, Sheerness (1824–29) by Edward Holl.

[3] Turpin C. Bannister, "Bogardus revisited," *Journ. Soc. Arch. Historians*, Vol. 15, 1956, pp. 12–22, and Vol. 16, 1957, pp. 11–19.

[4] William Fairbairn, *Treatise on Mills and Millwork*, Part II, London, 1863.

[5] W. Knight Sturges, "Cast iron in New York," *Arch. Review*, Vol. 114, 1953, pp. 233–237.

THE BOAT STORE, SHEERNESS, (1858–60)

structurally on all four elevations and with interior iron framing.[1] There were, on the other hand, several multi-storey buildings of this period in which iron framing was used throughout the interior and in one or two external walls—the other walls being of brick. The load-bearing walls solved the stability problem but, nevertheless, this type of construction is of interest since it marks an increasing use of structural ironwork in city buildings. A particularly successful example, architecturally speaking, is the four-storey building, with shops on the ground floor, at the corner of Jamaica Street and Argyle Street in Glasgow, to which Professor Hitchcock has drawn attention.[2] Construction began in 1855 and, when nearing completion, the *Illustrated London News* (1 March 1856) gave a good description of this "novel edifice." The two street fronts (facing east and south) are entirely of iron and glass, the columns being about 20 ft. apart, whilst the north and west "gable" walls are of brick. The interior framing consists of columns, in line with those in the street walls, supporting iron girders and beams with timber joists and flooring. Apparently the design was carried out by Robert McConnell, the contractor for the ironwork.

In none of these buildings, however, do we see a clearly expressed iron frame, as in the Boat Store. And the true origins are more probably to be found in single-storey shed-type structures such as the Hungerford Fish Market (1835) and various greenhouses. At least there can be no doubt that these provided the precedent for the Crystal Palace, which must be given the distinction of being the first great rectilinear iron-framed building.[3] The original design was produced by Joseph Paxton with the assistance of W. H. Barlow in June 1850. Fox, Henderson & Co. submitted a tender on 10 July and they were awarded the contract 16 days later. The working drawings, for a somewhat modified design, were then prepared in the incredibly short period of 7 weeks by Charles Fox and C. H. Wild with William Cubitt as consultant; the first column was set on 26 September and the building completed by the end of January 1851, with a labour force averaging about 1,600 men. Most of the structural iron was cast by the subcontracting firms of Cochrane and Jobson, the wrought iron was fabricated by Fothergill and the glass by Chance, Brotherton & Co.

In section the Crystal Palace comprised a central "nave" 72 ft. wide and 62 ft. high, flanked by "aisles" 24 ft. wide, two further "naves" 48 ft. wide and 42 ft. and 22 ft. high, each with an aisle 24 ft. wide. The total width was therefore 408 ft., whilst the length of the building was 1,848 ft. The roofs were carried on wrought-iron trellis girders of 72 ft. and 48 ft. span, but the longtitudinal and transverse bracing was provided by cast-iron trellis girders 3 ft. deep, rigidly fixed to the columns (Fig. 3). In addition, but only "as a measure of extra precaution," diagonal bracing was inserted in a few bays. The columns were essentially hollow cylinders with four "flats," giving the appearance of an octagonal section. The girders in the aisles of the central nave were arranged in three tiers, and those at the first stage supported a timber-floored gallery on timber beams and joists. A similar gallery was provided in the middle aisles on each side.[4] Apart from the extraordinary feats of design and construction, one of the most remarkable aspects of the structure was the portal bracing, achieved by the fixed-end girders. This system gave rise to much discussion at the time and was a decided novelty; at least as applied on so vast a scale.[5] But the entire Crystal Palace was virtually without

---

[1] The large five-storey store on Broadway, New York, built for A. T. Stewart and later owned by John Wanamaker, appears to have been of this type, with timber floors and joists. But the first portion of this building was opened in 1863 and it was not completed until about 1868 (A. Burnham, *Arch. Record*, Vol. 120, 1956, pp. 273–279).

[2] H. R. Hitchcock, "Early cast iron façades," *Arch. Review*, Vol. 109, 1951, pp. 113–116.

[3] For earlier works, including those by Paxton, see P. Morton Shand, "The Crystal Palace as structure and precedent," *Arch. Review*, Vol. 81, 1937, pp. 65–72, and H. R. Hitchcock, *Early Victorian Architecture in Britain*, London, 1954 (Chaps. 15 and 16). Also N. Pevsner, "Early iron curvilinear hothouses," *Arch. Review*, Vol. 106, 1949, pp. 188–189.

[4] An excellent brief account, with many contemporary illustrations, is given by C. H. Gibbs-Smith, *The Great Exhibition of 1851*, London, 1950.

[5] See the discussion at the Institution of Civil Engineers, lasting three evenings, following the paper by M. D. Wyatt, January 1851. See also Appendix I.

THE BOAT STORE, SHEERNESS, (1858–60)

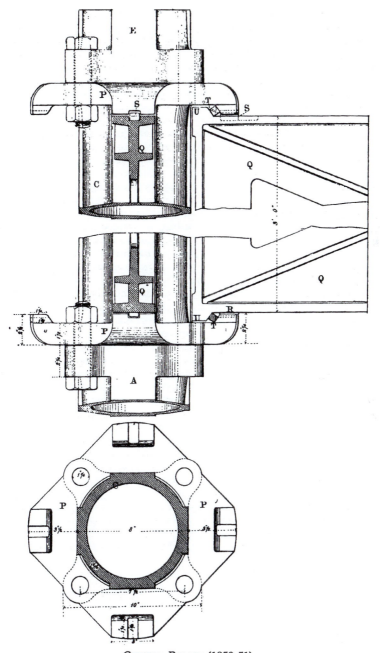

CRYSTAL PALACE (1850-51).
Fig. 3.   Detail of Column-Beam Connection.

69

THE BOAT STORE, SHEERNESS (1858–60)

precedent, and its success led, almost at once, to a number of great iron-framed structures which could hardly have been imagined a few years before.

Here we may merely note the construction of similar exhibition buildings in New York and Dublin, both completed in 1853, and Les Halles in Paris, the major part of which was erected 1854–57. We may also mention, again, that Greene was inspired by the Crystal Palace to design the Portsmouth Smithery (1851–54), with the same contractors (Fox, Henderson & Co.) and a closely related structural vocabulary; whilst the Chatham No. 7 Slip (1852–54) although showing more of Greene's personality, still retains unmistakable features of the 1851 structure. Another descendant was the Museum of Science and Art on Brompton Road. Erected in 1856 by Charles D. Young & Co.[1] under the direction of William Cubitt, this was the first of the South Kensington museums and colleges built in accordance with the Prince Consort's plan, on land purchased by means of the surplus funds of the Exhibition. The cross section consisted of a nave and two aisles, all 42 ft. wide, with three light wrought-iron truss roofs supported on cast-iron columns 26 ft. high. The aisles contained a floor carried on two rows of columns at 14 ft. centres with longitudinal wrought-iron plate girders and similar cross beams at 7 ft. centres, and timber joists running longitudinally 2 ft. 4 in. apart (Fig. 4). The wall columns were H-section, spaced every 7 ft., but all the others were of circular section. The wall panels were corrugated iron backed by wooden boarding, with windows on the ground floor, whilst the roof was also corrugated iron with monitor skylights. Longitudinally the structure was stiffened by spandrel brackets at the beam-column connections, but transversely there seems to have been no specific provision for wind bracing. Put up during wartime, at minimum cost, and regarded as a temporary building, the museum was nicknamed "The Brompton Boilers" and its utilitarian appearance may have had the effect of damping contemporary enthusiasm for iron architecture. It also had no pretence of being fireproof.[2] But the framing plans of the museum and the Boat Store are so similar that Greene possibly copied this aspect in designing his Sheerness building. In most other respects, however, the Boat Store is greatly superior.

We have, in fact, now considered the known antecedents of the Boat Store. And what stands out is the extraordinary advance made by Greene in this design. Bogardus had, so far as one can tell, built a four-storey iron-framed building 10 years before, but by comparison it is a period piece. The importance of the Crystal Palace is beyond all question, yet it was not strictly a multi-storey structure and it certainly had no resemblance to a modern steel-frame building. The South Kensington museum was little more than a large triple shed with mezzanine galleries. Then, suddenly, at Sheerness, we find a completely iron-framed building almost in the modern idiom; a clear-cut four-storey elevation, structurally explicit and with entirely logical detailing; yet attractive, even beautiful, in the functional tradition of the old water mills, especially in Kent and East Anglia, and the timber-framed and boarded sheds in the Dockyards themselves.[3] And it is, I think, Greene's greatest contribution that he developed this synthesis of the older, reasonable, style of the millwright and shipwright with the new possibilities of structural iron.

Perhaps the chief criticism of the Boat Store is the use of corrugated iron for the wall panels; since brick panels would have provided better insulation and a more weatherproof construction. In 1855, however, Bogardus erected a cast-iron frame shot tower 175 ft. high, only a few hundred yards from his factory in New York, for the McCullough Shot and Lead Co. This tower had eight iron columns and nine stages of horizontal beams carrying 12 in. thick brick panels; probably the first example of such construction. And in the following year he built another shot tower, rising to a height of 217 ft.

---

[1] Young also supplied the ironwork for the Dublin Crystal Palace of 1853. For this building and the South Kensington Museum, see Hitchcock, *op. cit.*
[2] Nor was the Crystal Palace fireproof.
[3] See J. M. Richards, *The Functional Tradition*, especially for the mills at Halstead, Essex (eighteenth century) and at Chilham, Kent (*c.* 1800), also the timber storehouses at Chatham (1809).

THE BOAT STORE, SHEERNESS (1858–60)

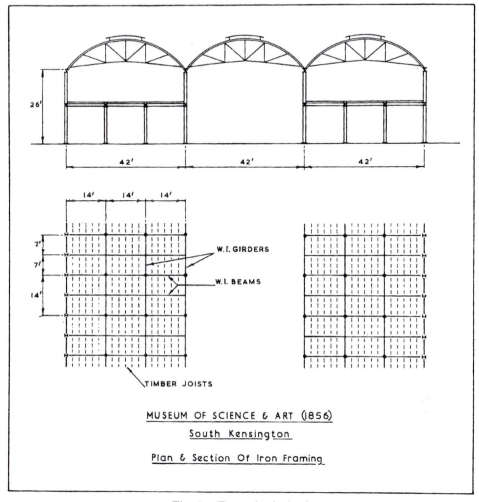

Fig. 4. (Drawn by Author.)

in Beckman Street.[1] Almost opposite the Bogardus factory, and practically within the shadow of the McCullough tower, Daniel Badger had his Architectural Iron Works, where George H. Johnson was employed from 1852 until he left to set up on his own in 1862. In that year a grain elevator 125 ft. by 107 ft. in plan and effectively five storeys high, was built to Johnson's design for the Pennsylvania Railroad in Washington Avenue, Philadelphia; and, probably in 1861, another almost identical one for the U.S. Warehouse Co. at Atlantic Dock, Brooklyn.[2] The walls of these elevators consisted of

[1] These towers are fully described by Professor Bannister (*loc. cit.*).
[2] Some details are given in *Illustration of Iron Architecture made by the Architectural Iron Works of the City of New York*, New York, 1865.

THE BOAT STORE, SHEERNESS (1858–60)

iron columns and beams with brick panels, almost certainly derived from the Bogardus shot towers, but now used in a structure which can be considered more as a "building" in the usual sense of the term—although the interior obviously comprised a series of grain bins. The object of this form of construction was to achieve a relatively fireproof elevator.

The next step was clearly to combine Johnson's walls with the iron-framed and brick-arch floors of the English textile mills; or, from another point of view, to use the Sheerness frame in conjunction with fireproof floors and brick wall panels. This was achieved by Hippolyte Fontaine in a magnificent six-storey warehouse, with a length of 630 ft., erected in 1864–65 at the St. Ouen docks by the side of a canal basin just off the River Seine in the northern suburbs of Paris.[1] The walls were constructed with cast-iron columns, at 13 ft. centres, and beams carrying 15 in. thick brick panels, each containing a window. The floors, which were test loaded to 600 lb. per sq. ft., consisted of hollow-brick arches, haunched with concrete, springing from 20 in. deep wrought-iron plate girders: the latter framing into the external columns and spanning 27 ft. between two rows of internal columns in the total width of 82 ft. across the building. Lateral rigidity was derived from the column-beam connections, as at Sheerness.

Visually, the St. Ouen warehouse was of little significance; but structurally it completes the development initiated at Derby and Shrewsbury and continued by Fairbairn, Bogardus, Johnson, Paxton and his associates, and by Greene. The multi-storey iron-framed building with incombustible walls and floors had been achieved. It led, finally, to the creation of the first masterpieces of modern architecture, in Chicago, in the 1890's.

ACKNOWLEDGMENTS AND POSTSCRIPTS

I am greatly indebted to Mr. L. G. Harris, Civil Engineer in Chief, Admiralty, and to Captain P. Chavasse for the most courteous way in which they placed the facilities of their Establishments at my disposal. Members of the staff at Pinner and at Sheerness were exceptionally helpful. I wish to record my particular thanks to Mr. A. H. Attrill who, with his intimate knowledge of the plans and drawings in his care at the Admiralty, has contributed much to this research. And it was Mr. D. W. Wyatt who, on my first visit to Sheerness, produced some of the original drawings which started the whole train of investigation. I am also most grateful to Mrs. Baden Powell for generously lending me many prints, and her thesis, and for several stimulating discussions on architectural matters. Miss Carlotta Hacker has given invaluable assistance, especially in the sections on Colonel Greene and Henry Grissell, whilst Mrs. de Maré and my wife have helped with the photography and measurement of the Boat Store. It was, however, my friend Mr. Eric de Maré who "lit the candle." Without his keen eye for beauty, often in rather unlikely surroundings, this remarkable building would have remained virtually unknown.

Finally, I am glad to be able to add that it has been scheduled by the Ministry of Housing and Local Government as a "building of special architectural or historic value"; and that Mr. de Maré's superb photographs, some of which have been used, with his very kind permission, to illustrate this Paper, will be placed in the National Buildings Record library. The dockyard is to be taken over by a civilian firm on 31 March 1960.

APPENDIX I

NOTES ON STRUCTURAL ELEMENTS

Portal Bracing. The principal key to the structural design of the Boat Store is to be found in the fact that lateral stability is provided entirely by the rigid connections between the beams and columns.

---

[1] A. W. Skempton, "Evolution of the steel frame building," *The Guilds Engineer*, Vol. 10, 1959, pp. 37–51.

THE BOAT STORE, SHEERNESS (1858–60)

More usually, at this time, portal bracing was achieved by spandrel brackets or by "arched" girders. The former were used in the Hungerford Fish Market (1835) by Charles Fowler—possibly the earliest important free-standing iron-frame (single-storey) structure of the trabeated form—and became very popular. Arched girders were adopted by Robert Stephenson in the train shed for Euston Station (1838) and they, also, were thereafter widely used. Both schemes allowed scope for decorative treatment. Bracing girders of rectangular aspect were perhaps first used in the Crystal Palace (1850) where they were of the open trellis type. Girders of the same type were extensively employed by Greene in the Chatham No. 7 Slip Roof (1852). The modern form of portal bracing, using solely a rigid joint between columns and a solid web beam of normal proportions, was first introduced by Greene in the Boat Store, so far as I am aware.

H-Section Columns. The connections for portal bracing are far more readily effected if the beams can be bolted to the flange or through the web of an H-section column, than is possible with a circular column. The connections in the Crystal Palace, although ingenious, are clumsy compared with Greene's details in the Chatham No. 7 Slip, where H-columns were used probably for the first time, and in the Boat Store. Morever, eccentric loading is inevitable in the external columns and also in columns carrying a travelling crane. An H-section is therefore also more appropriate for these positions in a building.

It is regrettable that Greene's calculations have not survived, for the design of the eccentrically-loaded columns of 45 ft. unsupported length at Chatham would be of great interest.

I-Section Beams. Cast-iron beams were usually simply-supported at their ends and, in this condition, the lower flange had to be larger than the upper flange. This was well known and where Greene used such beams as in the chain Testing House at Sheerness (1856), he followed the accepted proportions. With end-fixity, however, the negative bending moments, giving tension in the top flange, are of the same order as the positive moments. Thus the equal flanged I-section beams in the Boat Store are logical, as well as being more elegant than the traditional cast-iron section.

Plate Girders. The calculation of rivetted wrought-iron plate girders was placed on a scientific basis by the classic research of Fairbairn and Eaton Hodgkinson in connection with the design of the Conway and Britannia tubular bridges, for which Robert Stephenson was engineer. This work was carried out between 1845 and 1847 and the results were published in the Report of the Royal Commission on the Application of Iron to Railway Structures (1849). They were also given in great detail, together with an admirable treatment of continuous beam theory by William Pole, in Edwin Clark's notable book on these bridges.[1] No difficulty should therefore have attended the design of the girders in the Boat Store; but the 30 ft. span was considerable, in building construction, at this time.

Corner Columns. A rectangular hollow section was, I believe, uncommon in the 'fifties, although it later became widely used (for example, in most of the early Chicago skyscrapers). The device of allowing rainwater from the gutters to run down inside hollow cast-iron circular-section columns had long been practised.

Corrugated, Galvanised Iron. Corrugated iron had been employed in roofs since the 1830's and galvanising dates, effectively, from about 1840.[2] The combined product came extensively into use soon afterwards.

Roof Truss. Triangulated iron trusses can be traced back to a design by William Murdock for a roof erected in 1810 at the Soho foundry, of 27 ft. span. This form of construction received a great

---

[1] Edwin Clark, *The Britannia and Conway Tubular Bridges*, 2 vols., London, 1850.
[2] H. W. Dickinson, "A study of galvanised and corrugated sheet metal," *Trans. Newcomen Soc.*, Vol. XXIV, 1943, pp. 27–36.

THE BOAT STORE, SHEERNESS (1858–60)

impetus with the advent of railway stations and a very fine example is Robert Stephenson's roof at Derby (1840) with a span of 52 ft. Greene's 82 ft. truss at Chatham, however, is the most impressive I have seen. The Boat Store roof can be admired for the appropriate differentiation between tension and compression members and the delicate detailing.

Foundations. The columns at Chatham No. 7 Slip, with an unsupported height of 45 ft., were embedded in concrete to a depth of 10 ft., thereby achieving a good degree of end-fixity. At the Boat Store the maximum unsupported length was only 12 ft. Thus no special measures were required and the columns were merely flat-ended, bearing on a granite block. The pile foundations were perfectly normal, and continued the tradition established in 1814 at Sheerness when John Rennie began the construction of the docks.

APPENDIX II

LIST OF DRAWINGS FOR THE BOAT STORE, SHEERNESS

I. *Drawings prepared at Somerset House,* signed G. T. Greene, and dated when sent to Sheerness. The draughtman's initials are given together with the serial number. Each drawing is headed SHEERNESS YARD, New Boat Store.

Drawings sent to Sheerness 28 April 1858:—

—	—	General Plan[1]
2810	C.D.A.	Details of Foundations

Drawings sent to Sheerness 11 November 1858:—

2811	M.T.C.	Plan of Ground Floor
2812	C.D.A.	Plans of first, second and third Floors
2813	—	Roof Plan
2814	W.H.M.	Elevations
2815	W.H.M.	Sections
2816	M.T.C.	Details of Internal and External Standards
2817	J.W.C.	Details of Intermediate and Corner Standards
2818	M.T.C.	Details of Sashes, Cill, Corrugated Iron and Plinth for Filling between Standards
2819	W.H.M.	Details of Roofs—Principals and Gutters
2820	C.D.A.	Details of Roofs—Hip Connections and Gable Fittings
2821	C.D.A.	Details of Roofs—Skylight, Ridge, etc.
2822	C.D.A.	Details of Cast Iron Girders
2823	C.D.A.	Details of Wrought Iron Girders

Drawings sent to Sheerness 9 July 1859:—

3375	M.T.C.	Details of Cradle
3387	M.T.C.	Details of Traveller and Boat Truck
3388	C.D.A.	Details of . . . West End

Drawings sent to Sheerness 3 November 1859:—

3518	E.L.W.	Sketch of Cast Iron Shoe to receive Joists (and details of timber flooring)

[1] Now existing only as a tracing made in 1901 from the original paper tracing then "perished and destroyed." The date and signature were included, but not the serial number or draughtsman's initials.

THE BOAT STORE, SHEERNESS (1858–60)

II. *Drawings prepared at Sheerness,* signed by F. (Frederick) Turner, Clerk of Works, and John W. Johnstone (Assistant Clerk of Works).

28 April 1858   Part General Plan showing in red the site of New Store Boat House, and also the proposed site for re-erecting the centre portion of present Wooden Boat Shed.

21 May 1859   Plan showing the proposed manner of forming the floors.

1 February 1860   Sketch showing proposed Sliding Doors for West End.

DISCUSSION

Mr. H. CLAUSEN said that Professor Skempton had referred—in his notes on the building of the Crystal Palace in 1850—to the incredibly short time in preparation of the working drawings of this vast and unique structure. Perhaps he might be allowed to amplify this from information straight from the horse's mouth? That of Mr. Charles Fox, the senior partner of the main contractors, Messrs. Fox & Henderson.

On 21 June 1851, when the Great Exhibition was in full swing, speaking at a dinner given in his honour by his fellow citizens of Derby, he said:

"It was now that I commenced the laborious work of deciding upon the proportions and strengths required in every part of this great and novel structure, so as to ensure that perfect safety essential in a building destined to receive millions of human beings—one entirely without precedent, and where mistakes might have led to the most serious disasters. Having satisfied myself on these necessary points, I set to work and made every important drawing of the building, as it now stands, with my own hands, and it was no small source of gratification to me, when asking Mr. Cubitt (the Committee consultant) to look over the drawings I had prepared, to find that he not only had no desire to suggest alterations, but expressed entire approval of them all."

(They took possession of the site in Hyde Park on 30 July 1850 and started to lay out the various parts of the building. Continuing his speech:—)

"The drawings occupied me about eighteen hours each day for about seven weeks, and as they went from my hand Mr. Henderson prepared the ironwork and other materials required in the construction of the building. As the drawings proceeded the calculations of strength were made, and as soon as a number of the important parts were prepared, such as the cast iron girders and wrought iron trusses, we invited Mr. Cubitt to pay us a visit to our works at Birmingham to witness a set of experiments in proof of the correctness of these calculations."

(These trials were made on 6 September 1850, four times the design load was needed before fracture; and work was pushed on rapidly. He went on to say:—)

". . . so that on the 26th of September we were able to fix the first column in its place. From this time I took the general management of the building under my charge, and spent all my time on the works—feeling that, unless the same person who had made the drawings was always present to assign to each part as it arrived on the ground its proper place in the structure, it would have been impossible to finish the building in time for the opening on the 1st of May. I am confident that this would have been impossible if any other course had been adopted."

It is no longer practicable for the senior partner of a large contracting firm to spend 18 hours a day on his own drawing-board for 7 weeks, and then go and spend several months as his own clerk of the works on the site, but the speed and efficiency with which these vast projects were carried out was only made possible by first-class professional leadership, especially in the design and planning stages.

THE BOAT STORE, SHEERNESS (1858–60)

When it is recalled that at that time there were no telephones, no typewriters, no means of reproducing engineering drawings except tracing them by hand; and that on the site the only hoisting and lifting gear was pole masts with rope tackles—and either hand winches or horse teams to do the hauling—their achievements appear even more incredible.

Mr. R. J. SUTHERLAND asked if the Author could give some information on the history of the wrought-iron beam. Was any case known of a wrought-iron beam made before Hodgkinson and Fairbairn's experiments in 1845? Fairbairn and Stephenson took out a patent in 1846 for hollow wrought-iron plate girders; this implied that they thought they were the first in the field.

Professor SKEMPTON said he knew of no rolled wrought-iron beams being used earlier than 1845. In that year, it is said that small wrought-iron beams were rolled and used in France, but they were still something of a novelty in 1850.

Replying to a further question from Mr. Sutherland, who asked if the corner columns at Sheerness were used directly as rainwater pipes, or had they a pipe inside, Professor Skempton said he could not examine the inside of the columns but there was nothing on the drawings to indicate a pipe, nor would this be necessary with cast-iron.

Dr. S. B. HAMILTON said that the French beams mentioned were small, used mainly for ceilings, and not meant to carry any serious weight. The difficulty was to make from small puddled blooms a single piece of considerable size, and for that reason rolled wrought-iron beams were seldom used until forging with the steam hammer (invented by James Nasmyth in 1839) had become standard practice. There was no great urge to make wrought-iron beams when from 1800 onwards good cast-iron ones could be made more cheaply. For long spans after about 1850 the plate girder was the solution; it was made from angles and plates rivetted together.

Dr. Hamilton said that he was grateful to Professor Skempton for having cleared up this most important period in the history of structure and it would be very difficult for anyone to upset the careful analysis of sequence given in the Paper. This lucid Paper was a great achievement, and the incidental notes on Greene and Grissell, people of considerable importance to this history, who had hardly been heard of, were most useful.

Mr. J. FOSTER PETREE doubted whether the flooring was of old ships' planking or decking; not decking, for if it came out of an old ship it would probably not be of the dimensions quoted. Old hull planking would be worn, perhaps waterlogged, not flat, and certainly not suitable for making flooring. In 1859 the French produced the "Gloire" ironclad and virtually made the navies of the world obsolete overnight. At about that time the Admiralty had bought large stocks of ships' timber and, though they went on building wooden ships for some time, some of this timber might have been used for Dockyard buildings.

Mr. A. H. ATTRILL said he had seen drawings at Portsmouth of buildings appreciably older (end of eighteenth century) where the builders had not been above using masses of timber, presumably intended, but perhaps found unsuitable, for ships. With regard to the Smithery at Portsmouth, which Professor Skempton had thought to be inspired by the Crystal Palace: over the years the ironwork had failed to stand the strain and has been replaced piecemeal by modern steelwork; today only the shape of the original building survives.

Mr. REX WAILES said that ships' timbers were used in old watermills in Hampshire and on the south coast.

Dr. C. DAVISON said that all knew how Bessemer in 1855 patented his new steel-making process and how the cheapened steel gradually became more and more employed in constructional work. He was curious to know when steel had so far replaced cast-iron that it became the principal material for building construction. Twenty years ago he tested high-grade cast-iron for a firm and

THE BOAT STORE, SHEERNESS (1858–60)

found that the presence of small blowholes, coupled with the lack of homogeneity in the casting, made it necessary to employ high factors of safety in design work. Had Professor Skempton discovered any values for the factor-of-safety as employed by the early builders of cast-iron buildings?

Mr. L. T. C. ROLT said wrought-iron rails were used in 1824 on the Stockton and Darlington railway, from Birkenshaw's patent; old ships' timber from Portsmouth made good sleeper blocks for the same railway.

He said that in the building of the Britannia tubular bridge, great difficulty was experienced with the materials; all had to be trued up and cut on site. In the conditions prevailing there was much hesitation in putting up wrought-iron buildings; special workmen had to be engaged.

There was, he thought, a drawing in Brunel's sketchbooks at Bristol, showing the kitchen of the prefabricated hospital for the Crimea (about 1854) which Brunel insisted should be entirely of iron, although most of the rest of the building was of wood.

Mr. Rolt said that two bad railway accidents prompted the enquiries into the use of cast-iron in bridges. One was the Dee bridge, where a badly designed girder failed. The other was the collapse of a cast-iron girder on the Brighton line, near Norwood. In the accident report, which he had seen, the failure was said to be due to an unsuspected blow hole in the girder. Blow holes did occur, but only in large girders.

Mr. L. G. HARRIS said that, as Colonel Greene's successor, he had much appreciated the opportunity to help Professor Skempton in the preparation of a fascinating Paper. There was, at the Admiralty, a lot more history into which he could delve. The amusing thought occurred to him that perhaps in a hundred years' time Professor Skempton's successor might be looking into drawings produced by him: it would be found that he had not done all the working drawings with his own hand!

Mr. P. H. J. BAKER said that in the photographs and drawings of the 30 ft. girders in the Boat Store there was no evidence of increased thickness of flanges over the central part of the span as is the present practice. Would Professor Skempton comment on this? What, if anything, is known of the manner in which these structures were designed?

The CHAIRMAN (Mr. A. STOWERS), asked whether the three travelling girders, which spanned the nave of the Boat Store, were cranes or parts of machinery for pulling the boats along. He said that Sir William Fairbairn in his *Treatise on Mills and Millwork* (4th ed., 1878, pp. 398–407) gave a detailed description with four drawings of the small cornmill, with three pairs of stones, which was shipped to Constantinople and erected there for the Seraskier Halil Pasha in 1842. It was specified "that the building should be entirely of iron that it might not be burnt to the ground by the fires which so frequently occur in the Turkish capital." The same drawings, but to a larger scale and fully dimensioned, had been published in *The Engineer and Machinist's Assistant* by David Scott (1847) from which Fairbairn quoted.

The Chairman added that the artist's drawing of the "Brompton Boilers" in *The Illustrated London News* of 1857 was reproduced without engineering details in *A Short History of the Science Museum* by Frank Greenaway, published by H.M.S.O., 1951.

Professor SKEMPTON thanked Dr. Hamilton for his remarks, but said there might well be other iron-framed structures still not discovered.

He said a factor of safety of four, on the ultimate strength, was widely used, but it was sometimes as low as three. These figures were often mentioned in the Royal Commission of 1849. Steel was first used in buildings in 1885. Until that time cast-iron was employed for columns and, from about 1850, wrought-iron for beams.

Replying to Mr. Baker, it was absolutely standard practice to increase the depth or flange width of cast-iron beams at their mid span, when simply supported. In the Boat Store, however, the beams had a considerable degree of end-fixity. Thus the negative end moments were comparable in

THE BOAT STORE, SHEERNESS (1858–60)

magnitude to the positive mid-span moments, and it would not be logical to increase the mid-span section.

Asked by Mr. CLAUSEN if, where the cast-iron members were bolted together, the meeting faces had been machined, or faced, or rough-cast, or just put in with iron cement, Professor Skempton said it was difficult to reply as the joints were painted over. Iron cement had not been used, however.

Mr. WAILES said no machine existed at that time by which the facing could economically be done.

Dr. S. B. HAMILTON (Hon. Editor) wrote as follows:

In a store shed building of 1811 in London Docks, on a site liable to uneven settlement, molten lead was run into joints between certain cast-iron structural members. Sheet lead may well have been used for a similar purpose, but he could not recall an actual example (*Trans.*, XXI, 151).

Rust cement was used, as late as 1857, in bolted joints between members of the cast- and wrought-iron structure of the Reading Room at the British Museum. A clearance of about an inch was deliberately left between the faces of members to be joined. The bolts were presumably tightened against temporary packing or wedges until the space had been filled with the cement. No sign of movement or distress was observable when the structure was exposed in the 1920's (*The Structural Engineer*, 1949, XXVII (4), 187 f.).

PLATE VI

SHEERNESS BOAT STORE. Exterior View

PLATE VII

SHEERNESS BOAT STORE
Fig. 1. General Interior View

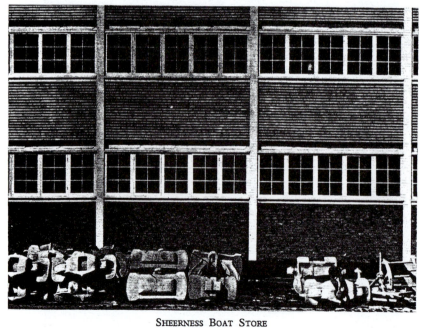

SHEERNESS BOAT STORE
Fig. 2. Detail of Exterior

PLATE VIII

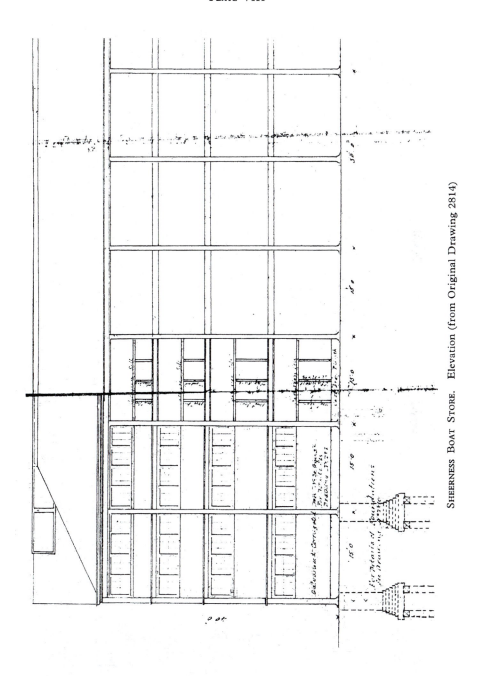

SHEERNESS BOAT STORE. Elevation (from Original Drawing 2814)

Plate IX

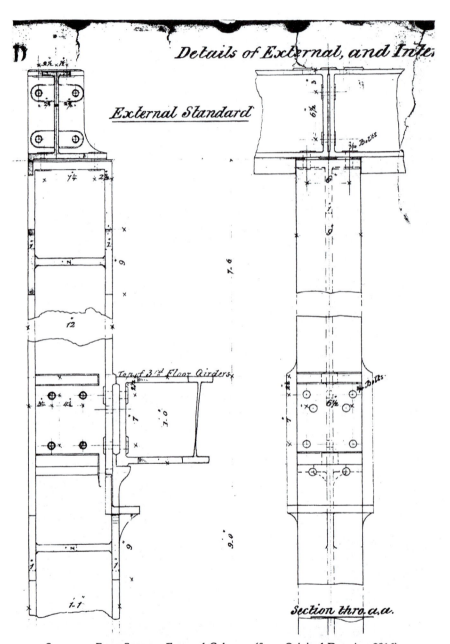

SHEERNESS BOAT STORE.   External Columns (from Original Drawing 2816)

PLATE X

SHEERNESS BOAT STORE
Fig. 2. Corner Column

SHEERNESS BOAT STORE
Fig. 1. Interior View of Wall

PLATE XI

SHEERNESS BOAT STORE. View of Second Floor

PLATE XII

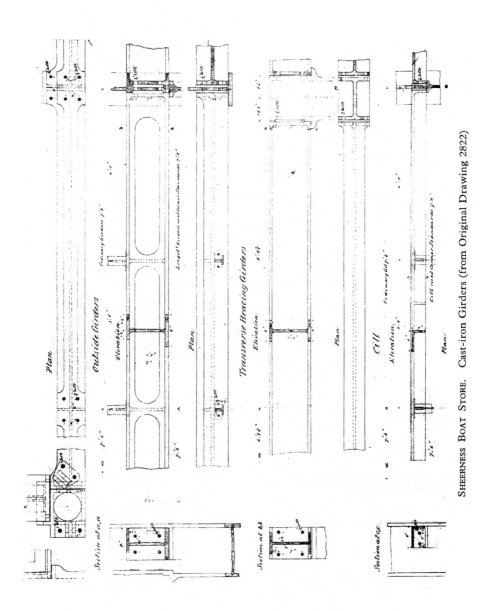

SHEERNESS BOAT STORE. Cast-iron Girders (from Original Drawing 2822)

PLATE XIII

SHEERNESS BOAT STORE
Fig. 2. Detail of Connection

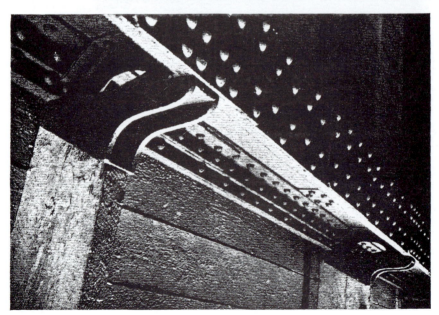

SHEERNESS BOAT STORE
Fig. 1. Wrought Iron Girder

PLATE XIV

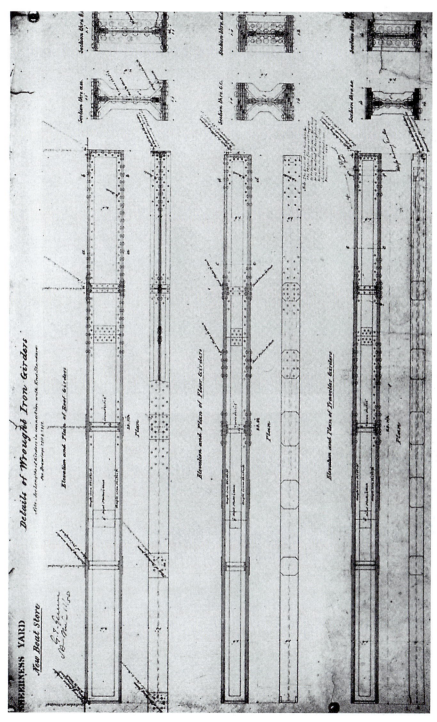

SHEERNESS BOAT STORE. Wrought Iron Girders (from Original Drawing, 2823. Note Greene's Signature.)

PLATE XV

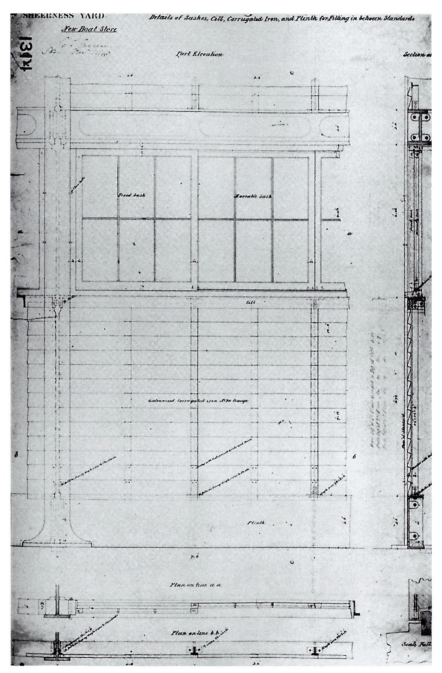

SHEERNESS BOAT STORE.   Details of Wall Construction (from Original Drawing 2818)

3

Bogardus revisited

Turpin C. Bannister

Part I : THE IRON FRONTS

JUST A CENTURY ago American architecture was entering a new era, its Age of Iron. Iron, the preeminent hallmark of the Industrial Revolution, had become by the middle of the nineteenth century sufficiently available and economical in the United States, either by importation or by domestic production, that its widespread use for building construction was at last practicable. Soon its strength would make possible the realization of that age-old dream, the skyscraper, but first it was to be exploited for its incombustibility and the ease with which it could be cast into almost any desired shape. These seductive qualities encouraged a state of mind which deserves the name of Ferromania.

For most historians, the prophet, apostle, and patron saint of Ferromania has been James Bogardus.[1] Now that a century has passed since he entered the American scene, it seems an appropriate time to assay more completely the man, his work, and his place in our architectural evolution.

Bogardus was born at Catskill, New York, in 1800.[2] Throughout his youth, the thriving town could offer excellent stimuli to an inquisitive mind. Fulton's *Clermont* steamed past its dock when the boy was but seven. Amos Eaton, later to found the first American engineering school, the Rensselaer Institute, was a Catskill lawyer who from 1810 on gave public lectures on scientific subjects.[3] At Catskill, Bogardus was apprenticed to the local watchmaker who trained him to become expert in the difficult crafts of engraving and die-sinking.

The prospects of Catskill, however, declined as the Erie Canal began to siphon off its back-country trade, and around 1825 Bogardus left home to try his fortune in New York City. There his industry and bent for mechanics were evidenced by a series of prizes and patents for clocks, a "ring-flyer" for cotton spinning, an eccentric sugar mill, a dry gas meter, a metal mechanical pencil, and a machine for engraving filigreed watch dials. He was firmly established by 1831 when he married Margaret, daughter of the Rev. Archibald McClay. In 1836 he went to London, apparently to promote his engraving machine. With it he engraved Queen Victoria's portrait, and in 1839 he won $2000 for applying the apparatus to the production of

TURPIN C. BANNISTER, *a founder of the Society, was the first editor of the* JOURNAL.

postage stamps. No doubt this prize financed the continental tour which he took before his return to New York in 1840.[4]

During the 1840's Bogardus sought to exploit commercially his eccentric sugar mill. He improved it and applied it to other materials, such as rice and white lead for paint. He shared a shop at 40 Eldridge Street, near Grand, and lived nearby at the corner of East Broadway and Pike.[5] His product was composed of parts made of cast iron, but, instead of casting them himself, he probably found it more economical to buy the rough castings from nearby foundries and to confine his own operations to finishing and assembly. Apparently the business prospered, since in 1848 he changed his listing in the city directory from *machinist* to *eccentric mill maker*.[6] In the previous year, his shop proving too small, Bogardus decided to erect a new factory at the eastern corner of Centre and Duane Streets, opposite several foundries which could supply him with castings (Fig. 1).[7]

By the summer of 1847 Bogardus exhibited a model of the new building which he proposed to construct entirely of iron, a material with which he was intimately familiar.[8] No doubt the great fires of 1835 and 1845 had so impressed him that he chose iron primarily for its incombustibility.[9] The foundation was laid in May, 1848,[10] and we can suppose that immediate fabrication and erection of the superstructure was intended.

Nevertheless, Bogardus soon postponed his own project to construct an iron front for the drugstore of John Milhau at 183 Broadway, between Cortlandt and Dey Streets (Fig. 2). We must assume that the internal structure employed the usual brick party walls and timber beams, but the façade, five stories high and four bays wide, was of cast iron. Its erection took only three days.[11] It featured piers with engaged Roman Doric columns at each story, spandrels with double panels enclosing applied ornaments, and fascias and a cornice frieze which sported appliquées of elliptical arch motifs. The correspondence with Bogardus' own building suggests that he used the same patterns. Indeed, he may well have delayed his own work in order to procure the patterns at a customer's expense. Assuming that the lot had a standard width of 25 feet, each of the four bays would then have been slightly more than 6 feet wide, a scale typical of Bogardus' first structures. Milhau's façade, completed in 1848, was thus the first iron front, not only of Bogardus, but of New York as well.[12] The building disappeared during the skyscraper boom soon after 1900.

Further delay arose when Edgar H. Laing ordered iron fronts for three stores to be built on his coal yard at the northwest corner of Washington and Murray Streets, in the wholesale district close to the Hudson River (Fig. 3). Work began February 25, 1849, and was finished in two months.[13] The internal structure was again composed of masonry and timber.[14] The bays of the four-story cast-iron façades repeat the design of the Milhau drugstore. We are indebted to Walter Knight Sturges for his discovery that these fronts are still standing, though they have lost most of their applied ornaments and are now disfigured by a crude modern marquee. It is of interest to note that, although only 150 tons of iron were needed, the castings were subcontracted to four different foundries: the West Point, Burden's, the Novelty Works of Stillman, Allen and Co., and William L. Miller whose furnace shared Bogardus' address at 40 Eldridge Street.[15] Bogardus' function seems to

have been confined to supplying the patterns and to superintending erection.

On May 3, an item in the *Evening Post*, obviously inspired by Bogardus, extolled the advantages of cast-iron fronts "constructed . . . to secure the greatest strength with the least material . . . cast and fitted so that each piece may be put up as fast as it is brought to the ground. They may be taken down, removed, and put up again in a short time . . . nearly three feet of room is gained over buildings put up with brick. They admit more light, for the iron columns will sustain the weight that would require a wide brick wall. They combine beauty with strength, for the panels can be filled with (ornamental) figures to any extent." [16] These arguments were readily accepted; by the summer of 1849 at least eight more iron façades were under way, but apparently by other builders than Bogardus.[17] Competitive exploitation had already begun.

Soon afterward we may assume that Bogardus completed his own factory. His handsome lithographed advertisement of it amply proves that its component castings were identical with those of the Milhau and Laing façades (Fig. 4). The building provoked immediate interest, even across the

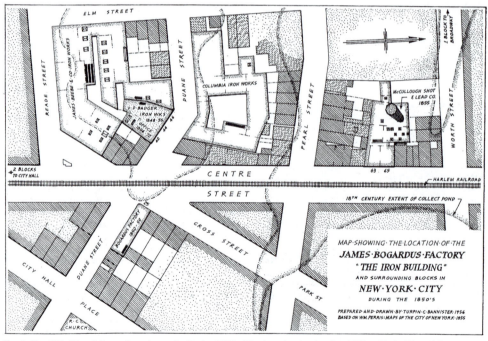

Fig. 1. New York. Map of Centre Street ironworks district, 1850's. (Bannister drawing, based on William Perris, *Maps of the City of New York*, 1st ed., 1852, III, Maps 25, 28; 3rd ed. 1857–62, I, Map 14)

Fig. 2. New York. John Milhau Drugstore, 183 Broadway (at left), 1848. (*King's Photographic Views of New York*, p. 257)

Fig. 3. New York. Edgar H. Laing Stores, northwest corner of Washington and Murray Streets, 1849. (Huson Jackson, *A Guide to New York Architecture, 1650–1952*, courtesy Reinhold Publishing Corp.)

Atlantic. On April 12, 1851, the *Illustrated London News* published a brief description and a crude woodcut of it. Unfortunately, the building stood for only a decade. In November, 1859, when Duane Street was widened, the factory was carefully dismantled in order to prove Bogardus' boast, but there is no hint that he reerected it for either his new office at 207 Canal Street or his workshop at Elm and White.[18] Perhaps the famous structure ended on the used-house market, but more probably it was melted up and recast for a later model, a final argument which Bogardus had not advanced.

Until the recovery of the Milhau and Laing stores, Bogardus' factory was thought to have been the first iron front. In recent years more thorough investigations have denied priority to all three. For, on July 27, 1847, when, according to Bogardus, his own project was only in model form, the *Cincinnati Daily Commercial* under the headline CAST IRON HOUSES reported, "We are informed, by good authority, that a block of three-story buildings are to be erected in this city [and] the entire front [is] to be of cast iron! The plates for the same are already being cast." [19] By some inscrutable editorial channel this item reappeared on September 25 in the London *Builder*.[20] Unfortunately, the location and maker of these fronts were not recorded.[21] Nevertheless, the report is entirely plausible since in the previous year, 1846, Gardner Lathrop's Cincinnati Iron Foundry had advertised iron "building fronts." [22] Moreover, Miles Greenwood later claimed that his Eagle Foundry, the largest in the West, had cast such fronts since 1843.[23] While no contemporary corroboration or executed examples have thus far been found, Greenwood's reputation for probity and his interest in fire prevention and incombustible construction make the claim highly credible.[24]

In his new factory Bogardus looked west across Centre Street to the shop of another claimant to priority in iron fronts. This was Daniel D. Badger who became his most energetic rival (Fig. 1). Born at Portsmouth, New Hampshire, in 1806, Badger learned the iron trade there and opened his own business in Boston in 1829.[25] No doubt stirred by Cyrus Alger, head of the great South Boston Iron Works, who from 1830 on promoted the idea of iron buildings, Badger erected in 1842 in Washington Street a store front with cast-iron columns and lintels which he later asserted to be the "first Iron Front in the United States." [26] A year later he bought from Arthur L. Johnson of Baltimore a patent for rolling iron shutters, a device for shop windows which required the shop front to be constructed with hollow cast-iron piers.[27] In 1846 Badger moved to New York to promote his shuttered fronts among merchants alarmed by the increasingly frequent conflagrations in the commercial district. In 1847 he established his factory at 44–46 Duane Street, possibly on the strength of a large contract to furnish shutters for A. T. Stewart's vast marble emporium on Broadway at Chambers.[28] In 1849

Badger listed himself as producing rolling shutters and iron store fronts. Bogardus did not add "cast iron houses" to his directory notice until the following year.[29] Due to the efforts of these two men Centre Street henceforth dominated the career of the American iron front.

Apparently Badger in his claim of priority chose to disregard the difference between his single-story shop fronts and Bogardus' whole façades, but in any case his Boston shop front was hardly a novelty in 1842. Alexander Jackson Davis had built one in 1835 for New York's Lyceum of Natural History, on Broadway between Prince and Spring, in order to reduce the usual heavy masonry piers and obtain larger display windows.[30] Davis was probably inspired by François Thiollet's 1832 publication of Parisian examples.[31]

There was still another predecessor building to which Bogardus was almost certainly indebted. In the summer of 1839 William Fairbairn, the famous British iron master, visited Constantinople to advise the Turkish government on the modernization of its arsenals, docks, and industries. This led to an order for Fairbairn to supply a steam flour mill for the army.[32] To house the machinery, Fairbairn prefabricated in his shops at Millwall, London, a three-story iron building, 27 by 50 feet (Fig. 5). The framework was entirely of cast iron; the lower spandrels were of the same material, while those above were of wrought iron. The roof was of corrugated iron sheets. Cast-iron beams and columns carried the floors and roof. Only the foundations and a low interior wall supporting the machinery were of masonry.[33] Before being shipped to Constantinople in 1840, the assembled structure was exhibited to the public at Millwall. It is entirely probable that Bogardus personally inspected this extraordinary structure before his return to New York, but, even if he did not, he could hardly have escaped during the next several years the ample accounts of it reported by the popular and technical press. In 1842–43 British progress in iron buildings had been promptly noted by newspapers in both New York and Cincinnati.[34]

The first American iron façade had preceded Bogardus by exactly two decades. In 1828 the Pennsylvania frontier coal-mining village of Pottsville celebrated its incorporation as a borough by inaugurating its first financial institution, the Miners' Bank.[35] When an appropriate building was constructed in 1829–30, two of the directors who were residents of Philadelphia secured the architectural services of John Haviland of that city. Following current Philadelphian models, Haviland designed a small structure with walls and vaults of brick. For the two-story façade, however, he intended decorative ashlar, but, finding no suitable local quarry, he substituted cast-iron plates which, when painted and sanded, produced the "very beautiful and uniform texture of stone" (Fig. 6).[36] This solution was probably prompted in part by the fact that another director, Benjamin Pott, was the son of John Pott, promoter of

Fig. 4. New York. Bogardus Factory, the *Iron Building*, Centre and Duane Streets, 1848–49. (Ackerman lithograph, courtesy of the Museum of the City of New York)

Fig. 5. Constantinople. Iron Flour Mill, 1839–41. (Bannister reconstruction)

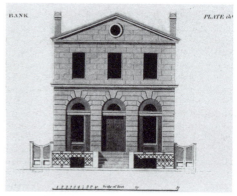

Fig. 6. Pottsville, Pennsylvania. Miners' Bank, 1829–30. Elevation. (John Haviland, *An Improved and Enlarged Edition of Biddle's Young Carpenter's Assistant*, Plate 60)

the town and owner since 1807 of the local Greenwood Foundry which doubtless supplied the castings.[37] But Haviland also surely knew of similar uses of metallic veneering. He had no doubt seen the iron-faced Narva Triumphal Arch at St. Petersburg, Russia, just completed by Quarenghi and Staroff when he visited that city in 1816.[38] Moreover, the bronze-revetted Vendome Column built by Napoleon at Paris in 1806–10 had attracted wide attention among architects. Haviland may also have read of the recent Parisian vogue for cast-iron shop fronts.[39] In any case, the bank and its façade were widely reported and no doubt stirred the imagination of both Alger and Badger in Boston and Bogardus in New York.[40]

While Bogardus was thus in no sense the inventor of the iron front, his work appeared at a moment when the state of technology, need, and taste combined to favor its acceptance and exploitation. The earliest example of this reaction outside New York was the Penn Mutual Life Insurance Company's Office, erected between April, 1850, and September, 1851, in Philadelphia at the northeast corner of Third and Dock Streets.[41] Next to the Laing Stores in New York, it is the oldest existing iron front in the United States. Its architect, G. P. Cummings, furnished an astylar design with wide piers and small windows originally intended for execution in masonry. News of Bogardus' work led to the substitution of iron, but, though purchase of a Bogardus front was considered, a contract for local castings was finally let. Inexperience led to delay, especially when the Third Street side, discovered to overreach the lot line by three inches, had to be taken down and refitted.[42] The resulting building contrasts markedly with the lightness and openness of Bogardus' products. It would be interesting to know what Haviland, still living at the time, thought of this mid-century revival of his idea of two decades earlier.

From modest beginnings and small-scale initial designs the iron front soon blossomed into large and luscious effulgence. Widespread acceptance came in part from the fact that the first examples and the enthusiastic claims of foundrymen now convinced previously hesitant owners and architects of the safety and economy of iron.[43] Metallic veneering soon became fashionable, especially for commercial structures. Bogardus pressed home his argument that the casting process at last made the richest aristocratic styles available within the limited budgets of the bourgeoisie.[44] Iron thus joined Walpole's cast stone, Nash's stucco, Inwood's terra cotta, and the ubiquitous *papier mâché* as one of those characteristic substitute materials symbolic of the nineteenth century's yearning for low-cost *haute couture*. In no other age has architectural respectability been more fervently sought. Only a few purists challenged the emulation of eclectic and masonry forms in iron, and even fewer seemed to appreciate its potentialities of litheness and openness.[45] Paxton's Crystal Palace and its

progeny quickly subsided before the taste for traditional effects. To Bogardus, Badger, and their rapidly multiplying competitors the iron front was primarily an opportunity for business exploitation. They swam with the current of dominant desire and, on the whole, found it profitable and easy exercise.

Bogardus had just occupied his new factory when in April, 1850, he associated with Hamilton Hoppin to win his first out-of-town contract to erect the large iron front of the Sun Building in Baltimore. No doubt the owner, A. S. Abell, had decided to use metal on the recommendation of his New York architect, R. G. Hatfield.[46] Badger supplied either rolling shutters or some of the castings.[47] The building was occupied in September, 1851. Except for similar bay widths, Hatfield's design differed decidedly from Bogardus' earlier fronts (Fig. 7). The ground story, occupied by shops, presented segmentally arched bays separated by deep, narrow, panelled iron piers over which a thin projecting fascia was supported by console brackets. This astylar treatment formed a curiously weak base for the vigorous display above. The four upper stories were given gradually diminishing heights and were grouped visually into two double stages by the introduction of arched windows in the third and fifth levels. The piers received strong emphasis through the use of three superimposed orders, each slenderized by projecting pedestal and entablature blocks. The verticals ended in the top story with statues above which large consoles jutted to carry the massive crowning cornice Thus, the full panoply of the then novel Baroque vocabulary was recruited to obtain a surprisingly vertical accent paralleling contemporary Gothic treatments such as had been used in the Jayne façade in Philadelphia. In the lush Sun design Hatfield established a prototype which was to be much admired and followed in the next two decades.

Cast-iron architecture received a powerful stimulus early in 1852 when Thomas Ustick Walter chose it for rebuilding the new Library of Congress within the U. S. Capitol itself.[48] It is interesting to note that of the eight bids submitted for the work seven came from New York State. Bogardus and Hoppin were among these, but lost the contract to their Centre Street neighbors, Janes, Beebe and Co., who during the next decade went on to furnish 4,454 tons of castings for the Capitol dome as well (Fig. 1).[49]

Perhaps Bogardus' best known iron façade was that erected in 1854 for the Harper Brothers Printing Plant facing Franklin Square in New York (Fig. 8).[50] The building replaced one lost in a disastrous fire. John B. Corlies, the architect and builder, designed the new plant to secure maximum safety against fire and also to reduce construction time to the minimum. The cast-iron front met both of these conditions, and to cut its fabrication schedule still further, Bogardus had the castings of the four upper stories made from the patterns of Hatfield's Sun Building in Baltimore. For the ground story, however, a stronger treatment, with elegant Corinthian columns and entablature, was substituted. Luckily, the 6½-foot width of the twenty bays of the 130-foot front meshed neatly with the internal structural system which Corlies determined.

Although Hatfield's approval to duplicate the Sun Building design was doubtless procured, the case raises an interesting professional problem. Since working drawings for a commission remain the property of the architect as "instruments of service," did iron architecture make it necessary for him to control the patterns as well? The possibility of similar duplication in other cases also emphasizes the need for caution in attributing the design of an iron front to a specific architect.

In 1858 Bogardus published an advertising pamphlet written for him by John W. Thomson, a teacher, and entitled *Cast Iron Buildings, their construction and advantages*. The text sums up all of his previous arguments and in addition lists more than 30 executed projects constituting a considerable accomplishment over the preceding decade. About half were located in New York and it is notable that Bogardus had already supplied fronts not only to clients in Philadelphia, Baltimore, and Washington, but also as far afield as Chicago, San Francisco, and Havana.[51] The Cuban commission was a tremendous warehouse for the Santa Catalina Company, 400 by 600 feet, and 50 feet high. It was reported in October, 1859, that it would still require two years to complete the contract.[52]

No doubt Bogardus' pamphlet was a natural reaction to the cessation of building in the 1857 panic and to the growing rivalry furnished by the increasingly successful Daniel Badger. In 1852, or soon after, Badger had employed, as manager of his new architectural department, a young and energetic English builder, George H. Johnson, who was later to play an important role in the development of terra cotta fireproofing for iron buildings.[53] By 1855 Badger's business required expanded production facilities which he obtained on East 14th Street between Avenue C and the East River. During the next year he incorporated his firm as the Architectural Iron Works of New York.[54] In 1857 he erected the monumental five-story façades of the E. V. Haughwout and Company's Store which still stands serenely on the northeast corner of Broadway and Broome Street (Fig. 9).[55] J. P. Gaynor, the architect, skillfully quoted Palladio in the bay motif of a window arch on a small order between piers with engaged Corinthian columns. Each story is separated by strong entablature and pedestal bands and the whole is crowned by a handsomely bold entablature. With its original light stone-tinted paint creating rich patterns of transparent shadows, it must have been one of the finest examples of the Renaissance Revival.

Iron front construction, for all of its novelty and economy, was actually a rather simple problem for firms skilled in making complex machinery. Before long, foundries throughout the country rushed to supply the growing market.[56] In New York, the Cornell, James L. Jackson, Excelsior (George R. Jackson), and Aetna Iron Works soon came to be very active in the field.[57] John B. Cornell, for example, erected in 1859–60 the largest and best known of all iron fronts, the A. T. Stewart Store (later Wanamaker's) on Broadway between Ninth and Tenth Streets for which John Kellum was the architect. Stewart proudly likened its four white-painted Renaissance façades, 85 feet high and 961 feet long, to "puffs of clouds." [58] By December, 1854, even the Pacific Foundry of San Francisco was advertising its building fronts.[59] Increasing interest likewise provoked a number of patents for iron construction.[60] However, none of those granted by 1860 was particularly significant; some were ingenious but impractical; others were obviously inspired by the desire of newcomers to obtain competitive advantage from the legal recognition implied.

It is beyond our scope to trace in detail the subsequent course of Ferromania. During the Civil War, even the North's need for munitions caused little curtailment. Indeed, President Lincoln ordered work on the Capitol dome to continue as a morale-building precaution.[61] When peace finally came, a building boom of record proportions loomed. Though the iron front was by then an accepted type of construction, Bogardus, now approaching the age of seventy, no longer was to be its presiding genius. Leadership passed to Badger and his Architectural Iron Works. In 1865 Badger issued a handsome catalog which listed 604 executed projects, of which 549 were single-story store fronts and 55 were façades of from two to six stories.[62] There had been erected in New York and Brooklyn 383 of the store fronts and 36 of the façades. The catalog illustrates many designs of excellent quality, perhaps because so many of them had been furnished by competent architects.[63]

The last great wave of iron fronts in New York came in the 1880's with the conversion of Mercer and Greene Streets, from Canal north to Houston, to serve as the city's principal wholesale dry goods district.[64] Block after block of towering lofts transformed quiet residential streets into metallic canyons. They add measurably to New York's remaining iron frontage which in 1943 still totalled, south of 14th Street, an impressive 2.75 miles.[65] Not until around 1890 did the fashion subside before more stringent building codes, the urge for greater height, and the new taste for Richardson's masonic Romanesque.

Thus, from the standpoint of the iron front alone, it appears that Bogardus, whatever he contributed to its popularization, most certainly did not invent, initiate, or monopolize it. While it cannot be proved that he knew of Haviland's or Fairbairn's work, it is very difficult to believe that he did not, because all the permissive factors suggest that he did. If he had claimed its invention while knowing the Pottsville bank and the Turkish flour mill, it would be difficult to acquit him of deliberate misrepresentation.

But did he make such a claim? The truth is that he did not. Actually, in his fullest advertisements, he described himself as "Architect in Iron; originator, constructor, and patentee of iron buildings; and manufacturer of the eccentric mill." It is interesting to note that this phrasing with the keyword "originator" appeared for the first time in the city directory of 1858, perhaps in response to Badger's growing competition and counterclaim. Although the

Fig. 7. Baltimore. Sun Building, 1851. (Courtesy of the Enoch Pratt Free Library)

Fig. 8. New York. Harper and Brothers' Printing House, Franklin Square façade, 1854. (Brown Brothers)

same statements recurred in a series of notices in the *Architects' and Mechanics' Journal* during the following year, the word "originator" was henceforth absent from subsequent directories until it was repeated in 1872 and 1873, the last two editions before his death on April 13, 1874.[66] Before 1858 he was content to confine his title to "machinist," or "eccentric mill maker," or "iron manufacturer," or "manufacturer of cast iron houses," or "Architect in Iron; constructor and patentee of Iron Buildings." [67]

Therefore it is clear that Bogardus never considered the iron front itself as more than a lucrative commercial product. On the other hand, his use of the term "Iron *Buildings*" indicated his interest in them as complete units, rather than in just their façades. But he did not even claim *iron buildings* as an invention in his patent, No. 7337, dated May 7, 1850; it was simply entitled "Construction of the Frame, Roof, and Floor of Iron Buildings" (Fig. 10). Drawn up as he was still finishing his own factory, it shows (upper left) a two-story version of the identical design he had used for Milhau, Laing, and himself, except that all applied ornament is omitted. The floor beams, seen in the sections, have interest in that each has a wrought-iron rod inserted in the lower ends of a cast-iron arch, forming a sort of trussed arch. Since wrought iron is markedly higher in tensile strength than cast iron, these beams saved considerable metal. Bogardus did not claim this as his own idea; indeed he could not, for John Gardner, a Berkshire engineer, had patented it in Britain in December, 1848, and had published it in the *Civil Engineers' and Architects' Journal* in 1849.[68] The resemblance between the two is striking.

Actually Bogardus claimed only three innovations. First, his method of bolting columns and girders through end flanges. Second, the tongue-and-groove jointing of his flooring sheets. And, third, the interlapping of his roofing plates. None of these was at all revolutionary or even important. Thus, the patent itself does nothing to bolster any pretension to great original contributions.

Moreover, it is significant that Bogardus, in his 1858 pamphlet, made only passing minor references to these innovations. He claimed special virtue for his bolted connections as overcoming vibration and expansion hazards. The flooring sheets would not permit fire to spread to other stories.[69] In contrast to these very general arguments, he stressed that the trussed arch principle, which he did not claim as his own, had been adopted by Corlies for the Harper Printing Plant. Here, however, the casting was greatly elaborated by complex ornamentation.[70] Apparently these trussed-arch girders aroused some general interest since, as soon as the Harper plant was completed, the New York Wire Railing Works was already picturing both plain and fancy versions in its catalog.[71] In any case, the joists supported on these Harper girders explain why trussed arches had no lasting significance, for these joists were rolled wrought-iron sections, 7 inches deep, developed by Abram Hewitt at Cooper and Hewitt's Trenton Iron Works and the first American examples of sufficient size to satisfy the requirements of building spans.[72] They, rather than the trussed arches, were prophetic of the floor systems of future skyscrapers.

If we assume that Bogardus constructed his factory according to his patent drawings, it becomes clear that it would be his use of iron for the whole ensemble—walls, floors, roof, and partitions—on which he must rest his claim as "originator of iron buildings." Stated in such terms, Haviland and his iron veneer would obviously be eliminated. Badger likewise could not compete because he claimed to have built only an iron store front in 1842. Bogardus probably would not have considered William Strickland's iron market house, erected in Philadelphia in 1834, as satisfying his definition since it had only a single story and therefore no iron floors.[73] He would have the same objection to the one-story sheet-iron prefabs which Britain had exported so diligently throughout the '40's. Thus, for him, Fairbairn would be the closest contender since his Turkish flour mill had iron walls, roof, and floor beams. But Fairbairn needed no partitions and the published sections of his mill show floor panels between the beams too thick to look like iron.[74] Unfortunately, Fairbairn did not describe these panels and, despite his statement that only the supporting pier of the machinery was of masonry, there remains the possibility that he formed the panels of segmental arches in brick or on some other non-metallic system. If indeed this was the case, Bogardus' claim would then be vindicated, but only by a few floor plates. It could hardly rest on slenderer grounds.

This conclusion is predicated on the assumption that Bogardus built his factory in conformity with his patent specification of an "iron building." In his 1858 pamphlet he called the structure "the first complete cast-iron building in America and in the world," but it is curious that, while he discoursed at some length on the details of the exterior walls, he remained singularly inexplicit about its internal construction. The suspicion that it perhaps was not as "complete" as he would have us believe is certainly not allayed by the *New York Sun's* report of its dismantling in 1859: "his building has been taken down piece by piece, even to the ornaments and *timbers*."[75] It is difficult to understand what role "timbers" could legitimately play in the world's "first complete iron building"! Perhaps the most charitable view we can take is that Bogardus desired to erect his factory wholly of iron, but, for some reason falling short of his goal, preferred for promotional purposes to present it as fulfilling the ideal exemplified in the patent which followed its completion by several months. If this argument seems excessively legalistic, we must remember that Bogardus was an enthusiastic promoter and

a very shrewd business man primarily concerned with selling his product in an extremely competitive mid-nineteenth century market. To him the desire of mid-twentieth century historians for a precise and complete record would probably seem a droll and irrelevant sport. Nevertheless the final irony is that no later building built by him according to his patent specification has thus far come to light.

It is clear that the reputation heretofore accorded Bogardus has arisen almost exclusively from the attribution

FIG. 9. New York. E. V. Haughwout and Company Store, 488–492 Broadway, at Broome Street, 1857. (Courtesy of the Otis Elevator Company)

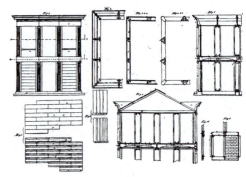

FIG. 10. Patent No. 7337, by James Bogardus, 1850. Drawings.

Bogardus Revisited; Part I, The Iron Fronts 19

to him of a creative role in the evolution of the cast-iron front. Closer study of the record reveals that this estimate has been based on a too-uncritical acceptance of claims he made in the heat of commercial rivalry. It is now apparent that, while his energetic part in popularizing iron fronts is demonstrable, his pretensions to innovating them must be evaluated in context and drawn from more than a self-laudatory advertising pamphlet. If this was his total contribution to American architecture, the importance previously bestowed upon him must be radically reduced.

But this was not the case, for in several works only recently recognized it can be shown that, perhaps inadvertently and without realizing their eventual significance, Bogardus achieved results which justify for him an honorable, if unsuspected, place in the main stream of architectural history. Part II of this study will present the evidence on which this well-deserved rehabilitation can be based.

1. A particularly adulatory account is contained in Sigfried Giedion, *Space, Time and Architecture* (Cambridge, Mass., 1941), pp. 129–134; a preliminary account is contained in Turpin C. Bannister, "Some Early Iron Buildings in New York," *New York History*, Vol. 24, No. 4 (October, 1943), pp. 518–24.

2. *Dictionary of American Biography*, "James Bogardus" by Carl W. Mitman, which was based principally upon obituaries in the *New York Herald* (April 14, 1874) and the *Scientific American* (May 2, 1874).

3. Palmer C. Ricketts, *Amos Eaton, Author, Teacher, Investigator* (Rensselaer Polytechnic Institute, Engineering and Science Series, No. 45 [Troy, 1933]), p. 9; H. S. Van Klooster, *Amos Eaton as a Chemist* (R.P.I., Eng. and Sci. Ser., No. 56 [Troy, 1938]), p. 5.

4. *DAB, loc. cit.*

5. *Doggett's New York City Directory, 1847–48.* In 1845 his shop was at 87 Eldridge.

6. *Ibid.*, 1848–49.

7. Bogardus always gave his address as "Centre, corner of Duane." Fig. 1, based on William Perris,' *Maps of the City of New York* (1st ed.; 1852), Vol. 3, Maps 25, 28; (3rd ed., 1857–62), Vol. 1, Map 14, shows that only the eastern corner provided a plot conforming to later views of the factory. Moreover, the indication on the Perris maps of a boiler (shown as a black rectangle) and a hazardous occupancy—not present on the other three corners—proves its use for industrial purposes. Bogardus no doubt preferred the general address to the more exact 25 Cross Street, which, being only one block long, would be less well-known. Curiously, both the first and third editions of the Perris maps show the factory as of brick ("Second Class") construction, but iron fronts were still too new to merit the separate classification they later received. The Milhau drugstore at 183 Broadway and the Tatham Works at 82–84 Beekman Street likewise appeared as brick buildings. The whole neighborhood represented in Fig. 1 disappeared in the 1920's with the creation of Foley Square.

8. James Bogardus, *Cast Iron Buildings, their construction and advantages* (New York, 1858).

9. The "Great Fire" of December 16–17, 1835, destroyed nearly 700 buildings in the seventeen blocks between Wall and Broad Streets and the East River. On July 19, 1845, more than 300 buildings in the same area burned (I. N. Phelps Stokes, *New York Past and Present* [New York, 1939], pp. 78–79).

10. Bogardus, *op. cit.*

11. *Moses King's Handbook of New York City* (Boston, 1892), pp. 806–7; *Moses King's Photographic Views of New York* (Boston, 1895), pp. 256–7; I. N. Phelps Stokes, *The Iconography of Manhattan Island* (New York, 1915–28), III, 883, Pl. 24A, b (1856 lithograph by W. Stephenson of the west side of Broadway, between Cortlandt and Fulton Streets, including the Milhau front).

12. The date of 1848 is established by a Milhau letterhead reproduced in *King's Photographic Views* (p. 256), and by Milhau's location at 183 Broadway in that year (*Doggett's New York City Directory*, 1848–49). Bogardus, *op. cit.*, lists Milhau as a customer. Reference to the priority of the Milhau front is given in Henry Ericsson, *Sixty Years a Builder* (Chicago, 1942), p. 152.

13. *History of Architecture and the Building Trades of Greater New York* (New York, 1899), II, 168–170, quoting *New York Evening Post*, May 3, 1849, in which the name is given as *Lang. Dog-*

gett's *New York City Directory, 1846–47* lists Edgar H. Laing and Co. with coal yards also at 61 Leonard, 13th and Hudson, and 21st and Ninth Avenue.

14. Huson Jackson, *A guide to New York Architecture, 1650–1952* (New York, 1952), p. 7. In 1954 the ground floor of 258 Washington Street was occupied by the Tom Tramutola Corp., produce dealers.

15. *History of Architecture . . . of Greater New York*, II, 169. A fine lithograph view of the Novelty Works, as of about 1850, is reproduced in color in John A. Kouwenhoven, *The Columbia Historical Portrait of New York* (New York, 1953), p. 205.

16. *History of Architecture . . . of Greater New York*, II, 169.

17. *Ibid*, II, 171. One is designated as being located on Broadway near Fulton. This might mean the Milhau drugstore, but, if so, the date is a year too late. In Bogardus' pamphlet (*op. cit.*), the list of customers, except for Milhau and Laing, does not include any others whose buildings appear to have been constructed by this time (cf. n. 51).

18. *Architects' and Mechanics' Journal*, I (1859). The October issue (p. 23, and an advertisement) still gave the Centre and Duane address. In November (pp. 47, 50), removal to the new locations was reported. In 1860, Bogardus' new office was listed at 198 Canal and in 1861 at 200 Canal where it remained until his death (*Trow's New York City Directory*).

19. Vol. 8, No. 97, p. 2. The item was copied by the *Daily Gazette* on the following day (Vol. 21, No. 6209, p. 2).

20. Vol. 5, No. CCXLII, p. 464.

21. On August 5, 1847, Winthrop B. Smith and Co., publishers and booksellers, were reported to have enlarged their Main Street store to five stories and doubled width, and "with new cast iron fronts" (*Daily Times*, Vol. 15, No. 2177, p. 3), but this could mean only ground-story shop fronts of iron with masonry walls above. Other blocks of stores for Millius, Loring, Dexter, and the Methodist Book Concern were noted on August 24 as improvements in 1847, but without mention of iron (*Cist's Advertiser*, p. 3, quoted from the *Daily Gazette*).

22. [*J. A.*] *Robinson and Jones' Cincinnati Directory for 1846*, p. 509. Lathrop was listed in 1840 as a pattern-maker originally from Connecticut (D. H. Shaffer, *The Cincinnati, Covington, Newport, and Fulton Directory for 1840*, p. 256).

23. Charles Cist, *Sketches and Statistics of Cincinnati in 1859* (Cincinnati, 1859), p. 279. Greenwood first listed iron fronts among his products in 1850 (*Williams' Cincinnati Directory and Business Advertiser for 1850–51*, p. 53).

24. Greenwood was born in 1807 at Jersey City, New Jersey. In 1817 the family moved to Cincinnati where, after a brief attempt at farming on the Indiana frontier, the boy supported his invalid father by various menial jobs. In 1825 father and son joined the Owenites at New Harmony where the latter took charge of the mill's steam engine. After a sojourn in Pittsburgh to learn the foundry trade, he managed the community factory. After the colony disbanded in 1828 Greenwood returned to Cincinnati and in 1832 established the Eagle Iron Works. By 1850 he was the largest iron manufacturer in the West. In 1843 the burning of a large packing plant opposite the foundry, and in 1847 the destruction of his own shops by fire impressed Greenwood with the urgent need of incombustible buildings. In 1852 he won for the city its first paid fire de-

partment and built for it the first successful steam fire engine in the United States. His plant was a primary Northern arsenal during the Civil War. He founded the Ohio Mechanics' Institute and served as president of the company which built Roebling's Ohio River Suspension Bridge. He died in 1885. (*DAB*, "Miles Greenwood"; *Appleton's Cyclopaedia of American Biography* [New York, 1900], II, 758; M. Joblin and Co.: *Cincinnati past and present* [Cincinnati, 1872], pp. 101–5.) By 1859 Greenwood iron fronts had been erected in St. Louis, New Orleans, Chicago, Memphis, and Nashville (Cist, *Sketches*, p. 279).

25. J. Leander Bishop, *A History of American Manufactures from 1608 to 1860* (Philadelphia, 1868), III, 206–7.

26. *Illustrations of Iron Architecture made by the Architectural Iron Works of the City of New York* (New York, 1865), p. 4.

27. Patent No. 2554, dated April 11, 1842.

28. *History of Architecture . . . of Greater New York*. II, 167; *Illustrations of Iron Architecture*, p. 28.

29. *Doggett's New York City Directory*, 1849–50, 1850–51.

30. Roger H. Newton, *Town and Davis, Architects* (New York, 1942), p. 184. A view is given in Herman L. Fairchild, *History of the New York Academy of Sciences* (1887).

31. François Thiollet, *Serrurerie de fonte et de fer recémment exécutées* (Paris, 1832). Plate 20 illustrates three single-story fronts in the Rue Vivienne, No. 12, designed by Billaud.

32. William Pole, ed., *Life of Sir William Fairbairn, Bart.* (London, 1877), p. 174; Samuel Smiles, *Industrial Biography, Iron workers and Toolmakers* (London, 1863), p. 330; William Fairbairn, *Useful Information for Engineers* (2nd ser.; London, 1860), p. 226.

33. Pole, *op. cit.*, quoting Fairbairn's paper in *Minutes of Proceedings, Institution of Civil Engineers*, 1843, p. 125; William Fairbairn, *Treatise on Mills and Millwork* (London, 1865), pp. 252–4. William Fairbairn, "On Iron as a Material for Building and Decoration," a paper read June 10, 1844, before the Royal Scottish Society of Arts, cited for special thanks, not printed in the Society's *Transactions*, but published in abridgment as "On the Uses and Adaptation of Iron as a Material for Building," *Civil Engineers' and Architects' Journal*, VII (June, 1844), 249. Iron construction was adopted primarily as a safeguard against the notorious fires of Constantinople where most buildings were of timber and Moslem fatalism made fire-fighting more than casual.

34. *New York Evening Post*, Aug. 12, 1842; *Daily Cincinnati Gazette*, Vol. 16, No. 4916, May 23, 1843; the *Journal of the Franklin Institute* reprinted almost immediately similar items from numerous British publications; even the trade periodicals were surprisingly active in this regard. During the early 1840's, French and Belgian sheet iron houses were noted in many American journals.

35. *History of Schuylkill County, Pennsylvania* (Albany, N.Y., 1881).

36. John Haviland, *An Improved and Enlarged Edition of Biddle's Young Carpenter's Assistant* (Philadelphia, 1833), p. 45, Plate 60; Turpin C. Bannister, "The Architectural Development of the Northeastern States," *Architectural Record*, Vol. 89 (June, 1941), p. 74.

37. *History of Schuylkill County*.

38. Piotre Artamof, *La Russie, historique, monumentale, et pittoresque* (Paris, 1862), I, 56; Paul Planat, *Encyclopédie de l'Architecture et de la Construction* (Paris 1888–93), "Staroff"; Architectural Publication Society, *Dictionary of Architecture* (London, 1853–92), "St. Petersburg." The arch was of granite faced with iron plates cast by the English engineer, Clark, who was governor of the Imperial Iron Foundry.

39. Thiollet (*op. cit.*, Pl. 21) shows the two-story front of the Café de Malthe, built on the corner of the Rue and Boulevard St. Martin by the architect, Paul Lelong, *fils*. No date is given, but, since Thiollet certainly offered it in 1832 as *à la mode*, it probably was concurrent with the Pottsville bank.

40. *Hazard's Register of Pennsylvania*, April, 1830, p. 232 (quoting the *Pottsville Advocate*), and July, 1830, p. 400 (quoting the *Miners' Journal*). Since Haviland inserted it in his 1833 edition of Owen Biddle's *Young Carpenter's Assistant*, which down to the Civil War remained the most influential American handbook

on building construction, it gained prompt and wide recognition.

41. The discovery, documenting, and publicizing of the Penn Mutual and its importance were accomplished by Charles E. Peterson (*Journal of the Society of Architectural Historians*, Vol. IX, No. 4 [December, 1950], pp. 24–25).

42. *Ibid.*

43. Both Bogardus (*op. cit.*) and Badger (*Illustrations of Iron Architecture*) stressed the prejudice they had met against the structural use of cast iron due to the failure of certain British structures and the fear that it would crush, melt, crack, and attract lightning.

44. Bogardus claimed to have conceived the reproduction of richly modelled historic styles while in Italy in 1840 and thought that "Their general introduction would tend to elevate the public taste for the beautiful and to purify and gratify one of the finest qualities of the human mind." He noted that elaborate designs increased the cost very little, and rationalized that the only danger lay in ornamental buildings which lacked structural stability (*op. cit.*).

45. The critical arguments culminated in December, 1858, in the papers read before the American Institute of Architects by Henry Van Brunt (pro) and Leopold Eidlitz (con). These were discussed in the *Scientific American* and the *Architects' and Mechanics' Journal* (Vol. 1, [1859], November, pp. 28–9; December 3, 31, pp. 51–2, 83). A rejoinder in the latter (December 24, p. 77) was signed "Vindex," who was surely Bogardus himself.

46. J. T. Scharf, *History of Baltimore, City and County* (Baltimore, 1881), p. 621 and illustration opposite p. 618; G. W. Howard, *The Monumental City, History, Resources, and Biography* (Baltimore, 1872), p. 57; Richard H. Howland and Eleanor P. Spencer, *The Architecture of Baltimore, a Pictorial History* (Baltimore, 1953), p. 88, Plate 65. The building was destroyed in the great fire of 1904.

47. *Illustrations of Iron Architecture*, p. 23.

48. Turpin C. Bannister, "The Genealogy of the Dome of the United States Capitol," *Journal of the Society of Architectural Historians*, Vol. VII, No. 1–2, (January–June, 1948), pp. 1–31; *Documentary History of the Construction and Development of the United States Capitol Building and Grounds* (Washington, 1904), pp. 341–4.

49. *Doc. Hist.*, pp. 348, 1027. The highest bid, submitted by Erastus Corning of Albany, was for $87,636; Bogardus asked $72,-518, but Janes, Beebe and Co. easily won the contract at $59,872.

50. "The Harper Establishment, or How the Story Books are Made" (in Jacob Abbott, *Harper's Story Books* [New York, 1855 (?)]); *Visitors' Guide to Harper and Brothers Establishment* (New York, 1891); J. Henry Harper, *The House of Harper* (New York, 1912), pp. 92 ff.

51. New York customers: Milhau; Harper and Brothers; the McCullough and Tatham shot towers (described later in this paper); and the following stores (dates and addresses deduced from changes in *Doggett's New York City Directory* (1850–56) and *Trow's New York City Directory* (1857–60):

1851? [O.] Blunt and Syms, guns, 177 Broadway [or 1858 at 300 Broadway]
1854 H[enry S.] Sperry and Co., clocks, 338 Broadway
F[rancis] Hopkins and Brothers, glass, 61 Barclay
Emigrant Industrial Savings Bank, 51 Chambers [Robert J. Dillon, lawyer, also listed, was vice-president of the bank, and, therefore, probably not a direct purchaser].
1855 Charles O'Connor, tailor, 129 Cedar
Christal and Donahue, paints, 226 Pearl
John H. Sherwood, shoes, 9 Park Place
Spofford and Tileston, commission merchants, 29 Broadway
1856 McKesson and Robbins, drugs, 91 Fulton
1858 George [W.?] Bruce, hardware, 39 Warren
Douglass Robinson, insurance [?], 33 Pine
William H. Munn, lawyer, is also listed, but no building can be deduced, unless he was connected with Munn and Co., publishers of *Scientific American*. This is plausible since this journal often advocated iron buildings.

It is curious that Bogardus did not list one of his largest New

York projects, the Thompkins Market-Seventh Regiment Armory, Third Avenue, Sixth and Seventh Streets. Theodore Hunt built the vast three-story iron hall, 135 by 225 feet, in 1856–60 from plans by Bogardus and Lafferty (Stokes, *Iconography*, V, 1865, 1870, 1888; *King's Handbook*, pp. 496, 749, 754).

52. *Architects' and Mechanics' Journal*, I (October, 1859), 23.

53. A. T. Andreas, *History of Chicago* (Chicago, 1886), p. 87. Johnson was born in 1830 at Manchester and learned the building trade with the Manchester builders, Robert Neil and Sons. In 1849 he established his own business.

54. Bishop, *op. cit.*, p. 204.

55. *Illustrations of Iron Architecture*, Pl. 3. The building is now occupied by the Broadway Manufacturers' Supply Co. Its passenger elevator, the first commercial installation, was furnished by Elisha Graves Otis.

56. At Baltimore in 1851 Bogardus' Sun Building immediately stirred Hayward, Bartlett and Co., leading stove manufacturers, to open an architectural iron department (Ferdinand C. Latrobe, *Iron Men and their Dogs* [Baltimore, 1941], p. 18). The firm supplied part of the ironwork for the Harper Building in New York, and in 1856 shipped 265 tons of iron fronts to that city (*ibid.*, p. 22). In 1870 it sent a three-story front for the Corbett Building, 531 SW First Avenue, Portland, Oregon (*ibid.*, pp. 14–15). By 1872 it had cast at least eight fronts for Baltimore buildings, and others for Richmond, Raleigh, New Orleans, and Galveston (Howard, *op. cit.*). Also in 1851 Williams and Adams' Novelty Iron Works of Cincinnati began to compete with Lathrop and Greenwood in manufacturing "house fronts" (Cist, *Sketches*, p. 199).

57. *A History of Real Estate, Building, and Architecture in New York City during the last quarter of a century* (New York, 1898), p. 459.

58. *Loc. cit.; Architectural Record*, I (1891–2), 244; *History of Architecture . . . of Greater New York*, II, 164–6. Kellum had previously used many Badger fronts (*Illustrations of Iron Architecture*, pp. 25–33).

59. *The Pacific* (San Francisco newspaper), December 29, 1854. I am indebted to Charles E. Peterson for contributing this item.

60. During the 1850's, the following U.S. patents related to iron front construction were granted:

1. 1851, No. 7951, Joseph Banks, New York: Improved connexion for the Beams and Columns of Iron Buildings. (A system of interlocking lugs and flanges cast in the members of iron fronts.)
2. 1851, No. 7993, Simon Willard, Cincinnati: Construction of Metallic Buildings. (Floors, walls, and roofs of wrought-iron sheets with bent flanges.)
3. 1853, Michael B. Dyott, Philadelphia: Improvement in Facing or Veneering Buildings. (Cast-iron plates fastened to masonry by spikes driven through flanges. Joints waterproofed by cement.) (Apparently an application only. Noted in *Report of the U.S. Commissioner of Patents* [1853], p. 286.)
4. 1854, No. 10,756, Stephen Colwell, Philadelphia: Using Iron for Buildings. (Iron skeleton units, joined by H-shaped keys, covered by iron plates.)
5. 1854, No. 11,290, Charles Mettam (architect), New York; Construction of Iron Houses. (System of jointing of cast-iron members.)
6. 1854, No. 11,509, Amos J. Saxton, Brooklyn: Mode of Constructing Iron Buildings. (Elaborate system of interlocking joints of iron structural members without use of bolts, rivets, or nails.)
7. 1854, No. 11,809, Bernard J. LaMothe, New York: Iron Building. (Members formed by laminated plates or bands.)
8. 1855, No. 13,379, D. D. Badger, New York: Iron House. (System of connecting cast-iron members by flanges.)
9. 1856, No. 14,208. Harriet V. (William D.) Terry, Boston: Mode of Constructing Cast-Iron Buildings. (System of cast-iron boxes, plates, and ties to form hollow walls.)

10. 1859, No. 22,542. A. J. Bowers: Iron Column. (Sides of square column joined by wedges.)

61. I. T. Frary, *They Built the Capitol* (Richmond, 1940), p. 194.

62. *Illustrations of Iron Architecture*, pp. 23–35. The company had the great advantage of producing store fronts, with its patent rolling shutters, which were in strong demand for masonry-walled structures. Badger's prosperity, unlike Bogardus', was therefore not entirely linked with multi-story iron façades.

63. Of the 419 projects in New York and Brooklyn, architects were named for 174. Those most frequently named were (Griffith) Thomas and Son, J. B. Snook, R. G. Hatfield, (John) Kellum, J. F. Duckworth, and S. A. Warner, but James Renwick and Richard Upjohn were also represented. Many other fronts, though listed without architects, may well have been so designed. Almost all of the multi-storied façades had architects. However, Badger's stock designs were also of high quality; most of these were created by George H. Johnson whose taste and skill were amply proved by his five-story Gothic façade built in 1860 for the Grover and Baker Sewing Machine Company, 495 Broadway, just north of the Haughwout Store (Kouwenhoven, *op. cit.*, p. 326). The fact that Hanford was officially the architect of this building suggests that some practitioners took the easy course of securing design service, in addition to production, from Badger's firm (*Architects' and Mechanics' Journal*, I [October, 1859], p. 23). This extra service may well explain the increasing success of the Architectural Iron Works. Another factor was probably Badger's emphasis of architects' names in his list, a courtesy which Bogardus apparently neglected.

64. *History of Real Estate . . . in New York City*, pp. 125–7; but the trend had already started by 1865 when Badger listed a five-story front designed by Kellum and built for A. T. Stewart at 18 Mercer (*Illustrations of Iron Architecture*, p. 31).

65. G. W. Bromley and Co.: *Atlas of the City of New York, Borough of Manhattan* (Philadelphia, 1931), Pls. 1–32.

66. *Trow's New York City Directory*, 1858 to 1873; *Architects' and Mechanics' Journal*, I, October, November (p. 50), 1859, and several subsequent issues. A peculiarly exaggerated claim was made for Bogardus in 1851 in the *National Intelligencer* (reported and countered in the *Scientific American*, VI [June 28, 1851], 325) which asserted that he had initiated the principles of cast-iron construction, spread them in Britain during his stay there, and thus inspired Paxton and his Crystal Palace! The *Scientific American* deprecated such obvious chauvinism and cited in refutation several early cast-iron bridges and the cast iron lighthouse built in 1824 at Glasgow (see n. 88).

67. *Doggett's New York City Directory*, 1845 to 1850; *Rode's New York City Directory*, 1852; *Trow's*, 1854 to 1857.

68. XII (1849), 250.

69. This argument recalls the purpose of the iron fire plates for the covering of ceilings which David Hartley patented in England in 1773 (Winchcombe Saville Hartley, *An Account of the Invention and Use of Fire-Plates* [London, 1834]; Great Britain, H. M. Patent Office, *Alphabetical Index of Patentees and Applications for Patents of Inventions* [London, 1854], p. 254). The fact that Hartley's book appeared only two years before Bogardus' arrival in London suggests that he could easily have known it.

70. Abbott, *op. cit.*, p. 25. The girders were manufactured by James L. Jackson (*ibid.*, p. VIII).

71. Issued 1855. A copy is in the Landauer Collection, New-York Historical Society. I am indebted to Charles E. Peterson for bringing this item to my attention.

72. Abbott, *op. cit.*, p. 32 ff.; Allan Nevins, *Abram S. Hewitt, with Some Account of Peter Cooper* (New York, 1935), pp. 86, 101, 111, 114–116.

73. Agnes A. Gilchrist, "Market Houses in High Street," in Luther P. Eisenhardt, ed., *Historic Philadelphia, from the Founding until the Early Nineteenth Century* (*Transactions, American Philosophical Society*, Vol. 43, Part 1), (Philadelphia, 1953), pp. 305–9.

74. Fairbairn, *Treatise on Mills and Millwork*, pp. 252, 254.

75. Reprinted in *Architects' and Mechanics' Journal*, I (November, 1859), 47.

Part II : THE IRON TOWERS

THE PARADOX OF James Bogardus has been that thus far his reputation for influencing the course of American architecture has been based on a misguided evaluation of his least significant accomplishment, the cast-iron front. He himself was responsible in large part for this misconception because he emphasized these façades in his advertising pamphlet of 1858, and because he failed to call attention to other works which led directly to an achievement of major importance. If Bogardus' contribution is to be properly judged, it is necessary to assess his whole production.

One project which has achieved considerable renown was the proposal which Bogardus submitted in 1852 for New York's Crystal Palace (Fig. 11). The design called for a huge circular hall at least 400 feet in diameter which would have filled Reservoir Square (now Bryant Park), the western half of the two-block site facing Sixth Avenue between Fortieth and Forty-second Streets. In the center a cast-iron circular tower, about 75 feet in lower diameter, was to rise in thirteen open stories to a height of 300 feet. A four-story cast-iron front ringed the 1200-foot outer circumference. The resulting annular hall, with an internal span of about 150 feet, was to be covered by a sheet-iron roof hung from link chains slung radially between tower and outer wall.[76] It was easily the boldest project offered in the competition.[77]

It is obvious that Bogardus' roof was inspired by current interest in suspension bridges. In 1845 John Roebling had built a suspended canal aqueduct over the Allegheny River near Pittsburgh. The following year he completed the Monongehela Bridge in the same city. By 1849 Roebling had erected four more canal aqueducts, and Charles Ellet had gained fame for a Niagara footbridge and his Ohio River span at Wheeling. In 1851 Roebling had begun the first successful railroad suspension bridge, that across the Niagara Gorge.[78] No doubt Bogardus had also seen or read of earlier British and French examples. Was he the first to apply the suspension idea to a building? The answer is "No," for by 1840, the year in which he had visited France, there was under construction at the Brittany naval base at

Lorient a suspended iron roof, 140 feet in span, over the mast shop of the arsenal (Fig. 12). Moreover, in the same year this roof was illustrated in the fifth edition of Sganzin's *Cours de Construction,* a standard engineering text well known in the United States.[79] It is significant that Bogardus did not contemplate hanging his roof on wire cables, already being marketed by Roebling, but proposed link-chains such as were common in British practice and actually used for the similar span of the Lorient atelier.[80]

Of the supporting elements, the outer wall obviously stemmed from Bogardus' experience with cast-iron fronts. Its greatest interest lay in the ingenious circular plan which, acting as a self-bracing ring, would, theoretically at least, not have required any guys or buttresses to resist the inward pull of the radial roof chains. It was, however, the 300-foot central tower which formed the most prophetic part of the design. Although framed towers in timber were certainly no novelty, and although Trevethick in 1832 and Buckingham in 1848 had proposed towers built of iron, Bogardus' cast-iron skeleton was more than an idle dream because it was based on his own practical experience during the previous year. The Crystal Palace project has been cited as evidence of Bogardus' inventive genius, primarily because of its suspended roof. Its true merit is now seen to lie, not in fundamental innovations, but rather in achieving an imaginative architectural synthesis of current structural ideas.

There remain to consider five Bogardus structures which he himself never regarded as worth comment. The first three he did not even mention in his 1858 pamphlet; he listed the owners of the last two but without naming the works themselves.

The first two were fire alarm bell towers for the city of New York. The conflagration of 1845 had proved once more that prompt alarm and the immediate despatch of equipment were vital necessities, and· that the old system of isolated lookouts and bells on a few public buildings could no longer be tolerated in a metropolis. In 1847, on recommendation of the chief engineer of the city fire department, the Council authorized the linking of the five existing lookout stations to department headquarters by telegraph.[81] In 1850 the city was divided into eight fire

Part I: Bogardus and the Cast-Iron Front *appeared in the December 1956* JOURNAL.

districts and several new timber bell towers were erected.[82] Some of these timber structures promptly burned.[83] Bogardus immediately proposed that such towers should be built of cast iron and the Council ordered one to be erected on 33rd Street near Ninth Avenue. It was finished by mid-August, 1851 (Fig. 13).[84] The tower was decagonal and about 100 feet high with six open stages of iron columns and horizontal beams. An iron spiral stair mounted to the enclosed lookout-at the top. The bell, the largest in the continent and the fifth largest in the world, hung in the fourth stage.[85] It is obvious that this structure was the prototype of the 300-foot central tower of Bogardus' Crystal Palace proposal of 1852. In 1853 Bogardus and Hoppin built a second iron bell tower for the city near the corner of Macdougal and Spring Streets.[86]

The third structure was a lighthouse, almost identical in size and construction to the New York bell towers (Fig. 14). It was fabricated in 1853 for the Dominican Republic and was erected at the mouth of the Ozama River to mark the harbor of the capital, Santo Domingo (Ciudad Trujillo).[87] Bogardus' adaptation of the iron bell tower construction to lighthouses reveals once more his alertness to recent developments. Although the use of cast iron for such structures had been proposed as early as 1799 by Robert Stephenson and by Captain Joseph Brodie, R.N., and Joseph Couper, iron founder of Leith, for Bell Rock in the Firth of Tay, the first to be constructed, in 1824, was a small 30-foot high tower on Broomielaw Quay, Glasgow.[88] In 1834 William Tierney Clark erected another small one on the town pier at Gravesend.[89] Three years later, when Bogardus was in London, Captain Sir Samuel Brown, R.N.,

proposed a 90-foot cast iron lighthouse for Wolf's Rock, near Land's End.[90] During the 1840's several towers on this larger scale were achieved. The first was built in 1841–42 by Alexander Gordon, engineer to the London commissioners, on Morant Point, the easternmost tip of Jamaica, West Indies. Its nine tiers of flanged cast-iron plates formed a 100-foot tower shaped like a conical masonry tower.[91] Several others subsequently employed this frameless, plate construction.[92] More pertinent to Bogardus' iron-framed towers was the beacon constructed in 1843 at Black Rock harbor, on the south end of Block Island, Long Island Sound. It was 34 feet high and had a structural frame of wrought iron.[93] In the following year in Britain a similar frame, but of cast iron enclosed with wrought iron plates, was used by Walker and Burges for the 60-foot Point of Air lighthouse at the mouth of River Dee, northwest of Chester.[94]

It is clear, therefore, that Bogardus' towers take their place in a sequence which he must have known from a steady stream of publications during the 1840's. While his projects were visually lighter and more characteristic of iron because he omitted the usual enclosing jackets, this choice was determined by economy and not aesthetics. His Santo Domingo tower was "arranged to receive iron pannelling should it ever be found desirable to enclose it."[95]

The final pair of Bogardus' structures are towers for the manufacture of gun shot. In such towers molten lead was poured through a sieve at an upper level; the falling drops congealed into shot as they fell down the shaft and were caught and cooled in a large tank of water at the bottom. The gauge of the sieve and the height of fall controlled the

FIG. 11. Bogardus' Project for the New York Crystal Palace, 1852. (Benjamin Silliman, Jr., and C. R. Goodrich, *The World of Science, Art and Industry.*)

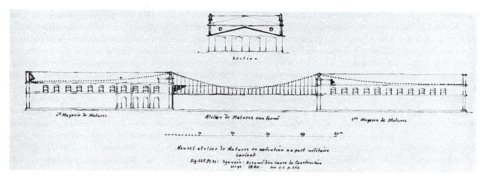

Fig. 12. Lorient. Naval Arsenal, Mast Shop, c. 1840. (Sganzin, *Cours de Construction*, Plate 51, Fig. 265)

size of the pellets. Such towers were commonly about 200 feet high, built of massive brick masonry, and shaped somewhat like an overgrown factory chimney. Perhaps the best known early example is the Phoenix Shot Tower which still stands majestically at Front and Fayette Streets in Baltimore. Its date is 1828 and its height 246 feet.[96]

Early in 1855 in New York James McCullough, president of the McCullough Shot and Lead Company, decided to move his business from Front Street to 63–65 Centre Street, a block north of Bogardus' factory and on the west side of the street (Fig. 1). This decision led to two difficulties. First, a traditional brick tower with its excessively thick lower diameter would leave little work space in the modest shop surrounding its base. Second, the site selected could hardly have offered worse soil conditions to support a tremendous load of vertical masonry because it lay exactly in the middle of the former Collect Pond which, though it had been obliterated by miscellaneous fill, flowed on (and to this day still flows on) in an underground drain to the Hudson.[97] Bogardus immediately came to the rescue, and in two months—from August 15 to the middle of October— built a tower uniquely slender and light.[98] Atop a firm foundation of brickwork, $4\frac{1}{2}$ feet thick and 18 feet deep, the superstructure rose 175 feet. The octagonal shaft was $15\frac{1}{2}$ feet in outside diameter at the top, but the base was only 25 feet, about half the usual dimension. To achieve this result, Bogardus had used eight cast-iron corner posts, tied together at the eight interior platform levels by horizontal cast-iron members. The resulting framework was thus based in principle upon his fire alarm towers but stood almost twice as high and almost two-thirds the height of his Crystal Palace project. More important, however, was the fact that the sides of this cage were then enclosed with 12-inch-thick panels of brick supported entirely by the framework. That this was indeed the case is clearly revealed in the photograph made just before the tower was taken down in 1908 (Fig. 15).[99] It reveals that, in order to make the catch basin at the base of the tower easily

accessible from the shop in which it stood, the enclosing panels had been omitted entirely in the ground story.

Here, at one stroke, Bogardus anticipated the iron-skeleton, curtain-walled skyscraper of the next generation. It antedated Préfontaine's warehouse at the St. Ouen Docks by a decade.[100] Saulnier's Turbine Building for the Menier Chocolate Company at Noisiel-sur-Seine was sixteen years in the future.[101] All that Bogardus' tower lacked to equal the final structural solution of the skyscraper was to protect the ironwork from fire by imbedding it within the masonry. Nevertheless, Bogardus did not invent curtain-wall construction. Examples lay all around him. Consciously or subconsciously, he adapted a principle widely used in medieval half-timbered construction. In the 1860's, when French architects adopted the same iron-framed, masonry panelled system, in naming it their term for "half-timber," *pan de bois*, with great lucidity became *pan de fer*.[102] Did Bogardus reason thus? He may well have done so, since the better-built wood-framed houses of his day still commonly used brick nogging. His contribution was simply to combine the framework of an iron lighthouse with a masonry jacket.

The second tower, for Tatham and Brothers, was built the following year at 82 Beekman Street (Fig. 16). The crowded site called for repetition of Bogardus' previous solution. Each of eight columns rested on a massive brick foundation pier weighing 30 tons, joined to its neighbors by inverted arches. On this was erected the 217-foot tower.[103] Again, the columns were joined by girders, but, although they too supported the enclosing brickwork, they were hidden inside these walls. No doubt this change came from a desire to protect the iron girders and their bolts as much as possible from the weather. In doing so, however, Bogardus inadvertently moved closer to later fireproofing principles. The tower was demolished in 1907.[104]

The slender verticality of these towers made them conspicuous landmarks.[105] In 1860 McCullough illuminated his with candles at its forty windows to celebrate the visit of Edward, Prince of Wales. But their plans did not permit public visits for observation, and so they remained aloof utilitarian curiosities. Yet we should ask whether they were only idle aberrations or whether they deserve a place in the main stream of structural evolution.

Unfortunately, the record is not definitive. Nevertheless, it is significant that in 1855 George Johnson was working in Badger's office at 42 Duane Street, only a block and a half south of McCullough's tower (Fig. 1). It is inconceivable that he would have neglected such a unique opportunity to follow its erection. Leaving Badger's employ in 1862, Johnson opened an architectural office in New York, but after the end of the war worked briefly in Richmond and with Hayward, Bartlett and Company in Baltimore.[106] In 1869 he moved to Buffalo to erect a fireproof brick grain elevator on a system which he patented.[107] This experience stirred his interest in recent French patents for fire-resistant floors of hollow tile and iron beams and early in 1871 he visited Paris to study them.[108] On his return to New York, he and Balthasar Kreischer obtained a patent on a similar system.[109] Immediately after the Chicago fire in October, Johnson rushed there to promote his tile and the following spring won its adoption for the Kendall Building which was designed by John M. Van Osdel, for whom a decade earlier Johnson had erected several of Badger's

Fig. 13. New York. Fire alarm bell tower, 33rd Street near Ninth Avenue, 1851. (*Illustrated News*, Vol. 1, 1853, p. 61)

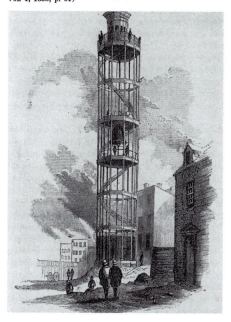

iron fronts.[110] When the Chicago boom subsided in 1874, Johnson returned to New York, but failed to stir interest in his product. Finally, in September, 1877, he again came to Chicago and with his son set up a company to make and install the tile. After his death late in 1879 his son helped form the Ottawa Tile Company which was later to become the well known Pioneer Fire-Proof Construction Company.[111]

Meanwhile, in the late '70's, some Chicago architects were seeking means to raise the ceiling of Loop structures without forfeiting valuable light and rental space to excessively massive bearing masonry. In 1879 William LeBaron Jenney took the initial step in the five-story first Leiter Building. In it he introduced rectangular cast-iron columns on the inner faces of the east and west walls and piers to support the timber girders of the floor system. On the façades each bay had triple windows divided by two cast-iron mullions which ran vertically as continuous columns from foundations to roof. The brick spandrel panels under these windows were carried on cast-iron lintels supported by the mullion-columns and, at the ends, by the main piers of masonry.[112] In the eastern façade facing Wells Street it would have required only the moving of the rectangular iron columns to the center of the masonry piers and the bolting of the ends of the spandrel lintels to these columns to achieve a true curtain wall carried upon a skeleton frame. Late in 1883 Jenney incorporated these final steps in his design for the nine-story Home Insurance Company's Office Building which was erected during the following year.[113]

Inevitably, an advance so fundamental to the development of skyscraper construction has encouraged many speculations with regard to the milieu of ideas out of which Jenney created his final culminating solution. Without detracting in any way from the crucial role of this remarkable man, it is usually recognized that most great technical innovations have arisen out of the partial and hesitant contributions of many experimenters. Indeed, this was Jenney's own view.[114] For this reason, therefore, Jenney's background and contacts assume uncommon significance and interest. He had studied at the Lawrence Scientific School; in 1856 he had earned the diploma in civil engineering of the *Ecole centrale des arts et manufactures* in Paris; he had returned to France in 1858–59 for business, study, and travel; and he had had excellent experience in railroad building and as General Sherman's chief engineer during the Civil War. For many years he was the only Chicago architect to attend the annual conventions of the American Institute of Architects normally held in eastern cities. Moreover, the fact that Jenney had served as Professor of Architecture at the University of Michigan during the academic year 1876–77 suggests both that he undertook a serious analytical review of current structural developments in preparation for his lectures and that he enjoyed stimulating association with an excellent engineering faculty.[115]

Two suggested sources of Jenney's inspiration have a strong apocryphal flavor. William B. Mundie, assistant from 1884 and, after 1891, partner in Jenney's firm, believed that Jenney first recognized the advantages of skeleton construction when, as a youth on a voyage in one of his father's whaling ships, he observed in Manila the strength of native bamboo-framed huts.[116] On the other hand, Henry Ericsson, who built the Manhattan Block for Jenney and therefore knew him well, relates that Jenney was impressed with the lithe strength of skeleton construction when he witnessed his wife lay a heavy book upon a wire birdcage.[117] Even if such romantic rationalizations contain a grain of truth, they deal solely with one phase of the problem, the skeleton alone. In any case, such sources were surely superfluous in a city where dwelling construction had for half a century been dominated by that most dramatic application of the skeleton principle, the balloon frame![118]

The crux of the problem was more than just the skeleton frame; it was the combination of this frame with an enclosure, and the building of the whole system in incombustible materials. Jenney's specific motives in attacking the problem were three-fold. First, he had long desired to

Fig. 14. Santo Domingo (Ciudad Trujillo), Santo Domingo, Lighthouse, 1853. (*Illustrated News*, Vol. 1, 1853, p. 133)

improve the natural lighting of office buildings.[119] Second, he wished to reduce the weight of masonry bearing walls and thereby simplify foundation and settlement problems as well.[120] The third motive came to focus in April, 1883, when the first great strike of Chicago bricklayers revealed the alarming stranglehold which that group had acquired over all large-scale commercial building in Chicago.[121] The first of these factors resulted in the wall columns and mullions of the Leiter Building; the other two inspired renewed effort during the designing of the Home Insurance Building.

In facing these problems, Jenney most certainly did not work in a vacuum. He had kept well informed by reading American and foreign, and especially French, technical journals.[122] It seems highly probable that he had learned with little delay of the St. Ouen dock warehouse and the Menier Turbine Building, published in 1865 and 1873, respectively.[123] Likewise, he may well have studied in the mid-'seventies the stimulating and prophetic second volume of Viollet-le-Duc's *Entretiens sur l'architecture*, in which appeared in 1872 the challenge: "A practical architect might not unnaturally conceive the idea of erecting a vast edifice whose frame should be entirely of iron, and clothing that frame, preserving it by means of a casing of stone." [124]

Notwithstanding these timely possibilities, there remains the question of a specific stimulus. This may well have stemmed from Bogardus because it seems highly probable that Jenney knew the McCullough and Tatham shot towers. After returning from Paris late in 1856 he was in New York at least twice during the following winter, only a few months after their completion. He was there again in April, 1858, and in 1860 on business as an engineer for the Bureau of American Securities, and he returned to the city in 1866 to accept the vice-presidency of two New York companies which operated coal mines in northern Pennsylvania.[125] Thus, with his absorbing interest in structures, it is difficult to believe that he failed to note Bogardus' soaring landmarks. In 1868 Jenney came to Chicago and soon established himself as an architect.[126] His first important commercial building was the Portland Block in 1872 and this was followed by the Lakeside Block in 1873 and the Crilly Building in 1878. Since height had not yet become an architectural passion, he adopted for these structures the prevailing mode of heavy bearing masonry for exterior walls.[127] But, although Jenney was already endeavoring to provide adequate natural light for the offices in these blocks, the required masonry piers strictly limited window size. In 1879 the Leiter façades corrected this defect and even exceeded the large glass areas already attained in some iron fronts.[128] The emphatic demand of the officers of the Home Insurance Company for maximum light provided Jenney with the final incentive to create his full solution of skeleton frame and curtain wall.[129]

It is tempting to suppose that George Johnson helped to

Fig. 15. New York. McCullough Shot and Lead Company, 63–65 Centre Street, Shot tower, 1855. View during demolition in 1908. (Courtesy of the New-York Historical Society, New York City)

Fig. 16. New York. Tatham and Brothers, 82 Beekman Street, Shot tower, 1856. (Courtesy of the Charles A. Schieren Company)

refresh Jenney's recollection of Bogardus' towers. Perhaps between October, 1871, and early 1874 when he was in Chicago installing his tile fireproofing in the Kendall Building and the Cook County Courthouse and Jail, or between September, 1877, when he returned to form his tile-making company, and his death late in 1879, Johnson recognized the basic similarity between the problems solved by Bogardus' towers and those inherent in the new tall buildings of Chicago, and suggested their applicability to the Chicago situation. No doubt it was only coincidence that the Home Insurance Building, the first of the new breed, was, with its height of 179 feet, only four feet higher than the McCullough tower, and that both had the same number of stories, but the correspondence does indicate analogous structural conditions and techniques. No record survives that Johnson and Jenney discussed Bogardus' towers, but it is difficult to believe that they lacked opportunities to do so. In promoting his product, Johnson must surely have visited frequently all of the city's important architectural offices. It may well have been Johnson's efforts that led Jenney, four years after Johnson's death, to adopt hollow tile fireproofing for the Home Insurance Building. Thus, though detailed confirmation is absent,

the surmise of such contact does not violate credibility. The conjunction of persons, interests, experiences, and motives seems too compatible to lack meaning.[130] If Jenney knew the New York shot towers—either with or without Johnson's help—and it seems entirely plausible that he did, Bogardus' neglected orphans comprise a new and important element in Jenney's technical equipment, take on unexpected significance in the evolution of modern architecture, and paradoxically become their creator's greatest claim to architectural fame.

In summary, the evidence presented in this investigation seems to deny Bogardus the fundamental inventive genius once accorded him. But, if he formulated no new, epoch-making principles, he did exhibit amazing alertness and receptivity in adapting to his purposes, and with admirable alacrity, the rapidly expanding technology of his day. Thus, he was an intriguing representative in the field of mid-nineteenth-century building construction of that phenomenon, the inspired mechanic, who has done so much in every age to apply science and technology to the needs of daily life. To this activity he brought a restless energy often considered typical of the new American nation. He was a born promoter and exploiter. Indeed, it is his enthusiastic vitality which now most arouses our sympathy and interest. If this role is less dramatic than that previously conceived for him, it is still one that is highly creditable. For, in the last analysis, he popularized iron fronts so effectively that the fashion for them reached almost every city in our land. To this we can now add the likelihood that he contributed, through his long-neglected towers, to the realization of our national architectural symbol, the skyscraper. Perhaps the best measure of Bogardus' true place in the evolution of our architecture is that he has required and received a century afterward so long an essay to define it.

76. Benjamin Silliman, and C. R. Goodrich, *The World of Science, Art, and Industry* (New York, 1854).

77. Other competitors were: Sir Joseph Paxton, whose proposal was singularly undistinguished; Andrew Jackson Downing, who suggested a huge canvas-covered, iron-ribbed dome; J. W. Adams, who conceived a large octagonal dome supported on ribs made of bundles of gas pipes; and Leopold Eidlitz, who also offered a suspended roof (Horace Greeley, ed., *Art and Industry as Represented in the Exhibition at the Crystal Palace, New York, 1853–54* [New York, 1853], pp. xi–xii). The iron and glass hall actually erected was designed by Karl Gildemeister (1820–69), a native of Bremen who worked for some years in New York as an artist and architect (Planat, *op. cit.*, "Gildemeister, Karl"; *Trow's New York City Directory*). For this project he took as partner Georg Johan Bernhard Carstensen (1812–57), a Dane who had laid out in 1843 and then managed Copenhagen's favorite pleasure park, Tivoli (*Illustrated News*, I [1853], 11; II, 46; Greeley, *loc. cit.*; *Dansk Biografisk Leksikon* [Copenhagen, 1934], IV, 558–61). Carstensen's role was apparently that of a cosmopolitan "idea" man and it was he who, drawing upon extensive Spanish and North African travels, initiated the building's exotic mélange of Saracenic ornament.

78. David B. Steinman, *The Builders of the Bridge* (New York, 1945), pp. 85, 90–99, 103–5, 161–9.

79. Joseph-Mathieu Sganzin (1750–1837), eminent French civil engineer, was from 1798 professor at the Ecole Polytechnique and from 1803 *Inspecteur général des Ponts et Chaussées*. Ordered by Napoleon to publish his lectures, his *Cours* first appeared in 1807. ("Notice of the life and services of the late M. Sganzin," translated from *Annales des Ponts et Chaussées*, 1837, in *Journal of the Franklin Institute*, Vol. 22, 2nd series, 1838, p. 123.) A second edition was issued in 1809, a third in 1821, and a fourth in 1838. The Lorient suspended roof was noted in the fifth edition (1840) as then under construction (I, 350, Pl. 51, Fig. 265). An English translation of the third edition was published in Boston in 1827, with a second in 1828, and a third in 1837 (H.-R. Hitchcock, *American Architectural Books* [3rd ed.; Minneapolis, 1946]). The Lorient roof may also have inspired Joseph Aloysius Hansom, London architect, to propose in 1842 a Metropolitan Music Hall, the roof of which was to hang from chains suspended from four corner towers to form "the largest room in the world" (*Mechanics' Magazine* [London], Vol. 35 [1842], p. 265, quoted in J. C. Loudon, *Encyclopaedia of Cottage, Farm, and Villa Architecture* [2nd ed.; London, 1846], p. 1251). Since both of these publications had an enormous distribution, it is not impossible that Hansom's project may also have stimulated Bogardus. All of these may indeed owe a general debt to the *Rotonde du Panorama*, built in 1839–40 at Paris by the architect, Jacques-Ignace Hittorff. (J.-I. Hittorff, *Description de la rotonde du Panorama des Champs-Elysées* [Paris, 1842]; *Revue Générale* (Daly), II [1841], 500, 511, Pl. 27–31). The filiation was not direct since the Parisian roof rested *upon* suspended iron rods rather than being hung *from* iron chains.

80. Roebling began the manufacture of wire rope at Trenton late in 1849 (Steinman, *op. cit.*, p. 141).

81. Lowell M. Limpus, *History of the New York Fire Department* (New York, 1940), pp. 184–5. The stations were located atop City Hall, the Merchants' Exchange, and the Jefferson, Centre, and Essex markets. The alarm bell on the roof of City Hall is seen in Edward Burckhardt's panoramic drawing (reproduced in Kouwenhoven,

op. cit., p. 191). Three bells, each larger than before, had cracked in 1836, 1838, and 1848, until finally in 1849 a bell weighing five tons was installed with a striking apparatus which rotated the bell slightly at each stroke (Stokes, *Iconography*, V, 1817). It should be noted that New York's first telegraph line, to Philadelphia, was completed in 1846 (Stokes, *New York, Past and Present*, p. 79).

82. Limpus, *op. cit.*, p. 199

83. The Jefferson Market tower, Sixth Avenue at Tenth Street, burned July 29, 1851. It was rebuilt in timber (Stokes, *Iconography*, V, 1835). A woodcut view of this tower is given in Limpus, *op cit.*, p. 198. A contemporary photograph is in the De Voe scrapbook at the New-York Historical Society.

84. Stokes, *Iconography*, V, 1835.

85. *Illustrated News* (New York), I (1853), 61.

86. *Ibid.*; Stokes, *Iconography*, V, 1847; Limpus, *op. cit.*, p. 257; *Harper's Weekly Magazine*, February 28, 1874, with views drawn by Winslow Homer (reproduced in Kouwenhoven, *op. cit.*, p. 341).

87. *Illustrated News*, I (1853), 133, with a woodcut view. The octagonal tower rose, in four open stages, about 17 feet in diameter, and a fifth stage somewhat smaller, to a height of 75 feet. It cost $6000, f.o.b. New York.

88. Letter of John Rennie (*Civil Engineers' and Architects' Journal*, XII [1849], 77–9); Robert Stephenson, *Report to the Commissioners of the Northern Lighthouses* [1800], p. 440; *Glasgow Mechanics' Magazine and Annals of Philosophy*, I (1824), 162.

89. Peter Paterson, "An Account of the Cast-Iron Lighthouse Tower on Gibbs' Hill in the Bermudas" (*Minutes of Proceedings, Institution of Civil Engineers*, IX [1849–50], 182. Statement by Alexander Gordon during discussion); "Memoir on William Tierney Clark" (*Ibid.*, XII [1852–3], 153).

90. *Journal of the Franklin Institute*, XIX (2nd series, 1837), 55, quoting *Mechanics' Magazine* (London).

91. *Civil Engineers' and Architects' Journal*, IV (1841), 333–4.

92. Gibbs' Hill, Bermuda, 106 feet high, designed 1842, erected 1844–45, by Alexander Gordon (Paterson, *loc. cit.*); harbor at Galle, Ceylon, 80 feet high, 1846, by Gordon (Architectural Publication Society, *Dictionary of Architecture*, "Lighthouses, Iron"); Fasnet Rock, southwest Ireland, 86 feet, 1848–54 (W. H. D. Adams, *Lighthouses and Lightships* [New York, 1870], pp. 204–6); Middleton Point, Saugar Island, at the mouth of Hooghly River, south of Calcutta, Bengal, 70 feet high, designed by Cowper for East India Company, cast 1850 by Fox, Henderson Company (*Civil Engineers' and Architects' Journal*, XIII [1850], p. 309).

93. *Journal of the Franklin Institute*, VI (Series 3, 1843), 385–90. It was designed by Captain W. H. Swift of the Corps of Topographical Engineers, and the ironwork was fabricated by Cyrus Alger of Boston.

94. *Civil Engineers' and Architects' Journal*, VII (1844), 208, 293.

95. *Illustrated News*, I (1853), 133.

96. WPA Writers' Program, *Maryland, a Guide to the Old Line State* (New York, 1940), p. 228, and photograph following p. 282; the operation of this tower is shown in *Illustrated News* (New York), I (1853), 244–5. It rivalled Europe's tallest, the 249-foot tower at Villach, Austria. The walls of the Phoenix tower at grade were 4 feet, 6 inches thick. In 1853 there were six shot manufacturers in the United States: two in New York, and one each in Philadelphia, Baltimore, St. Louis, and Lead Mines (now Austinville), Wythe County, Virginia (*ibid.*). Thomas Jackson's shot

tower at Lead Mines was a square 75-foot tower built of stone about 1820 (WPA Writers' Program, *Virginia, a Guide to the Old Dominion* [New York, 1940], p. 478). The Chicago Shot Tower Co., organized by Eliphalet W. Blatchford in 1867, erected a typical masonry tower at 40 North Clinton St. (*Industrial Chicago* [Chicago, 1891], II, 427; woodcut view in *A Business Tour of Chicago* [1887], p. 85).

97. The original shore line is shown by the Landmark Map, Battery to Franklin Street, reproduced in Stokes (*Iconography*, III, Pl. 174) and apparently based on Ratzer's map of 1766 (I. N. Phelps Stokes, *American Historical Prints* [New York, 1933], p. 22, Pl. 20) which Stokes characterized as extremely accurate; in the Taylor Roberts map of 1796 (*ibid.*, p. 42, Pl. 36–b), which Stokes also described as accurate, the pond was already considerably reduced by filling; by about 1811 it finally disappeared (Stokes, *New York, Past and Present*, p. 25). Haviland's Halls of Justice, "the Tombs," 1838, rested its Egyptian Revival mass on the same fill in the block just to the north. The pond drained originally through a small brook to the East River, but at the time of filling a cut was dug to divert the flow of the springs west to the Hudson via the canal which later became Canal Street (Fremont Rider, *New York City, a Guide Book for Travelers* [2nd edit.; New York, 1924], p. 198).

98. *New York Daily Times*, October 1, 1855, cited in Stokes, *Iconography*, V, 1862, and reported in *The Builder* (London), XIII (December 15, 1855), 616.

99. Demolition was due to the construction of the Interborough Subway which curves northwestward from Centre Street into Lafayette (Elm) Street, passing directly under the site of the tower. After the Civil War, the plant had been bought by the Colwell Lead Company.

100. *The Builder* (London), XXIII (1865), 297; Roger H. Newton, "New Evidence on the Evolution of the Skyscraper," *Art Quarterly*, IV (Winter, 1941), 56–69.

101. *Encyclopédie d'Architecture*, III (Sér. 2, 1873), 116–120; VI, 91–3; Russell Sturgis, *Dictionary of Architecture and Building* (1901), "Iron Construction" by W. R. Hutton; Sigfried Giedion, *Bauen in Frankreich, Eisen, Eisenbeton* (Berlin, 1928), p. 46. The use of this construction arose because the building housed waterpowered machinery and was erected on piers across the Marne River.

102. Planat, *op. cit.*, "Pan de fer."

103. *New York Daily Times*, December 18, 1856, cited in Stokes, *Iconography*, V, 1865.

104. It was taken down between May 25 and June 5 to make way for an addition to the adjoining Schieren building (*New York Sun*, January 2, 1907, cited in Stokes, *loc. cit.*). The main building at 82 Beekman has an iron front which was probably furnished by Bogardus. Bogardus did not follow the custom of other iron works in placing a signature plate on the front, but the scale and detail of this front seem similar to his work.

105. Panoramic views showing either or both towers: aerial view, woodcut in *Harper's Weekly*, November 19, 1870, shows the Tatham tower from a station point which apparently was the top of the McCullough tower, and at the center of the lower edge just reveals the upper story of the building which replaced Bogardus' Factory (reproduced in Kouwenhoven, *op. cit.*, p. 332); both towers appear in a photographic panorama taken by W. W. Silver in 1874 from the roof of the Post Office (copy in the New York-Historical Society; reproduced in Stokes, *Iconography*, III, Pl. 155a); *King's Handbook* gives photographs taken about 1890 from the dome of the World Building looking north up Centre Street with the McCullough tower at mid-distance (p. 54), and looking southeast toward the Tatham tower (p. 62).

106. Andreas, *op. cit.*, III, 87.

107. The Niagara and Plympton Fireproof Grain Elevator (*ibid.*); Johnson was copatentee with George Milsom of Patent No. 87,679, dated March 9, 1869. It should be noted that in 1859 Badger and William S. Sampson had received Patent No. 24,424 for an iron grain elevator, and that Badger had erected two such elevators, each 107 by 125 feet and five stories high, one for the U. S. Warehouse Company, Atlantic Dock, Brooklyn, and one for the Pennsylvania Railroad on Washington Street, Philadelphia.

In his 1865 catalog Badger named Johnson as the architect of both (*Illustrations of Iron Architecture*, pp. 23, 34).

108. Andreas, *op. cit.*, III, 87.

109. Patent No. 112,926, dated March 21, 1871.

110. Andreas, *op. cit.*, III, 88. Van Osdel (1811–91) had first come to Chicago in 1836 as a builder. During the winter of 1840–41, he was in New York as associate editor of the *American Mechanic* (which after a hiatus became in 1845 the *Scientific American*). Ericsson (*op. cit.*, pp. 134, 184, 287; no source is cited, but he had known Van Osdel well) states that Van Osdel "worked with Badger on his [Badger's?] iron front idea." In 1840 Badger was listed in *Adam's Boston Directory* as a partner (or employee) of A. Richardson and Co., saw makers, but he did not appear in the 1841 and 1842 issues. Neither was he listed in New York in these years, but it is still possible that he may have been in New York and met Van Osdel. In 1841 Van Osdel returned to Chicago and two years later became a partner of Elihu Granger in a foundry and machine shop. In 1845, at the request and guarantee of a group of Chicago builders, Van Osdel opened the city's first architectural office (Ericsson, *op. cit.*, p. 135; *Industrial Chicago*, I, 594). Due to his interest in iron, his professional designs came to include an increasing amount and diversity of iron (Ericsson, *op. cit.*, p. 184). Van Osdel and Johnson, as Badger's agent, are credited with the introduction of iron fronts in Chicago in 1856 (*ibid.*, pp. 151–7; Thomas E. Tallmadge, *Architecture in Old Chicago* [Chicago, 1941], p. 109). In that year they furnished fronts for: the Allen Robbins block of stores at the southeast corner of South Water and Wells, 231 foot frontage, 5 stories (*Illustrations of Iron Architecture*, p. 24, Pl. 54); and two five-story groups with uniform façades opposite each other on Lake Street east of State Street: the north side, 136 feet long, built for five owners, Frederick Tuttle, Jason McCord, George Collins, Tuthill King, and S. P. Skinner (Ericsson, *op. cit.*, pp. 151–2; *Industrial Chicago*, I, 102, plate opp. p. 154; II, 384; *Illustrations of Iron Architecture*, Pl. 70), and the south side, 135 feet long, for Cornelius and William Price, J. W. Waughop, M. D. Gilman, and Thomas Church (Ericsson, *op. cit.*, p. 153; *Industrial Chicago*, I, 384). The latter two made Lake Street "the finest architecturally in the city, with scarcely a rival on the continent" (Ericsson, *op. cit.*, p. 151; two views in Jevne and Almini, *Chicago Illustrated*, portfolio in the Chicago Historical Society), and comprise a late commercial survival of the English "terrace" idea. In 1857 Van Osdel designed five five-story fronts: Daniel McElroy, southwest corner of Randolph and Dearborn; M. O. Walker; William Jones; Peter Page; and Alexander Lloyd, northwest corner of Randolph and Wells (Ericsson, *op. cit.*, pp. 155–6). Ericsson (p. 156) states that Van Osdel let the contracts for these façades to local foundries, but that the panic of 1857 led Jones and Page to curtail orders, and Lloyd, who paid $11,256.85 to N. S. Bouton for his façade, was ruined in the crash. Badger, however, in 1865 listed Lloyd as a customer, and also J. Link (*Illustrations of Iron Architecture*, p. 24, Pls. 7, 19), the latter being located at La Salle and Lake (*Industrial Chicago*, I, 117). Moreover, in 1858 Bogardus (*op. cit.*) listed four Chicago customers: Isaac H. Burch, A. G. Burley and Co., Peter Page, and Tuttle. If the attribution in 1868 of all Chicago iron fronts, 1100 feet of frontage, to Van Osdel was correct (*Biographical Sketches of the Leading Men of Chicago* [Chicago, 1868], p. 94), it suggests that the Bogardus fronts were erected before 1856, because the priority of the Robbins front by Badger is based on the fact that it appears as the first item in the first of three extant volumes of Van Osdel's office record books (now in the Chicago Historical Society). A five-story Burch Block, destroyed in the 1871 fire, stood on the southwest corner of Wabash and Lake streets (photograph in Paul Gilbert and Charles L. Bryson, *Chicago and Its Makers* [Chicago, 1929], p. 322), but only the first floor store fronts appear certainly to be of iron. The duplication of Frederick Tuttle in both the Bogardus and Badger lists may mean that Tuttle, with his numerous real estate interests, had used an iron front before his 1856 Lake Street building. Bogardus' front for Page could be either that erected in 1857 or an earlier one. No iron-fronted building survived the fire of 1871, but twenty new iron façades were erected in 1872, many replacing earlier examples (Ericsson, *op. cit.*, p. 211; *Industrial Chicago*, II, 385–6).

111. Andreas, *op. cit.*, III, 88.

112. William B. Mundie, "Skeleton Construction, its origin and development applied to Architecture" (Manuscript written in 1932 and recorded by *Chicago Architectural Archives Project*, under sponsorship of the Burnham Library of the Art Institute of Chicago and the Department of Architecture of the University of Illinois, Microfilm Roll No. 23) pp. 14–15; Frank A. Randall, *History of the Development of Building Construction in Chicago* (Urbana, Illinois, 1949), pp. 13, 88–9; Carl W. Condit, *The Rise of the Skyscraper* (Chicago, 1952), pp. 112–3. In 1888 two more stories were added. The building, now known as the Morris Building, still stands at 200–208 West Monroe Street, at the northwest corner of Wells. The working drawings were microfilmed by the Chicago Architectural Archives Project.

113. Mundie, *op. cit.*, pp. 32–9; Randall, *op. cit.*, pp. 105–7; Condit, *op. cit.*, pp. 114–6, 133; Tallmadge, *op. cit.*, pp. 193–7. The building stood on the northeast corner of Adams and LaSalle Streets. It was demolished in 1931. In 1890 two more floors had been added. The working drawings were microfilmed by the Chicago Architectural Archives Project.

114. Report of a committee for the Field Estate, quoted in Tallmadge, *op. cit.*, p. 196. Mundie (*op. cit.*, pp. 10–11) emphasized that "Jenney was always opposed to any statement that spoke of skeleton construction literally as an invention . . . it was the evolution of principles . . . though it remained for Mr. Jenney to apply throughout an entire building what had been done before only in small parts of buildings. Architects had occasionally been obliged to build an iron column into a masonry pier where the load was too great for the masonry, and Mr. Jenney had done this several years before in the Fletcher and Sharp Bank Building in Indianapolis, in order to gain light." It should be noted that, in citing the age-old use of the skeleton principle, Jenney adopted the best possible defense against the false pretensions of Buffington's claim to priority (see n. 122). Mundie also records (pp. 95–6), apropos Buffington's patent of 1888, that "Jenney often stated that the question of applying for a patent occurred to him at the outset, but what was done as a whole (in the Home Insurance Building) had often been done in a single pier; he did not think that the patent, if attacked, could be successfully defended. Still he regretted he had not made the application, as it would have established conclusively his priority."

115. An autobiographical statement covering the period to the end of the Civil War is recorded, along with Jenney's scrapbook, in Microfilm Roll No. 11, *Chicago Architectural Archives Project; Industrial Chicago*, I, 602; *DAB*, "William LeBaron Jenney," by Carl W. Mitman.

116. Randall, *op. cit.*, p. 12, based on Mundie, *op. cit.*, pp. 10–11. Jenney himself did not mention this observation in his autobiographical statement, but his later lectures at the Art Institute on primitive and historical buildings and his articles in the *Inland Architect* indicate that he appreciated such examples as illustrating fundamental principles.

117. Ericsson, *op. cit.*, pp. 217–8, which may be an elaboration of the general statement by Mundie (*op. cit.*, p. 11).

118. Walker Field, "A Reexamination into the Invention of the Balloon Frame," *Journal of the Society of Architectural Historians*, Vol. 2, No. 4 (October, 1942), pp. 3–29. Mundie (*op. cit.*, p. 11) also offers this analogy.

119. Mundie, *op. cit.*, pp. 11, 16, 27.

120. Ralph B. Peck, *History of Building Foundations in Chicago* (University of Illinois Engineering Experiment Station, Bulletin Series No. 373 [Urbana, Illinois, 1948]), p. 19.

121. Ericsson, *op. cit.*, pp. 62, 67–71, 216–8.

122. Mundie notes (*op. cit.*, p. 4) that Jenney was "an intense student and inveterate reader" with special interests in archaeology and metallurgy.

123. See nn. 100 and 101.

124. *Discourses on Architecture*, trans. Benjamin Bucknall (Boston, 1881), p. 128. Due to Jenney's command of French, he was not dependent on the English edition of this work. The claim of Leroy S. Buffington that he invented skyscraper construction after reading this passage in 1881 has been thoroughly discredited (Dimitri Tselos, "The Enigma of Buffington's Skyscraper," and Muriel B. Christison, "How Buffington Staked His Claim," *Art Bulletin*, Vol. 26, No. 1 [March, 1944], pp. 3–24).

125. Autobiographical statement and letters in Scrapbook (*Chicago Architectural Archives Project*, Microfilm Roll No. 11).

126. In 1868 the firm of Jenney, Schermerhorn, and Bogart laid out the new suburban town of Riverside, designed by Frederick Law Olmsted and Calvert Vaux. It also designed several city parks in west Chicago. In 1869 the firm of Loring and Jenney built Grace Episcopal Church.

127. The Portland Block had seven stories and the Lakeside Building six (Randall, *op. cit.*, pp. 62, 82; Mundie, *op. cit.*, pp. 13, 28–9).

128. Mundie, *op. cit.*, p. 27. The building was nicknamed "the conservatory."

129. *Ibid.*, p. 16. It should be noted that since 1879 the main office of the company in New York had been located at 117–119 Broadway, near Cedar Street, not many blocks from the McCullough and Tatham towers.

130. This hypothesis naturally raises two questions: first, why did not Bogardus' towers bear fruit on Manhattan itself? and second, why, if Johnson acted as catalyst, he did not stimulate Van Osdel to adopt Bogardus' construction? As to the second, the answer seems to be that Chicago's needs in 1856 had not yet exceeded the limits of traditional masonry structures and that Johnson himself at that time was preoccupied with selling iron fronts for such buildings. As to New York, the explanation apparently lies in the fact that the development of business properties was not constricted by land hunger, as in Chicago's Loop district, until the turn of the century.

4

The development of fireproof construction in Great Britain and the United States in the nineteenth century

Sarah Wermeil

Introduction

Although the word "fireproof" has disappeared from the builder's lexicon, nineteenth century architecture and engineering journals routinely discussed fireproof construction. To modern ears, "fireproof building" is an oxymoron, since, as I am frequently told, it is the contents of a building that burn, not the structure. But this is true only for certain buildings – in fact, only for fireproof buildings. The vast majority of homes in the United States are not fireproof and burn very well. On the other hand, new buildings in city centres generally are fireproof, as they are compelled to be by building laws. Today, because most buildings which the public can enter are, in the nineteenth century sense, "fireproof", there is no reason to distinguish them from "non-fireproof" buildings, and so the designation has fallen out of use. The predominance of fireproof buildings is a twentieth century phenomenon. In 1800, only a handful of buildings that could be called fireproof existed in Great Britain and the United States. By the end of the century, fireproof construction was standard for tall buildings in the United States, a type which increasingly dominated the downtowns of large American cities, and a great variety of systems for constructing fire-resisting buildings was available in both nations. As fireproof buildings replaced buildings of ordinary construction, the danger of general conflagration decreased. After the first decade of the twentieth century, the era of great urban conflagrations in the United States was over.

What, then, is a fireproof building? In nineteenth century terms, it was a building constructed of incombustible materials; in other words, wood was not used structurally or if used, was protected with some non-inflammable material. The discarding of wood applied particularly to the interior of structures – to the spanning parts – since exterior walls were easily made incombustible. Indeed, since the seventeenth century, public authorities in London and Boston, Massachusetts, for example, required that walls of buildings in the town centres be made of brick or stone, as a fire protection measure.[1] Yet the interiors of even masonry-walled buildings – the floors, partitions, and roofs – were made of wood, as well as the window frames, doors, cornices, and so forth, which could communicate a fire on the outside of a building to the inside.

Despite steady development in practice, and contrary to popular belief, a fireproof building conferred no magic immunity from harm. "Fireproof construction must not be understood to mean a mode of constructing buildings in which no fire can arise; nor does it even imply that the buildings so called fireproof are absolutely safe from destruction or damage by fire", *Building News* explained in 1861. Rather, "fire-proof construction ... is little more than construction in which incombustible materials only are employed."[2] Likewise, Peter B. Wight, an American architect and authority on fireproof construction, observed in 1879 that "the most that can be attained by the best known systems of fire-proofing – and this is the main thing after all – (is) the preservation of the constructive portions of a building".[3] In so defining the term, neither writer meant to minimise the importance of fireproof construction but rather to caution what a fireproof building could and could not do. Fireproof buildings were intended to check the spread of a fire and eliminate the structure itself as a source of fuel. The building should be designed so that the floors and roof act as horizontal firebreaks, just as masonry party walls and parapets made

The Development of Fireproof Construction

vertical firebreaks. By creating fire-resisting compartments, and thus containing a blaze, a fireproof building bought time, for occupants to escape and firefighters to do their work. Thus, fireproof buildings had to be more than merely compositions of uninflammable materials, and they had to be backed up by a means of suppressing a fire. Ideas about what constituted best or prudent practice changed over the course of the century, as understanding of the performance of materials and the relative value of certain design features and fire protection appliances increased.

In this paper, I trace the development of, and attempt to account for differences between, fireproof construction practices in Great Britain and the United States in the nineteenth century. To know what in theory constituted the best fireproof construction I rely on contemporary authorities – the architects, engineers, fire insurance underwriters, and construction materials manufacturers who studied, worked on, and wrote about fireproof buildings.

Fireproof Buildings Before Iron and Brick Arched Floors

The British engineer Charles Sylvester, commenting on developments in structural fire protection in an 1819 pamphlet, wrote that before the introduction of the iron and brick system, fireproof buildings had been made "with ceilings and roofs of stone". Already in the mid-eighteenth century the architectural writer Batty Langley proposed a solid masonry building system "to prevent the sad consequences of fire in dwelling-houses". It consisted of "brick floors, with arches, groined, or coved ceilings", as well as stucco trim, stone staircases, brick interior partition, and lead covering for the roof.[4] Whether or not dwellings were built this way, at least some small industrial buildings at the Royal Dockyards were constructed with brick vaulted roofs for fire protection. Also at the dockyards, cellars in buildings for holding flammable stores were covered with brick vaults.[5] While evidence is very scanty as to how extensively the system was used in Britain, it is probably safe to take Sylvester's word that "such buildings are very uncommon, very expensive, and the principle upon which they are constructed is not at all adapted for the common purposes of life".[6] However, vaulted cellars continued to be built in Britain in the nineteenth century for secure storage.[7]

In the last quarter of the eighteenth century, fires occurred in London with "alarming frequency", prompting calls for public intervention.[8] In the first significant revision of London's building laws since the Great Fire over one hundred years before, the Act of 1774 added metal, artificial stone (concrete), and tile to the list of materials allowed in exterior walls, which materials came to be the principal ones used in new systems of fireproof construction.[9] At this time in Britain, however, no one had yet proposed a substitute for wood in floors (save for impractical vaults).

Rather, invention went in the direction of better protecting wood, thereby creating fire barriers. One invention, patented by David Hartley in 1773, wrapped wood floor members in thin sheets of iron called "fire-plates".[10] Although Hartley tested his invention in a building known as the Fireproof House, the plates were a way of making ordinary construction slower burning, not of making a fireproof, or incombustible, building. The plates were used in public and industrial buildings – for example, at storehouses in the Royal Dockyards in the 1780s[11] – and dwellings. While Hartley's plates seem to have gone out of use by the turn of the century, some building owners continued to wrap sheet iron around wood structural members for fire protection. For example, in 1807, the roof timbers of an existing corn mill, which became a wing of the new fireproof Armley textile mill in Leeds, were wrapped in thin sheets of iron.[12] A second proposal was an application of a kind of concrete, such as was used to deaden floors, to fire protection. In 1778, Lord Mahon proposed that the spaces between joists be filled with a mixture of lime, sand, and chopped hay to a depth of about one and one half inches.[13] Like Hartley's plates, this system could be applied to existing buildings. In the same vein, building owners sometimes placed plaster around beams and under flooring with the idea of making floors more fire resistant. But

Sara Wermiel

such measures could create structural problems. While common lime plaster was found not to exclude air from wood, plaster (a natural material, so of varying compositions) could cause dry rot unless the wood beneath was ventilated, as could sheets of iron tightly wrapped around wood.[14] Various methods for protecting wood were improvised over the years: wire lath and plaster, paints made with alum, interlocking tile plates, and slabs of "fibrous plaster". But to make a truly fireproof building a substitute for wood had to be found.

By the 1790s, just as British building owners started experimenting with iron joinery, solid masonry fireproof buildings began to appear in the United States. The masonry system continued to be the method of building fireproof in the United States until the late 1840s. Unlike in Britain, where extant examples suggest that such buildings were small, the American masonry fireproof buildings were relatively large public buildings. Commissioned by federal and state governments for the most part, they often were several storeys high, with floors formed of brick barrel or intersecting arches carried on exterior walls and interior partitions or columns of stone or brick, levelled with concrete, and covered with stone or terracotta tiles. The system probably was first used in Philadelphia, where a prominent early example was the Bank of Pennsylvania, designed in 1789 by Benjamin Latrobe. Latrobe had recently immigrated to America, having apprenticed and practised architecture in his native England, and probably brought knowledge of this method of construction with him.[15] Latrobe's apprentices, Robert Mills and William Strickland, and Strickland's student Thomas U. Walter, went on to design most of the fireproof buildings erected in the United States in the first half of the nineteenth century.

Robert Mills was especially prolific, designing many fireproof buildings while serving as architect and engineer for the state of South Carolina in the 1820s, and later as architect and engineer for the national government. Several of his fireproof custom houses and court houses still stand, as do his Treasury, Patent Office, and Post Office buildings in Washington, DC, the last three built between 1836 and 1842. (Fig 1.) Despite his experience designing such buildings and attempts at innovation, Mills was unable to overcome the limitations of the system. For example, in the U.S. Treasury building, he tried to make the exterior walls thinner by constructing the floor arches with "hydraulic cement", which he believed "constitute them like

Fig 1: Stone columns and fireproof vaults in the Old U.S. Patent Office, Washington, D.C., built 1836–40 (Collection of the National Portrait Gallery, Smithsonian Institution).

The Development of Fireproof Construction

one mass of masonry, relieving the lateral, and increasing the perpendicular press of the arches".
This building became the target of a Congressional committee, inquiring whether it was unsafe
and Mills incompetent.[16] While politics and professional rivalry muddled the investigation,
nevertheless it seems that there was no settled practice for constructing such buildings. And
indeed, these cave-like buildings were not very practical. An unhappy resident of Newburyport,
Massachusetts, described Mills' damp custom house fifty years after it was built: "...there was not
in the city a more dreary and desolate place than the Custom House".[17] But although
unsatisfactory as buildings, they undoubtedly were fire resistant.

Fireproof Construction in Britain, 1790–1860

The search for less expensive and more practical systems for constructing horizontal fire barriers,
principally floors, went in several directions in Britain in the late eighteenth century. One was
brick floors, springing from cast iron beams; a second was floors of hollow clay products,
supported by walls or iron beams; and a third was floors of concrete, with or without embedded
iron joists. Iron first began to be used for structural members at this time. Improved methods of
smelting iron ore, using coke rather than charcoal, spread rapidly in the last quarter of the
eighteenth century, contributing to a much increased output of pig iron and its use for a greater
variety of purposes, including construction materials. Iron was considered fireproof because it
could not burn, and became an important component of the new systems of fireproof
construction.

Iron and Brick

In the 1790s, the iron and brick arch system of construction, which came to define fireproof
construction, was introduced by William Strutt and Charles Bage in their multi-storey,
mechanically powered textile mills. A considerable literature on the history of this system in mill
buildings in Great Britain is available, so I shall only mention a few points about them.[18]
Fireproof mills appeared in the major textile areas of Lancashire and Yorkshire, though because
they were much more expensive to build than ordinary timber mills, only well capitalized
manufacturers built them.[19] Often fireproof mills were built to replace mills that had burned
down. Not until the end of the nineteenth century did fireproof construction become standard for
new mills.

   The mills were built with bearing walls of brick or stone, typically in a rectangular shape. Cast
iron beams ran across the narrow dimension, resting on the exterior walls and in between on one
or two rows of cast iron columns. Brick segmental arches, which sprang from the beams, were
levelled with sand, ash[20] or "hard rubbish" and at this time were paved with tiles or flags.[21] The
shallow arches reduced the thickness of the floor but created narrow bays. Improvements in beam
design were in the direction of using metal more efficiently and creating wider bays, but all
beams had an angle or flange projecting from their lower portions to start brick arches or carry
the skewbacks for an arch. Typically, the roofs of fireproof mills were built of wood, covered
with slates.

   A second system of fireproof mill construction, developed perhaps to increase the span
between beams as well as to reduce the weight and depth of the floors, consisted of an
iron framework filled in with large flag stones, making a flat floor. A number of mills and
warehouses constructed this way date from the 1820s and 1830s, of which the Beehive
Mill, Manchester, is an extant example.[22] Also in the 1830s, a Mr. Farrow patented a version of
this type of floor, using small wrought, rather than cast, iron joists in the shape of an inverted T
such as were being rolled in France, on which were placed stones of the depth of the joist, which

Sara Wermiel

could form either the floors or roofs of fire-resistant buildings. These floors were used in some sugar refineries – a very hazardous business.[23] However, experience soon showed that stone was not a satisfactory material for fireproof buildings, since most kinds could be badly damaged in a fire.[24]

Space in textile mills and warehouses could be compartmentalized with relative ease; not so the non-industrial buildings which were constructed with brick and iron fireproof floors, beginning in the 1820s and 1830s. Mills needed vertical openings for little besides the stairways, lifts, power, water service, and heat pipes, all of which could be walled off from the main floor, or in the case of staircases, put in a separate tower. Architects of public and institutional buildings, the type which tended to be built fireproof, generally relied on the incombustibility of the materials to protect the buildings rather than compartmentalizaion.[25] Charles Barry designed a number of buildings in which incombustible materials were used for the sake of fire protection, but the buildings as a whole probably were not conceived as fireproof structures. For example, only after his design for the Houses of Parliament was accepted did the Government order the building to be built fireproof. This was accomplished "by substitution of iron girders and brick arches for ordinary floors, and iron roofs instead of slated coverings" – the latter modelled on roofs of public buildings in France, according to the architect's son, Edward Barry. He also described the floors of the tower as "fire proof receptacles for records and papers of value".[26] Thus the building was compartmentalized where necessary, but not generally. Office buildings, not containing the kinds of flammable contents found in warehouses or mills, were considered low risk structures. Parts of Charles Barry's Reform Club (1838-41), such as the floors over the basement where the kitchen was located and over the first floor, were made of iron beams and brick arches; and the public stairways were enclosed, though whether this was for fire protection, I can not say. At the same time, the servants' stairs, roof, some partitions, and finishes were made of wood, so the building was not thoroughly fireproof.[27]

Hollow Tile

A 1793 report of a committee of architects, which tested David Hartley's and Lord Mahon's fireproofing systems, mentioned a hollow tile which also could be used for fireproof floors: "Arches of Cones, or Bricks, or Tiles ... will answer the purpose, but they are more weighty and expensive." Tile is the general name for materials made of fired clay, with the exception of brick. "The advantage arising from the use of Cones, when compared with Bricks, is their superior lightness (being twice the bulk and only half the weight) and their being applicable to Arches of a very small rise".[28] The cones referred to were made by a pottery near London. The top floor of William Strutt's fireproof mill in Derby, under construction in that year, was made of hollow pots manufactured in Britain. Pots also formed the top floor, of two other pioneer fireproof buildings: a warehouse in Milford built in 1793, and West Mill in Belper built in 1795.[29]

The pot idea probably came from France, where floors of brick arches carried by timber beams – like those first introduced in Britain by Strutt, save for the shape of the beam – were being built in the late eighteenth century. Benjamin Franklin described them in a 1771 letter: "In some of the Paris Buildings the Floors are thus formed. The Joists are large and square, & laid with two of their Corners up and down, whereby their sloping Sides afford Butments for the intermediate Arches of Brick. Over the whole is laid an Inch or two of Loom, and on that the Tiles of the Floor..." The joists were tied with iron bars and a ceiling under the joists made of lath and plaster. "But it is heavy, taking up more Room, requires great strength of Timber and is I suppose more expensive than Boards".[30] It may have been the longer experience

The Development of Fireproof Construction

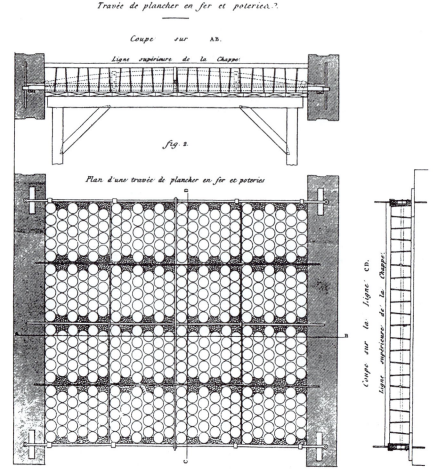

Fig 2: French method of constructing a floor of hollow pots and iron beams (from Charles Eck, *Traité de Construction en Poteries et Fer*, 1836).

French builders had with these heavy floors that prompted a search for a lighter structural clay product. At any rate, hollow pots – a rediscovery of an old method of construction – appear in about the 1780s, and soon were used in conjunction with rolled iron in a system of fireproof construction known as "poteries et fer". The pots, wrote architect Charles Eck in his 1836 treatise on the system, in combination with iron, created very light, solid and absolutely fireproof masses, and could be used in the construction of partitions, roofing, vaults, floors and stairs. He illustrated examples of the system, as used in theatres, government buildings, and market halls in France.[31] Several kinds of tiles are illustrated in Eck's book, but the "cone" type was narrower at one end than the other; they were placed alternately right side up and up side down to form a flat floor, or narrow side down to form an arch. The pots were made by hand, thrown on a potter's wheel. (Fig. 2)

Sara Wermiel

Hollow pots springing from stone skewbacks resting on iron beams were used for fireproof floors in buildings in England from about the 1790s to the 1840s, including several government buildings, a mansion or two, and the domed roof of Soane's Bank of England. But they were never used in as many buildings, or applied to as many structural purposes, in Britain as in France. This may be because, as built in Britain, they offered no great advantage over brick: pot floors were relatively deep and average spans, at 4½ – 7½ feet, were less than those of brick arch floors.[32] In addition to pots, hollow bricks also were used in France and a couple hollow brick systems were introduced in Britain, but they were little used.[33]

John Webster, in his comprehensive 1890 survey of fireproof construction materials, was probably correct when he suggested that the ability to produce hollow tiles by machine was important to the success of this system. He gave 1845 as the date of the first successful tile forming machine.[34] But there is evidence of machine-made hollow tiles at an earlier date, though the specific product may not have been widely used. In the 1830s, a builder, James Frost, introduced square, hollow tubes "made by a machine" for constructing floors and flat roofs. The "machine" may have been like the sewer pipe press used to make hollow tiles in the U.S. some five decades later. Frost's tubes, 2½ inches square and a foot long, were laid flat in two layers at right angles to each other, bonded with a "cement" of chalk and clay, and topped with mortar. While the floors were only perhaps 6-7 inches deep and comparatively light, they were not designed to have intermediate supports, so apparently were intended for small rooms.[35] The desideratum of lightness combined with greater span was not accomplished until Joseph Bunnett patented his hollow tile system in 1858.

Concrete

Probably the first fireproof concrete floor in Britain was that installed by Henry Fox in the 1830s at his private asylum near Bristol. The floors of this building are made of cast iron joists, of inverted T section, with heavy laths resting on the bottom flange, forming a permanent centering. A layer of mortar covered the laths, and then a thicker layer of mortar mixed with an aggregate, followed with a finish layer of lime and sand.[36] Although patented in 1844, the system seems not to have been used until some years later, after Fox joined with James Barrett, a building contractor, who promoted the system. Barrett claimed his floor weighed 78 pounds per foot, comparable to a floor made of half-size brick arches but about two-thirds the weight of full-size brick arches. By his calculation, in 1853, a 63 x 28 foot mill floor built his way cost about 40 per cent less than a brick and iron floor.[37] In the 1850s, Barrett began using rolled iron joists rather than cast iron; however the joists continued to be closely spaced, about 1½ feet apart. The eventual product, known as the "Fox and Barrett" floor, was installed in hospitals, residences and office buildings.[38]

Also by the 1850s, French methods of constructing concrete floors began to receive attention in Britain. For example, in 1854, H. H. Burnell read a paper at the R.I.B.A. on the French "iron floors". He described two systems used in Paris, both of which consisted of closely spaced rolled iron joists which carried small iron bars; the iron was covered with plaster. These floors apparently had not been developed in France as a fire protection measure; rather, they were improved versions of floors which came into general use following a carpenters' strike in the previous decade.[39]

Thus, in Britain by mid-century, the cast iron and brick arch system was well established, a number of patented systems of floor and roof construction were in use, and certain principles of fireproof construction – the concept of compartmentalization and the need for fire breaks in wall cavities – had been discussed in print in several places.[40] However, few kinds of buildings were built fireproof – mainly prominent government and institutional buildings, the better capitalized textile factories, some warehouses, and model housing. London's building laws did not require any building to be wholly fireproof. Rather, the Building Act of 1844 codified the tendency to concentrate fireproof materials

The Development of Fireproof Construction

where they might, theoretically, do the most good. Thus access ways in the public building class, and stairs in multi-unit buildings in the dwelling class, were required to be fireproof. Large buildings such as warehouses could not exceed 200,000 cubic feet, although openings in party walls between warehouses were allowed, if protected with iron doors.[41]

In American cities, such building regulations as existed were concerned with exterior materials of construction. Very few fireproof buildings existed, mainly the solid masonry type, built mainly for government or institutional owners. Manufacturers did not build fireproof buildings. Iron and brick construction was just beginning to be taken up. Not until the 1840s did American iron production increase to the point where it could be used extensively in building construction. Before this time, cast iron columns were imported.[42]

Introduction of the Iron and Brick Fireproof Building in the United States, 1850 – 1870

The American production of castings for buildings increased considerably by mid-century, as urban foundries – what became known as architectural iron works – began to manufacture building facades, columns, lintels, stairways and so forth. In the late 1840s, a few fireproof buildings modelled on the British iron and brick fireproof non-industrial type were commissioned by government clients. By 1854, one of the nation's leading iron manufacturers – Trenton Iron Works in Trenton, New Jersey – succeeded in rolling T shaped beams, referred to by contemporaries as "deck beams" since they were shaped like those used in iron ships.[43] This new product came on the market at a propitious time, when the U.S. Congress was busy voting approbations for the construction of government buildings in newly settled regions as well as replacements for out-dated buildings in the East. Between 1854 and 1857, about seventy custom houses, court houses, post offices, marine hospitals, and specialised buildings were authorised. All were fireproof, and all were built with internal iron structures, using the new beams from

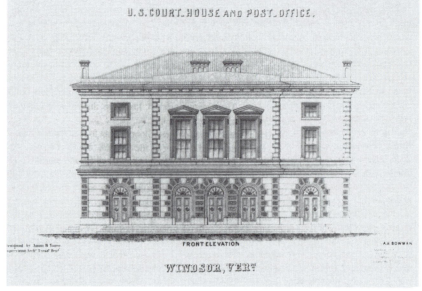

Fig 3: Court House at Windsor Vermont (from *Plans of Public Buildings*, 1856).

Sara Wermiel

Fig 4: Workroom on the upper floor of Harper's Publishing House, 1855 (from Jacob Abbot, *The Harper Establishment*, 1855).

Trenton. Also, interestingly, all were built from designs of one architect, Ammi Burnham Young, who was employed by the U.S. Treasury Department – the agency responsible for building these structures (Fig. 3). Unlike the masonry system, the iron and brick system also began to be used by owners of commercial buildings to a comparatively large extent.

The girders used in the American iron and brick buildings came in a variety of sections. One of the earliest was in the form of an arch made of cast iron with the ends tied by a rod of wrought iron (Fig. 4). This girder was used in the Harper Brothers' publishing house of 1855 and one of the first brick and iron fireproof buildings in the U.S. to use "solid" – as contemporaries called them – wrought iron beams. The girders designed for the Treasury Department buildings were made of rolled plates, channels, and double beams. Girders could be manufactured in large sizes, such as the 30 inch deep, 41½ foot, 6,600 pound girder shipped from Trenton in 1857. The dimensions of rolled beams increased rapidly, from a 7 inch deep bulb headed beam to a 9 inch I shaped beam about two years later (Figs. 5-6). Both sizes weighed about 31 pounds per foot, and could be made in lengths of 20 feet and more.[44] As with rails, the long lengths were made by "piling" and rolling puddled bar iron. Other mills began producing rolled iron beams, although only the largest were able to do so. These products were developed primarily for fireproof buildings. At this time, the firms that bid on contracts for manufacturing and erecting the iron work in these buildings were architectural iron works.[45] They or the builder (often a masonry contractor) ordered the rolled beams and girders from the few companies that made them, and then iron workers from the foundry firm did the set up.

11

The Development of Fireproof Construction

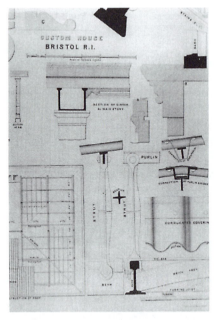

Fig 5: Ironwork in the Custom House at Bristol, Rhode Island (from *Plans of Public Buildings*, 1856)

Fig 6: Typical American iron and brick fireproof floor (from J.K. Freitag, *The Fireproofing of Steel Buildings*, 1899)

By the time American iron and brick fireproof buildings began to be built, the system had fallen out of favour for new institutional buildings in Great Britain, although it continued to be the system for constructing industrial buildings until the end of the century. Nevertheless, the American system differed from the British iron mill in a number of respects. First, American floors were made of iron girders carrying smaller iron joists, with brick arches springing from the joists. British mills used girders only, and therefore required more columns. Second, the brick arches in the government buildings usually were filled with cement concrete, like the arches in the earlier masonry fireproof buildings. Concrete did not begin to be used in this way in British mills until the 1860s.[46] Third, the roofs of the American buildings were made of iron, with cast and rolled iron supports and corrugated iron covering (Fig. 7). The roofs of British mills usually were framed in wood. Lastly, as little wood as possible was used in the American buildings: thus the window frames and stairways were made of iron, and floors were covered with stone or tile. The buildings also were supplied with iron shutters unlike British fireproof mills.

Sara Wermiel

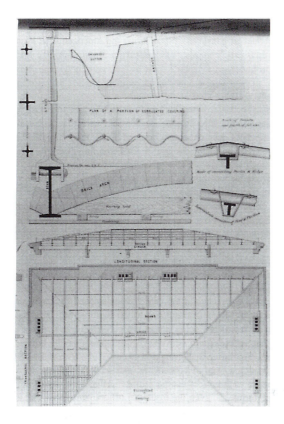

Fig 7: Details of the roof, Custom House, Portsmouth, New Hampshire (from *Plans of Public Buildings*, 1856).

Why wrought iron beams, which were available in Britain in the 1840s, were not more used in British iron and brick mill buildings – as joists, as in the non-industrial buildings, or as girders – is something of a mystery. Even the most exemplary plants, for example the huge integrated mill in Yorkshire built 1850-53 by William Fairbairn for Titus Salt, was constructed with cast iron beams carried on columns.[47] Fairbairn's important book on the construction of fireproof buildings, published in 1854, discussed the superiority of wrought iron over cast iron for beams, but did not suggest that they might be used as joists in combination with girders.[48] The girder and beam system began to be used in railway warehouses in Manchester in the later 1850s or 1860s[49], and in textile factories in Lancashire by the last decade of the century.[50] Nevertheless factories throughout the century continued to use cast iron.

Fireproof buildings were built around the country, but especially in New York, which was located near to Trenton. The example of the government buildings undoubtedly helped popularize the system. Fireproof buildings built for commercial clients in the 1850s and 1860s include the American Exchange Bank, Continental Bank, Hupfel's Brewery, Metropolitan Gas Works, and Mutual Life Insurance Co. Building in New York City; the Chicago Historical Society and the Tribune Building in Chicago. Nevertheless, the number of fireproof buildings constructed was small. Iron was still an expensive material in America compared with wood. Moreover, American-made rolled beams were sold at fixed prices, and imported iron was taxed.

The Development of Fireproof Construction

Construction of iron and brick buildings slowed after 1857, when the nation's economy took a dive, and dried up in the first part of the 1860s during the American Civil War and the inflation that followed.

Rise of Fireproofing – the 1870s

Already in the 1840s in Britain, iron was under attack as a building material. James Braidwood, Superintendent of the London Fire Brigade, argued that cast iron beams and columns when used in large buildings with open expanses, staircases, and wells, and filled with combustible goods, "are not, practically speaking, fireproof'. Cast iron, he observed, was liable to fail for many reasons, including flawed casting or weakness from over- loading; girders, when expanded by the heat of a fire, could push out walls; iron tie rods might give when softened in a fire; and heated iron might fracture when cold water was thrown on it. "For these and similar reasons, the firemen are not permitted to go into warehouses supported by iron, when once fairly on fire".[51]

Braidwood met his death in 1861, crushed by a falling wall while fighting what was perhaps London's most serious conflagration since 1666 – the Tooley Street fire. The fire started in and spread among the dreaded iron warehouses, many of which had been very well built. Calls for new laws to protect the public typically follow such tragedies. Parliament passed the Metropolitan Fire Act, providing for a fire department under government administration to replace the organization Braidwood led, which was financed by fire insurance companies. However, no clamour was raised for revisions to the building regulations. Rather, criticism of structural iron increased. The Tooley Street fire showed dramatically what could happen to iron in a serious blaze. As a *Building News* reporter described the fire scene: "The greater part of the premises...now lie in shapeless hills of bricks, broken and half-melted columns, girders, iron doors... Such a heap of broken ironwork as that here collected is seldom to be seen – girders from two to three feet deep are broken into short lengths, others, half melted, have run into strange forms..."[52] Even the insurance offices considered iron a more dangerous material than wood.[53] The solution to the iron problem was either to avoid using it, or to protect it.

In the iron-avoidance camp was the redoubtable Capt. E. M. Shaw, who next headed London's firefighting organization and repeated his predecessor's warnings about the unreliability of iron. He wrote that hardwood posts with girders and joists filled with cement were preferable to iron combined with brick.[54] Shaw, in fact, was highly sceptical of the idea of fireproof construction. He condemned the use of stone, the usual material for making stairways in London in compliance with the Building Act, and thought hollow brick could crack when the heated air in the cavity expanded.[55] He recommended limiting the size of buildings – height and volume – instead of trying to make them fireproof. Regarded as a hero and unimpeachable authority, his views were cited and echoed by writers in the architectural press for years to come. As the architect T. Hayter Lewis concluded in a 1865 paper: "Nothing short of diminishing the size of warehouses and other such buildings, or protecting them with brick arches or brick piers (as in solid masonry buildings), will render them secure; ...the common method of brick arches on iron girders is the most dangerous that can be used."[56]

By the mid-1860s several new methods of building fireproof floors came on the market, most of which were made of concrete, a less expensive material in Britain than clay products. British inventors also addressed the problem of how to protect iron beams. Iron columns received less attention, perhaps because the new fireproof floor systems tended to be used in situations where walls and partitions rather than columns and girders carried the floor slabs. In an 1872 article in *Building News* on "how to build scientifically with the aid of modern inventions," a

Sara Wermiel

writer listed Phillips' and Dennett's fire resisting floors as the kinds most generally used.[57] Phillips' floor was like Fox and Barret's, with small T iron replacing wood lath between rolled iron joists, and the concrete made with Portland cement.[58] But with joists spaced two feet apart, the floor required a great deal of iron. Dennett's consisted of gypsum combined with an aggregate to make "Nottingham concrete", and was shaped in an arch usually, but was not reinforced with iron although it sometimes was built between iron girders. This floor was used in a "long list of buildings", including government buildings, St. Thomas's Hospital, and at least one Yorkshire mill in the 1870s.[59] As well, a type of concrete arch floor, unreinforced like Dennett's, or with reinforcement when constructed flat for landings or corridors, made by W. B. Wilkinson & Co. was installed in railway stations, a building at Edinburgh University, and "in many warehouses and stables".[60] These new floors led one writer to exclaim: "What changes have not come over the meaning of fire-proof! Among my early experiences no building was considered fire-proof that had not iron joists and brick arches ... Now it is generally admitted that no floor can be called ... fire-proof that has iron used in its construction – such is the present position of iron".[61] Somehow, though, these new truths had passed by mill designers and owners, as they continued to build with iron, unprotected.

That iron is unreliable in a fire was amply demonstrated to Americans by the fire which consumed Chicago in 1871. It occurred a few weeks before the annual convention of the American Institute of Architects (A.I.A.), and was a hot topic at the meeting. Peter B. Wight, an architect with a great interest in fire protection, visited Chicago shortly after the fire and reported to the meeting on lessons learned from the destruction of Chicago's fireproof buildings. Wight held the cast iron columns responsible for the failure of the fireproof Post Office, believing that they shattered. Iron was again put to the conflagration test the following year, when the centre of Boston, Massachusetts, burned down. After surveying the Boston wreckage, R.G. Hatfield, an architect with an interest in technical aspects of construction, concluded "all iron had been proved untrustworthy; cast iron, however, had stood much better than wrought iron".[62] How did iron behave in a blaze?

American architects lacked technical information regarding new construction systems and materials. As one complained in 1869, architects did not have the means to test new products for themselves (though they often required manufacturers to perform load tests on items ordered, as did British architects), and manufacturers did not divulge complete information about their products.[63] Another remarked a few years later, "notwithstanding our seventy years' experience in iron, we now really know very little with certainty as to its action under varying circumstances of stress".[64] How American architects got information is still a question. The A.I.A. chapter and annual meetings were venues for discussing such topics and the New York chapter collected product samples, but the organisation was elitist and only a small number of all building designers were members. The papers read at the annual meeting were published in Proceedings. The first American architecture magazine to survive for more than a few years began publication in 1876, and it printed the papers given at A.I.A. meetings and articles on technical subjects. No doubt designers also relied on the material manufacturers, and the handbooks they published, to a great extent. Some read British periodicals. While still scanty, by the 1870s the sources of information on technical matters for architects at least were growing.

And their interest in fireproof construction was great, judging from the number of articles on the topic appearing in *American Architect and Building News* and the patents for fireproof materials – or, now, "fireproofing" materials, as the age of structural protection rather than incombustibility had arrived. Though the men who wrote the articles about fireproof construction were well acquainted with British hostility to iron, they also believed that

The Development of Fireproof Construction

the strength of iron, especially columns, was indispensable; rather, they too made the distinction between incombustible and fireproof, and emphasized that iron had to be protected. As Wight wrote in 1878, in an approving comment on the plans for a new city building in Chicago: "In its constructive features the materials are not alone incombustible – a word too often mistaken for fire-proof – but are to be made fire-proof in the true acceptation of the term. All the iron- work is to be protected".[65]

Two great problems of fireproof construction – how to make it affordable and how to protect iron – led to two different styles of fireproof building in the United States in the 1870s, both of which made use of an old material, clay, employed in a new way. The iron and brick fireproof building was very heavy, requiring extra material in the exterior walls and foundations. One way to lighten floors was to use hollow tiles rather than bricks. From this idea, the system of fireproof construction which became standard practice in America until the first decade of the twentieth century evolved. However rolled iron girders and joists were still very expensive, in part, contemporaries believed, because of price fixing by the manufacturers, the "mill pool", as well as tariffs on imported beams.[66] A more economical method of fire resisting construction was to protect ordinary wood floors by suspending ceiling tiles from them. A number of products for this purpose began to be patented in the 1870s. With respect to protecting iron, attention was first directed to protecting iron columns, perhaps because iron columns were used in buildings of all types, whereas iron beams were used principally in the few thoroughly fireproof buildings. Several methods were patented to protect columns; beam coverings were not used until the 1880s.

Tile fireproofing products first came into commercial use in the fireproof buildings constructed after the Chicago fire. Some months before the fire in 1871, George H. Johnson, a manger with the Architectural Iron Works in New York (and English by birth) and Balthasar Kreischer, a manufacturer of brick products, patented a large tile which spanned between iron floor beams. Their tile was shaped like a tile patented about 15 years before by the German born engineer and architect Frederick Peterson. Peterson's tile is unlike the pots, tubes and hollow bricks used in England. The Patent Office illustration shows a one piece unit, resting on the lower flanges of beams of Hodgkinson section, with an arched top and flat bottom. According to Peter Wight, these tiles were only ever used in the first storey of the Cooper Institute, designed by Peterson and built in the 1850s, where they were set between double 6 inch channel bars bolted together, 2 feet 6 inches on centre; they were made by hand of semi-fire clay.[67]

It was not this tile but one patented by Johnson a year later, in the shape of hollow voussoirs, that Johnson installed in the Kendall Building (1872-73) in Chicago, along with hollow block partitions, in the first instance of the use of this material in America.[68] (Fig. 8) Hollow voussoir-shaped tiles were being manufactured in France in the late 1860s.[69] Although the French blocks generally had interior webs, unlike the Chicago floor, they were probably the inspiration for Johnson's floor. Johnson may have received help selling the idea of hollow tile floors from the example of a 12 foot wide terracotta arch made from blocks sent over from England, put up on a

Fig 8: Hollow tile floor, as used in the Kendall Buildings, Chicago, 1872 (From J.K. Freitag, *The Firproofing of Steel Buildings*, 1899).

16

Sara Wermiel

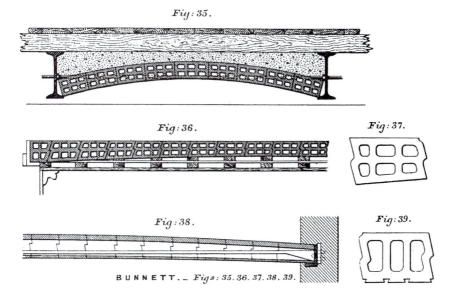

Fig 9: Joseph Bunnett's patent hollow tile floors (from *Minutes of the Proceedings of the Institution of Civil Engineers*, 1890–1).

vacant lot in Chicago after the fire.[?] (Fig. 9) Joseph Bunnett, inventor of this floor, patented his system some 13 years before, and it had been used in Grosvenor Hotel and the London and Brighton Railway Station, Pimlico.[71] His interlocking blocks tied with an iron rod could form spans of 21 feet, with a rise of only 2¾ inches. The blocks came in two patterns, one for a "side-pressure" arch – with the hollow cavity running perpendicular with the tie rod – and the other, an "end to pressure" arch – with the cavity running parallel to the tie rod. The tiles were made by machine, with the clay pressed through dies. Whether Bunnett ever sold his blocks in the United States is not known, but he made no headway in Chicago, in part because local firms had entered the hollow tile business, and in part because, in the hurry to rebuild Chicago, "there was no time to study up the subject" of fireproof building.

For owners who could not afford to build with iron – and most were in this group – inventors devised a new version of wood protection, à la Hartley and Mahon, in the form of interlocking ceiling tiles. A number of patents for such tiles were granted in this decade.[72] In addition, patents for the materials of which tiles were to be made were granted. Materials used in making tiles included ordinary clay, fire clay, and mixtures of different kinds of clay. The Fire-proof Building Co. of New York manufactured tile from a mixture of "French cement", plaster, and coke breeze, according to methods used in France. In Chicago, a method of making porous terracotta invented by the architect Sanford Loring and patented in 1874, consisted of clay mixed with sawdust or other vegetable matter which burned out in the firing.[73] Porous tile could be nailed and sawed, and was used rather than lath and plaster for ceilings under floor joists.

The problem of protecting iron columns was first addressed in the United States by Peter Wight and his partner William Drake (English by birth) who in 1874 patented a method of protecting cast iron columns of cruciform section with insulating wedges.[74] For larger columns, Wight came up with the idea of having small flanges cast on to cylinders to hold tile wedges.

17

The Development of Fireproof Construction

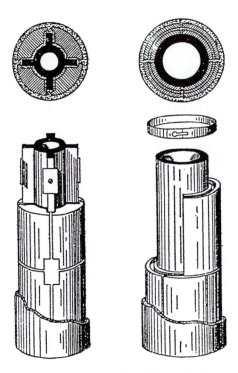

Fig 10: Peter Wright's systems of column foreproofing (from J.K. Freitag, *The Fireproofing of Steel Frame Buildings*, 1899)

Columns of this type were used in the 1880s in a variety of buildings. The tile wedges also were used to cover Phoenix columns, which were made of sections of rolled iron with flange joints. To meet the specifications for federal government buildings, which did not allow the flanged cast iron columns, Wight developed a system of tile rings with a groove, held in place with iron band.[75] (Fig. 10)

Many of these inventions appeared after the 1873 Panic and were not used in buildings in the 1870s, due to the general economic slowdown during the rest of the decade. Nevertheless, ideas for improving hollow tile floors continued to be patented, and the system developed in the direction of wider spans, made possible with terracotta of new compositions and the placement of reinforcing webs inside the blocks. Several New York area companies, in addition to Johnson's Illinois-based firm, entered the business, including Huvelman, Haven & Co. and the Fire-Proof Building Co. Tile manufacturers were the contractors for installation, although some also sold their products to builders, and their line of business came to be known as "fireproofing". Although these companies advertised in the national architectural press, few owners outside of New York City and Chicago (with the exception of the federal government) bought their products.

Why Americans did not adopt any of the concrete floor systems used in Britain, or even use concrete for making walls as was tried in the Peabody workers' houses in London in 1871, was a mystery to the British. In building construction, "concrete" of varying compositions, not always including cement, was used in America for foundations to some extent before the 1880s, and for

Sara Wermiel

levelling brick arches. A type of fireproof floor made of concrete or mortar poured over sheet iron plates, with or without corrugations, flat or arched, had been installed in a few buildings in America.[76] C.C. Dennett obtained a U.S. patent for his concrete arch in 1870.[77] But a writer in 1869 remarked that Americans lacked an understanding of "management of the material in large masses", and users found they ended up spending as much as if they had used brick.[78] Production of Portland cement did not begin in the United States until the 1870s, and even as domestic production increased, far more cement was imported, from England and Germany, at great expense, than was manufactured locally. As late as 1896, about twice as many barrels were imported as were produced in America.[79] The architect Richard Hunt, writing in 1877, believed, "with the experience gained by the more general use of these materials (concrete and beton) in this country, the same (uniform) results will undoubtedly be attained" as were achieved in Europe.[80] On the other hand, tile had much to recommend it. Clay was abundant in America, whereas concrete was a cheaper alternative to brick in Britain. In this period, tile floors took less time to install than did concrete floors, which was a selling point for time-conscious Americans.[81]

British inventiveness in the decade of the 1870s was also stimulated by the Chicago and Boston fires. Archibald Dawnay, "one of the pioneers of the flat or suspended concrete floor", began working on a concrete floor in 1868 when rolled iron joists were first imported to Britain.[82] His floor was a flat slab of cement concrete reinforced with bars or small joists of iron, and could be used to create spans up to 20 feet. It was used in "over 3000 buildings". Another slab, made of rolled joists embedded in concrete but with no other reinforcement, was patented in 1871 by Homan and Rodgers.[83] The Liverpool architect, Lewis Hornblower, invented a method of constructing floors, partitions and roofs which combined iron rods, hollow tiles, and concrete made of Portland cement and aggregate. The iron rods ran through tile tubes, between which larger tiles were suspended, forming a permanent centring which was covered with concrete.[84] This system was used in the Manchester Pantechnicon, the Liverpool Corn Exchange, and several buildings in Glasgow.[85] Hornblower also invented a method of fireproofing iron columns and girders in existing buildings by covering them with fire-clay tubes held in place with Portland cement concrete. Another form of column protection, available from Dennett and Co., consisted of concrete laid on to cast iron columns, held in place by longitudinal strips of corrugated iron or wire mesh on wood strips.[86] The objection to such coverings was that they increased the diameter of the column.

While London architects may have abandoned iron and brick arches for fireproof construction, mill architects did not. Some innovations were introduced to increase the span and reduce the depth of arches, for example A. H. Stott's iron column brackets, patented in 1871.[87] Iron in mills rarely was protected, a fact noticed by American fire insurance officials who visited English fireproof mills.[88] American mills in the nineteenth century rarely used structural iron, since large dimension wood for columns and beams was much less expensive.

The First and Second Waves of American Skyscrapers

The American economy picked up at the beginning of the 1880s, and the new fireproofing products were adopted in new buildings constructed in the brief booms that punctuated the decade. Production of fireproof products increased as new hollow tile, or "fireproofing" companies entered the business. The flat or curved arched floors made of terracotta were called "American floors" in Britain. Many of the buildings constructed in this decade were "office buildings", practically a new type of structure. Rental space in the commercial city before this time could be found in lofts comparable to what were called warehouses in Britain, which lacked facilities for the convenience of tenants. But demand for office space, coincident with the growing number and scale of some businesses, increased to the extent that ever larger buildings

The Development of Fireproof Construction

could be profitably filled; the new buildings had to have elevators, lavatories, and appointments to attract tenants. Even owners who built for their own use occupied only a few floors of their buildings and rented out the rest.[89] Such speculative office buildings apparently were not being built in Britain to the same extent.

American fireproof building of the 1880s was constructed of either incombustible materials or with wood floors protected with terracotta ceiling tiles. Many buildings were constructed in both styles until mid-century, after which they thoroughly incombustible style came to be preferred for first class buildings. A fire in the Grannis Block, a fireproofed wood floor type of building, in 1885 helped turn the tide in favour of using iron and tile exclusively for office buildings in Chicago. As Henry Ericsson, a builder and later building commissioner for the city, recalled: "In a real sense, more was learned from the burning of the Grannis than from the great fire of 1871; at least, its lessons were taken to heart and tenants became aware and alert as regards the perils of fire".[90] Also, the first wave of tall building construction had begun, and concerns were being raised over the safety of buildings which stood beyond the effective reach of fire hoses. By mid-decade, laws were passed both in New York and Chicago which forbade the constructive use of wood in buildings over a certain height within the fire limits.[91] After mid-decade, then, the progress of the tall building and the fireproof building became completely entwined. Tall buildings had to be built fireproof, by law if for no other reason, and fireproof buildings had to be tall, in order to return a significant rent to make their higher cost of construction affordable.

The story of the tall building has been told many times, but the fact that it is also the story of the fireproof building is not always appreciated. The tall fireproof buildings of the early 1880s were impressive for their height, but also for their weight. One of the first skyscrapers, the ten storey Montauk in Chicago (1878-82), was completely fireproofed by Wight Fireproofing Co. It was also notable for having rail grillage foundations on isolated footings, a new type of foundation made necessary because of the depth of bedrock under the city.[92] With grillage foundations, a heavy building would settle on the upper layers of clay, but evenly and not too far, and the basement would still have room for mechanical equipment. As Peter Wight explained the connections between fireproofing, height, weight and foundations in 1893:

> "The use of steel (rails in) foundations, and later of steel- framed constructions, are the natural outcome of the use of light hollow fireproof blocks. In order to build fireproof structures and make them pay, they must be many storeys higher, so as to decrease the relative cost of the land to the improvement. Building higher on compressible soils necessitated economy in weights. Hollow materials only made this feasible. It was then found that the heights of buildings could be increased more and more by using steel frames, but only in case those frames were protected by the light fireproof material. Hence the latest and most improved buildings contain very few bricks, the exteriors being of cellular terracotta, and the interior faces of the exterior walls of hollow fire-clay blocks."[93]

In 1883, construction began on the pioneer skeleton building, the Home Insurance Building in Chicago. It was actually of a type of construction that came to be known as a "cage", meaning that the frame carried the floors but the walls were self-supporting. Putting columns in the piers was a way of reducing the size and weight of the piers. This building was fireproofed by Wight. In the second half of the 1880s, many cage buildings were built in Chicago and New York.

The second wave of tall buildings, beginning at the end of the 1880s, was characterised by the introduction of the skeleton system and steel. Architects were aware of the potential advantages of steel, but had rarely used it before 1890, both because of cost and because of doubts about the reliability of Bessemer steel, then the principal kind.[94] But as steel prices fell in the 1890s and

Sara Wermiel

production of open hearth steel increased, they began to use it to a greater extent. Cast iron continued to be used for columns, especially in cage-style buildings. But in the skeleton-style building – in which the exterior walls as well as floors are carried by the metal frame – rolled steel began to be used for the entire frame. Tile floors were standard for such buildings, with the end-pressure type gaining favour after well publicised tests of tile arches in 1890.[95] Although a number of concrete floor systems had been introduced, they were adopted to the largest extent in San Francisco, presumably because English Portland cement there was relatively cheap. These developments allowed buildings to be constructed ever taller. In major cities, tall buildings had to be fireproof. Indeed, building codes had the effect of spreading and standardising this system of construction. The codes in Boston, New York and Chicago, for example, contained much technical information, which gave guidance on such matters as the loads to be assumed in designing floors and roofs, the strength of wrought-iron and steel beams and cast iron columns, and formulas which should be used.[96]

The State of Structural Fire Protection at the Close of the Century

No similar surge of interest in new materials of construction occurred in Great Britain, although inventors continued to patent ideas for fireproof products in the last two decades of the century. Again, most of the fireproofing systems used concrete. Two systems, perhaps the most commonly used ones, combined hollow tile, in end-pressure, and concrete.[97] Homan and Rodgers' flat floor, patented in 1885, used hollow tubes which were shaped like trapezoids, spanning between rolled beams, and were covered in concrete. A similar idea was introduced by Mark Fawcett in 1888, and consisted of tile tubes with arched tops and flat soffits, laid diagonally on joists and covered with concrete. The tiles allowed an air space under the beam soffit.[98] These floors saved the cost of centring and were light: however, as joists were placed two feet apart, they required a good deal of iron compared with American hollow tile floors. Nevertheless, the Fawcett Ventilated Building Co. floors were installed in a number of American buildings, especially in Philadelphia and other Pennsylvania cities.[99]

Despite the variety of systems available for building fireproof, the kinds of buildings in which they were used continued to be those owned by institutions and government, textile factories and some warehouses. Americans found the British complacent about fire protection, as their relatively better fire record might lead them to be. For example, a writer who compared the English and American fire services found that the number of fires in London and New York was the same (in 1885) even though London had three times the population, five times the number of buildings, and three times the land area.[100] Yet the city's better fire loss record could not be due to its fire service, which he found very slow in responding to calls.

Rather than requiring that new buildings be constructed fireproof, London authorities relied on size limitation. The warehouse class of buildings had been limited to 200,000 cubic feet in the 1844 Building Act; 216,000 in the 1855 Act; and up to 450,000 cubic feet with permission and then limited to 60 feet high in the London County Council Act passed 1890, with a general height limitation of 90 feet plus two storeys in the roof. The architect Horace Cubitt compared London's laws with those of New York and Boston, and found American laws contained far more rules governing construction: fireproofing of certain buildings, stricter egress requirements, and detailed regulations for safe construction.[101] With respect to fireproof building in Britain, he noted that "the greater proportion of the best class of buildings (in Britain) are now erected of fire-resisting construction, but entirely at the option of the owners, professional opinion here apparently not having yet reached the point of considering compulsory measures desirable." A comprehensive revision of London's building laws in 1894 reduced the allowable height of buildings as a fire safety measure, with no objection from the R.I.B.A. committee formed to advise the code writers. But not everyone found this strategy satisfactory. Edwin O. Sachs, an

The Development of Fireproof Construction

architect and a leading figure in Britain's early fire protection engineering movement, was critical of London's Fire Brigade and of building construction in London. He helped form the British Fire Prevention Committee, an organisation devoted to increasing the adoption of "preventive measures" by conducting independent tests of materials, methods and appliances; publishing papers and reports; collecting information on fire prevention; and holding meetings.[102]

This committee got started following a tragedy, the fire in London's Cripplegate in 1897. Cripplegate was a district of warehouses that had been rebuilt in the 1870s, but the best practices of the period had not been observed, and the buildings were never updated. In a report about the fire, Sachs wrote that there were no fireproof buildings in the burned area: no fire-resisting doors, no protected iron work "as is generally understood today, either by plaster or terra-cotta", no fire shutters or sprinklers. Many buildings in the area were combined horizontally, and the fire doors installed to protect wall openings failed in the fire.[103]

How does one account for the variety of systems available and the fact that traditional methods continued to be used? In answering this question, I take a hint from Marian Bowley, who pondered the problem of why British architects were slow to adopt the steel frame:

"(The) developments of modern steel frame construction and of reinforced concrete were not necessary to fulfil any obvious requirements in the country in the late nineteenth century. They offered new and better ways of providing buildings to perform functions already performed by existing buildings".[104]

Was fire safety a problem that was not being addressed? Or was anxiety about fire safety low? Did the fact that much land in Britain was leased rather than owned by those who owned the improvements discourage construction of more substantial buildings? Were British fireproof materials too expensive? I do not know the ultimate reasons, only its manifestations: a building law in London that did not require fireproof construction, and little agitation to allow fireproof skeleton buildings.

This situation changed in the first decade of the twentieth century, when new laws in London addressed fire safety, and allowed skeleton frame construction. Also in this decade in the United States, concrete came to be used to a much greater extent in fireproof buildings, following favourable reports of its performance compared with terracotta in the great fires in Baltimore and San Francisco. Thus British and American construction practice began to look more similar, after a century of developing differently.

Conclusion

British building designers and construction materials manufacturers were leaders in introducing fireproof construction systems in the nineteenth century. American practices were adapted from or anticipated by British systems. However, fireproof construction became much more general in America than in Britain at the end of the nineteenth century. The question I address is why, having pioneered so many fireproof building systems, British inventiveness slowed down and adoption never spread beyond a limited set of clients, while the variety of fireproofing systems in America increased and fireproof construction became standard for many kinds of buildings. I conclude that the difference stems from different levels of anxiety with respect to the likelihood of general conflagration, which was reflected in the different building laws in the two nations. In both countries, building laws originated in order to control fire. American cities, unlike British cities, suffered serious fires throughout the nineteenth century. The approach to the problem eventually adopted by American cities was to require that buildings over a certain height within designated fire limits, or of a certain type (e.g. theatres), be constructed fireproof. But tall buildings had to be fireproof not only because of building laws; as a practical matter, there was no other way to build them, and thus the progress of the development of the tall building and the fireproof building became thoroughly intertwined in the last two decades of the century. In

Sara Wermiel

Britain, a distrust of large buildings, as fire hazards, long was embodied in building laws. Just as the first generation of skeleton frame buildings was going up in the United States, the allowable height of buildings in London was reduced, in an 1894 revision to the building laws, as a fire safety measure. In short, most Americans accepted tall buildings but wanted them fireproof, a situation which encouraged research and development in the field of structural fire protection. Britons forbade tall buildings for the sake of fire safety, and could protect the buildings that were allowed with the methods already at hand. The century ended with the apparently paradoxical situation of American cities having both more serious fires and yet more buildings being constructed fireproof, using the latest practice.

ACKNOWLEDGEMENTS

The author is particularly indebted to Lawrance Hurst and Arnold Pacey for previous information and for their many valuable insights regarding nineteenth century construction practice.

References

1. C. C. Knowles and P. H. Pitt, *The History of Building Regulation in London 1189-1972* (1972); *Records of the Governor and Company of the Massachusetts Bay ...* (1854), pp.239-40.
2. *Building News*, 7 (5 July 1861), p.557.
3. *American Architect and Building News*, 5 (7 June 1879), p.179.
4. Batty Langley, *The London Prices of Bricklayers Materials and Works* (1749), p.246.
5. J. G. Coad, "Two Early Attempts at Fire-Proofing in Royal Dockyards", *Post-Medieval Archaeology*, 7 (1973), p.88.
6. Charles Sylvester, *The Philosophy of Domestic Economy* (1819), footnote pp.7-8.
7. For example, the warehouses on Cotton's Wharf and Depot Wharf, built between 1840 and 1860, which burned in the Tooley Street fire. *Building News*, 7 (5 July 1861), p.573.
8. Associated Architects, *Resolutions of the Associated Architects: with the Report of a Committee ... To Consider the Causes of the frequent Fires ...* (1793), p.ii.
9. Knowles and Pitt, *Building Regulations*.
10. Frank Kelsall, "David Hartley's Fireplates" (unpublished paper, March 1991).
11. Coad, "Two Early Attempts", p.89.
12. The Leeds Industrial Museum, *Armley Mills* (Leeds n.d.), p.6.
13. Associated Architects, *Resolutions*, Appendix No. 1.
14. Manufactureres Mutual Fire Insurance Co., *Special Report No. 10*, April 1, 1882.
15. *Macmillan Encyclopedia of Architects*, vol. 2 (New York, 1982).
16. House of Representatives, "New Treasury and Post Office Buildings", Report No. 737, March 29, 1838. Mills' quote from . p24.
17. Article in the *Herald* of 23 Nov. 1873, quoted in B. Woodman, *A Customhouse for Newburyport* (privately published, 1985), p.20.
18. Recent publications include: Ron Fitzgerald, "The Development of the Cast Iron Frame in Textile Mills to 1850", *Industrial Archaeology Review*, 10 (Spring 1988), pp.127-145; Colum Giles and Ian Goodall, *Yorkshire Textile Mills*, 1992; and Mike Williams with D. A. Farnie, *Cotton Mills in Greater Manchester* (Preston, 1992).
19. Jennifer Tann, *The Development of the Factory* (1970).

The Development of Fireproof Construction

20. Williams with Farnie, *Cotton Mills*, p.59.
21. Luke Hebert, *The Engineer's and Mechanic's Encyclopaedia* vol. 1 (1836), p.526.
22. Giles and Goodall, *Textile Mills*, p. 64; Williams with Farnie, *Cotton Mills*, p.61.
23. Hebert, pp.526-27.
24. For example, C. W. Pasley, *Observations on Limes...* (1838), p.168.
25. Edward Diestelkamp, "Architects and the Use of Iron", in Robert Thorne, ed., *The Iron Revolution* (1990), p.21.
26. Edward Barry, "An Account of the New Palace at Westminster", R.I.B.A. *Sessional Papers* (1857-58), pp.86, 90 – 91.
27. See descriptions in John Olly, "The Reform Club", *Architects' Journal*, 181 (27 Feb. 1985), pp.34-60.
28. Associated Architects, *Resolutions*, footnote on p. 11.
29. H. R. Johnson and A. W. Skempton, "William Strutt's Cotton Mills, 1793-1812", *Transactions of the Newcomen Society*, 30 (1955-56 and 1956-57), pp.179-205.
30. "Unpublished Letters of Benjamin Franklin", *The Pennsylvania Magazine*, 15 (1891), p.39 (cited in Philadelphia Museum of Art, Philadelphia, *Three Centuries of American Art*, (1976).
31. Charles Eck, *Traite de Construction en Poteries et Fer* (Paris 1836).
32. Pasley, *Observations*, p.164.
33. For example, Henry Roberts, hollow, wedge-shaped bricks, patented 1849, weighing with concrete fill 70 lbs/sq. ft., and William Fairbairn's jogged bricks, used at Saltaire Mills in 1854.
34. John J. Webster, "Fire-proof Construction", *Minutes of Proceedings of the Institution of Civil Engineers*, 105 (1890-91), p.264.
35. Pasley, *Observations*, p. 164, and Hebert, p.526.
36. Lawrance Hurst, "Fox and Barrett" (unpublished paper, March 1991).
37. James Barrett, *Minutes of the Proceedings of the Institution of Civil Engineers*, 7 (1852-53), pp.264-65.
38. Hurst, "Fox and Barrett".
39. William Ware, "On Middle-Class Houses in Paris and Central London", R.I.B.A. *Transactions* (1878), p.33.
40. For example, Builder, 7 (Nov. 1848), p.541.
41. Knowles and Pitt, *Building Regulations*, p.63.
42. P. B. Wright thought the first cast iron columns used in the U.S. had been imported from Scotland. (American Institute of Architcts, *Proceedings*, 1877.) At a meeting of the Polytechnic Club in New York in 1860, a Mr Godwin commented that he had seen cast iron columns imported to the U.S. "a good many years". (*Architects' and Mechanics' Journal, 2*, (5 May 1860), pp.41-43.
43. *Architectural Review and American Builders' Journal*, 2 (Aug. 1869), p.102.
44. Day books, order books, and shipping records, 1852-1865, Cooper & Hewitt Collection, Manuscript Division, Library of Congress.
45. All iron work contracts at federal government buildings built in the 1850s went to iron founders (National Archives, Record Group 121, entry 6 and 26); for the later period, William Fryer in *A History of Real Estate in New York City* (1898, reprinted New York 1967), p.498.
46. Williams with Farnie, *Cotton Mills*, p.106.
47. Fitzgerald, "*The Cast Iron Frame*", p.142-43.
48. *On the Application of Cast and Wrought Iron to Building Purposes* (1854).
49. A. J. Pacey, "Technical Innovation in some late Nineteenth-Century Railway Warehouses", *Industrial Archaeology*, 5 (1968), pp.364-372.

Sara Wermiel

50. Roger Holden, "Pear Mill, Stockport: An Edwardian Cotton Spinning Mill, *"Industrial Archaeology* Review" 10 (Spring 1988), p.163.
51. James Braidwood, *Fire Prevention and Fire Extinction* (1866), p.48.
52. *Building News*, 7 (5 July 1861), p.573.
53. Paper read by T. Hayter Lewis to the R.I.B.A., summarised in *Building News*, 12 (7 April 1865), pp.243-44.
54. From *Building News*, 12 (27 Jan. 1865), p.69.
55. *Building News*, 22 (29 March 1872), p.250.
56. *Building News*, 12 (7 April 1865), p.244.
57. *Building News*, 22 (29 March 1872), p.250.
58. *Building News*, 12 (29 Dec. 1865), p.925; *Building News*, 22, (29 March 1872), p.250.
59. *Building News*, 12 (7 April 1865), p.243; G. M. Lawford, "Fireproof Floors", Society of Engineers *Transactions for 1889* (1890), pp.45-46; Williams with Farnie, *Cotton Mills*, p.108.
60. Lawford, "Fireproof Floors", p.46.
61. *Building News*, 22 (29 March 1872), p.250.
62. American Institute of Architects, *Proceedings*, 1873, pp.18-19.
63. "The Office of the Supervising Architect: What it was, what it is, and what it ought to be", New York, 1869, signed "Civis".
64. N. H. Hutton, paper presented at 1873 A.I.A. convention, *American Architect and Building News*, 1 (5 Feb. 1876), p.43.
65. *American Architect and Building News*, 3 (8 Feb. 1878), p.43. 66. For example, Louis De Coppet Berg, *Architectural Record*, 1 (1891-92), p.461.
67. *Brickbuilder*, 6 (March 1897), p.54.
68. Patent 132, 292, Oct. 15, 1872, with W. Freeborn.
69. Wight, in *Brickbuilder*, 6 (March 1897), p.54.
70. *Brickbuilder*, 6 (March 1897), p.54.
71. Henry Eyton, *Journal of the Society of Arts*, 12 (20 Sept. 1864), p.722.
72. For example, 129,827, Isaac Hodson and William Brown and 133,448 Johnson and E. R. Hall, in 1872; 143,197, L. A Tartierre in 18 73; 156, 808, Henry Maurer in 1874.
73. American Architect and Building News, 1 (30 Dec 1876), p.421.
74. Peter Wight, writing in Brickbuilder, 6 (August, 1897), p.173.
75. 1874 patent 154 , 852 and 1878 patents 203, 972 and 204, 867.
76. Gilbert's patent ceiling, *Architectural Review and American Builders' Journal*, 1 (July 1868), p.62. The arched version was like a floor used by William Fairbairn in a refinery building, 1845; and the corrugated version was like Moreland's floor.
77. Patent 98,571, Jan. 4, 1870.
78. John Draffin, "A Brief History of Lime, Cement, Concrete and Reinforced Concrete", in *A Selection of Historic American Papers on Concrete 1876-1926* (Detroit: American Concrete Institute), p.11.
80. R. M. Hunt, "The Architectural Exhibits of the International Exhibition", *Reports of the United States Centennial Commission* (Philadelphia 1877-78).
81. *American Architect and Building News*, 16 (15 November 1884, p.232.
82. Arthur Cates, "Concrete and Fire-Resisting Construction", in R.I.B.A. *Sessional Papers* (1877-78), p. 308; Lawford, "Fireproof Floors", p.47.
83. Webster, "Fire-Proof Construction", p.267.
84. *Building News*, 22 (9 March 1872), p.193; 23 (8 Nov. 1872); 358–9.
85. Cates, "Concrete and Fire-Resisting Construction", p.298.
86. *Building News*, 26 (27 Feb. 1874), p.225.

The Development of Fireproof Construction

87. Roger Holden, "Pear Mill, Stockport: An Edwardian Cotton Spinning Mill", *Industrial Archaeology Review*, 10 (Spring 1988), p.163.

88. Edward Atkinson, "Report on English Cotton-Mills and Methods", New England Cotton Manufacturers' Association, *Proceedings*, October 31, 1883, pp.33-55; J. R. Freeman, "Comparison of English and American Types of Factory Construction", reprint from the *Journal of the Association of Engineering Societies*, remarks presented Sept. 17, 1890.

89. Gail Fenske and Deryck Holdsworth, "Corporate Identity and the New York Office Building, 1985-1915", in Ward and Zunz, eds., *The Landscape of Modernity* (New York, 1992), pp.129-159.

90. Henry Ericsson, *Sixty Years a Builder: An Autobiography* (Chicago, 1942), p.227.

91. *Inland Architect and News Record*, 4 (April 1887), p. 32; William Fryer, "The New York Building Law", *A History of Real Estate, Building, and Architecture in New York City* (New York, 1898, reprinted 1967), p.292.

92. Ralph Peck, *History of Building Foundations in Chicago*, U. of Illinois Engineering Experiment Station, Bulletin Series No. 373 (Urbana, Illinois, 1948).

93. *American Architect and Building News*, 41 (19 Aug. 1893), p.114.

94. G. Henning, "Notes on Steel", A.S.M.E. *Transactions*, 4 (1882/83), p.410.

95. *Brickbuilder*, 6 (May 1897), p. 99.

96. As discussed by Frank Kidder in *American Architect and Building News*, 37 (21 Nov. 1892), pp.97-100.

97. Lawrance Hurst, "The Age of Fireproof Flooring", in Robert Thorne, Ed., *The Iron Revolution* (1990), p.37.

98. Lawford, "Fireproof Floors", pp.49-52.

99. The Fawcett Ventilated Building Co. Ltd. 1898 trade catalogue in the collection of the Hagley Museum and Library, Wilmington, Delaware.

100. H. D. Purroy, "English and American Fire Services", *The Forum*, 2 (1886), pp.299-307. It is impossible to get an accurate picture of fire loss in the 19th century because of the lack of data.

101. *American Architect*, 89 (12 May 1906).

102. "Objects of the Committee", printed in British Fire Prevention Committee, *Redbooks*.

103. *Engineering News* (London), 65 (1898), pp.355-357.

104. Marian Bowley, *The British Building Industry* (Cambridge, 1966), p.34.

5

The development and use of
the tubular beam, 1830–1860

Stanley Smith

ABSTRACT

In the mid-nineteenth century, one response to the problem of creating large span structures was the development of the tubular beam. Early beams of this type, for moderate spans, were erected in the 1830s, but it was the construction of large tubes, with spans of over 400 ft (90 m), for the Britannia Bridge that brought this form of structure to the attention of a wider audience. Robert Stephenson and William Fairbairn, designer and detailer of this structure, developed the tubular beam and attempted to have this form of structure used more widely. By 1860, when the Great Victoria Tubular Bridge was opened across the St Lawrence River, in Canada, although many tubular beams had been used, this particular form of beam had fallen out of favour.

This paper discusses the differences between the first and last of these large-span bridges, some of the reasons for the changes in attitudes towards this form of structure; and how these were related to new ideas in structural design generally. An attempt is made to identify the people who questioned the economic viability and efficiency of the tubular beam in the technical press and at institutional meetings, and to offer some reasons why it fell from favour and exerted little influence on the subsequent evolution of large span structures.

INTRODUCTION

In 1844, the decision of the Directors of the Chester and Holyhead Railway Company to construct a bridge over the Menai Straits as part of the line connecting Holyhead, on the island of Anglesey, with the mainland rail network at Chester presented their engineer with a formidable problem. The expansion of the railway system in the United Kingdom in the 1830s and 1840s had required the provision of a large number of bridges across rivers, estuaries and channels such as the Menai, and had encouraged the use of new materials, especially cast iron and wrought iron for long span construction.

The Menai Straits posed a particular difficulty, owing to the Admiralty requirement for a clear headroom of 100 ft (30 m) and the minimum of supports obstructing the channel. This severely restricted the choice of structural solution; arches of timber, masonry or iron, even if capable of a 450 ft (145 m) span, would have restricted the headroom required, suspension structures would need high support towers for the cables and, in any event, because of their lack of stiffness as designed at the time, were not favoured by railway engineers in the United Kingdom. The lattice truss beam had not been used at that time for such large spans and was still being developed in the United States. The final choice, some form of rigid beam, was a familiar structural device in cast and wrought iron, but usually in some form of I shape, not capable of such a large span.

The solution adopted for the Britannia Bridge over the Menai Straits was a large wrought iron tube, with the train passing through it, originally intended to have suspension chains, but these were omitted when the bridge was built (Figure 1). It was a structure acclaimed at the time as an exceptional engineering achievement, and was exceptional too, in another sense, as it was the first occasion (for which there is documentary evidence) when the design proposals for a structure were developed and tested in such detail by means of a series of large-scale models by the railway engineer, Robert Stephenson and by the experienced fabrication contractor, William Fairbairn.

The tubular construction of both the Britannia Bridge and the smaller-span Conway Bridge across the river at Conway Castle attracted a great deal of publicity at the time and generated a high level of interest in the design of the tubular beam, which has continued until the present day. The impression given by this profusion of contemporary published material is that from this date the tubular beam form, both the Stephenson type, with the train passing through it, and the type evolved by Fairbairn, with tubular flanges, was widely accepted as a suitable method of spanning large spaces.

Yet within 15 years the tubular solution had started to fall into disfavour, and after 1860 very little more is heard about large span structures of this type. A study of the events that took place during this short period, between the rise and fall of the tubular beam, offers some interesting glimpses of the personalities of the people involved, and of the changes in attitude to the design and construction of tubes that were occurring. These changes can be readily identified in the technical description of the last large tubular bridge built, completed in 1859, the Great Victoria Bridge in Canada (Figure 2). This is well documented in a specially bound volume by James Hodges, *The Construction of the Great Victoria Bridge, Canada.*[1] It is profusely illustrated with coloured plates and engravings, prepared from photographs that were taken as the work proceeded, together with detailed drawings of both the stone and iron construction.

THE GREAT VICTORIA BRIDGE

From the start of the first masonry work in 1854, the Victoria Bridge took five years to complete and was a massive example of the wrought iron

102   *Development and Use of the Tubular Beam*

Figure 1   Portion of one of the tubes of the Britannia Bridge.

Source: Edwin Clark, *The Britannia and Conway Tubular Bridges*, 1850. All the illustrations are reproduced, with permission, from books in the Library of the Institution of Civil Engineers.

Figure 2 The Victoria Bridge.

Source: James Hodges, *Construction of the Great Victoria Bridge in Canada* (1860).

tubular beam, designed by Robert Stephenson, similar to the Conway and Britannia Bridges. The Victoria was part of the Grand Trunk Railway, designed to connect the eastern seaboard of Canada with the St Lawrence River and the Great Lakes. The engineer for the whole system was Robert Stephenson and the contractors were Jackson, Peto, Brassey & Betts. Schemes for the route of the line had been under discussion for some years, and the location for the crossing of the St Lawrence had been suggested in 1851 by Thomas Keefer[2] and surveyed together with the whole of the route in 1852. A report on the scheme was published in 1853, the year Robert Stephenson went to Canada and inspected the site of the bridge.[3]

By this time a detailed survey of the proposed crossing had been made by A.M. Ross,[4] the resident engineer for Stephenson, and the general form of the structure had been decided. From the very beginning, some form of tubular beam was proposed: in timber and iron by Keefer,[5] and as a large iron tube by the Stephenson office. In the event, the bridge was to consist of two wrought iron tubes, built side by side spanning between stone piers, with 24 spans of 242 ft and one central span of 330 ft. The total length was, with approach spans, nearly $1\frac{3}{4}$ miles.

The contractors had decided to manufacture the ironwork for the bridge (and other mechanical equipment for the line) in England and to ship it out to Canada for fabrication and erection.[6] It is clear that there were competent ironwork fabricators in North America at the time as some sections of the Grand Trunk were built by them, but presumably it was to retain control over quality and progress that the decision was taken to manufacture in England.

The contractors decided to set up their own plant for the work and in 1853 purchased a site at Birkenhead and started to erect the first sheds that were to become the Canada Works. That year the works manager, George Harrison, arrived from Canada and work was started. Within 12 months, 400 men were employed out of an ultimate total of 2,000; two locomotives had been shipped to Canada, and one 155 ft span was completed. The men in charge of the bridge works were William Evans and William Heap. When Peto went bankrupt in 1866 the latter took over the works. As a young man, Heap had worked for W. Evans, fabricators of Cambridge, on the construction of the Conway Bridge.[7]

The ironwork for the bridge was constructed from material purchased from various mills in England and rolled and punched in the works at Birkenhead. Each plate and rolled section was then numbered in accordance with the drawings, before being sent to Canada. The completed structure was inspected by Mr Bruce in December 1859, after Mr B.P. Stockman, who prepared the working drawings for the tubes, had checked them during a visit to Canada in 1858.[8] The official opening of the bridge by the Prince of Wales took place in 1860, when he drove the last rivet.[9] The rapid publication of Hodges' volume (put out in seven weeks) meant that the Victoria Bridge was perhaps better described than the majority of the structures of the time. It also means that we have a very comprehensive list of the people working on the site, including Samuel Ratcliffe and Edward Coulton, foremen riveters to James Hodgkinson, erector of the tubes, together with many other members of the contractor's site staff.[10]

A major problem was, of course, the Canadian climate: the extremely cold winter, with the river frozen over, and the spring, with high water conditions brought about by the thaw. For the masons this restricted the working season but as regards ironwork, once on site, it could be fabricated on land during the winter, carried to the site by rail in the summer and erected on a staging built between the piers (Figure 3), a much simpler operation than the system of jacks required for the large tubes at Conway and Menai. The approach spans, over the land at Menai, were built on what E. Clark described as 'whole timber scaffolding', which consisted of 12-inch or 16-inch square timbers up to 60 ft long.[11]

Although the holes in the plates were punched at Birkenhead, they were purposely formed undersize, and reamed out on site to permit some erection tolerance and to produce what was intended to be a good fit. Later criticisms suggest that this was not achieved and that the riveting, done by hand on site, always gave problems to such an extent that in later years a gang of riveters was required, working all the year round, to replace the rivets that fell out.[12]

The bridge differed in two major respects from the Conway and Britannia Bridges. First, the stiffness of the top was achieved with layers

Figure 3 The Victoria Bridge: erection of one span on scaffolding.

Source: James Hodges, *Construction of the Great Victoria Bridge in Canada* (1860).

of thin plates riveted together with longitudinal built up 'I' sections (formed of a plate with two angle irons fixed top and bottom), tied together with wrought iron straps and not, as at Menai, using cellular construction, (Figure 4). Second, the tubes were stiffened over the piers with projecting triangular-shaped fins at right angles to the main tube, described as diaphragms (Figure 5). Additional refinements, not present at the Menai Straits, were the provision of rails for a travelling cradle to run along the tube to allow inspection and painting, and a wooden roof on top of the tubes with an access walkway on it.

The six years between the completion of the Britannia and the start of the Victoria had seen some development in the mechanical equipment available for fabrication. Mechanical drills were specially designed to cut out the segmental corners of the rectangular smoke vents in the side of the tubes and to ream out the holes for the rivets.[13] At the Canada Works the rivet holes were formed by a Jacquard machine, where the pattern of holes to be punched was set by the insertion of wooden strips, operating on the same principle as the Jacquard loom. A similar machine, or perhaps the same one, had been used to punch the plates for the Conway Bridge. The machine was capable of punching rows of holes, 10 in line, through about one hundred $\frac{1}{4}$-inch thick plates each day.[14]

The construction of the Victoria was widely reported in the press. From June 1856, when *The Engineer* was first published, there was a magazine

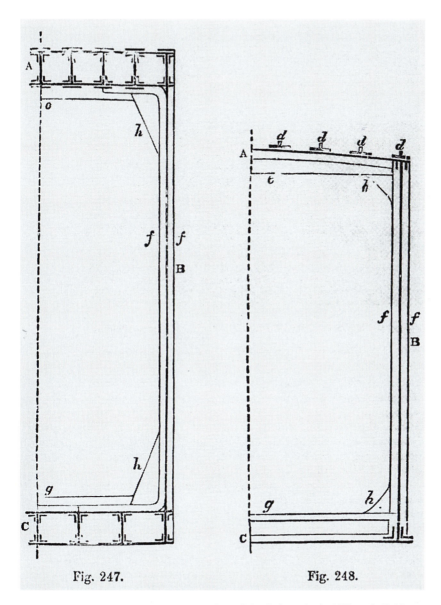

Fig. 247.   Fig. 248.

Figure 4   Comparison of the cross-section of the Britannia and Victoria Bridges.

Source: W.J. Maquorn Rankine, *Civil Engineering* (1926). This illustration appeared in every edition from the first in 1862.

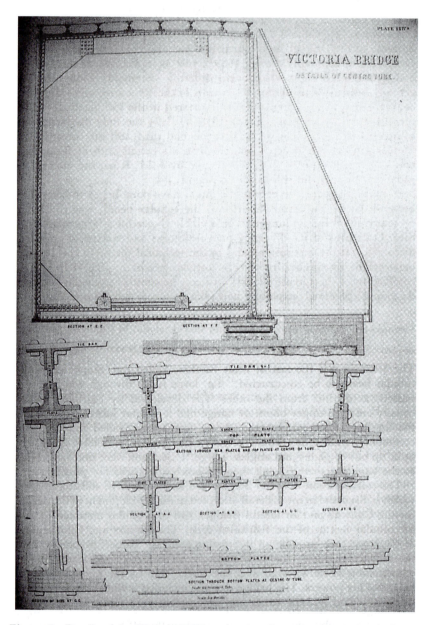

Figure 5 Details of the Victoria Bridge, showing fins over piers.

Source: James Hodges, *Construction of the Great Victoria Bridge in Canada* (1860).

108   *Development and Use of the Tubular Beam*

solely devoted to engineering matters as well as the older *Civil Engineer and Architects' Journal* and *The Builder*, all giving a great deal of space to the building of the bridge. Its construction was also covered in the *Illustrated London News*, especially during 1859.[15] Just as in the case of the Conway and Britannia Bridges, there were differing statements about who had actually been responsible for the design of the structure, and claims and counter-claims for the original idea appeared in the technical papers and the *Illustrated London News* during 1858–59.[16] By the time the bridge was completed in 1859, Robert Stephenson had died and his cousin, G.R. Stephenson, who had acted on Stephenson's behalf both at Birkenhead and in Canada, refuted the claims made by A.M. Ross, the man on the spot, that he was the responsible designer.

In many respects, the disputants might have done better to keep silent because the design under discussion, the tubular beam, was considered by many engineers no longer to be a viable choice for a large span structure. Criticisms of its efficiency and usefulness had started to appear in discussions at the institutions and in the technical press. In the 14 years between the first Fairbairn tests on tubular beams in July 1845 and the completion of the Great Victoria Bridge, the tubular principle had been developed, patented, exploited and then begun to fall from favour.

STEPHENSON AND FAIRBAIRN

The Victoria was the last of what Rankine called the 'Stephenson-type' tubular beam to be constructed;[17] i.e. large tubes through which a train passed, as distinct from the other type developed by Fairbairn, where usually only the upper boom or flange had a tubular form (Figure 6). In the literature of the time other beam forms were called tubular, most commonly, what today would be called box girders, a hollow component built up out of plates and angles. Large 'I' sections were not then rolled, so the later practice of using them in box girders was not possible.

The collaboration between Stephenson and Fairbairn, starting in 1845, which is discussed in more detail later, led to the development of the designs for the Conway and Britannia Bridges and to a patent obtained in 1846 for tubular beams of the Fairbairn type. The careers and achievements of these two men provide an interesting contrast. Robert Stephenson was the railway engineer, the civil engineer *par excellence*, responsible for the construction of railways all over the world, and by the mid-1840s at the height of his powers. His bridge designs included a whole series of girder bridges, plated girders, tubes and arches, but very rarely lattice trusses. The large-span trussed roofs built over the stations on lines for which he was responsible were usually designed in the offices of contractors.[18] Stephenson appears as the practical man, organizing and supervising very large contracts with efficiency and dispatch. He had a large office staffed with a group of talented engineers who translated his embryonic ideas into detailed drawings. For all his involvement in the professional affairs of the institutions at the Civils and Mechanicals, apart from his contributions

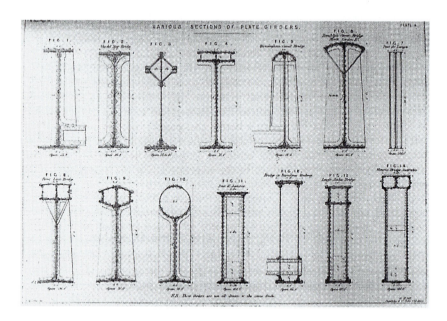

Figure 6 Examples of tubular beams proposed or constructed in mid-century.

Source: William Humber, *A Complete Treatise on Cast Iron and Wrought Iron Bridge Construction* (2nd edn, 1864).

to discussions and Presidential addresses, he never wrote or presented a paper expounding his ideas about design or describing his works. His only published writings were his contributions to the *Encyclopaedia Britannica* on Bridges and Roofs,[19] the first chapter in Clark's book on the Britannia tubes and various technical reports. In this latter respect William Fairbairn was a complete contrast, being a prolific writer of books and a presenter of papers to the British Association for the Advancement of Science, the Royal Society, numerous Literary and Philosophical Societies, the Institution of Mechanical Engineers and, up until about 1855, the Institution of Civil Engineers. In other ways as well, Fairbairn was very different. His early work had been as a millwright, a boiler-maker, the designer of the Lancashire boiler and a shipbuilder, as well as an ironwork fabricator and designer of structures. In present-day terminology he was more a mechanical than a civil engineer.

Over the years Fairbairn was involved in a series of experiments to establish the properties of materials, the strength of riveted joints and, in the late 1850s and early 1860s, the safety of steam-raising boilers. His experimental work, starting as early as 1838-9, was usually concerned with riveted structures of one form or another, frequently carried out in conjunction with people such as Hodgkinson and Unwin, and was well received in Europe. One of his main claims to fame was as a publicist for the use of iron in the construction of buildings and ships. This was a theme he developed in the books he wrote from the 1850s onward, such as *Useful Information for Engineers* (1855), *The Application of Cast and Wrought Iron to Building Purposes* (1854) and *A Treatise on Iron Shipbuilding* (1865).[20] All these volumes were reprinted and revised into the 1870s and 1880s but by the latter date received very unfavourable reviews in the technical press, critical of the use of out-of-date examples and discredited design constants.[21] Nevertheless, critics as pedantic as Todhunter and Pearson were prepared to admit in 1899 that Fairbairn's books and papers 'played a considerable part in developing a more rational scientific education for engineers'. The books were one of the earliest attempts to provide scientific information in a form suited to the abilities of the average artisan or the pupil in the engineer's office.

THE INTRODUCTION OF THE TUBULAR BEAM

The requirements of the railways in the 1830s and 1840s for long span structures coincided with the wider availability of wrought iron together with a growing battery of techniques for shaping, processing and joining the material, plus the mechanical plant to carry out some of these operations. For many railway engineers, this suggested the use of iron for all structures and, with very few exceptions, the end of the use of wood or masonry for large spans.

The increase in wrought iron output in the early years of the nineteenth century made possible developments such as the built-up beam section, the plate girder and the box girder, forerunner of the tube. As early as 1834 a box beam had been used at the Fairbairn works to form the paddle beam in a boat built for use in the Humber.[22] Maudsley and Field took out a patent in 1839 for a box beam for a similar purpose.[23] The first use of a box beam for a bridge on a railway seems to have been in 1840, on the Pollock and Gowan Railway. It was constructed by William Dixon, the owner of an ironworks, where similar beams had been used for some years.[24]

The box girder showed that it was possible to join plates of iron together to form a beam but it was not a tube in the accepted sense of the Stephenson or Fairbairn tubes, which had cellular flanges—sometimes both top and bottom, sometimes only the top—and one or two vertical webs. One of the earliest mentions of a tube is in a patent for a tubular mast taken out in 1800, but this was a composite structure of wood and iron.[25] In 1841 C.L.G. Eck illustrated the tubular construction of the floors at the Winter Palace in St Petersburg, which consisted of a series of elliptical tubes about 3 ft deep.[26]

When the Bill for the Chester and Holyhead Railway was before the Parliamentary Committee, several people giving evidence talked of an aerial tunnel over the Menai Straits,[27] but it was Robert Stephenson who put forward the most logical solution, which used a tube. In the chapter he contributed to the Edwin Clark book, Stephenson describes the various stages his ideas went through. It appears that the final solution developed from two basic concepts; the first was the cellular form that had been proposed in 1841 for a bridge at Ware but never used and the second arose from the idea of a suspension bridge with sides stiffened with a lattice structure, thus giving the semblance of a tube with the train passing through it. The formula for cast iron was used to give the general dimensions for this structure, considered as two very deep 'I' beams joined together.[28]

It was this claim of prior invention, by Stephenson of the tubular beam, that so incensed Fairbairn and which, together with assertions about responsibility for the development of the formula, the conduct of the tests at Millwall and payments for them and other items, was the cause of the acrimonious dispute between the two men. It was in April 1845 that Stephenson and Fairbairn first discussed the construction of the Britannia Bridge, when its form was to be that of a tube with side chains.[29] By July 1845 tests had started at Millwall on elliptical and circular tubes, the forms favoured by Stephenson.[30]

In the early 1840s most engineers appear to have thought of beam design in terms of cast iron components with the bottom flange larger than the top to compensate for the poor tension-resisting properties of the material. The experiments of Tredgold and Barlow had resulted in a set of widely used constants for the design of cast iron beams and the ratio of the flange sizes to each other.[31] It was these design aids that Stephenson appears to have used in his early investigations and Fairbairn, judging by his later writings, hoped to produce a similar set of constants for the design of wrought iron tubes.

At this time Fairbairn's experience of the design and construction of riveted wrought iron structures, his experiments on riveted connections in 1838–9 and his work on boiler design and shipbuilding in iron all made him an ideal choice, perhaps the only choice at the time, for the type of investigation and development work that Stephenson required.[32] Fairbairn appreciated that the solution to the problems of the large tube would depend, in part, on the strength of the plates and the riveted joints but was not aware, nor it would appear were others, that the failure of the tube would be by buckling of the top. The solution was seen as the disposition of more material in the upper part of the tube, achieved at Conway and Britannia by the use of cellular construction which was also used for the bottom (Figure 7). The experiments that were carried out by Fairbairn, Hodgkinson and Clark at Millwall and Manchester started in 1845 on cylindrical tubes, then in late 1845 on rectangular tubes and finally from April 1846 until April 1847 on the one-sixth full size model which was modified after each test to produce additional strength (Figure 8). It is salutary to consider that these tests were taking place after July 1846, at a time when workshops were being erected on site, orders were being placed for material and contracts let for fabrication.[33]

Edwin Clark, an outsider in some respects as far as the engineering ethos of the time was concerned, having started his engineering career

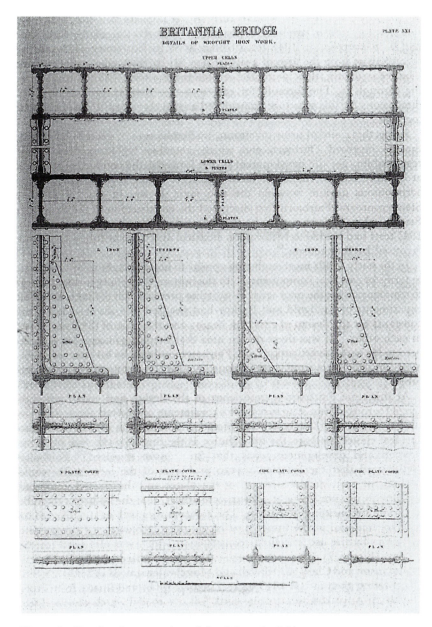

Figure 7   Details of construction of the Britannia Bridge.

Source: Edwin Clark, *The Britannia and Conway Tubular Bridges* (1850).

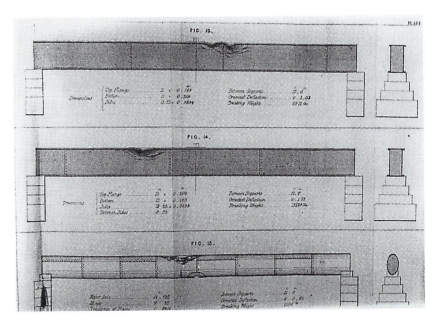

Figure 8 One of the sheets showing the results of the tests on the model beams, carried out at Fairbairn's Yard on the Isle of Dogs.

Source: William Fairbairn, *An Account of the Construction of the Britannia and Conway Tubular Bridges* (1849).

only in April 1846, expressed his admiration for the confidence that both Stephenson and Fairbairn had in the correctness of their ideas, and the certainty that the design would be successful.[34] They both demonstrated the result of experience of construction work, and the pragmatism of the practical man. In his book *The Britannia and Conway Tubular Bridges*, Clark neatly summarizes their attitudes as follows:

> We cannot but participate with Mr Stephenson in his unshaken confidence in the justice of the principles with which he had started in his inquiry, now confirmed by test of experiment; nor can we fail to admire the zeal with which Mr Fairbairn anticipates the results of the important investigation in which he was engaged, while his sanguine conclusions contrast forcibly with the abstract and minute deductions, the sceptical doubts and fears, of the exact Mathematician.[35]

This was written when Clark had had only four years' engineering experience. As the following discussion illustrates, more experienced engineers were less confident.

114   *Development and Use of the Tubular Beam*

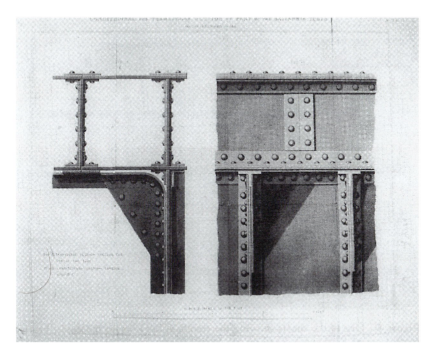

Figure 9   Britannia Bridge: detail of the vertical stiffeners.

Source: William Fairbairn, *An Account of the Construction of the Britannia and Conway Tubular Bridges* (1849).

What Fairbairn did introduce in the Conway Bridge, and later into his designs for boilers, was the use of stiffeners on the outside of the sides of the tubes (Figures 9 and 10). The early test tubes were constructed of plates simply overlapped and riveted together. Later, angle iron was used at the joint and in the finished construction and, because of the narrow width of the plates, these vertical side stiffeners occurred at approximately 24-inch intervals.[36] These thus acted to restrain the distortion of the tubes and assisted in the strength of the completed structure. From discussions in the 1850s at the Institution of Civil Engineers and elsewhere, it is clear that the strength of the sides was frequently ignored in the calculations and even when, later in the decade, computed by a formula, the choice of dimension always exceeded the calculated size to meet the practical requirements of fabrication.[37]

Owing to disagreements that developed between Stephenson, Fairbairn and the Directors of the Railway Company, Fairbairn's firm did not, as was originally intended, carry out any of the fabrication and erection work on the Conway and Britannia Bridges. However, in the subsequent 15 years, his firm built a substantial number of tubular beams based on the principles illustrated in the 1846 patent.[38] According to his biography, 100

Figure 10   Erection of the tubes on land.

Source: Edwin Clark, *The Britannia and Conway Tubular Bridges* (1850).

were constructed in the first five years, and by 1870 the number had reached 1,000.[39] The first was supposed to have been built for Vignoles on the Blackburn and Bolton Railway,[40] but throughout the 1850s and 1860s references appear noting Fairbairn-type tubes as far afield as Canada (several on the Grand Trunk and its feeders), France, Australia and Ireland.[41]

Some appreciation of the widespread use of the tubular beam can be seen in the *Minutes of Evidence of the Report of the Commissioners on the Application of Iron to Railway Structures*, published in 1849. The illustrated record sheets of the bridges identified show a remarkably large number that are based on the Fairbairn principle, some with cast iron top booms.[42]

The Stephenson-type tube, of massive proportions and large span, was not very widely used, certainly not by any designers outside the United Kingdom, although the form was suggested for a bridge in Germany.[43] Even Stephenson used the tube for only one other bridge in England, at Brotherton, and for the two bridges in Egypt, in the mid-1850s, prior to the design and construction of the final example in Canada in 1859.[44]

CRITICISM OF THE TUBULAR BEAM

Nine years before the completion of the Great Victoria Bridge in March 1850, the first doubts and criticisms about the tubular beam principle, and the basis for its design, were expressed at a meeting at the Institution of Civil Engineers. Again, in 1854 and 1855, more specific doubts were voiced about efficiency and suitability of the large Stephenson-type tubes, a theme that was taken up in the engineering press again in 1859 and 1860.

As each of these discussions occurred, the contestants in the arguments split into two distinct camps. In the first were Stephenson and Bidder in favour of the large tube, with a sub-group including Fairbairn who were backers of the small tubular beam; and in the second were their opponents, usually younger men, who favoured the truss or lattice as a solution for large span structures.

The first occasion when these doubts were articulated was on 12 March 1850 when Fairbairn presented a paper at the Institution 'On Tubular Girder Bridges'.[45] This was intended to be an explanation of the design basis of the Fairbairn-type tubular beam, in response to the refusal of the Inspectors of the Railway Board to approve the construction and design and to open for traffic a bridge designed and built by Fairbairn for John Fowler. In his introduction to the paper, Fairbairn notes that a difference of opinion appears to exist:

1. As to the application of a given formula for computing the strength of wrought iron girders;
2. As to the excess of strength that should be given to a tubular-girder bridge, over the greatest load that can be brought upon it; and
3. As to the effects of impact, and the best mode of testing the strength, and providing the security, of the bridge.[46]

He goes on to note how important it is, when introducing a new system of construction, to appreciate that safety depends not only on the correctness of the principle but also on the quality of the workmanship.[47] The discussion that followed the presentation of the paper indicates that for many people neither of these conditions had been satisfied. Not surprisingly, the three items listed about which differences of opinion existed—formula, factors of safety and testing—are still today matters for continuing discussion.

According to Fairbairn, the basis for the design of his tubular girder bridges was a formula that gave the proportion of the material to be disposed in the top and bottom for given depths, spans and breaking loads. The depths were based on a constant of one-thirteenth of the span for the spans of less than 150 ft and one-fifteenth for greater spans. The paper gives tables of loads, spans, depths and disposition of material and, in a footnote, states that 'the constant and table have been the basis for the dimensions of all the tubular girders constructed during the preceeding 18 months'.[48] Unfortunately, the design of the Torksey Bridge, around which discussion was to centre, did not quite comply with these criteria, but the 'beams

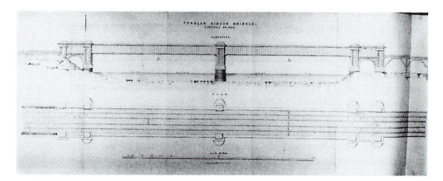

Figure 11 Torksey Tubular Bridge, plan and elevation.

Source: William Fairbairn: 'On Tubular Girder Bridges', *Minutes of the Proceedings of the Institution of Civil Engineers*, 1849–50, vol. 9.

are nevertheless sufficiently strong to render the bridge properly secure'[49] (Figures 11 and 12).

The paper was a relatively short one, only $8\frac{1}{2}$ pages long, but the discussion that followed continued for three evenings and was only finally concluded by a letter on 26 April. The discussion ranged over several other aspects that concerned mid-century designers such as government interference, the effect of impact blows, the position of the neutral axis and general beam theory, which are not primarily of interest here. Those parts of the discussion that were about tubular girders and the basis of Fairbairn's design contained a continual stream of adverse criticism. Nearly every speaker disagreed with Fairbairn's formula and his methods of deciding depth and load. George Bidder, a close colleague of Stephenson, seemed to take some satisfaction in pointing this out, no doubt reflecting the animosity that existed between the two men. Other speakers, such as Hodgkinson, had already disagreed with Fairbairn (at the BAAS meeting in Southampton in 1846 and over the credit for the formula used for the Conway and Britannia tubes) but nevertheless used this opportunity to suggest that the formula produced results that were unsafe. Dr Tate, who had been involved with the Millwall tests, disagreed with both.[50]

The discussion and the Inspectors' objections centred on the way the breaking load was calculated, the lack of consideration of the strength of the sides and the general standard of workmanship. It is clear from these comments that the problems of rigidity and resistance to compressive forces over the supports was considered by the Inspectors but not always by Fairbairn, and that the standard of workmanship, not commented on by any of the engineers present, had been of concern to the Inspectors.[51] The bad fit of rivets, oversize holes and distorted plates were problems that were to attract comment more and more as the volume of riveted ironwork increased.

118   *Development and Use of the Tubular Beam*

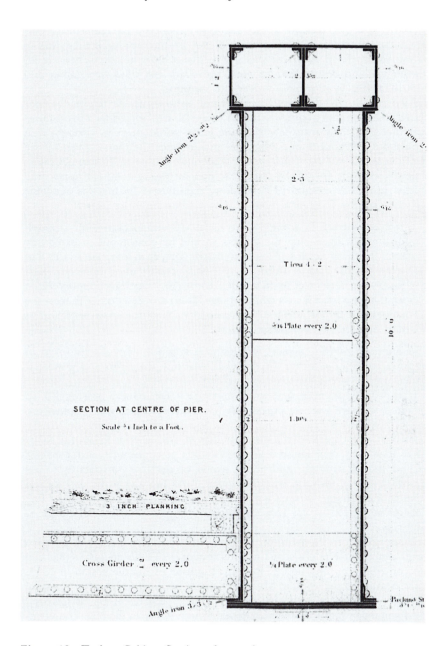

Figure 12   Torksey Bridge. Section of one tube.

Source: William Fairbairn: 'On Tubular Girder Bridges', *Minutes of the Proceedings of the Institution of Civil Engineers*, 1849–50, vol. 9.

Many of the comments made, especially those by Hodgkinson,[52] indicated the direction that the design of the Stephenson-type tube was to follow, to be seen in the Great Victoria Bridge, where the cells were omitted, thicker top and bottom flanges were provided, the sides were stiffer and additional fins were provided over the supports.

Two reasons for the Inspectors' refusal of approval for the bridge concerned their doubts about whether it could be considered as a continuous structure and their insistence that the permissible stress in wrought iron should not be more than 5 tons per square inch, the figure given by the *Report of the Royal Commission into the Application of Iron to Railway Structures*, a figure which many of the engineers present thought should apply only to cast iron.[53] A method of culculating continuous beams was available but not used by Fairbairn, who said in a footnote to his paper:

> It is considered by some engineers, as very important to the strength of these bridges, that the girders should be continuous or extending over 2 or more spans. This is no doubt correct to a certain extent and although the fact is admitted, yet this consideration is nevertheless purposely neglected, in these calculations; any auxiliary support of that kind acting merely as a counterpoise. It is considered safer to treat the subject on the principle of compassing each of the spans with simple and perfectly independent girders.[54]

The question of the correct permissible stress for wrought iron was to continue to be a matter for dispute until well into the 1870s and it was not settled until a stress for steel was agreed.[55]

It is worthy of note that after presenting the paper, presumably in person, Fairbairn was not present for the discussion (nor was Stephenson) and replied to his critics in a letter to Manby, the secretary. In this he defended his formula on the grounds that he had used it for all the tubes up to that date, had ignored any advantage of continuity, so the beams had additional strength, and that it would be perfectly satisfactory to use it until a better formula was developed.[56] As far as can be ascertained none of the tubular bridges being discussed failed in use. Following line closures in the 1970s, the Torksey Bridge continued in use as an unofficial footbridge.

It appears from the Minutes of Meetings that after this date Fairbairn never again spoke about structural matters at the Civils and after 1855 did not contribute on any topics. Perhaps the tone of the discussion in 1850, with so much disagreement about his ideas, left him feeling that many of his fellow engineers held him personally responsible for the Inspectors' involvement in matters of design detail, which many in the profession considered did not form part of the Railway Board's remit.

In a paper given to the Manchester Literary and Philosophical Society in 1850, very similar to the one given to the Civils earlier in the year, Fairbairn again justified the basis for his designs, described how the formula was based on experimental results and went on to say:

it appears preferable to adhere to a general formula, and to give the artificer a simple rule of extensive application, such as he may safely use without entering upon theoretical investigation which more properly belongs to the mathematician than the man of practical science.

From this it would appear that it was usual in the mid-century for the design of structures to be undertaken by people with limited skills in mathematics, who were not likely to be members of the Institutions.[57]

It is clear from the statements in these papers that Fairbairn and his contemporaries assumed that structures using a relatively untried, variable-quality material could be designed on the basis of a formula, a set of constants, that were derived from a very limited number of test results obtained by one experimenter. They also assumed that safety could be assured with a load that was some accepted fraction of the estimated failing load of the material established by a simple test. Fairbairn's view of the engineering profession's attitude to safe loads is given in the Manchester paper, where he notes that factors of safety of 3, 4, 5 and 6 were adopted, with the more timid engineers insisting upon 8 times.

Criticisms of the design and cost of the Victoria Bridge started in 1853 and Stephenson's visit to Canada in that year was partly to inspect the progress of the work there. In addition Stephenson prepared a report for the Directors of the Grand Trunk justifying the expense and time that were involved in the construction of the Victoria Bridge. The report was made public as soon as it was published in May 1854 and appeared in both the technical and public press.[58] In it Stephenson attempted to justify the choice of structure, the site chosen and the necessity for a bridge rather than some form of ferry; the last two points were defended on the grounds of the geography of the region, but the first point was more difficult to explain convincingly. Most of the argument revolved around the experience of the Menai bridges and the differences in approach adopted in England and North America respectively. Stephenson accepted that there was a difference of opinion as to the merits of trusses and suspension structures in America as against tubes and plated girders in the UK. In his view the structures erected on the former principles in America 'cannot be considered permanent, substantial and safe'.[59]

The next criticism, of the tubular beam in general and the Victoria in particular, occurred at the Institution of Civil Engineers in April 1855 during a discussion of a paper presented by James Barton, 'On Economic Distribution of Material in the Sides or Vertical Portion of Wrought Iron Beams'.[60] By this time, in Barton's view:

The laws which regulate the strains in the top and bottom of wrought-iron beams are now well ascertained and . . . can be determined with accuracy . . . ;

and their design in general was well understood. This was not the view that later commentators felt this particular discussion presented, exemplified in Todhunter and Pearson's judgement of 1893:

> Indeed the whole problem which engaged the minds of the practical men present as to whether the strains in the web of a girder are horizontal or inclined at 45°, seems to point to a painful want of theoretical knowledge in the English engineers of that day.[61]

Much of the discussion on the Barton paper concentrated on the comparison between the advantages of tubular and plate girders, Warren girders and lattice trusses and the mathematical design appropriate to each. After the main paper, Barton gave a description of the Boyne Viaduct, recently completed, a large lattice-type truss bridge, designed in Sir J. McNiel's office, with the construction on site supervised by Barton himself.

As was to be expected, the criticism of the large Stephenson-type tube, on the grounds of poor economic use of material compared to lattice trusses or Warren girders, was rebutted by Stephenson and Bidder. One contribution of the former to the discussion contained the phrase that caused Todhunter so much concern.

> He (Stephenson) entertained what might perhaps be considered peculiar notions with regard to the duties performed by the vertical portion of a common beam. In the theory of strains and resistances of a beam, the idea of a neutral axis, or line free from any strain, had been almost universally admitted by the profession, but he ventured to differ from that broad conclusion.[62]

Designers such as Barton, Blood, Doyne and Heppel, with experience of work in Ireland where a pragmatic basis for the design of lattice trusses had been developed, all considered the tubular beam and the plated girder to involve a very uneconomic and wasteful distribution of the material with no easy way available of calculating the strength of the sides or web of the beam. The disadvantages of the lattice truss were seen by Bidder and Stephenson as due to difficulties of erection and doubts about the accuracy of the calculations on which designs were based, in both instances criticisms that could equally well be levelled at tubes. Bidder's comment that the sides of tubular beams were always constructed thicker than the formula required emphasizes how much the size of structural components was based on rule of thumb and past experience and not on mathematical analysis.[63]

By the time this paper was presented in 1855 two other Stephenson tubes were either completed or nearly complete. They were both on the Alexandria and Cairo Railway in the Nile Delta, Egypt, of dimensions similar to those of the Britannia, but designed for the train to run on top of the tube, not through it. As at the Great Victoria, it appears that the cellular format at the top and bottom was omitted.[64] By 1855 sufficient details of the form and detail of the bridge to be erected on the St Lawrence had been published to permit the long discussion about the amount of wrought iron that would be used and for comparisons to be made with the quantities required in other forms of structure. The general tenor of the discussion that followed Barton's paper, spread over three evenings in April and May, is that the defenders of the tubular beam, principally Stephenson and Bidder, both in their mid-fifties, represented the old guard, while Barton, Blood, Doyne and Heppel, all in their thirties, represented the new, and wished to be considered part of the more theoretically educated engineering elite that was to be found outside the United Kingdom.[65]

Before criticisms appeared in the technical press about the work in Canada, it is clear that people other than engineers were having doubts about the cost and progress of the works. This is demonstrated by the journey to Canada made by Charles Hutton Gregory, at the request of the Chairman and Board of Directors of the Grand Trunk Railway, between April and July 1857, and the report he submitted about it.[66] The principal aim of the visit was to check that Jackson, Peto, Brassey & Betts, and Gzowski (a United States-based firm), the contractors, were complying with the terms of their contracts. Gregory inspected some 800 miles of railway, including hundreds of bridges, and in his report describes the forms of construction used. A substantial number were described as wrought iron tubes and girders, most of spans less than 100 ft. Unfortunately, it is not always possible to determine the location of all the bridges mentioned, but he does give information on standards of workmanship, levels of pay (50 per cent above UK rates) and the difficulties caused by the climate.

As the work on the Great Victoria neared completion criticisms started to appear in the technical press about the tubular beam and Stephenson's use of it. Journals such as *The Builder* and *The Civil Engineer and Architects' Journal* described in a straightforward way the construction of the bridge, but it was in *The Engineer*, just three years old, edited by Zerah Colburn (an expatriate American) that the most direct criticisms were put forward. These started in June 1859; more were to follow in August and December of that year and again in March 1860.

The two editorials in June, after describing the early history of the tube, and Fairbairn's involvement, concentrated on the high cost of tubes, an attribute for which they were famous, and the way this cost became a liability for the Railway Company, requiring expensive borrowed money to pay for it. Colburn suggested that an extra five minutes on the journey time between Chester and Holyhead could have allowed trains to travel across the Straits at 4 mph and so permitted the construction of a much cheaper bridge. The type recommended was of course the lattice, a form much more familiar to Colburn, with his railway engineering experience in the USA.[67]

The editorial of 19 August considered the very large weight of wrought iron and its cost in tubular bridges of the Stephenson type and the disadvantages of such beams for small spans, based on the effect of cost on the ratio of the number of piers to the size of span. It went on to argue that Stephenson's predilection for the rigid tube was mistaken and that the completion of the Roebling bridge at Niagara in 1854 demonstrated that a more elastic structure, with greater deflection, could still carry a very large moving load.[68]

In December the theme was pursued in the same vein, comparing the cost of the rigid tube with the number of piers that were required and suggesting that the total cost of the Victoria, £1,500,000, costing the Railway £75,000 in annual interest, was far too large for a company that 'had never enjoyed such circumstances or prospects as would justify such an outlay for such a purpose'. The alternative proposed was a lattice truss, and the editorial ended in true mid-Victorian fashion:

> As a work of engineering, we trust it will be the last in which the outlay is so disproportionate to the end. We say this with no wish to be severe but because such examples of extravagance are not creditable to our profession with which, after absolute and entire safety, economy should be the chief object of attainment.[69]

This demonstrated very clearly the change that had taken place with regard to economics in the years between the completion of the Britannia and the opening of the Victoria, and how the impressive unique solution to a large span problem was not always to be accepted without question.

Rumours of a failure in one of the piers of the Boyne Viaduct in 1860 were the starting point for an editorial, 'Railway Bridges', in the 9 March issue of *The Engineer*. After briefly describing the problems at the Boyne, Colburn goes on to discuss the failure of other rigid girder and tubular beam bridges (specifically the Torksey and the Spey) to receive Railway Board approval when first erected. It was contended that the experiments for the Britannia, which cost the Railway £7,000, had been perverted, in order to construct a formula 'favourable to the tubular system'. This assertion was based on the different results that were obtained when using the Fairbairn formula, compared with that evolved by Edwin Clark, whose results gave a safe load 25 per cent less than that calculated by the Fairbairn method.[70]

The author followed this with comments on the omission of cells from the top of the Victoria and the strange comments by Bidder and Stephenson in the discussion following Barton's paper in 1855, in the following terms:

> But when, in a single discussion in the year of grace 1855 among the most eminent engineers in the world, it was argued variously that beams exposed to transverse strains had no neutral axis; that all strains were horizontal and, again, that they were all diagonal, we might well have questioned the actual knowledge to which engineers had attained, as to the proper mode of proportioning beams.

The practice in Germany and Switzerland was cited as a recommendation for the use of the lattice system, together with the expected saving in the weight of ironwork that this form of construction allowed. The point was made that too often the suitability and safety of a beam was judged by the amount of deflection that occurs under a test load when in fact, for a less rigid structure than one with stiff sides, this was not an accurate measure of strength.[71]

One result of this editorial published on 16 March was a letter from Mr Alexander, the manager of the Canada Works, explaining why no cells were needed at the Victoria 'due to smaller spans', and attempting to make a more favourable comparison between the Victoria and the Boyne Viaduct. One advantage of the plated beam, according to Alexander, was the speed of fabrication and erection, it having taken only eight weeks to construct the centre span on the St Lawrence. This inevitably brought a response from Barton justifying again the supremacy of the lattice.[72]

In 1866 Zerah Colburn left *The Engineer* to edit a new magazine called *Engineering*, and in one of the first issues he wrote an editorial, 'Bridge Construction', where he again extolled the virtues of the lattice and the suspension bridge, noted the uneconomic use of material in plate beams and commented on Stephenson's insistence on mass in iron structures to resist the effects of impact and vibration. He also commented on the fact that for most builders 150 ft spans were the average, and that often fabricators found it difficult to find wrought iron that would resist the required breaking load of 24 tons.[73]

In September 1867 *The Engineer*, in an editorial entitled 'Dead Weight in Bridges', criticized the excessive amount of material in the Britannia, where only 40 per cent of the sides were resisting the stress, the other 60 per cent being required in the cover plates, angles and rivets needed for fabrication. It did, however, go on to note that even in a bridge such as the Charing Cross, of lattice construction with heavily plated booms (Figure 13), a great deal of dead weight occurs because of the fabrication technique adopted.[74]

By 1869, Colburn had changed the basis of his criticisms, and in an editorial on 12 March, in *Engineering*, discusses how the practicalities of construction affect design and influence the use of theoretical assumptions.[75] It is remarkable how long the arguments continued about the advantages of one structural form compared to another. In 1886 at the BAAS meeting in Birmingham, Shelford and Shield were still putting forward reasons for using lattice and arch trusses and citing American and Continental practice as examples to be followed.[76]

These criticisms of the tubular beam appeared to come primarily from two sources: first from a group of Irish engineers who were all practising, or had practised, in Ireland, and second from the American editor Zerah Colburn.

In the latter case it would seem likely that Colburn's experience in the United States would have made him familiar with lattice, pin-jointed structures and that the plated and riveted tube would have appeared a heavy, inefficient method of construction. The differences between American and UK practice, noted in the 1850s, were still sufficiently pronounced

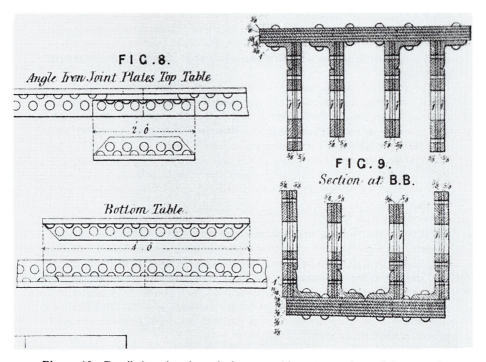

Figure 13 Detailed section through the top and bottom members of the trussed lattice beams of the Charing Cross (Hungerford) Bridge.

Source: William Humber, *A Complete Treatise on Cast Iron and Wrought Iron Bridge Construction* (1864).

for engineers such as Sheldon and Shields to bring them to the notice of the BAAS in 1886. Similarly, in 1895, Edward Barrington gave a paper to the Institution of Civil Engineers in Ireland on the topic, in which he pointed out that the early structures in the USA were of the truss form, and that the Americans considered pin-jointed trusses cheaper, quicker to build and requiring less work on site. This was in direct contrast to the practice in Canada, according to Gregory, who noted that the majority of bridges on the Grand Trunk, by either British or Canadian designers, were constructed of plates and tubes.

The criticism of the tubular beam by the engineers from Ireland is more difficult to explain. The most outspoken critics, Barton and Stoney, were obviously basing their views on their experiences in the design and construction of the Boyne Viaduct, but several other engineers who offered opinions, Anderson, Blood, Doyne, Heman, Heppel and Mallet, had all been involved in the design of truss structures of one form or another and, presumably, this provided the basis for their views. It is apparent that in some respects this group of engineers were different from their English contemporaries. Several had received a formal education in engineering, some at Trinity College, Dublin, where degree courses started in 1841, and in the papers that the members of this group presented to professional institutions in both England and Ireland all relied to some extent on some form of mathematical analysis as part of their explanation, a reliance not all that common at the time.

The engineering community in Ireland was relatively small. The Institution of Civil Engineers of Ireland had 100 members in 1849, which increased to about 200 by 1891. It is therefore worth noting that in this small group there were people prepared to disagree with the eminent engineers in London, even though it was from London that much of the engineering work in Ireland arose.

THE DEMISE OF THE TUBULAR BEAM

After the mid-1860s it appears that far fewer tubular beams were erected. There is no way of knowing how much this was because of the criticisms, described above, of the uneconomic use of material in plated and tubular girders or how much it was because of the defects inherent in the form of construction itself.

When Stephenson reported to the Directors of the Grand Trunk Railway in 1854, he said that the cost of maintenance of tubular beams was low and that it was easy to carry out. This does not seem to agree with what others had said about the subject. For instance in 1868, Edwin Clark, late of Stephenson's office, said that a man had been employed full time on the Britannia Bridge to identify the start of corrosion and instantly to repaint the damaged surface.[77]

Corrosion, both inside and outside the tube, due to condensation and the elements was only one of the practical disadvantages of the Stephenson type of tube that the supporters of the form chose to ignore. From the start the fumes and noise generated from the locomotive passing through were a problem and, at the Victoria, holes for ventilation were provided in the sides but apparently with little effect. Even if smoke fumes were bearable in an aerial tunnel 450 ft long, they were not in one nearly a mile long. The replacement of loose and missing rivets was another problem that continually plagued the Great Victoria and must also have caused problems on the Britannia. In Canada a riveting crew was employed full-time to remake failed joints and no doubt a similar provision was needed at the Menai to combat the effects of structural movements and temperature.[78] That large tubes could survive with constant and expensive attention is demonstrated by the life of both the Victoria and the Britannia. In the end they both had to be replaced owing to the effect of unforeseen circumstances: in the former because of the corrosive effect of brine dripping from refrigerated cars and in the latter because of fire.

With the exception of the difficulty caused by smoke and noise, all the other problems mentioned were to affect the Fairbairn tube as well, especially the inaccessibility of voids below track level, where constant repainting was needed but extremely difficult to achieve. During the 1860s, those tubular beams that were erected were all of this type and were mostly constructed in France, Canada and Australia.[79] It seems that in the United Kingdom the form was no longer seen as a viable alternative, a view confirmed by the comments in Benjamin Baker's book, *Long Span Railway Bridges*, published in 1867, where he identifies the box or tubular girder with plate webs as the most unfavourable type of large-span railway bridge, because of what he considered to be the very uneconomical amount of material required.[80]

No doubt criticisms of this type, and all those listed earlier, including cavilling at the massive appearance of this type of structure and the practical drawbacks inherent in the form, all contributed to make the tubular girder less and less attractive as a structural alternative.[81] Thus, after 20 years what had been hailed as a structural innovation ceased to be considered a worthwhile choice. There were two different reasons for the tubular beam's popularity, in spite of all its inherent drawbacks. The first has to do with the personalities involved. The second was the sheer volume of published material and the experimental investigations associated with it that appeared during the four years that the design and construction of the Conway and Britannia tubes were in progress, which afforded the tubular beam vast publicity.

Both Fairbairn and Stephenson were rising to eminence in their profession in the late 1840s and early 50s, holding institutional office, giving evidence to Royal Commissions, the subjects of laudatory biography. The schemes and ideas that they put forward or that had their backing would have seemed innovative and praiseworthy to their contemporaries.[82] To take a stand that was in direct opposition to their view would have required a great deal of courage and a willingness to disregard professional ridicule. Thus the reputation and position of these two men was a significant influence on the widespread acceptance of the tubular girder.

The two men, in spite of the contrasts in their backgrounds and aspirations, and the disputes that arose over the design of the Conway and Britannia tubes, were similar in one respect. They were both enthusiastic optimists, as Edwin Clark noted in the passage quoted earlier. Clark's view of Fairbairn was much influenced by his loyalty to Stephenson and, as the annotations in his personal copy of Fairbairn's book indicate, he did not think highly of the latter's theoretical knowledge. His comment about Fairbairn's claim that it was his formula that was the only one used in the design of the Conway tube was, 'This is entirely false'; on other topics, 'A mass of egotistical representation', and to Fairbairn's claim to 'have never thought of failure', the comment 'Ignorance is bliss'.[83] For Clark, with an extensive mathematical background, Fairbairn's reliance on experience and the minimum of mathematical analysis tended to undermine his confidence in the latter's conclusions. When Unwin was asked by Pole to write about the 'Scientific position' of Fairbairn after his death, this aspect of the latter's character was described as follows:

> He did not appear to me to accept with firmness anything which he had not confirmed by his own observations of experiment. His

thorough reliance upon direct experiment made him willing to under-
take any investigation likely to throw light on doubtful points of
practical science, and when he had once formulated the results of his
experiments he relied on them with a remarkable absence of doubt or
hesitation and applied his conclusions in practice with a courage that
would have sometimes seemed rashness to anyone more conversant
with theoretical considerations.[84]

The discussions about the design of the Conway and Britannia tubes
and the attempts by Fairbairn to justify his tubular girder formula were
the source of a substantial volume of written material setting out several
approaches to beam design. Clark's book of 1850, although superficially
about the Conway and Britannia tubes, contains in fact 90 pages about the
principles of beam design and 80 pages about the strength of materials and
the nature of the forces that they resist. There were, in addition, sections
contributed by Pole and Wild on strength and deflection. This large body
of material was one of the most easily accessible collections available to
engineers at the time and, it is suggested, accounts for the re-occurrence
of references to the Menai bridges and the associated experiments that
continued to appear in books such as those by Rankine and Wray, written
for the use of practising engineers much later in the century.[85]

The descriptions of the experiments in both Clark and Fairbairn, the conclusions that were drawn from them and the contributions by Hodgkinson
were much admired in Europe and are referred to in various later Continental works such as Saint-Venant's edition of Navier's *Leçons*.

CONCLUSION

Although later theorists would disagree with the conclusions that were
drawn in the late 1840s, and the design formula then proposed was discredited, the approach of Fairbairn and Stephenson to the problem of the
design of very large beams using an untried material, by means of direct
experiment, was one that appears to have had the approval of the majority
of the engineers of the time. The work of these two men and all the people
who assisted them, using techniques derived from other forms of construction, especially Fairbairn's shipbuilding experience, made it possible
to construct a very large span structure. Thus the principles evolved for
the design of tubular beams at the Menai Straits were of some importance in developing a more rational approach to structural design, even
though the completed structures themselves were not the forerunners of
a series of long span bridges of similar design and form. As the century
progressed, the better understanding of the forces acting in a spanning
structure, and the availability of new material, steel, meant that the preferred solution to the problem of the large span was to be found in the
development[86] of trussed lattice beams, lattice arches and suspension
structures.

The practicalities of construction meant that the correctness of the
formulae used was always obscured by the effect of additional material

or physical effects that were not understood. This did not, until 1855, suggest to contemporary designers that the use of a limited number of tests as a basis for design had any major disadvantages. The problem of describing how structures perform in practice and what effect workmanship, quality of material and fabrication restrictions have on structural strength is still one that is of concern to designers.

In the case of tubular girders some of these effects were resolved with the developments that took place from 1855 onwards. The construction, in 1860, of a multi-spindle drill meant that up to 80 holes at a time could be *accurately* drilled in the wrought iron plates required in a built-up plated boom. This meant that the rigidity required could be achieved by riveting together layers of plates, often totalling 4 inches in thickness, and the drilling and riveting of only one plate, as in the tubular form, was no longer an advantage. The advent of steam and hydraulic riveting machines meant that joints could be made more accurately and soundly and the availability of better-quality wrought iron, and later steel, provided a material with more reliable and standard qualities. Again, more efficient rolling mills meant that large-size 'I' sections could be produced, thus making the built-up plate girder less necessary.

The construction of the Hungerford Railway Bridge, at Charing Cross Station, London, in 1863-4 demonstrated the advantages of the changes that had occurred. Although some engineers might not consider it economic, it was a lattice bridge with heavily plated booms, diagonal braces and struts and was built to a very high and much admired standard of workmanship.[87] All these developments meant that, until the twentieth century and the advent of a new jointing technique, welding, the tubular girder was a far too labour-intensive, uneconomic use of material for spanning structures although, as Benjamin Baker demonstrated in the Forth Bridge, the tubular form was well suited to resist high compressive loads (Figure 14, overleaf).[88]

Notes and References

1. James Hodges, *Construction of the Great Victoria Bridge in Canada* (London, J. Weale, 1860). The photographs were taken by Notman of Montreal.

2. Thomas C. Keefer practised in Canada. See *Dictionary of Canadian Biography* Vol. 11 and F.N. Boxer, *Hunter's Handbook of the Victoria Bridge* (Montreal, Hunter & Pickup, 1860).

3. Hodges, *op. cit.* (1).

4. Hodges, *op. cit.* (1).

5. Boxer, *op. cit.* (2).

6. 'Description of Works at Birkenhead', *Illustrated London News*, 1859, 34: 234. See also pp. 176-8 for general description of bridge.

7. 'Canada Works', *Civil Engineer and Architects' Journal*, 1853, 16: 276, and 'The Canada Works, Birkenhead', 1854, 17: 252.

8. Hodges, *op. cit.* (1).

9. 'Mr Hodges' Account of the Great Victoria Bridge, Canada', *The Builder*, 1860, 18: 665-6.

10. Hodges, *op. cit.* (1).

11. Hodges, *op. cit.* (1), and *General Description of the Britannia and Conway Tubular*

130   *Development and Use of the Tubular Beam*

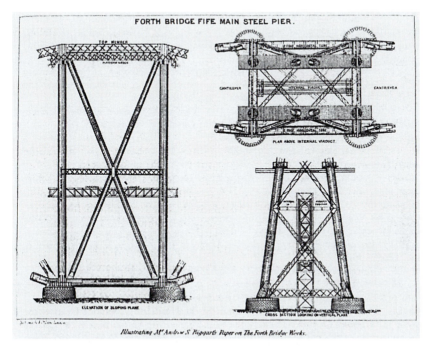

Figure 14 Detail of the tubular supports to the Forth Bridge.

Source: Andrew S. Biggart: 'The Forth Bridge Works', in *The Report of the British Association for the Advancement of Science* (Aberdeen, 1885).

Bridges, published with permission of Robert Stephenson by a Resident Engineer (London, Chapman & Hall), 1849.

12. J.A.L. Waddel, *Bridge Engineering* (New York, John Wiley & Sons, 1916), 23.

13. Hodges, *op. cit.* (1).

14. The machine used for the plates of the Conway Bridge is described in 'The Jacquard Punching Machine', *Civil Engineer and Architects' Journal*, 1848, 11: 224–6, and that used for the Victoria in 'The Jacquard Punching Machine', *The Builder*, 1860, 18: 291–2.

15. *Illustrated London News*, 1854, 24: 474, report in 'Epitome of News', and 1859, 34: 176–8.

16. *Illustrated London News*, 1859, 35: 260, 300, 313, 505.

17. William John Macquorn Rankine, *A Manual of Applied Mechanics* (London, Griffin, Bohn & Co., 1861), 366–7.

18. The roofs at Euston, Birmingham New Street, Sheffield, Paddington, and many others were designed and built by Fox Henderson. Others were designed and erected by other contractors.

19. *Encyclopaedia Britannica* (8th edn, Edinburgh, Adam & Charles Black), vol. 12, 575–610. No mention of Fairbairn's contribution to the design and testing of tubes is made.

20. William Fairbairn, *Useful Information for Engineers* (London, Longmans Green, 1855). *On the application of Cast and Wrought Iron to Building Purposes* (London, John Weale, 1854). *Treatise on Iron Shipbuilding: Its History and Progress* (London, Longmans Green, 1865).

21. *Engineering*, 1870, 10: 6. Review of Fairbairn's *Applications of Iron to Building Purposes*, 4th edn. Adverse criticisms had appeared earlier, see *Civil Engineer and Architects' Journal*, Vol. 20, on Fairbairn's, *Useful Information*.

22. Reported by Andrew Murray, in *Theory and Practice of Ship Building* (Edinburgh, 1861), 77. A box beam was used in a paddle steamer after 1836, when Murray was Fairbairn's partner at Millwall.

23. J. Maudsley, Patent No. 8,060, 7 May 1939, Construction of Marine Steam Engines.

24. 'Tubular Bridges', *Civil Engineer and Architects' Journal*, 1849, 12: 57, a paper given by T.L. Donaldson at RIBA on 22 January 1849. Description of a bridge on the Pollock and Gowan Railway erected by Andrew Thompson and constructed by William Dixon, an ironfounder, who was reported to have used box beams for some years on the access bridges to blast furnaces. This is also recorded by W.J. Macquorne Rankine, in *Applied Mechanics* (Edinburgh, Charles Griffin & Co., 1864), 366.

25. George Smart, Patent No. 2,415, 1800, Tubular Masts, Yards, etc.

26. G.L.K. Eck, *Traité de l'application du fer, de la fonte et de la tôle*, 1841: 49–50. I am indebted to J.G. James's research papers for this reference.

27. *The Builder*, 1845, 3: 237, a report of the House of Commons Committee where Mr Randell proposed to carry the railway over the Menai Straits 'by means of a huge tube composed of sheet iron'. In *Mechanics' Magazine*, 1845, 43: 162, 248, 325 there are three letters by John de la Hope, of Liverpool, about a submarine tube of wrought iron.

28. Stephenson mentioned the bridge at Ware, at a dinner in Conway, reported in *The Builder*, 1848 6: 272, which angered Fairbairn. In the chapter he contributed to Clark's book, Stephenson makes it clear that the bridge was not built in a tubular form: see Edwin Clark, *The Britannia and Conway Tubular Bridges* (London, Day & Son and J. Weale, 1850), 25. For a modern discussion of the design of the bridge see Nathan Rosenberg and Walter G. Vincenti, *The Britannia Bridge: The Generation and Diffusion of Technical Knowledge* (Cambridge, Mass., MIT Press, 1978).

29. William Fairbairn, *An Account of the Construction of the Britannia and Conway Tubular Bridges* (London, John Weale and Longman, Brown, Green & Longmans, 1849), 12.

30. See Fairbairn *op. cit.* (29), and Edwin Clarke, *The Britannia and Conway Tubular Bridges* (London, Day & Son, 1850).

31. Thomas Tredgold, *Practical Essay on the Strength of Cast Iron and other Metals* (London, J. Weale, 1842) and Thomas Tredgold, *Elementary Principles of Carpentry*, with appendix by P. Barlow (London, Lockwood & Co., 1840).

32. Some of the research work undertaken by Fairbairn was as follows: 'An Experimental Enquiry into the Strength of Wrought Iron Plates and their Riveted Joints' in *Philosophical Transactions of the Royal Society*, 1859, 5: 677–725. (The experiments described had been conducted in 1838.) 'An Experimental Enquiry into the Strength and Other Properties of Cast Iron', *Transactions of the Literary and Philosophical Society of Manchester*, 1842, 6: 103 (read in 1837). 'On Some Defects in the Principles and Construction of Fireproof Buildings', *Minutes of the Proceedings of the Institution of Civil Engineers*, 1847, 7: 213–24.

33. See Fairbairn and Clark, *op. cit.* (29, 30).

34. Edwin Clark (1814–1894) entered the Stephensons' office in March 1846, and went to the Menai Straits in April. After two and a half years at Cambridge, he had travelled extensively, and had taught mathematics at various schools.

35. As Clark, *op. cit.* (30), 155.

36. See drawings in Fairbairn, *op. cit.* (29).

37. This point is made very clearly in James Barton's paper, read to the Institution of Civil Engineers in 1855. See later notes.

38. William Fairbairn, Patent, No. 11,401, 1846, 'Improvements in the Construction of Iron Beams'.

39. See William Pole, *The Life of Sir William Fairbairn, Bart.* (London, Longmans Green & Co., 1877; David & Charles reprint 1970), 212–13.

40. See G.D. Dempsey, *Tubular and Other Iron Girder Bridges*, Virtue Bros., (London, 1984).

41. See *The Engineer*, 1866, 22: 467–78. Hammond River Viaduct, European and N. American Railway, Canada, *The Engineer*, 1860, 9: 225. Great Western (Canada) Railway, Desjardins Bridge; at Aigullion (1856), Moissoc (1856) and the Pont de la Quodrontaine, Lyon (1853), France; Penrith, NSW (1886), Saltwater River, NSW (1860) and Menagle Viaduct (1862), Australia; and the bridge over the River Suir in Ireland, reported in *The Engineer*, 1856, 1: 336. It has been possible to identify individual bridges with help provided by Michael Chrimes, Librarian at the Institution of Civil Engineers and through access to the research notes of J.G. James held there.

42. Prior to taking verbal evidence, the Commissioners required each railway to submit a return of the iron bridges on its routes. Of about 200 bridges recorded, 22 can be identified as of tubular construction, either by written description or drawing. See Public Record Office, MT8/1, Record of Iron Bridges 1847.

43. By Fairbairn for a bridge in Prussia.

44. The bridges in Egypt were on the Alexandria and Cairo Railway at Kaffra Azzayat, see *The Engineer*, 1859, 7: 439; and at Benha, see *Civil Engineer and Architects' Journal*, 1853, 16: 425. In P. Westmacott, *A Short History of the Development of the Engineering Industry in Tyne and Neighbourhood*, published in 1863, it is stated that R. Stephenson & Co. had built 38 wrought iron bridges. I am indebted to J.G. James's research notes, *op. cit.* (41), for this information. A useful summary of the use of tubular girders is contained in S. Tyson, *Industrial Archaeology Review*, 1977/8, No. 2, 'Notes on the History, Development and Use of Tubes in the Construction of Bridges', 145–53. Paul N. Wilson: 'The Britannia Tubular Bridge', *Industrial Archaeology*, 1972, 9: 229–41 gives information about the bridge in the twentieth century.

45. William Fairbairn, *Minutes of the Proceedings of the Institution of Civil Engineers* 1849/50, 9: 'On Tubular Girder Bridges', 233–287.

46. William Fairbairn, *op. cit.* (45), 233.

47. Fairbairn, *op. cit.* (45), 234.

48. Fairbairn, *op. cit.* (45), 239.

49. Fairbairn, *op. cit.* (45), 237.

50. Fairbairn, *op. cit.* (45).

51. *Op. cit.* (45), 280, and Public Record Office, MT 6/9/5. A letter from Capt. Simmons to Capt. Harness dated 20 February 1850 reports a further inspection of the bridge and sets out the reasons for refusing to allow the bridge to be used. Most of this letter was printed in *Minutes of Proceedings*, *op. cit.* (45), 280–1. One of the parts omitted was Simmons's reference to the reliance on the results of tests under controlled conditions and observations on site, with a bridge in use.

52. Fairbairn, *op. cit.* (45), 253.

53. *Report of the Royal Commission into the Application of Iron to Railway Structures* (London, HMSO, 1849).

54. Fairbairn, *op. cit.* (45), 237.

55. Board of Trade, Committee on Steel. The decisions about permissible stresses were set out in *Railway Structures* (Use of Steel), 27 March 1877, and in the *Requirements of the Board of Trade When Making a Railway*, 1877, Part B, para. 17. A copy of this document is in the Public Record Office, RAIL 1053/169.

56. *Op. cit.* (34), 276.

57. William Fairbairn, 'On the Security and Limit of Strength of Tubular Girder Bridges Constructed of Wrought Iron', 1851, 9: 179-95, *Memoirs of the Literary and Philosophical Society of Manchester*. The quotation is on p. 186.

58. 'Grand Trunk Railway of Canada, Victoria Bridge, Montreal', *Civil Engineer and Architects' Journal*, 1854, 17: 211-12.

59. *Op. cit.* (58), 212.

60. James Barton, *Minutes of the Proceedings of the Institution of Civil Engineers*, vol. 14, 1854/5, 'On the Economic Distribution of Material in the Sides of Vertical Partitions of Wrought Iron Beams', pp. 443-90.

61. Isaac Todhunter and Karl Pearson, *A History of the Theory of Elasticity and of the Strength of Materials*, Cambridge University Press, (Cambridge, Vol. I, 1886, Vol. II 1893). Dover Reprint 1960. See Vol. II, part 1, p. 680.

62. Barton, *op. cit.* (60), 469.

63. Barton, *op. cit.* (60), 481.

64. *Civil Engineer and Architects' Journal*, Vol. 16, 1853, p. 425, 'Bridge at Benha', *The Engineer*, Vol. 7, 1859, p. 439, 'Bridge over Nile at Kaffre Azzayat'.

65. Barton, *op. cit.* (60).

66. Charles Hutton Gregory, *Report to the Chairman and Directors of the Grand Trunk Railway Company of Canada*, 15 August 1857.

67. 'Railway Bridges', *The Engineer*, 1859, 7: 138, 389-90.

68. 'Railway Bridges', *The Engineer*, 1859, 8: 138.

69. 'The Victoria Bridge', *The Engineer*, 1859, 8: 431.

70. 'Railway Bridges', *The Engineer*, 1860, 9: 157-8.

71. *Op. cit.* (70).

72. *The Engineer*, 1860, 9: 170-1 and Barton's reply pp. 188-9.

73. 'Bridge Construction', *Engineering*, 1866, 1: 32.

74. 'Dead Weight in Bridges', *The Engineer*, 1867, 24: 231-2.

75. 'Experience in Design', *Engineering*, 1869, 7: 173.

76. W. Shelford and A.H. Shield, 'On Some Points for the Consideration of English Engineers with Reference to the Design of Girder Bridges', *British Association for the Advancement of Science 1861*, *Transactions of Sections*, 427-83.

77. Edwin Clark, 'Durability of Materials', *Minutes of the Proceedings of the Institution of Civil Engineers*, 1867-8, 27: 578.

78. J.A.L. Waddel, *Bridge Engineering* (New York, John Wiley & Sons, 1916), 23.

79. *Op. cit.* (41).

80. Benjamin Baker, *Long Span Railway Bridges* (London, E. & F.N. Spon, 1867), 8.

81. 'Form in Design', *Engineering*, 1866, 1: 85; 'Bridge Construction', *Engineering*, 1866, 1: 32.

82. *Op. cit.* (53) Minutes of Evidence.

83. A copy of W. Fairbairn, *An Account of the Construction of the Britannia and Conway Tubular Bridges*, signed by Edwin Clark, with pencil margin notes, is part

134   *Development and Use of the Tubular Beam*

of the collection in the Library of the Institution of Civil Engineers. The notes quoted appear on pp. 22, 32 and 21.

84. Pole, *op. cit.* (39), 463.

85. W.J. Macquorne Rankine, *Civil Engineering* (Edinburgh, Charles Griffin, 1862), and Col. Henry Wray, *Some Applications of Theory to the Practice of Construction*, (Chatham, RE, 1872).

86. Comments on standard of workmanship in Harrison Hayter, 'Charing Cross Bridge', *Minutes of the Proceedings of the Institution of Civil Engineers*, 1862-3, 22: 512-39.

87. For information about later developments, see William Addis, *Structural Engineering: The Nature of Theory and Design* (Chichester, Ellis Horwood, 1990).

88. Andrew S. Biggart, 'The Forth Bridge Works', *British Association for the Advancement of Science, Transactions of the Sections*, 1885: 1193, and 'On the Manufacture of the Girders Used in the Forth Bridge', *Transactions of the Institutions of Engineers and Shipbuilders in Scotland*, 1888-9, 32: 37-65.

6

Surviving cast- and wrought-iron bridges in America

Eric Deloney

Only 74 cast- and wrought-iron bridges survive of the thousands built between 1840 and 1880. They were a type that spanned the gap between wood and steel. This article chronicles these irreplaceable structures that derived from both a craft tradition and scientific engineering. They were the products of country blacksmiths and "state-of-the-art" bridge works; the designs of crafters, millwrights, and mechanics—unschooled "apple-tree engineers"—and the first specialist to emerge from the engineering profession— the bridge engineer. They exemplify fundamental American values of craft, entrepreneurialism, and creativity. They helped Americans cross thousands of streams and rivers, reach new markets, and create new businesses as the frontier moved west. These artifacts of the American landscape, both urban and rural, are threatened with extinction if not saved soon.

The Phoenix Bridge Works lies nestled in the Schuylkill valley about an hour out of Philadelphia on the Reading Railroad. In the 1870s, Phoenix was one of the few establishments where the birthing of a bridge could be observed from raw iron ore to the finished product.[1] Established in 1790, it was at the forefront of progress in the iron and steel industry during the 19th century. It began modestly as America's first nail works. With the advent of railroads, it began to roll iron rails. Phoenix then parlayed this technology into rolled structural shapes, including the famous Phoenix column.

Several individuals engaged by the works were prominent engineers, inventors, and manufacturers: from 1813–21 the owner and superintendent was Lewis Wernwag, builder of the "Colossus" (1812), the longest wooden trussed-arch bridge ever constructed; George Walters built the first blast furnace to recycle exhaust gases to preheat the blast and generate steam; John Fritz, inventor of the three-high rolling mill, the machine that revolutionized the iron industry, installed rail-rolling equipment for Phoenix; and Samuel Reeves patented the Phoenix column in 1862 and wrote one of the first printed bridge specifications in 1864.[2]

I begin this essay with the Phoenix Bridge Works because

its experience parallels the development of iron bridge building in America. Extending from the earliest years of iron bridge construction, its products became so well known by the 1880s that the Phoenix bridge was used throughout the western hemisphere.[3] Bridge companies like Berlin, Canton, Chicago, Detroit, Keystone, King, National, Pencoyd, and Phoenix had reached as high a state of perfection as any industry in the 1880s. Advanced engineering and assembly practices enabled American bridge companies to compete successfully in world markets with a pin-connected, wrought-iron bridge product called the "American system" by foreign competitors. Progressive shop practices, standardized parts, and labor-saving pinned, rather than riveted, connections that enabled quicker erection at remote sites ensured that the prices quoted by American bridge manufacturers were the lowest and their completion dates the earliest.[4]

These manufactories, however, are not the subject of this article. I am interested in promoting the importance of the actual product, the fabricated cast- and wrought-iron truss bridge. Fewer than 75 survive. The significance of the Phoenix bridge is that it represents the penultimate development of this bridge type, a structure that evolved over a 40-year period, 1840–80. Hayden Bridge (1882) of Springfield, Oregon, when recorded by the Historic American Engineering Record in 1990, was virtually unaltered, complete in every detail, a distinctive example of the "American system" bridge at the end of the 1880s (figures 1, 2).

Though companies like Phoenix dominated the market, many industrial towns boasted manufacturers that made and repaired iron implements for the agricultural industry. Some were not much larger than village blacksmiths—family operations of fathers, sons, grandfathers, and uncles. Others were owned by risk-taking industrialists beset with promoting a certain bridge patent and keen on making profits. The proliferation of iron bridge companies coincided with two important events: industrialization of the iron industry and western settlement. Larger furnaces and improved technology drove down the price of iron, resulting in a product that was competitive, cost-effective, and practical. Canals, turnpikes, and railroads delivered pioneers and immigrants to the heartland of America, creating an overwhelming need

Industrial Archeology

Figure 1. *Hayden Bridge (1882), spanning the McKenzie River near Springfield, Oregon, was the Phoenix Bridge Works' major entry into the fiercely competitive fabricated-bridge market of the 1880s. Originally built by the Central Pacific Railroad to span Bear River near Corrine, Utah, it was moved 1,000 miles to Oregon by the Southern Pacific in 1911 and re-erected. It remained in service on a logging railroad until 1979.* Jet Lowe, HAER photographer.

for farm-to-market roads and bridges by the thousands. Not surprisingly, most of the surviving bridges are located in those states—Ohio, Iowa, Indiana, Illinois, Pennsylvania, and New York—where bridge manufactories operated and which still maintain an agrarian economy: the East and Midwest, with a few scattered in New England and a few more in the mountain West.

The fabricated metal truss bridge is one of the most important developments of American building technology. As much a marketing phenomenon as a technological feat, fabricated metal trusses symbolize fundamental American values of craft, entrepreneurialism, and unbridled invention and creativity. Marking the desire to improve technology, hundreds of patents were granted. Many went to trained engineers, but most went to the crafters, millwrights, and mechanics who recognized a need and sought engineering and manufacturing solutions to the demand for inexpensive and easily erected bridges.

In the early 1970s, industrial archeologists working with the Historic American Engineering Record recognized that America's historic bridges were threatened by massive federal and state programs created to repair America's aging highway system. These also were the nascent years of historic preservation, a movement created by local citizen groups to fight the devastation urban renewal and interstate highways wrought on the historic built environment. At that time, historic industrial and engineering resources were not part of the venue considered worthy of preservation. HAER

was established in 1969 to compile an everlasting record of these resources and, by extension, to educate the nation of their values. In the event these resources could not be saved, HAER drawings, photographs, and written data ensured that a permanent record would be available in the Library of Congress.

We have nearly succeeded in eliminating this single distinguished artifact of engineering and manufacturing technology; these technological gems of the American landscape are threatened with extinction. Metal truss bridges are an endangered species vulnerable to floods, spring freshets, and other acts of nature. But by far the greatest threat is the hand of man in the form of reckless drivers, and until recently county engineers, transportation planners, and indifferent citizens. Awareness and appreciation of historic bridges have increased since the 1980s. More and more transportation planners and bridge engineers recognize the value of historic bridges and work with local communities and preservation groups to save them. Despite these advances, however, many in county and state transportation departments and individual citizens do not appreciate the value of old bridges and do nothing when they are threatened.

The First Iron Bridges

The world's first iron bridge was cast in 1778 by Abraham Darby and John Wilkinson at the Coalbrookdale Ironworks in England. Erected over the River Severn in 1779, the

Surviving Cast- and Wrought-Iron Bridges in America

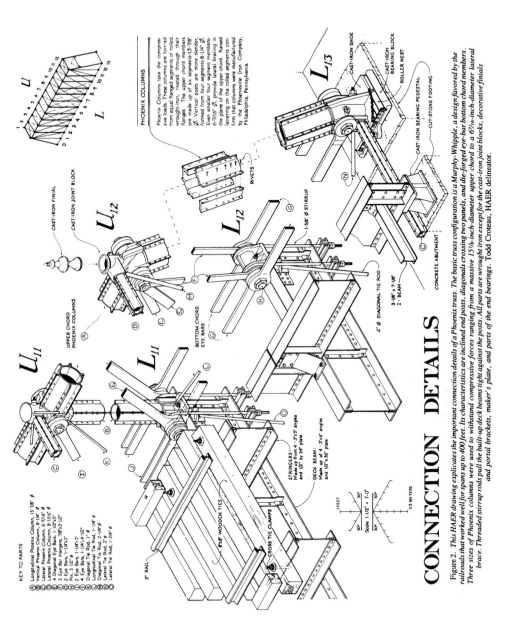

CONNECTION DETAILS

KEY TO PARTS

Ⓐ Longitudinal Phoenix Column, 15-7/8" ⌀
Ⓑ Vertical Phoenix Column, 8-1/4" ⌀
Ⓒ Lateral Phoenix Column, 6-7/16" ⌀
Ⓓ Lateral Phoenix Column, 8-1/16" ⌀
Ⓔ 4 Diagonal Eye Bars, 1-1/2"x5"
Ⓕ 2 Eye Bar Hangers, 1-1/2"x5"
Ⓖ 2 Eye Bars, 1-1/4"x5"
Ⓗ Pin, 3-1/2" ⌀
Ⓘ 2 Eye Bars, 1-1/4" ⌀
Ⓙ 4 Eye Bars, 1-1/4"x4-1/2"
Ⓚ Diagonal Tie Rod, 1" ⌀
Ⓛ Longitudinal Tie Rod, 1-1/4" ⌀
Ⓜ Diagonal Tie Rod, 2-1/4" ⌀
Ⓝ Lateral Tie Rod, 2" ⌀
Ⓞ Lateral Tie Rod, 1-3/4"s ⌀

PHOENIX COLUMNS

Phoenix Columns take the compressive loads. These columns are formed from equal flanged segments of rolled wrought-iron, riveted through their flanges. The upper chord members are made up of six segments—15-7/8" ⌀. Vertical posts are more slender, formed from four segments 8-1/4" ⌀. Even smaller four segment members—6-7/16" ⌀, provide lateral bracing in the plane of the upper chord. Raised lettering on the rolled segments confirm that columns were manufactured by the Phoenixville Iron Company, Philadelphia, Pennsylvania.

CAST-IRON FINIAL
CAST-IRON JOINT BLOCK
UPPER CHORD PHOENIX COLUMNS
BOTTOM CHORD EYE BARS
RIVETS
1-3/8" ⌀ STIRRUP
2" ⌀ DIAGONAL TIE ROD
I-BEAM
CAST-IRON SHOE
CAST-IRON BEARING BLOCK
ROLLER NEST
CAST-IRON BEARING PEDESTAL
CUT-STONE FOOTING
CONCRETE ABUTMENT

STRINGERS: Made up from 4 - 3"x5" angles and 1/2" by 24" plate
DECK BEAM: Made up of 4 - 3"x6" angles and 1/2"x30" plate

8"x8" WOODEN TIES
CROSS TIE CLAMPS
5" RAIL

Scale 1-1/2" = 1'-0"
1 FEET
0.5 METERS

U L
U_{12} L_{12} L_{13}
U_{11} L_{11}

Figure 2. *This HAER drawing explicates the important connection details of a Phoenix truss. The basic truss configuration is a Murphy-Whipple, a design favored by the railroads that worked well for spans up to 400 feet. Its characteristics are inclined end posts, diagonals crossing two panels, and die-forged eye-bar bottom chord members. Three sizes of Phoenix columns were used to withstand compressive forces ranging from a massive 15⅞-inch-diameter upper chord to a 6⁷⁄₁₆-inch-diameter lateral brace. Threaded stirrup rods pull the built-up deck beams tight against the posts. All parts are wrought iron except for the cast-iron joint blocks, decorative finials and portal brackets, maker's plate, and parts of the end bearings. Todd Croteau, HAER delineator.*

19

Industrial Archeology

bridge was designed not by an engineer, but an architect, Thomas Farnolls Pritchard of Shropshire. Engineering did not materialize as a profession until the middle of the 19th century when building got so complicated that society demanded a specialist who understood the subtleties of material behavior when a structure was subjected to stress.[5] Industrial entrepreneurs Darby and Wilkinson engaged architect Pritchard to design a bridge to provide passage, but more important, to demonstrate the versatility of the miracle material of the Industrial Revolution—cast iron. Though 100 feet is a modest span by today's standards, the Iron Bridge's construction revolutionized bridge design at the end of the 18th century.

To place American developments in perspective, we need to cross the Atlantic to the young republic, where a revolutionary Englishman, Thomas Paine, was espousing not only "common sense" and the "rights of man," but also unprecedented ideas on iron bridges capable of spanning 400 feet. Renowned throughout the world as a political philosopher and champion of individual rights, Paine, like Benjamin Franklin and Thomas Jefferson, was a Renaissance man whose interests knew few bounds. In addition to being a social philosopher, he was a bridge designer. Though English-born, Paine was the first in America to recognize iron's potential as a building material. Multitalented and gifted with special insight, he perceived that the traditional materials of bridge construction, stone and wood, were deficient: stone was poor in tension, and with wood it was difficult to fabricate tension splices in the bottom chord. Paine proposed a cast-iron arch of 400 feet to span the Schuylkill in Philadelphia in a single reach.

Today, skeptical historians doubt that a radical philosopher, untrained in the building arts, could possibly have conceived a workable plan.[6] However, Paine's design was favorably reviewed by the French Academy of Sciences in Paris in 1787; it was patented in England in 1788. With the help of the Walker brothers, a family of iron founders in Rotherham, England, he erected a 110-foot prototype and displayed the bridge for several weeks on the Leasing Green in Paddington. Despite these concerted efforts, with the outbreak of the French Revolution, Paine reverted to his original passion of politics and never completed his iron bridge invention.[7] (See figures 3, 4, 5.)

The same Walker brothers who built Paine's prototype built the next important iron bridge, the 236-foot cast-iron arch span over the River Wear at Sunderland. For nearly 200 years this bridge was attributed to Paine. Only in the last 20 years has it been definitively attributed to Thomas Wil-

son, who built several cast-iron arches, including the Rio Cobre Bridge (1800) in Jamaica, the oldest iron arch in the western hemisphere (figure 6).

After Paine's advocation of iron for bridges at the end of the 18th century, the material was not considered again in the United States until the 1830s, when both Ithiel Town and Colonel Stephen Harriman Long suggested that their patents for parallel chord wooden trusses could be fabricated as easily in iron. It was August Canfield, however, a West Point graduate working in Paterson, New Jersey, who patented the first iron bridge in America in 1833. Though not a practical design, the combination of two materials, cast and wrought iron, marked a trend that would last for 40 years.

Dunlap Creek on the Cumberland (National) Road in Brownsville, Pennsylvania, is the next chronological step in the development of American iron bridge technology. Completed in 1839, it is an evolutionary anomaly. This remarkable structure picks up on the cast-iron arch designs of Wilson and Telford in England and de Cessart and Polonceau in France. The bridge most relevant to Dunlap Creek is not Darby's cast-iron arch at Coalbrookdale or Wilson's cast-iron frame at Sunderland but the five elliptical cast-iron arch tubes that formed the structure of Antoine Remey Polonceau's Pont du Carrousel, completed in 1834 over the Seine in Paris.

Dunlap Creek was designed by Captain Richard Delafield of the Army Corps of Engineers who was building the Cumberland Road, one of America's first public works projects. The five hollow cast-iron arch tubes, bolted at their flanges, span 80 feet. Rather than a truss, Delafield's design followed European precedents of the cast-iron arch. I theorize that Delafield, through his West Point education, must have been influenced by iron arch bridge building, then the rage in England, France, and Russia.[8]

Polonceau's Pont du Carrousel, though much more complicated in its detailing and spandrel infill, is essentially the same—five tubular elliptical arch ribs of iron (figure 7). Delafield might have seen a drawing of Polonceau's arch in one of the technical journals of the time or been aware of it through his engineering professors at West Point. Dunlap Creek is a simplification of Polonceau's design, eliminating details difficult to pattern, much less cast, in molten iron. Simple details were worked out between Delafield and his pattern maker and foundryman, resulting in arch segments that could be easily cast and erected.

Surviving Cast- and Wrought-Iron Bridges in America

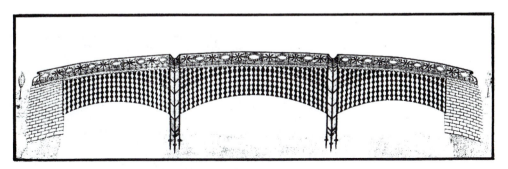

Figure 3. *One would think some illustration or reference would have been printed while Paine's bridge was displayed on the Leasing Green in Paddington. To date, this drawing located in the Science Museum and another at Sir John Soane's House and Museum, both in London, are the only known drawings of the bridge. I was shown this drawing while researching Paine's bridge-building activities at the Science Museum in 1971. It is captioned "Given to Isaac Dodds in 1833 by Samuel Park, Esq. This design made and executed by Thomas Paine at the Holmes works at Rotherham in the office of the model shop about the year 1800." Clearly a vernacular drawing, it is hard to discern Paine's written patent description in this graphic.* Courtesy Science Museum, London.

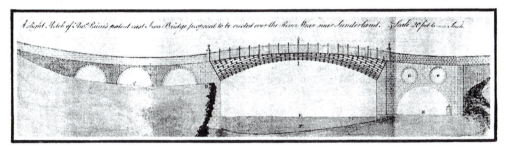

Figure 4. *The other drawing was discovered by Ted Ruddock (author of* Arch Bridges and Their Builders, *Cambridge University Press, 1979) at the Soane Museum. It is a proposal for the famous bridge over the River Wear at Sunderland that used parts from Paine's prototype bridge at Paddington and is the clearest depiction of Paine's intentions with iron bridges.* Courtesy Sir John Soane's House and Museum, London.

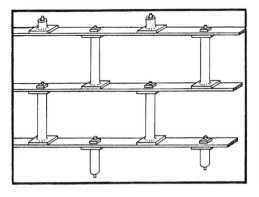

Figure 5. *Conjectural drawing by J. G. James of Paine's system of curved 4-by-1-inch wrought-iron bars, spaced vertically by radial two-foot-long cast-iron tubes connected with threaded rods and square nuts, based on LeRoy's 1787 description of Paine's 400-foot span. LeRoy was spokesman of the group from the Paris Academy of Sciences that reviewed Paine's bridge in 1787.*

21

Industrial Archeology

Figure 6. *The Rio Cobre Bridge (1800) survives today as a pedestrian bridge in Spanish Town, Jamaica.* Eric DeLony, photographer.

The bridges that followed the cast-iron arch configuration of Europe were the Chestnut Street Bridge (1861–66) over the Schuylkill, designed by Strickland Kneas, city engineer of Philadelphia, and the decorative cast-iron arches in New York's Central Park that Calvert Vaux and J. Wrey Mould built to separate equestrian and pedestrian traffic. These surviving cast-iron arches comprise the best collection of decorative iron-arch bridges in the United States.

In 1860, another arch of cast-iron construction was erected by Montgomery C. Meigs over the Rock Creek on the Washington aqueduct system. The bridge is unique in that it served the dual purposes of carrying Pennsylvania Avenue and delivering water to the citizens of Washington. This was accomplished by two four-foot-diameter cast-iron pipe sections bolted through their flanges, forming an arch that carried both road and water. Several historians have pointed out the similarity of the Rock Creek bridge to the Dunlap Creek structure and drawn the conclusion that Meigs's design may have been derived from Delafield's. Both engineers were familiar with each other's work through their employment in the army corps.[9]

Early Railroad Combination Bridges

This group of structures returns us to the mainstream of American bridge development—parallel chord trusses of composite cast- and wrought-iron construction, a form that evolved from composite timber and iron trusses like the Howe and the Pratt during the 1840s. By the 1840s, iron bridge technology had made impressive strides driven by the thundering impact of railroads. Spark-belching locomotives with ever-increasing weights and the vibration of fast-moving trains demanded bridges that were fireproof, stronger, more rigid, and essentially maintenance free. While the lower costs of timber bridges were advantageous to the early, struggling railroads, engineers realized that the initial cheapness of wooden bridges was only a short-term investment. Wooden bridges were susceptible to fire and rapid decay when left uncovered and required constant inspection, repairs, and adjustments.

Richard Osborne, a London-born Irish emigrant engineer working for the Philadelphia & Reading Railroad, built the first American all-metal railroad bridge in 1845. James Mill-

Surviving Cast- and Wrought-Iron Bridges in America

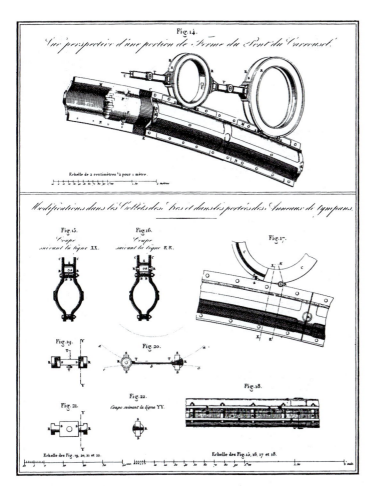

Figure 7. *Details of Polonceau's Pont du Carrousel showing the intricate elliptical arch tube and spandrel ring castings. The most interesting design features are the bitumen-impregnated laminated wooden staves reinforcing the arch tubes. Notice sur le nouveau système des ponts en fonte, suivi dans la construction du Pont du Carrousel (Paris, 1839).*

holland built the first wrought-iron plate girder in 1846, a bridge type far advanced for its time, for the Baltimore & Susquehanna Railroad at Bolton Station, Maryland. Nathaniel Rider patented (1845) and built multiple-intersection trusses of cast and wrought iron for the New York & Harlem and Erie railroads in 1846.[10] This was followed by an iron Howe truss built by Frederick Harbach on the North Adams branch of the Boston & Albany Railroad near Pittsfield, Massachusetts, in 1847. But the consistent use of all-iron bridges on a railroad was first embraced as standard practice in 1851 by Benjamin Henry Latrobe, Jr., chief engineer for the Baltimore & Ohio.

Amazingly, several of America's oldest all-iron railroad bridges survive, the oldest being the West Manayunk Bridge (1845), followed by Halls Station (c1846), and three from the Pennsylvania system built c1854. The first two were designed by Richard Boyse Osborne, CE, for the Philadelphia & Reading, a dynamic railroad that under the direction of Moncure Robinson built many innovative structures. The Manayunk Bridge was built originally on a subsidiary of the Reading, the Little Schuylkill & Susquehanna (Catawissa) Railroad, and spanned 34.2 feet over a stream south of Flat Rock Tunnel near Manayunk, Pennsylvania. It consisted of three lines of trussing carrying two tracks (figure

23

Industrial Archeology

8). The bridge remained in use until 1902 when it was retired. One of the trusses was donated to the Smithsonian Institution and today is part of the *John Bull* locomotive exhibit.[11]

The other Osborne-designed bridge is Halls Station, presently the oldest surviving all-iron railroad bridge still in service, though its use is vehicular, not rail. Halls Station provides access to a private farm. Osborne used Howe trusses rendered in iron: cast-iron diagonals in compression, wrought-iron verticals in tension, with upper and lower chords of wrought-iron bars. Egyptian Revival, at the time a fashionable design motif, embellished the cast-iron diagonals.

Three other early iron railroad bridges survive, two as vehicular crossings over the Main Line of the Pennsylvania at Villanova and Ardmore and a third in pieces at the Railroaders Memorial Museum in Altoona. (A fourth at Ronks was destroyed in 1993.) These bridges were designed by Herman Haupt and are tied cast-iron arches stiffened by Pratt trusses. Haupt adapted the Pratt truss to iron, with verticals in compression and diagonals in tension, and then integrated a tied cast-iron arch onto each truss[12] (figure 9).

Two metal trusses dating from the mid-19th century survive from the Baltimore & Ohio system. One is a double-span Bollman truss built c1869 for the Main Line, then moved

Figure 8. *The only known view of the Manayunk Bridge in rail service at its original location on the Little Schuylkill & Susquehanna (Catawissa) Railroad was part of the collection of bridge photographs used to teach Cornell University engineering students. When this picture was taken, the trusses only served as railings, with the heavy timber structure doing all the work. The photographs were given to the university by John C. Trautwine III on May 1, 1900.* Robert Vogel collection.

Surviving Cast- and Wrought-Iron Bridges in America

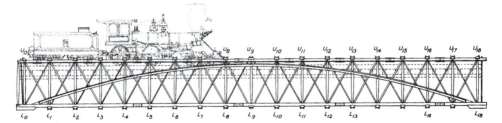

Figure 9. *Profile view of Haupt's arch-strengthened truss of 103-foot-span originally erected at Vandevander, Pennsylvania, c1854, as part of a five-span crossing on the Pennsylvania Main Line. One span was moved to Thompsontown in 1889 where it remained in service till 1984 when it was placed in the exhibition yard of the Railroaders Memorial Museum in Altoona.* Christine Theodoropoulos, HAER delineator.

Figure 9a. *This Howe truss survives as a towpath trail bridge on the former Union Canal near Reading, Pennsylvania. Built in 1869, it once carried traffic across the West Branch of Perkiomen Creek at Rush's Mill in Hereford township, Berks County. Construction of the bridge in 1869 has been attributed by HAER historian Robert Hadlow to Simon Dreibelbies, a local farmer and hotel operator. The details of the connections resemble a patent (no. 78,797) taken by John L. Foreman, a master carpenter in the Reading Railroad shops in Pottstown, Pennsylvania, indicating possible connection with Foreman and the Reading Railroad.* Joseph Elliott, HAER photographer.

to Savage Mill in Maryland 18 years later (figure 10). The other dates from 1871 and originally was one of seven bridges built on the line to Pittsburgh. Like the Savage bridge, it was moved from its original location—over Wills Creek in Somerset County—and placed on a township road over the same Pittsburgh line in 1910, providing access to a farm north of Meyersdale, Pennsylvania. Both the Savage and Meyersdale bridges were built by Wendel Bollman after he left the railroad and started his own company, the Patapsco Bridge & Iron Works in Baltimore.[13]

The Fink truss, patented by Albert Fink in 1854, was another iron truss used by the B&O and later the Louisville & Nashville when Fink became chief engineer of that line in

1857. His major work was the Ohio River bridge at Louisville (1870) that used 25 Fink deck trusses and two channel spans of a different kind. Fink trusses were also used on highways and the best surviving example was built in 1858 by the Trenton (N.J.) Locomotive & Machine Works for Hunterdon County to cross the South Branch Raritan River at Hamden in west-central New Jersey. When it was destroyed the evening of October 2, 1978, the result of an automobile accident, this left only three Fink trusses. Zoarville Station Bridge (1868), a hybrid of a Fink designed by Charles Shaler Smith, president and chief engineer of the Baltimore firm of Smith, Latrobe & Company, is on old Route 212 over Conotton Creek, Zoarville, Ohio, where it was moved in 1905. Abandoned in the 1940s, originally it

Industrial Archeology

was one of three spans over the Tuscarawas River in Dover, Ohio[14] (figures 11, 12). A deck Fink of composite wood-and-iron construction, dated c1870, has been restored as a pedestrian bridge in a park in Lynchburg, Virginia, and another, dating from 1851, was restored as a footbridge in a park in West Chester, Pennsylvania.

Figure 11. *Portal of Zoarville Station Bridge (1868) designed by C. Shaler Smith while a partner in the firm of Smith, Latrobe & Company, Baltimore; the only Fink through-truss surviving in the United States.* Joseph Elliott, HAER photographer.

Figure 10. *View of the cast-iron stanchion at mid-span of the restored Bollman bridge at Savage, Maryland, showing the wooden housing of the anchor block, an intricate hollowed-out casting where all the diagonals to each of the five panel points are pinned.* Eric DeLony, photographer.

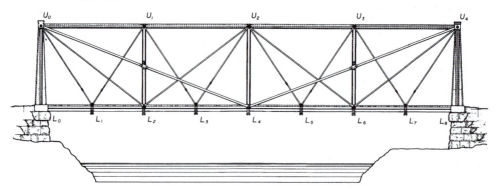

Figure 12. *Profile showing the Fink configuration of the Zoarville Station Bridge. The upper chord and vertical end posts are 8-inch- and 6-inch-diameter Phoenix columns.* Chris Payne, HAER delineator.

Surviving Cast- and Wrought-Iron Bridges in America

Only two cast- and wrought-iron bridges survive from New England's railroads: the Riverside Avenue Bridge (1871) in Greenwich, Connecticut, and the Pine Creek Park Bridge (1872) in Fairfield. Riverside Avenue Bridge, originally one of six spans on the New York, New Haven & Hartford's crossing of the Housatonic at Stratford, was designed by Francis C. Lowthorp, built by the Keystone Bridge Company, and replaced in 1884 when engine loads exceeded its capacity. Re-erected 10 years later in Greenwich and recently rehabilitated, the bridge still stands as a vehicular crossing over the railroad's Main Line. As elaborate in its decorative castings and ornamentation as the B&O bridges, this Whipple truss of 164-foot span is the only surviving bridge where web diagonals actually pass through openings in the vertical columns. This was a simple detail that was not adopted by other engineers even though it did concentrate the lines of stress directly in-line with the centerline of the trusses[15] (figure 13). The Pine Creek, also a Keystone company bridge, was built in 1872 for the Boston & New York Airline Railroad, later absorbed by the New York, Haven & Hartford, as an approach span to the drawbridge crossing the Connecticut River at Middletown.

All of the other railroad survivors are products of the Keystone Bridge Company of Pittsburgh and display the split-column design patented in 1862 by company engineer Jacob Hays Linville and J. L. Piper. The detail was used on the Steubenville Bridge over the Ohio, which in 1864, with a channel span of 320 feet, was the longest span truss bridge in America.

The oldest surviving Keystone bridges are located in Dubuque County, Iowa, and date from 1868. One spans White Water Creek and another that spanned Cloie Branch was moved by the county engineer to a bike path. Both originally were railroad crossings of the Mississippi, later converted to vehicular use.[16] The next oldest is the Kessler Bridge, which may be as old as the Iowa bridges. Its original location is unknown; it was re-erected in Watertown Canyon in 1903 on the Denver, South Park & Pacific Railroad, and in 1935 it was converted to vehicular use. In the last 10 years, the bridge was re-erected over the South Platte River in Bailey, Colorado. The other Keystone bridges are located in Stewartstown, Pennsylvania, Vicksburg, Mississippi, and Fairfield, Connecticut. The only one still in railroad service is the Stewartstown Bridge (1870), a pony-truss originally used on the Northern Central Railroad to cross Jones Falls in Baltimore and then moved to the Stewartstown Railroad in 1885[17] (figure 14). The Fairfield, Connecticut, bridge was re-used in 1890 as a highway overpass of the New York, New Haven & Hartford Railroad in Fairfield, and moved again in 1979 to its present location as a trail bridge in a wetlands conservation area.[18] These former rail bridges survive only because they were removed from rail service

Figure 13. *The Riverside Avenue Bridge (1871) exhibits a number of details that are textbook examples of railroad bridge construction for this period: elaborately decorative portals, tapered circular cast-iron compression members, wrought-iron diagonal rods arranged in a Whipple pattern, and built-up wrought-iron deck beams of riveted angles and plates.* State of Connecticut Department of Transportation, Office of Environmental Planning.

27

Industrial Archeology

Figure 14. *The trusses of the Stewartstown Railroad Bridge (1870) are decorative, serving as railings while the railroad is carried by plate girders. Linville's design is essentially wrought iron other than the cast-iron joint blocks at the connection and bearing points.* Joseph Elliott, HAER photographer.

to vehicular crossings, a common practice once a bridge had outlived its capacity to carry ever-increasing locomotive loads.

Bowstring Tied and Trussed Arches

By far the largest category of cast- and wrought-iron bridges remaining are bowstrings, both tied and trussed arches, of which 22 survive.[19] Though similar in appearance, these can be two subtly different structural systems. In both types, the bottom chord ties the ends of the arch together, similar to the string of a bow. In the tied arch, however, partial loading produces bending in the arch. In the trussed arch, partial loading causes loads in the web members. The bowstring is an extremely efficient form providing reasonable strength compared to the weight of material. Bowstrings, not to be confused with cast-iron arches so common in Europe, were used almost exclusively in America for vehicular crossings. They were one of the common proprietary designs that competed in the highway bridge market during the years immediately preceding and following the Civil War. The configuration was the basis of numerous patent applications with nearly an equal number of patents granted for the profile of the upper chord member. The first widely accepted all-metal bridge design was Whipple's cast- and wrought-iron bowstring truss bridge.

All 22 surviving bowstrings are vehicular bridges, though historically the form was used for railroads in Europe. Isambard Kingdom Brunel's Windsor Bridge (1849) over the Thames, which is still in service on the former route of the Great Western Railway, is a tubular wrought-iron arch truss of 187-foot span. Robert Stephenson's Newcastle High Level Bridge, built in the same year and still in service, was a double-decked structure consisting of six cast-iron tied arches of 125-foot span each.

The earliest designs and details for a tied arch, the use of metal in bridge trusses, eye-bar tie-rods, and the suspension bridge were all explained in detail in 1617 by a Venetian holy man and philosopher, Faustus Verantius, and illustrated in his book *Machinae Novae*.[20] Robert Fulton illustrated an early design for an iron bowstring in his treatise of 1796.[21] But the oldest surviving bowstring in the United States is an 1851 Whipple cast-iron arch in Chili Mills near Rochester, New York.

Squire Whipple was a pivotal figure in the development of iron bridges in America. Born to a farmer and mill owner in 1804 in Hardwick, Massachusetts, he studied engineering at Union College in Schenectady, New York, graduating in 1830 with a bachelor's degree. He went to work as a rodman and leveler on the Baltimore & Ohio Railroad and later as a surveyor on the Erie Canal.[22] On August 22, 1840, he

Surviving Cast- and Wrought-Iron Bridges in America

conceived a plan for a cast-iron arch; it was erected over the Erie Canal at Utica, New York. Letters of patent were issued April 24, 1841. Whipple designed the bridge exclusively for the Erie Canal enlargement, but the design was so successful that it was adapted by the canal commissioners as standard (figures 15, 16). Whipple truss spans by the hundreds also found use on common roads.[23]

Two interesting and distinctly different types of Whipple trusses survive from this early period: a former Erie Canal towpath change bridge relocated to Palmyra, New York, and a Pratt pony-truss bridge providing access to a private residence south of Ilion, New York. The first, known as Aldrich's Crossover Bridge (1858), has a slightly arched, tubular cast-iron upper chord of seven panels with hipped end posts. The other has a cast-iron upper chord similar to Whipple's classic bowstring, but the truss is a parallel chord Pratt configuration rather than an arch. Both have his sculpted cast-iron joint blocks and looped, wrought-iron tension rods for the lower chord.[24]

Whipple remained a pivotal figure in the evolution of iron truss bridges. In 1847, he published *A Work on Bridge Building,* the first American book, and possibly the first in the world, on truss analysis. Members were sized on the analysis of the forces they carried based on equilibrium in every joint, a uniformly distributed dead load, and moving live load. In the same year Whipple proposed the trapezoidal truss, a configuration similar to the Pratt but with the diagonals extending over two panel points rather than one, and inclined end posts. More will be said about this type in the next section.

The next oldest bowstring surviving is the former Upper Pacific Mills Bridge (1864) of Lawrence, Massachusetts, a Moseley tied arch patented in 1857. Though not of composite materials other than the cast-iron shoes, it is included here because it is important to know when the all-wrought-iron and riveted bridge was phased into American bridge technology. Moseley is credited with introducing riveted wrought-iron tubular construction to the United States, a structure type common in Europe but not in the United States until the 1880s when composite construction was replaced. Twenty years later wrought iron was replaced with steel.[25]

The bridge is a tied arch with the arch, triangular in section, of riveted wrought-iron boiler plate. The arch tie is a wrought-iron strap hung from narrow strips of iron riveted to the upper chord member. Aside from the triangular upper chord, the most interesting feature of the bridge is the reverse curved member located in the truss's web. Computer model-

ing by the HAER team that documented the bridge in 1990 proved that the reverse curve member prevented deflection of the upper chord under a moving load. This Moseley bridge was restored by engineering students at Merrimack College, North Andover, Massachusetts, under the direction of Professor Francis Griggs.

Three other Moseley bowstrings survive: one providing a pipe chase to a mill in Claremont (1870), New Hampshire, and another dismantled and stored in Bennington, Vermont (c1860). Another surviving Moseley is the Hare's Hill Road Bridge (1869) near Kimberton, Pennsylvania, a tied arch. Moseley called it a "wrought-iron lattice girder bridge" and patented it in 1866 as an economic alternative to his tubular bowstring[26] (figure 17).

Another distinctive bowstring design is Henszey's wrought-iron arch bridge, built the same year as Moseley's lattice girder. Research by the HAER team that documented this bridge revealed that it was based on an 1869 patent of Joseph G. Henszey of Philadelphia and, like Hare's Hill Road, is the only surviving example (figure 18). The bridge was built by the Continental Bridge Company of Philadelphia, a firm organized to market and build Henszey's patent wrought-iron arch truss.[27]

Other bowstrings surviving from the formative years of iron bridge construction include the inventions of David H. Morrison and two brothers, Jonathan and Zimri Wall, all significant figures in the remarkable coterie of Ohio bridge inventors and fabricators during this period. The oldest is the Moulton Angle Road Bridge, a Morrison bowstring of 1864, patented in 1867. The bridge has eight cast-iron cruciform arch segments, seven feet long, butt-jointed and bolted at their ends for a total length of 54 feet. Originally located in Wapakoneta, Ohio, moved to New Knoxville in Auglaize County, the bridge was relocated again in 1985 to the village of New Bremen, where it was erected over the Miami & Erie Canal. Egypt Pike Bridge (1877), patented in 1874 and 1875 by the Wall brothers, is the earliest surviving work of the Champion Iron Bridge Company, the only Ohio bridge company still in business.[28]

One bowstring that survives in Ohio and Indiana had an upper chord that was completely different from the Whipple or Moseley. It was designed with a lattice configuration. The originator was Joseph Davenport, who worked for the Russell Bridge Company and then established the Massillon Bridge Company, both located in the small manufacturing town of Massillon, Ohio. Davenport received a patent for his bowstring in 1868 and marketed it as a "patent Howe

Industrial Archeology

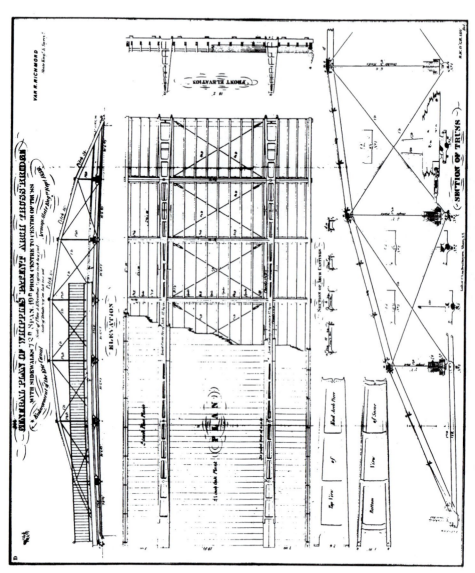

Figure 15. *General plan of Whipple's patent arch truss bridge of 72-foot-span published in the New York Annual Report of the State Engineer & Surveyor on Canals for 1859.*

Surviving Cast- and Wrought-Iron Bridges in America

Figure 16. *Where the horizontal, vertical, and diagonal members met at the bottom chord connection, Whipple devised a sculpted cast-iron connecting block to receive the ends. Though Whipple devised one of the first scientifically designed bridges, this detail, including the forged bottom chord rods, shows the craft hand of the pattern maker, founder, and blacksmith.* Joseph Elliott, HAER photographer.

Figure 17. *Rather than a triangular upper chord of riveted boiler plate, Hare's Hill Road Bridge (1869) uses two Z-bars riveted to a 12-inch-deep plate that follows the curve of the upper chord. The entire web is filled with 2¼ by ¼-inch iron straps spaced one foot on center diagonally in a lattice pattern. The lower chord is a 14½ by ⅜-inch-thick wrought-iron strap. The bridge is deceptively modern in appearance, looking more like a European-style lattice girder than a thick-membered American truss.* Eric DeLony, photographer.

Industrial Archeology

Figure 18. *The Henszey bridge (1869) is interesting both because of its similarities to the Moseley design and its peculiarities. The Henszey patent follows Moseley's precedent of all wrought-iron construction and riveted rather than pinned connections. The cast-iron shoes at the ends of the truss are standard, but the cast-iron strut block and tension-rod assembly that attempts to induce a reverse stress in the lower chord are unusual. Other curious features of the bridge are the two Phoenix sections giving the upper chord its half-circle profile.* Eric DeLony, photographer.

truss-arch bridge." As the name implies, the upper chord is built-up of curved wrought-iron straps separated by a web of threaded rods, tubes, and angle blocks arranged in a Howe pattern (figures 19, 20). Surviving examples include: the County Engineer's Garage Bridge (1872), a span of 72 feet carrying South Market Street over Beaver Creek in Lisbon, Ohio; a bridge in the Martinsville vicinity of Clinton County, Ohio; Paint Creek Bridge (c1875), a Massillon-built bowstring carrying County Route 25W over Paint Creek about a quarter-mile east of Camden, Carroll County, Indiana; and Burton Lane Bridge (c1875), carrying County Route 189 over Indian Creek in Martinsville, Morgan County, Indiana.

While discussing Davenport, one should include his straight Howe truss. The oldest iron bridge in Ohio, dating from 1859, is based on this configuration. It was originally erected on a county road near Alliance, and moved to Massillon's Oak Knoll Park in 1899 when it had outlived its usefulness. This is the first metal truss bridge preserved in America.

Examples of Davenport's straight Howe truss survive as the Towpath Footbridge (c1872) over the Ohio & Erie Canal in the restored canal town of Roscoe Village, Coshocton, Ohio, and Sockman Road Bridge (1873), still in service near Fredericktown, Knox County. The designer/builder of the canal bridge has not been definitively attributed. Sockman Road Bridge, like Oak Knoll Park, was built by the Russell Bridge Company[29] (figure 21).

The "Eureka wrought iron bridge," built in 1874, was patented in 1871 by entrepreneurs William H. Allen and Oliver H. Perry, machinists and general jobbers who manufactured agricultural machinery and farm implements. Located just over the Iowa border in Beloit, Wisconsin, this bridge is a classic example of a fabricated iron truss built for farm-to-market roads.

The last two bowstrings in the survey were built late, in 1881, by which time bowstrings had largely been replaced by parallel chord trusses. This tied arch, with an upper chord

Surviving Cast- and Wrought-Iron Bridges in America

Figure 19. *Detail of the latticed upper chord of Davenport's bowstring made of wrought-iron straps separated by pipes and threaded rods seated in small cast-iron plates.* Joseph Elliott, HAER photographer.

shaped like an ellipse, was built by John L. Foreman, master carpenter for the Philadelphia & Reading Railroad at its Pottstown Shops. The Scarlets Mill Bridge carries the Horse-Shoe Trail over an abandoned Reading right-of-way just up the line from Scarlets Mill, Pennsylvania (figures 23, 24). Another structure, recently moved from Tank Farm Road near Macungie, Pennsylvania, is in storage at the Hugh Moore Historical Park and Museums in Easton, Pennsylvania. Ed Kutsch, a bridge historian who has been studying and photographing iron bridges since the 1950s, documented the bridge's service on canals. His sources are two undated drawings of the bridge by the Schuylkill Navigation Company. Foreman was awarded a patent in 1871 for a bottom chord connection that resembles the bottom chords of these two structures.[30]

Included in this section are four surviving bridges designed and patented by Charles H. Parker, chief engineer for the National Bridge & Iron Works of Boston. These are Parker trusses, not bowstrings, and they are primarily of wrought-iron construction. They are included because, like the Moseley, the Parker truss was advanced for its time, a forerunner of bridges to come.

For 1870, Parker's patent truss is extremely sophisticated and shows an implicit understanding of materials, structural analysis, and detailing that anticipates bridge design 20 years in the future. Like Moseley's, Parker's truss is all wrought iron other than cast-iron eyes at the connections between the verticals and the upper and lower chords, the thrust blocks (or shoes), and bolsters at the ends of the truss that protected them from traffic. Parker's truss has a curved upper chord like the Moseley, except for the inclined end

LAYMON ROAD BRIDGE
·1871·
WILMINGTON, OHIO

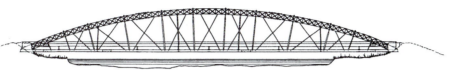

Figure 20. *Profile of Davenport's patent Howe truss-arch as represented in Laymon Road Bridge (1871), moved in 1991 to J. W. Denver Williams Park in Wilmington, Ohio.* Julie Willis, HAER delineator.

Industrial Archeology

Figure 21. *Though no longer clear spanning when this photograph was taken in 1992, Sockman Road Bridge (1873) was still in service.* Joseph Elliott, HAER photographer.

posts, Pratt bracing in the web, and wrought-iron bars for the bottom chord. His patent claim was not for these features, but for the inclined end panel, or hips, which allowed him to vary the length of the bridge without changing the rest of the structure. Parker's configuration resembles other truss types much larger in size, such as the Pennsylvania, petit, and camel-back. These bridges were used well into the 20th century as standard types by railroads and state highway departments[31] (figure 25).

Parallel Chord Trusses

In 1848, while pondering whether the arch form was the most economical, Squire Whipple, the father of iron bridges, "took some investigations and computations with the expectation of being able to demonstrate such to be the fact, but on the contrary the result convinced [him] that the trapezoidal form with parallel chords and diagonal members, either with or without verticals, was theoretically more economical than the arch"[32] (figures 26, 27).

The configuration Whipple was evaluating was the parallel chord truss, or the "trapezoidal" as he preferred to call it. Trusses have a long history extending back into antiquity. Vitruvius wrote the earliest extant description, but Palladio, an Italian architect, is attributed as the first to apply the

basic concept of transferring both dead and live loads to the abutments or piers in the truss form. The easiest visualized form to accomplish this was a rigid, self-supporting system of triangles. Palladio drew plans for several parallel chord trusses and published them in his *I quattro libri dell'architettura* (1570). He built several, all less than 100 feet.

For 200 years, from the 16th to the 18th century, wooden truss design was dormant. Then in pioneer America, in the late 18th and early 19th century, carpenter-engineers like Timothy Palmer, Lewis Wernwag, Theodore Burr, and Ithiel Town built truss forms predicated on intuition, pragmatic rules of thumb, and a craft tradition passed from master to apprentice. These bridges were improved on by craftsmen-engineers like William Howe and the father-and-son team of Caleb and Thomas Pratt, who patented trusses in the 1840s. Whipple built his first long-span trapezoidal truss in 1853. This configuration, also known as the Murphy-Whipple, Linville, or double-intersection Pratt, became standard for moderate- to long-span truss bridges, vehicular and rail, until the 1880s.

While Manayunk, Halls Station, and the Haupt trusses over the Pennsylvania Main Line are the oldest parallel chord railroad bridges in America, the oldest non-railroad parallel chord truss is a simple Pratt located in Hellertown, Pennsylvania. Built by Charles Nathaniel Beckel in 1860, the

Surviving Cast- and Wrought-Iron Bridges in America

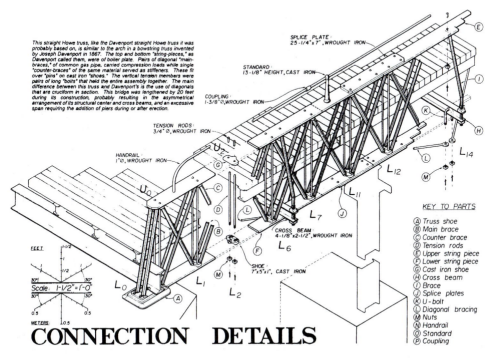

This straight Howe truss, like the Davenport straight Howe truss it was probably based on, is similar to the arch in a bowstring truss invented by Joseph Davenport in 1867. The top and bottom "string-pieces," as Davenport called them, were of boiler plate. Pairs of diagonal "main-braces," of common gas pipe, carried compression loads while single "counter-braces" of the same material served as stiffeners. These fit over "pins" on cast iron "shoes." The vertical tension members were pairs of long "bolts" that held the entire assembly together. The main difference between this truss and Davenport's is the use of diagonals that are cruciform in section. This bridge was lengthened by 20 feet during its construction, probably resulting in the asymmetrical arrangement of its structural center and cross beams, and an excessive span requiring the addition of piers during or after erection.

SPLICE PLATE : 25-1/4"x7", WROUGHT IRON

STANDARD : 13-1/8" HEIGHT, CAST IRON

COUPLING : 1-3/8"Ø, WROUGHT IRON

TENSION RODS : 3/4"Ø, WROUGHT IRON

HANDRAIL : 1"Ø, WROUGHT IRON

CROSS BEAM 4-1/8"x2-1/2", WROUGHT IRON

SHOE : 7"x5"x1", CAST IRON

FEET

Scale: 1-1/2"=1'-0"

METERS

KEY TO PARTS
Ⓐ Truss shoe
Ⓑ Main brace
Ⓒ Counter brace
Ⓓ Tension rods
Ⓔ Upper string piece
Ⓕ Lower string piece
Ⓖ Cast iron shoe
Ⓗ Cross beam
Ⓘ Brace
Ⓙ Splice plates
Ⓚ U-bolt
Ⓛ Diagonal bracing
Ⓜ Nuts
Ⓝ Handrail
Ⓞ Standard
Ⓟ Coupling

CONNECTION DETAILS

Figure 22. *Davenport's straight Howe truss, as detailed in this isometric drawing of the Sockman Road Bridge, is similar in construction to his Howe truss-arch except for the diagonals being cruciform in section.* Attila Kovacs, HAER delineator.

Figure 23. *This picture shows the cruciform cast-iron vertical posts, connecting blocks, and brackets that strengthened the ends of Scarlets Mill Bridge, details that were out-of-date by 1881.* Joseph Elliott, HAER photographer.

bridge is named for one of the many country lanes that crossed Saucon Creek in Lower Saucon Township. Walnut Street Bridge is one of three surviving Pratt trusses built by the Beckel Iron Foundry & Machine Shop of Bethlehem, Pennsylvania.

Before discussing these Pratt trusses, the few surviving Post trusses should be mentioned. Simeon S. Post, an Erie Railway bridge engineer, designed a bridge in 1865 that he called the "diagonal truss iron bridge." It enjoyed a brief period of popularity during the 1860s and 1870s, primarily by the railroads for long-span bridges. None of the railroad bridges survive, but two vehicular Post trusses dating from the 1870s are located in Lancaster, Massachusetts. One is a pony-truss, the Atherton Bridge, spanning 75 feet, 6 inches over the Nashua River and built by J. H. Cofrode & Company of Philadelphia. It used four-inch-diameter Phoenix columns for the web compression members. The other is a

Industrial Archeology

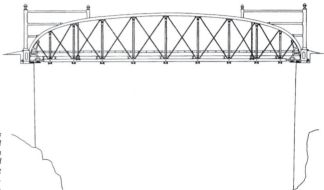

SCARLETS MILL BRIDGE
SCARLETS MILL · 1881 · PENNSYLVANIA

Figure 24. *Profile of Scarlets Mill Bridge showing the elliptical upper chord, Pratt bracing in the web, and the functionally detailed cast-iron post and pipe railing at the ends of the bridge.* Christine Ussler, HAER delineator.

Figure 25. *Elm Street Bridge (1870) was the subject of a major preservation row in Woodstock, Vermont, in 1977. The compromise between transportation officials and local residents was rehabilitation of the trusses as decorative guardrails, while the deck was widened and supported by four-foot-deep concrete girders to meet AASHTO standards. This view is of the pre-rehab bridge.* Donald Wiedenmayer, Vermont Department of Transportation.

Surviving Cast- and Wrought-Iron Bridges in America

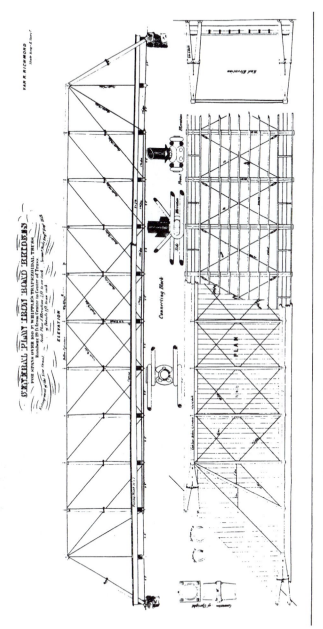

Figure 26. General plan of Whipple's trapezoidal truss published in the New York State Canal Engineer's report of 1859 shows the classic configuration that endured for long-span bridges for the rest of the century—parallel chords and inclined end posts with diagonals extending over two panels. The ultimate development was a bridge without the cast-iron compression members and connecting blocks, but, rather, compression members of wrought iron built-up from standard structural shapes riveted together, and forged eye-bar tension members that were pin-connected—a bridge of homogeneous materials and standard shapes capable of being simply supported up to 400 feet clear span.

37

Industrial Archeology

Figure 27. *Half of a stereoscopic view of an iron bridge nearly identical to the previous drawing even though it was erected on the Murphy-Whipple plan in 1856 for the North Pennsylvania Rail Road by the Pencoyd Iron Works, Philadelphia, John W. Murphy, Engineer. Though not clear in the photograph, the bottom chord appears to retain Whipple's looped rod and cast-iron connecting block rather than pin-connected eye-bars, which was Murphy's improvement on the Whipple trapezoidal truss.* Robert Vogel collection.

Post through-truss of 100-foot span, built a year later by one of the companies licensed to build Post trusses, the Watson Manufacturing Company of Paterson, New Jersey. It crosses the same river on Ponakin Road. Post never patented the inclined web configuration—posts leaning at an angle of 70 degrees toward the center—that is the distinguishing characteristic of his trusses, but in 1863 he did receive a patent for a joint box and pin, used in the through-truss and the Falling Rock Camp Bridge, that connected the top chord, posts, lateral struts, and diagonal braces.[33] The last of the surviving Post trusses, Falling Rock Camp Bridge, is located near Newark, Ohio. Little documentation has surfaced on this interesting structure. It was ordered by the Licking County commissioners from a bridge fabricator in Cleveland, Ohio, to span Brushy Fork Creek, c1872. Moved to its present site in 1931, this historic bridge provides access to a Boy Scout camp (figures 28, 29).

By the end of the 1870s, the Pratt and its variations dominated bridge types and was the preferred choice of bridge manufacturers and engineers. Walnut Street Bridge, the oldest surviving non-railroad parallel chord truss, is a through

Pratt of five panels spanning 55 feet. Several details distinguish it from the other Pratt truss spans. Most unusual are the cast-iron floor beams. Cast-iron girders saw extensive use on the railroads in England. Beckel's design shows that he understood beam action as implicitly as the English. The deck beams of the former Walnut Street Bridge in Hellertown were never reinforced (figures 30, 31).

Other interesting details include the round, tapered cast-iron upper chord members and web posts that resemble the compression members in Whipple's trapezoidal truss, and the "straining plate." This was a bridge connection detail patented in 1857 and 1860 by Francis C. Lowthorp of Trenton, New Jersey. It enabled the vertical post and horizontal floor beam to act as one, rather than as two separate units. In this detail, Lowthorp anticipated the rigid connection between vertical and horizontal members that became standard for modern truss bridges.[34]

The two other Beckel-built bridges that survive are identical Pratt pony-trusses. One is the Old Mill Road Bridge (1870), just a few miles upstream from Walnut Street, and the other

Surviving Cast- and Wrought-Iron Bridges in America

Figure 28. *Detail photo of the Falling Rock Camp Bridge (1872) showing the inclined web posts of the Post configuration.* Joseph Elliott, HAER photographer.

is the former City Line Road Bridge built in the same year. Both bridges have been preserved by Northampton County: the Old Mill Road *in situ* as part of a National Register historic district, and the City Line Road by moving it to Sand Island, now a Bethlehem city park, but once the site of Beckel's ironworks where the bridges were made.

Like Walnut Street, both bridges use Lowthorp's straining block and cast-iron floor beams. The deck beams of Old Mill Road Bridge worked without cracking until 1927 when they were reinforced with steel I-beams. Rather than cylindrical compression members, Beckel used octagonal castings for the upper chords and web posts. The lower chords are square eye-bars with forged heads rather than threaded iron rods used on the earlier Walnut Street Bridge.[35]

Barely 20 miles on the other side of the Delaware River in New Jersey are three more Pratt pony-trusses built by a competitor of the Beckel ironworks, William Cowin, pro-

prietor of the Cowin Iron Works of Lambertville, New Jersey. They display the same finesse as the Beckel bridges and incorporate details based on patents granted to Lowthorp. The bridges in Clinton and Glen Gardner were built in 1870; the New Hampton bridge was built two years earlier. All have octagonal compression members and wrought-iron eye-bar lower chords. Differences include tapered cast-iron I-section web posts and William Johnson's tension adjuster in the lower chord panel points. Another difference is vertical end posts on the Cowin bridges and inclined end posts on the Beckel bridges (figure 32).

Bridges aesthetics had reached as high a state of Victorian embellishment by the 1870s as any other mechanical contrivance. The extraordinary skills of the pattern maker and foundryman are exemplified in the Beckel and Cowin bridges. The pattern maker's art is beautifully translated into elaborate architectural moldings. The molder formed green sand around the patterns and assembled core boxes; the foundryman filled the molds with molten cast iron and "struck" the castings after hardening; and a finisher then filed the mold marks from the castings.[36]

Other surviving examples of cast- and wrought-iron Pratt truss bridges include the Mead Avenue Bridge (1871) of Meadville, Pennsylvania (Penn Bridge Works, New Brighton), the Kokosing River Bridge (1874) in Howard, Ohio (David Morrison's Columbia Bridge Works, Dayton), Lombard Street Bridge (1877), formerly spanning Baltimore's Inner Harbor and now stored in pieces at the Baltimore Streetcar Museum (Wendel Bollman's Patapsco Bridge & Iron Works in Baltimore), Upper River Bridge (1878) over the Ausable River in Keeseville, New York (Murray, Dougal & Company, Milton, Pennsylvania), and the Hardin City Bridge (1879), placed on the side of the road in Eldora, Iowa (Western Bridge Works, Fort Wayne, Indiana). Mead Avenue, Kokosing, and Hardin City are Whipple trusses—diagonals crossing two panel points. Lombard Street, like the Rock Creek Bridge in Washington, carried water in a cast-iron pipe that was shaped like a bowstring truss and served as the center support of the bridge. Mead Avenue is cocooned inside a Baltimore truss, added in 1937 to strengthen the bridge. These five round out the surviving cast- and wrought-iron parallel chord truss bridges of the Whipple and Pratt configurations built in the 1870s.

The last parallel chord truss dates from 1881, although its patent date was 1858. It is a lovely park bridge, like the ones in Central Park, providing pedestrian access to an island of the Winnipesaukee in Tilton, New Hampshire. Tilton

39

Industrial Archeology

FALLING ROCK CAMP BRIDGE · 1872
HICKMAN VICINITY, OHIO

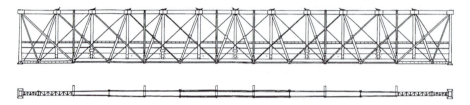

Figure 29. *Profile drawing of the Falling Rock Camp Bridge.* Julie Willis, HAER delineator.

Figure 30. *Beckel's Walnut Street Bridge (1860) that formerly spanned Saucon Creek in Hellertown, Pennsylvania. Though similar to Whipple's parallel chord truss, this bridge features Lowthorp's patented connecting block of 1857 (no. 17,684) and 1860 (no. 27,457). The cast-iron deck beams never needed strengthening in 110 years of increasing loads.* Joseph Elliott, HAER photographer.

Surviving Cast- and Wrought-Iron Bridges in America

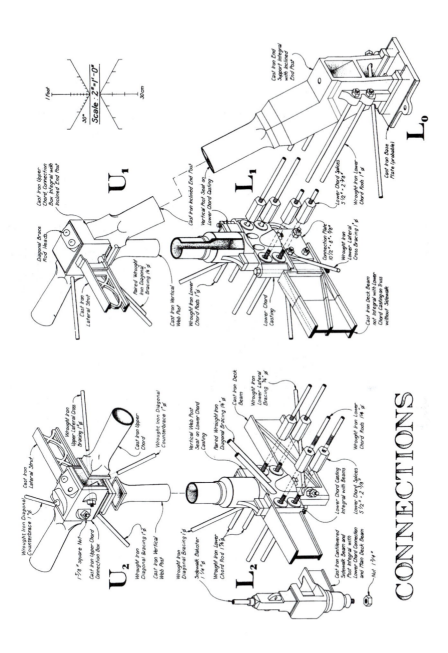

Figure 31. *Exploded isometric of the Walnut Street Bridge (1860) showing the intricate castings of the upper chord connections and Lowthorp's patented bottom chord connecting block. Monica Korsos, HAER delineator.*

41

Industrial Archeology

Figure 32. *The skills and craft of the pattern maker and founder are exemplified in the cast-iron end post, verticals, and upper chord of the School Street Bridge (1870), Glen Gardner, New Jersey, one of three surviving bridges fabricated by the Cowin Iron Works, Lambertville, New Jersey. Joseph Elliott, HAER photographer.*

Island Bridge was manufactured by Albert D. Briggs & Company of Springfield, Massachusetts, based on a design patented by Lucius Truesdell of Warren, Massachusetts. It consisted "of a series of horizontal chords in combination with diagonal and vertical braces by which the strain and tension of the various parts is neutralized by distributing them more evenly throughout the whole structure."[37]

Truesdell's truss is essentially an iron lattice, like Town's, braced by horizontal wrought-iron straps and vertical cruciform cast-iron braces. An interesting feature of the patent is a circular ring-clamp used to connect diagonals providing lateral bracing to the bottom chord. This ring-clamp became a standard detail of truss design.

Conclusion

The surviving cast- and wrought-iron bridges in America are an outstanding group of engineering and manufacturing structures, each representing a rare example of American bridge design and manufacturing prowess. Many are nationally significant and the loss of one is tantamount to a disaster since so few survive. Every effort should be made to save these bridges.

The bridges illustrate the intricate weave of technological transfer, theories of structural design, strength of materials, manufacturing technologies, marketing strategies, the struggle between professionalism and practical know-how, trans-

Surviving Cast- and Wrought-Iron Bridges in America

portation, western settlement, and bridge aesthetics. The near-comprehensive inventory of historic bridges in America permits comparative analyses and understanding of the themes historic bridges offer. The appended list of surviving cast- and wrought-iron bridges is based on these surveys. I would be grateful to readers who know of other examples and can send additional information, including photographs. To bridge enthusiasts, scholars, and individuals responsible for preserving the patrimony, I am not presuming that the subject has been exhausted or that the scholarly assessment of this branch of bridge engineering has been satisfied. Much remains to be researched, digested, and written about the historic bridges of America.

Why is Ohio so fortunate in having such a remarkable number of old metal truss bridges? One reason may be the number of bridge fabricators located in Ohio. Another may be that individual farmsteads reached a critical number exactly when metal truss manufacturing was at the peak of development. To address the farmers' need to get produce to market, miles of farm-to-market roads were built. Ohio, like many of America's midwestern states, is coursed by hundreds of rivers and streams. The solution to crossing these barriers was the fabricated metal truss—thousands were manufactured. Or it simply may be the dedicated work of one individual—David Simmons, historian with the Ohio Historical Society, who through his research, writing, and diplomatic persuasion has focused the attention of the state's citizens and, most important, its county engineers on the historic bridges of Ohio for the last 20 years.

Ohio has reached a point in its statewide bridge program where historic bridges, like the ones highlighted in this article, are being preserved by transportation officials and county engineers through an understanding of their cultural values and an appreciation of their engineering finesse. While other states may scoff at the idea of state highway departments being responsible for historic bridges, Ohio and a few other states have included the preservation of historic bridges as part of their day-to-day operations. The reality is that highway departments are the most qualified to accomplish this task. Bridges are engineered structures and require engineers who understand their behavior and have the knowledge and experience to fix them. A part of state governments' highway department funds should be dedicated to historic bridge preservation. Hiding behind the excuse that historic bridges are not the responsibility of highway departments ended in 1987 when Congress declared it to be in the national interest to save historic bridges that represent values of American engineering know-how, architecture, and manufacturing genius. This does not mean that every historic bridge can or should be saved, but concerted efforts must be extended to save the truly outstanding examples. Otherwise, little physical evidence will be available to future generations of this fascinating period of American engineering prowess.

Notes

1. Editors, "Iron Bridges and Their Construction," *Lippincott's Magazine*, January 1873, p. 13.
2. E. C. Kreutzberg, "Phoenix: One Hundred Years Old, Pioneer in Industry," *Iron Trade Review* 81, 8 (August 25, 1927):434.
3. "List of Wrought-Iron Bridges, Viaducts, and Piers Built and Now Building by the Phoenix Bridge Company, Successors to Clarke, Reeves & Company, from 1869 to 1885," *Album of Designs of the Phoenix Bridge Company* (Philadelphia: J. B. Lippincott, 1885), pp. 7–10.
4. Charles Evan Fowler, "Some American Bridge Shop Methods," *Cassier's Magazine* 17, November 1899–April 1900, p. 102.
5. One has only to look at the great works of antiquity to realize that "engineering" occurred before 1850. The mid-19th century was the period when a series of developments formalized the engineering profession. The American Society of Civil Engineers became the first professional engineering association in 1852, followed by the establishment during the 1860s of permanent, national associations for almost all the specializations within the field. In the late 1860s and the 1870s formal engineering education expanded from an exceptional activity to a program available to all through the new land-grant colleges.
6. J. G. James, "The Cast Iron Bridge at Sunderland (1796)," *Occasional Papers in the History of Science and Technology no. 5* (Newcastle upon Tyne: Newcastle upon Tyne Polytechnic, 1986), p. 4.
7. Emory L. Kemp, "Thomas Paine and His Pontifical Matters," *Transactions of the Newcomen Society* 49 (London, 1979), p. 21.
8. Zerah Colburn, "American Iron Bridges," *Proceedings of the Institution of Civil Engineers* 22 (1863). This informative article goes into extensive, detailed descriptions and evaluations of most of the important iron bridges built in America. Colburn points out the similarities between Polonceau's Pont du Carrousel and Delafield's Dunlap Creek (p. 540).
9. Frances C. Robb, "Cast Aside: The First Cast-Iron Bridge in the United States," in this issue of *IA*.
10. Victor C. Darnell, "The Pioneering Iron Trusses of Nathaniel Rider," *Construction History: Journal of the Construction History Society* 7 (1991):69.
11. Emory L. Kemp and Richard K. Anderson, Jr., "The Reading-Halls Station Bridge," *IA: The Journal of the Society for Industrial Archeology* 13 (1987):22–23.
12. Victor C. Darnell, "The Haupt Iron Bridge on the Pennsylvania Railroad," *IA: The Journal of the Society for Industrial Archeology* 14, 2 (1988):35–50.
13. Robert M. Vogel, "The Engineering Contributions of Wendel Bollman," paper 36 in *United States National Museum Bulletin 240: Contributions from the Museum of History and Technology* (Washington, D.C.: Smithsonian Institution, 1964).
14. William Michael Lawrence, "Zoarville Station Bridge," Historic American Engineering Record report OH-84, Washington, D.C., 1992.

Industrial Archeology

15. Bruce Clouette, "Riverside Avenue Bridge," National Register of Historic Places nomination form, Washington, D.C., 1976.

16. Clayton Fraser, historic bridge authority and consultant operating out of Loveland, Colorado, has inventoried the historic bridges of Iowa. I have him to thank for bringing these bridges to my attention.

17. Robert H. Hadlow, "Stewartstown Railroad Bridge," Historic American Engineering Record report PA-205, Washington, D.C., 1991.

18. Bruce Clouette and Matthew Roth, "Pine Creek Park Bridge (Mill Hill Road Bridge)," National Register of Historic Places registration form, Washington, D.C., 1991.

19. This count includes bowstrings representing early, developmental designs, not the "column, plate, and channel" bridges of the Wrought Iron Bridge Company of Canton, Ohio, or the "channel and plate" bridges of the King Iron Bridge Company of Cleveland, Ohio, which fall into the next chronological category—bridges essentially of all wrought-iron construction.

20. William Barclay Parsons, *Engineers and Engineering in the Renaissance* (Baltimore: Williams & Wilkins, 1939), pp. 490–492.

21. Robert Fulton, *Treatise on the Improvement of Canal Navigation* (London: I. and J. Taylor, 1796).

22. Information on Squire Whipple was obtained from Francis E. Griggs, Jr., *Call Him Squire: The Life and Times of Squire Whipple, 19th Century Engineer, the Father of Iron Bridges*, unpub. MS, Merrimack College, North Andover, Massachusetts.

23. "The Development of the Iron Bridge," *Railroad Gazette*, April 19, 1889. This article by the editors of the magazine was based on notes sent to A. P. Boller by Squire Whipple shortly before his death. Boller contemplated a history of iron bridge building and Whipple sent the notes as a contribution to that work (p. 253).

24. Little is known about these bridges. I thank Bill Chamberlin of Schenectady, New York, for bringing them to my attention.

25. Francis E. Griggs, Jr., with Lola Bennett, ed., "Upper Pacific Mills Bridge," Historic American Engineering Record report MA-72, Washington, D.C., 1991, p. 1.

26. William P. Chamberlin, PE, "Hare's Hill Road Bridge (Moseley's Wrought Iron Girder Bridge)," Historic American Engineering Record report PA-208, Washington, D.C., 1991.

27. William P. Chamberlin, PE, "Henszey's Wrought-Iron Arch Bridge (1869/1870)," Historic American Engineering Record report PA-209, Washington, D.C., 1991.

28. David A. Simmons, "Engineering and Enterprise: Early Metal-Truss Bridges in Ohio," *Timeline: A Publication of the Ohio Historical Society* (February–March, 1985):25.

29. Ibid., p. 18.

30. William P. Chamberlin, PE, "Scarlets Mill Bridge," Historic American Engineering Record report PA-210, Washington, D.C., 1991.

31. Dennis M. Zembala, "Elm Street Bridge," Historic American Engineering Record report VT-3, Washington, D.C., 1983.

32. "Development of the Iron Bridge" (n. 23 above), p. 253.

33. Patrick Harshbarger, "Addendum to Ponakin Bridge, HAER No. MA-13," August 1990, and "Addendum to Atherton Bridge (Bolton Road Bridge), HAER No. MA-17," August 1990, Historic American Engineering Record reports, Washington, D.C., 1990.

34. Robert W. Hadlow, "Walnut Street Bridge," Historic American Engineering Record report PA-206, Washington, D.C., 1991.

35. Robert W. Hadlow, "Old Mill Road Bridge," Historic American Engineering Record report PA-93, Washington, D.C., 1991.

36. Robert W. Hadlow, "West Main Street Bridge," Historic American Engineering Record report NJ-19, Washington, D.C., 1991.

37. Lucius E. Truesdell, of Warren, Mass., "Specifications of Letters Patent No. 21,388, dated August 31, 1858," U.S. Patent Office, Washington, D.C.

Appendix
Surviving American Cast- and Wrought-Iron Bridges

May 1994

1. **Dunlap Creek Bridge** (1839)
Old U.S. 40 over Dunlap Creek, Brownsville, Pennsylvania, Capt. Richard Delafield, engineer, John Snowden and John Herbertson, foundrymen.

2. **Philadelphia & Reading Railroad:**
Manayunk Bridge (1845)
National Museum of American History, Smithsonian Institution, Washington, D.C., Richard B. Osborne, engineer.

3. **Philadelphia & Reading Railroad: Halls Station Bridge** (c1846)
Private road over Conrail, Muncy, Pennsylvania, Richard B. Osborne, engineer.

4. **Main Street Bridge** (1851, 1874)
Main Street (formerly) over French Creek, Phoenixville, Pennsylvania, moved to Chester County park, Albert Fink, patentee.

5. **Whipple Cast- and Wrought-Iron Bowstring Truss Bridge** (1851)
Chili Mills, New York, Squire Whipple, patentee.

6. **Pennsylvania Railroad: Haupt Truss Bridge** (c1854)
Railroaders Memorial Museum, Altoona, Pennsylvania, Herman Haupt, engineer, Altoona Shops, Pennsylvania Railroad, builder.

7. **Pennsylvania Railroad: Haupt Truss Bridge** (c1854)
Spring Mill Road over Main Line, Villanova, Pennsylvania, Herman Haupt, engineer, Altoona Shops, Pennsylvania Railroad, builder.

8. **Pennsylvania Railroad: Haupt Truss Bridge** (c1854)
Church Road over Main Line, Ardmore, Pennsylvania, Herman Haupt, engineer, Altoona Shops, Pennsylvania Railroad, builder.

9. **Change (Aldrich's Crossover) Bridge** (1858)
Privately owned near Palmyra, New York.

10. **Davenport Truss Bridge** (1859)
Oak Knoll Park, Massillon, Ohio, Joseph Davenport, designer, Russell Bridge Company, Massillon, builder.

11. **Washington Aqueduct: Rock Creek Bridge** (1860)
Pennsylvania Avenue and Washington Aqueduct over Rock Creek, Washington, D.C., Montgomery C. Meigs, engineer.

12. **Whipple Cast- and Wrought-Iron Pony Pratt Truss** (c1860)
Private-access bridge over Gulf Stream to Lupinskis' residence, adjacent to NY 51, south of Ilion, New York.

13. **Walnut Street Bridge** (c1860)
Formerly spanning Saucon Creek, Hellertown, Pennsylvania, Charles N. Beckel, designer, Beckel Iron Foundry & Machine Shop, Bethlehem, builder.

14. **Murphy Road Bridge** (c1860)
Formerly spanning Walloomsac River, moved in 1958 to Bennington Museum, Bennington, Vermont, Thomas W. H. Moseley, designer, Moseley Iron Building Works, Boston, builder.

15. **Pine Bank Arch** (1861)
Central Park, New York, Calvert Vaux, J. Wrey Mould, designers.

16. **Bow Bridge** (1862)
The Lake, Central Park, New York, Calvert Vaux, J. Wrey Mould, designers.

17. **Bridge 28 (Gothic Arch)** (1864)
Central Park, New York, Calvert Vaux, J. Wrey Mould, designers, J. B. & W. W. Cornell Iron Works, New York, builder.

18. **Reservoir Bridge Southwest** (1864)
Central Park, New York, Calvert Vaux, J. Wrey Mould, designers.

19. **Upper Pacific Mills Bridge** (1864)
North Canal, Lawrence, Massachusetts, Thomas W. H. Moseley, designer, Moseley Iron Building Works, Boston, builder.

20. **Moulton Angle Road Bridge** (1864, 1985)
Over Miami & Erie Canal, Lions Club Park, New Bremen, Ohio, David H. Morrison, designer, Columbia Bridge Company, Dayton, builder.

21. **Reservoir Bridge Southeast** (1865)
Central Park, New York, Calvert Vaux, J. Wrey Mould, designers.

22. **Whipple Cast- and Wrought-Iron Bowstring Truss Bridge** (1867)
Normans Kill Private Way over unnamed stream that leads into the Normans Kill, Albany, New York, Squire Whipple, engineer, Simon DeGraff, builder.

23. **Zoarville Station Bridge** (1868)
Abandoned State Route 212, Zoarville vicinity, Ohio, Charles Shaler Smith, engineer, Smith, Latrobe & Company, Baltimore, builder.

24. **Cloie Branch Bridge** (1868)
Moved from road over Cloie Branch to bicycle path, Dubuque County, Iowa, Jacob H. Linville, engineer,

Industrial Archeology

Keystone Bridge Company, Pittsburgh, builder.

25. **White Water Creek Bridge** (1868)
Unidentified road over Whitewater Creek, Dubuque County, Iowa, Jacob H. Linville, engineer, Keystone Bridge Company, Pittsburgh, builder.

26. **Musconetcong River Bridge** (1868)
Unidentified road over Musconetcong River, New Hampton, New Jersey, William and Charles Cowin, designers, Cowin Iron Works, Lambertville, builder.

27. **Hare's Hill Road Bridge** (1869)
Hare's Hill Road over French Creek, Kimberton, Pennsylvania, Thomas W. H. Moseley, designer, Moseley Iron Bridge & Roof Company, Philadelphia, builder.

28. **Henszey's Wrought-Iron Arch Bridge** (1869)
Kings Road over Ontelaunee Creek, Wanamakers, Pennsylvania, Joseph G. Henszey, designer, Continental Bridge Company, Philadelphia, builder.

29. **Rush's Mill Bridge** (1869)
Union Canal Bicycle & Walking Trail over Plum Creek near Blue Marsh Lake, Reading vicinity, Pennsylvania, Simon Dreibelbies, builder.

30. **B&O Railroad: Bollman Truss Bridge** (c1869)
Abandoned B&O spur over Little Patuxent River, Savage, Maryland, Wendel Bollman, designer, Patapsco Bridge & Iron Works, Baltimore, builder.

31. **Union College (Cayadutta Creek) Bridge** (c1869)
Moved 1979 from Johnstown, New York, to Union College campus, Schenectady, New York, Squire Whipple, engineer, Shipman & Son, Springfield Center, New York, builders.

32. **Second Whipple Cayadutta Bridge** (c1869)
Spanning Cayadutta Creek, Fonda, New York, Squire Whipple, engineer.

33. **Shaw Bridge** (1870)
Van Wyck Lane (formerly the Old Albany Post Road), abandoned, over Claverack Creek near State Route 9H, Claverack, New York, Squire Whipple, engineer, J. D. Hutchinson, builder.

34. **Old Mill Road Bridge** (1870)
Old Mill Road over Saucon Creek, Hellertown, Pennsylvania, Charles N. Beckel, designer, Beckel Iron Foundry & Machine Shop, Bethlehem, builder.

35. **City Line Road Bridge** (1870)
Moved to Sand Island Park, Bethlehem, Pennsylvania, Charles N. Beckel, designer, Beckel Iron Foundry & Machine Shop, Bethlehem, builder.

36. **School Street Bridge** (1870)
School Street over Spruce Run, Glen Gardner, New Jersey, William and Charles Cowin, designers, Cowin Iron Works, Lambertville, builder.

37. **Stewartstown Railroad Bridge** (1870)

Stewartstown Railroad over Valley Road, Stewartstown, Pennsylvania, Jacob H. Linville, engineer, Keystone Bridge Company, Pittsburgh, builder.

38. **Atherton Bridge** (1870)
Bolton Road over Nashua River, Lancaster, Massachusetts, Simeon S. Post, engineer, J. H. Cofrode & Company, Philadelphia, builder.

39. **Elm Street Bridge** (1870)
Elm Street over Ottauquechee River, Woodstock, Vermont, Charles H. Parker, engineer, National Bridge & Iron Works, Boston, builder.

40. **(Lower) Rollstone Street Bridge** (1870)
Lower Rollstone Street, Fitchburg, Massachusetts, Charles H. Parker, engineer, National Bridge & Iron Works, Boston, builder.

41. **West Main Street Bridge** (1870)
West Main Street over South Branch Raritan River, Clinton, New Jersey, William and Charles Cowin, designers, Cowin Iron Works, Lambertville, builder.

42. **Monadnock Mills Bridge** (1870)
Workers' access to Monadnock Mills, Claremont, New Hampshire, Thomas W. H. Moseley, designer, Moseley Iron Building Works, Boston, builder.

43. **Watkins Glen Bridge** (c1870)
Park footpath over gorge, Watkins Glen State Park, New York, John L. Foreman, designer.

44. **Fairground Street Bridge** (c1870)
Fairground Street over Illinois Central Railroad, Vicksburg, Mississippi, Jacob H. Linville, engineer, Keystone Bridge Company, Pittsburgh, builder.

45. **Youngsville Airport Bridge** (c1870)
Airport Road over Brokenstraw Creek, Youngsville, Pennsylvania, Squire Whipple, engineer.

46. **Talcottville Bridge** (c1870)
Talcottville, New York, Squire Whipple, engineer.

47. **Vine Street Bridge** (c1870)
Vine Street over Central Vermont Railroad, Northfield, Vermont, Charles H. Parker, engineer, National Bridge & Iron Works, Boston, builder.

48. **Kessler Bridge** (c1870)
Unidentified road over South Platte River, Bailey, Colorado, Jacob H. Linville, engineer, Keystone Bridge Company, Pittsburgh, builder.

49. **Parker Truss Bridge** (187?)
St. Lawrence County, New York, Charles H. Parker, engineer, National Bridge & Iron Works, Boston, builder.

50. **Riverside Avenue Bridge** (1871)
Riverside Avenue over Northeast Corridor, Greenwich, Connecticut, Francis C. Lowthorp, engineer, Keystone Bridge Company, Pittsburgh, builder.

Surviving Cast- and Wrought-Iron Bridges in America

51. **Ponakin Bridge** (1871)
Ponakin Road over North Nashua River, Lancaster, Massachusetts, Simeon S. Post, engineer, Watson Manufacturing Company, Paterson, New Jersey, builder.

52. **North Village Bridge** (1871)
North Main Street over French River, Webster, Massachusetts, Charles H. Parker, engineer, National Bridge & Iron Works, Boston, builder.

53. **B&O Railroad: Bollman Truss Bridge** (1871)
Township Route 516 over Pittsburgh Branch, B&O (CSX), Meyersdale, Pennsylvania, Wendel Bollman, engineer, Patapsco Bridge & Iron Works, Baltimore, builder.

54. **Mead Avenue Bridge** (1871, 1937)
Mead Avenue over French Creek, Meadville, Crawford County, Pennsylvania, Penn Bridge Works, New Brighton, builder.

55. **Laymon Road Bridge** (1871, 1991)
J. W. Denver Williams Park, Wilmington, Ohio, Joseph Davenport, designer, Massillon Bridge Company, builder.

56. **Roderick Bridge** (1872)
Coshocton vicinity, Ohio, Squire Whipple, engineer, James W. Shipman, Coshocton Iron Works, builder.

57. **Pine Creek Park (Mill Hill Road) Bridge** (1872)
Over Pine Creek, Pine Creek Road to Old Dam Road, then north beyond park, Fairfield, Connecticut, Jacob H. Linville, engineer, Keystone Bridge Company, Pittsburgh, builder.

58. **County Engineer's Garage Bridge** (1872)
South Market Street over Beaver Creek, Lisbon, Ohio, Joseph Davenport, designer, Massillon Bridge Company, builder.

59. **Towpath Footbridge** (c1872)
Over Ohio & Erie Canal at Uppermost Triple Lock, Roscoe Village, Coshocton, Ohio.

60. **Falling Rock Camp Bridge** (c1872)
Newark vicinity, Ohio, similar to bridge by the Cleveland Bridge & Car Works, McNairy, Claflen & Company, proprietors.

61. **Tioronda Bridge** (1873)
South Avenue over Fishkill Creek, Beacon, New York, Glass, Schneider, and Rezner, designers, Ohio Bridge Company, Cleveland, builder.

62. **Sockman Road Bridge** (1873)
Sockman Road over Granny Creek, Fredericktown vicinity, Ohio, Joseph Davenport, designer, Russell Bridge Company, Massillon, builder.

63. **Howard (Kokosing River) Bridge** (1874)
Abandoned County Route 35 over Kokosing River, Howard, Ohio, David H. and Charles C. Morrison, designers, Columbia Bridge Works, Dayton, builder.

64. **Eureka Wrought-Iron Bowstring Arch-Rod Bridge** (c1874)
Moved to city park, Castalia, Iowa, William H. Allen and Oliver H. Perry, designers, Allen, McEvoy & Company, Beloit, Wisconsin, builder.

65. **Paint Creek Bridge** (c1875)
County Route 25W over Paint Creek, near Camden, Indiana, Joseph Davenport, designer, Massillon Bridge Company, Massillon, Ohio, builder.

66. **Burton Lane Bridge** (c1875)
Old Burton Lane (CR 189) over Indian Creek, Martinsville, Indiana, Joseph Davenport, designer, Massillon Bridge Company, Massillon, Ohio, builder.

67. **Lombard Street Bridge** (1877)
Stored at the Baltimore Streetcar Museum, Baltimore, Maryland, Jas. Curran, Baltimore Water Department, designer, Wendel Bollman, Patapsco Bridge & Iron Works, Baltimore, builder.

68. **Egypt Pike Bridge** (1877)
Pedestrian walk over Mud Run, New Holland, Ohio, Jonathan and Zimri Wall, designers, Champion Iron Bridge Company, Wilmington, Ohio, builder.

69. **White Bowstring Arch-Truss Bridge** (1877)
Cemetery Drive/Riverside Drive over Yellow Creek, Poland, Ohio, Glass, Schneider, and Rezner, designers, Wrought Iron Bridge Company, Canton, builder.

70. **Upper River Bridge** (1878)
River Street over Ausable River, Keeseville, New York, S. W. Murray, designer, Murray, Dougal & Company, Milton, Pennsylvania, builder.

71. **Hardin City Bridge** (1879)
Displayed alongside county road, Eldora vicinity, Iowa, Western Bridge Works, Fort Wayne, Indiana, builder.

72. **Tilton Island Park Bridge** (1881)
Pedestrian access to Tilton Island Park over Winnipesaukee River, Tilton, New Hampshire, Lucius Truesdell, designer, J. R. Smith, A. D. Briggs & Company, Springfield, Massachusetts, builder.

73. **Scarlets Mill Bridge** (1881)
Horse-Shoe Trail over abandoned Conrail (former Reading Railroad) right-of-way, Scarlets Mill, Pennsylvania, John L. Foreman, designer, Pottstown Shops, Reading Railroad, builder.

74. **Tank Farm Road Bridge** (1881)
Moved from Tank Farm Road over Conrail (former Reading Railroad) right-of-way, Macungie, Pennsylvania to Hugh Moore Historical Park and Museums, Easton, Pennsylvania, John L. Foreman, designer, Pottstown Shops, Reading Railroad, builder.

7

The designing of the Eads Bridge

John A. Kouwenhoven

When the Eads Bridge across the Mississippi River at St. Louis was completed in 1874 it was the largest and most important metal-arch structure ever built, and it still ranks as one of the world's great bridges.[1] Even before its completion it was internationally recognized as "the most highly developed type of bridge-building of the present day," in the design of which "the alliance between the theorist and the practical man is complete."[2] The history of its construction, written by Calvin M. Woodward, dean of the Polytechnic School of Washington University, is one of the classics of engineering literature.[3]

On opening day, July 4, 1874, the bridge was christened the Illinois and St. Louis Bridge; then, after the bankruptcy of the company that had completed it, it was for a time known formally as the St. Louis Bridge—the name Woodward used. But even while it was still under

JOHN A. KOUWENHOVEN has served as an advisory editor for *Technology and Culture* since the journal was founded. He dedicates this article in honor of Melvin Kranzberg.

[1] When the eminent bridge engineer David B. Steinman collaborated with Sara Ruth Watson on *Bridges and Their Builders* (New York, 1941), a historical narrative of bridge building from prehistoric times to the present, they devoted whole chapters only to the Eads Bridge, the Brooklyn Bridge, and the Firth of Forth Bridge. In Joseph Gies's *Bridges and Men* (Garden City, N. Y., 1963) only Eads and his bridge and the Roeblings and the Brooklyn Bridge get two chapters each.

[2] Editorial in *Engineering* (London) (October 10, 1873).

[3] C. M. Woodward, *A History of the St. Louis Bridge: Containing a Full Account of Every Step in Its Construction and Erection, and Including the Theory of the Ribbed Arch and the Tests of Materials* (St. Louis, 1881). All who have since written about Eads and his bridge, including Steinman, Watson, Gies, and a number of others, have depended almost entirely on Woodward for facts and conclusions relating to the technology, except Howard S. Miller, whose recent "Historical Appraisal" (in *The Eads Bridge*, Quinta Scott and Howard S. Miller [Columbia, Mo., and London, 1979]) provides fresh insights based on some fresh material. The manuscript records of the companies involved in building Eads Bridge were "lost" after Woodward used them. I found them in the 1950s (after fruitless searching elsewhere for several years) in a vault at the Terminal Railroad Association's headquarters in St. Louis and was allowed to make transcriptions and photostats (documents hereafter cited as TRRA files). Many of the records have since been turned over to the Missouri Historical Society for safekeeping and the original engineering drawings are now in the Washington University archives.

construction it was frequently called, as it is now officially named, the Eads Bridge, in recognition of the unique role of its chief engineer, James Buchanan Eads (1820–87). As his colleague W. Milnor Roberts said in the spring of 1869, Eads was "different in position from Chief Engineers in general, not merely from being the *projector* as well as the designer of the work, but because he [was] one of the largest owners, and one who [had] induced the subscriptions." After ten months' service as Eads's associate engineer, in full charge of operations while Eads was on sick leave, Roberts was well aware that, as he told Eads, "the Bridge, in its inception, in its plan, and in its noble battle against very fierce and extreme opposition, is eminently yours."[4]

Eads's position as chief engineer was different also in that he had no prior experience in bridge engineering, having spent his life hitherto chiefly in association with people who thought of bridges over navigable rivers as obstructions to commerce, not as desirable objects to build.[5] It is of interest, therefore, to try to determine in what sense he really was the "designer" of his bridge and how he became qualified to be its chief engineer.

So far as I have been able to discover, Eads first became interested in the problems of bridging the Mississippi in the spring of 1866, and his interest at that time was solely in making sure that if a bridge were built it would not be a serious obstacle to river traffic. He was then forty-six years old, and most of his adult life had been spent in enterprises concerned with river transportation. In 1839, as a young man of nineteen who had already demonstrated considerable mechanical and commercial aptitude, he had become what was known as a "mud clerk" (second clerk, under the clerk, or purser) on the fine steamboat *Knickerbocker,* whose Captain was E. W. Gould.[6] The *Knickerbocker* was in the Cincinnati-St. Louis-Galena trade. Less than a year after Eads

---

[4]Roberts to Eads, May 5, 1869, J. B. Eads Collection, Missouri Historical Society, St. Louis, Missouri. Roberts (1810–81) was one of the greatest and most admirable civil engineers of the 19th century and should be made the subject of a full biography. He was appointed Eads's associate engineer on July 9, 1868, and served until the end of April 1870. He made no contribution to the design, so far as I know.

[5]There is no adequate biography of Eads. Aside from a few biographical articles (those published in his lifetime are the most useful) and some obituaries, the only publications of consequence are a brief book by his grandson Louis How (*James B. Eads,* Riverside Biographical Series, no. 2 [Cambridge, Mass., 1900]) and Florence Dorsey's *Road to the Sea: The Story of James B. Eads and the Mississippi River* (New York, 1947), which is rather offhandedly documented and much given to romanticized imaginings. The most important of Eads's own writings are included in *Addresses and Papers of James B. Eads* (St. Louis, Mo., 1884), which were edited by his son-in-law Estill McHenry.

[6]Fifty years later Gould published his garrulous but invaluable chronicle *Fifty Years on the Mississippi; or Gould's History of River Navigation* (1889; reprint ed., Columbus, Ohio, 1951). For Eads's service on the *Knickerbocker* see pp. 483–85, 592–94.

joined her crew, the *Knickerbocker* was sunk by a snag near Cairo while laden with a large cargo of lead from the mines at Galena. The loss of this valuable cargo impressed Eads with the necessity for devising machinery that would facilitate salvage operations, and by 1841 he had designed the first of the diving-bell boats, or "submarines" as he called them, with which he built up the salvage and wrecking business that made him a wealthy man.[7]

Basically these submarines were adaptations of the double-hulled snag boats which Henry Miller Shreve had perfected in the 1820s and 1830s.[8] But Eads personally planned them, supervised construction, and designed much of the machinery with which they were equipped. Correspondence between Eads and his wife in the late 1840s and early 1850s is full of references to his work on the new submarines he was building,[9] and from these letters it is clear that Eads did more than suggest general ideas to be carried out by skilled professionals. In November 1850, for example, when Eads was in St. Louis designing a powerful centrifugal pump for use on *Submarine No. 4,* his wife, then at his parents' home near Le Claire, Iowa, wrote that she hoped he would not have to stay in town to superintend its construction and thus miss another Christmas with the family. Surely, she thought, his "minute drawings and directions" would be sufficient for the workmen who would make the pump.[10]

As Captain Gould said in his 1889 history of navigation on the Mississippi,[11] the crude and unwieldy diving-bell boats at first used in the salvaging business presented an open field for Eads's mechanical genius, "which soon resulted in improved boats, and machinery."

[7]James D. McCabe, Jr., "James B. Eads," in *Great Fortunes, and How They Were Made* (Philadelphia, New York, and Boston, 1871), pp. 211–12; How, pp. 9–20.

[8]Louis C. Hunter, *Steamboats on the Western Rivers* (Cambridge, Mass., 1949), pp. 193–94.

[9]Through the courtesy of James Eads Switzer, a grandson of Eads, I was permitted to make transcripts of the 213 letters in the correspondence between Eads and his first wife, Martha Dillon Eads, 1844–52.

[10]Martha Eads to Eads, November 22, 1850. The pump, like those Eads later used in constructing the foundation of the west abutment pier of his bridge (see James B. Eads, *Report of the Chief Engineer, October 1870* [St. Louis, 1870], p. 4) was a steam-powered centrifugal pump of the kind recently invented by James Stuart Gwynne and patented by him in 1851. Eads had acquired the sole right to use pumps of Gwynne's type "on the Mississippi and its tributaries," and his use of them on *Submarine No. 4* "inaugurated a new era in the business of wrecking on Western rivers" (Taylor and Crooks, *Sketch Book of St. Louis* [St. Louis, 1858], pp. 115–16). An illustrated paper about Gwynne's centrifugal pumps was published in the *Transactions of the American Institute . . . for the Year 1852* (Albany, N.Y., 1853), pp. 104–7. Gwynne exhibited them at the first world's fair, London, 1851 (see *Official Descriptive and Illustrated Catalogue of the Great Exhibition . . .* [London, 1851], 3:1441).

[11]See n. 3 above.

Within a few years Eads and his partner, William S. Nelson, had "an immense collection of working stock, of every improved construction, and every piece of it bore evidence of Capt. Eads' genius and master mind." The whole culminated in the construction of *Submarine No. 7*, which, Gould says, "for ingenuity of device, and concentration of mechanical power" excelled all predecessors and anything that had been constructed since.[12] Equipped with derricks, diving bells, and two Gwynne centrifugal pumps, she was capable of raising the largest steamboats.[13] A comparison of the accompanying 1858 lithograph of the *No. 7* (fig. 1) with the 1870 lithograph of the "Construction Works and Machinery" for sinking the caisson and laying the masonry of the east pier of Eads Bridge (fig. 2) suggests that Eads drew heavily on his earlier experience as a designer when he undertook the bridge job.

There had, of course, been new problems to face, among them the design of the travellers (the system of movable pulleys) by means of which the stones for the pier's masonry were lifted off barges tied alongside the construction boats and carried to the spot above the caisson where they were lowered for the masons to place in position. Eads had first experimented with the design of such travellers when his men were laying the foundations of his first pier, the west abutment, on the St. Louis levee early in 1868. As he said in his 1868 report, "the large framework and machinery" for laying stone, "designed to expedite the construction of the channel piers," was erected over the west abutment in order "to have the machinery fairly tested and its manipulation fully understood before using it on the piers, where so much depends on the celerity of operations."[14]

By the time he wrote those words (in May 1868) the machinery, driven by one engine, was capable of placing 500 tons of stone in position in a ten-hour day, and its performance gave "entire satisfaction." But there had been difficulties. In the diary of Benjamin Singleton, the engineer in charge of work on the levee, there is the following entry under date of February 28, 1868: "Have trouble with hoisting apparatus. Eads designed a traveller to be used in laying stone and made a mistake in putting a friction clutch on the hoist instead of on the traveller rope, and the friction clutch slips just where

[12]Gould, p. 486.

[13]Taylor and Crooks, pp. 116–17. In 1861–62 Eads converted this vessel into the ironclad gunboat *Benton*, which Admiral Mahan called "the most powerful fighting-machine" in Flag-Officer Foote's river squadron, of which she became the flagship. See A. T. Mahan, *The Gulf and Inland Waters* (New York, 1883), pp. 11–12; and *Official Records of the Union and Confederate Navies*, ser. 1, vol. 22 (Washington, 1908), pp. 773–77.

[14]Eads, *Addresses and Papers*, p. 510.

FIG. 1.—Steam-powered "Submarine" designed by Eads in 1856 to facilitate salvage operations (lithograph from Taylor and Crooks, *Sketch Book of St. Louis* [St. Louis, 1858]).

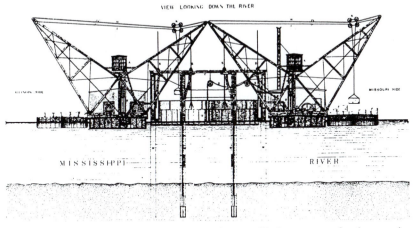

FIG. 2.—Eads's apparatus for sinking the caisson and laying masonry for the east pier (from C. M. Woodward, *A History of the St. Louis Bridge* [St. Louis, 1881]).

it is needed most to hold stone in proper place. I have urged him to let me change them, but his obstinacy knows no bounds. He will have his own way at whatever cost."[15]

I do not know how the problem of the slipping clutch was solved. Singleton may have been right in thinking Eads's original design of the traveller was faulty, or he and his men may simply not yet have learned how to control the mechanism properly. In any event, Singleton was not alone in thinking Eads was obstinate in his insistence upon his own designs; many who thought they knew more about bridge building than he did learned, as did Singleton, that he could be stubborn about having his own way. And usually, if not always, his own way was based upon firsthand knowledge of the conditions to be met and of the materials and methods required to meet them. If this meant going against precedent or against the opinion of recognized authorities, he stubbornly persisted.

But to return to Eads's career on the river before he became interested in bridge building: it was during his years of active participation in the wrecking business that he acquired the intimate firsthand knowledge of the action of the river's currents that caused him later to insist that the piers of his bridge should be founded on bedrock even though the nation's most eminent engineers had decided it was unnecessary. When, in the summer of 1867, Eads's bridge company was still being challenged by a rival group that claimed the exclusive right to build a bridge at St. Louis, the head of the rival group—a Chicago bridge contractor named Lucius B. Boomer—convened a board of civil engineers to consider Eads's plans. This Committee on Foundations and Piers included E. S. Chesbrough, constructor of the lake tunnel of the Chicago waterworks; William J. McAlpine and his brother Charles L. McAlpine, who had been associated in building a bridge over the Harlem River in New York, where they did pioneering work in employing the pneumatic process in sinking foundations; and William Sooy Smith, who had sunk the pneumatic foundations for the bridge across the Missouri at Omaha. The committee concluded that, since bedrock was so far below the river's bed, it was

[15]This diary, the original manuscript of which I have been unable to trace, is known to me only in the form of a mutilated clipping I found by chance, and transcribed, in the morgue of the *St. Louis Post-Dispatch* in October, 1956. (I was given access by courtesy of Donald Grant, then one of the paper's distinguished correspondents.) The clipping was undated and its source was not indicated. The heading, partly flaked away, was: DIARY [approximately thirteen letter spaces missing] GE, which I assume to have been DIARY OF THE BRIDGE. From its contents it is clear that the diary was that of Benjamin Singleton, whose supervision of the early work on the west abutment pier is mentioned in Eads's 1868 report, reprinted (without the important appendices) in Eads, *Addresses and Papers*, p. 510, and in Woodward, pp. 17 and 33.

altogether safe to build foundations which were "entirely in-dependent of any support to be gained from it." Piers carried down through the sand to a point below the limit of the current's scouring power, which they fixed at a maximum of 45 feet below low water, .could, they officially concluded, be safely supported by wooden or iron piles driven firmly into the sand.[16]

To Eads such a conclusion was absurd. He knew from personal experience that in time of flood the sand over bedrock was scoured to a depth much greater than 45 feet. As he later said in his first report as chief engineer, "I had occasion to examine the bottom of the Mississippi, below Cairo, during the flood of 1851, and at sixty-five feet below the surface I found the bed of the river, for at least three feet in depth, a moving mass, and so unstable that, in endeavoring to find footing on it beneath the bell, my feet penetrated through it until I could feel, though standing erect, the sand rushing past my hands, driven by a current apparently as rapid as that at the surface."[17]

But experience had also taught Eads that the deepest scour—perhaps even to bedrock itself—occurred not in flood time but during low water, in the winter when the river at St. Louis froze over with a crust of ice 10–15 inches thick. On two occasions in his years on the river he had undertaken to cut a channel in the ice through which he could remove from the gorged ice one of his diving-bell boats to a place of safety: "The surface ice being removed from the canal and hauled off on its sides, I found the quantity of submerged ice which continually arose, when that in sight was removed, was so great that the supply seemed inexhaustible."

Eads understood, then, that when the narrowed river at St. Louis was solidly frozen, "backing up," or raising, the water in the wide unclosed stretches above the city 10 or even 20 feet above its former level, the currents sweeping below the ice were greatly in-creased in force. Floating ice from the open stretches above the city was constantly being carried under the solid crust, forcing the accel-erated current to cut deeper into the sandy bed. "As rapidly as the latter is cut away," he wrote, "fresh supplies of ice are driven under, and thus the mass continues to grow in depth and the current to be directed nearer to the rock."[18]

Piers erected in the channel of the river would, he knew, facilitate

---

[16]See *Proceedings and Report of the Board of Civil Engineers Convened at St. Louis, in August, 1867* (St. Louis, 1867). These proceedings were summarized and discussed in Major G. K. Warren's *Report on Bridging the Mississippi River (Annual Report of the Chief of Engineers for 1878*, app. x3 [Washington, 1878]), pp. 1058–60.

[17]Eads, *Addresses and Papers*, pp. 490–97.

[18]Ibid., p. 498.

the formation of an ice gorge at the bridge in winter, and they would certainly tend to hold that gorge in place until the sand was scoured out around and between them "to an unknown depth." "For these reasons [he reported to the directors of the bridge company] I have maintained and urged that there is no safety short of resting the piers for your Bridge firmly upon the rock itself. On no other question involved in its construction does my judgment more fully assure me that I am correct. . . ."[19]

* * *

As I indicated earlier, I know of no evidence that Eads concerned himself with the problems of bridging the river at St. Louis before the spring of 1866. In 1865 a group of St. Louis men (Eads not among them) had acquired a charter from the state of Missouri and a supplementary charter from Illinois to build such a bridge, and in December of that year Senator Benjamin Gratz Brown of Missouri introduced a bill in the U.S. Senate authorizing its construction. Brown's bill was referred to the Committee on Post Offices and Post Roads, whose chairman reported it back to the full Senate in March 1866 with a substitute bill as an amendment. This bill provided that the bridge might be a pivot or other form of drawbridge or else one of continuous spans. If the latter, its bottom chord was to have an elevation not less than forty feet above the city directrix[20] and spans not less than 250 feet long or, if a drawbridge, not less than 100 feet on each side of the pivot.

Eads and his rivermen associates knew that a bridge with such low and narrow spans would materially interfere with navigation. His salvage firm, Eads and Nelson, had been involved in salvaging the cargo and hull of the *Effie Afton* after she collided with the piers of the first railroad bridge across the Mississippi—the ill-fated and badly designed drawbridge built at Rock Island by Lucius B. Boomer in

---

[19] Ibid., p. 499. From the very beginning, Eads had intended to go to the rock with his channel piers. That was part of his plan as reported in the St. Louis papers some weeks before Boomer's board of engineers convened (see, e.g., *St. Louis Democrat* [July 21, 1867]). However, he did not at first intend to carry his east abutment pier, on the East St. Louis shore, to bedrock. The cost of doing so would have been very great, and he believed a pile foundation could be adequately protected from the action of the current with rip-rap stone. But his complete success in founding the deepest of the two channel piers (the east pier) on rock determined him to do the same with the east abutment, "thus terminating forever all doubts as to the absolute stability of each one of the four great piers" (see his third report, October 1870 [*Addresses and Papers*, pp. 564–65]).

[20] A curbstone at the foot of Market Street indicating the "high water" of 1828, which was the datum plane for all city engineering in St. Louis.

1855–56.[21] And many steamboats and barges had been damaged on the piers of this and other bridges since that first memorable episode.

Thus it was that in April 1866, when the Senate was considering the substitute bill opposed by the rivermen, Eads became chairman of a committee appointed by the St. Louis Chamber of Commerce to consider what restrictions on bridge building "were really demanded by the marine interests" and what those interests could concede to "the requirements of land transportation in crossing the river [while preserving] a comparatively uninterrupted navigation." Eads, reporting for the committee at a meeting in the Merchants Exchange on April 18, proposed a resolution (adopted unanimously) that Congress should be asked to pass a general law requiring that all bridges crossing the river "shall have a clear height of fifty feet over the main channel, between the lowest part of the bridge and high water mark, measured in the center of the span." Further, that all bridges below the mouth of the Missouri (which of course included any bridge at St. Louis) "shall have one span of 600 feet or two spans of 450 feet each," and that no suspension bridge or drawbridge of any type should be permitted.[22]

The committee recommended those unusually long spans because Eads had assured them arches that long were entirely practicable, even though straight-chord trusses increased in weight so rapidly in proportion to length that their great cost made them virtually impracticable. "It was for this reason," Eads later said, "that in defining the height the words '*measured in the center of the span*' were inserted by this committee."[23]

Few if any experienced bridge engineers in 1866 would have so confidently assured the members of the committee that a 600-foot

---

[21]The suit brought against the bridge by the *Effie Afton*'s owners was a landmark case, in which Abraham Lincoln, one of the lawyers for the railroad, argued so impressively that the trial ended in a hung jury—in effect a victory for Chicago and the railroads over St. Louis and the rivermen. Eads's connection with the case came to light only in 1963 when the Davenport Public Museum acquired some letters revealing that Eads and Nelson's agent recovered the *Effie Afton*'s freight. See the *Davenport-Bettendorf Times-Democrat* (January 20, 1963); also G. K. Warren, pp. 1033–40; Albert J. Beveridge, *Abraham Lincoln* (Boston, 1928), pp. 598–605; and Lincoln's concluding address to the jury as reported in the *Chicago Daily Press* (September 24, 1857) and reprinted in *Collected Works of Abraham Lincoln*, ed. Roy P. Basler (New Brunswick, 1953), 2:415–22.

[22]*Missouri Republican* (April 19, 1866). The act of Congress authorizing a bridge at St. Louis, as finally passed and approved July 25, 1866, included the requirements Eads's committee had suggested as to the height of the spans but reduced the length by 100 feet, calling for one span of 500 feet or two of 350 feet (U.S. Congress, House, *Executive Document No. 194*, 43d Cong., 1st sess. [1866], p. 9).

[23]Eads, "Review of the U.S. Engineers' Report on the St. Louis Bridge," *Addresses and Papers*, p. 83.

544   *John A. Kouwenhoven*

arch was "entirely practicable." No bridge had ever been built anywhere of such long span, except a few suspension bridges, and Congress had forbidden suspension bridges at St. Louis.[24] To be sure,
Thomas Telford, the great Scottish engineer, had proposed a cast-
iron arch of 600-foot span back in 1801, but no arch actually constructed had spanned more than 400 feet, and no trusses even that
long had yet been erected. Work had begun on a truss bridge over the
Leck river at Kuilenburg (Culenborg) in Holland, whose main span
was to be almost 500 feet, but that was 100 feet less than Eads wanted
Congress to require for the main channel span at St. Louis, and many
experienced American bridge engineers doubted that even the
Kuilenburg bridge was practicable.[25]

Eads's confidence in the feasibility of 600-foot spans can be explained, I think, partly by his lack of practical acquaintance with
bridge engineering and partly by his considerable firsthand knowledge of the properties of iron and steel. The same civil engineers who
said in 1867 that it was unnecessary to go to bedrock to provide safe
foundations at St. Louis also asserted that there was "no engineering
precedent" for the 500-foot spans for which Congress finally settled
and which Eads (as they knew) had by that time determined to build.[26]
From the professional bridge engineer's point of view this was a simple statement of fact, as we have seen. But to Eads, whose ideas about
bridge building had not yet been trammeled by what practical bridge
engineers and contractors called "the custom of the trade," there were
ample precedents, including Telford's unrealized 600-foot arch. As
he said in his rebuttal to the 1867 report, surely Telford's assertion in
1801 that a cast iron arch of 600 feet was practicable furnished "some
'engineering precedent' to justify a span of 100 feet less in 1867."

> When we take into account [he continued] that the limit of the
> elastic strength of cast iron in compression is only about 8,000
> pounds to the square inch, and that in cast steel it is at least seven
> or eight times greater, and consider the advance that has been
> made in the knowledge of bridge building since the days of Tel-

[24]There was considerable distrust of suspension bridges at the time, despite the
success of Roebling's bridges at Niagara and Cincinnati. Many suspension bridges here
and in Europe had collapsed, including Charles Ellet's great bridge over the Ohio River
at Wheeling, whose main span was more than 1,000 feet long (see David B. Steinman,
The Builders of the Bridge [New York, 1945], pp. 170–73).

[25]Even in 1869, after the Kuilenburg bridge was completed, E. S. Chesbrough told
Major Warren that it had not been used long enough, in his opinion, to be pronounced
a "safe precedent," and William Sooy Smith still thought 500-foot spans were "barely
practicable. They may or may not prove permanently safe and reliable" (Warren, pp.
1070, 1072).

[26]Ibid., p. 1067.

ford, it is safe to assert that the project of throwing a single arch of cast steel, *two thousand feet* in length, over the Mississippi, is less bold in design, and fully as practicable, as his cast iron arch of 600 feet span.[27]

What mattered to Eads was not the precedent of some bridge already erected, whose plans need only be copied or modified. To him it was clear that where data on materials and workmanship in spans so great were not supplied by structures of equal magnitude, what was required was "such thorough acquaintance with the strength of materials as experience and experiment alone can furnish, together with a knowledge, obtained by careful study and observation, of the laws which guide us in the combination of these materials."[28]   By 1866 he had acquired considerable acquaintance with the strength of materials and knowledge of the laws governing their combination. Throughout the Civil War and since, he had been in close contact with men in the Naval Ordnance Bureau and Bureau of Steam Engineering who knew as much about the qualities of iron and steel as anyone in America. He had built a fleet of ironclad gunboats and seven double-turreted iron river monitors which played an important part in the Union campaign to open the Mississippi from Cairo to New Orleans and in Admiral Farragut's victory at Mobile Bay.[29] Hitherto overlooked sources give us a clearer notion than we have had of his substantive role in the design of these vessels and their armament.

In all this work, as in the later work on the bridge, he had expert professional assistance. One of the young civil engineers in his drafting room was George P. Herthel, Jr., a graduate of Rensselaer Polytechnic Institute who had also studied in Berlin and Carlsruhe Polytechnic schools.[30] But it was the naval constructor Edward Hartt whose assistance was most important to him in the early stages of the work, as he handsomely acknowledged some years later in a letter to Gustavus Vasa Fox, who had been assistant secretary of the navy when

[27]Eads, *Addresses and Papers,* p. 513.

[28]Ibid., p. 514.

[29]See Fletcher Pratt, *Civil War on Western Waters* (New York, 1956), pp. 14–23, 37, 129–30; and How (n. 5 above), pp. 22–41. As Pratt says, the turrets Eads designed for his river monitors later became the standard type on American warships. For Eads's controversy with John Ericsson over turret design see Eads's letters on the subject dated June 4, 1867, December 4, 1869, and January 29, 1870, in *Addresses and Papers,* pp. 467–80.

[30]See William H. Bryan, "The Engineers Club of St. Louis: Its History and Work," *Journal of the Association of Engineering Societies* (February 1900). pp. 161–62. Herthel later organized a patent agency which handled some of Eads's inventions, including the sand pump employed in the sinking of the piers for the bridge (see Letters Patent no. 105,056, July 5, 1870).

Eads was building his ironclads and monitors. "This gentleman [Hartt] you may remember was sent here as inspector of the hulls I built for the Gov't. They were iron and this was a novel matter with me. Hartt was so zealous in hurrying their construction that he frequently worked for days at a time in my drawing room making detail plans of various parts of the work and in this way greatly aided me and did labor I would have had to pay others, much less competent, for doing."[31]

As to Eads's role in developing the turrets for his monitors, we have a letter he wrote Assistant Secretary Fox on April 14, 1864, about the tests to which his turret on the monitor *Winnebago* had been submitted in the presence of Chief Engineer James W. King of the navy's Bureau of Steam Engineering. Eads was seriously ill at the time and confined to his house.

> It gives me great pleasure [Eads wrote] to inform you that Mr. King called to say to me yesterday that my steam turret had been thoroughly tested and was a most complete and triumphant success. He said he should write to you today and in a few days after make an official report of the whole thing.[32] He characterized the experiments he had made with it yesterday as being the most important made for many years in the Navy.
>
> It has been a matter of great regret to me that so much delay has occurred in bringing this matter to its present state of perfection and demonstration. Much of it has been owing to my ill health, but more to those difficulties which attend most of our workers in iron at the present time. Besides this there were in the machine itself so many objects to be attained, surrounded with difficult conditions, all of which had to be reconciled and so simplified as to admit of practical opperation [*sic*], that I found it required an amount of thought and time I had underestimated, and which will scarcely be credited in looking at the simplicity which it now presents. The vessel in which it was to be placed was so shallow as to necessitate the guns dropping on both sides of the vertical cylinder. This spread them wider apart than was desirable and left less room on the platform. The ports were to be strongly closed and quickly opened, and to be readily moved out of the way if their machinery were disabled. The guns to have great elevation and depression, and be moved out and in by machinery that should be operated by the engineer and yet be

[31] Eads to G. V. Fox, January 8, 1871, Fox Papers, New-York Historical Society, New York, N.Y. I am indebted to Ari Hoogenboom for calling my attention to these and other Eads letters in the Fox Papers.

[32] King's official "Report to the Navy Department of the Eads Steam Turret" was dated at Washington, April 30, 1864.

automatic. The platform likewise moving automatically so that it could not jam the guns by careless raising when loading, nor by sinking when they were in their ports if the engineer was confused; and yet to be entirely under his will at all other times— these and many other desirable ends were to be attained and the whole to be done by machinery of the simplest kind and least liable to derangement.

This labor is now over and cannot present itself again in any others that may be built.[33]

As to Eads's knowledge of the properties of steel, I do not know whether or not steel parts were employed in any of his turrets or gun carriages during the war, but the navy men with whom he worked may well have directed his attention to this relatively new material. Cannon were made and tested as early as July 1, 1861, of steel puddled in Troy, New York, and Trenton, New Jersey, and forged, bored, and rifled in New York City.[34] Henry Augustus Wise, a naval commander who joined the Naval Ordnance Bureau in 1862 and became its chief in 1864, had secretly investigated Krupp's manufacture of steel weapons.[35] And early in 1863 Assistant Secretary Fox was urging John Ericsson to get his associates in the *Monitor* project to build a Bessemer steel works.[36]

In the years after the war Eads continued to work on the design of naval turrets and the steam mechanism for handling heavy guns. There are records of tests of his steam gun carriage on the Hudson River in the spring of 1867 which were so satisfactory that ordnance bureau chief Wise (now Captain) wrote to inform Eads that the Department of the Navy was releasing him from "all pecuniary obligations concerning it."[37] It is quite probable, then, that when in 1866

[33]Eads to Fox, April 14, 1864, Fox Papers.

[34]*The New American Cyclopaedia,* ed. George Ripley and Charles A. Dana (New York, 1863), 15:76.

[35]Wise became acting chief in 1864 and was not officially chief until 1866 (see *Who Was Who in America: Historical Volume* [Chicago, 1963], p. 591).

[36]See Victor S. Clark, *History of Manufactures in the United States* (New York, 1929), 2:19.

[37]This letter, dated May 29, 1867, was found for me in 1958 by Mildred Mott Wedel in the National Archives, War Records Division, Old War Records Branch, Record Group 74, "Miscellaneous Letters, Navy Ordnance." Eads's achievements as a designer of naval armaments have been largely ignored. Further designs were described in a report he made to the secretary of the navy, February 22, 1868 (U.S. Congress, House, *Executive Document No. 327,* 40th Cong., 2d sess. [1868]), and in illustrated articles published in *Engineering* (London) (August 28 and September 4, 1868). A monitor turret was exhibited by the navy's ordnance bureau at the Centennial Exhibition, Philadelphia, 1876. It was equipped with two 15-inch guns, one mounted on Eads's carriage "by which it was run out and otherwise regulated by steam" and the other on

Eads told his fellow rivermen in the St. Louis Chamber of Commerce that 600-foot arches were entirely practicable, he based that statement on solid knowledge of the properties of iron and steel. But there is no evidence that he yet had any thought himself of designing a bridge at St. Louis or elsewhere. That idea did not, I think, occur to him until almost a year later.

*   *   *

Early in 1867 there were rumors in St. Louis that a group of men who had in 1865 procured a charter to build a bridge were about to sell out to people who did not want a bridge to be built. Eads presided at a meeting in the Merchants Exchange at which a committee was appointed "to obtain information with respect to legislation . . . upon the subject of bridging the Mississippi," and the man he appointed as chairman of that committee was Dr. William Taussig, a physician turned banker who had been an associate of his since gunboat days.[38]

At a meeting at the Exchange about a month later, with Eads again in the chair, Taussig read his report. It concluded by quoting a long, evasive letter from Judge John M. Krum, chairman of the group who controlled the charter, which ended with the assertion that "anyone who has sense enough to go from one house to another ought to know that the *corporators* of a chartered company cannot sell out, for they have nothing to sell."[39]

When Taussig sat down, Eads said he was sorry Judge Krum could not have attended the meeting, as there were some matters his letter did not fully explain. It was true, of course, that the corporators had no right to sell out a charter, but they might, Eads observed, "empower certain parties to open books and receive subscriptions, and create stockholders," and those stockholders *would* own the charter. "If the stock was subscribed by parties outside of St. Louis it might fall

---

an Ericsson carriage "worked by hand power, taking the united effort of four men to direct its movements" (see J. S. Ingram, *The Centennial Exhibition Described and Illustrated* [Philadelphia, 1876], p. 134; and Centennial Commission, *Official Catalogue, Department of Machinery* [Philadelphia, 1876], p. 69).

   [38]The reader will have to take this on faith. Documentation of Taussig's long association with Eads, dating back to 1849 or 1850, is in my possession but would occupy too much space here.

   [39]A detailed report of this February 16 meeting appeared in the *Republican* the next day. Incidentally, two years later Judge Krum demanded and got $6,500 for his share of the ownership of the charter in question (manuscript minutes of the July 9, 1869, meeting of the directors of the Illinois and St. Louis Bridge Co., TRAA files [n. 3 above]).

into the hands of the enemies of St. Louis," or of "parties who are opposed to the building of a bridge," in which case there might be a delay of many years before any bridge was built.

I am not sure, but I suspect that it was at this meeting, or just prior to it while Eads and Taussig were looking into the matter of the charter, that Eads determined to take the bridge project in hand. At all events, ten days later Eads and a group of his intimate friends and close business associates had subscribed for $300,000 worth of stock in the company holding the charter, and on March 23 Eads dominated a meeting of the stockholders at which his old and dear friend Charles K. Dickson was, on his motion, elected president and he himself designated engineer-in-chief. Soon afterward Taussig was appointed solicitor. By July 11, 1867, Eads had so far determined his plans that he was able to submit estimates of the cost of the bridge he proposed to build, its approaches, the tunnel that would be required under the streets of downtown St. Louis, and the property that would have to be condemned. His plans and estimates were approved, and he was authorized "to commence active operations" and "to open negotiations with some party, for the construction of the Bridge and approaches."[40]

There is no need to unravel here the long and complex corporate history of the company that built the bridge.[41] The point I want to establish for present purposes is that between mid-February and mid-July 1867 Eads had worked out plans for his bridge detailed enough to serve as the basis for cost estimates.

In the later stages of this initial planning he was ably assisted by Henry Flad, a German-born and German-trained civil engineer whom Eads selected as his chief assistant soon after the stockholders' meeting of March 23. Flad was forty-three in 1867 and had had considerable experience in railroad construction. Born near Heidel-

---

[40] See bound volume of manuscript records, "Charters and Proceedings, St. Louis and Illinois Bridge Co.," pp. 25, 26, 30, 39, TRRA files. The probable reason for Eads's unwonted desire that a bridge be built was that he had recently become interested in several railroad enterprises that were of interest also to the officers of the Pennsylvania Railroad. This aspect of Eads's career has been completely ignored by his biographers. The reader will find references to it in my article, "Eads Bridge: The Celebration," *Missouri Historical Society Bulletin* 30 (April 1974): 159–80 (republished in *The Eads Bridge*, catalog of an exhibition prepared by the Art Museum and the Department of Civil Engineering, Princeton University, 1974, pp. 48–73). Some particulars are given in my commentary on "Downtown St. Louis as James B. Eads Knew It . . . ," *Missouri Historical Society Bulletin* 30 (April 1977): 181–95 (esp. items 8, 13, 14, 23, 31, 46).

[41] It is told in Woodward, pp. 12–31, with the omission of important details too "hot" to publish while the participants were alive and without some material details that were unavailable to Woodward but have come to light since, as my notes, I trust, make clear.

berg, he was educated in civil engineering at the University of Munich, after which he worked for the Bavarian government on projects for the improvement of the river Rhine. During the revolution of 1848 he served in the Parliamentary army as captain of engineers; after the defeat of the Parliamentary forces he escaped to France and thence to the United States in the fall of 1849. He worked during the 1850s on construction of the western end of the Erie Railroad, then on the Ohio and Mississippi Railroad from Cincinnati to East St. Louis, and finally on the St. Louis and Iron Mountain Railroad from St. Louis south to the iron mines at Pilot Knob. During the Civil War he served with distinction as an engineer with the Union forces, building fortifications and rebuilding railroads, and was mustered out as a full colonel at the end of 1864. In the spring of 1865 he became chief assistant engineer of the St. Louis Board of Water Commissioners under James P. Kirkwood, the renowned builder of the Brooklyn waterworks who had been hired to design new waterworks for St. Louis.

Just when Eads first met Flad I am unable to say. In the memoir published after Flad's death in the *Transactions* of the American Society of Civil Engineers (of which Flad had been president in 1886–87) it is said that the two men met while Eads was engaged upon plans for gun carriages and turrets and Flad was assistant engineer under Kirkwood. The rooms then occupied by the water commissioners being larger than they needed, Eads had requested and been granted space in which to place a draftsman at work, and this was followed by frequent discussions between Eads and Flad on engineering matters "which led to mutual recognition of each other's abilities and laid the foundation of a life-long friendship."[42]

This dates their meeting sometime before March 1867, when Kirkwood relinquished his appointment and Flad became a member of the Board of Commissioners which hired Thomas Jefferson Whitman (Walt Whitman's brother) as Kirkwood's successor.[43] It may have been through George P. Herthel, the young draftsman who had worked for Eads in the gunboat days, that the meeting came about, since Herthel and Flad worked together in 1866 designing and erecting the first hydraulic elevators in St. Louis.[44] Herthel may well

[42]Robert Moore, Joseph P. Davis, and J. A. Ockerson, "Memoir of Henry Flad," *Transactions of the American Society of Civil Engineers* 42 (December 1899): 561–66. Davis (chief engineer of AT&T in the 1890s) had been Thomas Jefferson Whitman's assistant on the St. Louis waterworks in 1867–69 and was treasurer of the Engineers Club of St. Louis when it was founded in 1868 with Flad as president (see Bryan [n. 30 above]).

[43]M. L. Holman, "Water Works, City," in William Hyde and Howard L. Conard, *Encyclopedia of the History of St. Louis* (New York, 1899), 4:2471–72.

[44]Bryan (n. 30 above), pp. 161–62.

have been the draftsman for whom Eads found space in the water commissioners' office. At all events we know that as early as April 1867 Flad was engaged in surveys connected with the location of Eads's bridge.[45]

It is certain, I think, that Eads had formed tentative plans and had made the decision to use steel before he hired Flad to assist him. By the end of March he had publicly proposed plans for a double-decked bridge with three arched spans of steel, each approximately 500 feet long, with the railroad on the lower deck running into a tunnel under the city.[46] But these plans were still rudimentary when, in May and June, Eads corresponded with Jacob Hayes Linville, bridge engineer of the Pennsylvania Railroad, whose empire-building vice-president, Tom Scott, was a director of Eads's company. Eads had shown a very rough "sketch" of his proposed bridge to Linville when he was in Philadelphia in late April or early May. On June 3 he sent Linville tracings of the drawings then on hand. These, he indicated in a letter dated three weeks later, "had no dimensions of parts on them, and exhibited no completed system of bracing, neither horizontal, vertical or transverse. Nothing in fact but a method of bracing between the four arched ribs, and the struts and tension rods shown between the arches and the top member, the position, number and size of which had not been determined nor the counter bracing shown." The depth and form of the braced arch ribs had not yet been determined, but the ribs themselves consisted "of four rectangular bars of steel of large section, apparently about four by six inches."[47]

However, as Eads told Linville in his letter of June 24, he had been "for some time considering upon the propriety of substituting a ribbed arch in the place of the braced arch shown on the plan I sent you."

[45]The manuscript ledger of the St. Louis and Illinois Bridge Co. records payment to Flad of $41.60 "for surveying" on April 15, 1867, the same day that $400 was paid to R. B. Lewis, whom Eads described in his 1868 report as "a gentleman of great experience and high reputation as a locating engineer, and for many years in the service of the Pennsylvania Railroad" (Eads, *Addresses and Papers*, p. 482).

[46]These plans are mentioned in a letter written on April 4, 1867, by Isaac Sturgeon, president of the North Missouri Railroad, published in a pamphlet entitled *Alton & St. Charles County and the St. Louis & Madison County Bridge Companies Consolidated* (n.p., n.d.). A copy was bound into a volume of pamphlets relating to Eads Bridge that belonged to Henry Flad and was loaned to me by his granddaughter, Mrs. Towner Deane of St. Louis. Eads's 500-foot spans conformed to the requirements of the law Congress had finally passed July 25, 1866 (U.S. Congress [n. 22 above]). By using three such spans he was able to bridge the 1,500-foot river with only two piers standing in the stream to interfere with navigation.

[47]The name of the Pennsylvania's vice-president, Thomas Alexander Scott, is not in Woodward's index and appears but once in the text (p. 15), without mention of his connection with the railroad. The first quotation is Eads to Linville, June 24, 1867; the other is Linville to Eads, June 13, 1867 (TRRA files [n. 3 above]).

In the longest span [515 feet] it would be about 8 feet wide, composed of an upper and lower rectangular steel rib retained in their relative positions by a system of diagonals between them, somewhat after the plan of the bridge at Coblentz on the Rhine. It would not be deep enough to prevent some tension on the lower member, nor so deep as to create much strain from excessive temperature in the upper one. It would be supported on a central pivot or joint at each pier, as in the Coblentz bridge, but on a better method.

The reference to the Coblentz (Koblenz) bridge in connection with the change of plans Eads was considering is especially interesting because a long illustrated article about that bridge had been published more than two weeks earlier in *Engineering* (London), a paper Eads knew well.[48] The bridge had been completed in 1864, but was currently in the news because the drawings for it were then on display at the Paris Universal Exhibition. *Engineering* called it "one of the finest and most interesting structures of its kind in Europe," which "in beauty of appearance . . . is equal to any modern railway bridge in existence" (see fig. 3). Eads must surely have noted that comment, for he had persistently asserted in his correspondence with Linville that he chose the arch form because it would be "more commodious and attractive" than any truss bridge, and that "strength with durability, and beauty with economy" could best be achieved by that form.

FIG. 3.—The Coblentz (Koblenz) railway bridge, with structural details (wood engraving from *Engineering* [London] [June 7, 1867], facing p. 586).

[48]*Engineering* (London) (June 7, 1867), p. 586.

By the end of July, when large drawings of his bridge were on display at the Merchants Exchange, it was widely publicized that Eads had chosen a style "somewhat similar to" or "resembling" the Koblenz bridge, but with an upper highway deck and a lower deck for a double-track railroad instead of the single railway deck at Koblenz, and with much longer spans.[49] Essentially this was the design Eads would present ten months later in his first published report as chief engineer. Of the three spans the center one would be 515 feet long and the other two 497 feet. Each span would be formed of four ribbed arches of cast steel, having a rise of about one-tenth of the span, and each ribbed arch would consist of "two ribs placed seven feet apart, one above the other, and strongly braced between with diagonal steel braces." Though the upper and lower steel ribs were now only 7 feet apart, instead of 8 as when Eads wrote to Linville on June 24, they were still, I assume, rectangular in section; as late as November 1867 Eads was still looking for manufacturers capable of making steel bars 28 feet long of 3- by 6-inch section.[50]

By that time Eads had added to his engineering staff a young German-trained assistant named Charles (Karl) Pfeifer. Pfeifer had come to America early in 1867, at the age of twenty-four, with excellent training in engineering and mathematics and had settled among the Germans in St. Louis. It was presumably through Henry Flad that

[49]See the articles about Eads's plans published in the St. Louis and out-of-town papers at this time. The *Democrat*'s article of July 21, 1867, was quoted at length in the *Chicago Tribune* of July 23, and the *Republican*'s of August 5 was reprinted entire in the *East St. Louis Gazette* of August 8. It is not, I think, just to say as Miller (n. 3 above) does that Eads downplayed the influence of the Koblenz bridge on his design "until his own bridge was almost completed" (p. 90).

[50]In early November 1867, the general manager of Park Bros. & Co.'s Black Diamond Steel Works in Pittsburgh told J. Edgar Thomson, president of the Pennsylvania Railroad, that he had no facilities for making bars of the size Eads had named (3 by 6 inches, 28 feet long) and that "an entire new mill, foundations, Engines, Steam Cranes & c would be necessary before they could touch the order" (Andrew Carnegie to Eads, November 9, 1867). Carnegie, who had resigned as superintendent of the Pennsylvania's Pittsburgh division in March 1865, had since been headquartered in Pittsburgh to oversee some of Thomson's and Thomas A. Scott's investments in various enterprises, including the Keystone Bridge Co., and was soon to take charge of their investment in the bonds of Eads's bridge company. His press copy of his letter to Eads is among the Carnegie Papers in the archives of the United States Steel Corporation, Pittsburgh. After many years of unsuccessful attempts to get access to these papers I had the good fortune to enlist the aid of the late George Ketchum, a highly respected citizen of Pittsburgh, well known to the officers of U.S. Steel. Through his intervention I received permission in 1973 from the secretary of the corporation to go through all Carnegie's letter books and other papers of the years involved in the building of Eads Bridge and to transcribe, and in some instances make photocopies of, those relating to the building and financing of the bridge. There are hundreds of them, a few of which were used (and occasionally misapprehended) by Joseph Frazier Wall in *Andrew Carnegie* (New York, 1970).

he came to Eads's attention. He was appointed assistant engineer on August 19, 1867, and thereafter worked closely with Flad on the mathematical investigations and calculations for the bridge.[51] As Eads said in his 1868 report, several months of patient labor were spent by Flad and Pfeifer "in investigation of the arch with spandrel bracings, the ribbed arch with pivoted ends (as in the Coblentz bridge), and with fixed ends, and of various depths." But so far as I have been able to discover Pfeifer played no part in the designing of the bridge aside from his extremely sophisticated mathematical computations of the necessary dimensions of its constituent parts—dimensions which Eads sometimes disregarded, as we shall see.[52]

I have not ascertained when or how Eads decided to abandon the rectangular ribs and adopt instead the tubular form described in his first report. It must have been after early November 1867 and before the end of April 1868 when he sent "plans in detail and data for computation" to Julius W. Adams, vice-president (and later president) of the American Society of Civil Engineers, who was soon to serve on the board of consulting engineers convened by John A. Roebling to pass upon his plans for the Brooklyn Bridge.[53] The plans sent to Adams were substantially those Eads published in his first report, which was dated June 1, 1868 (though much of it had appeared in the newspapers in May), and which specified that the upper and lower ribs of the arches (now again spaced 8 feet apart) would consist of "two parallel steel tubes, nine inches in diameter, placed side by side."[54]

[51]The date of Pfeifer's first employment on the bridge comes from Singleton's diary (n. 15 above).

[52]For a full discussion of Pfeifer's and Flad's computations and how they led to Eads's decision to use the ribbed arch with fixed ends rather than the arch pivoted at the ends as at Koblenz, see Woodward, chap. 26. See also Charles Pfeifer, "The Theory of Ribbed Arches," *VanNorstrands Eclectic Engineering Magazine* (June 1876). Most of what I know about Pfeifer comes from his granddaughter Katherine Pfeifer Chambers of Overland, Missouri, with whom I corresponded in 1957. The rest comes from Woodward (who frequently mentions his work as a supervisory engineer during the construction of the bridge piers); the manuscript records of the bridge company; and an obituary in the *St. Louis Globe-Democrat* (February 18, 1883).

[53]Steinman (n. 24 above), pp. 316–17, and David McCullough, *The Great Bridge* (New York, 1972), pp. 21–23. Eads sent the plans and data to Adams on April 29, 1868, with the request that Adams carefully examine them in detail and judge if they were "entirely safe, practicable and judicious," as we learn from Adams's twelve-page reply, dated June 4, 1858, which is among the bridge company records in the TRRA files (n. 3 above). Adams had been listed as a member of the board of engineers assembled by Lucius Boomer, whose *Report* (n. 16 above) was artfully modulated to produce the impression that Eads's plan to build 500-foot arches was impracticable. But Adams "took no part [in the deliberation of the convention], not having been present," as he later told Major G. K. Warren (Warren, pp. 1067–68).

[54]Eads, *Addresses and Papers,* p. 505.

The only testimony we have as to who should be credited with these tubular arched ribs comes from Carl Gayler, another German-trained civil engineer, who worked in Eads's drafting room under the chief draftsman, William Rehberg. Gayler did not enter the employ of the bridge company until 1869 or 1870, at least a year after the decision to use tubes had been made, and his comments on the subject were not made until many years later, when he was the sole survivor of Eads's engineering staff.[55] But he would have been unlikely to underestimate the contributions of his fellow Germans on the staff.

Writing in 1909 Gayler said that "an unprecedented amount of labor and time" had been spent in merely proportioning the bridge, and that "this proportioning, this designing of our bridge, was the exclusive work of Jas. B. Eads."[56] And twenty years later, at a banquet given in his honor by the Engineers Club of St. Louis, he gave specific instances of the ways in which Eads dominated the design process. He recollected well, for instance, how Carl Pfeifer (Gayler's brother-in-law) "had made a sketch of what he considered a proper cross-section for the chords of the arches, all in the European style: plates and angles riveted together" and how Eads promptly vetoed it. "Tubes, safely enveloped, had been one of his earliest conceptions," Gayler said. "Eads just loved this part of the work and all the minutest details of the tubes with their couplings and pin connections, the skewbacks and anchor bolts, all of it to the last ⅛ of an inch are the work of Eads, of course always subject to Pfeifer's established effective areas."[57]

John A. Roebling, whose suspension spans at Niagara and Cincinnati had won him international recognition and whose plans for the Brooklyn Bridge had recently been accepted, had expressed the belief that the best form in which to employ iron for upright arch bridges was the cylindrical. "I venture to predict," he had said, "that the two great rival systems of future bridge engineering will be the inverted and upright arch—the former made of wire, and the latter of pipe, both systems rendered stable by the assistance of lattice work, or by stays, trusses and girders." But Roebling thought it worthy of notice

---

[55] Gayler's obituary in the *St. Louis Globe-Democrat* (September 3, 1933) says he was born in Stuttgart in 1850 and came to the United States in 1870, but an article about him in the *Post-Dispatch* (February 27, 1927) says he was employed by the bridge company "from the summer of 1869 . . . until the completion of the bridge, five years later." Company records for 1874 indicate that Gayler was a draftsman in the engineering office on a salary of $125 per month. For an example of his work see pl. 2, "Section of East Pier and Caisson," in Eads, *Report of the Chief Engineer, October, 1870* (St. Louis, 1870).

[56] Carl Gayler, "Bridge Designing," *Journal of the Association of Engineering Societies* 40, no. 3 (March 1909): 114.

[57] Carl Gayler, speech prepared for an Engineers Club banquet, typescript dated January 28, 1929, Gayler Papers, Missouri Historical Society.

"as a curious professional circumstance" that iron cylinders had "never been used in arching, although proposed on several occasions."[58]

Actually they had been used, by a man well known to Eads, in a bridge that may have suggested to him not only the tubular form for his ribs but also the novel method by which he built up the tubes. It has been pointed out before that Eads may have been influenced by the "water-pipe bridge" constructed in 1858 as part of the Washington, D.C., aqueduct by Captain Montgomery C. Meigs of the army engineers.[59] It was Meigs, then quartermaster general, who in 1861 had given Eads the contract to build the first of his ironclad gunboats, and it is entirely possible that Eads saw Meigs's pipe bridge on one of his many visits to Washington. But whether or not he had ever seen the bridge, he must surely have seen the article about it, and the drawings of it, published in *Engineering* (London) May 3, 1867, while he and Flad were working on their earliest designs. As shown in figure 4, Meigs's 200-foot span was supported by two arched tubes, each composed of seventeen straight lengths of cast-iron pipe. This pipe, 4 feet in diameter, was made in 12-foot pieces with flanged, slanted ends which when bolted together intersected on a plane parallel to a radius of the ideal circle of which the arch was a segment. Through these arched tubes, supporting the roadway, the water of the aqueduct flowed.

As I have said, Meigs's bridge may have reminded Eads of the advantages of the hollow cylinder as a strucural form; in any event we know that he investigated the possibility of using steel pipe for his arches. In his first report he referred to the fact that cast-steel tubes had been "recently drawn cold by hydrostatic pressure in France, from steel expressly prepared for the purpose," but he had found that the process had not been carried "to any extent beyond the production of gun barrels." To avail himself of the advantages of the tubular form of construction he had therefore proposed "to have the steel rolled for the arches in bars of nine feet length, and of such form that ten of them shall fill the circumference of a nine-inch lap-welded tube 1 inch thick, in the manner that the staves of a barrel fill the hoops."[60]

[58]Quoted in L. U. Reavis, *Saint Louis: The Future Great City of the World* (St. Louis, 1870), p. 104.

[59]See, e.g., David P. Billington, *Structures and the Urban Environment* (Princeton, 1978), p. 31, n. 8. An earlier iron-tube bridge had been erected at Brownsville, Pa., in 1836, but I have no reason to think Eads (or Meigs, for that matter) knew of it (see Carl Condit, *American Building Art* [New York, 1960], pp. 184, 320).

[60]Eads, first report, *Addresses and Papers*, pp. 527–28.

In the course of design changes during the next two years the dimensions and details of Eads's tubes were altered considerably, but the idea of using staves enveloped in an encircling steel hoop remained constant. And that idea may, it seems to me, have been suggested by the fact that, as originally built, Meigs's cast iron pipes had been "lined with staves of resinous pine, 3 in. thick, to prevent the freezing of the water." This pine-stave lining had later been removed—because it was unnecessary and because the bridge was much less affected by temperature changes when the water was allowed to flow in contact with the metal of the pipes—yet the mention of it in *Engineering* may well have been what suggested to Eads the possibility of forming his steel tubes as he did.[61]

As indicated earlier, the design of the bridge in May 1868 specified that the upper and lower ribs of the arches would each consist of two such tubes, 9 inches in diameter. By February 1870 (when a contract for the construction and erection of the superstructure was made with the Keystone Bridge Co. of Pittsburgh) Eads had substituted a single tube 13 inches in diameter for the two smaller tubes.[62] A few months

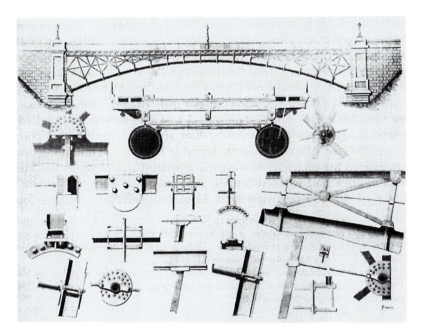

Fig. 4.—Montgomery C. Meigs's "water-pipe bridge," Washington Aqueduct (from *Engineering* [London] [May 3, 1867], p. 447).

[61]"Water-Pipe Bridge, Washington Aqueduct," *Engineering* (London) (May 3, 1867), p. 448.

[62]Woodward, p. 67.

later the diameter of the tubes was increased to 16 inches, and finally, toward the end of 1870 or early in 1871, the 18-inch tubes actually used in the bridge had been adopted.[63] And by this time the number of staves composing the tubes had been decreased from ten to six, while their length had been increased from 9 feet to approximately 12.[64]

Such changes obviously required, and were interdependent with, changes in all the subsidiary elements of the great spans. In renegotiating his contract with Keystone in February 1871, Eads had to discuss changes in forty-six separate categories, one of which (the ninth in the numbered sequence) was concerned with the extra compensation Keystone was entitled to "by reason of increased diameter of the tubes from 16″ to 18″, the introduction of stay bolts, the substituting of steel for iron in the enveloping tubes and laps, the wrot [sic] iron bands at the ends of the tubes, and the change of 'grooves' instead of 'screws' for the coupling joint and increased cost of turning off the corrugation of channel bars."[65]

Though there is no reason to question Carl Gayler's assertion that Eads was personally responsible for designing "the minutest details of the tubes with their couplings," this does not mean that Eads made detailed engineering drawings of any parts of the bridge or of the machines and devices used in building it. Like many great engineers he could not draw very skillfully, though he communicated his ideas to his draftsmen in crude sketches.[66] What those sketches were like is suggested by figure 5, showing the only drawing by Eads that is known to exist. It is scrawled on the back of a memorandum, in Eads's handwriting, of the agreement he had arrived at with James Harrison, a director of Boomer's rival bridge company, containing their suggestions for amicably settling the disputed rights of the two companies. They had worked out the agreement in Washington late in January 1868 and returned to St. Louis together.[67] During the jour-

---

[63]See the "memoranda" of a conference between Eads and G. B. Allen of the bridge company and two representatives of the Keystone Bridge Co., St. Louis, February 6, 1871, in the minutes of a special meeting of the directors of the bridge company February 13, 1871, TRRA files (n. 3 above).

[64]The length depended on whether the tube was to be used in the upper or lower member of one of the ribbed arches of the center span or in the upper or lower member of a side span (Woodward, pl. 29).

[65]See n. 63 above.

[66]George Stephenson, who designed every detail of the Liverpool and Manchester Railway in 1825–30—locomotives, bridges, tunnels, roadbed, and track—made none of the working drawings for these things. They were made by his principal draftsman, Thomas Gooch, who got his instructions from Stephenson either by word of mouth or what he called "little, rough hand sketches on letter paper" (see Samuel Smiles, *The Life of George Stephenson* . . . [New York, 1868], p. 295).

[67]See the *Democrat's* report, January 30, 1868, that they were returning together after

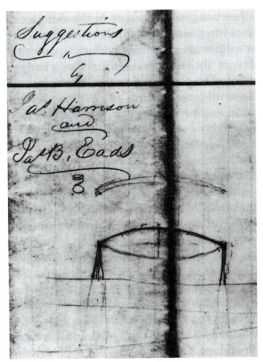

FIG. 5.—The only known example of a drawing by Eads. The sketch is of an upright arch and a suspended arch between piers extending down to sloping bedrock. The curved lines just below Eads's signature probably represent the upper and lower ribs of the ribbed arch.

ney, as I suppose, Eads was explaining to Harrison why he was convinced that an upright arch bridge could be constructed out of the almost untried metal, steel, even more economically than a suspension bridge, then regarded as the most economical form for long spans—giving the same reasons he presented a few months later in a long section of his first report, "Suspension and Upright Arch Bridges."[68] At any rate this crude sketch or one much like it was probably the basis of the figure numbered 11 in that section of the report.[69]

arranging a settlement. Harrison was the iron expert in the St. Louis firm of Chouteau, Harrison, & Valle, which in 1865 had become partners in the Kelly Process Co., at whose experimental works in Wyandotte, Mich., the first "Bessemer" steel in America was made in the fall of 1864 (see "Iron Making in Pennsylvania," in *Pennsylvania and the Centennial Exposition* [Philadelphia, 1878], 1, pt. 2: 56–58). Here is another possible source of Eads's knowledge of steel.

[68]Eads, *Addresses and Papers,* pp. 519–27. It is worth noting that at this time the British Board of Trade forbade the use of steel in bridges. Not until three years after Eads Bridge was completed was the ban removed (see H. Shirley Smith, *The World's Great Bridges* [New York, 1953], pp. 76, 85).

[69]Eads, *Addresses and Papers,* p. 522.

A number of the changes Eads made in the design of the tubes, as in the design of less important structural members, were suggested by the mechanics or engineers associated with companies that fabricated the various parts of the superstructure. The change from screw threads to grooves in the coupling joints of the tubular ribs was, as I recently discovered, the suggestion of William Sellers, the distinguished mechanical engineer who was president of the Franklin Institute from 1864 to 1867 and who, it now appears, was one of the principal owners of the Wm. Butcher Steel Works in Philadelphia, the recently established firm to which Keystone awarded the subcontract for most of the steel used in the bridge. In a letter written the day before the Eads company signed the contract with Keystone, Andrew Carnegie told Eads that "Mr. Sellers [on behalf of Butcher] made us a bid for the steel tubes complete, provided you accepted some changes in mode of constructing—He has a plan which avoids screws altogether & cast iron also which he says will save considerably in material (as you of course lose in cutting threads) & make a better job—But it increases Cost per lb."[70]

Sellers's connection with the Butcher Works, and with the great Philadelphia banking house of E. W. Clark and Company—which gave an urgently needed loan of $250,000 to Eads's bridge company only on condition that President Thomson and Vice-President Scott of the Pennsylvania Railroad (and their agent Carnegie) see to it that Butcher got the steel contract—has not hitherto been made known. Nor did the officers of Eads's company know of the connection. When Carnegie was in New York on March 7, 1870, about to embark for England to negotiate the sale of $2.5 million of the Eads company's first mortgage bonds, which he and Thomson and Scott had "taken" at 90 percent of face value, he telegraphed E. W. Clark and Company, begging them not to inform the treasurer of Eads's company "about our confidential efforts to throw the steel contract your way. . . . no one knows about it in St. Louis and no one should know."[71]

[70]Carnegie to Eads, February 25, 1870, Carnegie Papers. The awesome difficulties the Butcher Works encountered in fabricating the grooved steel couplings Eads designed in response to Sellers's suggestion are recounted at length in Woodward, pp. 122–56.

[71]I should mention that at the end of William Sellers's term as president of the Franklin Institute, the institute's *Journal* published a "puff" about the steel works and its general superintendent, William Butcher (*Journal of the Franklin Institute* 54 [November 1867]: 293–94). The active partners, apparently, where Samuel Huston, president, and Sellers, who had "no more regard for [Butcher's] opinion, or his promises than if he were totally unknown to them" (Carnegie to Eads, October 18, 1870). But E. C. Clark of E. W. Clark & Co. was also a partner (Carnegie to William Butcher, September 15, 1870). On October 1, 1871, Butcher was replaced by William F. Durfee, who had been superintendent of the Kelly Process Co.'s experimental works (see "Iron Making in Pennsylvania") where he established "the first analytical laboratory built as

At any rate, Eads's readiness "to receive suggestions and advice upon the details, methods of construction &c" had been well known to Carnegie and the officers of the Keystone Company from the beginning. More than six months before Keystone took the contract to erect the superstructure, Carnegie had told Jacob Linville that Eads wanted "the suggestions of practical men like [John L.] Piper [Keystone's general manager] . . . and is disposed to do anything reasonable upon questions of detail."[72] And when Keystone complained, after almost a year of work under the contract, that Eads had not yet provided all the working drawings, Dr. Taussig, chairman of the bridge company's executive committee, reminded them that Eads had made many changes "in accordance with the suggestions and views of your Engineers" and that "the calculations, drawings, tests etc. required for these changes necessarily consume time."[73]

Changes resulting from the awarding of the steel contract to the Butcher Works, under pressure from Thomson and Scott (and Scott's "little white-haired Scotch devil," as Carnegie had been proud to be called a few years earlier),[74] were the cause of enormously costly delays. As Howard S. Miller has recently pointed out in the only study of Eads Bridge to add significantly to what was embodied in Woodward's classic study, the Butcher Works failed repeatedly to make the anchor bolts and staves which were the principal steel members of the bridge, and it was only after Eads arranged to have Butcher licensed to make chrome steel under Julius Bauer's 1865 patent that suitable bolts and staves were produced. As Miller also points out, the story of Eads's decision to use chrome steel was confusing at the time and has grown even more confusing since. From the data available to him Miller concluded that, far from being a bold innovator in employing structural alloy steel, Eads was at most "a metallurgical pioneer by default." Chrome steel was, Miller thinks, Eads's "second choice, an unknown material that looked promising only after carbon steel had made such a poor showing" (i.e., in early August 1871) and about which he knew little except what came from "the company's advertising circulars."[75]

The data I have assembled do not support those conclusions. They

---

an adjunct to steel works" in this country, and who in 1869, at the American Silver Steel Co. in Bridgeport, made the first successful application in the United States of the newly invented Siemens reverberatory-regenerative furnace to the puddling of iron (see *Appleton's Cyclopedia of American Biography* [New York, 1892], 2:271). In June 1873, after the bankruptcy and reorganization of the Butcher Works, Sellers became the president.

[72]Carnegie to Piper, June 14, 1869, and Carnegie to Linville, June 19, 1869, Carnegie Papers.

[73]William Taussig to Carnegie, January 7, 1871, Carnegie Papers.

[74]Carnegie, *Autobiography* (Boston and New York, 1920), p. 72.

[75]Scott and Miller (n. 3 above), pp. 110–13, 115.

562   *John A. Kouwenhoven*

indicate that Eads knew a good deal about chrome steel. He had
furnished thirty-two samples of it to David Kirkaldy, the pioneer of
steel testing in Great Britain, in 1868.[76] He had tried to interest Tom
Scott of the Pennsylvania Railroad in investing in the chrome steel
process early in 1869 and had himself, I am reasonably sure, been an
investor in the Chrome Steel Works in Brooklyn (which had been set
up by the American Tool Steel Company, of which Bauer was the
chemist).[77] He had provided Kirkaldy with more samples to test on
April 7, 1869, at about the same time that he arranged to have Henry
Flad and his old friend James W. King (now a commodore) of the
navy's Bureau of Steam Engineering spend forty-eight hours in the
closest inspection of the works, on Eads's personal pledge "that Mr.
Haughian's [the superintendent] trade secrets should not be revealed."[78] And he had, at a meeting of the directors of his bridge
company on May 12, 1869, presented a "memorandum of agreement" he had worked out with the American Tool Steel Company (of
which the Brooklyn Chrome Steel Works was an offshoot), which
induced the board of directors to pass a resolution that it preferred
"to contract with the American Tool Steel Co. for Twelve hundred
tons of steel with the privilege of all the steel they may require in the
construction of their bridge; provided the material furnished be of
first class quality, and the price not greater than that charged by any
other manufacturer for a similar article."[79]

It seems likely that Eads's attention had first been directed to

[76]Eads to William M. McPherson, president of the bridge company, February 12,
1872, quoted in Woodward, p. 116.

[77]Scott, when considering this investment, had asked Carnegie to find out, in
Pittsburgh, what the pioneer steel maker William Coleman thought about the process.
Later he had his private secretary, R. D. Barclay, instruct Carnegie to visit the Chrome
Steel Works and report on the plant, equipment, and personnel. Carnegie wrote to
Scott about Coleman's opinion (he was skeptical) on March 8, 1869, and sent his report
to Barclay on March 29, 1869. Though "not pretending to know about the Steel
Manfr," Carnegie reported that "the Steel I saw every where, looked well, I examined
bars at every part of the shops & believe they are making a good steel. . . ."

[78]Flad and King "weighed out the proper mixtures, placed them in the crucibles,
melted them, cast the ingots, and had the steel finished by the hammer," after which
they made "an elaborate and confidential report" to Eads (see Eads's October 1, 1871,
report in *Addresses and Papers*, p. 593).

[79]Manuscript minutes of the directors' meeting (see n. 3 above). The Chrome Steel
Works were described in an article, "Chrome Steel," *Iron Age* (January 19, 1871), pp.
1–2. See also L. P. Brockett, "The Manufacturing Interests of Brooklyn and Kings
County," in *The Civil, Political, Professional and Ecclessiastical History and Commercial and
Industrial Record of the County of Kings and the City of Brooklyn*, ed. Henry R. Stiles (New
York, 1884), 2:697–98; and *Half Century's Progress of the City of Brooklyn* (New York,
1886), p. 127. Much work remains to be done on the history of chrome steel and the
people and companies involved in it.

chrome steel by the naval engineers with whom he worked so closely during the war and after—perhaps by Captain Wise, chief of the ordnance bureau.[80] Edward Fithian, chief engineer of the navy throughout the war and for some years thereafter, was convinced that chrome steel had "uniform texture in large or small masses," and performed "three or four times more work than the best tools of carbon steel."[81] It was, as we have seen, Commodore King, who had supervised the testing of Eads's turret and had been with Eads in Europe inspecting naval dockyards and ironclads in the fall of 1864,[82] who went with Flad to investigate the chrome steel process in the spring of 1869. Furthermore, just before Eads arranged for C. P. Haughian of the Chrome Steel Works to teach Butcher how to make steel of Bauer's patented mixture, Eads had appointed as his chief inspector of iron and steel (at Butcher's Philadelphia works) Henry W. Fitch, who as a first assistant engineer in the navy had been assigned to special duty in charge of Eads's gun-carriage at Fort Hamilton, New York, from June 1869 to June 1871 and had now been granted one year's leave of absence from the navy at Eads's special request.[83] Finally, it is worth noting that the president of the Chrome Steel Company (organized to run the Brooklyn works) was William W. W. Wood, chief engineer of the Brooklyn Navy Yard, which lay southward across the street from the steel works located at the corner of Kent Avenue and Keap Street—an interesting juxtaposition.[84]

Clearly Eads had good reason to say, as he did, that before the contract with Keystone or the subcontract with the Wm. Butcher Works were made, he was satisfied that chrome steel "possessed qualities eminently suited for the bridge superstructure," and that even though Krupp, and Petin Gaudet and Company, and "some of the most eminent steel makers in America" had assured him that crucible carbon steel could readily be made to meet his specifications, he did not

[80]See nn. 35 and 37 above. Wise retired as chief in 1868 because of ill health and went to Naples, Italy, where he died April 2, 1869. We know that Eads went briefly to Naples in October or November 1868, where he may have seen Wise (Henry T. Blow to Eads, December 22, 1868, J. B. Eads Collection, Missouri Historical Society).

[81]Quoted in a generally skeptical article, "Chrome Steel?" in *Mines, Metals and Arts* (December 2, 1875), p. 135.

[82]See Eads to Assistant Secretary G. V. Fox, October 4, 1864, Fox Papers, New-York Historical Society.

[83]Woodward, pp. 83–84. Fitch's prior service is documented in the National Archives (n. 34 above).

[84]There is a brief biographical sketch of Wood in *Appleton's Cyclopaedia of American Biography* (New York, 1889), 6:598–99, which does not mention his connection with the Chrome Steel Works.

at any time hesitate "to express [his] belief that the chrome-steel was most likely to meet the requirements of the Bridge."[85]

The changes in materials used, like the changes in the detailing of the tubes discussed earlier, important as they were in a structural sense, had little effect on the overall appearance of the bridge. But there were other changes of greater visual consequence.

As presented in Eads's first report (1868) the bridge was to have a center span of 515 feet and side spans of 497 feet, supported by masonry piers whose upstream and downstream faces were to be rounded, as were those of the Koblenz bridge. At some point the piers were redesigned as shown in the undated drawing reproduced as figure 6, perhaps at the suggestion of George I. Barnett, a St. Louis architect of considerable distinction who had rebuilt and enlarged Eads's own house in 1866, making it into a fashionable Italianate villa, and who in 1870 drew up the designs for a Grand Union Passenger Depot in the "Franco-Italian" style, which Eads and Taussig hoped to erect a couple of blocks west of the St. Louis end of the bridge.[86] By the summer of 1870, however, when the piers had been built above low water level, the final design (fig. 7) had been worked out.

By this time the length of the spans had also been changed. The center span was now to be 520 feet and the side spans 502, a 5-foot increase in the length of each arched rib or a total increase of 15 feet in the length of the superstructure between piers. Such an increase would one might suppose, require that the piers be spaced farther

---

[85] J. B. Eads, *Report of the Chief Engineer, October 1, 1871* (St. Louis, 1871), pp. 11–12 (also in *Addresses and Papers*, p. 593). After Haughian returned to Brooklyn, Butcher and his successor, William F. Durfee, had considerable difficulty with production of suitable chrome steel for the anchor bolts and couplings, and in the end it was chiefly in the tube staves (the principal supporting members of the structure) that chrome steel was used. It is of course true, as Miller (n. 3 above) says, that short of analyzing samples from each of the 6,216 staves, there is "no way to know just how much of the 'world's first chrome steel structure' was actually chrome steel" (p. 116). But the available data are reassuring. Early in 1928 J. N. Ostrum, a consulting engineer, drilled 1-inch inspection holes in the bottom of each of the tubes in the arches, and "analysis of the drillings revealed the steel to be a high carbon chromium steel extremely low in sulphur" (see "Eads Bridge Pronounced Safe," *Railway Age* 84 [1928]: 1442–43; and E. E. Thum, "Alloy Bridge Steel Sixty Years Old," *Iron Age* [September 20, 1928], pp. 683–86, 733–34). The carbon content of the drilling averaged .79 percent, the sulfur .009 percent, and the chromium .61 percent. Miller (p. 117n) gives the results of analyses made fifty years later of samples from a tube damaged by the collision of a towboat in 1973 which averaged carbon .641 percent, sulfur .022 percent, and chromium .453 percent. No sample ever taken from any one of the 1,036 tubes in the arches has revealed an absence of chromium. We need not hesitate to credit Eads with the first major application of any kind of structural alloy steel anywhere in the world.

[86] Woodward, p. 144; *The City of St. Louis and Its Resources*, a pamphlet published by the *St. Louis Star-Sayings* (1893), p. 140; and *Description and Plans of the Proposed Grand Union Passenger Depot in St. Louis* (St. Louis, 1871), p. 13.

FIG. 6.—South elevation of the west abutment pier, as redesigned in late 1868 or early 1869 (original drawing, probably by William Rehberg, from the files of the Terminal Railroad Association of St. Louis, now in the Washington University archives).

apart than originally planned. Yet the increase in span lengths was not planned until after the location of the abutments and the two river piers had been determined and work had begun on their foundations.[87]

Neither Woodward nor any subsequent writer who has discussed Eads Bridge seems to have noticed this puzzling aspect of the development of the design. But here again we can get a useful clue from Carl Gayler's reminiscences. Gayler was troubled by the fact that when the test loads were applied to the finished bridge in 1874 and the first

---

[87]The driving of the piles for the east pier breakwater began about August 12, 1869; so by then the location of the river piers had been definitely established (see Eads's report, *Addresses and Papers,* p. 544).

Fig. 7.—South elevation of west abutment pier, as finally designed and as constructed (detail of drawing by W. P. Gerhard, lithograph by Julius Bien, in C. M. Woodward, *A History of the St. Louis Bridge* [St. Louis, 1881], pl. 11).

train had covered the east span, "the east span arch sank and the center span rose: *the East river pier had bent.*"

I will give you the history of those River Piers [he continued]. Mr. Pfeifer, like the accomplished Engineer he is, has laid out one of those piers correctly with the pressure lines of the different assumed loadings laid off, the lower end of the pressure lines striking the bottom within safe distance from the face of the Pier, as the law directs. When Eads comes to see the drawing (I was standing right there) he marks off with a pencil a slice of two or three feet thickness the whole height of the Pier. It was the artist in Eads who protested, and his artistic side led him into this blunder. Eads, true enough, didn't want the pier too slim, but he wanted above all a graceful looking pier. . . .

Poor Pfeifer argues and protests in vain. Eads is his Superior and that ends the controversy.[88]

This was written almost sixty years after the event, and Gayler's memory played him false on a number of details.[89] But the specificity of the picture of Eads slicing "two or three feet" off the thickness of the pier as Pfeifer had drawn it is, to me at least, convincing. And if Eads did, indeed, slice say 2.5 feet off each side of the two river piers and off the river faces of the two abutment piers, that would have added 5 feet to the distances between them—exactly the amount by which the length of each of the three spans was in fact increased.

In any event, the center span of 520 feet with side spans of 502 feet had been adopted as part of what Eads referred to in his report of October 1870 as "modifications in the general arrangement of the arches and in the details of their construction, which will considerably improve the architectural appearance of the Bridge and simplify its fabrication." The principal changes, he said, were the use of the single cast-steel tube of 18-inch diameter, instead of two of 9 inches, in forming the upper and lower members of each of the four ribbed arches composing each span, and the spacing of the upper and lower tubes 12 feet apart instead of only 8 feet. But even more important, visually, was the raising of the railway so that in no place would it appear below the soffit of the arches as it did in the original design. In that design the railway was 8 feet lower than the center of the 515-foot middle span, a flat line slicing off the upper segment of the arch. In the revised design, with the lower tubes 12 feet instead of 8 feet below the upper tubes (thus deepening the ribbed arches by 4 feet), it was necessary to raise the level of the railway only 4 feet to keep it entirely above the soffit of the middle span's arches.

If the railway had been kept at this level over the side spans, it would have had to descend precipitously over the arcaded approaches at either end of the bridge proper. To lessen the approach grade it was necessary that the tracks should descend gradually each way from the center of the bridge, which would cause them to fall below the

[88]See Gayler Papers (n. 57 above).
[89]The test loads were not applied on July 4, as he says, but on July 1 and 2 (see Woodward, pp. 197–200).

soffit of the side spans even though their ribs had also been deepened 4 feet. To avoid this, Eads lowered the shore ends of the side spans by placing the skewbacks (which received the thrust of the tubular ribbed arches) 18 inches lower on the abutment piers. By so doing he lowered the centers of the side spans 9 inches, permitting the gradient of the railway to be correspondingly lower toward the ends of the bridge. Raising the tracks above the arch soffits would, Eads said, "unquestionably improve the appearance of the structure," and the lowering of the shore ends of the side spans would also be an architectural improvement since "the effect upon the eye caused by it, will be somewhat similar to that produced by the camber of the bridge."[90]

These changes, like the trimming of the width of the piers, were primarily the work of what Carl Gayler called "the artist in Eads." And, as Eads acknowledged, they involved "the necessity of revising the former investigations and results [so carefully worked out by Flad and Pfeifer], so as to ascertain the difference in the strains, and to determine the alterations required in the sectional areas of the various members of the structure." And this, in turn, required that Rehberg, Gayler, and the others in the drafting room produce "an entirely new set of detail and general drawings." No wonder there were delays that gave Keystone a plausible excuse for their own delays in erecting the bridge. It is nevertheless appropriate, I think, to close this discussion of Eads as a designer by quoting the climax of Taussig's unpublished defense of his colleague during the controversies with Keystone in 1871:

> I cannot be made to believe [Taussig wrote to Carnegie] that he has embodied anything in his plans for theory's sake. Genius, as a general thing, never permits itself to be fettered by theories, and I take it that his genius is more of a creative than of a theoretical turn. Nor do I believe that he has added anything unnecessary to his plan for the sake of show or display. Our conversations on this point have been too frequent, and his endeavours to cheapen the cost too evident to me on many occasions. Apart from his own very heavy investment in the enterprise, every impulse of his would induce him to guard the interests of his Company in that respect, just the same as if he had not a Dollar invested in it. He is a noble character, as well as a noble Engineer.[91]

[90]Eads's October 1870 report, *Addresses and Papers*, pp. 577–78. Miller's account of these changes is quite misleading (p. 136).

[91]Taussig to Carnegie, January 7, 1871, Carnegie Papers.

8

Tay Rail Bridge centenary:
some notes on its construction

J.S. Shipway

This Paper describes the history, design and construction of the Tay railway bridge. The design and construction of the present bridge are so inextricably bound up with the failure of its predecessor in the disaster of 1879 that any description of it must begin with the story of the earlier first effort to bridge the Tay. Although everyone has heard of the disaster, perhaps few know the facts of an event which seems to have gripped public imagination as no other has done since. The Paper begins with a description of the design and construction of the first Tay Bridge, which was a few feet shorter than two miles long, by far the longest bridge in the world at that time. The events leading to its fall in a gale on 28 December 1879 are outlined, together with the findings of the public inquiry, and the new conditions set out for the construction of the present bridge. The ingenious construction methods for the new bridge, employed by the contractor, William Arrol of Glasgow, are described. The construction took five years from 1882–87, and the bridge celebrated the centenary of its opening on 20 June 1987.

The first Tay Bridge 1871–79

The Tay Bridge was designed for the North British Railway by Thomas Bouch (1822–1880), an experienced engineer with many successful bridges to his credit, including two similar in design to the Tay Bridge in the North of England, which carried railway traffic until they were dismantled in 1962. For most of his engineering life, Bouch held the view that contemporary structures were over-designed, and he introduced considerable refinement of material into both his masonry and iron bridges.

2. Bouch planned his Tay Bridge to carry a single line of railway (Fig. 1). Owing to difficulties with the construction of the foundations, the original 89 spans were modified to 85; thirteen of these were navigation spans, higher and larger than the others; eleven of these spans were 245 ft and two were 227 ft; the remainder of the bridge had spans of between 67 ft and 164 ft. The bridge deck was laid on top of the smaller spans but ran through the girders of the navigation spans (Fig. 2); the same arrangement holds today in the rebuilt bridge. In the disaster of 1879, only the navigation spans fell; the rest of the bridge remained standing but was dismantled later.

Bridge foundation

3. The Tay is a shallow estuary nearly two miles wide at Dundee, with many sandbanks and a water depth which rarely exceeds 50 ft. Borings in the river showed sand and gravel overlying rock at a depth of about 20 ft below the river bed. Elsewhere there was a stiff clay. It was planned to found each pier on the rock

SHIPWAY

Fig. 1. The first Tay Bridge, 1878

TAY RAIL BRIDGE CENTENARY

Fig. 2. Engine within navigation span of the first bridge

SHIPWAY

or clay by caisson construction, and the piers themselves were to be of solid brickwork for their full height to the underside of the girders. The girders themselves were of the well-tested double triangular design so loved by the Victorians.

4. The bridge contract was let on 1 May 1871 to Charles de Bergue & Co. Work began from the Fife shore, and pushed slowly out into the river. After 14 piers had been constructed, it was found that the rock was no longer solid, but took the form of shelves of conglomerate 3 ft or 4 ft thick interspersed with sand. As a result of the borings, the shelves of conglomerate had mistakenly been identified as bedrock, which in fact existed at increasingly greater depth as the distance out from the shore increased. Caisson sinking proved extremely difficult owing to the presence of the conglomerate and random boulders. It was obvious that founding on rock further out into the river would be impracticable, and therefore the piers would have to be built on weaker material.

5. The brick piers were heavy and applied about 8.5 tons/ft^2 on the rock, which was considered too high a bearing pressure for sand. Bouch apparently made no load test on the sand; instead he rapidly redesigned the piers to consist of groups of cast iron columns on a larger base, giving a pressure of about 3.75 tons/ft^2 on the sand.

Ironwork of the piers

6. The cast iron columns formed a group of six in an elongated hexagonal shape, the longer dimension being in the line of the river. The batter on the ironwork was negligible and the bracing consisted of slender criss-crossed flat straps, giving the tall piers an appearance of spidery slenderness. The columns themselves were slender, with diameters of 15 in and 18 in, and cast in lengths of 10 ft joined by bolting through flanges. The bracing was bolted at one end to lugs cast on the column. The other end had a cotter connection to similar lugs, to allow tightening (Fig. 3).

7. At about this time, Charles de Bergue fell ill; as a consequence, his firm was unable to continue the work and he asked to be relieved of the contract. A new contract was let on 26 June 1874 to a Middlesborough firm, Hopkins Gilkes & Co. This firm had previously done satisfactory work for Bouch elsewhere and was well known to him.

8. A feature of the new iron work of the piers was the holding-down bolts. Bouch seemed to have no real idea of the forces they were to resist and anchored them in two courses of masonry. The bolts themselves were capable of taking a load of 200 tons, but their anchorage at most gave a resistance of 6 or 7 tons.

Completion of the bridge

9. A temporary foundry was set up on the Fife shore and the casting of the ironwork was started. Pier construction proceeded slowly across the river, and the girder spans were floated out and erected. By September 1877, the first train passed over, although the bridge was not formally opened until 1 June 1878. After work on the approaches was completed, the bridge was inspected and passed by the Board of Trade: the Inspector was Major-General C. S. Hutchinson, RE. The bridge was tested according to his instructions, by running six coupled goods engines over it and measuring the deflexions of the girder spans. The loading applied by the engines was nearly 1.5 tons/ft run. In his report Hutchinson observed, among other points, that

TAY RAIL BRIDGE CENTENARY

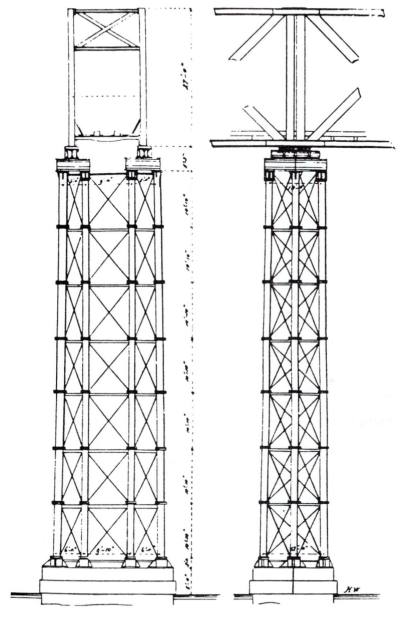

Fig. 3. Typical pier of first bridge (from Edinburgh & Leith Engineer's Society Vol. III, Session 1876–77)

SHIPWAY

> The lateral oscillation was very slight and the structure showed great stiffness.
> The ironwork has been well put together, both in columns and girders.
> I would suggest 25 mph as a limit which should not be exceeded.
> I should wish if possible to have an opportunity of observing the effects of a high wind, when a train of carriages is running over the bridge.

He made some minor criticisms regarding slack places in the rails and the preservation of the gauge, but that was all. Queen Victoria crossed the bridge in June 1879 and knighted Bouch for his work. In the meantime, Sir Thomas was already busy with his design for a railway bridge over the Forth, and foundation construction had already begun at Inchgarvie island.

Troubles loom

10.   All was not well with the Tay Bridge, however. The cast iron columns had been filled with concrete and were said to be cracking in various places. The winter of 1878–79 was exceedingly cold, and contemporary accounts state that the concrete was expanding and bursting the columns, and also that the iron was cracking by shrinking on to the concrete.

11.   Furthermore, many of the lugs holding the bracing were snapping off, a consequence, it was said, of having been burned on afterwards instead of being cast integral with the column. The bracing itself was loose in places because the cotter connection was vulnerable to vibration. Local enthusiasts timed the trains as they raced the ferry, and found that they were travelling at over 40 mph.

12.   Bouch had the cracked columns strapped with iron bands, and seemed not to worry since, he claimed, Brunel had had the same trouble at Chepstow. Repairs were also carried out to the bracing by the contractor's foreman, who (it transpired later) had an uneasy conscience about the casting, and did the repairs at his own expense without informing Bouch. The bridge maintenance continued in this haphazard fashion and the railway company seemed unaware of the situation.

The disaster

13.   The 28 December, 1879, was a Sunday, and on that day a strong westerly gale sprang up, of the kind which occasionally sweep the central plain of Scotland. It was recorded locally as being force 10 or 11 on the Beaufort scale, or about 60–70 mph. This is not a particularly severe gale, and has been exceeded many times since. It seems certain that had the bridge not fallen in 1879 it would have succumbed to other stronger gales at a later date.

14.   The train in the disaster was the evening train from Edinburgh to Dundee, consisting of an engine and six carriages with 75 passengers on board. It passed punctually on to the bridge at 7.14 pm. Its lights were seen to disappear but for a time no one realized what had happened. Later, in the darkness, the station staff from Dundee made their way out on to the bridge and discovered the navigation spans had fallen into the river, taking the train with them (Fig. 4). There were no survivors.*

15.   The 13 navigation spans had been of continuous construction, arranged in groups of 5, 4 and 4, reading from the south. The engine and coaches were found

---

* There was a survivor. This was the railway engine. It was retrieved from the bed of the river and had a useful life for many years afterwards. It was known among railwaymen as 'The Diver'.

TAY RAIL BRIDGE CENTENARY

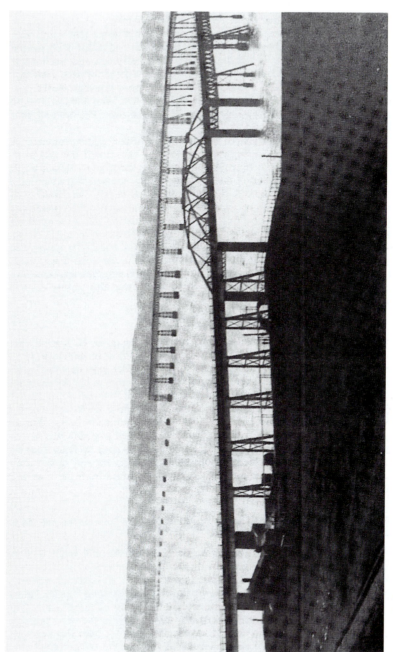

Fig. 4. Fallen navigation spans of first bridge, 1880

1095

SHIPWAY

inside the fourth and fifth spans of the first group; the throttle of the engine was fully open, which suggests that the driver had had no warning.

16.   Various theories were put forward to explain the disaster. Inspection of the shattered pier columns shows the cast iron to have been badly cast, with patched blowholes, uneven thickness of metal in the walls of the columns, and boltholes for connection flanges and bracing cast in by the use of tapered formers, instead of being bored true after casting. The tapered holes gave poor bearings for the bolts, resulting in loose fastenings. Fissures in the columns had been filled in and disguised by a mixture of iron filings and lead, and painted over. The holding down bolts were inadequately anchored.

17.   An interesting explanation put forward by the former resident engineer was that the weight of the train in the penultimate span had caused the end of the continuous section to lift off its bearings sufficiently for the wind to blow it off the pier. Since the engine was found in the end span, it was assumed that its momentum could have carried it forward to that position during its fall. The details of the bearing showed no holding-down attachment and this theory looked possible. A simple calculation will show, however, that since the dead weight of the span was around 300 tons, the live load in the penultimate span necessary to reduce the end reaction to zero would have been 2400 tons, assuming full continuity under dead load, which is unlikely to have been achieved. Even the test load train on the bridge totalled only 370 tons per span, and the train in the disaster must have weighed considerably less. It seems unlikely, therefore, that this feature contributed to the disaster.

The Inquiry

18.   A Court of Inquiry was set up, the panel consisting of: W. H. Barlow, then president of the ICE; Colonel W. Yolland, Inspecting Officer of Railways; H. C. Rothery, Commissioner of Wrecks. The most significant fact to be exposed by the Inquiry was that Bouch had taken little notice of wind forces in his design of the structure. The Astronomer Royal had suggested a wind force of 10 lbs/ft^2; however, Bouch must have known that, at that time, the French were using a figure of 55 lbs/ft^2 and the Americans 50 lbs/ft^2. Bouch's explanation was that the train had been blown off the rails, and had so damaged a girder that it had collapsed and brought down the piers. He supported this with evidence that the last two coaches were much more seriously damaged than the rest of the train. This seemed an improbable cause, but the girder was raised from the river and inspected. It showed little more than score marks.

19.   The Inquiry stated that

> The fall of the bridge was occasioned by the insufficiency of the cross bracing and its fastenings to sustain the force of the gale.

However, much speculation has continued since as to whether this really was the cause of the disaster. An examination of the mode of failure of the ironwork showed that the majority of the 12 collapsed piers failed at the base; the masonry of the pier tops was torn up by the holding down bolts, suggesting that the failure may have been due to overturning rather than to failure of the bracing. The Inquiry calculated that, with the holding-down bolts as built, the wind pressure required to overturn the bridge would have been 40 lbs/ft^2. Under this pressure, the stress in the bracing would have been as high as 23 tons/in^2. When tested after the disaster, specimens of the bracing failed in a range between 21–25·6 tons/in^2.

TAY RAIL BRIDGE CENTENARY

This suggests that failure of the bracing and the holding-down bolts may have been simultaneous. However, 40 lbs/ft^2 is an extremely high wind pressure to apply uniformly over the length of even one span, and it may be that the poor quality of the patched ironwork in the columns played a part in triggering the failure (Fig. 5).

The present Tay Bridge 1882–1987

New beginnings

20. Although the first Tay Bridge had been in operation for only 18 months, it had more than demonstrated its usefulness. The North British Railway was determined to replace the bridge as soon as possible, and introduced a Bill in the Parlimentary session of 1880 to allow it to do so. The company also decided on a double-line bridge, which meant the new bridge would have to be considerably wider and more substantial than the first.

21. The directors of the North British referred the question of the reconstruction to Mr W. H. Barlow, an eminent engineer who was President of the ICE and who had assisted in the completion of Brunel's Clifton suspension bridge in the 1860s. He was appointed Engineer for the new bridge, and was assisted by his son, Crawford Barlow, who in 1888 presented a paper on the design of the new bridge to the ICE.

22. Barlow's first task was to determine how much, if any, of the first bridge could be incorporated in the second. He set up a series of loading tests on the piers, and investigated scour effects in the river bed at their bases. He made a new series of borehole investigations at 500 ft intervals across the Tay in line with the piers of the first bridge. He then sank a trial cylinder where the foundation appeared weakest (silty sand) and loaded it to a gross bearing pressure of 7 tons/ft^2. This produced an initial settlement of 5·25 in, which did not increase, although the test load was kept in place for three months.

23. As a result of these investigations, Barlow was able to draw up various alternative proposals and estimates for the reconstruction as follows

(a) widening of the first bridge on one side
(b) widening of the first bridge on both sides
(c) constructing a new single-line bridge parallel to the first and bracing the two structures together
(d) constructing a completely independent new bridge.

24. It was found that, if the piers of the first bridge were to be used, protection works against scour would have to be constructed, since, in places, the foundations had not been carried deep enough into the bed of the river. Owing to the various forms of the piers, these works would be of considerable difficulty and complexity. Further, the ironwork of the superstructure was suspect, the bracing and holding-down details were weak, and it was not advisable to increase the weight on the existing foundations. The girder spans, however, were in the main considered to be in good order.

25. These considerations led Barlow to recommend to the directors the construction of a new bridge completely independent of the first. If the spans of the new bridge were kept the same, many of the girders of the old spans could be re-used which would result in a significant saving in cost. If the line of the new bridge was sufficiently close to the old bridge, it could be used as a useful staging

SHIPWAY

Fig. 5. Fallen span and remains of pier ironwork, 1880

and means of access for men and materials. The girder spans could also be more readily transferred to the piers of the new bridge.

26. The North British directors accepted Barlow's recommendations for a new bridge located 60 ft upstream from the first, and the necessary plans were deposited for Parliamentary approval in May 1881. This was less than 18 months after the fall of the first bridge, and it will be seen that events had moved quickly towards the restoration of the rail link with Dundee and the North-East.

27. After the plans had been deposited, representation was made to the company that, in view of public opinion expressing fears about the safety aspect, the new bridge should be rebuilt at a lower level. The North British was anxious to restore public confidence, and the navigation headroom requirements were investigated further, resulting in the lowering of the height of the navigation spans from 88 ft to 77 ft above high water. Another consequence of public safety considerations was that the bridge was designed for a wind pressure of 56 lbs/sq ft (Fig. 6).

28. The Bill obtained the Royal Assent in July 1881. 'The New Tay Viaduct Act', as it was called, contained two rather curious clauses.

> Every cylinder foundation of the piers of the viaduct shall be properly tested to at least 33% above the maximum weight to which it will be subjected, and to the satisfaction of the Board of Trade.

The other clause related to the disposal of the first bridge.

> The Company shall remove the ruins and debris of the old bridge and all obstructions interfering with the navigation caused by the old bridge, to the satisfaction of the Board of Trade.

29. The first provision was inserted because Barlow had stated in his evidence before Parliament that he proposed to test every cylinder foundation. It was therefore made compulsory by the Act, and resulted in the endless transference of thousands of tons of iron kentledge from pier to pier for test purposes, which must have resulted in much unnecessary labour and cost to the project.

30. The seemingly innocent wording of the second clause was interpreted by the Board of Trade to mean that the remains of the first bridge would be cleared before the new bridge was begun. However, when the contract documents for the new bridge were being prepared, the assumption had been made that the old bridge would be available for use as a staging and means of access during construction, and its removal before the work started would be disastrous, particularly since the girder spans were to be re-used in the new work (Fig. 7).

31. The Board of Trade blindly stated its case, and intimated that it could not consent to the start of the works until the old bridge was removed. This unexpected decision stopped all proceedings for some time and it was not until the beginning of June 1882 that the matter was resolved and construction allowed to begin.

32. Tenders had been invited during 1881, and that of William Arrol & Co., Glasgow had been accepted in October of that year. This firm had a high reputation for bridge work, and was later to complete the Forth Railway Bridge in 1890 and Tower Bridge, London, in 1895. (The firm still continues in existence in Glasgow to the present day. Arrol himself was knighted after the successful completion of the Forth Bridge, and died in 1913.)

Barlow's design and Arrol's opportunity

33. It should be noted that Barlow was left little scope or freedom to design the new bridge: the span lengths were all fixed by those of the old bridge; the old

SHIPWAY

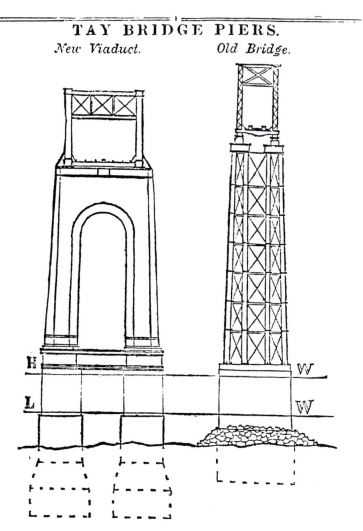

TAY BRIDGE PIERS.

New Viaduct.   *Old Bridge.*

We are indebted to Messrs Barlow, Son, & Baker, Engineers of the undertaking, for the sketch reproduced above of the Cross Section of the new Viaduct, showing the relative positions of the new work and the old Bridge. The massive character of the new structure as compared with the old is obvious at a glance, especially (1) the greater lateral stability from the substitution of twin piers for the single pier below, and the increased width for the double line of rails above ; and (2) the greater vertical stability from the diminished height of the superstructure and the arched formation at the upper junction of the piers.

Fig. 6. Comparison of piers of first and present Tay Bridge (from Dundee Advertiser, 18 October 1881)

TAY RAIL BRIDGE CENTENARY

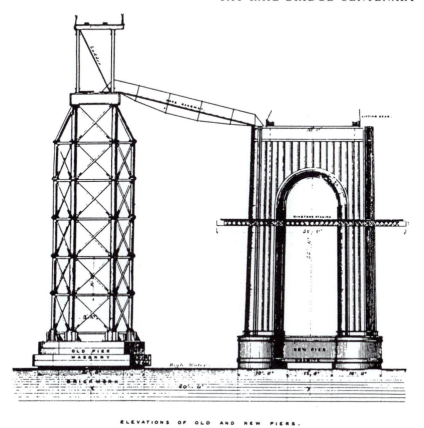

ELEVATIONS OF OLD AND NEW PIERS.

Fig. 7. Access to new bridge from first bridge during construction

girder spans were to be re-used wherever possible; even the navigation spans, which fell in the disaster, dictated the span lengths of the new, because of the need to keep the new piers in line with the old.

34.   Therefore, Barlow was left mainly with the design of new piers and new girders for the navigation spans (Fig. 8), and it was Arrol who distinguished himself in the construction of the new bridge. He devised ingenious floating plant for sinking the piers, for transferring the girder spans of the old bridge, and for transporting and raising the new navigation spans. The bridge was begun in June 1882 and completed five years later in June 1887. This compares with the seven years it took to build the old bridge (1871–78), although it consisted of only a single line of railway. However, Arrol was undoubtedly helped by the fact that the existing spans of the first bridge could be used for access to the new.

Description of the new bridge
35.   The bridge is 10 711 ft in length; of this length, 8396 ft is in a straight line running very nearly north-south. The centre-line is 60 ft distant from and parallel

SHIPWAY

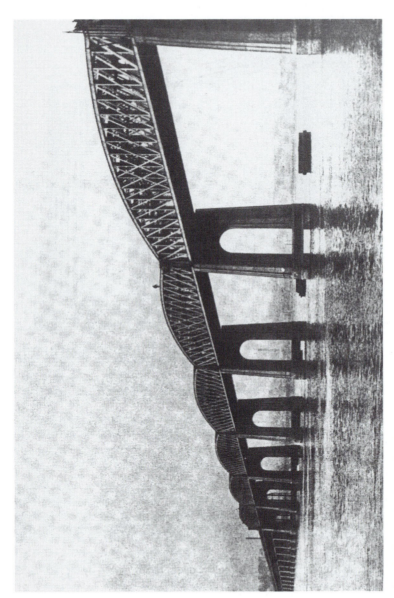

Fig. 8. Present bridge navigation spans

1102

to the line of the old, except at the northern end where the curved portion had to be adjusted to line in with the existing arrangement at the station. This resulted in a curve of 21 chains radius. From the abutment at the south end there are 85 piers: piers 1–28 form the south approach to the navigation spans; piers 28–41 are the navigation spans; piers 41–85 form the north approach. The south approach is on a gradient down to the north of 1 in 762, the navigation spans are level, and the remainder of the bridge is on a gradient of 1 in 113·5.

36.   The main portion of the bridge over tidal water consists of 74 spans; i.e. piers 4–78. The spans over this section are the same as in the old bridge, and are as follows.

> South approach: 1 span of 118 ft; 10 spans of 129 ft; 13 spans of 145 ft
> Navigation spans: 11 spans of 245 ft; 2 spans of 227 ft
> North approach: 1 span of 162 ft; 11 spans of 129 ft; 24 spans of 71 ft; 1 span of 56 ft

These spans (except the navigation spans) contained the undamaged girders of the old bridge which were to be re-used in the new bridge. The track was laid on the tops of the girders of the approach spans, but ran through the girders of the navigation spans to give the necessary clearance for shipping of 77 ft. Many of the approach spans are in continuous groups of up to four spans, unlike the navigation spans, which are all arranged to be simply-supported and do not follow the continuous arrangement employed in the old bridge.

The design and construction of the piers

37.   Each pier consists of two parts: an underwater supporting structure of brick and concrete; and a superstructure of wrought iron supporting the bridge girders.

38.   The underwater structure consists of two circular columns of brickwork enclosing a concrete core, generally about 16 ft dia. and 32 ft apart (Fig. 9), but varying in size according to the spans and loads supported. These columns were built up inside wrought-iron cylinders constructed for the purpose of penetrating the river bed to the required depth, which were left in position to become part of the permanent works. The columns were widened out at the base to a maximum of 23 ft dia. to allow the bearing pressure to be restricted to 3·5 tons/ft^2 on the sand. Above highwater level, the columns were connected by a horizontal member of concrete and brickwork about 7 ft deep, which gave added strength to resist the pressure of ice, which occasionally appears in considerable quantities in the Tay.

39.   The iron cylinders were built on shore and sunk to their required position by means of a remarkable pontoon designed by Arrol. There were four pontoons altogether, varying in size according to the pier construction. Each pontoon had four legs which could be raised or lowered hydraulically to found on the river bed. Once the pontoon was sitting firmly on its four legs, it could be raised hydraulically clear of the water to provide an extremely stable and secure working platform (Fig. 10). This ingenious device was the forerunner of what is known in today's oil industry as a 'jack-up platform', but it was invented in the 1880s by Arrol.

40.   The pontoon was located at each pier position, and the iron cylinders were let down through two rectangular openings and sunk to their required positions. The pontoon carried steam cranes, concrete mixers and all the necessary plant, men and materials for constructing the brick and concrete pier columns. Weights

SHIPWAY

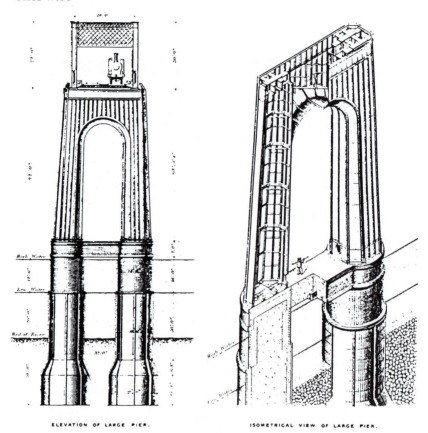

ELEVATION OF LARGE PIER.   ISOMETRICAL VIEW OF LARGE PIER.

Fig. 9. Typical pier construction of present bridge

had often to be applied to the cylinders to force them to the required depth, while the sand was excavated by grab from inside.

41.   When the pier columns were completed, they had to be test-loaded according to the terms of the Act. This was accomplished by means of iron blocks, each weighing half a ton, of which no fewer than 30 000 were required. Each of the largest piers had to carry a test load of 2438 tons. The total placing and uplifting of test loads amounted to 94 122 tons in all, and very considerable labour was involved. Levels were taken before and after loading. The maximum settlement recorded was 7·02 in at pier 62; the average settlement of all the piers was 1·37 in. Pier 6, on rock, was also test-loaded to abide by the Act, but no settlement was recorded.

42.   When testing had been completed, the wrought-iron superstructures were erected. They were constructed first at Arrol's works in Glasgow, then taken apart and re-erected on the piers at site. The upper part of each pier consisted of two hollow octagonal legs joined at their tops by a connecting arch, and were con-

TAY RAIL BRIDGE CENTENARY

Fig. 10.   Jack-up barge devised by Arrol for pier construction

SHIPWAY

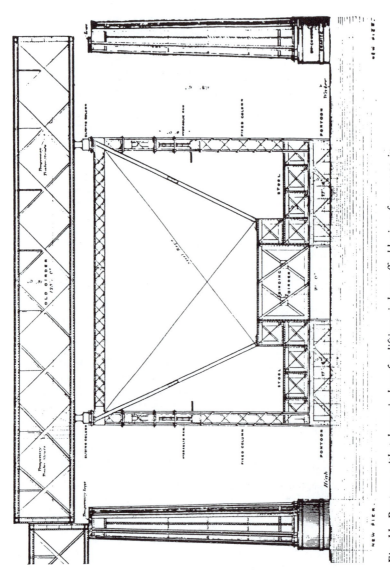

Fig. 11. Pontoon with telescopic legs for lifting girders off old piers for re-use in present bridge

structed from the jacked-up pontoons as a working platform. The pier legs and arch are constructed of angle-irons and other steel sections, plated over on the outside and stiffened by means of internal diaphragms at vertical intervals of 10–13 ft. Each leg is held down by eight holding-down bolts, of 2·5 in dia. and 20 ft in length, securely anchored in the brick and concrete (Fig. 8).

43.   In a published description of the bridge, Crawford Barlow remarked

> In these superstructures of the piers the plates not only act as bracings to the vertical members of the frameworks, but also assist in carrying the vertical pressures. Although this arrangement may have the objection of presenting a larger surface to the wind, it is to be borne in mind that the wind can only act on the outside surface, and there is no second surface for it to act on, as would be the case if they were constructed of open framework. The strain on the ironwork of these superstructures, due to vertical pressures, produces no greater stress than 2·2 tons/in^2 on any part of the metal.

The design and construction of the girder spans

44.   The design of the north and south approach spans was conditioned by the re-use of the girders of the old bridge. The old bridge had carried only a single line of railway and the girders were inadequate to carry the double line of the new bridge unaided. Therefore, additional new girders were incorporated in each of the approach spans of the new bridge.

45.   One pair of girders was available for all the approach spans except the two end ones between piers 4/5 and 77/78. These girders became the outer girders of the new spans, two new inner girders being added. The old girders were therefore loaded to something less than their calculated capacities. The new girders are very similar in appearance to the old, being of the same double triangular form, but rather heavier in section on account of the greater loads carried.

46.   The four girders in each span are connected at their top chords by the trough flooring forming the bridge deck. Horizontal and vertical bracing is also incorporated to provide a rigid and secure structure.

47.   Arrol employed specially designed pontoons to lift the old girders off their bearings on the old piers. The girders were supported on telescopic legs on the pontoons which could be adjusted in height according to the state of the tide. The girders were lifted off the old piers by the rising tide (often in as short a time as 15 min) moved upstream 60 ft, and lowered on to their new bearings by adjusting the telescopic legs (Fig. 11).

48.   The new girders were constructed on shore and were transported out to their locations by means of a special travelling gantry running on the newly-positioned pairs of old girders (Fig. 10).

49.   The new navigation spans were larger than the approach spans: 11 were of 245 ft and two of 227 ft. They were manufactured in Glasgow and taken apart for transport to the Tay, where they were assembled on the south shore. Each span was assembled complete and floated out to its position, using the same pontoons as had been employed for lifting off the old approach girder spans. Each span, weighing more than 500 tons, was landed on the pier tops and carefully jacked up in short lifts to its full height. Openings in the pier plating and a special ladder structure within allowed lifts of 15 in by hydraulic jacks. The lifting operation for all the 13 spans was completed without incident, which speaks volumes for the organization and ingenuity of all concerned (Fig. 12).

50.   Provision for expansion and contraction is by rocker bearings at approx-

SHIPWAY

1108

Fig. 12. Floating out the last of the navigation spans of the present bridge

TAY RAIL BRIDGE CENTENARY

imately 500 ft intervals. Over this length, the variation in length has been found to be about 1·65 in for a range of temperature of 55°F.

51.   The material of the new girders was wrought iron, and the new material, namely steel, was not yet in widespread use, although it was used for the decking. The wrought iron used had an ultimate tensile stress of 22 tons/in^2, and the steel in the decking had a corresponding stress of 27 tons/in^2.

52.   The stresses in the new girders did not exceed 5·0 tons/in^2 in tension and 4·8 tons/in^2 in compression, which are modest compared with the stresses that would be allowed in steel structures today. (The stresses in the pier superstructures due to vertical loading were even more modest at 2·2 tons/in^2.)

53.   In connection with the arrangements for expansion and contraction, it was considered desirable to make provision against any possible tendency for the girders to travel in the direction of the downhill gradient towards the north. To prevent this, the four girders at the south end are fastened by means of a strong anchorage bedded 10 ft into the brickwork of the abutment; while at 38 places along the viaduct, the girders covering one span in each group of girders are bolted firmly down to two piers. As a result of these measures, the amount of separation which can take place between any two groups of girders is limited. No tendency for the girders to travel has been found.

Completion of the bridge

54.   The Board of Trade inspected the bridge on 16, 17 and 18 June, 1887. One of the Inspectors was the same Major-General Hutchinson who inspected the old bridge before the disaster. The test load consisted of eight coupled engines on each track, giving a distributed load of about 3 tons/ft run on the bridge. Under the load, the deflexion on one of the navigation spans (245 ft) was only 1·38 in.

55.   The results of the tests were considered satisfactory and the bridge was opened to traffic on Monday, 20 June, 1887.

56.   The cost was £670 000, compared with £350 000 for the first bridge. Some economy was achieved by the use of the girders from the old bridge, but it will be seen that the North British Railway spent over one million pounds bridging the Tay, no mean sum in those days.

57.   The number of fatal accidents throughout the work was 13 men over the course of five years. The number of men employed on the bridge varied between 100 and 900. Accidents arose mainly from the individual recklessness of the men themselves, and not from negligence or carelessness in carrying out the works.

Acknowledgements

58.   The Author is indebted to the staff of ScotRail for assistance given in visiting the bridge and in preparing the Paper, in particular to Mr D. Hill-Smith and Mr P. Jolliffe.

59.   Several of the illustrations were provided by Mr Roland Paxton, Vice-Chairman of the ICE Panel for Historical Engineering Works.

Bibliography

1. Report of the Court of Inquiry, Tay Bridge Disaster, 1880.
2. BARLOW C. *The New Tay Bridge*, Spon, London, 1889.
3. BARLOW C. The Tay Viaduct, Dundee. *Proc. Instn Civ. Engrs*, 1888.
4. INGLIS W. The construction of the Tay Viaduct, Dundee. *Proc. Instn Civ. Engrs*, 1888.
5. SMITH D. W. Bridge Failures. Proc. Instn Civ. Engrs, Part 1, 1977, **62**, May, 257–281.

SHIPWAY

Conversion factors

1 in	25·4 mm
1 ft	0·305 m
1 ton	1·016 tonnes
1 ton/ft run	3·335 tonnes/m-run
1 ton/ft^2	109·4 kN/m^2
1 ton/in^2	15·44 N/mm^2
1 lb/ft^2	0·049 kN/m^2
1 mph	1·609 km/h

9

The Forth Railway Bridge centenary, 1890–1990: some notes on its design

J.S. Shipway

The design and construction of the Forth Railway Bridge was a massive project extending over at least 10 years; a comprehensive treatment is outside the scope of a single paper. This Paper therefore addresses the design aspect only, on which little material is extant, and none at all in the *Proceedings* of the ICE of that time. Some notes are included on design in general; the early proposal of Sir Thomas Bouch to bridge the Forth at Queensferry is dealt with; the previous history of cantilever bridges and the early design of Fowler and Baker are outlined. Foundations were straightforward—this Paper is mainly concerned with the super-structure. The evolution of the present form of the bridge is described, with materials and stresses adopted, and some notes on the method of calculation. It is shown that the design of the bridge evolved in a particular manner due to the simultaneous occurrence of a number of factors, each of low probability.

Introduction

In civil and structural engineering the term 'design' is often used without strict observance of its true meaning. Sometimes we use it when we mean calculation or analysis of a structure, but in reality a structure is analysed and calculated only after the design has been chosen, however tentatively. The design of a structure is its form, its shape, its basic concept. When this is decided, calculations are made to establish whether it can be constructed, and to estimate the cost. This is only the start of the design process. The analysis and calculation check may mean many revisions, or the scrapping of the initial idea altogether and a new start. The path of engineering design is often, therefore, a slow, irregular and halting journey: sometimes, however, the right solution emerges at the start and little adjustment is required, depending on how inspired the designer happens to be.

2. The ability to foresee difficulties and advantages in the realization or construction of the design is essential to the process. This requires experience as well as insight and understanding. There is a close connection between the idea and the means of achieving it—the engineer must have a knowledge of how things are constructed and made.

3. Civil engineering has advanced throughout the years in the employment of new materials and new technology as they have been developed, and in the understanding of the behaviour of structures through analysis and calculation. In general, a design should make the most of available technology, but it will also be limited and influenced by available technology, including the materials available. The design must engender the confidence of the user—this was a major difficulty after the collapse of the Tay Bridge in 1879.

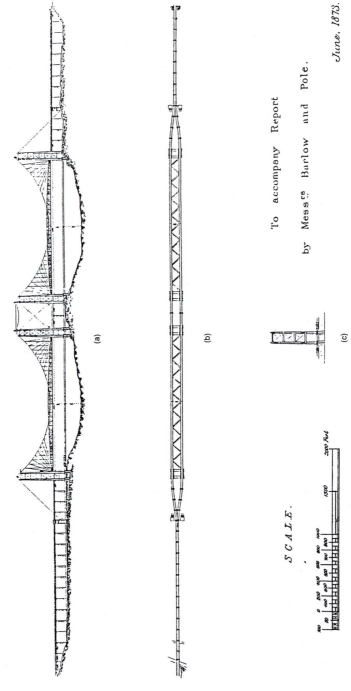

Fig. 1. Proposed Forth Bridge by Thomas Bouch, 1873: (a) general elevation; (b) plan; (c) transverse elevation

FORTH RAILWAY BRIDGE CENTENARY

Early proposals—Bouch's bridge of 1873

4.   A design for a bridge to span the Forth was prepared by Sir Thomas Bouch in the early 1870s (Fig. 1), and the first foundation pier was begun in 1878. Bouch was not the first engineer to prepare a design for this purpose, but his was the first design to reach the stage of construction, and was the first proposal for a railway bridge at Queensferry; previous proposals had been made for sites above and below Queensferry.

5.   Bridging the Forth at Queensferry meant thinking big. In 1818, an Edinburgh civil engineer, James Anderson, startled the public with proposals for his suspension bridge with spans of 2000 ft, and the engineers for the present bridge gave Bouch the credit for the ' bold proposition to cross the Forth in two spans of 1600 ft '. Bouch's design must have been taking shape in his mind for many years before construction started, for its feasibility was the subject of a private independent report by two eminent engineers, W. H. Barlow and William Pole, as early as 1873.

6.   Suspension bridges are much more flexible than any other form of bridge. The cable or chain is the main support member—its curve distorts easily under uneven loading and causes disturbing oscillations and sag unless steps are taken to prevent it. This can be resisted by introducing stiffening, either of the chains themselves or by a deep braced girder forming the deck. These methods apply the loads to the chains in a more uniform manner, and reduce the deflexion and distortion of the shape of the chain.

7.   Bouch thought in terms of a stiffened suspension bridge to carry rail traffic. Many suspension bridges had been built to carry the road traffic of those days, which consisted mainly of horses and carts and carriages. This load was very much lighter and more evenly distributed than the weight of a railway engine and a loaded train: in the 19th century only one stiffened suspension bridge to carry rail traffic was built—that over Niagara in the USA by Roebling in 1855 (Fig. 2). The span of the bridge was 821 ft, and it lasted for 42 years. In 1845 Stephenson planned to carry rail traffic over the Menai Straits by utilizing one side of the carriageway of Telford's suspension bridge. This idea proved impractical, and instead he developed the concept of the Menai tubular bridge, which was to incorporate suspension chains to assist the tubes in carrying the loads from rail traffic. However, it was found on further investigation that the massive tubes were sufficient to carry the rail loading by themselves, and the chains were never constructed, although the towers were built to accommodate them. The Menai tubular bridge was the largest rail bridge in the UK at that time, and had two main spans of 460 ft (Fig. 3).

8.   The spans of 1600 ft over the Forth proposed by Bouch were enormous, and it was natural that his first thought was to reduce the weight of his structure. This no doubt influenced him strongly towards the stiffened suspension bridge. He produced four designs on this principle, which are illustrated in Westhofen's book (Fig. 4). Many suspension bridges of the day had a sag/span ratio for the chains of approximately 1 : 10, and three of Bouch's designs incorporated chains and stiffened chains of this form. The fourth design, however, included chains with a sag/span ratio of about 1 : 4, which meant a sag of around 400 ft for the spans of 1600 ft. The clearance required for shipping was 150 ft, so that the towers required to support the chains and deck were nearly 600 ft in height, i.e. higher than the present road bridge towers (550 ft). This was the design favoured by Bouch, upon which construction had begun (Fig. 1).

SHIPWAY

Fig. 2. Suspension bridge carrying rail traffic. Roebling, 1855

FORTH RAILWAY BRIDGE CENTENARY

Fig. 3. Menai tubular bridge, 1856

1083

SHIPWAY

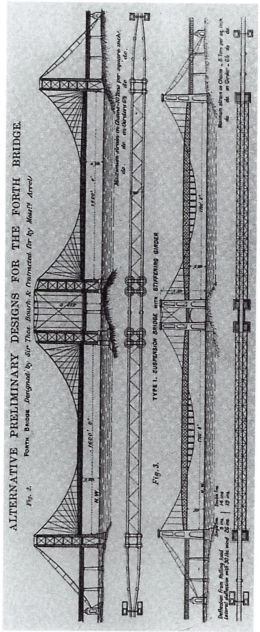

Fig. 4 (above and facing). Alternative designs for the Fourth Bridge by Thomas Bouch

FORTH RAILWAY BRIDGE CENTENARY

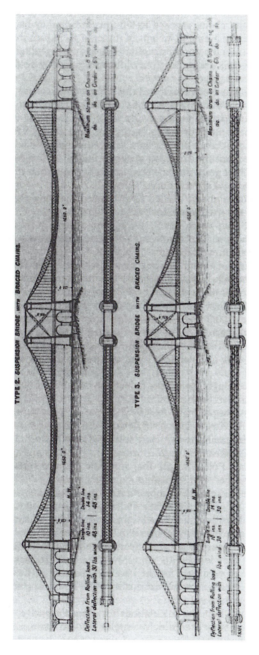

Fig. 4—continued

9. Bouch evidently chose this low sag/span ratio to reduce the stresses in the chains, which were of steel and stressed to 10.0 tons/in^2, high for those days. His three other designs had chains stressed to 8.0 tons/in^2: as they had less sag, they must have had a greater area and weight of material to reduce the stress to this figure. For comparison, a maximum stress of 7.5 tons/in^2 was adopted for the steel of the present Forth rail bridge, but only after prolonged negotiation with the Board of Trade by the engineers.

10. It is not clear why Bouch favoured this design, with its very large cable sag implying increased length of chains, height of towers, load on foundations, resistance to wind, and, of course, increased cost. Also, the large sag meant that the chains themselves were more prone to oscillation than chains with a shallower profile. The usual elegant curve of the chains generally lends suspension bridges an attractive appearance, but the large sag of the chains on Bouch's bridge made it look cumbersome. There were no supended side spans to match the 1600 ft main spans; this was also an awkward feature.

11. Distortion of the chains was to be precluded by tying them in position with radiating chain ties fixed to the ends of the stiffening girder. These ties were to assist the stiffening girder, which was 50 ft deep at mid-span, 18 ft deep at the ends, and of lattice construction. Also, the chains were anchored to the stiffening girders at their midpoints—an unusual feature.

12. Wind pressure for design purposes was assumed to be 10 lbs/ft^2, on the advice of the Astronomer Royal. This figure was also approved by Barlow and Pole in their report on Bouch's design in 1873, and seems to have been the norm for design in the UK at that time. Bouch separated the rail tracks in his bridge to two distinct structures 100 ft apart, bracing them to provide a rigid system against the horizontal forces of the wind. The chains for each of the two 1600 ft spans were anchored separately, so that the loading on one span did not affect the other. Temperature effects were also carefully assessed and suitable provision was made accordingly.

13. The design seemingly gained Parliamentary and Board of Trade approval without any detailed investigation other than the private report by Barlow and Pole, and construction began in 1878, with William Arrol of Glasgow as contractor. After the fall of the Tay Bridge in 1879 work was discontinued, and only the single foundation pier remains today. Had Bouch's design been completed it might have proved difficult and expensive to construct, owing to its multiplicity of small members. Barlow and Pole thought that it would require 'great accuracy in manufacture and erection', and seemed to indicate a lingering doubt on its fitness for its purpose: 'While we raise no objection to Mr Bouch's system, we do not commit ourselves to an opinion that it is the best possible'. A modern day writer (Professor H. J. Hopkins) was more forthright and less kind when he commented that the design was 'painstakingly laboured to the point of being an oddity'.

14. In the past, bridges of two or four spans have been considered unattractive aesthetically because they formed an 'unresolved duality'. Bridges of three spans or five spans have been proposed for the sake of appearance. It can be seen that Bouch's design embodied an unresolved duality of awkward appearance in a way that the present bridge does not.

15. It is interesting that the calculations for Bouch's bridge, with its many degrees of redundancy, were exceedingly complex, and he was assisted by a Cambridge mathematician, Allan D. Stewart (see below). When the bridge construction was abandoned, Stewart transferred his allegiance to Fowler and Baker, and

FORTH RAILWAY BRIDGE CENTENARY

became their chief assistant on the cantilever design. His name appears on the commemorative plaque on the present bridge.

Revised proposals by Fowler and Baker, 1881

16.   After the Tay bridge disaster in 1879 the public and the press were loud in their criticism of Bouch's Forth Bridge design, and there was a massive loss of faith in the project. It soon became known that new and stringent regulations were to be introduced by the Board of Trade to control standards, and it was obvious that Bouch's design would have to be revised, particularly as it was designed for a wind pressure of only 10 lbs/ft².

17.   The Railway Board formally abandoned Bouch's design on 13 January 1881 (i.e. a full year after the disaster), which indicates that they gave careful consideration to the matter. They cancelled the existing contracts and paid compensation where necessary. A formal Abandonment Bill was placed before Parliament, but a bridge, tunnel or some fixed means of communication across the Forth was still considered necessary, and the Abandonment Bill was withdrawn before it was passed.

18.   New proposals for a bridge were invited from the Board's consulting engineers, Sir John Fowler, W. H. Barlow and T. E. Harrison. From these emerged a design proposal based on what was then called the 'continuous girder principle'. This entailed a continuous girder with definite breaks at chosen points of contraflexure. These breaks, or hinges, made the bridge form easier to calculate and build, and transformed it into a series of cantilevers and suspended spans rather than a continuous girder. This type of bridge had many advantages over the original stiffened suspension bridge, being more rigid and stable under construction. The original proposal was modified by Fowler and his junior partner, Benjamin Baker, to the form that we know today.

19.   The original design had cantilever arms based on N-girder or Pratt truss panels with large 500 ft suspended spans in between (Fig. 5). The Fife and Queensferry cantilevers were not completely stable under construction until the landward arms had been completed. The revised design had a cantilever structure based on the double-triangular form, and shorter suspended spans of 350 ft. The Fife and Queensferry cantilevers were also designed to be selfsupporting at all stages of construction. This is the bridge we know today—the revised arrangement gave the impression of stability and strength.

20.   These proposals gained the approval of the Board, and on 30 September 1881 Fowler and Baker were instructed to proceed with their design. A model 13 ft long was prepared specially for the House of Commons. (As late as 1955 this model was on public view at the Institution of Civil Engineers in London.) A new Bill passed through Parliament and received Royal Assent on 12 July 1882. Thus, within 18 months of the abandonment of Bouch's design a new bridge was well on the way.

21.   Influenced by the widespread popular fears aroused by the Tay bridge failure, Parliament imposed many restrictions, including a new wind loading of 56 lbs/ft². It instructed the Board of Trade to inspect every stage of construction, no doubt mindful of the poor quality of ironwork inherent in the earlier disaster. The most important consideration was that the bridge 'should gain the confidence of the public, and enjoy a reputation of being not only the biggest and strongest, but also the stiffest bridge in the world'. By 'stiffness' they undoubtedly meant lack of

SHIPWAY

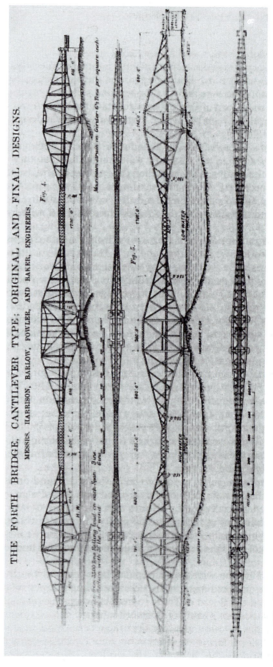

Fig. 5. The Forth Bridge: original and final design by Fowler and Baker, and others

1088

FORTH RAILWAY BRIDGE CENTENARY

noticeable movement or deflexion under the passage of the trains or the violence of the winds.

22. In the 18 months of discussion between the abandonment of Bouch's design and the acceptance of Fowler and Baker's, the following criteria emerged as the basis of design of the bridge

> (a) the maximum attainable rigidity, both vertically under the rolling load and laterally under wind pressure
>
> (b) facility and security of erection, so that at any stage the incomplete structure would be as secure against a hurricane as the finished bridge
>
> (c) that no untried material be used in the construction, and that no steel be used which did not comply with the requirements of the Admiralty, Lloyds and the Underwriters' Registry
>
> (d) that the maximum economy be attained consistent with the fulfilment of the preceding conditions.

The proposed continuous girder bridge by Fowler and Baker complied more fully with these criteria than the previous stiffened suspension design.

23. Baker himself (on whom the main burden of design and supervision fell) had strong views on the requirements of a design, and as early as 1873 had stated in a lecture:

> Of all the numerous practical considerations and contingencies to be duly weighed and carefully estimated, before the fitness of a design for a longspan railway bridge can be satisfactorily determined, *none are more important* than those affecting facility of erection.

24. From the above, it can be seen that the design of the Forth Bridge evolved in a particular form because of the simultaneous occurrence of a number of factors, each of low probability. These factors (and constraints) were

> (a) the existence of a group of railway companies with the desire and the financial means to bridge the Forth
>
> (b) the existence of the Queensferry site, with its high ground on either side allowing the necessary headroom, its wide deep-water channels precluding all but the largest spans, and the presence of rock and hard boulder clay offering suitable foundation material for a major bridge
>
> (c) the availability of a new material, i.e. steel, of reliable quality, quantity and price
>
> (d) the existence of engineers of the required towering vision, ability and courage to develop the design and bring about its realization.

The present form of the bridge

25. The present form of the Forth Bridge is familiar to everyone, and we think of cantilever bridges of all types as being commonplace. But it was not always so. Before 1881, when Fowler and Baker put forward their proposals, the cantilever bridge was unknown in Britain; the designers of the new bridge were continually asked to justify it. This was important, as there would ultimately be no point in a bridge that did not inspire confidence in those who would be using it.

26. In particular, Baker was asked about his novel use of 'cantilevers'. He explained that the term means no more than 'bracket', and that an ordinary balcony or shelf is a form of cantilever. There was nothing novel even in the design of cantilever bridges; they had been built in China more than 200 years before, and

SHIPWAY

Fig. 6. Road bridge at Newcastle, 1871 by Thomas Bouch

1090

FORTH RAILWAY BRIDGE CENTENARY

probably earlier than that. There were also more recent examples of road and railway bridges in Europe and the USA built on the same principle, including a strange hybrid type of braced structure which Bouch had built across the Tyne at Newcastle in 1871 (Fig. 6).

27. As early as 1867, Benjamin Baker (then aged 27) had published a series of articles in *The Engineer* advocating the use of cantilevers supporting a girder system as the most effective means of providing bridges of long span. He and his senior partner Fowler had some experience of designing such bridges, for in 1864 they had proposed a bridge of 1000 ft span on the cantilever system for a railway crossing of the Severn. The span was subsequently reduced to 600 ft with 300 ft side-spans, and a contract was let for the works, which did not proceed due to financial problems. Again in 1871 they had prepared designs and estimates for a second proposal to cross the Severn in two spans of 800 ft each, but in this case also the design did not reach the construction stage. Fowler had taken part in a discussion on a Paper to the ICE as far back as 1850 on a continuous girder bridge at Torksey over the river Trent, which showed that even at that early stage, 30 years before the Forth bridge design, he had an accurate grasp of cantilever principles.

28. In addition to Fowler and Baker's designs, other engineers in Europe and the USA had produced at least three cantilever bridges before 1883.

(a) In 1866 the Bavarian engineer Heinrich Gerber was granted a patent for a design known as the 'Gerber girder', or in English speaking countries, a cantilever girder. This was a continuous girder over several spans in which hinged joints were inserted so that the harmful influence of minor settlement of supports was eliminated. The first bridge built by Gerber employing this system was in Germany over the river Main at Hassfurt in 1867. This had a central span of 426 ft (Fig. 7)

(b) In 1876 the Cincinnati Southern Railway crossed the Kentucky river by means of a cantilever bridge which had three equal spans of 375 ft. This was designed by an eminent American engineer, C. Shaler Smith (Figs 8 and 9).

(c) In 1883, the year work began at the Forth, a notable cantilever bridge was completed over the Niagara river in the USA by another leading American engineer, C. C. Schneider. This had a total length of 910 ft, was 239 ft above the water, and had a main span of 495 ft. It had pin-connected members, and was constructed in the amazingly short time of 10 months (Fig. 10).

29. There was also Bouch's bridge of 1871 at Newcastle (Fig. 6) which had main spans of 240 ft, braced with tension members from the tops of towers over the piers. These ties were fixed at the third point of the spans, and gave the bridge the appearance of a modern cablestayed structure or a cantilever bridge by Riccardo Morandi.

30. One of the basic questions affecting the form of the structure was the length of the cantilever arm in relation to the length of the suspended span. This was the subject of elaborate investigation by Baker, as it was known to have a pronounced effect on the economy of the design as well as on the method of erection. He chose lengths of 681·75 ft and 346·5 ft respectively (Fig. 11), giving a ratio of 1·96. But the first proposal by Fowler and Baker had a ratio of 1·23 due to the long suspended span of 500 ft (Fig. 5).

SHIPWAY

Fig. 7. Cantilever 'Gerber' bridge at Hassfurt, Germany, 1869

FORTH RAILWAY BRIDGE CENTENARY

Fig. 8. Cantilever bridge over the Kentucky River, 1876

SHIPWAY

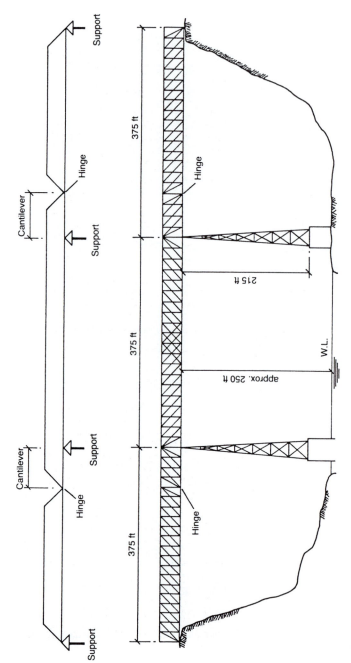

Fig. 9. Articulation diagram for Kentucky River bridge

FORTH RAILWAY BRIDGE CENTENARY

Fig. 10. Niagara Cantilever Bridge—1883

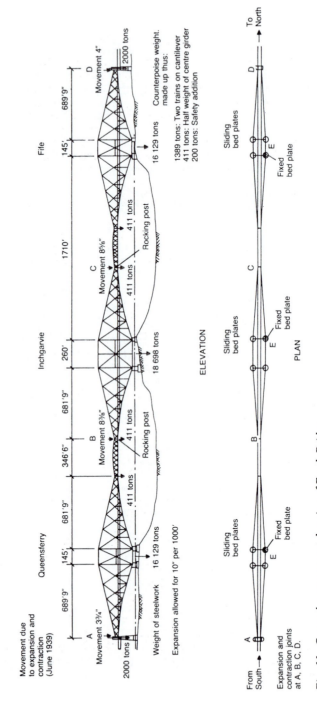

Fig. 11. General arrangement drawing of Forth Bridge

FORTH RAILWAY BRIDGE CENTENARY

31.   In the Quebec cantilever bridge of 1917 the ratio is 0·91, arising from a suspended span of 640 ft in a main span of 1800 ft (Fig. 12). This length of suspended span was so heavy that it had to be floated out and lifted into position, whereas Baker's smaller suspended spans could be constructed by cantilevering out from each side and joining up at mid-span. At Connel Ferry, Oban, completed in 1903, the ratio is even lower at 0·64 (Fig. 13). Thus, the Forth Bridge has rather short suspended spans compared to other designs of the period, but they look right.

32.   Another feature of the bridge affecting its form was Baker's decision to have a small number of large, rather than a large number of small, structural members. Bouch's 1873 suspension bridge design illustrates the latter case. The towers and stiffening girders were of lattice construction, generating many connections and a probable substantial maintenance problem had it been built, owing to its multiplicity of members (Fig. 4). Baker's choice of few but large structural members was emphasized by his selection of tubes for the compression members of the bridge. These struts were up to 343 ft long and 12 ft in diameter, yet appear of slender proportions and even matchstick-like from a distance. (The vertical tubes over the piers have a length/breadth ratio of 28·6, as compared to 21·5 for a match) (Fig. 14).

33.   Tubes were chosen because they are known to be the most efficient shape for a compression member, curved surfaces being much less prone to buckling than flat surfaces. Baker accepted that they would cost more to construct, but that this would be outweighed by the structural advantages. Nevertheless, the interpenetrations of the curved tubes at the skewbacks and elsewhere were extremely complex and difficult to design and detail as well as to construct.

34.   Baker had to decide at an early stage how best to take the wind forces to the foundations, and he did this by introducing bracing between the tubular members, both in the webs and in the lower chords of the cantilever. The lattice girders in the upper chords and diagonals are unbraced. This arrangement led the wind forces to the piers by the shortest route; the tubular members were of course designed to accept this extra loading.

35.   Careful provision was made for temperature movement (see Fig. 11). Also, Baker left three of the four skewbacks at the base of each cantilever tower free to move. Only one skewback in each group was fixed (Fig. 11). This was to allow the tremendous compression forces at the base of each cantilever arm to be resisted by the horizontal strut joining them. If this movement had not been allowed, the forces would have produced an overturning effect on the respective pier foundations.

36.   Perhaps the most noticeable feature of the bridge, however, is the 'Holbein' straddle, i.e. the wide base of the cantilevers tapering to narrow widths both vertically and horizontally. The German artist, Hans Holbein, was wont to straddle the feet of male subjects in his pictures. Sir John Fowler knew this: when he met James Nasmyth of steam-hammer fame by chance at a Holbein exhibition in London after the Tay bridge failure, he remarked that the bridge would not have fallen had it had a straddle to its piers resembling Holbein's characteristic pose. Hence the Holbein straddle, which resulted in a batter of about 1 : 7·5 throughout all the vertical members. This arrangement gave an impression of great stability, but also gave rise to much complexity in drawing and detailing, and in construction (Fig. 15).

SHIPWAY

Fig. 12. Quebec Bridge of 1917

FORTH RAILWAY BRIDGE CENTENARY

Fig. 13. Connel Ferry Bridge, Oban, 1903

SHIPWAY

Fig. 14. Inchgarvie tower, Forth Bridge (note the superfluous upper central vertical member, not present in Baker's later original design (Fig. 5))

Materials and allowable stresses

37. In the late 1870s when the Forth Bridge was being designed, steel remained a comparatively untried material for bridges, although it had been employed since the 1850s in several ships, including the 'Columba', the most famous of all the Clyde steamers, which was built in 1878 and queened it on the Clyde for more than 50 years. Steel was considered a new material, and some engineers had reservations about its brittleness as compared to that of wrought iron. It was also impossible to define its character completely by chemistry and ingredients, and testing of specimens was necessary to obtain sufficient proof of its quality and strength.

FORTH RAILWAY BRIDGE CENTENARY

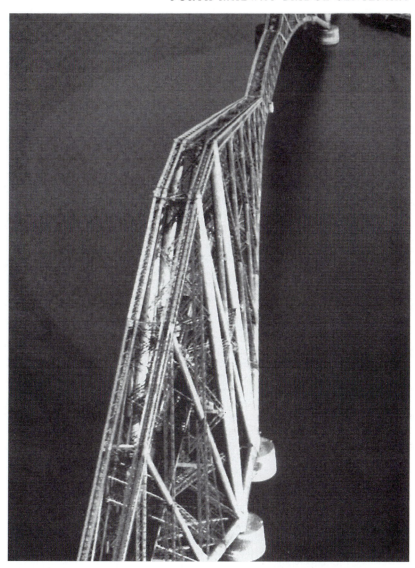

Fig. 15. Inclined structure of Forth Bridge: the Holbein straddle

38. In the rebuilding of the Tay bridge conservatism held sway, and wrought iron was used. Corresponding maximum stresses of 5·0 tons/in^2 in tension and 4·80 tons/in^2 in compression were adopted. However, steel could offer a 50% increase on these working stresses, and was obviously a great attraction where long spans were concerned, as its weight differed little from that of wrought iron.

SHIPWAY

Fowler and Baker therefore approached the Board of Trade to find out the maximum stress which could be adopted in design. At that time the Board was allowing 6·5 tons/in², but Baker showed that by improving the quality of the steel, 7·5 tons/in², i.e. a quarter of the ultimate strength of the steel would be reasonable, and the Board accepted this figure. Its figure of 6·5 tons/in² had been based on steel with an ultimate strength of 26 tons/in², whereas Baker proposed a minimum of 30 tons/in² for the bridge. Nowadays, BS 449 would allow a working stress in tension of 10·6 tons/in² on a steel of this ultimate stress.

39. Baker was aware of the dangers of fatigue, and limited the stress in the wind bracing, which was subject to alternate tension and compression, to 5·0 tons/in². Elsewhere on the bridge the working stress was to be 3·33 tons/in² if the stresses alternated in this fashion. He recognized that in the case of a hurricane the repetitions of stress would be few and far between, and so allowed a higher stress.

40. The Board of Trade regulations for the use of steel in the bridge were minimal, simply stating that the working stress should not exceed 25% of the ultimate. No distinction was made between tensile and compressive stress, or between stresses produced by dead and live load, either alone or in combination. Fowler and Baker therefore derived their design rules for stresses by careful thought and experiment, and their caution and insight has been amply repaid in the 100 year life of the bridge so far. Fatigue has not been a problem in the main structure, but has necessitated some repairs to the internal viaduct. In the latter, of course, live load plays a much greater part than dead load, although in the main structure the reverse applies.

41. In the construction of the tubes and other members, Baker insisted that as far as possible all plates and bars were to be bent cold. Where heating was essential, no work was to be done on the material after it had fallen to a 'blue' heat. He also insisted that the steady pressure of hydraulic riveting was to be used in place of hammering wherever possible, and that annealing would be required if the steel had been overworked in any way. He allowed no punching of holes or shearing of edges, and specified that all plates were to be planed at the edges, and all holes drilled. In particular, holes were to be drilled through multiple thicknesses of plates and angles after assembly.

42. These recommendations show the care with which Baker considered his material and its interconnection. Nothing was left to chance; painstaking attention to detail prevailed throughout. Having chosen the quality of steel and the working stresses, Baker then designed his structure boldly and confidently to the set limits.

43. Incidentally, the Author has not been able to locate any mention of Baker employing extra material or thickness to allow for the effects of corrosion in such an exposed location. In the event, his confidence in the effective maintenance of the bridge was not misplaced; it has been exceedingly well painted and maintained over the last 100 years.

Analysis—forces in the struts and ties

44. None of Baker's published papers give any hint of the methods used in calculating the structure. His book 'Long span railway bridges', published in 1873, does not go into structural analysis or stress calculation; it outlines general principles. Recourse to the Mitchell Library in Glasgow, where some of the original Arrol drawings are stored, indicated that no calculations have been filed. It has

FORTH RAILWAY BRIDGE CENTENARY

therefore not been possible to locate any relevant calculations, but the method of calculation is known.

45.   As mentioned above, Baker was assisted in his calculations by a Cambridge mathematician named Allan D. Stewart who had earlier assisted Bouch in his calculations for the stiffened suspension bridge. For this rather more complex bridge, Stewart is known to have used what he called 'diagrams of forces' evolved by Professor Clerk Maxwell (1831–1879), a well-known physicist of the 19th century, whose work embraced many fields. Clerk Maxwell evolved the load displacement method and reciprocal theorems in 1864 for analysing structures.

46.   Allan Stewart presented a Paper to the ICE in 1892 on 'Stresses and deflections in braced girders'. In those days the words 'stress' and 'strain' were commonly used where 'force' is the equivalent term today, and the paper is actually about forces and deflexions. In it, Stewart shows how a method of calculation which he calls 'the principle of elastic forces' can be applied to double triangular girders and other redundant structures with great accuracy, and states that this method was used in the calculation of the Forth Bridge structure. He also gives an example of its use for calculation of deflexion at the counterweighted shore arms of the Fife and Queensferry cantilevers. Stewart's name appears on the plaque on the bridge as Fowler and Baker's chief assistant, and there seems little doubt that he was responsible for the basic calculations for the Forth Bridge.

47.   It will be noted that the bridge is almost entirely composed of girders of the double triangular arrangement of an even number of panels in each span, i.e. the approach girders, the central suspended spans, and the cantilever arms. This form of truss, if the upper and lower chords are straight, is calculated approximately by separating the double triangular system into two single systems, each loaded with 50% of the total load, then superimposing the two results for the total forces in the members. Textbooks of the period claim that this method gives accuracy to within 5% of a more rigorous redundant structure analysis such as Allan Stewart's method. When the upper or lower chord of the girder is curved, however, it is more difficult to apply because of the resulting 'kinks' in the members of the single systems, and a more detailed method of analysis is required.

48.   In calculating the wind effects, Baker assumed the circular form of the tubes to give a reduction in resistance of 50% as compared to a flat surface. He also took the wind force on the leeward structure as being equal to that on the windward structure; an assumption on the safe side. The assumption regarding the streamlining effect of the tubular surface is almost exactly that quoted in CP3 today.

49.   In the cantilevers Baker gave figures of 3300 tons for the dead load and train test load, and 2900 tons for the wind force in the central lower chord strut, giving a total of 6200 tons. The net area of this strut is 830 in^2, giving a stress of 7·47 tons/in^2. The strut has a slenderness ratio of about 29, being 12 ft in diameter with $1\frac{1}{4}$ inch plating and 145 ft long, but restrained by some fixity at the ends. The allowable total stress was 7·5 tons/in^2, lower than would be allowed today, and no additional 25% increase was allowed for wind loading (Fig. 16).

50.   The greatest load on a lattice girder tie member in the top chord is approximately 3800 tons. No wind load was taken on these members, which makes the calculation rather easier. The area in tension is 506 in^2, giving a tensile stress of 7·50 tons/in^2. The vertical column over the skewback is 343 ft high, 12 ft in diameter and the shell is of plating $\frac{5}{8}$ inch thick. The area in compression is about 468 in^2, and Baker gives a force of 3280 tons in the strut, i.e. about 7·0 tons/in^2.

SHIPWAY

The strut has a slenderness ratio of about 34, being braced at mid-height. The slenderness ratio is thus higher than the central lower chord strut, which may account for the slightly lower stress shown in the calculation. Baker states in his paper to the British Association that no attempt was made to calculate temperature effects in the bridge members, although of course ample provision for temperature movement was made in the bridge as a whole (Fig. 11).

51.   The method of using influence lines for forces in members, widely used in railway bridge work, was derived in Germany by Weyrauch as early as 1873 and first appeared in the English language in 1887 in a paper to the American Society of Engineers. Its use was slow to develop in this country, and it is unlikely that influence lines were used in the calculation of any of the members of the Forth Bridge. They would have been of little use in the calculation of forces in the cantilevers, but might have had some application in the girders of the approach spans, or in the decking and the internal viaduct.

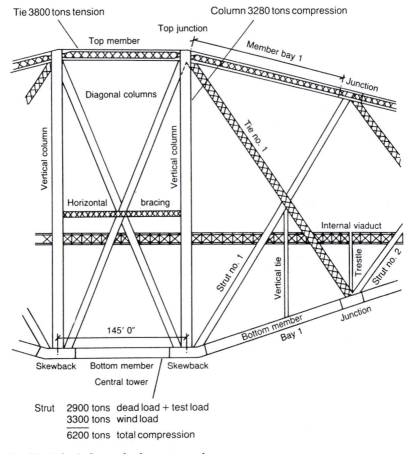

Fig. 16. Baker's figures for forces in members

FORTH RAILWAY BRIDGE CENTENARY

52. The magnitude of the structure and the forces deriving from it takes it beyond the range of simple modes of calculation which are customary in structures of a more ordinary kind. Influences which are usually small and can be handled easily have in this case to be carefully studied, particularly the dead load of the tubes and other members spanning between the panels, stiffness of the joints, torsion effects in the cantilevers due to trains on one line only, and the effects of the wind bracing on the tubes where the bracing does not reach a base reaction point. The locked-in stresses due to erection procedures would add to these problems, as would temperature effects of many kinds including sunshine on one side only of the bridge.

53. Baker forecast that the heaviest train traversing the bridge would not deflect the 1700 ft span more than 4 inches. In this he was remarkably accurate, as a deflexion of $3\frac{1}{2}$ inches has actually been measured on the bridge. He also calculated that a wind pressure equivalent to 30 lbs/ft^2 over the entire 1700 ft span would bend the bridge laterally less than 9 inches. He did not give a figure for a pressure of 56 lbs/ft^2, perhaps because it was unlikely that such a pressure would ever act over the whole structure.

54. It is interesting that Baker in his public lectures up to the year 1885 gave the estimate for the weight of steel in the cantilever structures of the bridge as totalling 42 000 tons, excluding the approach viaducts. In a lecture in 1887 he gave the figure as 45 000 tons, after erection of the steelwork had begun. However, the final figure given by Westhofen is 51 000 tons, 21% higher than the original estimate.

55. Westhofen wrote of alterations to the design and the increase of cross-section in various parts. The extra steel may have been necessary because of the weights of the cranes and other plant on individual members during erection, where cantilevering out over long lengths took place. The internal stiffening to the great tubes may not have been refined in detail, and perhaps the internal viaduct was not fully designed at the estimating stage. Other complex interpenetrations of tubes such as the 12 skewbacks are unlikely to have been fully detailed at that stage either, and may have required more steel than allowed for. There are many reasons why the original estimate may have been low, but if Baker used a figure of 42 000 tons in his calculations, he must have designed with a good margin in hand to allow for an increase in dead load of 21% for the cantilever structure of the bridge. Digesting these figures has been a fascinating exercise, but suggests that the Forth bridge is not so over-designed as is often supposed!

56. Most views of the bridge are from the shore close by, where foreshortening gives it a heavy appearance. Seen from the road bridge, however, the railway bridge is slender and graceful, leaping like a greyhound over the vast span of water between the cantilevers. In spite of the constraints of high wind loads and low steel stresses, Baker achieved a graceful and elegant design (Fig. 17).

Conclusion

57. This necessarily brief review of the origins and design of the Forth Bridge has tried to show something of the thinking behind it, and the boldness, original thought and painstaking care which went into its design. It is a beautiful bridge, second to none in the world, and our country is the richer because of it. Long may it survive to inspire others with its majesty and grace!

SHIPWAY

Fig. 17. The gossamer bridge: delicate ana.

FORTH RAILWAY BRIDGE CENTENARY

Acknowledgements

58. The Author is indebted to the staff of ScotRail for assistance in visiting the bridge and in preparing this Paper, in particular to Mr W. D. F. Grant, Area Civil Engineer, Scotland South-East. He is also indebted to Mr Roland Paxton, Chairman of the ICE Panel for Historical Engineering Works, without whose assistance and encouragement the Paper would never have been written.

Bibliography

1. HARRIS A. J. Civil Engineering considered as an art. *Proc. Instn Civ. Engrs*, Part I, 1975, **58**, 15–23.
2. INSTITUTION OF STRUCTURAL ENGINEERS *The aims of structural design.* The Institution of Structural Engineers, London, 1969.
3. BARLOW W. H. and POLE W. *Report on the Forth Bridge designed by Thomas Bouch.* Hugh Paton and Sons, Edinburgh, 1873.
4. WESTHOFEN W. *The Forth Bridge.* Moubray House Publishing, Edinburgh, 1989, Centenary Facsimile Edn (first published by Engineering Magazine, London, 1890).
5. HOPKINS H. J. *A span of bridges.* David and Charles, Newton Abbot, 1970.
6. BAKER B. The Forth Bridge. *J. Iron Steel Inst.*, 1885, No. 11.
7. BAKER B. The Forth Bridge, Lecture to the British Association, 1882.
8. BAKER B. *Bridging the Firth of Forth.* Lecture to the Royal Institution, 1887.
9. STEWART A. D. Stresses and deflections in braced girders. *Proc. Instn Civ. Engrs*, 1892 **109**, 269–287.

Conversion factors

1 in	25·4 mm
1 ft	0·305 m
1 ton	1·016 t
1 ton/ft run	3·335 t/m run
1 ton/ft^2	109·4 kN/m^2
1 ton/in^2	15·44 N/mm^2
1 lb/ft^2	0·049 kN/m^2
1 mph	1·609 km/h

10
L'entreprise Eiffel
Bertrand Lemoine

Résumé

Gustave Eiffel, « le magicien du fer » constitue un cas exemplaire de réussite entrepreneuriale. Centralien, il mène à bien, comme ingénieur, les travaux du pont de Bordeaux. Etabli à son compte, d'abord associé avec Seyrig, il obtient à l'étranger de retentissants succès — pont Maria Pia sur le Douro, gare de Budapest —, tout en s'implantant précocement en Indochine. Damant le pion aux plus grosses entreprises de l'époque, il réalise en métropole de très importants ouvrages — viaduc de Garabit, coupole du Grand Equatorial de Nice, Tour Eiffel —, grâce entre autres à ses appuis franc-maçons. Impliqué dans le scandale de Panama, il se retire des affaires et consacre ses dernières années à la météorologie, à la radiotélégraphie et à l'aérodynamique.

Abstract

Gustave Eiffel, the « iron wizard », is an exemplary case of entrepreneurial success. A graduate of the French Ecole Centrale, he was responsible for the engineering work on the Bordeaux bridge. Setting up his own firm, initially in partnership with Seyrig, he scored outstanding successes in foreign markets — the Maria Pia bridge over the Douro, the Budapest railway station —, while staking out early on strong positions in Indochina. Stealing a march on the larger, leading firms of the time, he secured on the home front contracts for schemes of major importance — the Garabit viaduct, the Nice Grand Equatorial observation cupola, the Eiffel Tower —, a helpful factor in this respect being the support he could enlist among his connections in masonic circles. Implicated in the Panama scandal, he retired from business involvements, and his final years were devoted to work on meteorology, wireless telegraphy and aerodynamics.

Il y a incontestablement un mythe Eiffel, celui d'être « un magicien du fer », à qui l'on attribuerait volontiers tout ce qui ressemble à une charpente métallique, comme Vauban se voit créditer moult fortifications bastionnées. Ce mythe est en partie fondé, mais Eiffel n'a donc pas seulement été un grand ingénieur, un inventeur de formes, dont la Tour qui porte son nom serait l'éclatant et ô combien visible chef d'œuvre. Son parcours qui allie réussite technique et réussite commerciale est en effet un modèle du genre. Autant qu'un inventeur brillant, Eiffel s'est révélé un véritable chef d'entreprise, capable de transformer ses conceptions les plus audacieuses en réalité bâtie, doué de volonté et d'ambition, un homme d'affaires avisé sachant prendre des risques calculés dans un environnement économique particulièrement favorable, marqué par le développement des chemins de fer et l'essor de la construction métallique. L'histoire de l'entreprise Eiffel s'identifie certes avec celle de son fondateur [1]. Mais, au-delà de l'épopée individuelle, l'étude de la fondation et du développement de l'entreprise montre de façon exemplaire comment le succès est venu de la conjonction de l'innovation technique, notamment dans les procédés de construction, de la maîtrise des coûts de fabrication, du contrôle systématique de la qualité des produits, de la mobilisation de

---

1. Sur la biographie personnelle d'Eiffel, voir F. Poncetton, *Eiffel, le magicien du fer*, Paris, 1939. Sur sa carrière, voir G. Cordier, *A propos de l'œuvre de Gustave Eiffel*, Paris, 1978 (dactyl.), B. Lemoine, *Gustave Eiffel*, Paris, Hazan, 1984 ainsi que H. Loyrette, *Gustave Eiffel*, Paris, Payot, 1986.

compétences et de capitaux grâce au charisme du fondateur, de l'organisation exemplaire de la production, de l'attention aux termes des contrats, de la politique relationnelle et de la constante recherche d'appuis bien placés. Bien qu'il eût rapidement développé l'entreprise qu'il avait fondée, Eiffel ne fut jamais en mesure d'égaler les géants de la construction métallique pour ce qui est du tonnage des constructions, restant plutôt aux environs du sixième ou huitième rang des entreprises françaises, abstraction faite du « coup » que constitua le canal de Panama. Mais s'il a pu jouer dans la cour des grands, c'est grâce à une meilleure capacité d'innovation, aux brillants ingénieurs qu'il a su découvrir ou débaucher. C'est aussi par un sens aigu des relations commerciales et de sa propre publicité, qui a focalisé sur sa personne et sur son nom les succès de l'entreprise. Ce sont enfin des qualités d'organisateur et de gestionnaire hors pair, un sens évident des affaires qui en font un très grand entrepreneur.

L'INGENIEUR

Eiffel est né à Dijon en 1832 d'une mère gestionnaire active du commerce de bois et charbons dont elle avait hérité, et d'un père autodidacte convaincu, qui lui communiquera son esprit aventureux et sa soif d'apprendre. Après des études sans éclat au collège royal de Dijon, le jeune Gustave monte à Paris pour préparer au collège Sainte-Barbe le concours d'entrée à Polytechnique. Il échoue à l'oral, mais intègre en 1852 l'Ecole Centrale des Arts et Manufactures en qualité d'admissible à l'X. Moins prestigieuse et de plus récente création que son aînée, l'Ecole Centrale a aussi une vocation plus « industrielle ». La soixantaine d'élèves que compte alors chaque promotion se répartit en deuxième année en quatre grandes options : métallurgie, mécanique, constructions civiles et chimie. Eiffel choisit cette dernière, parce qu'il espère prendre la succession de son oncle maternel à la tête d'une fabrique de peinture installée à Pouilly-sur-Saône. Il présente ainsi son mémoire de fin d'études sur la construction d'une usine chimique, et sort en 1855 de l'Ecole au treizième rang sur quatre-vingt. Il laisse également huit cent francs de dettes chez son logeur à Paris, rue Saint-Gilles, que sa mère couvrira, non sans reproches. Elle lui avance également le montant d'un abonnement à l'Exposition universelle, qu'il visite à plusieurs reprises. Hasard ou destin ? La famille se brouille avec l'oncle, et après un cours passage en stage non rémunéré chez son beau-frère Joseph Collin, directeur des forges de Châtillon-sur-Seine, Eiffel rentre, par l'intermédiaire d'une relation d'affaires de sa mère, au service de Charles Nepveu, un ingénieur-constructeur inventif et prolixe, établi au 36 rue de la Bienfaisance à Paris, à proximité de la gare Saint-Lazare. Nepveu, qui a pour raison sociale la « Construction de machines à vapeur, outils, forge, chaudronnerie, tôlerie, matériel fixe et roulant pour chemins de fer, travaux publics », dispose également d'un atelier annexe à Clichy où il construit des wagons [2]. Eiffel devient rapidement son homme de confiance, et met à profit ces premiers mois d'activité pour compléter sa formation en suivant le dimanche les cours d'économie de Frédéric Le Play et des cours du soir au Conservatoire des Arts et Métiers.

Eiffel a pu constater que Nepveu est « considéré comme un homme très distingué par une foule de personnages éminents dans l'industrie et les sciences », et que « ses

---

2. Sans être un personnage de premier plan, Nepveu est à l'époque un ingénieur d'une certaine notoriété. Il est membre du Comité de la Société des Ingénieurs Civils, et s'est fait une spécialité des fondations en rivière à l'air comprimé.

ateliers et affaires sont considérables » [3]. Eiffel est plus particulièrement chargé de l'étude des fondations en rivière, avec emplois de presses hydrauliques pour le fonçage de tubes à l'air comprimé, qui avait fait un an plus tôt l'objet d'une communication de Nepveu à la Société des ingénieurs civils. Eiffel aura bientôt l'occasion de mettre en œuvre ce procédé.

Mais les affaires de Nepveu ne sont pas au plus haut. Comme le remarquera Eiffel, son capital est insuffisant et il doit assurer une trésorerie difficile par l'escompte de traites auprès des banques, qui ne tarderont pas à l'abandonner. N'ayant pu assurer la paye de ses ouvriers, Nepveu disparaît le 12 mai 1856, non sans recommander Gustave à l'un de ses amis les plus intimes, Emile Trélat, professeur au Conservatoire des Arts et métiers, futur fondateur de l'Ecole Spéciale d'Architecture et franc-maçon. Nepveu reparaît, et Eiffel est placé par ses soins à la Compagnie des chemins de fer de l'Ouest, où il a l'occasion d'étudier un petit pont en « tôle » de 22 mètres pour le chemin de fer de Saint-Germain. C'est le premier pas d'Eiffel dans une grande carrière de constructeur de ponts, et notamment pour les chemins de fer qui se développent à une vitesse fulgurante. Il apprend ici son métier d'ingénieur-constructeur, se familiarisant avec une technique toute neuve mais qui trouve déjà ses applications.

PREMIERES ARMES

Quelques mois plus tard, il commence avec Nepveu, en dehors de ses heures normales de bureau, l'étude du pont ferroviaire sur la Garonne à Bordeaux, en vue de présenter une offre pour sa construction. Cet ouvrage stratégique conçu par l'ingénieur en chef de la Compagnie, Stanislas de la Roche-Tolay, doit lier les réseaux d'Orléans à ceux du Midi, construits par les Pereire. Dans le même temps, Nepveu cède son affaire à la Compagnie belge de matériels de chemins de fer dirigée par Pauwels. Outre l'usine de Clichy, le principal actif est constitué par le marché probable du pont de Bordeaux sur lequel Nepveu semble avoir eu de sérieuses assurances [4]. Eiffel rentre alors en décembre 1856 chez Pauwels comme « chef d'études des travaux de l'usine » de la nouvelle succursale française de la compagnie. Après la signature du contrat du pont de Bordeaux, le 4 janvier 1858, Eiffel est chargé par Nepveu de la mise au point des plans d'exécution et des commandes de fourniture, avant de partir pour Bordeaux diriger les travaux. Long de 500 mètres, cet ouvrage est l'un des plus importants alors construits en France. Ses fondations sont réalisées grâce à l'emploi de caissons à l'air comprimé, technique qui deviendra l'une des spécialités d'Eiffel. Il révèle sur ce difficile chantier ses capacités de technicien, d'organisateur et de meneur d'hommes. Il s'assure également de la confiance de personnalités de premier plan, tels que les frères Péreire, Raphaël Bischoffsheim, administrateur de la Compagnie du Midi, Léon Courras, secrétaire général du Réseau central, ou Wilhelm Nordling, ingénieur en chef du Paris-Bordeaux.

Eiffel devient en 1860, après l'achèvement du pont de Bordeaux et le retrait de Nepveu, ingénieur de la Compagnie des Matériels de Chemin de Fer. Laroche-Tolay lui confie la réalisation de divers ouvrages pour la Compagnie des Chemins de fer du Midi,

---

3. Lettre d'Eiffel à sa mère, 13 février 1856, Musée d'Orsay, Fonds Eiffel.

4. Nepveu semble en effet bien informé de l'état d'avancement du projet dès juillet 1856, alors que la Roche-Tolay ne remettra officiellement son avant-projet qu'en mars 1857. Voir G. Cordier, *op. cit.*, p. 87.

notamment le viaduc de Paludate à Bordeaux et un pont sur la Nive à Bayonne. Puis il le recommande à Jean-Baptiste Krantz, alors agent de travaux de la Compagnie d'Orléans en résidence à Périgueux pour préparer l'ouverture du réseau central. Eiffel se voit alors confier la réalisation de plusieurs ponts sur la ligne de Périgueux, notamment à Capdenac et à Floirac. Il sillonne le sud-ouest et s'affirme comme l'homme de confiance de la société Pauwels. Il passe directeur de l'usine de Clichy en octobre 1862.

A peine installé à Clichy, il constate que la situation de la société n'est guère brillante. « Il y a peu de travaux et ceux que nous avons sont mal payés » écrit-il le 8 mars 1863. Eiffel commence à ménager ses arrières et songe à s'installer à son compte. Il obtient même en février 1864 de la Compagnie du Midi d'être personnellement substitué à la Compagnie du matériel des chemins de fer pour la construction de la halle de la gare de Toulouse, et finit par obtenir d'être licencié fin 1864.

LA FONDATION DE L'ENTREPRISE

Il s'installe alors comme ingénieur-conseil au 14 de la rue de Saint-Petersbourg. Outre son indemnité de licenciement et le marché de la gare de Toulouse, il escompte la vente de 33 locomotives à l'Egypte, en association avec un certain Lambert. Eiffel se rend sur place en avril 1865, mais « s'ennuie affreusement et déplore le temps qu'on perd ici dans l'inaction ». Ses bonnes relations avec Krantz, qui vient d'être nommé directeur des travaux de l'Exposition Universelle de 1867 lui permettent d'obtenir un premier contrat important. Eiffel doit s'occuper des essais de la charpente métallique que l'entreprise Gouin [5] prépare pour la Galerie des machines [6]. Plus concrètement, il obtient en janvier 1866 la commande de la partie métallique de la galerie des Beaux-Arts. Le marché est modeste, 300 tonnes de métal pour 200 000 francs, mais la charpente est « extrêmement simple et ne présente pas d'éventualités ni de risques à courir ». Pour assumer cette commande et s'établir de façon solide comme entrepreneur, il reprend des ateliers de chaudronnerie installés à La Villette. Après quelques mois comme « ingénieur-constructeur », Eiffel franchit une nouvelle étape. Il fait l'acquisition en novembre 1866 d'un bail de douze ans pour de nouveaux ateliers à Levallois-Perret. Sa nouvelle raison sociale devient alors « constructeur » [7]. Cette acquisition est entièrement financée par un prêt de son beau-père. Eiffel a déjà 50 000 francs de cautionnements bloqués et doit en outre équiper sa nouvelle usine [8].

A trente-quatre ans, voici donc Eiffel chef d'entreprise, avec une expérience déjà solide, des ateliers bien équipés et des relations bien placées. Il ne lui manque qu'un fonds de roulement à la hauteur de ses ambitions. La famille y pourvoiera pendant deux ans encore, jusqu'à ce qu'il trouve un associé qui lui apportera les moyens nécessaires. Les affaires rentrent doucement mais sûrement : la charpente de la synagogue de la rue

5. Fondée par Ernest Gouin en 1846 avec des soutiens financiers importants, cette entreprise est alors l'une des toutes premières de France. Elle prendra en 1872 le nom de Société de construction des Batignolles.

6. Eiffel y conduit une série d'épreuves consignées dans un *Mémoire* publié en 1867 dans lequel il détermine une valeur expérimentale du coefficient d'élasticité du métal dans les poutres composées.

7. Apparaît aussi sur son papier à en-tête « les travaux exécutés par lui-même en qualité d'entrepreneur » : le pont de Bordeaux (*sic* !), les ponts de Capdenac et de Floirac, les halles des gares de Toulouse et d'Agen et ses travaux à l'Exposition.

8. Il rachète à Pauwels une partie du matériel de l'usine de Clichy pour 45 000 francs, soit l'équivalent de la « dot » reçue de ses parents. Il empruntera en outre 30 000 francs à son père en 1867 pour faire face à ses fournitures.

des Tournelles, dont l'ossature métallique est apparente, et celles des églises Notre-Dame des Champs et Saint-Joseph à Paris. Puis plusieurs usines à gaz à Paris, une série de 42 petits ponts pour le Grand central, un client avec qui il conserve d'étroites relations.

Mais c'est l'adjudication après concours de deux viaducs de grandes dimensions à Rouzat et Neuvial sur la Sioule qui lancent véritablement l'entreprise. Quatre grands viaducs doivent être construits sur la ligne Commentry-Ganat concédée en 1863 à la Compagnie d'Orléans. Eiffel emporte le marché des deux plus petits face à la concurrence des trois grands de la construction métallique de l'époque : Cail, Gouin et Schneider. L'innovation apportée par Eiffel porte moins sur la conception même des projets, dus à Nordling, ingénieur en chef de la Compagnie d'Orléans, que sur le mode de construction par lançage du tablier préalablement construit sur la rive, procédé qui allait rencontrer un grand développement par la suite [9]. Si Eiffel a su faire jouer ses relations au sein de la Compagnie d'Orléans, la crédibilité technique et financière de son offre lui assurent ici un double succès, financier et « d'amour-propre ». « J'ai réussi à me faire admettre aux côtés des grands constructeurs, ce qui était déjà fort honorable pour un établissement comme le mien » écrit-il le 8 juin 1867. Cela lui assure un an et demi de sécurité.

Il développe son entreprise en s'associant en octobre 1868 avec Théophile Seyrig, sorti trois ans plus tôt major de l'Ecole Centrale. Seyrig n'apporte pas seulement sa compétence technique, mais aussi 126 000 francs d'argent frais sur le capital total de 200 000 francs. La société ainsi formée a pour raison sociale « Gustave Eiffel et Cie ». Son double statut, de commerce en nom collectif en ce qui concerne Eiffel et en commandite simple à l'égard de Seyrig, assure les pleins pouvoirs à Eiffel, seul gérant [10]. Bien que majoritaire, Seyrig n'a que le droit de demander un emploi dans la maison, « sans pouvoir prendre aucune part dans la gérance ou la direction », tout en recevant cependant 38 % des bénéfices. Seyrig sera beaucoup plus qu'un associé discret. Il dirigera avec brio le bureau d'études de l'entreprise, et concevra notamment le viaduc du Douro à Porto, l'une des plus belles réalisations de l'entreprise.

LE DEVELOPPEMENT DE L'ENTREPRISE A L'ETRANGER

Ainsi commanditée, l'entreprise peut assurer un volume de travaux qui tourne autour du million de francs annuels. La recherche de nouveaux marchés, face à la rude concurrence métropolitaine, pousse Eiffel à prospecter le Pérou, où les Péreire ont des intérêts. Il traite fin 1869 pour 800 000 francs une série de ponts pour les Chemins de fer du Midi sur la ligne de Brive à Tulle.

Eiffel traverse sans trop de dommages la guerre de 1870 et cherche à consolider son entreprise, en France d'abord en réalisant de nombreux ponts, notamment ceux des lignes Latour-Millau et Chinon-les Sables d'Olonne, dont le viaduc de Thouars, des charpentes ou des gazomètres. Il tente aussi de s'installer durablement en Amérique du Sud, en particulier au Pérou et en Bolivie, où, grâce aux efforts de son homme de confiance Lelièvre, il espère construire la Douane de Callao, soit un marché de huit à

---

9. Pour éviter tout risque de renversement des piles, Eiffel a mis au point un système de châssis à bascule munis de rouleaux actionnés par des leviers.

10. Voir contrat passé entre Eiffel et Seyrig, Musée d'Orsay, Fonds Eiffel, ARO 1981, 1914, pièce 1.

dix millions de francs. Eiffel profite de cette circonstance pour doubler le capital de l'entreprise [11]. Il construit des ponts, des jetées, des gazomètres et même des églises préfabriquées en métal, comme celle d'Arica à la frontière chilienne [12]. Le décès prématuré de Lelièvre le 28 novembre 1873 mettra fin à cette aventure américaine.

Eiffel marque un nouveau point dans l'accroissement et la diversification de ses activités en construisant en 1875-1877 la gare de l'Ouest à Pest en Hongrie. Il obtient l'entreprise générale de la gare pour un montant de 2 822 000 francs, à réaliser en deux ans. C'est la plus grosse affaire qu'il ait eu à traiter jusqu'alors. La présence de Nordling à la tête des chemins de fer autrichiens depuis 1875 n'est sans doute pas étrangère à ce succès.

Les charpentes métalliques restent cependant le terrain de prédilection de l'entreprise. Elle le prouve en remportant en mai 1875 un concours international pour la construction d'un important viaduc de chemin de fer à Porto, lancé par la Compagnie Royale des Chemins de Fer Portugais, où l'on retrouve encore les Péreire. Lauréat face à Gouin, Fives-Lille et une entreprise anglaise, Eiffel montre qu'avec une solution originale et inventive, on peut réduire considérablement les prix de revient habituels pour ce genre d'ouvrage : il est trois fois moins cher que le plus coûteux des concurrents [13] ! Le pont affecte la forme d'un arc de 160 mètres d'ouverture, portant un tablier droit, prolongé vers les rives par un viaduc sur piles métalliques. Comme l'explique Seyrig, le véritable concepteur du projet, « cet arc d'une forme tout à fait spéciale était appuyé sur une simple rotule aux naissances et sa hauteur allait progressivement en augmentant jusqu'au sommet, de manière à affecter la forme d'un croissant » [14]. L'arc est monté sans aucun échafaudage directement à partir des rives, reprenant une technique inaugurée par J. Eads au pont de Saint-Louis [15]. Il n'a fallu que six mois pour réaliser cette prouesse technique, autorisée par la parfaite qualité de la préparation des éléments à l'usine de Levallois-Perret et la rigueur des calculs, effectués à l'aide de tables de logarithmes à sept décimales. Cette réussite marque l'entrée d'Eiffel dans le club des grands constructeurs, et sa renommée internationale va désormais aller croissante. Avec le contrat de la gare de Pest signé deux mois plus tôt, Eiffel quadruple son chiffre d'affaires annuel. C'est le début de la prospérité. Il peut s'implanter durablement dans la péninsule ibérique, où il construit beaucoup de ponts à la fin des années 1870 : en Espagne, ceux de la ligne de Gérone ; au Portugal, ceux de la ligne du Minho. L'ouvrage le plus important est celui de Vianna do Castelo, dont le tablier long de 563 mètres est lancé à partir des rives, un nouvel exploit technique. Le marché s'élève à 1 823 000 francs, soit 50 % de plus que le pont du Douro.

Cherchant à exploiter le succès de Porto, Eiffel répond en mai 1876 au concours

---

11. Seyrig réinvestit 74 000 francs et Eiffel anticipe sur ses bénéfices pour 116 000 francs, ce qui met les deux associés à égalité. Lelièvre, qui dispose de la signature d'Eiffel, sera intéressé aux bénéfices pour un montant de 10 %. *Renouvellement du contrat entre Eiffel et Seyrig, 11 octobre 1873*, Musée d'Orsay, *ibid.*, pièce 2.

12. D'autres églises seront exportées par l'entreprise, à Tacna au Pérou, à Manille, et à Santa-Rosalia au Mexique, après avoir été présentée en 1889 à l'Exposition Universelle.

13. Les prix varient en effet de 8350 francs au mètre courant à 2930 francs. Cette différence de prix paraît tellement surprenante au maître d'ouvrage, qu'une commission est nommée pour vérifier les calculs et la constructibilité du projet.

14. T. Seyrig, *Le pont du Douro à Porto*, Paris 1878.

15. Des câbles en acier retenaient les parties de l'arc progressivement construit en surplomb sur la rivière, jusqu'à la jonction des deux demi-arcs à la clef. La coordination de l'exécution est à mettre au compte d'Emile Nouguier, ingénieur civil des Mines, qu'Eiffel avait débauché de chez son concurrent Gouin en début de chantier. Eiffel recrute aussi de la même façon Jean Compagnon, chef monteur de grande valeur, qui fera partie de la même loge maçonnique que Nouguier, loge affiliée au Grand Orient de France. Voir *Le Tout-Paris maçonnique*, Paris, Hemmelin, 1896.

ouvert pour l'Exposition Universelle de 1878. Il propose un pont couvert passant au dessus du pont d'Iéna, appuyé sur une arche métallique semblable à celle du Douro. Eiffel croit au succès : « Un travail de ce genre me mettrait au rang des premiers constructeurs d'Europe » [16]. Le projet est primé, mais refusé par le préfet de la Seine parce qu'il aurait obstrué la vue sur le palais du Trocadéro. Eiffel devra attendre la prochaine exposition universelle pour réaliser une œuvre à la hauteur de ses ambitions. Il obtient néanmoins la construction du grand vestibule d'accueil, un morceau de choix de 3000 tonnes de fer, soit dix fois ce qu'il avait réalisé en 1867. Il construit également le pavillon de la Ville de Paris et celui de la Compagnie parisienne du gaz, deux édifices qui associent une ossature métallique à un remplissage en brique. Il montre aussi à l'Exposition des dessins et maquettes de ses réalisations, notamment un modèle au 1/50e du pont de Porto.

A côté de la construction de nombreux ouvrages d'art en France, en Espagne, en Roumanie, en Algérie, en Espagne, avec notamment la construction d'un grand pont sur le Tage sur la ligne de Cacérès, Eiffel poursuit la diversification de son activité en réalisant en 1879 la dernière tranche de l'agrandissement des magasins du Bon Marché, dont la structure est entièrement métallique, puis, deux ans plus tard, l'imposant hall de bureaux du siège du Crédit Lyonnais à Paris. Sa notoriété est maintenant bien établie et depuis Pest, Porto et Vianna, son chiffre d'affaires annuel tourne autour de cinq millions.

LA NOTORIETE INTERNATIONALE

Le succès du viaduc de Porto apporte à Eiffel la commande directe d'un ouvrage semblable sur la ligne Marvejols-Neussargues dans le Cantal. L'avant-projet est dressé par le jeune ingénieur des Ponts et Chaussées chargé de la ligne, Léon Boyer, avec l'idée d'économiser le détour de quelques kilomètres de voie ferrée et surtout de coûteuses rampes à travers les gorges de la Truyère. Eiffel est sollicité pour la réalisation, et une décision ministérielle du 14 juin 1879 lui confie l'exécution du marché de gré à gré, y compris les maçonneries [17]. Seule ombre au tableau, Eiffel se brouille avec son associé Seyrig. Celui-ci veut sans doute sa part du pactole, d'autant plus que c'est au fond son idée qui est exploitée à Garabit. Toujours est-il qu'Eiffel décide brutalement le 30 juin 1879 de rompre le contrat qui les associait, alors qu'il restait neuf ans à courir [18]. Il est remplacé quatre mois plus tard par Maurice Koechlin, un jeune ingénieur des chemins de fer de l'Est frais émoulu du Polytechnicum de Zurich. La première tâche de Koechlin sera de faire les calculs de Garabit, avant d'assurer la direction du bureau d'études de l'entreprise.

Le projet de Garabit diffère par quelques détails de celui de Porto : la forme de l'arc

16. Lettre d'Eiffel à sa mère, 11 juin 1876, Musée d'Orsay, Fonds Eiffel.

17. Cette procédure exceptionnelle est justifiée par l'administration par la perte de temps qu'occasionnerait un appel d'offres et par les garanties que donne l'exemple du Douro : « Il serait d'ailleurs peu équitable dans l'espèce de confier les travaux à d'autres que M. Eiffel quand c'est son pont sur le Douro qui a donné aux ingénieurs l'idée de franchir la vallée de la Truyère par un nouveau tracé dont l'Etat doit retirer finalement une économie de plusieurs millions ». Cité par G. Cordier, op.cit., p. 454.

18. La répartition de l'actif en cours s'étendra jusqu'en 1891, après des velléités de procès en 1882-1884 de la part de Seyrig, qui contestait le partage des bénéfices. Seyrig aura finalement retiré un bénéfice de 800 000 francs de l'association. Il poursuivra une brillante carrière d'ingénieur, en construisant le pont routier Luiz Ier à Porto, à côté du pont Maria Pia.

n'est plus circulaire mais parabolique, les supports du tablier sont plus rapprochés du sommet de l'arc et les arbalétriers des piles sont transformés en caisson à claire-voie, ce qui facilite l'entretien de l'ouvrage. Le montage est achevé en novembre 1884, là aussi sans échafaudages, si ce n'est un léger pont de service au-dessus de la gorge. Les deux moitiés de l'arc sont construites en porte-à-faux, et clavetées à leur jonction au centre. Comme l'a souligné Eiffel, il fallait une très grande précision de fabrication, de mise en place et de calculs : « Nous y sommes arrivés avec une précision presque mathématique » [19]. Le résultat est un magnifique ouvrage, qui franchit la vallée à 122 mètres d'altitude, avec une légèreté incomparable. L'élégance de l'arc se retrouve dans tous les détails, impeccablement réalisés. Ce succès ouvre la voie à la tour de trois cents mètres, qui sera conçue et réalisée avec les mêmes méthodes de calcul et d'exécution, et qui plus est par la même équipe d'ingénieurs et de techniciens.

Eiffel et ses ingénieurs montrent encore leur capacité d'invention en obtenant l'adjudication en octobre 1879 d'un pont routier de 553 mètres à Cubzac sur la Dordogne. Du fait de la fragilité des piles en fonte héritées de l'ancien pont suspendu, Eiffel décide de ne lancer que trois travées de chaque côté de la rive. Les deux travées centrales sont montées en porte-à-faux, une première en France. La technique du lançage n'est d'ailleurs pas exempte de risques, ainsi qu'Eiffel en fait l'expérience au viaduc d'Evaux sur le Tardes, dont le tablier est précipité dans le vide par une tempête dans la nuit du 26 au 27 janvier 1884, sans toutefois que la responsabilité de l'entreprise ne soit en cause.

Les années 1880 sont pour l'entreprise une période d'intense activité. Eiffel remporte en 1880 le concours international pour la construction du pont de Szeged en Hongrie, un bel ouvrage doté d'arches surbaissées articulées aux naissances. Mais il perd l'adjudication d'un nouveau pont à Porto, un concours remporté par son ex-associé Seyrig désormais intégré à une société néerlandaise. Parmi quantité de ponts construits par l'entreprise, celui de Morannes en 1885 est le premier ouvrage en acier construit en France. Quelques années plus tard, ce matériau aura complètement supplanté le fer. Le pont de Montélimar, également en acier, possède une membrure supérieure parabolique, une forme qui se répandra à la fin du siècle. Eiffel a cependant réalisé la plupart de ses ouvrages en forme de poutres droites très classiques, faciles à calculer et à construire. Il n'a cherché à innover sur la forme que dans les grands concours et les circonstances exceptionnelles, où il n'était pas tenu de respecter des projets conçus par d'autres ingénieurs. Parmi ces projets se distinguent la structure intérieure de la statue de la Liberté, un pylône en fer qui porte par l'intermédiaire d'une ossature légère la mince peau de cuivre du colosse, et la coupole métallique de l'observatoire de Nice construite en 1886. Pour la rendre plus facilement mobile, Eiffel avait imaginé de la faire flotter sur une cuve annulaire remplie d'eau additionnée de sel pour prévenir les effets du gel. L'entreprise réalise aussi de gros bénéfices avec la mise au point d'un système de « ponts portatifs », c'est-à-dire vendus en pièces détachées pour l'exportation. Très simples de conception et réalisés avec un nombre limité de pièces différentes, ces ponts étaient livrés avec une notice de montage et pouvaient être assemblés en quelques heures par un personnel non qualifié. De très nombreux exemplaires ont été vendus par l'entreprise à travers le monde, et ce jusque vers 1940, sous des formes variées adaptées aux por-

---

19. Eiffel, *Les grandes constructions métalliques*, conférence à l'Association française pour l'avancement des sciences, Paris, Chaix, 1888, p. 16.

tées et aux usages demandés par les clients, notamment militaires. Cette invention s'est révélée extrêmement lucrative pour Eiffel. Couvert par des brevets, il avait la faculté de traiter les marchés pour un prix tournant autour de 90 centimes le kilo départ usine en 1885. A titre de comparaison, c'est exactement le prix payé pour Garabit, grand arc compris.

LA TOUR DE MONSIEUR EIFFEL

En 1884, Eiffel atteint à l'âge de 52 ans la parfaite maîtrise de son art. L'Exposition Universelle de 1889 va lui donner l'occasion de parachever son œuvre de constructeur. Alors que rien n'était encore décidé, certains songent à un monument qui marquerait de façon spectaculaire l'exposition projetée dans un contexte de crise économique pour commémorer le centenaire de la Révolution française, et en particulier une tour de grande hauteur. Nouguier et Koechlin, « en s'entretenant entre eux de l'Exposition Universelle projetée pour 1889, se demandent ce qui pourrait être fait pour donner de l'attrait à cette exposition », et ils ont l'idée d'une tour très haute [20]. Koechlin fait un croquis, date du 6 juin 1884, qui représente un grand pylône formé de quatre poutres en treillis écartées à la base et se rejoignant au sommet, liées entre elles par des poutres métalliques disposées à intervalles réguliers. C'est une extrapolation hardie à la hauteur de 300 mètres – soit l'équivalent du chiffre symbolique de 1000 pieds – du principe des piles de ponts que l'entreprise maîtrise alors parfaitement. Nouguier et Koechlin soumettent alors le projet à leur patron, « qui déclare n'avoir pas l'intention de s'y intéresser mais qui toutefois donne l'autorisation à ses ingénieurs d'en poursuivre l'étude ». Ils s'adjoignent l'architecte Stephen Sauvestre pour mettre en forme le projet : il relie les quatre montants et le premier étage par des arcs monumentaux, destinés à la fois à accroître l'impression de stabilité que doit donner la Tour et à figurer une éventuelle porte d'entrée de l'Exposition, place aux étages de grandes salles vitrées, agrémente l'ensemble de divers ornements. A la vue du projet ainsi « décoré » et rendu habitable, Eiffel change complètement d'attitude, juge l'idée tellement intéressante qu'il s'empresse de prendre le 18 septembre 1884 un brevet aux noms d'Eiffel, Nouguier et Koechlin, « pour une disposition nouvelle permettant de construire des piles et des pylônes métalliques d'une hauteur pouvant dépasser 300 (trois cents) mètres » [21]. Eiffel rachètera par la suite à ses collaborateurs la propriété exclusive du brevet, y compris pour l'étranger, contre une prime de 1 % sur les sommes qu'il recevrait pour la construction de la dite tour [22]. Le génie d'Eiffel n'est donc pas d'avoir inventé la tour : c'est de l'avoir réalisée et de lui avoir donné son nom.

L'essentiel du projet est défini quelques mois plus tard et représente un compromis entre le schéma initial et le projet décoré. Mais alors qu'Eiffel s'efforce de discréditer un projet rival de tour en maçonnerie proposé par l'architecte Jules Bourdaix, Edouard Lockroy, le nouveau ministre du Commerce, lance le 1er mai 1886 un concours d'idées ouvert aux architectes et aux ingénieurs français ayant pour objet de provoquer la manifestation d'idées d'ensemble pour l'Exposition. Le programme invite, entre autres, les concurrents à « étudier la possibilité d'élever sur le Champ de Mars une tour en fer à

20. Koechlin, Résumé historique de l'origine de la Tour Eiffel, note manuscrite, publié dans Les Koechlin vous parlent, n° 33, Meudon, juin 1989, p. 4. Le dessin original dressé par Koechlin est conservé au Polytechnicum de Zurich.
21. Brevet n° 164 364 du 18 septembre 1884.
22. Contrat entre Eiffel, Nouguier et Koechlin, 12 décembre 1884, archives de la famille Koechlin.

base carrées de 125 mètres de côté à la base et de 300 mètres de hauteur ». C'est une référence quasi explicite au projet d'Eiffel, qui a d'ores et déjà convaincu les autorités du bien fondé de sa conception. Cent sept concurrents soumettent des projets, la plupart intégrant le dessin de la tour proposé par Eiffel. Les trois premiers prix sont attribués à Dutert, Formigé, Eiffel et Sauvestre, qui reçoivent chacun une commande importante pour l'Exposition, Eiffel recevant bien entendu la Tour de trois cents mètres. Le projet est alors une nouvelle fois redéfini dans sa conception architecturale. La décoration est simplifiée, l'ampleur des arches limitée, la dimension des salles couvertes est réduite. Par contraste, la structure s'affirme comme l'élément prépondérant de la composition. Une convention entre Eiffel, l'Etat et la Ville de Paris est signée en janvier 1887 octroyant à Eiffel en son nom propre une concession d'exploitation de vingt ans et une subvention d'un montant d'un million cinq cent mille francs, couvrant à peine le quart du coût de la construction. Soucieux de protéger son entreprise mais aussi de se réserver l'entière paternité et les bénéfices du projet, Eiffel crée en effet le 31 décembre 1888 une société anonyme au capital de cinq millions destinée à réunir le reste du financement nécessaire. Une moitié des fonds est apportée par un consortium de trois banques, l'autre par Eiffel lui-même sur sa fortune personnelle. Le coût des ascenseurs fera cependant encore augmenter le budget d'un million.

Les travaux ont à peine commencé que paraît dans le numéro du 14 février 1887 du journal *Le Temps* la fameuse « Protestation des artistes contre la Tour de M. Eiffel ». Eiffel y répond en faisant valoir la beauté intrinsèque que possèdera selon lui la tour : « Parce que nous sommes des ingénieurs, croit-on donc que la beauté ne nous préoccupe pas dans nos constructions et qu'en même temps que nous faisons solide et durable, nous ne nous efforçons pas de faire élégant ? Est-ce que les véritables fonctions de la force ne sont pas toujours conformes aux conditions secrètes de l'harmonie ? » Eiffel considère sa Tour avant tout comme une œuvre technique. S'il la compare implicitement aux pyramides d'Egypte, qui ne sont « après tout que des monticules artificiels », c'est pour mieux en faire ressortir le caractère à la fois trivial et exceptionnel, en marge des créations artistiques de l'époque, envers lesquelles il a d'ailleurs une attitude très conventionnelle. Ses maisons, ses meubles, ses tableaux, le décor de sa vie intime révèlent en effet un bourgeois parfaitement intégré à la culture dominante de son siècle. Pour Eiffel, l'esthétique de la Tour n'est pas d'avant-garde, elle est simplement ailleurs que là où on la cherche. Elle est à la fois purement rationnelle, abstraite, référencée aux lois de la science, et morale, « symbole de force et de difficultés vaincues ».

Les critiques ne tardent pas cependant à diminuer à mesure qu'avance le montage de la Tour. C'est une merveille de précision. Deux des piles reposent sur des fondations situées en dessous du lit de la Seine. Il a fallu recourir à des caissons métalliques étanches, où l'injection d'air comprimé permettait aux ouvriers de travailler sous le niveau de l'eau. Le montage des piles commence le 1er juillet 1887. Toutes les pièces tracées au dixième de millimètre arrivent de l'usine de Levallois-Perret déjà préassemblées par éléments de quatre mètres environ [23]. Si elles présentent un défaut quelconque, elles sont aussitôt renvoyées à l'usine et jamais retouchées sur le chantier. Les deux tiers des 2 500 000 rivets que comprend la Tour sont posés en usine, le reste sur

23. Les 12 000 pièces de la tour ont ainsi nécessité 700 dessins d'ingénieurs, 3000 dessins d'atelier, qui ont occupé 40 dessinateurs et calculateurs pendant deux ans. Par ailleurs 150 ouvriers ont travaillé à Levallois-Perret à la préparation des pièces.

place par une équipe d'environ 150 ouvriers sur le site, très bien encadrés par des vétérans des grands viaducs métalliques. Douze échafaudages provisoires en bois de trente mètres de hauteur étayent les piles du premier étage, puis de nouveaux échafaudages de 45 mètres sont nécessaires pour soutenir les grandes poutres du premier étage. Au-delà, les pièces sont montées par des grues à vapeur spéciales qui grimpent en même temps que la tour. La partie la plus délicate du chantier est la jonction des quatre grandes poutres du premier étage. Eiffel a prévu des « boîtes à sable » et des vérins permettant de régler la position de la charpente métallique au millimètre près. Deux des piles sont également montées sur vérins hydrauliques, de façon à pouvoir les soulever légèrement et rattraper ainsi le jeu qu'il pourrait y avoir à la jonction des quatre piles et du premier étage. Après la mise en place, ces vérins ont été bloqués. Le jonction a lieu le 7 décembre 1887, et la tour est achevée quinze mois plus tard.

Le succès n'est pas seulement technique, mais aussi populaire. La Tour n'est pas encore achevée que déjà on la reconnaît comme une extraordinaire réussite, non seulement digne de figurer comme l'entrée monumentale de l'Exposition, mais aussi comme le symbole même de la puissance de l'industrie, chef-d'œuvre absolu de l'art des ingénieurs de cette époque. Elle reçoit deux millions de visiteurs pendant l'exposition. Eiffel est promu officier de la Légion d'Honneur. Il est, à 57 ans, multi-millionnaire, et peut s'offrir un somptueux hôtel particulier à Paris, où il règnera en patriarche sur une nombreuse maisonnée, et plusieurs maisons à Sèvres, à Beaulieu sur la côte d'Azur, à Vevey en Suisse. Il est élu président de la Société des Ingénieurs civils.

Eiffel n'assume plus à partir de 1890 que la présidence de son entreprise, la direction effective étant aux mains de Koechlin et de son gendre, le polytechnicien Adolphe Sailes [24]. Eiffel prend des vacances, à Evian, en Suisse et s'offre même une croisière en Méditerranée. L'entreprise étudie à cette époque trois projets importants qui n'aboutiront pas. Eiffel propose en 1890 de construire à ses risques et périls un métro à Paris, qui formerait une grande boucle de douze kilomètres passant par les grands boulevards, la rue de Rivoli et les quais rive droite. Toujours en 1890, un autre tunnel de grande envergure est étudié par l'entreprise. Alors que les travaux du tunnel sous la Manche ont été interrompus depuis pour des raisons stratégiques, et que Schneider associé à Hersent projete de franchir la Manche par un gigantesque pont en acier, Eiffel préfère défendre la solution d'un tunnel formé de deux tubes métalliques de sept mètres de diamètre simplement posés sur le fond de la mer. Ce procédé serait moins cher, moins difficile à construire, moins dangereux pour la navigation et serait plus facile à détruire pour la Marine britannique qu'un tunnel foré. Eiffel est par ailleurs sollicité par son ami l'astronome Janssen pour étudier la construction d'un observatoire au sommet du Mont-Blanc. Les sondages entrepris révèlent une épaisseur de neige trop importante, et les travaux sont suspendus fin 1891.

L'AVENTURE DE PANAMA

Lorsqu'en 1889 Eiffel reçoit les dividendes de la gloire, il est aussi engagé dans l'aventure du canal de Panama, qui aboutira au plus grand scandale financier du siècle. Deux ans plus tôt, alors que venaient d'être réalisée la jonction des poutres au premier

---

24. Hormis Eiffel, les deux plus gros actionnaires de la nouvelle Compagnie des Etablissements Eiffel sont alors la Banque internationale de Paris et la Société Générale, déjà présentes dans la société de la Tour.

étage de la Tour, Eiffel a signé le contrat le plus important mais aussi le plus risqué de toute sa carrière d'entrepreneur. Il avait déjà été associé en 1879 lors du Congrès international d'études sur le canal interocéanique de Panama à un projet de canal entre l'Atlantique et le Pacifique comportant une écluse de très grande dénivellation et passant par le Nicaragua [25]. Mais l'initiateur du projet, Ferdinand de Lesseps avait opté pour un canal à niveau passant par l'isthme de Panama. Les travaux commencés en 1882, s'étaient rapidement heurtés à des difficultés inextricables. On commençait à réaliser que le canal à niveau rêvé par de Lesseps n'était qu'une utopie. Boyer, l'ingénieur du Garabit, avait ainsi comme tant d'autres, succombé à la fièvre jaune cinq mois après son arrivée à la tête des travaux du canal. A la demande du remplaçant de Boyer, le polytechnicien Philippe Bunau-Varilla, Eiffel étudie en 1886 un avant-projet de canal doté d'écluses de 15 mètres de dénivellation. Les portes métalliques peuvent être déplacées par flottaison au moyen de ballasts. Entre temps, un milliard et demi ont déjà été engloutis, dont la moitié seulement affectée aux travaux. La Compagnie semble alors se ressaisir, et le concours d'Eiffel est officiellement sollicité. Il a non seulement déjà étudié un avant-projet, mais il jouit d'un grand crédit moral et technique et « présente d'exceptionnelles garanties » selon sa propre expression. La Tour commence à sortir de terre et le nom d'Eiffel est connu du public : cela facilitera les souscriptions aux emprunts nécessaires. Après de « longues hésitations », Eiffel accepte le 10 décembre 1887 de signer le contrat de construction des écluses enfin reconnues nécessaires pour le canal. Le montant total est fabuleux : 125 millions de francs, soit plus de quinze fois le prix de la Tour. Il s'engage à livrer dix écluses dans un délai de trente mois. Si l'on songe qu'Eiffel a construit 80 000 tonnes de charpente métallique au cours de sa carrière, dont la moitié sous forme de ponts, représentant un chiffre d'affaires global de 70 millions, on comprend qu'il ait pu à la fois hésiter et se laisser tenter par cet énorme contrat qui doit lui laisser 25 % de bénéfices. Eiffel joue banco : « Non seulement mon nom, non seulement ma fortune, mais même ma vie, en quelque sorte, étaient en jeu dans cette colossale entreprise » [26]. En contrepartie, il obtient d'énormes avantages financiers et de solides garanties, notamment des conditions de règlement exceptionnellement favorables, qui l'assurent d'encaisser son bénéfice dès le commencement des travaux [27].

Les chantiers sont donc ouverts dans un délai record. Moins d'un mois et demi après la signature du contrat, alors que la construction de la Tour bat son plein, des milliers d'ouvriers s'activent déjà sur les chantiers de terrassement des dix écluses. Les portes métalliques sont aussi mises en fabrication. Mais à la suite de l'échec d'une ultime souscription d'emprunt, la Compagnie du canal est mise en liquidation le 4 février 1889. L'énorme faillite de la Compagnie de Panama a lésé trop de petits épargnants et les irrégularités de gestion ont été trop nombreuses pour que l'on en reste là. Le scandale aboutit en novembre 1892 à l'inculpation pour escroquerie de Lesseps père et fils, des administrateurs de la Compagnie ainsi que d'Eiffel lui-même. En fait, on lui en veut surtout d'être l'un des seuls à s'être enrichi dans cette affaire. Eiffel était pourtant dans son droit, même si le contrat de travaux était très avantageux pour lui

---

25. Projet étudié avec les ingénieurs Pouchet et Sautereau.

26. *Note de M. G. Eiffel sur son contrat d'entreprise des écluses du canal de Panama*, Paris, Chaix, 1892.

27. Les pièces relatives au contrat d'Eiffel sont conservées au Musée d'Orsay, fonds Eiffel. Voir B. Lemoine, *op. cit.*, p. 106 et suiv.

et s'il avait été paradoxalement favorisé par l'arrêt prématuré des travaux, ayant perçu des avances supérieures aux travaux réellement effectués [28].

Cette inculpation atteint profondément Eiffel dans son honneur et dans sa dignité. Elle ternit la gloire immense dont il se préparait à recevoir les fruits, même si Panama a fait de lui un homme comblé de richesses. A soixante ans, Eiffel est las des luttes du monde des affaires. Il démissionne de sa présidence de l'entreprise le jour même de l'ouverture de son procès, le 19 janvier 1893, demandant « expressément à ce que son nom disparaisse de la désignation de la Société » [29] pour la garantir des suites pouvant résulter de son éventuelle condamnation. L'entreprise prend alors le nom de Société de construction de Levallois-Perret, qu'elle conservera jusqu'en 1937. Malgré l'absence de bases juridiques sérieuses, Eiffel est condamné à deux ans de prison, et à 2000 francs d'amende. L'arrêt est cassé par la Cour de Cassation en invoquant la prescription des faits reprochés, ce qui met fin à toute poursuite.

Après la fin de sa carrière d'entrepreneur, Eiffel poursuivra une vie active, occupée par des recherches scientifiques expérimentales menées avec méthode. Il se passionnera pendant les vingt huit dernières années de sa vie pour trois domaines scientifiques d'avant-garde, tous trois liés à l'usage possible de la Tour, son « œuvre principale » dont il lui faut en démontrer l'utilité, car sa durée de vie n'a été fixée qu'à vingt ans : la météorologie, la radiotélégraphie et l'aérodynamique. Des communications militaires sont établies en 1903 avec les forts des environs de Paris, et un an plus tard avec l'Est de la France. Une station radio permanente est installée sur la Tour en 1906, ce qui assure définitivement sa pérennité. Les dernières années de sa vie sont marquées par des expériences d'aérodynamique menées dans la soufflerie qu'il a fait construire en 1911 à Auteuil. Sans doute davantage que dans la météorologie, Eiffel a trouvé là le champ d'application de sa vocation tardive de savant. Il est mort le 27 décembre 1923, onze ans trop tôt pour assister à la première émission de télévision, lancée du haut de la Tour qui l'immortalise.

---

28. Sur les 69 millions perçus par Eiffel, après 3 millions remboursés au liquidateur, il reconnaît un bénéfice net d'au moins 15 millions, et même 19 si l'on inclut les profits réalisés par l'usine de Levallois-Perret sur les fournitures métalliques, l'expert nommé pour la liquidation lui en reconnaissant pour sa part 23,5 millions.

29. « Procès-verbal de l'assemblée générale de la Compagnie des Etablissements Eiffel », 1er mars 1893, Musée d'Orsay, Fonds Eiffel.

11

The Galerie des Machines
of the 1889 Paris world's fair

John W. Stamper

When the Galerie des Machines was completed for the Paris International Exposition of 1889, it was the largest wide-spanned iron-framed structure ever built (fig. 1). Described at the time as "one of the wonders of the construction age," it is still seen today as representing the revolutionary development of iron-building technology during the course of the 19th century.[1] Spanning 364 feet 2 inches with twenty giant three-hinged arches, it not only embodied a unique way of covering a large space, it also enclosed a larger area than any previous building—over 900,000 square feet.[2]

The construction of the Galerie des Machines and other structures of the exposition, particularly the Eiffel Tower, was a remarkable political and economic achievement for the French government. The cost of the fair, nearly 47 million francs, with about one-fifth of that ($1.5 million in 1889 dollars) going toward the Galerie des Machines, was a small price to pay for a country that wanted to represent itself

---

[1]William Walton, *Chefs-d'oeuvre de l'Exposition Universelle de Paris, 1889* (Paris, 1889), p. xii.

[2]The principal sources of technical information on the Galerie des Machines are: "Exposition Universelle," *Bulletin de la Société d'Encouragement pour l'Industrie Nationale* 3 (1888): 628–57; "The Paris Exhibition," *Engineering* 45 (April 27, 1888): 419–20; 45 (June 1, 1888): 534–37; 47 (May 3, 1889): 415–54; "Exposition Universelle; chronique des travaux," *La Construction moderne* 2 (August 6, 1887): 509–11; 2 (August 13, 1887): 520–22; 3 (July 28, 1888): 501–4; Louis Gonse, "Exposition Universelle de 1889: L'architecture," *Gazette des Beaux-Arts* 2 (July–December 1889): 484–86; "Les Fermes de l'Exposition de 1889," *Le Génie civil* 13 (May 5, 1888): 1–3; "Les Travaux de l'Exposition," *Le Génie civil* 13 (September 22, 1888): 321–24; 13 (August 4, 1888): 211–14; "L'Architecture en fer à l'Exposition de 1889," *Le Génie civil* 15 (July 6, 1889): 185–89; and William Watson, *Paris Universal Exposition, 1889, Civil Engineering, Public Works, and Architecture* (Washington, D.C., 1892), pp. 832–61.

FIG. 1.—Interior of the Galerie des Machines. (Arthur Drexler, ed., *The Architecture of the École des Beaux-Arts* [New York, 1977], p. 453.)

favorably in the centenary year of its Revolution.[3] It came at a time when unprecedented advances were being made in French industry. The average annual rate of growth of the country's industrial products and investment during the Third Republic exceeded that of all other sectors of the French economy. During the 1880s, industrial investment replaced basic investment in construction, public works, and

[3]"Exposition Universelle de 1889," *L'Architecture* 2 (1889): 45; "Le Palais des Machines," *Le Génie civil* 15 (May 1889): 15; "The Paris Exhibition," *Engineering* 48 (December 13, 1889): 698–99; Watson (n. 2 above), p. 860; E. T. Jeffery, *Paris Universal Exposition: 1889* (Chicago, 1889), pp. 56–57; and "Rapport du directeur des travaux," *L'Exposition de Paris de 1889* 6 (1889): 42–43.

transportation as the leading element of investment activity. In addition, there was a shift of the working population to factory labor as industry gained an increasing proportion of the country's employment, capital, and production.[4] The implication of economic and political superiority over rival countries like England was a dominant concern in France throughout the 19th century and helps explain the concentration of economic and technological resources not only on the fair of 1889 but in three previous international fairs and dozens of smaller industrial expositions.[5]

From the beginning, such fairs had required some sort of large exhibition hall to house displays of products of the country's industry, science, and art. The first of these fairs was conceived in 1798, and the government constructed a building in the middle of the Champ de Mars, a former military parade ground on the south side of the Seine in the seventh *arrondissement*. This first industrial fair contained 110 exhibits from the country's leading manufacturing companies, its purpose being to demonstrate that French industrial progress and prowess had not been impeded by the turmoil of the Revolution, the drain of foreign wars, and continuing economic crises. A second and larger exposition was held in 1801, and a third the following year, both taking place in the courtyard of the Louvre. Fairs continued to be held every three or four years, with a consistently increasing number of exhibitors.[6]

The first of France's international fairs, held in 1855, was located in the Palais de l'Industrie constructed on the Champs-Élysées. Designed by J. M. V. Viel, with a span of 157 feet and a length of 630 feet, it embraced the largest area to date covered by an iron-framed structure without intermediate supports.[7] Initiated by Napoleon III during the Crimean War, this exhibition was intended to strengthen the Second Empire's prestige and to demonstrate advances made in French industry. Among the exhibits that attracted the most attention were the machines, cranes, and excavators that made possible Baron Haussmann's renovation of Paris.[8]

Twelve years later, in 1867, a second international exposition was held, this time on the Champ de Mars in an oval-shaped building of

[4]Patrick Hutton, ed., *Historical Dictionary of the Third French Republic, 1870–1940* (New York, 1986), pp. 749–51.

[5]"The Paris Exhibition," *Engineering* 47 (May 3, 1889): 415; Walton (n. 1 above), p. vii; and Jeffery (n. 3 above), pp. 21–22.

[6]Walton (n. 1 above), p. viii; Blake Ehrlich, *Paris on the Seine* (New York, 1962), p. 342; and Paul Greenhalgh, *Ephemeral Vistas: The Expositions Universelles, Great Exhibitions and World's Fairs, 1851–1939* (Manchester, 1988), p. 6.

[7]Leonardo Benevolo, *History of Modern Architecture* (Cambridge, Mass., 1971), 1:103.

[8]Walton (n. 1 above), p. viii; see also Benevolo (n. 7 above), 1:103.

seven coaxial galleries with overall dimensions of 1,608 by 1,266 feet. Designed by J. B. Krantz and Gustave Eiffel, the span of the main outer gallery was 115 feet.[9] It enclosed a series of coaxial oval sheds, with an open colonnaded courtyard in the center. Avenues radiated like the spokes of a wheel through the ovals, and spaces between were assigned to the different countries so that visitors making a tour of each oval could compare the products of each country.

A third international exhibition was held in 1878 to demonstrate that the Third Republic was secure and prosperous enough to rival the industrial production of the Second Empire. It was housed in yet another building on the Champ de Mars, again designed by Krantz. The Palais de l'Industrie was a rectangular building that measured 2,316 by 1,115 feet, with a large gallery surrounding a series of interconnected sheds. Like that of 1867, its largest span was 115 feet. The Trocadéro Palace, designed by J. D. Bourdais and G. J. A. Davioud, was built for this fair on the opposite bank of the Seine.[10] All of the exhibitions were presented by their organizers as giant demonstrations of progress, especially in science and technology, which it was hoped would in turn promote more inventions and discoveries and greater international understanding.

Such was the case of the 1889 fair. Planning for the event started in 1884, during the presidency of Jules Grévy (1807–91), France's first truly republican president. A longtime opponent of Napoleon III, he was a member of the National Assembly in 1848–51 and again in 1871–75. He was elected president in 1879 and reelected in 1885.[11] It was Grévy's administration, on the recommendation of the minister of commerce, Édouard Lockroy, that established an exposition commission to begin planning the fair and selecting architects and engineers for its major buildings.[12] Adolphe Alphand, an engineer and administrator who had been the principal organizer of the 1867 and 1878 fairs and was now the director of works of the city of Paris, was put in charge of overseeing the fair's planning.[13] Georges Berger, who also had been involved with the 1867 and 1878 fairs, was appointed

[9]Mario Labò, "Industrial Exhibitions," *Encyclopedia of World Art* (New York, 1961), 5:282–93; "Paris Universal Exhibition, 1867," *The Builder* 24 (February 10, 1866): 105; and "The Machinery Department of the Paris Universal Exhibition," *The Building News* 13 (March 9, 1866): 150.

[10]Labò (n. 9 above), p. 285; see also "The Paris Exhibition," *The Engineer* 45 (January 11, 1878): 20.

[11]James Cooke, *France, 1789–1962* (Hamden, Conn., 1975), p. 273.

[12]C. Yriarte, "Les Origines et le plan de l'Exposition," *L'Exposition de Paris de 1889* 2 (1889): 10–11; and see Jeffery (n. 3 above), pp. 30–33.

[13]Walton (n. 1 above), p. xiv; Jeffery (n. 3 above), p. 32; and "M. Alphand," *L'Exposition de Paris de 1889* 6 (1889): 42.

334   *John W. Stamper*

director-general of the fair to handle day-to-day operations and organization.[14]

Sources of funding were arranged through the French government, the city of Paris, and a private investment group headed by Albert Christophle, president of the Crédit Foncier. The purpose of this private investment group was to guarantee a substantial sum of money to the government in the event that the expenses incurred exceeded the initial estimates. It was intended that the French government, which would have chief control over the undertaking, would be completely repaid by the influx of visitors, and that the city of Paris would be repaid by an increase in local tax revenues, while the loan of the investment group would be secured with the receipts taken at the gate and from an exhibition lottery.[15]

In 1885, the exposition commission invited French architects and engineers to submit proposals for the plan of the fair and its buildings. A total of 107 entries were received by May 1886. The first prize of 4,000 francs was awarded to three separate entrants: the architects Ferdinand Dutert and Jean Formigé, and the engineer Gustave Eiffel.[16] The final plan of the fair was prepared by Adolphe Alphand; it combined the best elements of the three winning proposals.[17]

The designer of the Galerie des Machines, Ferdinand Dutert (1845–1906), was a graduate of the École des Beaux-Arts and winner of the Prix de Rome in 1869.[18] He conceived the idea of the building, prepared the plans, and supervised the placement of decorative details during construction. The engineer was Victor Contamin (1840–93), a professor at the École Centrale des Arts et Manufactures. He prescribed the dimensions, did the structural calculations, and supervised

[14]Jeffery (n. 3 above), p. 32.

[15]"The Paris Exhibition" (n. 5 above), pp. 417; Jeffery (n. 3 above), pp. 60–66; and see Yriarte (n. 12 above), p. 11.

[16]The second prize of 3,000 francs was allotted to Cassien, Nachu, DePerthes, and Rolan. The third prize of 2,000 francs was given to Ballu, Fogiau, Hochersau, Paulin, Pierron, and Vaudoyer; see "The Paris Exhibition" (n. 2 above), p. 417.

[17]E. Rivoalen, "Expositions," *Encyclopédie de l'architecture et de la construction*, ed. Paul Planat (Paris, 1900), p. 460.

[18]Ferdinand Dutert had studied with the aging Louis Hypolite Lebas and the younger Ginan. He later became a renowned teacher himself at the École. He designed numerous buildings in Paris, including galleries for the Museum of Natural History in 1896, that were significant for their exposed metal structure and a decorative system based on the forms of plants and animals. See Arthur Drexler, ed., *The Architecture of the École des Beaux-Arts* (New York, 1977), p. 450. See also Louis Hautecoeur, *Histoire de l'architecture classique en France* (Paris, 1957), 7:400; and Adolf Placzek, ed., *Macmillan Encyclopedia of Architects* (London, 1982), 1:617–18.

the erection of the girders and general framework.[19] It is not explicit in the available contemporary literature on the fair which of these men was responsible for the unique configuration of the Galerie's arches. It is known that Dutert's initial design proposed covering the space with several smaller spans as in the earlier machinery halls on the Champ de Mars. He then proposed an elliptically formed roof with fixed-end trusses, which proved to be difficult for Contamin to calculate. Finally, the statically determinate three-hinged arch configuration was derived; it allowed Contamin to effectively size the structural members using a series of calculations that took into account the horizontal, vertical, and moment forces acting on the building.[20] At one point in the planning process, Dutert prepared an alternate drawing of the building showing the bases of the arches clad with stone (fig. 2). This was done to appease fair organizers who were uncomfortable with the radically tapered lower panels and hinge connections.[21] In the end, however, Dutert and Contamin succeeded in having their structurally expressive frame approved.

After the plan was finalized, a large bureaucracy was established to carry out the fair. A committee with 300 members and twenty-two subcommittees was formed to oversee every aspect of construction and management. The process was interrupted in 1887, though, when Jules Grévy was forced to resign his presidency over a scandal centering on his son-in-law, Daniel Wilson.[22] Grévy was replaced by Sadi Carnot (1837–94), a political moderate whose father, Sadi Carnot, Sr., formulated the second law of thermodynamics, and whose grandfather, Lazare Carnot, was important in French revolutionary history. An engineer by training, Sadi Carnot, Jr., was elected to the National Assembly from the Côte d'Or—a post he held until 1876.[23] He was appointed undersecretary for public works in 1879, and the following year he was put in charge of public works, a position that would have involved him in the initial planning for the fair. When he became

[19]Contamin was assisted by Charton, joint engineer-in-chief; Pierron, engineer; and Escande, who had charge of the details of the metalwork. Frances Steiner, *French Iron Architecture* (Ann Arbor, Mich., 1984), p. 99; Watson (n. 2 above), p. 833; and "The Paris Exhibition," *Engineering* 45 (June 1, 1888): 537.

[20]Banister Fletcher, "Construction Details of the Late Paris Exhibition," *Building News* 1 (March 21, 1890): 402–4.

[21]Ibid.

[22]Cooke (n. 11 above), p. 273.

[23]Sadi Carnot was an 1863 engineering graduate of the École des Ponts et Chaussées. See Cooke (n. 11 above), pp. 58–59; see also E. Franceschini, "Carnot, Marie-François-Sadi," in *Dictionnaire de Biographie Française*, ed. M. Prevost and Rowan d' Amat (Paris, 1956), 7:1186–87.

FIG. 2.—Galerie des Machines plan showing stone cladding of the arch bases. (*Engineering* 47 [May 3, 1889]: 466.)

president of the Republic in 1887, he turned his attention to matters of foreign policy and defense while still seeing to it that the concept of the fair was realized.[24]

Construction of the buildings for the fair was carried out from May of 1887 to May 1889.[25] The Galerie des Machines was located along the southeast side of the exposition grounds, at one end of the site's central axis and opposite the 984-foot Eiffel Tower (fig. 3). Adjoining the Galerie on the northwest side were the lower roof structures of the Industrial Exhibition Galleries, and beyond that, flanking a central open park space, were the twin buildings of the Fine Arts and the Liberal Arts. The Eiffel Tower, located next to the river, dominated the entire site. At its base, the Pont d'Iena led across the river to the horticultural and agricultural exhibits and to the Trocadéro.

The Galerie measured 1,407 feet long by 460 feet wide. It stood 143 feet high at the apex and 77 feet at the eaves. On either side of the 364-foot-2-inch main space were galleries 48 feet in width formed by arcades and attached to the principal arches. Each end of the building was composed of the gabled form of the main arches, with vertical mullions aligned with the framing members of the glazed roof panels. The facade at the north end contained a large arched entranceway framed in iron and flanked by pediments. The whole building was decorated with colored glass, mosaic work, paintings, and ceramic bricks, so that the great metal skeleton became essentially the frame of an enormous jewel box.[26]

The principal material of the building's structure was to have been steel, but the decision was made at the last minute to use iron instead. There is considerable confusion about this on the part of architectural historians, most of whom assume it was built of steel since that is what was mentioned by contemporary journalists before the opening of the fair. William Watson, an American engineer who wrote a thorough report on the fair after it closed, states that the idea of using steel was abandoned "on the two-fold ground of expense and the necessity of hastening the execution of the work."[27] The price of iron was about two-thirds that of steel in 1889, although the production process of steel was rapidly improving and its price was going steadily down.

[24]Cooke (n. 11 above), pp. 58–59.

[25]Watson (n. 2 above), p. 836.

[26]For general descriptions of the Galerie des Machines, see Jeffery (n. 3 above), pp. 53–54; Drexler (n. 18 above), p. 452; Gonse (n. 2 above), pp. 484–86; "La Galerie des Machines," *Figaro-Exposition 1889* (Paris, 1889), pp. 111–12; and F. G. Dumas and L. De Fourcaud, *Revista de la Exposición Universal de Paris en 1889* (Barcelona, 1889), pp. 23–184.

[27]Watson (n. 2 above), p. 834.

FIG. 3.—Aerial view of the Champ de Mars. (*Engineering* 45 [June 1, 1888]: 534.)

While there was an ample amount of steel being produced, most of it was used for military purposes, especially for shells and armor.[28]

The building's principal arches were noteworthy not just because of their size but because of their three-hinged construction as well. Pin connections at the center and at each end of the arches made them statically determinate, and therefore it was possible to accurately calculate the forces at their supports.[29] A structure is determinate if it has no more than three resolvable forces: a vertical, a horizontal, and a bending force. A fixed arch is indeterminate because it has six forces: two vertical and two horizontal components plus a bending moment at each end. These forces are caused by the weight of the structure itself and by concentric wind and snow loads. The degree of indeterminacy in this case is three because there are three more unknown forces than there are equations to solve them. The longest-span fixed-arch building in the world at the time was St. Pancras Station in London (1867), designed by William H. Barlow.[30] It was 239½ feet wide and 100 feet high, with continuous latticed ribs rising directly from the platform level to a point at the apex, a configuration complementing well the Gothic style of the headhouse. The rib ends were tied below the tracks and platforms by iron rods 3 inches in diameter. This helped counteract the outward thrust of the arches but did not allow any freedom of rotation that might be caused by thermal expansion or slight movement of the supports.[31]

The introduction of hinges eliminates bending moments and thus reduces the number of equations required to solve the structure. It also alleviates problems of movement and expansion. A two-hinged arch is indeterminate to the first degree because there are two pairs of horizontal and vertical components, or four unknowns. The earliest recorded two-hinged arch was used in a bridge over the Canal Saint-Denis near Paris (1858) at the passage of the North Railway. Built of wrought iron with a span of 147½ feet, it had a hinged connection

---

[28]The 1889 iron production in France totaled 809,000 tons, while steel production totaled 626,000 tons. See Bertrand Lemoine, *L'Architecture du fer; France: XIXe Siècle* (Paris, 1987), p. 20.

[29]Eugène Hénard, "L'Architecture en fer à l'Exposition de 1889," *Le Génie civil* 15 (July 6, 1889): 185–89; and Max de Nansouty, "Le Palais des Machines," *Le Génie civil* 14 (March 16, 1889): 320–21.

[30]Carroll L. V. Meeks, *The Railroad Station* (New Haven, Conn., 1964), p. 84; and "The St. Pancras Station," *Engineering* 4 (August 23, 1867): 148.

[31]Meeks (n. 30 above), pp. 84–85; and Rowland Mainstone, *Developments in Structural Form* (Cambridge, Mass., 1983), p. 224.

at each abutment.[32] It was soon followed by a second two-hinged arch bridge over the Canal Saint-Denis at La Villette, this one with a smaller span of 137½ feet.[33]

Because the bending moment in a two-hinged arch is zero at the hinges and maximum at the center, Gustave Eiffel employed a crescent-shaped form in his two-hinged Maria Pia Bridge over the Douro River in Portugal (1875–76) and the Garabit Viaduct over the Truyère River in France (1880–84). Built of wrought iron, their spans are 525 feet and 538 feet, respectively, considerably more than the Canal Saint-Denis bridges or St. Pancras Station.[34] Eiffel's bridges stand in sharp contrast to the giant fixed steel arches of the Eads Bridge in St. Louis (1868–74), which are very deep at the supports where the moment is greater, and smaller near the summit where the moment is less.[35]

In a three-hinged arch there are no bending moments either at the end supports or the apex. This allows for the size of the structure to be noticeably reduced at these points. The first known use of this system appeared in Austria in a small iron bridge over the Wien River (1864).[36] It was followed by the Radetzky Bridge in Laibach (1866) with a span of 98 feet 5 inches, and the Stieger Bridge in Vienna (1869) with a span of 99 feet 5 inches.[37] All these were built of cast iron. A number of more immediate precedents for the three-hinged arches of the Galerie des Machines were found in train sheds built in Berlin and Frankfurt. J. W. Schwedler built two—the East Station in Berlin (1867) with a span of 119 feet, and the Frankfurt am Main Station (1887), with three spans of 183 feet each.[38] Johann Eduard Jacobsthal designed the Alexanderplatz Station in Berlin (1880) with a three-hinged arch span of 123 feet.[39] Such three-hinged arches offered several advantages over two-hinged or hingeless arches: not only were calculations determinate as opposed to indeterminate, but the amount of stress was not significantly affected by differential set-

---

[32]The engineers of the Canal Saint-Denis Bridge were Couche, Mantion, and Salle. See Georg Mehrtens, *Vorlesungen über Ingenieur—Wissenschaften* (Leipzig, 1908), 2:350, 650; and Steiner (n. 19 above), p. 99.

[33]Steiner (n. 19 above), p. 99.

[34]Joseph Harriss, *The Tallest Tower: Eiffel and the Belle Époque* (Boston, 1975), pp. 43–44.

[35]"The St. Louis Bridge," *Engineering* 13 (January 5, 1872): 6–7; 13 (January 19, 1872): 40–41; and C. M. Woodward, *A History of the St. Louis Bridge* (St. Louis, 1881).

[36]Mehrtens (n. 32 above), pp. 350–51, 651.

[37]Ibid., pp. 332, 351, 361.

[38]Sigfried Giedion, *Space, Time and Architecture* (Cambridge, Mass., 1970), p. 270; and Meeks (n. 30 above), p. 171.

[39]Meeks (n. 30 above), pp. 80, 171.

tlement of the abutments, and the joints allowed for expansion and contraction with temperature changes.[40]

Despite the criticism of some contemporaries, like the Belgian engineer Arthur Vierendeel, who complained that the lack of traditional proportion in the arches "produces a bad effect . . . the girder is not balanced . . . it has no base . . . it starts too low . . . the eye is not reassured . . . and the supports are too empty," this three-hinged arch system was the logical culmination of the developing use of the scientific process taking place in building design during the second half of the 19th century.[41] Other critics recognized the significance of the building's structure. One journalist wrote, "Never before, in the opinion of engineers of all countries who have visited it, has a building, proportionately to its vast dimensions, been constructed with such a wonderous combination of solidity, lightness, and grace, the general effect being enhanced by the flood of light freely admitted to all parts of the palace."[42]

The building's principal arches were spaced 70½ feet center to center of the hinges. Exceptions to this were the end bays, which were 83 feet 2 inches center to center, and the central bay of 86 feet 7 inches. The arches were connected longitudinally at the summit by two ridge girders and on each roof face by five girders spaced 34 feet 8 inches center to center. The arches were connected along the sides by iron trusses at the floor level of the side galleries and by arched ironwork rising to the height of the main eaves. Three smaller intermediate arches were placed between each of the principal arches, following the outline of the roof and attached to the longitudinal girders. To these were bolted small girders, sash bars, and framing for the roof covering.[43]

Each principal arch was composed of flanges and web members fastened by rivets (fig. 4). The distance between the inner and outer flanges at the base was 12 feet 2 inches, a distance that gradually diminished to 9 feet 10 inches at the crown. The flanges were a double-T construction consisting of a 30-inch-wide wrought-iron plate and two perpendicular 17-inch plates. These double-T flanges were connected by upright and diagonal wrought-iron web members composed of angle irons, T-irons, and flat plates. Layers of extra stiffening plates

[40]Steiner (n. 19 above), p. 99.

[41]Giedion (n. 38 above), p. 273.

[42]Watson (n. 2 above), p. 833; published originally in *Galignani's Messenger* (July 1889).

[43]"The Paris Exhibition" (n. 5 above), p. 453; Watson (n. 2 above), pp. 840–42; "Exposition Universelle; chronique des travaux," *La Construction moderne* 2 (August 6, 1887): 509–10; "Exposition Universelle," *Bulletin de la Société d'Encouragement pour l'Industrie Nationale* 3 (1888): 636–37.

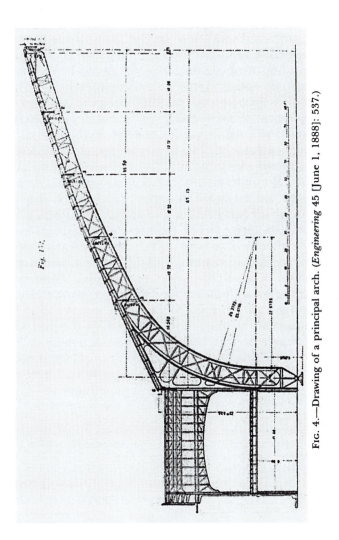

FIG. 4.—Drawing of a principal arch. (*Engineering* 45 [June 1, 1888]: 537.)

were attached to the inner and outer flanges at the curve, where the bending stress was greatest. The spandrel filling at the haunches of each arch had the same construction as the arch itself, with a 30-inch double-T flange (fig. 5). The uprights were simply a prolongation of those of the principal arch.[44] Each arch was divided into twenty-four alternating large and small web panels. Those at the head and foot were augmented by additional strengthening plates.[45] The head panel was composed of two large diagonals of double-T-iron with a series of supplementary webs and strengthening plates (fig. 6). The bottom panel was quite plain, with two massive triangular webs strengthened by two supplementary plates.[46] The pin connection of cast-iron bearings was bolted to a 0.8-inch-thick plate at the bottom of the lower panel.[47] The bedplates and cast-iron bearings had to be made strong enough to support a vertical load of 412 tons and a horizontal thrust of 115 tons.[48] No underground tie-rods or skewbacks were used.

Foundations for the principal arches consisted of large masonry piers measuring 23 feet by 11½ feet and 12 feet deep. These piers rested on 20-inch-deep concrete footings that varied in size according to the soil conditions. The largest were over 700 square feet in area. Some of the foundations, located on the site of a former gravel pit, were placed on wooden pilings 30 feet deep and 13 inches in diameter.[49] Interspersed with these foundation piers was an extensive system of underground pipes for water, steam, and drainage.[50]

The construction of the building was a very complex and costly process involving numerous contractors and subcontractors. The work of erecting the arches was divided between two principal contractors, each putting up ten of the arches in its own manner. One company assembled each arch in four sections on the ground and then raised

---

[44]"The Paris Exhibition" (n. 5 above), p. 454; Watson (n. 2 above), pp. 840–42; "Exposition Universelle" (1887) (n. 43 above), pp. 509–10; "Exposition Universelle" (1888) (n. 43 above), pp. 636–37.

[45]Drexler (n. 18 above), p. 452.

[46]"The Paris Exhibition" (n. 5 above), p. 456; Watson (n. 2 above), p. 843; "Exposition Universelle" (1888) (n. 43 above), p. 639; "Exposition Universelle," *La Construction moderne* 2 (August 13, 1887): 520–22.

[47]"The Paris Exhibition" (n. 5 above), p. 456; Watson (n. 2 above), p. 843; "Exposition Universelle" (1888) (n. 43 above), p. 639.

[48]Watson (n. 2 above), p. 843; "Exposition Universelle" (1888) (n. 43 above), p. 639.

[49]The weight on the ground at each foundation was calculated to be about 6,000 pounds per square foot. The foundations were constructed by Manoury-Gruselle & Company for a cost of 20,000 francs. See "The Paris Exhibition" (n. 5 above), pp. 456–57; Watson (n. 2 above), pp. 837–40; "Exposition Universelle" (1888) (n. 43 above), pp. 642–43.

[50]Watson (n. 2 above), p. 836.

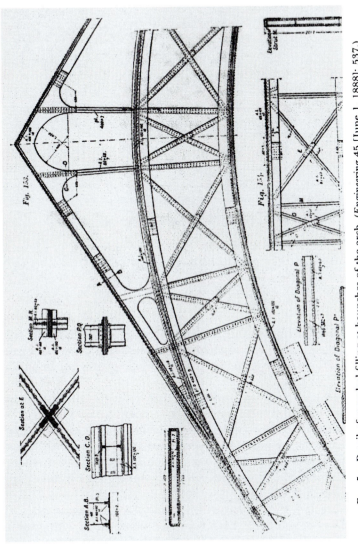

FIG. 5.—Detail of spandrel filling at haunches of the arch. (*Engineering* 45 [June 1, 1888]: 537.)

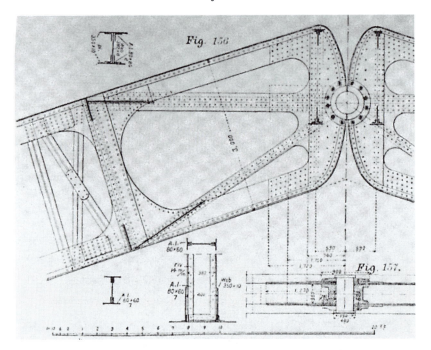

FIG. 6.—Details of head connection. (*Engineering* 45 [June 1, 1888]: 537.)

it into place, with the only on-site riveting required being at two intermediate joints. The scaffolding consisted of a tall central gantry, as high as the middle of the roof, and two side platforms, all mounted on wheels so that they could be moved forward on rails. The lower portion of each arch was attached to the bedplate, and the free end was raised by pulleys and winches. The upper halves of the arch were then hoisted directly into place (fig. 7). The other company followed a procedure that required constructing a narrow scaffolding spanning the entire width of the space, assembling sections of the arch on the ground, and raising them and riveting them together in place on the scaffolding.[51]

Once erected, the immense iron frame was sheathed in glass, zinc-covered wood, and brick. Each roof face was enclosed with glass from the center ridge to a point about 40 feet from the eaves, covering about four-fifths of the roof surface. Only the two end bays were solid.

[51]The firms responsible for the erection of the girders were the Fives-Lille Company and the Cail Company. See "The Paris Exhibition" (n. 5 above), pp. 458–59; "Exposition of 1889," *Le Génie civil* 13 (May 5, 1888): 1–2; 13 (August 4, 1888): 211–12; 13 (September 22, 1888): 1–3.

346 *John W. Stamper*

Fig. 7.—Construction of the arch at the pin connection. (*L'Exposition de Paris de 1889* [Paris, 1889], p. 4.)

Standard panels used in the roof measured 6½ feet long by 1½ feet wide.[52] The walls of the side aisles flanking the main space were built of red and white brick, and the arched windows were filled in with glass surrounded by a green border. The ceilings of these aisles were in decorated plaster.[53]

The gable end forming the main entrance from the Avenue de la Bourdonnais was flanked by two iron towers about 100 feet high, one containing a stairway, the other an elevator. These, along with the

[52]"Exposition Universelle de 1889: Le Palais des Machines," *L'Architecture* 2 (1889): 173–76, 232–36.
[53]"The Paris Exhibition" (n. 5 above), p. 460.

facade, were richly decorated with the coats of arms of countries taking part in the exhibition. Two great statues, one representing steam, the other electricity, also decorated the entrance.[54]

When the Galerie des Machines opened to the public on May 6, 1889, it was filled with all aspects of French industry (fig. 8), ranging from machinery for agriculture and food processing to equipment for clothmaking, papermaking, woodworking, construction, and generating electricity. Pumps, dynamos, transformers, engines, hydraulic elevators, and even windmills were on display. About one-fourth of the space in the building was devoted to exhibits from other countries, including Switzerland, Belgium, the United States, and England.[55]

Because much of the machinery in the Galerie des Machines required steam power for its operation, a number of steam generators were set up in adjacent buildings. Underground tunnels ran beneath the floor of the Galerie for steam and water mains, with connections being made through the floor directly to the machinery.[56] In addition, there were twenty-eight electric motors used in the Galerie to operate four rotating shafts that ran the length of the space. These lineshafts were supported partly by double cast-iron columns and partly by bearings suspended from the lattice girders connecting the columns.[57]

A further innovation that made visits to the building a unique experience for 19th-century Parisians was the installation of elevator systems and an overhead moving walkway running the length of the space. The exterior elevator tower flanking the building's entrance facade and smaller elevator towers located inside at each end gave access to two traveling cars (fig. 9) that were installed on tracks above the exhibits to carry visitors through the building.[58] The experience of riding one of these cars and viewing the building and its exhibits was best described by the sculptor Raymond Duchamp-Villon, who wrote of his impressions as a thirteen-year-old boy: "I remember very clearly the hallucinatory passage through the brightness of the nave in a traveling crane, above whirlpools of reptilean belts, creakings, whistles, sirens, and black caverns containing circles, pyramids, and cubes."[59]

[54]Ibid., pp. 459–60; Watson (n. 2 above), p. 861.

[55]"The Paris Exhibition" (n. 5 above), pp. 494–95; Watson (n. 2 above), p. 835.

[56]"The Paris Exhibition" (n. 5 above), p. 496; Watson (n. 2 above), p. 835.

[57]There were 148 double columns, spaced 36 feet 9 inches center to center, and 14 feet 8 inches high. See "The Paris Exhibition" (n. 5 above), p. 495; and "Exposition Universelle" (1888) (n. 43 above), p. 645.

[58]"The Paris Exhibition" (n. 5 above), pp. 460, 491; Drexler (n. 18 above), p. 142; Watson (n. 2 above), p. 835; and "Les Ponts roulants," *L'Exposition de Paris de 1889* 17 (June 22, 1889): 136.

[59]Giedion (n. 38 above), p. 269. Originally published in "L'Architecture et le fer," *Poème et Drame* (January–March 1914).

348   *John W. Stamper*

Fig. 8.—View of the exhibits from the balcony. (*L'Exposition de Paris de 1889* [Paris, 1889], p. 225.)

In addition to its structural and mechanical innovations, the Galerie des Machines was one of the earliest major exhibition buildings to be completely equipped with electric light fixtures. A total of eighty arc lamps in groups of five were suspended from the main girders, while the center of the space was lighted by a large six-lamp fixture. The side galleries were lighted by 200 arc lamps, and some 730 incandescent lamps were grouped around the stairways. The central gardens of the Champ de Mars also were lighted, as was the central space of

FIG. 9.—View of the elevated traveling walkways. (*L'Exposition de Paris de 1889* [Paris, 1889], p. 436.)

the Industrial Exhibition Galleries. Electricity for these lights was provided by three power stations containing electric motors and dynamos.[60]

The use of electrical lighting in halls of this kind had been experimented with in previous exhibitions held in London, Glasgow, and
Manchester, their organizers recognizing the need to attract people
to the exhibitions at night. No attempt had been made to light the
grounds of the 1878 Paris Exhibition, however, as cheaply produced
electricity was still unknown. An electrical exhibition was held in Paris
in 1881, in which incandescent lighting was shown for the first time
on a large scale.[61] This was the first exhibition to be kept open at
night, and its success led to the decision that a large part of the 1889
exposition would be lighted and would remain open late to the public.

The Galerie des Machines was a profound technical achievement.
Although the three-hinged arch had been developed several years
earlier, it had not been used to vault such a span. Most important,
however, was the fact that the Galerie des Machines was designed with
a delicate balance between structural necessity and artistic graceful-
ness and refinement to such perfection that it readily became the
proud bearer of French honor and respectability. It awed its visitors
and impressed on them France's achievements in science and industry—the goal that had been paramount in all previous exhibitions.
The Galerie, along with the Eiffel Tower, stirred national pride and
confidence in French ability to accomplish material wonders as millions of visitors found their way to the gaily decorated and brightly
illuminated buildings on the Champ de Mars. The exhibition succeeded, at least in the eyes of the French, in restoring the country's
political prestige and proving that it was among the leading nations
of the world.

The Galerie des Machines was destined to serve again as a major
exhibition hall in France's next great world's fair, that of 1900. It did
so, however, in a radically altered state. A huge rotunda, or *Salle des
Fêtes,* was erected in the middle of the space, thus obliterating completely the line of the arches and their hinged connections at the
floor.[62] The remaining spaces on either side of the rotunda were
devoted to food and agricultural exhibits. After the fair, the building
was used intermittently until it was demolished in 1910.

The concept of the three-hinged arch remained popular for only
a short time in the construction of exposition buildings and railroad

[60]"The Paris Exhibition" (n. 5 above), pp. 494–95.
[61]Ibid.
[62]"The Paris International Exhibition of 1900," *Engineering* 68 (December 15, 1899):
761.

train sheds, those structures whose spans exceeded that for which simple trusses could be economically employed. The greatest rival of the Galerie des Machines was the Manufactures and Liberal Arts Building of the 1893 World's Columbian Exposition in Chicago (fig. 10). Designed by George B. Post and engineer Edward C. Shankland, its span of 368 feet was 3 feet 10 inches wider than the Paris building.[63] It was also much taller, its height at the apex being 206 feet, a result of its more purely arched form. This was the last of the great exposition buildings, however, as planners of subsequent world's fairs preferred more and smaller individual pavilions, each independently representing a single national or corporate exhibitor.

The use of the three-hinged arch saw its biggest proliferation in wide-spanned train sheds during the 1890s, especially in the United States. The Jersey City Station of the Pennsylvania Railroad (1892), designed by C. C. Schneider and William H. Brown, had a three-hinged arch span of 252 feet 8 inches, which exceeded by more than 100 feet the longest previous simple roof truss span in the country.[64] It was followed by the Reading Railroad Station in Philadelphia (1893) with a span of 259 feet, and the Broad Street Station, also in Philadelphia (1894), with a span of 300 feet 8 inches.[65] According to Carroll L. V. Meeks, author of *The Railroad Station: An Architectural History*, the latter was the widest single-span train shed ever built anywhere at any time.[66] As with large exposition halls, construction of these vast train sheds waned, railroad companies finding them too costly to build and maintain. The three-hinged arch continued to be employed on a smaller scale in gymnasiums, aircraft hangars, and armories until the mid-1920s, but it eventually disappeared altogether as proponents of In-

[63]*Chicago Tribune*, September 23, 1891, p. 9; Titus Karlowicz, "The Architecture of the World's Columbian Exposition" (Ph.D. diss., Northwestern University, 1965), pp. 123, 343; and Donald Hoffmann, "Clear Span Rivalry: The World's Fairs of 1889–1893," *Journal of the Society of Architectural Historians* 29 (March 1970): 48–50.

[64]The longest simple roof truss span at the time was in the train shed of the Central Railroad of New Jersey Station, Jersey City. Its span was 142 feet 4 inches. See Mansfield Merriman and Henry Jacoby, *A Textbook on Roofs and Bridges* (New York, 1920), 4:170; "The New Terminals of the Pennsylvania Railroad at Jersey City," *Engineering News* 26 (September 26, 1891): 276; Meeks (n. 30 above), p. 88; and Walter G. Berg, *Buildings and Structures of American Railroads* (New York, 1893), pp. 431–36.

[65]The Reading Station was designed by Wilson Brothers & Company of Philadelphia. See "The Philadelphia & Reading Terminal Railroad Station, Philadelphia, Pa.," *Engineering News* 29 (February 2, 1893): 98; and Berg (n. 64 above), pp. 436–46. The Broad Street Station was designed by William H. Brown and William H. Pratt. See "The Broad Street Station Trainshed: Pennsylvania Railroad, Philadelphia," *Engineering News* 29 (June 1, 1893): 508–9; and Berg (n. 64 above), pp. 381–86.

[66]Meeks (n. 30 above), p. 88.

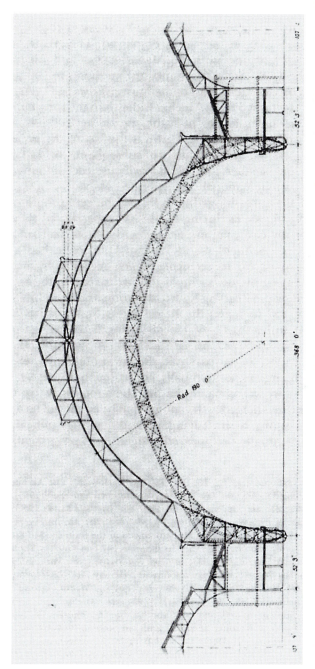

FIG. 10.—Comparison drawing of the Galerie des Machines and the Manufactures and Liberal Arts Building of the 1893 World's Columbian Exposition. (*Engineering* 52 [October 23, 1891]: 470.)

ternational Style architecture evolved a clear preference for flat rather than arched roofs.

The use of three-hinged arches met a similar fate in bridge construction, though a few notable examples were built in both Europe and the United States after the turn of the century. Carl Condit identifies as a classic example the Minneapolis, St. Paul & Sault Ste. Marie Railway bridge over the St. Croix River near New Richmond, Wisconsin (1910–11). Designed by Claude A. P. Turner, it has a span of 350 feet; its central hinge is not a pin connection but rather a sliding joint designed to lock into a rigid unit under the weight of the train, thus causing it to act intermittently as a two-hinged rather than a three-hinged arch.[67] The form of the three-hinged arch most frequently used in bridges, including those in reinforced concrete by Robert Maillart, came to have a horizontal upper chord and a curved or bent lower chord.[68] These so-called spandrel braced arches proved useful in the design of highway bridges, although they were eventually considered too flexible to withstand the vibrations and uneven loadings of railroad use. The culminating achievement of the three-hinged arch occurred with Robert Maillart's famous Salginatobel Bridge (1930), a graceful reinforced concrete structure that surpassed even the Galerie des Machines for sheer awe-inspiring boldness and structural purity.

[67]Carl Condit, *American Building: Materials and Techniques from the First Colonial Settlements to the Present* (Chicago, 1968), p. 229.
[68]Merriman and Jacoby (n. 64 above), p. 179.

12

The two centuries of technical evolution underlying the skyscraper

Carl W. Condit

We can no longer argue that the Home Insurance Building was the first skyscraper (Fig. 1). It was not. Then the question is, what was? Part of my purpose is to demonstrate that there is really no such thing as the first skyscraper, although we can certainly make a case for the emergence of the potential form. My chief argument against the claim for the Home Insurance Building is that it rests on an unacceptably narrow idea of what constitutes a multistory high-rise commercial building. Such a structure is a great deal more complex than what has always been claimed. I am going to use the word *skyscraper* for convenience, but it applies to any large multistory commercial, public, or residential building regardless of its shape or height.

An adequate history of the development of the skyscraper, its urbanistic and economic antecedents, its genesis, its design and construction, and its evolution over the past century, must rest on four fundamental aspects of this particular kind of building—namely, place, structure, utilities, and form. For years historians paid almost exclusive attention to external form, though in recent years a few have become interested in its structure and its history. But that leaves the other two aspects out of the equation, and in the case of utilities our neglect has been unfortunate. An account of the development of building utilities as part of technological history has yet to be written, since it consists

12   History of Tall Buildings

Fig. 1 Home Insurance Building, Chicago (1885)

of a handful of articles and one book, which treats only a very limited aspect of its subject. The purpose of this paper is to describe in a condensed form the historical development of modern building technology over the full period of time in which that evolution took place. In short, the historical growth of all the technical factors that underlie the ultimate skyscraper form and continue to be an organic part of that form will be traced. There are about a dozen parallel and successive lines of evolution, which may be grouped under four primary headings: structure, safety, internal transportation, and habitability. All these characteristics must be inherent in the skyscraper or any other kind of large multistory building that is used by a number of people on a regular, sustained, daily basis. It is impossible to treat these dozen or so aspects in strictly chronological terms. They overlap to such an extent that it will be necessary first to organize them topically, then to give each major area a broadly chronological survey.

STRUCTURE

Iron Framing

Structure is the oldest technico-material aspect of building, without which there would be no building at all. We rightly think of the iron frame—that is, a frame of ferrous metals of various kinds—as an essential characteristic of high-building construction and it is on this basis that buildings like the Home Insurance and the Tacoma in Chicago, for example, are given the place they have in architectural history. There was certainly nothing new about the iron frame, which had been used for more than a century when the Home Insurance Building was placed under construction. The first multi-story building in which floors were supported by iron columns was the Calico Mill in Derby, England, built in 1792–1793 by William Strutt, who was a practical builder trained neither in architecture nor engineering. It was late in the nineteenth century before such formal training became the rule rather than the exception. The first iron columns had appeared twenty years before Strutt's mill was constructed, having been introduced initially in St. Anne's Church, Liverpool, in 1772. Iron columns were quickly supplemented by iron floor beams. Charles Bage provided full interior iron framing in the Benyon and Marshall Flax Mill, in 1796–1797, at Shrewsbury, England (where Falstaff played dead on the battle field, *Henry IV*, Part I). Iron columns were introduced into the United States by Benjamin Latrobe, one of the great creative engineer-architects during the formative years of post-colonial building. The particular work was a church in Washington, D.C., constructed in 1808. The first iron roof truss was built by William Murdock for a foundry in Soho, London, in 1810. This truss was also the first metal framework in which there was a precise distinction between wrought iron and cast iron elements on the basis of stress, the wrought iron being used for members subject to tension and the cast iron for those under compression. A long series of experiments

14   History of Tall Buildings

carried on by William Fairbairn and Eton Hodgkinson established the basis for this distinction in scientific terms.

Moving rapidly through the chief milestones in the development of iron framing, we might argue that the Crystal Palace in London, 1851, was the best known and the most important. It was followed by the warehouses of the St. Ouen Docks in Paris, 1864–1865, designed by Hippolyte Fontaine, a builder and inventor who helped to develop the first practical electric motor in 1873 in collaboration with Théophile Zenobe Gramme. If our sole criteria for the skyscraper are height and structure, then the warehouses of the St. Ouen Docks would have to take precedence over everything else. They were the first fireproof, iron skeleton, curtain-walled, multistory buildings ever built. The entire dead load, internal floor loads, and live loads are carried entirely on a frame of deep wrought iron girders, smaller cast iron beams, and cast iron columns, together supporting concrete floors designed for a loading factor of 31.12 KPa (650 psf), more than enough for a whiskey warehouse and almost enough for a locomotive. Discussing the United States we turn back a few years in our chronology. Daniel Badger and James Bogardus, both of New York, began respectively in 1846 and 1848 to build multistory structures with cast iron fronts and internal cast and wrought iron frames. By the mid-1860s in Europe and the United States many of the essential features of the skyscraper structure were in place, but it was the United States that first exploited them.

Wind Bracing

A subsidiary but important aspect of structure is one to which an inordinate amount of attention has been paid in the past one hundred years, yet it goes far back into history. Wind bracing was a medieval invention, first introduced for wood construction in the large timber-framed house and barn as they reached maturity in the fourteenth and fifteenth centuries. The common system was knee-bracing, supplemented in larger structures by truss framing of various kinds. The structural system of the mature Gothic cathedral was braced against horizontal forces, the key element being the flying buttress, which is in fact a strut designed to transmit loads across the aisles to the tower buttresses on the periphery of the structure. The scientific investigation of the interrelations between wind velocity and wind pressure and the consequences of this pressure for the behavior of structures began in 1664 with the experiments of Robert Hooke, who worked in all areas of the physical sciences.

Hooke's pioneer work was carried on in the eighteenth century by John Smeaton, creator of the Eddystone Lighthouse and one of the great builder-engineers of his age. Smeaton began his investigations in 1759 and was concerned with the relation between wind velocity and pressure in the action and design of windmills. The French physicist and meteorologist Jean Charles

Borda in 1763 continued these experiments, which went on through the remainder of the eighteenth century and came to a focus in practical building with the design of French lighthouses beginning in 1832. Experiments continued throughout the nineteenth century and into the twentieth, leading in an irregular way to the formula that we use today for the relation of pressure and velocity — $P = 0.00256V^2$ — an empirical formula that is not susceptible to dimensional analysis but represents an accurate numerical relationship.

The curious thing is that it was more than 150 years before the scientific investigations began to bear fruit in iron-framed building. First, wind bracing in the form of knee braces was used in all large vaulted structures of wood, most conspicuously in churches. If you explore the space between the vault over the nave and the gabled roof of a large colonial church — Christ Church, Philadelphia; St. Paul's Church, New York; or St. Michael's, Charleston, S.C.; for example — you will find a complete system of bracing often in the form of ship's knees, so-called because of their use in the frames of wooden vessels. It was finally introduced for iron construction in the Hungerford Fish Market, London, in 1835, developed further as a proto-portal as well as double-diagonal bracing in the Crystal Palace of 1851, and as full portal bracing in the Royal Navy Boat Store, Sheerness, England, in 1858–1860.

At this stage we reach a mystery, and I am sorry that I cannot yet unravel it. Henry H. Quimby was the authority at the end of the nineteenth century on windbracing — its history, its applications in building, the accumulated theory, and pioneer uses. Quimby said that bracing was introduced into iron-framed buildings in the United States with the first use of wrought iron columns. These would have been Phoenix columns, the flanged wrought iron column invented in 1861. We are reasonably sure that the first building to be constructed with wrought iron columns was the Brown Brothers Bank in New York, 1863. We know nothing about the bracing in it, or whether it even had any, yet we are compelled to recognize Quimby as the voice of authority (Quimby et al., 1892–93). The ruling view at the time was that if buildings had external bearing walls of masonry, which all of them did except for the two warehouses mentioned, the weight was sufficient to render the internal framework and hence the whole building stable against the wind, so that bracing was regarded as unnecessary. As late as 1893 Adler and Sullivan's Stock Exchange Building in Chicago contained no wind bracing. The Tacoma Building, another candidate for the status of first skyscraper, had a kind of bracing in the form of shear walls of brick extending through the height of the structure. Nevertheless, by the end of the Civil War we know that the necessity for bracing in an iron-framed building was at least recognized.

Foundations

A third category under the heading of structure is that of adequate foundations. Piling goes back to classical antiquity and is described by

Vitruvius, but the watertight caisson of timber sheeting appears to have been a development of the late eighteenth century. There are illustrations in the *Encyclopedie*, the great French compendium of all the arts and sciences of the age. The pneumatic caisson was the invention of Thomas Lord Cochrane of England in 1830. It was introduced in the United States by a builder named L. J. Fleming in 1852 and was developed into its mature form by the pioneer foundation engineer William Sooy Smith. It was given its most conspicuous demonstration by James B. Eads in his St. Louis bridge (1868–1874) and was soon recognized as essential for laying down and supporting the foundations of all large bridges and buildings in unstable, water-bearing soil.

SAFETY

Fireproofing

Under the heading of safety I want exclusively to emphasize fireproofing, although safety factors are involved in all the technical aspects of building. We can follow the history of fireproofing in detail once we come to a decisive and unambiguous starting point. But there was a long antecedent history which began in the late eighteenth century. The overriding reason for tracing these origins to the Age of Enlightenment is that it was also the period of the Industrial Revolution and a new symbiotic union of science and technology. The French builder Ango introduced hollow clay pots into plaster flooring apparently in part to lighten the floor, perhaps the beginning of reinforced concrete because wrought iron beams were incorporated in the plaster work. But there is equally good reason to believe that the aim was to introduce trapped air and a refractory material of low thermal conductivity into the floor. Ango was followed by St. Far, who is credited with building the flooring of an entire house in this way in 1785.

The mature and progressive development of fireproofing began with the construction of the Cooper Union in New York. In 1854 Frederick A. Peterson, its architect, introduced the hollow clay pots into the concrete that leveled up the floor arches spanning between wrought iron beams. The decisive step toward a scientific understanding of fireproofing came with a paper delivered by Peter B. Wight before the New York chapter of the American Institute of Architects on April 6, 1869. In his paper Wight pointed out for the first time that because a mill, bank, or any other kind of commercial building is built with iron columns and beams, concrete floors, and brick walls, it does not follow that the building is proof against destruction by fire (Wight, 1876; 1878). That has been demonstrated again and again, and if you think the lesson has been finally learned you are very much mistaken. The original Metropolitan Fair and Exposition Building in Chicago was destroyed by fire in January 1967, although it was constructed with reinforced concrete walls resting on steel rigid frames. It was supposedly a fireproof building, but it was filled with combustible materials that burned at a temperature as high as 2,500°F. Nobody needs to know very much to explain what happens when the temperature of any ferrous metal is raised to 2,000°F or higher.

A long series of experiments on the relation of loss of strength to rise in temperature was necessary to establish accurate data. What happens to the strength of exposed iron or steel at elevated temperatures? At what point can it no longer be counted on to carry the load imposed upon it? How can it be protected from rapid absorption of heat? Maturity came in fireproofing techniques with the invention of hollow tile cladding for iron columns and beams by George H. Johnson and Balthasar Kreischer in 1871. Their invention was first applied to the iron frame of the Kendall Building in Chicago during the following year. The necessity for this kind of protection was finally recognized, but unfortunately the collapse of the Exposition Building in Chicago was not the last case of the destruction of a supposedly incombustible building. A few years ago a similar case took a very high toll in life as the result of a hotel fire in Las Vegas.

INTERNAL TRANSPORTATION

The third primary heading is internal transportation. When buildings passed five stories in height it was no longer possible to ask people to climb the stairs, especially if it was a prestigious office or department store block. Some other way had to be found for moving from one floor to another, and the solution again came from strictly utilitarian structures. The first power-operated elevators were introduced into English mills about 1835. England was far ahead of any other country in the century from the mid-eighteenth to the mid-nineteenth, but by the latter date it was being rapidly eclipsed by the United States and Germany in technology and industrial development. The first elevator was a primitive device, an open wooden platform bounded by rails that was hoisted by ropes in a brick-lined shaft. Hoisting was accomplished by winding the ropes around sheaves connected to the belted shafting of the mill. The apparatus was a homely and unsafe contrivance for the vertical movement of heavy loads and the workers responsible for the task.

Among the obvious defects of early mill elevators was the absence of any means to prevent or slow the free fall of the platform in the event of a cable rupture. The first safety brake, oddly enough, came before the invention of a practical elevator suitable for the movement of passengers. The inventor, Elisha Graves Otis, is perhaps the foremost name in the entire history of elevator technology. He developed an effective though primitive safety brake in 1851, an invention that logically falls in the second category, safety, as well as internal transportation. People were understandably reluctant to rise even a single floor in an elevator if there was a likelihood that it would fall to the basement floor. Otis achieved the second and perhaps decisive step with the invention in 1855 of an elevator moved by a separate steam-powered drum.

18   History of Tall Buildings

He made the first workable installation of an enclosed steam-driven car with safety brake in the Haughwout Building, New York, in 1857. Three years earlier, in the New York Crystal Palace, Otis had given his highly melodramatic demonstration of safety: He raised the elevator four floors and cut the cable from which it was suspended. He didn't come to a gentle stop, but it was better than falling to the bottom of the shaft.

The hydraulic elevator was the invention of two men working independently, Cyrus Baldwin of Boston in 1870 and William E. Hale of Chicago in 1873. We have heard a great deal about builders, developers, architects, and engineers in Chicago, but only one historian has ever mentioned the Hale elevator, and his work has yet to be published. The Hale machines were installed in the Tacoma Building, which has been offered as a better candidate for first skyscraper than the Home Insurance.

The electrically powered elevator had its primitive beginning in 1880 with a demonstration model built by Ernst Werner von Siemens, one of the great creative figures in the pioneer age of electrical technology. A much improved form with more promise for practical use was introduced by Frank Julian Sprague in the Park Row Building, New York, in 1897. Sprague's name ought to be well known: He was the chief creator of electric railroad traction in the United States. But Otis was already at work on a much superior model, having begun his experiments as early as 1890 and having made his first practical installation in 1894. Before the end of the decade he had produced an elevator with all the essential characteristics of the modern machine—the direct-drive electric motor, the cable drum, the counter-weights, the safety brake, and a system of controls that made it possible to provide smooth starting and stopping.

HABITABILITY

The last major category is called habitability, meaning all that makes a building healthy, comfortable, and usable to those who must work or live in it. The importance of this category is underscored with a little more emphasis than previously shown. The overwhelming majority of people who use a building do not care how it was constructed. They do not care how the building was erected, what it was made of, whether it has a riveted-steel or a welded-steel frame, or a reinforced concrete frame, whether it has bearing walls or curtain walls, whether masonry or any other material. But they are vitally concerned for quite understandable, absolutely essential human reasons with whether the building is comfortably heated, whether it has an adequate plumbing and water supply system, whether there are enough plumbing fixtures to serve the users, whether all the factors together guarantee the reliable operation of fixtures, and whether ventilation and air-conditioning provide reasonable comfort for all.

Central Heating

Once more we have to go back to the Industrial Revolution. Central hot air heating was introduced by William Strutt in the Belper textile mill in 1792. Steam heating was another creation of the prolific team of Matthew Boulton and James Watt, who made the first installations in mills placed under construction in 1802. The heating unit was simply a system of parallel pipes fixed to the walls of the mill. Everyone knows the name of James Watt: In a series of patents granted between 1769 and 1790 Watt developed the double-acting reciprocating steam engine with automatic valve and speed control, the first such feedback control or servo-mechanism. Matthew Boulton, primarily a builder, was his entrepreneurial partner. Like the elevator, the first heating systems were crude installations, hardly satisfactory for prestige buildings designed to bring high rents and big returns for their owners. In America the mechanical inventor and mill-builder Oliver Evans first used exhaust steam from boilers to provide the source of heat, around 1811 for his earliest installations. Improvements were slow in coming. Closed-circuit high-pressure hot-water heating was essentially the achievement of Jacob Perkins in England around 1831. He had developed a closed-circuit system in which water under pressure could be raised far beyond the boiling point. Pipes were so hot as to be dangerous to touch, but they gave off plenty of heat. One does not have to know very much about the thermodynamic behavior of fluids under high temperatures to know what might happen if a small fracture occurred in one of the pipes. The water would immediately flash into steam and the whole building would be blown up. It happened to locomotives year after year on the railroads.

A preferable system, a closed-circuit, low-pressure steam-heating system, was primarily the work of Joseph Nason in the United States, and again a series of experiments and innovations took place over a number of years around the mid-century. The chief safety advantage of steam heating is that the pressure may be reduced much below the atmospheric in a closed-circuit system. Nason was awarded the contract for heating the Capitol in Washington, finally completed in 1864 after construction that extended over a period of 72 years. All the essential equipment for a reliable steam heating system—boiler, valves, pumps, piping, controls—could be found described and illustrated in the 1861 catalogue of Morris, Tasker and Company of Philadelphia, the leading suppliers at the time.

Plumbing

After heating, plumbing follows as the most important utility. A building is simply unusable without plumbing equipment, without hot and cold running water, toilets, lavatories, fountains, and if it is a hotel or apartment building, bathtubs and showers. Three factors had to be brought together at the requisite level of maturity for a reliable plumbing system: first, a pressure water supply; second, the necessary fixtures with valves, faucets, seals, and traps; and third, piping. An early and for long an isolated pressure water supply system, with steam-operated pumps, was built in England in 1712. The primitive steam engine was the type invented by Thomas Savery in 1698. To the best of my knowledge the first metropolitan water supply system constructed on a scale adequate to the needs of the new commercial and industrial city of the nineteenth century, was the Croton Aqueduct and Reservoir of New York, 1839–1842, one of the many achievements of John B. Jervis in the formative years of American engineering. The gravity water supply system with its associated siphons and storage facilities provided water at a 30 m (100-ft) head, sufficient for the plumbing equipment that was to come in the city within the next few years.

The flush toilet and the lavatory, with associated valves, seals, and traps, appeared in the latter part of the eighteenth century, but the history of this area of technology has scarcely been touched. One of the important figures in the development of the toilet was Joseph Bramah, the foremost locksmith of England in the full tide of the Industrial Revolution. Benjamin Latrobe is again an important figure in American technology. In the same year in which he introduced the iron column, he built a house with the bathtub, lavatory, and toilet in the same room, making possible the centralized plumbing stacks necessary in a multistory building. He was thus responsible for the curious use of the word *bathroom* in the United States: When you ask your hostess where the bathroom is she does not assume that you plan to take a bath.

With respect to piping, the traditional cast-iron type was clumsy, oversized, and difficult to work, especially in large multiple installations. Wrought iron pipe was seen to be far superior, and once more it was Morris, Tasker and Company who were responsible for its first manufacture. As in the case of heating, all the essential equipment—fixtures, piping, vales, boiler—could be found in the Morris Tasker catalogue of 1858.

Artificial Lighting

The origins of artificial lighting bring us back once again to the eighteenth century. The first coal-gas illuminant to supply multiple fixtures was installed by William Murdock in his own home at Redruth, England, in 1779. The first multiple installation for a large multistory building came with the construction of the Philips and Lee Mill at Salford, England, in 1802. Boulton and Watt were the builders of the mill and William Murdock installed the lighting system. Electric street lighting in its early form depended on Humphrey Davy's invention of arc lighting in 1813, but it was slow in superseding the almost universal gas lighting, which was introduced initially in London in 1814. in Baltimore, 1817, for the first American installation, and in New York,

1825. The proponents of arc lighting, however, were an enthusiastic lot, and by mid-century they were recommending it for universal application, interiors, exteriors, and anything in between. Before very long incandescent lighting was to take the place of all previous forms. Electrical illumination goes back to the experiments and discoveries of Galvani, Volta, and Faraday, whose names are enshrined in the daily vocabulary of electrical technology. After many experiments conducted from 1879 to 1884 practical incandescent lighting was finally realized by Thomas Edison in the United States and Joseph Swan in England.

All large multistory buildings with electric lighting systems incorporated their own generating plant, but as we move toward the end of the nineteenth century these gradually gave way to the purchase of electricity from a central power station. The ancestor of them all was the Edison Station on Pearl Street in New York, opened in 1882, in preparation not only for the incandescent light but the newly invented telephone as well.

Ventilation

The subject of induced-draft ventilation is virtually a closed book. We have only two names, one at the ancestral origins, the other at the beginning of the period of maturity. The French physicist and meteorologist Jean Théophile Desaguliers in 1736 introduced hand-operated centrifugal fans into the holds of naval vessels. The boys who were paid to operate them were called *ventilateurs*, which is the beginning of the technology and the vocabulary of ventilation. Probably the single best known name in the United States was Benjamin Franklin Sturdevant. In a series of experiments initiated in 1855 Sturdevant developed a steam-operated power-driven fan by means of which he could blow air into ducts throughout an entire building. An early installation of great size is in the Cooper Union, New York, where a fan of 3.5-m (12-ft) diameter supplies forced-draft ventilation to the entire building.

CONCLUSION

It is no coincidence that the primary inventions came from England, to some extent from France, and that most of them found their practical expression in the United States. It was in this country that fireproofing, central heating, and reliable plumbing equipment found their first full use. If one is going to choose the buildings that are the milestones, there is no question that the hotel was the decisive building type. Hotel standards in the United States rapidly rose above the level in England and on the Continent except for a few aristocratic spas, where only royalty and the rich might have stayed.

The first hotel to embody the plumbing techniques I have described was the Astor House, 1838–1842, in New York, the building of which coincided with the construction of the aqueduct system that made its plumbing installation possible and workable. An even more advanced work was the Fifth Avenue Hotel, 1857, in New York, marked by the highest standards of utilities and the first hotel elevator equipped with a safety brake. Meanwhile, the builders of the English Houses of Parliament, 1837–1860, had raised the Victoria Tower at one end to a height of 101 m (331 ft) by means of an internal iron frame and external bearing walls of masonry. As I said earlier, if the sole criterion for the first skyscraper is iron skeleton, fireproof, curtain-walled, multi-storied, concrete-floor construction, then the warehouses of the St. Ouen Docks in Paris, 1864–1865, are the obvious candidates. But without utilities the building is uninhabitable for human beings, so that it must be equally obvious that the warehouses do not qualify as skyscrapers, anymore than does the Victoria Tower.

If there is a building in which most of the technical factors I have described — structural system, elevators, pressure plumbing, central steam heating, multiple illuminating fixtures connected to a central supply — are present at the requisite level of maturity and reliability, a high-rent prestige building, it is the Equitable Life Assurance Building of New York, 1868–1870. The architects were Arthur Gilman and Edward Kendall, who, while the building was in the process of design and was expected to cost a fortune, called in George B. Post, a civil engineering graduate of New York University, as a consultant. Post radically revised the structural system: The court walls were treated as true curtain walls supported on an iron skeleton. Other changes followed, and the total cost was reduced by $330,000 as a consequence, but with no sacrifice to the elegance of this Second Empire palace clothed in granite and marble.

To show his gratitude to Post, the Equitable president, Henry B. Hyde, invited the engineer-architect to occupy the office at the highest level of the building, at the highest rent, double the going rate for New York office space. It was height that gave the building its prestige, and the elevator that made it readily accessible. And all this was translated into financial terms for Post: When he needed larger quarters he sold his Equitable lease for $6,000, the equivalent of about $180,000 today. For the first time, first-class commercial building was defined not only by architectural design but by elevators, plumbing, heating, and lighting as well. And we now know, thanks to very recent research (Larson, 1981), that the same company's new building in Chicago, originally known as the Kendall and erected in 1872–73, was in one respect even more advanced than its New York predecessor. It was in this building that Johnson and Kreischer installed the first tile cladding for iron columns and beams. The guarantee of safety against destruction by fire and the easy movement from floor to floor provided by the elevator emboldened Hyde to add two more stories to the height of the company's New York counterpart. If we are tracking down the origins of the skyscraper we have certainly reached the seminal stage in New York and Chicago around the year 1870.

REFERENCES/BIBLIOGRAPHY

Badger, D. D., 1865
  ILLUSTRATIONS OF IRON ARCHITECTURE, MADE BY THE ARCHITECTURAL IRON WORKS
  OF THE CITY OF NEW YORK, Architectural Iron Works, New York.
Bannister, T. C., 1956 and 1957
  BOGARDUS REVISITED, Journal of the Society of Architectural Historians, 15:4, December,
  pp. 11-22; 16:1, March, pp. 11-19.
Bixby, W. H., 1895
  WIND PRESSURES IN ENGINEERING CONSTRUCTION, Engineering News, 33:11, March,
  175-184.
Bogardus, J., 1856
  CAST IRON BUILDINGS: THEIR CONSTRUCTION AND ADVANTAGES, J. W. Harrison, New York.
Brooks, M. A., 1912
  REMINISCENCES OF THE EARLY DAYS OF FIREPROOF BUILDING CONSTRUCTION IN NEW
  YORK CITY, Engineering News, 68:22, November 28, pp. 986-987.
Bruegmann, R., 1978
  CENTRAL HEATING AND FORCED VENTILATION: ORIGINS AND EFFECTS ON ARCHITEC-
  TURAL DESIGN, Journal of the Society of Architectural Historians, 37:3, pp. 143-160.

Condit, C. W., 1974
  THE WIND BRACING OF BUILDINGS, Scientific American, 230:2, February, pp. 92-105.

Ferguson, E., 1976
  A HISTORICAL SKETCH OF CENTRAL HEATING, 1800-1860, Charles E. Peterson, ed., Building
  Early America, Chilton Book Co., Radnor, Pa., pp. 165-185.

Larson, G. E., 1981
  FIRE, EARTH AND WIND: TECHNICAL SOURCES OF THE CHICAGO SKYSCRAPER, Inland
  Architect, 25:7, September, pp. 20-29.

Morris, Tasker and Company, 1858
  PRICE LIST, Morris, Tasker and Company, Philadelphia, Pa.
Morris, Tasker and Company, 1861
  ILLUSTRATED CATALOGUE, Fourth Edition, Morris, Tasker and Company, Philadelphia.

Otis Elevator Company, 1953
  THE FIRST HUNDRED YEARS, Otis Elevator Company, New York.

Quimby, H. H., et al., 1892-1893
  WIND BRACING IN HIGH BUILDINGS, Engineering Record, 26:25 (19 Nov 1892), p. 394; 27:5
  (31 Dec 1892), p. 99; 27:7 (14 Jan 1893), p. 138; 27:8 (21 Jan 1893), pp. 161-162; 27:9 (28
  Jan 1893), p. 180; 27:13 (25 Feb 1893), p. 260; 27:15 (11 Mar 1893), pp. 298-299; 27:16
  (18 Mar 1893), p. 320.

Skempton, A. W., 1858-1860
  THE BOAT STORE, SHEERNESS (1858-1860), AND ITS PLACE IN STRUCTURAL HISTORY,
  Transactions of the Newcomen Society, Vol. XXXII, pp. 57-78.
Skempton, A. W., 1959
  EVOLUTION OF THE STEEL FRAME BUILDING, Guilds Engineer, Vol. X, pp. 37-51.

Vogel, R. M., 1961
  ELEVATOR SYSTEMS OF THE EIFFEL TOWER, 1889, United States National Museum Bulletin
  228, Washington, Smithsonian Institution.
Vogel, R. M., 1976
  BUILDING IN AN AGE OF STEAM, Charles E. Peterson, ed., Building Early America, Chilton Book
  Co., Radnor, Pa. pp. 119-134.

24   History of Tall Buildings

Webster, J. C., 1959
    THE SKYSCRAPER: LOGICAL AND HISTORICAL CONSIDERATIONS, Journal of the Society of
    Architectural Historians, 18:4, December, pp. 126-139.
Wight, P. B., 1876
    THE FIRE QUESTION, American Architect and Building News, v. 1 (17 June 1876), pp. 195-
    197; (24 June 1876), pp. 203-205; (1 July 1876), pp. 211-212.
Wight, P. B., 1878
    THE FIRE QUESTION, American Architect and Building News, v. 3 (2Mar 1878), p. 76.

13
Toward a better understanding of the evolution of the iron skeleton frame in Chicago

G.R. Larson and R.M. Geraniotis

William Le Baron Jenney and the Home Insurance Building have been given a pivotal position in many of the early histories of modern architecture, a reputation that has been consistently embroiled in controversy during the building's 100-year history. The context of the Home Insurance Building in Chicago's commercial building milieu immediately prior to Jenney's design of 1884 reveals that tall buildings constructed before the Home Insurance Building were called skyscrapers. Many of these earlier buildings, in fact, were even taller than the final height of the Home Insurance Building. A technical analysis of Jenney's final structural design reveals that it was neither conceived nor detailed as a rigid, independent iron frame. A recently discovered article on the potential of iron framing published by Chicago architect Frederick Baumann in March 1884, before Jenney even started designing the Home Insurance Building, not only disputes Jenney's reputation as the "father of the iron skeleton frame," but also exposes the antiquated nature of Jenney's actual structure and detailing.

Fig. 1. William Le Baron Jenney, Home Insurance Building, Chicago, 1884. Exterior (J. W. Taylor, IChi-00989; Chicago).

THE ISSUE of the origin of the skyscraper and the role played by William Le Baron Jenney's design of the Home Insurance Building (Fig. 1) in Chicago has been the subject of considerable discussion, especially during the last few years as the building's centennial (1984) first approached and has now past. The Home Insurance Building has been credited by various authors as being everything from the first iron skeleton-framed building to the first skyscraper, and Jenney has consequently gained the reputation of being the "father of the skyscraper."[1] Actually, when one reads contemporary professional literature and examines the structure that Jenney designed, it is readily apparent that the Home Insurance Building was not the first building in Chicago to be called a skyscraper, nor did Jenney conceive or detail its structure as an independent iron skeleton frame. In fact, as will be documented, Jenney was not even the first Chicago architect to articulate the concept of an iron-framed skyscraper.[2]

---

1. A recent article by Theodore Turak attempted to confirm Jenney's priority of invention by comparing letters uncovered in the records of the American Institute of Architects to the unpublished recollections of Jenney's partner, William B. Mundie. Theodore Turak, "Remembrances of the Home Insurance Building," *JSAH*, 44 (1985), 60–65.

2. For the development of iron skeletal framing in America prior to the 1871 Chicago Fire see: Gerald R. Larson, "Fire, Earth and Wind—Part I," *Inland Architect*, 25 (September 1981), 20–29, and "Fire, Earth and Wind—Part II," *Inland Architect*, 27 (January/February 1983), 31–37.

40   JSAH, XLVI:1, MARCH 1987

Fig. 2.   Solon Spenser Beman, Pullman Palace Car Building, Chicago, 1883. Exterior (J. W. Taylor; Chicago Historical Society).

The term skyscraper, as used to describe a tall building, dates from at least 1884, when the 2 August 1884 issue of the Chicago magazine *Real Estate and Building Journal* contained an article, "High Towers and Buildings," which stated that "Veritable skyscrapers have been springing up here during the past couple of years almost with mushroom rapidity."[3] In addition to three towers designed by W. W. Boyington, the article also listed eight buildings that it considered to be skyscrapers, three of which (S. S. Beman's Pullman Palace Car Building, 165' [Fig. 2]; Boyington's Royal Insurance Building, 164' [Fig. 3]; and Burnham and Root's Insurance Exchange Building, 160' [Fig. 4]) were not only taller than the projected height of 159' for the Home Insurance Building,[4]

3. "High Towers and Buildings," *Real Estate and Building Journal*, (2 August 1884), 364.

4. In descending order of height, the skyscrapers were Boyington's Tower of the Board of Trade, 303'; Boyington's Water Works Tower, 175'; Boyington's twin towers of the La Salle Street Station, 170'; Beman's design for Marshall Field's ill-fated 13-story office building which would have topped the existing height record for a building of 165'—that of Beman's Pullman Building; Boyington's Royal Insurance Building, 164'; Burnham and Root's Insurance Exchange, 160'; Jenney's Home Insurance Building 159'; Burnham and Root's Counselman, Calumet and Montauk Buildings, 145'. Ibid.

Fig. 3.   W. W. Boyington, Royal Insurance Building, Chicago, 1883. Exterior (Gilbert and Bryson, *Chicago and Its Makers*; Art Institute of Chicago).

but were also already completed by August 1884, when the Home Insurance Building was only two stories out of the ground and its exterior iron work had not yet started to be erected.[5] Therefore, Chicago's local professional press at the time identified skyscrapers as buildings that were built not only prior to and taller than the Home Insurance Building, but also did this before the iron members in the Home Insurance Building's exterior were publicly announced or erected. Consequently, the iron skeleton frame was not intrinsic to the original Chicago definition of "skyscraper;" the Home Insur-

5. *Real Estate and Building Journal* of 26 July 1884 (p. 352) reported that the first floor of the Home Insurance Building was nearing completion. The first published account of Jenney's intention to use iron members in the exterior of the Home Insurance was contained in the September 1884 issue of *Inland Architect* (p. 24), which also stated that the construction had reached the third floor, the point where the exterior iron was to begin erection.

Fig. 4. Burnham and Root, Insurance Exchange Building, Chicago, 1884. Exterior (*Inland Architect* July 1885; Art Institute of Chicago).

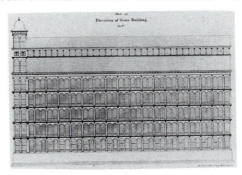

Fig. 5. Daniel Badger and George H. Johnson, U.S. Warehousing Grain Elevator, Brooklyn, 1860. Elevation (Badger, *Illustrations of Iron Architecture;* Art Institute of Chicago).

ance Building was not considered to be the first skyscraper in Chicago; and Jenney was not the designer of Chicago's first skyscraper. Boyington, Beman, and Burnham and Root had already built more and taller skyscrapers before Jenney and the Home Insurance Building ever entered the scene.

As early as 1892, Peter B. Wight, in the March issue of *Inland Architect,* began to link the technique of iron framing that Jenney used in the Home Insurance Building to the iron-framed buildings of James Bogardus and Daniel Badger that had been erected more than 30 years prior to the re-emergence of exterior iron framing during 1884 in Chicago:

But while this system of building is new as applied to business structures, it is not entirely novel. There is a grain elevator in Brooklyn [Badger's U.S. Warehousing Grain Building, 1860 (Fig. 5)], that was erected 30 years ago, the exterior of which is constructed of a cast iron framework filled in with a light wall of brick, the iron showing on the outside. There is also a shot tower in New York City [Bogardus' shot towers for the McCullough Shot and Lead Company, 1855, and the Tatham and Brothers Company, 1856] which was built about the same time in the same manner.[6]

6. Peter B. Wight, "Recent Fireproof Building in Chicago—Part II," *Inland Architect and News Record,* 19 (March 1892), 22.

In fact, the only departure from standard construction of the early 1880s in the Home Insurance Building was in the two street façades.[7] The two rear masonry bearing party walls that ran the entire height of the building and the interior iron cage (Fig. 6) were typical for the period. In fact, even the first two floors of the street fronts consisted of rusticated granite piers, battered from 4'–0" thick at the base to 2'–10" at the third floor. Upon these were set story-high, hollow rectangular cast iron columns (Fig. 7), bolted one on top of another to support the upper seven floors and roof. The columns were filled with concrete[8] and surrounded with brick, which created a solid cross section in the building's exterior piers. Rather than describing this technique as wrapping or enclosing the iron column with a masonry skin, Jenney stated that he embedded the column within the masonry pier: "a square iron column was *built into* [emphasis added] each of the piers in the street fronts."[9] This conceptual difference from modern skeletal framing is even more evident in the way Jenney used the exterior masonry to stiffen the assembly of iron columns, mullions, and spandrels.

7. To ascertain the actual detailing of Jenney's structure, Larson examined Jenney's working drawings for the Home Insurance Building now on microfilm at The Art Institute of Chicago. He also examined the four-columned bay fragment that is in the collection of Chicago's Museum of Science and Industry.
8. Theodore E. Tallmadge, *The Origin of the Skyscraper—The Report of the Field Committee,* Chicago, 1934, 12.
9. "As it was important in the Home Insurance Building to obtain a large number of small offices provided with abundance of light, the piers between the windows were reduced to the minimum." William Le Baron Jenney, "The Construction of a Heavy, Fireproof Building on Compressible Soil," *Inland Architect and Builder,* 6 (December 1885), 100.

42   JSAH, XLVI:1, MARCH 1987

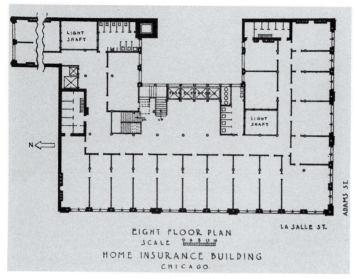

Fig. 6.   Jenney, Home Insurance Building, typical floor plan. (Tallmadge, *The Origin of the Skyscaper;* Art Institute Chicago).

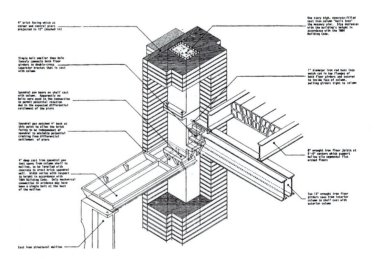

Fig. 7.   Jenney, Home Insurance Building. Reconstruction of the structural detailing of the exterior piers. (Drawing by Deborah Cohen and Maxwell Merriman).

The columns were cast with projecting shelf brackets to receive the appropriate horizontal framing members. Two 12-inch wrought iron I-beam floor girders sat on the ledge at the interior face of the column. These were loosely bolted to the column by a single bolt that passed through each of the girder webs and a projecting bracket which was also cast with the column. As a good amount of tolerance was needed for site erection, the holes were larger than the bolt, leaving the connection with a considerable amount of play. Therefore, Jenney incorporated a clamp consisting of a one-inch diameter wrought iron rod that was bent at one end and placed into a notch cut in the top flange of both girders. At the other end, the clamp was bolted to the column by a nut placed inside the column, thereby pulling the girders tight to the column face. The floor girders supported eight-inch wrought iron I-beams at five-foot centers, within which were placed hollow tile floor arches.

To support the windows and masonry spandrels between the piers, cast iron lintels in the form of four-inch-deep hollow pans, also filled with concrete like the columns, spanned from a column shelf bracket to an intermediate cast iron mullion. The cast iron lintels were as wide as the masonry spandrel walls that were constructed on top of them. As if the street fronts were still considered to be bearing walls, the spandrels, for no other conceivable reason, increased in thickness along with the piers, as required by the building code, from 20 inches in the top three floors to 24 inches in floors 5–7, to 28 inches in floors 3 and 4.

The cast iron lintels were not one continuous piece that spanned between the columns but were in halves that joined over the mullions. The lintel pans were evidently not bolted to either the column shelf brackets or the mullions, but simply rested on the bearing surfaces, apparently relying on the supported masonry knee wall, which was bonded into the masonry pier, to hold the iron armature in place laterally. The lack of bolts may have been a technique on Jenney's part to impart some rotational flexibility at the column/spandrel connection to accommodate differential settlement of the piers.[10] This flexible joint was augmented by notching the front of the iron lintel pan back four inches which allowed the pier's exterior face brick to continue past the lintel without actually sitting on it and minimized the potential of the face brick to crack if an iron spandrel rotated due to the settlement of an adjacent pier.

Therefore, the pier's brick facing (which was 12 inches thick in some locations) was continuously self-supporting from the granite piers at the third floor and was not supported at each floor on the iron column, as was the contention of the Field Committee.[11] If it was Jenney's intention to support the pier's brick facing on the frame, why did he intentionally notch the lintel pans precisely where they could have offered critical support to the facing as it turned the corner? While the iron lintels carried the weight of the masonry spandrels to the iron mullions and columns, the structure created by the lintel pans, mullions, and columns was far from being a rigid, self-supporting iron skeleton that independently carried its masonry envelope at each floor, which the Home Insurance Building was later claimed to have been.

This brings up the first of two extremely important points of interpretation. Jenney did not make the intermediate iron mullions a continuous vertical line of support to the foundation for two reasons. Principally, he wanted to avoid the inevitable uplift problems experienced by the lesser-loaded intermediate piers in buildings of the period. This resulted from the heavier-loaded major piers settling at a greater rate than the smaller mullions, transferring more and more load to the smaller mullions and usually creating major cracking in and around them.[12] The easiest way to avoid the problem was to prevent the mullions from becoming a continuous line of bearing by transferring the mullion loads over to the main piers before they reached the ground. If this could be done in a series of transfer beams, the mullion loads would be relatively uniform, and therefore the mullion cross section would not have to increase as the columns did, keeping the windows as large as possible.

Therefore, Jenney placed transfer beams (Fig. 8) to carry the mullion loads to the piers, immediately above the cast iron lintel pans at the fourth floor (four 7-inch I beams), sixth floor (three 15-inch I-beams), ninth floor (two 12-inch I-beams), and roof (two 15-inch I-beams). These transfer beams also nominally tied the columns together laterally (especially at the roof), thereby creating what one might call a skeleton. However, if it was Jenney's intention to actually create a rigid iron skeleton frame in the street fronts, these beams should have been introduced at every floor. The framework as built was not rigid independent of the masonry, for the columns in floors 6–8 extended unbraced for three stories. Since the lintel pans were not bolted to the columns, their action in this vein was negligible at best. Consequently, without the masonry

10. "As the building must settle . . . the first settlement must be uneven, therefore every care must be taken to make the construction elastic." Ibid.

11. The Trustees of the Estate of Marshall Field, Sr., planned to demolish the Home Insurance Building in 1931 in order to erect the 46-story Field Building designed by Graham, Anderson, Probst and White. With hopes of gaining a special historical prominence for the site of the new building, they assembled a respected committee of six architects, a contractor, and a realtor, to ascertain the true construction of the Home Insurance Building during its demolition.

12. For a complete description of this problem see Frederick Baumann, *The Art of Preparing Foundations*, Chicago, 1873, 17–22.

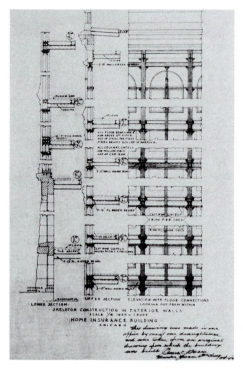

Fig. 8. Jenney, Home Insurance Building. Elevation of structural iron members in the exterior, showing the location of the transfer beams at Floors 4, 6, 9, and roof (Jensen & Halstead, Ltd., Chicago).

and the concrete filling, the exterior iron framework was not inherently rigid, and it would have been very difficult, if not impossible, to erect it "two or three floors ahead of the brick walls."[13]

This raises the second point of judgment: the actual intent and role of the masonry in the pier and the corresponding stability of the iron frame independent of the masonry. It can be argued that most of the pier masonry was supported on the iron columns because of the manner in which it was constructed around the lintels. However, the 4-inch exterior facing, which increased to 12 inches at the corner and entrance piers, enjoyed no similar support as the lintel pans were notched back at the piers to allow the facing to be independent of them, thereby allowing the facing to be continuous from

the granite walls for eight stories. Jenney went so far as to specify a very conservative technique of bricklaying to achieve a stronger-than-usual assembly to keep the cross section of the masonry piers to a minimum. Selected hard-burned brick was used with a strong cement, not lime, mortar and was laid up in very tight, solidly packed joints. This would have been entirely unnecessary if Jenney was supporting the face brick at each level.

We can therefore conclude from at least five points that the iron framework in the Home Insurance Building was not conceived or erected by Jenney as a modern skeletal frame that is entirely self-sufficient and independent of its masonry enclosure. First, he initially did not refer to the masonry as a covering but always stated that he embedded the iron column within the masonry pier in order to reduce its size and maximize the amount of daylight. Second, as the lintel pans were not bolted to the columns, rigidity of the mullion/lintel assembly was gained through the masonry spandrel wall. Third, the exterior brick facing of the piers was not supported on the iron column at any point; therefore, it was continuously bearing from the granite piers. Fourth, as the columns typically extended laterally unbraced for two stories (the spacing of the mullion transfer beams), and in the middle of the building for three stories, they relied solely on the rigidity of the spandrel masonry interacting with the masonry pier for lateral stability. Finally, without the rigidity of the two rear masonry bearing party walls and the masonry piers, the iron frame with its loosely bolted and clamped connections could not have resisted any wind loads. Therefore, the historical significance of the Home Insurance Building's structure is that it was the first extensive use of iron in the U.S. in the exterior of a multistory building to support a portion of its masonry enclosure since Badger's Grain Elevators of 1860 and 1862.

Because of the later controversy surrounding the Home Insurance Building and the issue of the origin of the iron skeleton frame, Jenney's professional position in the Chicago architectural scene of the early 1880s has been greatly inflated. The Home Insurance Building was not only Jenney's first tall building, but also his first major commission in the 11 years that followed the completion of the Portland Block and the Lakeside Building in 1873. To even better appreciate the fortuitous nature of his Civil War acquaintance with Arthur C. Ducat, the Chicago agent of the Home Insurance Company of New York, one must recall that the Home Insurance Building was Jenney's only tall building during the 16-year period be-

13. William Mundie, *Skeleton Construction, Its Origin and Development Applied to Architecture,* Roll 23, Chicago Microfilm Project, Art Institute of Chicago, frame 27. This disputes Mundie's recollection of not only the type of construction employed in the Home Insurance Building, but also the chronology of its erection. Mundie said that "the iron framework was up to the sixth floor of the building and two

or three floors ahead of the brick walls" in August 1884. Ibid. In reality, the ironwork did not start to be put into place until September 1884. "Our Illustrations," *Inland Architect and Builder,* 4 (September 1884), 24. As will be seen, this is not the only error contained in Mundie's unpublished manuscript of 1931, which throws suspicion on his accuracy and motives.

Fig. 9. W. W. Boyington, Chicago Board of Trade, Chicago, 1882. La Salle Street south from Adams Street, late 1880s (IChi-00253; Chicago Historical Society).

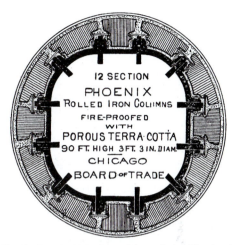

Fig. 10. Peter B. Wight, fireproofed wrought iron Phoenix columns in the Chicago Board of Trade Tower. (*Brickbuilder,* August 1897; Art Institute of Chicago).

tween the Portland Block and Lakeside Building and the Second Leiter Building of 1889.[14]

In stark contrast stand the records of Chicago's four premier firms, W. W. Boyington, John M. Van Osdel, S. S. Beman, and Burnham and Root, who were responsible for the vast majority of Chicago's early skyscrapers. Quite simply, Jenney no longer enjoyed the reputation he had had in the early 1870s, as one of Chicago's foremost office building designers. The true measure of the Jenney office's professional stature in the early 1880s is best exemplified with the Montauk Block of 1881. The owner of Jenney's Portland Block, Peter C. Brooks of Boston,[15] did not turn to Jenney when he was ready to build Chicago's first skyscraper, the ten-story Montauk Block. Instead, Brooks gave the honor to the young upstart firm of Burnham and Root, in association with Peter B. Wight, their former employer, who was to be the fireproofing contractor for the Montauk Block.

By this time, iron construction was being given more exposure in the local architectural press. Across the street from the Montauk, then under construction, Haverly's Theater was being erected. Although the exterior consisted of solid brick

walls, the supports of the galleries were all iron, leading the *Real Estate and Building Journal* in 1881 to state: "It is possible and feasible to construct the auditorium entirely of a light iron framework, which would make it practically fireproof, and every theater should be built this way."[16] The same issue contained an article on the newly constructed Cape Henry Lighthouse on Chesapeake Bay: "It is 155' from base to top, 30' in diameter at the base, 16' at the top. The exterior, which is octagonal in shape, is constructed of cast iron. Every story is solidly bolted together by heavy cast iron floor plates . . . 7,000 pounds of bolts were required."[17]

This article may well have been the inspiration for Chicago's tallest building, the Board of Trade Tower (Fig. 9), whose ironwork was a direct prelude to the Home Insurance Building. Designed by W. W. Boyington early in 1882, the tower was 303 feet high, although it was only 32 feet wide at its base. The mammoth tower was supported by the largest iron columns built during the 1880s. These were 12-sectioned Phoenix wrought iron columns (Fig. 10) that were 3 feet, 3 inches in diameter and 90 feet high and fireproofed with Wight's patented terra cotta casings.[18] As the base of the tower was only 32 feet wide, these columns must have supported some, if not all, of the masonry in the tower's exterior. If not, the thickness of the walls and the columns would have taken

14. Jenney admitted the importance of his prior relationship with Ducat in his success of gaining the commission for the Home Insurance Building: "In 1883, when the Home Insurance Company proposed to erect a building in Chicago, Ducat (who was the agent of the company in Chicago and the leading agent in the West) kindly recommended me to be their architect." Letter of William Le Baron Jenney, printed in Arthur C. Ducat, *Memoirs,* 65.

15. *Land Owner,* 5 (June 1873), 99.
16. "Theatre Construction," *Real Estate and Building Journal,* 23 (July 1881), 323.
17. "A Gigantic Lighthouse," Ibid.
18. Wight, "Fireproof Building," 22.

46   JSAH, XLVI:1, MARCH 1987

up almost all of the floor area at the ground floor.

In December 1883, three months before Jenney started to design the Home Insurance Building, the Board of Trade's columns were considered to be Wight's finest installation. In contrast to the ironwork of the later Home Insurance Building, for which Wight was also the fireproofing contractor, the Board of Trade Tower's iron was put in place before the masonry facing was added. The tower was under construction from December 1883 to August 1884, a period that parallels Jenney's gestation of the Home Insurance design for a site only two blocks north of the Board of Trade. In fact, the ironwork of the tower had been completed just before the first exterior iron columns of the Home Insurance Building were put into place.[19]

Even more revealing of the environment in which Jenney designed the Home Insurance Building is an article, "Improved Construction of High Buildings," in the 15 March 1884 issue of Sanitary News, recently uncovered by Dr. Geraniotis.[20] This article documents beyond the shadow of a doubt that Chicago architect Frederick Baumann had indeed clearly defined and articulated the concept of an independent iron-framed tall building before Jenney incorporated a watered-down version of the idea in the design of the Home Insurance Building. In 1873, Baumann had already established his reputation as Chicago's leading theoretician on construction with his pamphlet, The Art of Preparing Foundations, in which he was the first to clearly articulate the principle of the uniformly stressed, isolated pad foundation, Chicago's other important contribution to building construction.[21] Therefore, it comes as no surprise to find Baumann writing about the iron skeleton framed skyscraper prior to Jenney's design of the Home Insurance Building. As the newly discovered article is dated 15 March 1884, and moreover, it reports that Baumann

had already publicly presented his scheme, Baumann's first public discussion of his ideas would have necessarily preceded the article by, shall we say, at least two weeks to account for writing, editing, and printing. This, then, pushes Baumann's date conservatively back to at least 1 March 1884, if not even earlier. Such a date would confirm Baumann's statement that his ideas coalesced during the Home Insurance competition and also lends credence to his claim that he experimented with the idea in an 1883 design for a building at the Southwest corner of Clark and Jackson.[22]

In contrast, the first mention of the Home Insurance Building in Jenney's personal notes is dated 19 February 1884. The building at this date was to be only six stories plus a basement:

The basement story to be one step up from the sidewalk, similar to the Boreel Building [in New York]. . . . This would make the building 84′–5″ high [six stories plus basement], if another, [it] would be 96′, which is high enough and I would object to it being any higher. . . . The basement to be of some suitable stone to be decided upon. The rest of the building to be of brick with terra cotta or molded brick trimmings.[23]

When the building committee from New York arrived in Chicago during the first week in March (meaning they met after Baumann's initial presentation of his ideas) to review the competition drawings for the new building reported to be submissions by three different architects, they apparently had already increased the height of the building because a permit was obtained on 1 March 1884 for an eight-story plus basement structure.[24] The premature permit—for Jenney's design was not "officially" chosen for another two weeks—was forced by a pending building ordinance that threatened to limit the heights of all new buildings to 100 feet. Suspiciously, it was reported that even though the winner had not been chosen, the permit was taken out upon the plans of Jenney, and that he, upon the orders of the company (and undoubtedly at the encouragement of Jenney's friend, Ducat), had already begun to let the contracts for the cut stone and other materials.[25]

19. "Synopsis of Building News," Inland Architect and Builder, 4 (September 1884), 28.

20. "Improved Construction of High Buildings," Sanitary News, 3 (15 March 1884), 123. Baumann later published his ideas in a three-page pamphlet: Frederick Baumann, Improvement in the Construction of Tall Buildings, Chicago, 1884.

21. Frederick Baumann was born in Angermünde, East Prussia, on 6 January 1826. He studied architecture and building in Berlin, first at the Gewerbeschule and then at the prestigious Königliches Gewerbeinstitut. He also acquired extensive practical experience during periods of apprenticeship with master masons, master carpenters, and an uncle who was the government building inspector in Bromberg. Baumann joined many Germans in immigrating to the U.S. following the 1848–49 revolution. He traveled directly to Chicago, arriving in the summer of 1850. After working with John M. Van Osdel and Edward Burling, he formed a partnership with Van Osdel in January 1855, which lasted until the onset of the 1857 panic. Subsequently, he worked as a building contractor with August Wallbaum; he returned to architectural practice in 1864, eventually becoming a leading figure in the Chicago architectural community during the last third of the 19th century.

22. Letter, Frederick Baumann to Glen Brown, 14 December 1907, Archives, American Institute of Architects, Washington, D.C. as quoted in Turak, "Remembrances," 62. See also Baumann's autobiographical essay, "Life, Reminiscences, and Notes," Construction News, 4 (15 January 1916), 9.

23. Roll 9, Jenney Collection, Chicago Microfilm Project, Art Institute of Chicago, frame 424. Jenney's first entry that pertained to the Home Insurance Building correlates with the first published mention of the project which occurred in the 23 February 1884 issue of Real Estate and Building Journal (p. 88). This pushes Jenney's conceptualization period for the Home Insurance Building back to the Spring of 1884 and contradicts Jenney's failing memory in his later years when he claimed he received the commission in 1883; see n. 14.

24. Real Estate and Building Journal, 8 March 1884, 114.

25. "Architectural and Building Notes," Inland Architect and Builder, 3 (March 1884), 23.

The following month, *Inland Architect* reported that Jenney's design had indeed been chosen the winner from plans submitted by a half dozen of Chicago's best architects.[26] The design continued to be refined during the spring of 1884; the final height was set at 150 feet with nine stories plus basement on 28 April 1884.[27] Using Jenney's notes, it appears that as the building increased in height from the initial seven floors of 19 February, to the final ten stories of 28 April, he became concerned about the size of the masonry piers and most probably realized during the latter part of this period that he could keep the piers' cross section within reason by embedding iron sections in the piers. The first mention and calculation of the exterior iron columns in his notes is dated 17 April 1884, over a month after the article on Baumann's skeletal frame idea was published.[28] In fact, the erection of the iron in the street fronts was not started until September 1884,[29] over five months after the publication of the article describing Baumann's ideas.

The primitive nature of Jenney's iron framework is evident when compared to Baumann's ideas of modern skeletal framing:

The design is to erect on foundations a firm and rigid skeleton, or hull, of iron, and cover it at once with a proper roof. The enclosure, whether of stone, terra cotta, or brick, or any combination of these materials, may be erected at the same time the iron structure is being put in place. But the latter might proceed much faster than the former; while the hull might be roofed within two months, the enclosure might not have proceeded further than the fourth story. Thus there need be no delay to a steady progress. Derricks may be set on the roof for finishing the enclosure in a convenient manner. . . .

Mr. Baumann claims that this method would render the work more independent of the weather than by the usual construction; the erection of the iron hull is, in its nature, a rapid process. The practicability of erecting buildings on Chicago soil, twelve and more stories high, then becomes a fact. Light, the great desideratum in all city buildings, is secured, even on the lowest—the most valuable—floors, whereas, otherwise, the necessarily broad piers would be a hindrance. The piers may not only be made narrow, but shallow—twenty-seven inches at

the most, thus, again making a saving of light. [Was this not the exact logic Jenney used to explain his later design for the Home Insurance Building?]

The iron uprights are to be provided with a series of projecting brackets for the purpose of anchoring and supporting the parts forming the exterior enclosure. These supporting brackets will be so arranged as to permit an independent removal of any part of the exterior lining, which may have been damaged by fire or otherwise. [Contrast this with the lack of any structural support for the masonry facing in the piers of the Home Insurance as well as the structure's dependence on the masonry for rigidity]. The iron-floor girders are securely fastened [riveted fixed connections] to the outer posts at both ends. This imparts firmness to the structure; further, it increases the bearing strength of the girders at least to one-half of their usual strength. The iron floor-beams are fastened to the sides of the girders, and will gain thereby at least 20 percent in strength [compare Baumann's fixed connections to the friction clamp and single bolt used by Jenney]. . . .

Mr. Baumann holds that there will thus be a saving in the four most important items in construction—light, convenience, space and time. Structures wholly constructed of iron would in this light, be the most preferable, were it possible to clothe them with proper elegance, and were they proof against neighboring fires.[30]

The date of this article disputes William Mundie's claim that Baumann published his pamphlet on skeleton framing after he had allegedly intensely questioned Mundie, then a draftsman for Jenney, in the early summer of 1884 about Jenney's details for the Home Insurance Building while it was "under construction."[31] As construction didn't start until 1 May 1884,[32] Baumann's ideas had been already published for at least six weeks. The chronology of events surrounding the publication of Baumann's ideas and Jenney's initial thoughts for the Home Insurance Building contained in his own notebook suggest just the opposite of what Mundie later tried to prove. Apparently, Jenney used Baumann's ideas for the first time in the Home Insurance Building. Perhaps these points shed some light on the words of another Jenney employee, Elmer C. Jensen, who was always puzzled over the fact that "Major Jenney never made any claim that he had originated the skyscraper principle."[33]

26. "Synopsis of Building News," *Inland Architect and Builder*, 3 (April 1884), 42–43.

27. Roll 9, Jenney Collection, frames 426–434. Jenney's notes correlate with the 1 May 1884 start of construction as published in Tallmadge, *Field Report*, 10.

28. Jenney Collection, frames 426–443. The first shop drawing of the ironwork by the Dearborn Foundry was approved by Jenney on 24 May 1884. Ibid., 443. There is no evidence in Jenney's notebook to support Mundie's allegation that Jenney originally intended to use iron framing in all the walls but was prevented from doing so in the party walls by the City Building Commissioner. Mundie, *Skeleton Construction*, frame 25. Since the building permit was granted on 1 March 1884, a month and a half before the first mention of iron columns in Jenney's notes, Mundie's chronology once again appears to be faulty.

29. "Our Illustrations," 24.

30. "Improved Construction," 123.

31. Mundie, *Skeleton Construction*, frame 98. In fact, Baumann's article was published on 15 March 1884. Mundie was not even in Chicago then; he arrived two weeks later on 1 April 1884. Ibid., frame 4.

32. Tallmadge, *Field Report*, 10.

33. As quoted in Purcell, "First Skyscraper," 36. Although Purcell did not give the source of Jensen's quote, the essence of it was contained in an earlier article written by Jensen:

"Apparently Mr. Jenney either was not conscious of the important contribution he was making to the world at the time or his modesty prevented him from making any mention of it [the invention of the iron skeletal frame] in the press and technical papers." Elmer C. Jensen, "Origin of the Skyscraper—Part II, "*Union League*, October 1950, 17. Jensen entered Jenney's office in March 1885 as an office boy, becoming a partner in the firm in April 1905.

APPENDICES

APPENDIX I

Professor Larson presented a shorter version of this article in a paper delivered at the 1983 Annual Meeting of The Society of Architectural Historians in the session "Commercial Architecture Before 1914," chaired by Sarah Bradford Landau. Larson is working on a book, *Earth, Fire and Wind,* which documents architectural developments in Chicago prior to 1879. The Graham Foundation has helped to fund some of this research. Dr. Geraniotis is preparing a book on the German architects in 19th-century Chicago for the Architectural History Foundation. The authors would like to acknowledge the efforts of John Zukowsky, Curator of the Department of Architecture, The Art Institute of Chicago, in introducing the work of each author to the other. The joint results of Larson's research of Jenney's chronology during the design of the Home Insurance Building and Geraniotis' research which uncovered the article by Chicago architect Frederick Baumann have established the priority of events presented in this article.

APPENDIX II

On the key question of the piers' masonry facing, the Field Report stated: "In the important matter of the masonry piers, the conclusion is not so obvious. . . . Accordingly, the two typical piers were stripped or girdled, one midway between the fourth and fifth floors, and the other in the third story at the top of the window level. In each case the masonry was entirely removed for a space of two feet, completely exposing the column; the masonry piers above remaining undisturbed to the height of the remainder of the story on the fourth floor and a full story on the third floor. The stripping was left undisturbed and unshored until the building was wrecked down to that point, a matter of one day. No cracking of the piers or other failure of the masonry was apparent during the interval. This indicates to the Committee that regardless of Major Jenney's intention in the matter, and of the opinions of various commentators on the building, the piers, were, in fact, supported by the structural skeleton . . . the typical masonry pier was eight hundred square inches, and of this six hundred and forty square inches was supported directly by the cast iron lintels and the doubled twelve inch spandrel beams and the doubled twelve inch floor girders. The remaining one hundred and sixty square inches, one-fifth of the area, represents in typical cases the pier facing four inches in thickness and three feet, six inches in width. As this facing was bonded into the pier, it could not help but be supported by the corbel action from the main body of the pier. There was in addition, though unessential to its support, considerable adhesion to the iron columns to which the brickwork was closely pressed. Furthermore, at certain places stone lintels and stone belt cornices directly supported by the iron framing traversed the piers and was bonded into them, forming a cantilever and a beam action which aided in the support of the brick facing in the function of a shelf. An important exception occurs to the typical column design in the three street front corner piers. In these columns, at each floor, an iron flange extends four inches from the outside faces of the columns into the masonry pier, which at this point is twelve inches in thickness. This obviously was intended to support at least part of the pier." Tallmadge, *Field Report,* 14–15.

The Committee's interpretation of this last detail is in error, for this specific condition was the logical result of having to bolt the corner columns through flanges in the directions of both street fronts, which unintentionally forced the flanges to project into a corner pier's facing. This is quite evident when one examines the photo of the demolition (Plate III— Tallmadge, 22). Another error contained in the report was the Committee's extensive yet unconvincing explanation about the stone belt courses' structural capacity. Jenney's own words about the "cantilevered" stone lintels' potential to carry the masonry facing, which were even, surprisingly, reprinted in the Committee's report stated: "Stone lintels must have short bearings on the piers, that there may be some movement without fracture." Ibid, 32. Obviously, the short bearing of the lintel would have prevented any cantilever action and thus, no support to the masonry facing would have been available. Incredibly, the Field Report even contained a close-up photograph of the stone lintels in question that visually contradicted the committee's argument. This shows a vertical joint in the stone coursing directly over the corner of the masonry piers, the exact location where a joint could not occur if the committee's argument was correct. The location of this joint obviously would have prevented any beam action in the stone coursing, which would have been necessary to carry the pier's face brick as the Committee imagined. Ibid, 4.

Irving K. Pond also argued that the piers' facings were loadbearing and not supported on the frame, noting that "no masonry pier could have been installed until that immediately beneath was in place," Irving K. Pond, "Neither a Skyscraper Nor a Skeleton Construction," *Architectural Record* (August 1934), 32. The most cynical response to the Field Committee's attempt to prove the iron column's support of the masonry facing came from William G. Purcell in a letter to his partner George G. Elmslie:

"See the picture on page 21 where a small square cast iron column is seen, during demolition, to be supporting a few cubic feet of brick masonry which clings to it. Well, naturally, George, when they were taking down the building the brick piers ceased to support that which was no longer resting upon them and their reinforcing metal naturally had enough strength to hold up a cubic yard of rubble" . . . William G. Purcell, "First Skyscraper," *Northwest Architect* (January 1953), 5.

Steelwork in building: thirty years' progress

S. Bylander

BEFORE the year 1900 many skyscrapers had been erected in the United States of America and steel-frame buildings were quite usual there. Cast-iron bases and columns were much in use, while buildings of thirty storeys were considered high.

Meanwhile, steel-frame buildings were not general on the continent of Europe. Factories and railway stations were in prominence; sometimes light ornamental steel and glass structures occurred, such as the Kursaal in Ostend.

In England, steel-frame construction had not commenced in a general sense. The cast-iron column was in favour and internal steel beam framing and steel filler joists for thick breeze concrete floors. Most buildings were constructed in self-supporting brick walls and wooden joist floors.

The first steel-frame building of importance in London was the Ritz Hotel, erected in 1904 (*Figure* 1).

The external walls had to be of full thickness as required by the London Building Act, 1894, but they were carried on steel at each floor. The style, the details for pillar splices above the floor level, the top and bottom brackets on pillars connecting beams, and the framing generally, were the same as were used at that time in New York steel-frame buildings. This was the first building for which such steel detail design was adopted in London.

The floor construction consisted of 4-in. reinforced concrete floor slabs about 6 ft. span, and a 2-in. reinforced concrete ceiling slab about 6 ft. span; thus hollow floors and flush ceilings were obtained.

The erection of this steel-frame building did much to increase the agitation for revisions of the London Building Act. The new amendment Act for steel-frame buildings was completed by the London County Council in 1909, and until that time very little progress was made in the use of steel in building construction.

Before the issue of the 1909 Act, steelwork was mainly used for internal pillars and bres-

*Paper to be read before the Institution of Structural Engineers at the Institution of Civil Engineers, Great George Street, London, S.W.1, on Thursday, 14th January, 1937, at 6.30 p.m.

summers, or main girders, and girders over shop fronts. The pillars were usually in single storey lengths provided with caps and bases; the beams were laid on top of the cap, the next pillar resting on top of the beam, which type of pillar detail was only possible for very small loads owing to the weakness of the interposed beam web.

Cast-iron pillars were used to a great extent and also cast-iron bases to spread the load on the stone templates on the concrete.

The Piccadilly Hotel is, I think, the last example of cast-iron pillars for any large building in London.

Most buildings were designed on the private house style, adopting small windows in small bays or wall panels. Floors were mostly in wood, but for important buildings fire-resisting floors, using filler joist beams 2 to 3 ft. centres filled between with solid coke breeze or coal residue concrete floors having flush ceilings.

Later, solid reinforced concrete slab floors were used, aggregates being coal ash clean clinker mixed with broken brick.

For reason of difficulties experienced with expansion and weak floors, the coal residue concrete was superseded by stone concrete floors and hollow tile floors, commencing about 1908.

One interesting feature of the Ritz Hotel is the foundation cantilever girder with rocker pin. It was not customary in those days to use steel grillages and cantilever foundations. Party walls were mostly used, thickened and raised with ordinary spread foundations on each side and very seldom independent external walls supported on foundations entirely within the boundary lines of the site.

According to the 1894 Building Act it was not permissible to rivet the connection between beam and pillar, because the bressummers could not be fixed at the ends and provision had to be made for expansion by the use of oblong holes. This requirement was not insisted on by the authorities for the Ritz Hotel, and hence it was possible safely to erect this steel frame.

I have always contended that the connection between the pillars and the beams must be riveted and be strong so as to assure the

January, 1937   *THE STRUCTURAL ENGINEER*   3

Figure 1.   The Ritz Hotel, Steel Framing, February, 1905.
[*From " Supplement to the Builders' Journal & Architectural Record," March 1 ,1905.*]

About 1912, large bases, riveted to the pillar, were used (*see Figure* 3). This is a very effective type of base for heavy loads and simple to make.

For industrial buildings of one or two storeys and reasonably light loads, it was usual to make large and thin riveted bases with gusset pieces, but these could not be used for heavy loads, as the base plate was not strong enough to transmit the load to the concrete, although the large base was very useful for the introduction of anchor bolts where stability for high buildings was necessary.

The Ritz Hotel was built on the site previously occupied by Walsingham House in Piccadilly. When demolishing this building I noted with interest that it was built on a continuous plain concrete raft over the entire site 4 to 5 ft. thick. This raft had cracked and tilted several inches, showing that the subsoil had given way where heavy loads occurred, and distorted the raft, although the latter was very thick. From this it may be concluded that individual foundations and uniform pressure per square foot on the subsoil are to be preferred, and rafts are not reliable unless properly reinforced.

The authorities desired to widen Piccadilly, and in order to erect the Ritz Hotel it was necessary to extend the building over the foot pavement, and hence the Arcade (which is similar in design to the Ritz Hotel in Place Vendôme, Paris) has become a landmark in London.

Concerning foundations and concrete, a large building was erected in London about 1910 where I believe for the first time in London reinforced concrete individual foundations were used to support the steel pillars,

lateral stability of the building. Not only wind, but also loads placed eccentrically must be resisted.

The working stresses used were in accordance with the practice in New York at that time, as given in the Carnegie Steel Company's Handbook, issued 1897, namely, 16,000 lbs. per sq. in. for bending for plain beams and 15,000 lbs. for plated beams. The pillar stresses were 12,000 to 14,000 lbs. per sq. in. for usual sections of channels and plates.

In most of the early buildings after 1902, I used ordinary concrete foundations 12 to 18 ins. thick below the bottom layer of grillages. Two layers of grillages were used, and the 1-in. space between the flanges of the two layers was grouted with cement.

Cast-iron for bases 3 to 4 ft. square and 12 to 18 ins. high with metal 1 in. to 2 ins. thick were used for a few jobs (*Figure 2*), then for heavy loads cast-steel bases were introduced, because it was found that the cast-iron bases were not reliable.

Bylander, on Steelwork in Buildings.

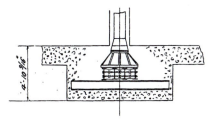

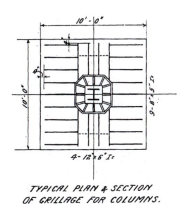

TYPICAL PLAN & SECTION
OF GRILLAGE FOR COLUMNS.

Figure 2. Detail of Cast Iron Base.

and the specialist in this case used in his calculations a pressure of 1,000 lbs. per sq. in. on the concrete under the steel base, and this building, after nearly thirty years, has not developed any noticeable weakness because of the high pressure on the concrete.

The first case where I used the now common reinforced concrete foundation for steel pillars was for Imperial House in Kingsway. Nothing in the Building Act governed the loads and stresses for reinforced concrete in those days. I used a pressure of 600 lbs. per sq. in. (38 tons per sq. ft.) under the steel bases and 600 lbs. per sq. in. for compression in the concrete, and 16,000 lbs. for tension in the steel reinforcement.

Since that date I have used similar foundations with 1 : 2 : 4 (¾ in. mesh) concrete, except that after the introduction of the London County Council Steelwork Code the maximum pressure allowed is 465 lbs. per sq. in. (30 tons per sq. ft.) instead of 38 tons per sq. ft.

I believe that the pressure on concrete under a well designed steel slab base can with safety be higher than ordinary stresses on concrete, provided that the grouting under the base is of good quality and reliable. Careless grouting will, of course, leave air pockets and cause unsafe work, while dry mortar forced in is good provided it is well supervised.

I find that neat cement or 1 : 1 cement mortar properly grouted and well worked in under the base, and using a head of grout not less than 4 ins. above the underside of the base, is the surest way of getting reliable work, particularly where access is difficult to ram in semi-dry mortar under the base. Further, the grout will spread the load around the edges of the base.

I have never used anchor bolts for pillar bases for ordinary multi-storey steel frame buildings, and I do not think they are necessary, but I always require that the first tier, or preferably two tiers, of pillars shall be completely erected and riveted in final position before grouting may take place.

The space between the concrete and the steel base should not be more than 1 in. and

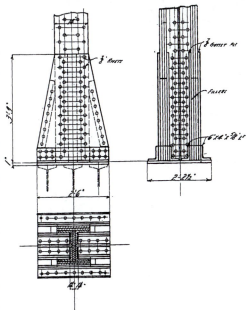

Figure 3. Detail of Steel Base.

Bylander, on Steelwork in Buildings.

January, 1937   *THE STRUCTURAL ENGINEER*   5

not less than $\frac{1}{2}$ in., and even this degree of accuracy is sometimes difficult to obtain. I find that if the grout after pouring is kept under water a better result can be obtained.

Before 1902 it was the usual practice to introduce pad stones (York stone) under bearings of steel beams in walls and piers, and to obtain improved contact by the use of felt or lead.

Wall plates are simpler to use and avoid the necessity for the builder to obtain special size stones and set same before the steel is fixed. I allowed a pressure of 200 lbs. per sq. in. under bearings on ordinary brickwork, but since the various regulations and codes were introduced this pressure has had to be reduced. I still think that for a small area in a brick wall it is permissible to use 200 lbs. per sq. in. under beam wall plates, if the brickwork is good quality in cement. If the plates are large the pressure must be reduced to the safe load on pier or wall.

Selfridge's building, east wing, was erected about 1906, before the passing of the Steel Frame Act. This was one of the first buildings of importance to be erected in London for commercial purposes having large bays or wall panels, the centres being 22 to 24 ft.

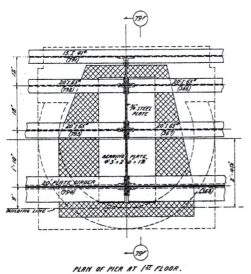

PLAN OF PIER AT 1ST FLOOR.

Figure 4. Selfridge's—Plan of Pier at first floor.

Bylander, on Steelwork in Buildings.

instead of the afore-mentioned small bays of 12 to 15 ft.

The external walls were made self-supporting and strengthened with piers and stone columns, and no steel pillars were introduced in the external walls.

The interior of the building was a complete steel frame with solid reinforced concrete floors.

When the building was extended after the passing of the 1909 Act it was not permissible to use external walls for carrying load, as all of the load had to be carried on a framework of metal. This is mentioned because I contend it should be permissible to make use of masonry piers for supporting load if they are strong enough, and even to-day I am in doubt if this is allowed for a steel frame.

I believe that Selfridge's building introduced a new aspect of building construction, and architects began to study a varied form of elevation, adopting larger panels and designs more suited to the steel frame type, and now many buildings can be seen in London of bolder design and more practical and yet, I believe it is said, very pleasing in appearance.

One interesting feature of the Selfridge's building, east wing, is the retaining walls for three basements for part of the building, the foundation extending about 65 ft. below the kerb level. This wall, I believe, is the highest retaining wall built at that time in reinforced concrete in London, and as evidence was not available to me at that time of the reliability of a bar lap in tension concrete, and as the main reinforcing bars could not be inserted in one length (about 90 ft. was required) I introduced 6-in. channels with bolted splices as part of the main reinforcement, and increased the thickness of the wall so as to reduce the amount of reinforcement required. The base was 25 ft. wide and the wall was constructed in a trench about 100 ft. long and 25 ft. wide, and satisfactorily fulfilled its purpose.

A $\frac{3}{8}$ in. crack occurred in the front area floor of the opposite building, but did not open further, proving that during the process of excavation it had not been possible to drive the timbers tight enough to take up the whole of the earth pressure.

At that time I worked out a scheme for a tower 35 storeys high supported on a large reinforced concrete base in the middle of the building. This, however, was never built, but it may be mentioned with interest for this

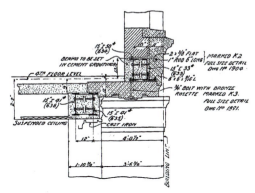

SPANDRIL SECTION AT 4ᵀᴴ FLOOR.

Figure 5.   Selfridge's—Spandril section at fourth floor.

reason, that it would not be possible to build a very high structure on the London clay as it would not be practicable to spread the foundations sufficiently. In this case the tower had to be placed in the centre of the building, because otherwise the foundations for the tower would extend into the street, and this was not possible on the Oxford Street front for reason of the existing "Tuppenny Tube."

Figures 4 and 5 show interesting details of the construction adopted in connection with walls and cornices for Selfridge's building.

A corner cornice-stone weighed 12 tons and had to be suspended on bolts at the end of a cantilever. Particular care was taken safely to support the stones projecting beyond the main wall face and to place the steel in cement mortar as protection against decay, and to cover the whole with asphalt to secure permanence as far as practicable.

It has many times occurred to me that some cornice-stones designed to balance over the front edge must have a precarious existence. Now and again it is reported that a cornice-stone has fallen, but it does not happen often.

This building was erected before the consent of the London County Council was obtained for increased cube, and the omission of cross walls.

An elaborate system of sprinklers was introduced. The distribution pipes were laid on top of the floor construction in concrete under the floor finish, and the filling was 5 ins. thick.

One interesting point I noted in connection with this filling, which was coke breeze, was that within a few weeks after laying, the pipes had in some cases corroded right through the full thickness and had to be replaced, but this corrosion ceased as soon as the building had dried sufficiently, and no further trouble was experienced. It indicates, however, the undesirability of using coal residue concrete for any purposes in connection with steel.

Selfridge's building is the first I have dealt with in London where the size of the floor panels repeats, thus enabling duplication of details and also the re-use of form work for floors. The forms for the floors were made in detachable boxes supported on soffit boards with hook-bolts to the bottom flange of the beams. After the concrete was set the boxes were lowered by the crane, the suspending rope passing through a hole in the floor. It was rolled to a new panel and hoisted into position again by the crane.

Details were made for every reinforcing bar. The bars were bent at the rolling mills and delivered in bundles ready for placing.

The east wing of Selfridge's building had internal division walls, and these were carried on steel and not self-supporting, to allow these walls to be taken down at a later date if and when the London County Council would permit of more than 250,000 cubic feet for each section of the building. The imposed floor load was 112 lbs. for retail shops.

The plans were fully dimensioned from the start, permitting steelwork detail drawings to be made at an early date to facilitate quick steelwork delivery.

For a certain part of the building the cube exceeded that permissible, and therefore in the basement a certain portion was separated by brick walls and not allowed to be used. At a later date these were removed, as well as the division walls, when a greater cube was permissible for the building.

It may be of interest to mention here that on the roof of Selfridge's building two steel towers were erected in 1925, about 150 ft. high above the roof, to carry the aerial for the first powerful British Broadcasting Corporation station. The machinery was housed in additional structures placed above the roof. The strength of the steel frame was carefully calculated, and the width of the towers at the roof was made large to lessen the load due to

Bylander, on Steelwork in Buildings.

wind. The towers were carefully assembled in the shops, the holes reamed in position and turned close-fitting bolts were used. These towers were dismantled five years later after a new Broadcasting Station had superseded this one in London.

The Waldorf Hotel erected about 1906 is not a complete steel-frame building, the external walls being self-supporting, but the interior of the building is carried on steel frame similar to the usual steel-frame structures. It was constructed very cheaply and the steelwork was calculated for an imposed floor load of 70 lbs. per sq. ft.

The floor construction consists of solid reinforced concrete floors, with 1¼ per cent. reinforcement, and the aggregate used was clean clinker and clean broken brick. A sloping roof was likewise constructed in solid reinforced concrete slabs, together with the dormers.

When I assisted in carrying out some alterations to this building recently, some of the floors were cut away, and it was noted with interest that the reinforcing bars had not corroded, although coke residue concrete was used. This, I believe, is due to the presence of broken brick which neutralises to some extent the injurious effect of the substance contained in the coal residue aggregate.

Figure 6.   The " Morning Post " Building, Strand, in course of construction, showing steel skeleton.

Bylander, on Steelwork in Buildings.

The "Morning Post" building erected about 1907 is a complete steel frame building (*Figure* 6), the external walls being of the 1894 London Building Act thickness and carried on steel. This building was erected after the construction of the new Aldwych, and the site is triangular in shape with rounded corners and the side to Aldwych is circular on plan. It therefore presented some difficulties in dimensioning, particularly for the steel frame building.

When detailing the steelwork for this building I introduced a method which I afterwards used with advantage for skew dimensions of connecting beams to pillars. For every pillar at every floor a full size sketch was made showing the crosspoint, i.e., the intersection of the centre line of the beam and the centre line of the pillar section. The dimensions for the crosspoint were ascertained by setting out same on paper full size to desired angle as shown on plan. This sketch therefore gave the necessary dimensions of ordinate and abscissa for these cross points for each pillar, and the length of the beam to cross points was ascertained by finding the hypotenuse in a triangle giving the ordinate and abscissa and sketched on a separate sheet (*Skew sheet*).

This method has the advantage of being very simple, and the position of the stiffener or connection on the pillar is selected to suit the practical convenience of riveting and fixing.

This method is simpler than ascertaining the centres of pillars and afterwards calculating the length of the beam.

In any case on the pillar details the cross points are given, and these dimensions are used for checking the length of the beam.

I am not aware of any case where a beam turned out to be the wrong length, proving that this method is reliable.

The curved walls at each corner of the building were carried on plate girders cantilevered from the pillar by large gussets or brackets in one piece with the plate girder. A view of the frame is shown on *Figure* 7.

The two basements of this building contained the printing presses and mechanical equipment, and the size of the building below the street was nearly the same as that above the street level.

The Calico Printers' Association building in Oxford Street, Manchester, erected about 1910, was a splendid example of modern build-ing for warehouses and offices. It was built as a complete steel frame, the length about 350 ft. and the width on plan about 250 ft. with internal courts for lighting.

One end of the building spanned the canal, and an interesting problem had to be solved in connection with the girders over this canal which are shown on *Figures* 8 and 9, picturing a girder carrying an extra heavy load near to one end, the depth being increased near the pillar to the full storey height to take care of the shear.

This building had ten storeys, the imposed floor load was 200 lbs. per sq. ft., and I believe this was the first large building in England constructed with hollow tile floors. I made many tests on solid reinforced concrete floors and hollow tile floors to ascertain the strength before the selection was made. The tests show that collapse took place due to yielding of the bars for a percentage of 0.6 per cent., while the concrete did not fail until reinforcement was $1\frac{1}{4}$ per cent. I believe it was the beginning of the introduction of hollow tile floors in place of heavy coke breeze fire-resisting floors, and this type of floor is now so generally adopted that one wonders why it was not used before, particularly when one considers that hollow tiles were made by the Romans, as may be seen from the relics at the Pump Room, Bath.

This building has large window areas, and the windows in the internal courts are set back in the various storeys so as to give better lighting to the lower floors.

In America up to 1900, hollow tile floor was greatly adopted, but not reinforced. Very small spans up to 6 ft. were practicable, and a thick floor sufficiently strong was the result of using about 12-in. deep beams.

The hollow tile industry was very efficient in supplying the needs, and there were no definite regulations defining the strength, but it was customary and considered necessary that the building should be fireproof, and naturally constructed light so as not unnecessarily to load up the steel.

In later years the reinforced concrete and hollow tile floor has superseded the thick plain hollow tile flat arch construction in the United States of America.

I believe that after the Baltimore fire it was ascertained that the concrete floor was superior for fire-proofing as compared with plain thick hollow tile.

Bylander on Steelwork in Buildings.

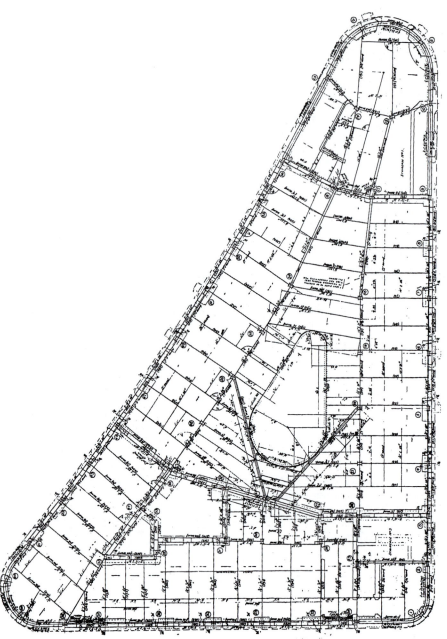

Figure 7. The " Morning Post."—First floor framing plan.

Bylander, on Steelwork in Buildings.

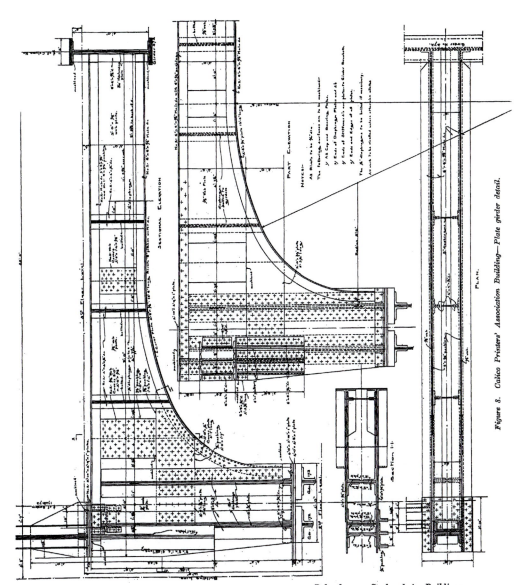

Figure 8.   Calico Printers' Association Building—Plate girder detail.

Bylander, on Steelwork in Buildings.

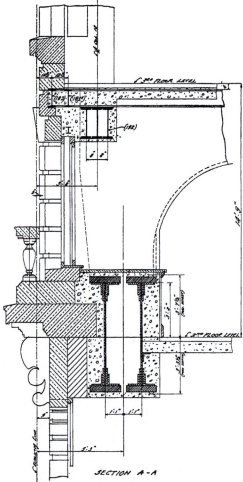

Figure 9. Calico Printers' Association Building—Spandril Section.

The Royal Automobile Club building in Pall Mall erected about 1911 is notable because of its beautiful design and plan. Being commenced before the 1909 Act it is not a complete steel-frame building, the front wall being self-supporting, but the remainder of the building is carried on steel frame.

The floor construction is reinforced concrete with plaster slab false ceilings. The haunching

Bylander, on Steelwork in Buildings.

to the beams under the floor slab was done by pre-cast blocks placed before the form work for the slabs was fixed.

The introduction of false ceilings or suspended ceilings facilitated the design of the decoration and the adoption of flush ceilings in the large rooms, and also a space for running pipes and ventilation ducts in connection with the large rooms.

The lowest basement being below the sewer level, an ejector chamber and machinery were introduced. A large swimming bath and plunge bath were constructed below the lower basement level, which is about 36 ft. below street level.

The foundations of the building are separate and independent of the swimming bath, which latter is constructed in reinforced concrete and lined with marble, subways being constructed all round the bath for pipes and mechanical equipment.

In order to meet the architects' requirements of small diameter decorative columns in the large rooms, steel pillar sections were made of angles and plates, and the outer flange plate was made narrow so as to reduce the diameter of the circle in which the steel pillar is confined. The pillars were cased in concrete and finished as decorative columns with scagliola.

The foundations were in plain concrete with grillages, and rested on sand and gravel, the excavations extending below water level, and some difficulty was experienced in connection with the deep foundations and the swimming bath.

At the back of the building there is a reinforced concrete retaining wall L-shaped 9 ins. thick at the top and 2 ft. 9 ins. thick at the base. The struts for the trench were left in during construction of the wall, the struts being afterwards withdrawn, the holes concreted and grouted, and the back asphalted.

Australia House, Strand, commenced 1912 was one of the first for which I designed the steel frame in accordance with the 1909 Act, and this is therefore a complete steel-frame building under this Act.

It contains exhibition rooms where the imposed load is 224 lbs. per sq. ft., and the majority of the floors are for offices with 100 lbs. imposed load.

The floors are in reinforced hollow tile (*Figure 10*), and a notable construction is that over the exhibition hall where the span is

12 *THE STRUCTURAL ENGINEER* *January, 1937*

24 ft. and continuous construction with deep haunches was adopted to obtain strength and rigidity. The external walls though carried on steel are not supported at each floor because of the external stone columns.

This building has large cornices carried on cantilevers on struts.

The foundations consist of reinforced concrete individual blocks supporting the bases of the pillars. The main staircase is constructed in reinforced concrete with flowing soffit and is semi-circular on plan. Some vertical shafts are constructed in 4 in. to 6 in. thick reinforced concrete.

Portland House in Tothill Street, Westminster, erected in 1913, has reinforced concrete spread foundations but not a raft, reducing the load on the soil, being the river bed or peat. The strips of raft were so designed as to obtain uniform load per square foot throughout. No settlement or difficulty has arisen, although the subsoil is of a soft nature.

Several office buildings in Kingsway, Westminster, Pall Mall, Oxford Street, &c., were erected on the steel frame principle with hollow tile or reinforced concrete floors. The steel frame system up to 1914 had rapidly developed and was in general use as an economical and practical type of construction.

The price of steel has an important bearing on the practicability of the steel frame. From 1902 to 1908 steel was cheap. I recollect the price being only about £8 per ton delivered, and a further £1 to 30s. per ton was charged for erection. The cost of erection was gradually increased as the span and the loads of steel members increased, and heavier cranes were required and speedier erection wanted, and the price of steel has now been more than doubled.

In this connection I would like to mention that for the erection of the Ritz Hotel I arranged for a purchase of a guy boom derrick with hoists from America, and an American

Figure 10. Australia House, showing hollow tile floor construction.

Bylander, on Steelwork in Buildings.

erector was employed to erect the steel on the lines of the American practice. As the London erectors were not used to the guy boom derrick it did not become popular, and the next buildings were erected by the use of the ordinary stiff leg derrick. Some twenty years later, however, the guy boom derrick has been introduced, and is now generally used as the best for handing steel on the site.

In America this type is used for the skyscrapers. The only heavy parts to be lifted as the steel goes up are the boom and the mast, the hoist remaining on the ground level.

The Manitoba Parliament building, completed 1918, is of particular interest as an example of the American type of building with foundations common to several of the Western States where rock (limestone) is found at a level of 50 to 150 ft. below the ground level. In this case rock was found at a level of 70 ft. below the street. All foundations consisted of circular piers in plain concrete extending down to rock.

The customary method of excavation for a circular pier in clay is to use steel flat rings and boards about 4 ft. long and 4 ins. wide as lagging. This is a cheap and good method. The lagging and the rings are removed as the concreting proceeds from the bottom. The capping of the piers is grillages and steel slab bases supporting the pillars.

In Canada at that time broad flange beams were obtainable from the United States. This section is very convenient and practicable, and I regret that in Great Britain it is not rolled.

The plan of the building is very simple, in the form of the letter " H." It is faced with Tyndale stone which is similar to Portland stone, and further it has a pleasing texture.

The floors were generally in reinforced concrete and the decorative rooms had suspended metal and plaster ceilings. The ceilings were suspended by means of $\frac{3}{16}$ in. diameter mild steel wires concreted in the floor slab at the upper end and bent round the lathing bars at the ceiling level. It proved a very simple and efficient type of construction for ceilings.

The dome, 235 ft. high, was placed in the centre of the building and was supported on four main piers (*Figure* 11). These piers were hollow and contained the lifts and the service shafts, and I designed the piers in reinforced and plain concrete.

No vertical reinforcement was provided. The concrete had to take the total load, the reinforcement was placed horizontally to distribute the load and to bind the various parts together.

On top of the piers were reinforced concrete caps and on these were set 6 ft. by 6 ft. by 8 ins. solid steel slabs to carry the main steel plate girders supporting the upper portion of the tower and the dome. These plate girders were exceptionally heavy, eight in number (*Figure* 12), placed under the external walls with a span of about 80 ft., the weight of each about 40 tons. They were brought to the site on a specially constructed railway track, and were hoisted by two A-frame derricks similar to two-leg mast cranes used at shipyards.

As one of these girders was hoisted the brake on one of the hoists failed to act, and the girder was dropped some 120 ft. I remember it because I was standing near. It cut through two stone arches about 3 ft. in thickness, cut off two railway axles about 4 ins. in diameter, and buried itself in the ground about 10 ft. below the surface. Although the section was very heavy, the flanges were badly bent. The damaged portions were cut out and repaired and the girder used.

The connecting of these girders together was done by reamering holes in position and placing turned and fitted bolts to transmit the heavy loads from one girder to the other efficiently.

The cement grouting under the steel slabs proved a difficulty, and tests were made and the method afterwards adopted which proved to be the most reliable. A 1-in. space below the slab was provided and four grouting holes through the slab. A dam was built about 6 ins. from the edge of the slab, very thick neat cement grout was used, and an excess amount poured in, and afterwards the grout was worked with a steel rod and the excess water escaped to the top, and the air bubbles were removed. Pressure grouting was first tried but abandoned.

I have since adopted this method, and believe it is the most reliable, particularly where access cannot be obtained for ramming-in cement-mortar in the cavity. It is important, however, that the grout should be quickly made, rather thick, and deposited quickly.

Another feature of concrete work in Winnipeg is the temperature conditions. In the building a portion of the concreting for the

Bylander, on Steelwork in Buildings.

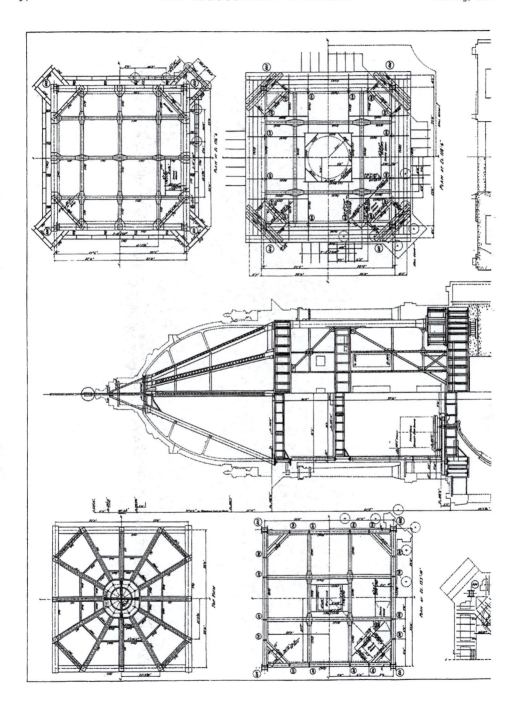

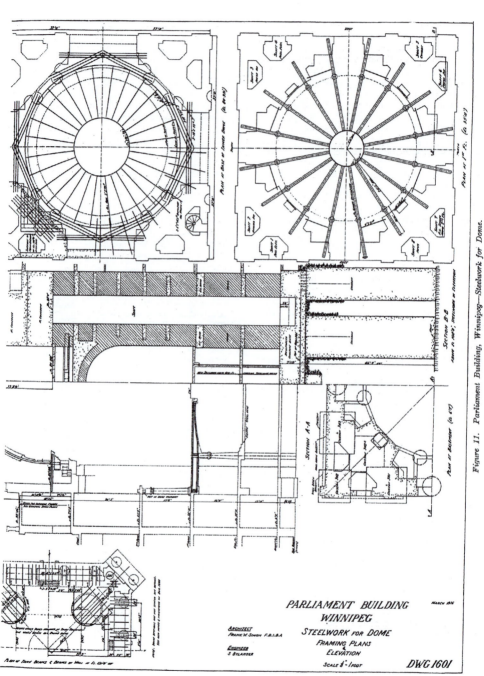

Figure 11. Parliament Building, Winnipeg.—Steelwork for Dome.

16   *THE STRUCTURAL ENGINEER*   *January, 1937*

tower for the dome was carried out during the winter. The working space was entirely enclosed, and warmed by steam radiators.

For a tunnel built between the power station and the building, however, the work was not enclosed during concreting, and yet it was carried out in a temperature of 30° F. below zero, the gravel and sand and water being warmed, and concrete mixed at a temperature of about 80° F. The concrete was deposited in fairly big quantities as quickly as possible, and after concreting it was covered over with boards and straw, and tarpaulins were placed so as to reduce heat losses. After 24 hours the concrete had partly set, and the temperature of it was then usually below the freezing point. The concrete was then frozen for two or three months until the spring, and it was found that this concrete hardened fairly well, in spite of being placed at such a low temperature.

I had test cubes made which were allowed to freeze immediately after pouring, and others which were kept at 60° F. and I found that the frozen concrete after six months would only develop about half the strength as compared with the 60° temperature matured concrete.

An office building for the Metropolitan District Railway was erected over St. James's Park Station in 1924. One interesting feature of this building is the supporting piers. The brick buttresses to the retaining walls were used to support this seven-storey building, and plate girders were placed over the station resting on these piers. The piers were strengthened by a U-shaped reinforced concrete casing 12 ins. thick which at the base was spread out to a foundation between the arches, and under the platform (*see Figure* 13).

Careful workmanship was insisted on, and the piers have proved to be effective.

The plate girders consist of single web with 30-in. wide flanges, and carry four rows of pillars in turn supporting the various floors over.

The floor construction is reinforced concrete, and the external walls are in brickwork.

Particular care was taken to obtain close-fitting bearing between the pillar bases and the plate girders.

The Bank building at 140, Leadenhall Street, erected about 1930, consisted of two basements with strong rooms, and one interesting feature of the construction is the under-pinning of the adjoining walls. Schroder's

Bank on the west side has a width of only about 30 ft. and a height corresponding to eight storeys, and the party wall had to be under-pinned one basement. This was done by introducing a common plain concrete foundation for the two walls in short lengths (*see Figure* 14). The existing pillar at the front was supported by means of heavy raking shore jacked up on a cradle on the street. The internal shores were carefully made, and splices were strengthened by steel plates so as to serve with reliability.

Reinforced concrete foundations were used with steel slab bases. The whole of the steelwork was riveted.

Floors were in solid reinforced concrete for the lower part, and hollow tile reinforced concrete for the upper part.

The Bank building at King Street, Manchester, is a steel frame building with thick external stone walls on an island site, erected 1930.

The sub-soil is hard brown clay and the whole site is covered with a reinforced concrete raft and enclosed with reinforced concrete retaining walls two storeys in height, thus forming a tank.

A feature of this building is the large spans necessitated by the banking hall on the ground floor. Heavy shallow girders were used at each floor to carry the floors, and were placed in alternate directions on each floor so as to distribute the load on the foundations evenly. The whole of the steelwork was riveted (*see Figure* 15).

Cunard House, London, erected in 1932, is a steel frame building on nearly an island site. It has two basements and part three, and is supported on individual foundations carried down to blue clay, and is enclosed with re-inforced concrete retaining walls two to three storeys in height.

The water level had to be lowered by pumping to enable the Contractor to carry out the concrete work.

One interesting feature of the steelwork construction here is the large trusses over the banking hall supporting two intermediate pillars, and permitting doors to be placed in the floor above the banking hall in the open panels of the truss. This truss was made up of channel shape riveted section for compression members, and single flats for tension members attached to large double gusset plates with turned and fitted bolts in reamed holes. The

Bylander, on Steelwork in Buildings.

January, 1937   *THE STRUCTURAL ENGINEER*   17

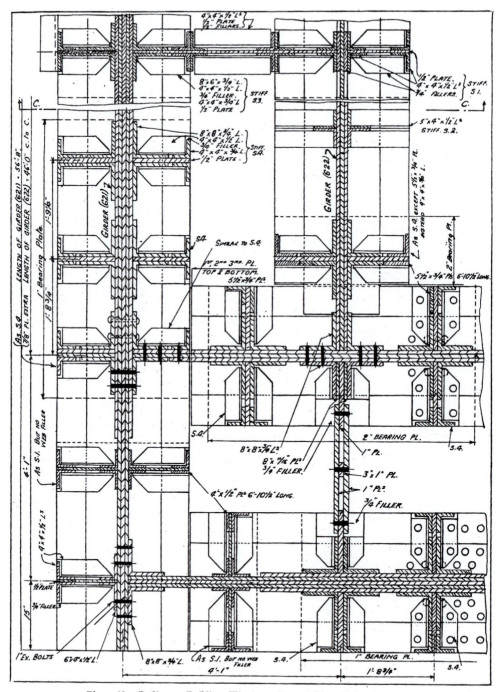

Figure 12. Parliament Building, Winnipeg—Plan of Plate Girders at support.

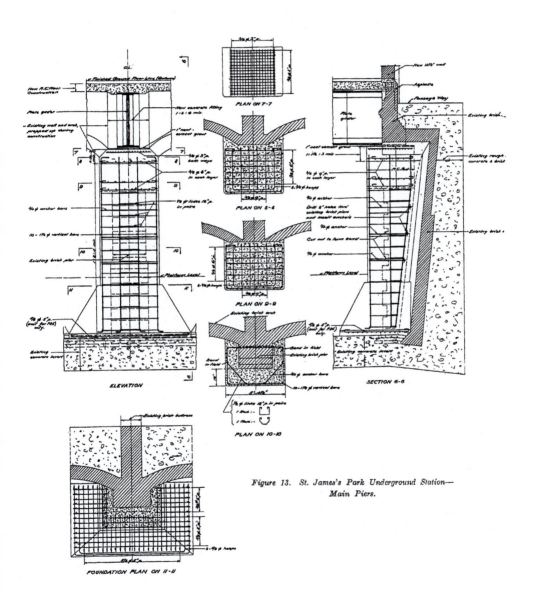

Figure 13. St. James's Park Underground Station—
Main Piers.

January, 1937   *THE STRUCTURAL ENGINEER*   19

total load, therefore, was carried on turned bolts (*see Figure* 16).

After 1920 many buildings were erected, and good progress was made with steel frame buildings. After this rush was over a depression set in, and the building industry concentrated on the revision of bye-laws and building acts to allow smaller imposed loads and increased stresses, both for steelwork and for reinforced concrete. Similar revision was made in the United States.

The Institution of Structural Engineers, through the Steel Committee, of which I was chairman, issued a report in 1927 which was in many respects accepted by the authorities, and later the British Standards Institution issued a report, "Use of Structural Steel in Building." The London County Council issued in the year 1932 a Steelwork Code authorising reduced loads and increased stresses. This code permitted of bolting a structure instead of riveting. The Steel Frame Act required site riveting. The permissible stresses in pillars were materially increased, while the increase in the permissible bending stresses for beams was only from $7\frac{1}{2}$ to 8 tons for tension.

As a result the designer was adopting these smaller loads and increased stresses. In many cases it was found that by reducing the imposed load to, say, 50 lbs. for offices, it was not possible to use these floors for other purposes, as would have been the case if they had been calculated for 100 lbs.

Later the load for the floor construction was increased by 50 lbs. per sq. ft. so that the total load on floor construction was 100 lbs. per sq. ft. to allow for partitions and local loads.

The original 50 lbs. per sq. ft. did not include for partitions, and 20 lbs. per sq. ft. was added for same, therefore the minimum would be 70 lbs. per sq. ft. for the steel frame.

The Steelwork Code being only a temporary regulation will probably be superseded by L.C.C. Bye-laws.

The steelwork trade has made a great effort to reduce the bye-law requirements and to reduce the cost. As a consequence of the depression the steel trade has further agreed to fix prices for steelwork in the interests of the trade. The result is that, although loads are reduced and stresses increased, the cost has gone up for steel-frame buildings, and reinforced concrete buildings are, as a result, being introduced as a competitor to the steel-

Bylander, on Steelwork in Buildings.

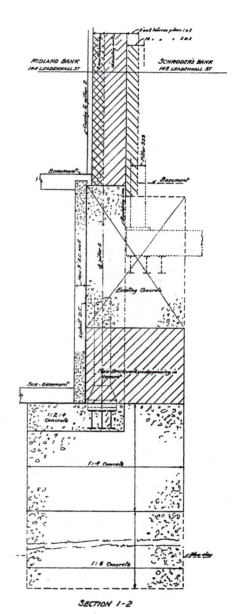

SECTION 1-2

Figure 14.   140-144, Leadenhall Street—Foundation Section.

Figure 15.   *Midland Bank, Manchester—Steelwork Framing.*

Bylander, on Steelwork in Buildings.

January, 1937   *THE STRUCTURAL ENGINEER*   21

frame building more than before. Steelwork previously dominated, at least in the large towns such as London where the working space on site is very small, it being usually more convenient and cheaper to adopt steel frame.

A great effort has also been made to introduce welded steel, but great progress has not been made in this method. Where specially suitable, welded steel has been used, and no doubt will continue to be used with great advantage. For instance, as published in *The Structural Engineer* in December, 1932, p. 521, heavy welded steelwork was used for the sun balconies for the Freemason's Hospital erected in 1932. This was a good example, not only of welded connections, but the whole section being welded instead of rolled.

The sun balconies 30 ft. in diameter, at the end of each block, are constructed in welded steel, the main sections being 12 by 12 with 1¼ in. flange plate and ½ in. web plate, made in the shop by electric welding, and connected on site by welding. This is the first building of importance in London where completely welded work was carried out.

As an interesting feature of welding may be mentioned the strengthening of an existing building having cast-iron columns, as shown on *Figure* 17 where the load of the cast-iron pillar was applied to grillage beams of steel rings and fins welded on to the cast-iron pillar.

Tests were made showing that a ⅜ in. weld between the steel ring and the cast-iron piece would fail at 16,000 lbs. per sq. in., and load one-quarter of this was allowed in the design.

It is not recommended to use welding on

Figure 16.   Cunard House—Main Truss.

Bylander, on Steelwork in Buildings.

22   *THE STRUCTURAL ENGINEER*   *January, 1937*

cast-iron, except in favourable conditions such as this when the steel ring was firmly held round the cast-iron pillar, and the weld was only subjected to compression and shear, and not to tension.

In some buildings the members are bolted together and afterwards the joints are strengthened by welding so as to be equivalent to riveted construction.

During recent years great progress has been made in the design and construction of residential flats on the steel-frame method, and here a special effort has been made to reduce cost of steelwork by using light loads, such as 40 lbs. imposed load plus weight of partitions. It has been found that the weight of partitions for a residential flat far exceeds the 20 lbs. per sq. ft. usually provided for temporary partitions in offices, the weight of partitions and fittings sometimes amounting to 30 or 40 lbs. per sq. ft.

High Tensile Steel. A lightly-constructed residential flat building, No. 35, Grosvenor Square, erected in 1935, was the first flat building erected in high tensile steel in London. The floor loads were in accordance with the Steelwork Code, and the material and working stresses complied with the British Standards Specification for high tensile steel, the brand " Chromador " being used. Twelve tons per square inch were used for the tensile stress, and generally the working stresses were 50 per cent. higher than for mild steel.

Clifton House in Euston Road is an example of a modern warehouse building erected 1936. It is a steel-frame building, high tensile steel being used. The steel for the whole height, seven storeys, was erected by a travelling crane, starting at one end of the building.

It is exceptionally simple on plan, the panels are alike permitting repetition of details.

The floors and the staircases are constructed in solid reinforced concrete, the external walls are in brickwork ornamented with bands of terracotta.

Owing to the design being completed before starting work, and good organisation and simple design, this building was erected in a remarkably short time, about six months.

A feature worth mentioning is that the reinforced concrete floor slab was completed with an accurate and level finish in one operation with the concreting. Dry cement and sand was sprinkled on the surface and levelled with a wooden float, temporarily protected by tar-

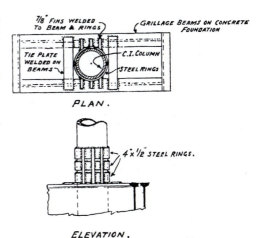

Figure 17. Strengthening of an existing building—Welding.

paulins, and afterwards covered with sand as a protection until the building was covered in and the wood block floor laid direct on the floor slab without screeding.

A pipe tunnel extends the whole length of the building connecting the boiler room in the basement.

Summarising the progress made in thirty years, I would say that the main progress has been in the general adoption of steel construction in place of masonry and brick construction.

Much progress has been made in the use of reinforced concrete as a skeleton, and amongst my work the Match Factory at Garston, Liverpool, is a good example of mushroom construction in reinforced concrete, and also Selfridge's warehouse in Paddington, London.

Grillages have been superseded by reinforced concrete bases, and the cast-iron pillar has been superseded by the steel pillar and the solid steel slab base or bloom, the latter being an immense improvement on the old type of base.

Buildings are provided with great open floor spaces, using bigger span designs. The framing is not much changed, except that one beam is usually provided in the external walls instead of two, as was the custom in America before 1900. Further, the floor spans have been increased owing to the introduction of hollow tile reinforced concrete

Bylander, on Steelwork in Buildings.

January, 1937   *THE STRUCTURAL ENGINEER*   23

floors. The filler joist solid concrete floor has been practically abandoned.

More attention is being given to the protection of the steelwork frame, and in many cases the steel beams and pillars in external walls are encased in concrete and not cased in brickwork. The Ritz Hotel and other buildings were cased in concrete as fire protection, but the external beams were embedded in the external walls without special concrete casing.

Much progress has been made in welding, but it is not yet generally adopted. I notice with interest during a visit to Germany this summer that the motor way viaducts were made of entirely electrically-welded continuous girders, the cross girders being welded to the main girders as well. It is a wonderful example of modern welded steel girders where the site welding has throughout been tested and examined by means of X-ray photography to assure reliable work.

A big change has taken place in the design and the stability of steel frame structure by allowing a wind load of about one-half of that prescribed in the 1909 Act, and further, that the authorities will not require calculations of the steelwork for resistance to wind if the height of the building is not more than twice its width, in the direction of the wind considered, therefore most buildings are exempt from wind calculations, but good designers nevertheless would verify that the connections between the horizontal and vertical members are such that they will, together with the brick walls, be efficient to secure a good lateral stability for the building.

Very much depends on the stiffness of the joints, and whether the connections are properly riveted or whether clearing bolts are used for connections.

While black bolts have been allowed to a great extent in clearing holes, the tendency is to require steel bolts with a closer fit and with bright heads and nuts, as a distinction from the black bolts which are often made of soft steel.

In important cases turned barrel-fitted bolts are required, in which case the heads and nuts need not be machined, as is the case with bright bolts. The essential requirement here is that the hole must be reamed to final size in position and the bolt made with close fit, about $\frac{3}{1000}$ in. tolerance. This type of bolt was used for the towers on Selfridge's building.

Bylander, on Steelwork in Buildings.

At the beginning of this paper I referred to steel-frame buildings thirty-six years ago in the United States. It is well-known that much progress has been made in thirty years. The Woolworth building of 55 storeys was at the time of its erection world-famous. Now it has been excelled by the Empire State building of 85 storeys, a height of 1,250 ft. above the kerb.

In England the most marked advance in building construction is the tendency to increase the size of the scheme for each building, and, where possible, a whole block is reconstructed, superseding many previous small buildings ; for instance, Cunard House, in the City.

In the City, where land is expensive, the tendency is to introduce two or sometimes three basements, requiring substantial retaining walls in reinforced concrete (*see Figure* 18). At this depth water trouble is encountered, which increases the interest of the design.

It will be noted that while the asphalt dampcourse was formerly usually applied to the outside of the wall, now the asphalt is applied on the inside of the wall and is retained by a reinforced concrete lining in order to facilitate making of a reliable dampcourse and also make repairs possible.

Sections of Steel Members. At the time of the erection of the Ritz Hotel the most favoured pillar section was channels and plates, or, for light sections, lattice channels which were, for instance, used for the pavilions for this building. For heavy loads plate and angle sections were used.

The English practice at that time was to use one or two rolled steel joists, but lately only one " I " beam with plates has become customary on account of the unsatisfactory connections resulting from the use of two " I " beams. The single " I " beam pillar section is also favoured because the new British Standard sections include heavier beams having a width of flange up to 8 ins. which were not obtainable thirty years ago.

In America the broad flange beam with a variable thickness of web and flange is in favour. The box section of channels has almost disappeared.

Formerly twin or triple compound girders were used, but now it is considered better to use single beam sections with or without plates stiffened by diaphragms.

24   *THE STRUCTURAL ENGINEER*   *January, 1937*

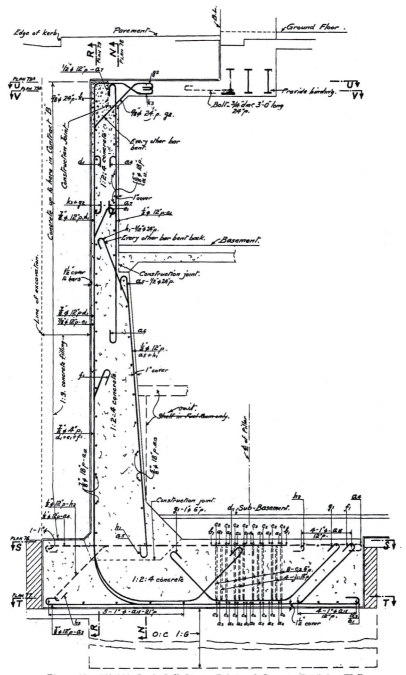

Figure 18. 140-144, Leadenhall Street—Reinforced Concrete Retaining Wall.

Bylander, on Steelwork in Buildings.

January, 1937   *THE STRUCTURAL ENGINEER*   25

For plate girder work likewise the double and triple web girders have disappeared because of the difficulty of manufacture.

An enormous advance has been made in thirty years in the method of manufacture. The high speed tool steels which are now available have increased the speed of drilling about three times. While formerly plates were generally punched it is now more usual to adopt " drilled through " holes. It may also be stated that the quality of workmanship, owing to drilled instead of punched holes, has been much improved, and instead of deducting the diameter of the rivet plus ⅛ in. for the holes owing to irregular and damaged edges in punched work, now the diameter of the hole only may be deducted in calculations.

ultimate strength of the material which I believe is the case. There is also a tendency to accept the fact that in certain details of construction the plastic yield may be exceeded with safety while formerly all calculations were made strictly within the elastic limit.

Since measuring instruments have improved in accuracy it is more generally recognised that the limit of proportionality is actually much lower than was formerly believed. The drop of the beam or the yield point seems now the best practical way of determining to some extent the elastic limit which is below the yield point.

Although high tensile steel has been on the market for a few years its use has not become general, probably because the price per ton

THE FOLLOWING TABLE SHOWS COMPARISON IN REQUIREMENTS FOR LOADS AND STRESSES.

	Floor loads, lb. per sq.ft.			Bending stress, tons per sq. in.	Pillar Stresses. Tons per sq. in.			Factor for beam stresses for beams without lateral support.		
	Flats.	Offices.			$l/r=60$	$l/r=90$	$l/r=120$	$l/b=20$	$l/b=30$	$l/b=40$
		Lower Floor	Upper Floor							
London Steel Frame Act, 1909	70	100	100	7.5	4.0	3.3	2.5	1.0	1.0	—
Steelwork Committee Report, 1927	60	100	80	8.0	6.0	4.5	3.0	1.0	0.8	0.6
London Code of Practice, 1932	40	80	50	8.0	5.9	4.3	2.9	1.0	0.8	0.6
Carnegie U.S.A., 1897 ...	70	70	70	7.2	5.4	5.4	4.6	1.0	0.9	0.8
Carnegie, New York, 1934 ...	40	100	50	8.0	6.7	5.6	4.5	0.9	0.8	0.6
* Institution of Structural Engineers: Report on Loads and Stresses, 1933 ...	40 ∝ 30	80	50	8.0 ∝ 9.0	5.9	4.3	2.9	1.0	0.9	0.8

* Note.—This (1933) report gives 40 lbs. per sq. ft., except 30 lbs. for bedrooms and bathrooms. Bending stresses 8 tons per sq. in., except 9 tons where embedded in reinforced concrete by specified method. Value of l/b given here is for 10 in. by 5 in. I 30 lbs.

Summarising the changes in thirty years, I would say that the loading of floors has not changed much; the loads now used are nearly the same as those used thirty years ago. Considering that the rolled steel is much more uniform and is mostly produced by the open hearth process under good control, I am of opinion that the working stresses could be increased and yet the same factor of real safety obtained as thirty years ago. I see no objection to the use of 10 tons as a unit stress for good design, correct loads and accurate calculations. I suggest, however, that pillar stresses be not more than three-quarters of beam stresses.

With this purpose in view, it is well to pay more attention to the yield point than to the

is more than for mild steel, thus reducing the saving due to higher allowable stresses.

Foundations. In latter years it has become usual and convenient to place the foundations of a building within the boundary lines so as not to interfere unnecessarily with the support of the adjoining buildings. A system of cantilever foundations is used, the load supported sometimes being as great as 500 tons, necessarily requiring several girders to cantilever the load. An example of this may be seen at the new building, Nos. 20-21, St. James's Square, London, being a steel-frame building, and also the large building in St. Andrew Square, Edinburgh, now being erected as a steel-frame building.

Bylander, on Steelwork in Buildings.

"STEELWORK IN BUILDINGS—THIRTY YEARS' PROGRESS."

Discussion on Mr. S. BYLANDER'S Paper.*

The CHAIRMAN (Mr. P. J. Black, L.R.I.B.A., M.I.Struct.E., Vice-President), introduced Mr. Bylander as one of the oldest members of the Concrete Institute, being in fact a Founder Member of the Institute, and said that he was regarded as one of the pioneers of steel-frame buildings. His paper was a very interesting retrospect and it showed the evolution of the steel-frame building:

Mr. GOWER B. R. PIMM, M.Inst.C.E., M.I.Struct.E., proposing a hearty vote of thanks to Mr. Bylander for his classic review of the development of structural steelwork, said he would not presume to criticise anything in the paper; but he expressed regret that Mr. Bylander had not mentioned a problem which was very much in mind at the moment, i.e., that of the sound-transmitting properties or, to coin a new word, the sound-transmitting "improperties" of buildings. He recalled that in one building recently he had heard a hammering noise, the location of which appeared to be just above his head. But on investigation he had found that it originated at a point four storeys below him and at a distance of about 40 ft. horizontally. He would not have believed that sound could have been so transmitted and not only transmitted, but actually intensified. He asked whether the increasing noise trouble had to do with the tendency to reduce the weight of buildings and to diminish the sizes of the members. Again, did Mr. Bylander consider that too much of the attention paid to the subject was being directed to the finding of remedies and palliatives for the noise nuisance, and that money which was being spent on providing remedies could sometimes be better spent on the structure itself? Mr. Bylander's views on the subject would be most valuable.

Mr. Bylander's reference to his tests on reinforced concrete in which he had found that the concrete had not failed until the percentage of reinforcement had reached 1¼, was very interesting and instructive, because some engineers had always felt that what was called the "economic percentage" of steel was quite a misnomer and was very much too low.

Mr. S. B. HAMILTON, M.Sc., M.I.Struct.E., A.M.Inst.C.E., seconding the vote of thanks, said that Mr. Bylander had given a number of most interesting examples, drawn from his own experience, which covered the major part of the history of steel frame building in this country. Mr. Hamilton hoped that the paper would be followed by others, presented by engineers who had been concerned with the rapid developments of recent times, so that while the pioneers were still alive and active, records could be published in "The Structural Engineer" of the stages by which all modern forms of building had developed.

When reading the paper one wondered whether as much attention was paid 20 years ago as was being paid to-day to some of the little fads of construction; and some of the recent reports of research committees

Read at a meeting of the Institution of Structural Engineers, in the lecture hall of the Institution of Civil Engineers, Great George Street, Westminster, S.W.1, on Thursday, January 14th, 1937. Published in "The Structural Engineer," Vol. XV (new series), No. 1, p. 2.

and institutions made one wonder how engineers 20 or 30 years hence would ever get a building designed at all. Yet many of the early designs were strikingly modern in appearance. That seemed to emphasise the fact that engineering was still mainly an art, and in that art the horse-sense of the engineer, and his ability to decide how far it was worth while to go with intricate calculations, was still an important factor. An account such as that given in the paper, of how one of our most eminent engineers had introduced and developed what was, to this country, a new form of building, was most interesting, and it was indeed a pleasure to second the vote of thanks.

The CHAIRMAN commented on the development of the steel-frame building. Starting with the old type of brick buildings, steelwork was introduced for floor and interior construction and then we approached the steel-frame support of the walls, still retaining the thick and heavy walls; and ultimately the Building Act of 1909 was passed, which definitely permitted the use of panel walls and lighter construction.

Mr. Bylander, he said, had to go carefully through all this period of the development of the steel-frame building, and thanks were due to him for some of the regulations relating to steel building. He had taken his full share in the work of the Institution in connection with the Steel Framed Building Regulations, and also with the Institution's "Report on Steelwork for Buildings" which was still used throughout the country and was a standard document.

Mr. Bylander had also shown how to deal with the cantilever foundation. In the earlier days one did not worry about encroaching upon the adjoining ground or even about going under a roadway, but in more recent years landowners would not permit of encroachment when dealing with heavy concentrated loads, and Mr. Bylander had had to study the problem of keeping his loads within his own land.

The arcaded footway at the Ritz Hotel, London, was referred to at the time of its construction as marking the beginning of a new era in the lay-out of London streets. It was thought at that time that we should have covered footways generally in important thoroughfares and thereby secure wider roadways for vehicular traffic; the Ritz Hotel, however, remains almost the only building in London where such provision has been made.

It was interesting to note Mr. Bylander's reference to the grouting of foundation slabs and bases, a problem to which he had devoted a great deal of thought. It was most important in connection with a steel-frame building, but in many cases it did not receive such careful consideration.

Finally, in a reference to St. James's Park Station, where Mr. Bylander had enveloped old brick piers with reinforced concrete, the Chairman asked whether the weight was carried partly on the brickwork or wholly by the reinforced concrete; it was not usual to utilise two such dissimilar materials.

Mr. C. S. GRAY, B.Sc. (Lond.), A.M.Inst.C.E., A.M.I.Struct.E., said that a historical résumé always interested him because it made him feel sorry for himself. In 1902, he said, engineers were unfettered

Discussion on Steelwork in Buildings.

and were allowed to do as they pleased; and Mr. Bylander's paper and his illustrations had shown what engineers could do under such circumstances. He wished that the paper had been carried a little farther forward and that Mr. Bylander had shown what he could have done to-day had he been free to do it; no doubt, he would then have demonstrated that he was still as much in advance of the times as he was in 1902.

Mr. A. B. DAILEY, M.I.Struct.E., A.R.I.B.A., commented on the statement in the paper that the concrete raft of the previously existing building on the site of the Ritz Hotel, which raft was 4 or 5 ft. thick, had cracked and tilted, indicating that there had been movement of the soil. Mr. Dailey asked whether the soil forming the foundation had consisted of clay or gravel; from the description given in the paper he presumed that it was clay. He recalled that at Barclay's Brewery site a raft which was 8 ft. thick had cracked. It had been constructed on material which was more or less river mud.

Mr. Dailey also commented on the large shutters that were used at Selfridge's building for the reinforced concrete floors, and said he had considered such shutters and had heard them recommended; but he asked whether any difficulty had been experienced, having regard to the size of the shuttering, in prising it away. It had occurred to him that there might be difficulty in getting the shuttering loose from the floor.

Another question he raised, and which related both to steelwork and to reinforced concrete, was that of permitting stresses beyond the elastic limit in the steel " in certain cases "; Mr. Bylander had carefully limited his remarks in that connection. Mr. Dailey said that he had always been of opinion that strains and stresses beyond the elastic limit did occur and should be allowed to occur, and that there should be a science of the matter which still needed proper study. At one meeting of the Institution, Mr. Stanley Vaughan had distinguished between " non-following " forces and " following " forces. The worst example of a following force would be that of a stanchion, which was liable to buckle; the greater the load applied to it, the more it would buckle and the conditions then became worse. A typical case of non-following force was that of continuous girder construction. The more the girder was strained at the point where the negative moment occurred—i.e., over the support—the less was the moment at that point, because being strained beyond the elastic limit, the thing was easing itself off before it failed, and, therefore, it did not fail. There were many such cases.

Mr. STANLEY VAUGHAN, B.Sc. (Eng.), A.M.Inst.C.E., A.M.I.Struct.E., commenting on the great interest of the paper, said that Mr. Bylander had not only attended at the birth of steel-frame buildings in England (which happy event occurred at the Ritz Hotel some 30 years ago), but he had also rendered valuable assistance in the development of steel-frame construction from its infancy to its present stage of maturity. But although the paper dealt with the " progress " of steel-frame construction during the last 30 years, a comparison of the steel frame for the Ritz Hotel with modern steel frames appeared to reveal comparatively little progress during that period. If one made comparison with motor car and aeroplane construction or almost any other form of engineering construction, the progress made in steel-frame construction seemed relatively small. This he suggested was largely due to the

restrictive influence of unrevised regulations. He recalled that when railways were introduced into England it was the custom for a man, carrying a red flag, to walk in front of each train. Also in the early days of steel-frame construction the authorities had introduced comprehensive regulations to prevent the misuse of that new form of construction, the governing statute being the 1909 Act. But whereas in the case of railways the man with the red flag had disappeared very quickly from the scene as soon as the progress of railways had made that course desirable and necessary, in the case of steel-frame building construction the " man with the red flag " had continued to impede progress until a very few years ago, i.e., the year in which the London County Council had granted waivers based on the Code of Practice for Steelwork. There had, of course, before this been a steady improvement of technique both on the part of the steel manufacturer and on the part of the designer; but he emphasised that there had been a complete lack of encouragement to any far-reaching developments owing to the continued application of a law which was originally introduced some 28 years ago to safeguard a new form of construction, but which was unfortunately left unaltered for so many years in spite of advances in knowledge and technique. But now that the Code of Practice for Steelwork had been recognised, he was convinced that with the greater freedom now permitted the development of the science of steel-frame construction would progress far more rapidly, and in fact this acceleration in progress was already operating.

Mr. Vaughan felt that Mr. Bylander had not put the spotlight on one or two of the outstanding points in the recent development of steel-frame construction, particularly the introduction of high-tensile steel and the use of welding. Although Mr. Bylander had referred to both, he had not perhaps stressed them so much as Mr. Vaughan thought their importance demanded, since they represented two entirely new branches of the development of steel-frame construction and offered great scope for progress. The use of welding for steel frames was now permitted by the authorities under certain conditions; and with this encouragement structural engineers were studying the problems involved and were developing that promising offshoot of steelwork construction. This development should result in structures which would not only be more scientifically proportioned in all their parts to the stresses and moments which they had to bear but which would in consequence gain in beauty.

Discussing the theoretical aspect of steel-frame construction, Mr. Vaughan said that in this field also there had been comparatively little progress during the first 25 years after the introduction of steel frame; indeed, not until the Steel Structures Research Committee had published the results of their labours during the last five or six years had we been able to form anything approaching an accurate idea of how a steel frame behaved under load. The Steel Structures Research Committee had relieved us of our ignorance. They had had facilities for making full-size tests on actual buildings, they had investigated the problems theoretically and practically, and they had produced an enormous amount of information, backed by theoretical research, which gave us an insight into the true behaviour of all the members forming a steel framework. All concerned with steel design were immensely

Discussion on Steelwork in Buildings.

indebted to the Steel Structures Research Committee in the first place for having been responsible for formulating the Code of Practice, the adoption of which resulted in a great advance in scientific accuracy and in economy in the design of steelwork. The Committee's final report published in 1936 contained further recommendations for design. These were based on the results of their exhaustive researches, but unfortunately they were so difficult to apply that if they were adopted unaltered they would, he feared, render the life of the designing engineer almost unbearable. Mr. Vaughan suggested that the final report of the Committee contained all the information required to enable a method of design to be evolved which although approximating closely to the actual results of the research could nevertheless be applied in the ordinary engineering office economically, quickly and accurately.

Mr. HUGH DAVIES, Hon. A.R.I.B.A., A.I.Struct.E., emphasised that the Institution was privileged to have a paper from Mr. Bylander, for he was a pioneer of structural engineering in England, and all concerned with structural engineering owed very much to the work that he had done in the early days. Probably there were not many at the meeting who could remember the early days when Mr. Bylander had first commenced to practise in this country and who could remember the doubts and difficulties in the path of the designer of steel structures at that time. Architects were not very happy in designing steel-frame and ferro-concrete buildings in those days, and some of the leading American people, such as McKim, Mead and White, and some of the French people, such as Hennebique and Mouchel, had been able to tell us how best to carry out work in steel and in reinforced concrete. The whole science of building in steel and concrete was then comparatively new and experimental. Mr. Davies recalled the need which had arisen at that time for the organisation of educational departments in which the subject could be taught, and the difficulty of finding experts to instruct the young men who came to the technical colleges seeking instruction in methods of building in steel and concrete. More than one of the men selected for that work subsequently became Presidents of the Institution of Structural Engineers, and they had done a great deal to lay the foundations of instruction in steelwork and ferro-concrete. Mr. Davies mentioned the matter particularly, because in those early days the instructors in steelwork were helped to a very large extent indeed by the work that Mr. Bylander was doing. He had very vivid recollections of the publication of the drawings of Mr. Bylander's early constructional work, and recalled that they were seized upon very gladly indeed by those whose business it was to organise instruction in the subject ; those drawings had played a great part in laying the foundations of structural knowledge for the benefit of those who had since become eminent engineers. The younger members particularly should acknowledge very fully indeed the substantial help which the profession had derived from Mr. Bylander and the very great debt that it owed to his past work. On that account it was an exceptional privilege to hear Mr. Bylander discuss the progress of structural engineering during the last 30 years.

Mr. H. V. CRABTREE, A.M.I.Struct.E., expressed his appreciation of Mr. Bylander's very interesting paper, and pressed Mr. Vaughan to explain more fully the problem of the " non-following " stresses.

Mr. H. J. DAVEY, M.B.E., M.I.Struct.E., said he personally entertained great respect for Mr. Bylander's work and was only too glad to be present to hear his clear and informative paper and to see the photographic records of some of the problems which the author had had to tackle. These afforded ample evidence of boldness in attack, and one can understand Mr. Bylander's recognition of the importance of inspection during the erection of the buildings shown and the value of a first hand knowledge of the materials actually used in the work and their mechanical properties, not to mention their possible imperfections.

It was at once a duty and a pleasure for a professional inspector to pay a tribute to a consulting engineer for a thorough exercise of inspection.

Mention of restrictions imposed by Government and municipal bodies in respect of the nature and qualities of steel for bridges and general building construction are arbitrary and confusing : the authority for the restrictions may be not uncharitably described as dependent more on the whims and fancies of a past generation than upon actual evidence available to-day. Mr. Davey had dealt personally with the inspection and testing of very heavy tonnages of steel produced in Great Britain and on the Continent and had found no reason for many years to suppose that Open Hearth steel was in any degree superior or more reliable than Bessemer Basic or Thomas Basic steel for structural purposes, whether bridges or buildings. To-day, there must be many bridges in wrought iron carrying heavy loads at high speeds where the mechanical properties of the iron would cause grave misgivings to the competent authority although the iron will probably continue to accept the loads and speeds for many years to come.

Mr. W. H. WOODCOCK, A.I.Struct.E., recalled an occasion on which Mr. Bylander was one of a party who had travelled to Middlesbrough in the early days of the development of high-tensile steel and had seen how wonderfully well such steel had withstood really cruel punishment. Mr. Bylander, he said, had come forward boldly and had used it, although its use had involved a great deal of fresh calculation, because the stresses were different from those applying to the steel used formerly. It was stated in the paper, that " although high-tensile steel has been on the market for a few years its use has not become general, probably because the price per ton is more than for mild steel, thus reducing the saving due to higher allowable stresses." One of the reasons given by some of the makers was that engineers did not like altering their calculations for the higher stresses which the use of high-tensile steel allowed. But the real reason was probably the opposite to that given by Mr. Bylander. The price of high-tensile steel had been fixed at a level which was too little above the price of ordinary steel, and the steelmakers had found that the economy in the amount of steel used was such that the profits they lost were far greater than those obtained from the higher price of high-tensile steel. Therefore, they did not push it, although they would make it to order, and presumably they would not push it until new prices were fixed. He personally had expected that high-tensile steel would come into general use and would replace all mild steel for structural purposes.

With regard to cement grouting under high pressure, Mr. Woodcock said he could not follow how Mr. Bylander had removed the air when grouting under the steel slabs of the Manitoba Parliament building (men-

Discussion on Steelwork in Buildings.

tioned on page 13). Having had experience of air locks in connection with such work, he said it seemed almost impossible to get the air out. Mr. Bylander had stated in the paper that the grout was worked with a steel rod and the excess water escaped to the top, and the air bubbles were removed ; but he had not stated how they were removed. It was interesting to hear that he had used neat cement 1 in. thick under high pressure.

Mr. HUGH DAVIES, Hon. A.R.I.B.A., A.I.Struct.E., discussing the future of structural engineering, said that one very important matter to which attention would have to be directed was that of earthquake-resisting construction. He mentioned it because he had received a communication from New Zealand (and it was being forwarded to the Institution) relating to the extreme importance of investigating the problems of structural engineering as they were affected by the lateral forces in earthquake shocks and the rolling motion resulting from earthquakes, and in that communication it was urged that the matter be investigated by the Institution. It was one of the newer problems in structural engineering, and one which members of the Institution might well regard as being of sufficient importance to warrant the fullest possible investigation.

Mr. STANLEY VAUGHAN, B.Sc. (Eng.), A.M.Inst.C.E., A.M.I.Struct.E., responding to the suggestion that he should describe what he had meant by " pursuing " and " non-pursuing " forces, said that a " pursuing " force was illustrated by reference to a tie-bar carrying a load in direct tension. As the load increased, the bar extended ; if the load were increased sufficiently, the yield point was reached, and any further increase of load beyond that point resulted in elongation and failure of the bar since the force is a " pursuing " one, that is to say, it continues undiminished throughout the full " drawing out " of the steel past the elastic limit. Thus, the continued increase of a " pursuing " force ultimately caused failure and consequently an adequate factor of safety on the yield point is essential.

To illustrate a " non-pursuing " force, he referred to a top or bottom cleat supporting a beam. If the beam were loaded, it tried to take up a small but definite slope at the end. If the cleat were very weak it would be forced to bend to the slope imposed on it by the beam and in so doing would pass its yield point. The beam, however, would have taken up its full slope and not only would it not tend to bend the cleat still further but it would resist any such increase. In other words the force on the cleat was " non-pursuing."

It is true that further loading of the beam would slightly increase the end slope, again to a definite and limited amount, and this would cause slight further yielding of the cleat, though clearly this would never even approach the 20 per cent. (or more) elongation which the cleat would stand before fracture. The increased force would still be " non-pursuing."

In such a case as this no danger was involved owing to the cleat material having passed its yield point. There was in fact no doubt that a considerable proportion of cleats in actual buildings are stressed beyond the yield point, but are nevertheless functioning perfectly satisfactorily and safely.

Mr. A. B. DAILEY, M.I.Struct.E., A.R.I.B.A., said it seemed to him that the problem of non-pursuing forces extended rather beyond the mere question of

the slope of cleats ; the subject could be enlarged to include all those cases in which the plasticity of the material was capable of preventing its breaking.

An instance which occurred to him was that of two beams, so connected that they deflected together. He had heard it claimed—though he did not guarantee, or even believe, that it was correct—that one could add together the section *moduli* of the two beams, even though the two beams were of entirely different depth. But although he thought that the statement was not correct, he believed there was something in it, and the question as to whether or not it should be allowed was one which could with advantage be investigated scientifically. He suggested that a great deal would be found to depend on the proportions of live and dead load, and whether the live load was subject to rapid and frequent change, also on whether the steelwork was encased or not. The question as to how far we could go outside the limits of mathematical calculations dependent on elasticity, had not been, in his opinion, sufficiently investigated.

Mr. BYLANDER, replying to the discussion, first expressed his gratitude for the kind way in which his paper had been received. He felt it an honour to have participated in the work of various buildings, and he did not wish to take all the credit for the progress described, as other engineers have done their share. He had not attempted in this paper to describe the work done by others, as he could only speak for himself.

Answering Mr. Gower Pimm concerning vibration, he could not give a simple and satisfactory statement. In order to avoid transmission of vibration one should try to sandwich different materials together, some of which would absorb sound or vibrations. The steel frame itself could not very well be designed in a manner to prevent sound transmission because the structure must be strong and rigid which is the main object. He instanced a case where vibrations occurred in a large span girder, not because the girder was too weak, but because the girder had a natural periodicity which was the same as that of an oil engine placed several hundred feet away ; therefore in dealing with vibrations, the first thing to look for was moving parts coinciding in periodicity.

Commenting upon remarks by Mr. Hamilton and other speakers with regard to research, education and experience, he said that as an engineer he felt strongly that the important thing is that a young man should receive an adequate and thorough training in theory for a start, then a few years' practical experience. If he is observant enough afterwards he will learn from what he sees and hears from others, and his best advancement in engineering knowledge is by practical observation. He instanced a few cases of failure which was research on a grand scale from which one should learn. Scientific research he considered was extremely valuable and because it is costly it is difficult to obtain. It cannot be too strongly emphasised that the results of scientific research are most valuable for the use of the engineer and should be strongly supported.

Replying to the Chairman's question concerning the strengthening of brick piers at St. James's Park Station by reinforced concrete, Mr. Bylander said the reinforced concrete would be strong enough without the brick piers to carry the load.

Commenting upon Mr. Gray's reference to the

Discussion on Steelwork in Buildings.

difference between bye-laws thirty years ago and those of to-day, Mr. Bylander said quite frankly that the bye-laws have not really troubled him very much, although many times he had spoken in disagreement of them, but his endeavour was to obtain bye-laws which were more suitable. The table in the paper shows the relative loads and stresses used during this period. He doubted whether it was wise for a building owner to erect a building for industrial and commercial purposes with a live load less than 100 lbs. per square foot, bearing in mind that it should include the weight of partitions and incidental alterations which he might wish to make. A building should not be restricted to one purpose only because a change in the use of a building often occurred.

Analysis of the change in thirty years as regards loads and stresses will show a relatively small change. In the Institution's report on steelwork prepared by a Committee of which he was the Chairman, the loads and stresses given in the table in the paper should read "inclusive of partitions." As partitions may be changed it has been a custom from the early days, as it is now, to make allowance in the live load to cover such partitions. The sub-division of rooms in most cases cannot be decided until after the erection of a building.

Replying to Mr. Dailey's question, Mr. Bylander said that the subsoil was sand under the foundation of the concrete raft for Walsingham House which stood on the site of the Ritz Hotel.

With regard to the yield of steel he was satisfied that if the steel used in structural engineering were absolutely brittle like glass and would not yield, many structures would fail because conditions and calculations are not always perfect. He instanced the setting of grillages. Safety much depended on the engineer responsible, and he was keen enough to watch the various phases of the work and to assure himself that fillers or packings were really there.

Although Mr. Vaughan suggested that little progress had been made in connection with steel-frame construction, Mr. Bylander emphasised that on the whole a great deal of progress had been made. It should not be forgotten that even prior to 1900 the problem of building construction was studied so thoroughly by very excellent engineers over a period of some twenty years that they really did know how to design structural steel. The progress was really made at the start.

We now use high tensile steel. He said that he had in hand the construction of three buildings in which high tensile steel was being used. He was not afraid of hard work, and he liked to use new methods where he could do so with reasonable safety.

He also emphasised that welded steel was an advancement, and instanced cases he had seen last summer of very important bridges in welded steel. He mentioned that high tensile steel is not suitable for welding. He agreed that welding must have a future before it. At first sight a welded member gave the impression of better work than a member made up of pieces and held together with rivets. The solid continuous work made a better appeal. There are, however, many difficulties in carrying out and examining welded work.

My Bylander agreed with Mr. Hugh Davies concerning education, that more should be done to give the young engineer a start and the right information and reliable books.

He agreed with Mr. Davey that thorough inspection

of the work was extremely important. It is no use making a careful design if the work is not properly carried out. Under certain circumstances it might hold up, but at some future time it might fail, therefore the engineer should assure himself that the construction was carried out as he had designed it.

Replying to Mr. Woodcock's question as to getting rid of air from cement grout, he said he had made experiments and had lifted the steel slabs after grouting and examined the result, and while air bubbles were not entirely removed the defective area resulting from air bubbles could be reduced to a very low amount. He emphasised the practical result obtained by moving a hoop iron through the grout while grouting.

With reference to yield of steel, Mr. Bylander said that the ideas of limit of elasticity are very different to-day from those of thirty years ago. The accuracy of instruments had improved so that to our terror we had found that the elastic limit had become much lower than had been expected and a deeper study of steel subjected to stress above the elastic limit is needed.

At the conclusion of the discussion, the CHAIRMAN again thanked Mr. Bylander for his paper and for his reply to the discussion, and he also thanked the meeting for the intelligent discussion that had been raised.

CORRESPONDENCE.

The Institution, whilst being at all times pleased to open its columns to correspondence, cannot accept any responsibility for the opinions expressed by correspondents.

To the EDITOR *of The Structural Engineer.*

SIR,—

THE DEVELOPMENT OF PADDINGTON STATION.

I have read the report of the discussion on the above paper in the current issue and note that the author in reply to one of my queries, states, " the foundations were designed to allow of two additional floors being added."

I should like to point out that I was fully aware of this, as the stanchions were made strong enough to take the extra loading. My query was with regard to the super load on the ground floor only and my argument was that by reducing this, as suggested, the weight of steelwork at and below the ground floor could have been reduced and the number of piles in the foundations cut down.

I think that the author in his reply, fails to appreciate the true purport of my remarks.
—Yours faithfully, J. McHARDY YOUNG.

Hampton Hill.

12th February, 1937.

Discussion on Steelwork in Buildings.

15

Steel frame architecture versus the London Building Regulations: Selfridges, the Ritz, and American technology

Jeanne C. Lawrence

Between 1906 and 1909, there unfolded an Anglo–American drama which had a significant impact upon retailing practice in London: an American businessman, H. Gordon Selfridge, arrived from Chicago in order to found a department store at the west end of Oxford Street. It would be, he declared, "the best thing of its kind in the world" [1]. Selfridge's enterprise was described as the "American Invasion of London" [2] by the daily and drapery trade presses, which accorded the venture extensive, and generally hostile, coverage as it evolved. However, the American methods of retailing thus ostensibly introduced to the British shopping and shopkeeping public were not the only trans-Atlantic innovations which Selfridge's "gigantic building" [3] brought to public attention. The success of his scheme was dependent upon the size and appearance of the store itself. Selfridge envisioned a truly monumental retail emporium which would help him to achieve his ultimate goal, that of raising "the business of a merchant to the Dignity of a Science." [4] (Fig. 1).

The modern methods of steel-frame and reinforced-concrete construction being used in Chicago and elsewhere in the USA at the turn of the century were critical to Selfridge's vision of an enormous, technologically-advanced department store. However, the London Building Regulations contained no provisions for structures of this kind, and therefore hindered the construction of buildings with the wide internal spaces and vast street-level windows which Selfridge desired, and with which his architects and engineers were familiar. These regulations were contained in the London Building Acts of 1894 and 1905. The 1894 Act incorporated all previous Acts from 1844 to 1893, and was aimed at the regulation of "widths of streets, lines of frontages, open spaces to dwellings, heights of buildings and projections therefrom, ventilation and height of habitable rooms and the control and prevention of the spread of fire" [5]. The London Building Acts (Amendment) Act 1905 required new buildings to be equipped with means of escape from fire [6].

The 1894 and 1905 Acts impeded the construction of the Selfridge building through their regulations for (1) fire prevention (which entailed restrictions placed on cubic footage between party walls) and (2) structural stability (for which the 1894 Building Act prescribed the required thickness of external walls). Although reinforced-concrete flooring could be used to create larger (yet fire-resistant) spaces, and structural steelwork could be employed to support the loads and stresses of a building (thus making load-bearing external walls unnecessary), the building regulations served

24 *Steel Frame Architecture*

LONDON'S BIGGEST SHOP: A COMING WONDER OF COMMERCIAL ENTERPRISE.

On a site covered upwards of one acre Messrs. Selfridge and Co. are building what will be the biggest shop in London. It will stand at the corner of Oxford Street and Duke Street, and will be built of Portland stone and steel throughout. The floor-space will measure more than eight acres. There will be six storeys above the level of the street and three beneath. The work will be completed next year.

FIG. 1. Selfridges as foreseen by the *Illustrated London News*, 25 July 1908.

to inhibit the erection of large structures whose interior and exterior appearance fully benefitted from these advances in technology.

The Building Acts were finally reformed after years of agitation by engineers, architects, and businessmen for legislation to allow the construction of large open premises supported by structural steelwork. The LCC (General Powers) Act of 1908 allowed greater cubical extent, and dealt with the uniting of buildings by openings in internal and external walls [7]. The LCC (General Powers) Act of 1909, popularly titled the Steel Frame Act, officially recognised steel-frame construction [8].

In the reform of the Building Acts to accommodate new construction methods, Selfridges department store played an important and instrumental role. The building was not solely responsible for legislative change. However, the highly publicised construction techniques employed by structural engineer Sven Bylander, first on the Ritz Hotel (1904–5) and then on Selfridge's daring commercial and architectural venture, were an important part of the process which led the LCC to take account of progressively more sophisticated methods of steel and reinforced-concrete construction. In effect, the Selfridge store was a transitional building, erected under the prevailing regulations, but with the knowledge that they were soon to change. H. Gordon Selfridge fully expected, and therefore anticipated, legislative reform; he consistently petitioned for waivers from the regulations, and, through his persistence, helped the building reforms come to pass. Selfridges department store therefore became the first large building in London to fully exploit steel-frame and reinforced-concrete construction so that both the interior and exterior of the building revealed the use of these modern methods of structural engineering.

Complex Foundations

At the Corner of Oxford Street and Duke Street, Mr H. G. Selfridge, formerly of Chicago, is erecting a large department store . . . It is aggressively big in scale and entirely at odds with everything else in Oxford Street, a matter which is not altogether to be regretted because Oxford Street is one of the ugliest streets in the world, and everything that pertains to architecture has been until recently conspicuous by its absence. (Francis Swales, 'Notes from Europe', *The American Architect* XCIV 28 October 1908, p. 140.)

Subsequent building programmes have altered and extended Selfridges premises, involving a number of architectural and building firms, and resulting in a tangled web of architectural history. Yet even as the first Selfridge premises (now the south-east wing of the building) opened to the public in 1909, the store was known to have had complicated origins. The entire enterprise was dependent upon a network of connections which linked together Selfridge, his business associates, and the architectural and engineering firms engaged to carry out the Selfridge store's construction.

Selfridge was no newcomer to the department store scene. He began his career as a sales assistant at Marshall Field's, Chicago's premier department store, in 1879, and become one of Field's junior partners in 1889 [9]. At Field's, Selfridge introduced amenities such as the ladies' tearoom and the cut-price bargain basement which were to become standard features of American department stores [10]. In 1904 Selfridge left Field's to go into business on his own, buying Schlesinger and Mayer's department store, the steel-frame building (1899–1903) designed by Louis Sullivan, which was

26   *Steel Frame Architecture*

located just down the street from Marshall Field's [11]. But Selfridge disliked competing with his old employer, and within a few months sold the store to Carson Pirie Scott & Co [12]. He next turned his attention to London, which he believed was in need of a progressive and modern department store [13].

Across the Atlantic, Harrods reigned over the vast London retail field which included Whiteley's (the self-proclaimed "Universal Provider"), D. H. Evans, John Lewis, John Barker of Kensington, and a number of other large drapery concerns. Most of these stores had evolved piecemeal from small shops, gradually adding departments and taking over neighbouring buildings; many had roots going back to the 1860s or even earlier. Purpose-built structures to house these retail establishments were, therefore, rare: in fact, despite its unified appearance, Harrods grandiose building of 1901–5 was actually a re-building, in stages, over the old existing structures [14].

Once in London, Selfridge secured English support for his "American Invasion". He entered into partnership with Samuel J. Waring, of Messrs Waring & Gillow, London's largest furniture and furnishings emporium, and highly successful interior decoration firm, with headquarters located at 175 Oxford Street [15]. The businessmen formed a company, Selfridge and Waring Ltd, "to purchase land and carry on the business of drapers, tailors, hosiers,..." [16] and Selfridge joined the board of directors of Waring & Gillow Ltd [17]. The partnership of Selfridge and Waring was short-lived: the company was dissolved in 1909, and Selfridge's new company, Selfridge & Co. Ltd, bought out Waring's interest in the venture with the understanding that the store would not sell furniture [18]. From 1906 to 1908, though, Selfridge and Waring Ltd had bought up a number of the property leases on the proposed Oxford Street/Duke Street site (owned by the Portman Estate), which was occupied by a "medley of small shops and private houses" [19].

Builders, Engineers and Architects

In addition to aiding Selfridge's enterprise, initially with both his capital and his knowledge of the London retail scene, Samuel J. Waring's interest in the venture extended to the building of the proposed store, for he also controlled a construction firm, the Waring White Building Co. Waring's partner in this business was James Gilbert White, an American engineer who had undertaken a number of large projects for English entrepreneurs in Australia. In 1900 White had founded an English branch of his firm, J. G. White and Co. Ltd, through which he supervised several power plant and electric railway works [20]. Waring and Gillow had entered the construction business in order to build their own new eight storey premises near Oxford Circus [21]. In 1904 Samuel J. Waring and J. G. White merged their interests to take construction contracts over from Waring & Gillow Ltd: these included, notably, that for the Piccadilly hotel which would become the Ritz. Two years later, the company re-registered as Waring and White (1906) Ltd, and took several contracts over from the Waring White Building Co., including that of 13 November 1906 for Selfridge and Waring Ltd to erect "Stores in Oxford Street" [22].

Chief engineer for the Waring White Building Co. was Sven Bylander, a Swedish-born structural engineer who had designed large steelwork buildings in Germany and America, prior to moving to London in 1902 [23]. Bylander designed the Ritz and Selfridges steel frames, and also that of the Royal Automobile Club (1910–11), in accordance with precedents set by Chicago and New York commercial high-rise architecture in the late nineteenth century, using, in fact, the Carnegie Steel Company's Handbook, issued in 1897 [24].

Selfridge also counted upon the expertise of Daniel Burnham's Chicago architectural firm. Burnham was the architect to whom Marshall Field consistently turned for his retail buildings and warehouse structures [25]. Selfridge, an integral member of the Field organisation for over 20 years, was well aware of Burnham's mastery of the technical requirements of department store construction such as fire-proofing, elevator placement and electric lighting [26]. Indeed, Burnham's reputation in this sphere had already spread far beyond Chicago; his firm had designed such stores as the New York Wanamaker Annex and the 1903 addition to Milwaukee's Gimble Brothers Department Store. In 1910 Gimbel's Department Store in New York would open their new D. H. Burnham & Co. designed premises, and likewise Philadelphia's new Wanamaker Building in 1911 [27].

Burnham's office supplied Selfridge with a complete set of drawings in 1906 [28]. During a trip to England in April 1907, Burnham visited Selfridge, perhaps to finalise plans for the store [29]. However, Burnham's firm was but the first of a series of "supernumerary cooks" [30] involved in the building's design. The Burnham elevation was soon altered by another American, Francis Swales. Swales modified the building's external appearance, including, as he explained, the introduction of triple windows in the friese, and "the change in style of detail from the neo-Grec to that of Louis XVI" [31]. A shrewd self-publicist, Swales praised his own contributions to the building's design in the *Architectural Record* [32].

Burnham's firm bowed out of the project altogether when the London building regulations, which required that commercial premises be split into cellular compartments of no more than 250,000 cubic ft each, became too difficult for them to deal with trans-Atlantically [33]. This measurement of a building's "cubical extent" meant "the space contained within the external surfaces of its walls and roof, and the upper surface of the floor of its lowest storey" (irrespective of horizontal divisions created by floors) [34]. The internal walls of a building (referred to in the Act as "party walls") could contain openings of no more than 7 ft in width and 8 ft in height, and, taken together, these openings could not exceed one half the length of the party wall in which they occurred. Such openings were required to be fitted with wrought iron doors or shutters to prevent the spread of fire; otherwise the two connecting spaces could not, taken together, exceed 250,000 cubic ft [35]. The 250,000 cubical extent limit could be waived, but the absolute maximum was 450,000 cubic ft. The D. H. Burnham & Co. plans submitted to the LCC in February 1907 showed divisions exceeding 450,000 cubic ft, and permission to erect the building was initially refused because "no power is given to the Council under the London Building Act 1894, to consent to the erection of buildings of the warehouse class with divisions of a greater cubical extent than 450,000 cubic ft" [36]. In order to realise Selfridge's vision of a spacious store, a London-based architect was needed, first, to petition the LCC for permission to divide the building into compartments of 450,000 cubic ft each; and, secondly, to alter the Burnham plans (presumably by adding more internal walls) in order to bring the cubical extent within the divisions down to the 450,000 maximum [37].

R. Frank Atkinson, Waring & Gillow's architect, was contracted to carry out the project. Like Waring, Atkinson had moved to London from Liverpool; in his case, he had studied architecture there [38]. The new store premises for Waring & Gillow which opened in June 1906 had been designed by Atkinson, who was, therefore, familiar with the process of erecting buildings on Oxford Street [39].

28 *Steel Frame Architecture*

Bypassing the Building Regulations

Atkinson's main diplomatic chore in London throughout 1907 and 1908 was petition-ing the LCC Building Act Committee on behalf of the Selfridge venture to exceed the regulations for structures of the "warehouse class" as defined and laid out in the London Building Acts of 1894 and 1905 [40]. According to the definition used in those acts:

> The expression 'building of the warehouse class' means a warehouse, factory, manufactory, brewery, or distillery, and any other building exceeding in cubical extent one hundred and fifty thousand cubic feet, which is neither a public building nor a domestic building. [41]

Structures corresponding to this description were not to exceed 250,000 cubic ft without party walls; hence the existing London department stores (including Harrods) each consisted of a series of separate, but interconnecting, rooms, like individual stores side by side, rather than departments within a single building [42]. It is worth noting that another large London drapery establishment, D. H. Evans, also petitioned the LCC for permission to exceed 250,000 cubic ft in divisions of their proposed Oxford Street extension throughout 1907 [43]. Pressure on the LCC therefore came from others in the drapery trade as well, quite possibly in response to the threat of increasing competition posed by Selfridge's much publicised grand scheme [44].

By 1907 the authorities were beginning to realise that adherence to this regulation was not always essential. *The Builder* noted in 1907 that during the 1905-6 construc-tion year 12 businesses had petitioned the London County Council for permission to exceed 250,000 cubic ft; six of the requests were granted, and six were refused [45]. In August 1907 *The Builder* reprinted an LCC Building Act Committee report which urged that the current regulations be amended "so as to remove all restrictions on the Council's power to allow increased cubical capacity for buildings of the warehouse class" [46]. The London and District Association of Engineering Employers had initiated the proposal, reasoning that "these restrictions made it almost impossible for engineering firms to carry out their work in London in accordance with modern requirements" [47]. The proposed amendment would give the Council discretionary power to allow for horizontal separations within buildings; openings in party walls; fire-resisting doors of materials other than iron; and the uniting of buildings through wall openings. Much of this proposal was eventually passed in the LCC (General Powers) Act of 1908, but first it was defeated on the grounds that "the erection in London of buildings of great cubical extent, not sub-divided by party walls, cannot fail to expose London to the risk of conflagrations . . ." [48]

Fear of Fire

The risk of fire was of great concern to the Council's Building Act Committee. As noted in *The Builder*, of 112 fires involving questions of structural safety which occurred within the London County boundaries in the year 1906, 97 occurred in buildings coming under the Council's building regulations; in these fires 24 lives were lost and 136 were endangered [49]. The Council clearly felt responsible for the structural safety of buildings coming under its jurisdiction, and was reluctant to pass any amendment which might result in further tragedies. Theatres, with their large crowd capacity, were notorious fire hazards. However, drapery houses too posed an especial threat, as fabrics, clothes and other dry goods were highly flammable. The danger was further heightened by the fact that in London a large proportion of drapery shop assistants lived-in, residing in crowded company-owned accommodation either on or very near the business premises. They were therefore spending 24 hours a day in a high-risk environment [50].

Widespread recognition of the need for fire legislation had resulted in the London Building Act (Amendment) Act of 1905. This Act required new buildings to be provided with so-called 'reasonable' means of escape in case of fire, and stipulated that plans and particulars be deposited with the Council before building work began [51]. Still, these new regulations lagged behind technological innovations in fire-proofing and building construction which enabled structures of greater cubical extent to be essentially safe from fire. Such advances included concrete flooring, encased steel framing, and rolling steel shutters in place of iron doors. These were understood to be particularly relevant to the construction of large commercial premises, a connection clearly made in 1907 when a spokesman for the LCC Building Act Committee stated that "the Building Act of London was obsolete", with the result that "restrictions placed on trade in London were too great" [52].

In addition to his repeated requests for greater cubic footage allowances, R. Frank Atkinson petitioned the Council for the use of rolling iron shutters to be used in place of iron doors for fire prevention, and also for wider and more numerous wall openings than the regulation allowance of 7 × 8 ft for interior walls. The interior openings Atkinson requested were 12 × 12 ft and the Building Act Committee eventually granted permission for them [53]. Atkinson's petition for exterior window openings equalling more than half the area of the external walls was also granted. However, the architect was not so lucky in his requests for greater building height. The maximum allowed under the 1894 act was 80 ft, and Atkinson therefore had to subtract two stories from the proposed building, leaving a total height of five floors above ground, with three basement floors [54]. Atkinson submitted the plans for the Selfridge store to the Council in early 1907. The Building Act Committee granted permission for exterior windows to exceed half the external wall area in June 1907; for divisions of the store to exceed 250,000 (but not 450,000) cubic ft in July 1907; and for internal openings to exceed the regulation size, along with the use of rolling iron shutters for fire prevention, in October 1908 [55]. Also at this time, and clearly related to Selfridge's and Atkinson's perseverance in petitioning for waivers from legislation, the LCC passed the London County Council (General Powers) Act 1908 [56]. Part III of this Act amended the 1894 Building Act, and allowed for horizontal divisions in buildings of the warehouse class, for cubic footage to exceed 250,000 (but not 450,000) cubic ft, and for the uniting of buildings by openings in party or external walls [57]. These changes had the effect of vastly increasing the legal limits of internal spaces bounded by walls. But there were still no regulations for reinforced-concrete and steel-frame construction.

The Steel Frame

Although still a new departure from traditional building methods, the internal steel frame was becoming more and more common in Chicago and New York by the turn of the century, but Britain lagged behind in its adoption [58]. Many architects resisted the use of steel in building construction because they dreaded the necessary study, or were reluctant to collaborate so closely with engineers [59]. The RIBA held up the process

30   *Steel Frame Architecture*

of legislation for new building methods by insisting that very definite rules, arrived at after much discussion and research, were needed in order to control builders [60]. Finally, it has been argued that the nature of Britain's design market, and the bifurcation of the architectural and engineering professions along the lines of building types and clients, hindered the acceptance of new building methods by providing no impetus (such as competition) for creativity or innovation [61].

Yet steelwork was definitely being employed, albeit in idiosyncratic ways. As Sven Bylander later noted, when he arrived in London in 1902 it was usual practice to "employ some steelwork in the internal part of the building only, or to carry the external wall at the first floor level on steelwork to permit large shop windows, and sometimes steel pillars were used to strengthen external walls", while little precaution was taken for the stability or fire protection of individual steel members [62]. One of Bylander's engineering colleagues affirmed that at that time "builders, in using steelwork in building simply piled one piece on top of another, stuck a few bolts in and called it constructional steelwork", a practice he described as "ironmongery" [63]. Because of the haphazard ways in which steelwork was employed, and the lack of standardisation in either methods or materials, it is virtually impossible to pinpoint the 'first' steel-framed building in Britain—although claims have been made for, among others, Robinson's Emporium in West Hartlepool [64].

The issue is further complicated by the fact that no standard *definition* of 'steel-frame construction' existed at the time—the term 'steel frame' was often used to describe any structure that employed some steelwork, in some way. The discrepancies in use of the term, and the ensuing difficulties in understanding just how various buildings had been constructed, were brought up in discussion at a meeting of structural engineers as late as 1913. There a speaker noted that a number of terms were used quite loosely in reference to steel construction, namely: "steel-cage construction", "interior skeleton", "steel skeleton", "skeleton construction", and "cage construction", and this lack of firm definition prevented one's understanding of exactly how and where the loads and stresses were being carried in buildings utilising structural steelwork [65]. At stake was the question of whether the steel frame supported solely (or primarily) the floor loads of a building which had self-supporting external walls, or whether the frame actually supported *all* loads and stresses, including those of the walls.

In early twentieth century London there was no real incentive to erect a steel-frame building with non-loadbearing external walls. This was because Part II of the 1894 London Building Act defined the necessary thickness of walls for large buildings: depending upon the height and length of the walls. Their base measurement was to range, for example, from 13 in. (for a wall of 25 ft or less in height) to 31 in. (for walls of between 100 and 120 ft in height and 45 ft in length); a taller or longer building would require even more substantial walls. Further, no wall was to be less in thickness than one fourteenth part of the height of the storey [66].

The Ritz and American Technology

The Ritz Hotel, the first London steel-framed building of "importance" [67], was designed with a "complete steel frame"[68] which carried all loads on steelwork, including the reinforced concrete fire-proof floor system. Still, the structure had also to conform to the LCC 1894 and 1905 Building Acts, and therefore the Ritz walls measured 39 in. in thickness at street level and 14 in. at sixth floor level [69]. The

J. C. Lawrence 31

hotel, designed by Mewes and Davis with Sven Bylander as structural engineer, and constructed by Waring White Building Co., was built in 1904–5, amidst great excitement in the architectural community [70]. The most minute details of the building's steel framework, and every 'Americanism' inherent in its construction, were fully recorded in the architectural press. *The Builder's Journal and Architectural Record* ran a lengthy series on the engineering side of the Ritz construction for a full year, from 28 September 1904 through 13 September 1905. Readers were assured that they would "be introduced to various methods employed in modern American contracting practice new to this country," because the hotel was "being erected under the management and supervision of men from the United States who have had wide experience of large building works there" [71] (i.e. J. G. White and Sven Bylander). Full details were provided of such innovations as the "American cranes" used in raising the steelwork, including "a derrick of American pattern specially constructed for the builders" with a 360° arc and, importantly, Bylander's standardised drafting procedures [72].

Bylander credited his method of preparing drawings to his experience in America, where "every office in good standing has a set of standard tables" which "are used throughout the office by each member, and this produces uniformity in methods and design" [73]. *The Builder's Journal* noted the significance of Bylander's system:

> We would particularly call attention to the great exactitude of the work, every dimension being figured on the drawings and nothing left to be scaled off; the elaborate nature and number of the drawings—this being no useless expense, because the drawing-office expenses form but a small percentage of the cost of the steel, and the German steelworks are thereby enabled to execute the work at a reduced price and without preparing templates, as is usual in English practice; and finally the careful way in which the details are standardized and facility of erection studied both to secure cheapness and to aid the execution being correct as designed. [74]

Numerous reproductions of the engineer's drawings and extensive photographic coverage of the Ritz frame as it went up testified to the interest in, and importance of, the new form of construction (Fig. 2). Two of the *Builder's Journal* articles included "Notes on the Steelwork by S. Bylander," in which the structural engineer explained how to read the accompanying framing plans, described the use of standardised parts which eliminated the need for on-site templates, outlined the numbering system used to distinguish each piece of steelwork, provided factual information on loads and stresses, and, importantly, reassured the public that "the construction practically conforms to the latest standards for steel-framed office buildings in America" [75].

Reinforced Concrete Construction

After the Ritz was completed and work on Selfridges had begun, a new professional organisation, the Concrete Institute, was founded to study and promote the use of reinforced concrete in construction. The birth of the Concrete Institute in 1908 (renamed the Institution of Structural Engineers in 1922) coincided with the creation, by the Institution of Civil Engineers, of a special committee to report on reinforced-concrete construction in response to prevailing doubts about its safety [76]. Just as the LCC building regulations hindered the adoption of steel-frame construction, so too did they inhibit use of reinforced concrete. Although several systems of this type of

32 *Steel Frame Architecture*

FIG. 2. The Ritz Hotel under construction (from *The Builder's Journal*, 12 April 1905).

construction were well known in Britain, and the Hennebique system in particular was commonly used outside London, the LCC regulations contained no provisions for the use of concrete in building [77]. New methods or materials could not be used unless a waiver was obtained, and the LCC had no power to grant waivers for the use of either reinforced concrete or structural steelwork [78].

In the absence of any regulations for concrete construction, the 1894 Building Act required that, as the Concrete Institute put it, "every building must practically be enclosed with brick or stone or concrete walls of an unnecessary thickness", whereas "by the use of reinforced concrete, as by the use of steel skeleton construction, this unnecessary expense may be saved" [79]. The Ritz Hotel was a victim of this legislation; although the building was constructed with a load-bearing steel frame, it was clad with masonry of loadbearing thickness, as if the steel frame were not there. Sven Bylander was a member of the Concrete Institute, which pushed for Council

J. C. Lawrence 33

authority to waive the existing Building Act rules where steel framing and/or reinforced concrete were involved, and agitated for the official recognition of these building methods in the LCC regulations [80].

Selfridges

In this atmosphere of increasing pressure for the repeal of antiquated legislation, and the enactment of new regulations appropriate to the erection of steel-framed buildings, the Selfridges department store was constructed along the lines of American high-rise technology. It incorporated a steel frame together with staircases, flooring, and one retaining wall of reinforced concrete [81]. In light of the Selfridge store's incubation as a Burnham design, the internal steel framework is entirely understandable. So, too, is Bylander's involvement in the project: not only was he chief engineer for Waring & White (1906) Ltd, the construction firm headed by Selfridge's short-lived partner, Samuel J. Waring, but his approach and methods had received wide publicity through the Ritz Hotel project. *The Builder's Journal* had promoted Bylander's "considerable experience in the design of steel-framed or skeleton buildings in the United States" [82].

Work on the Selfridge building progressed at exceptional speed: the structure was completed in twelve months, "the erection of the steelwork, amounting to 3000 tons, occupying less than half this time" [83]. Much of the facility with which Selfridges was erected was due to Bylander's organised system of preparing the engineering drawings and specifications, which enabled the steelwork to be cut (and in some instances shaped or riveted) in the shop (Fig. 3). For Selfridges, Bylander prepared 12,000 blueprints, and construction was carried on at the rate of about 125 tons per week; as Bylander noted, "The shop details prepared per week was equivalent to 100 tons of steel" [84]. (Figs 4 and 5 show interior and exterior views of the constructional steelwork).

The internal steel frame which Bylander designed for Selfridges corresponded to the building's exterior, as well as interior, appearance. The LCC regulation wall thicknesses for buildings of the warehouse class were bypassed, allowing not only much thinner walls, but far greater window area. Traditionally, the width of window openings had been determined by the safe span for a stone lintel [85]. At Selfridges the steel frame, combined with the use of cast iron window surrounds and entrances, allowed a much larger proportion of the facade to be taken up by windows. Very large plate glass windows were installed, some as large as 19 ft 4 in. long by 12 ft high [86]. In fact, the window area was greater than half the area of the external walls on both the Oxford Street and Duke Street frontages, and permission for this had been granted by the LCC in 1907 [87].

The steel frame carried the weight of the interior walls and the reinforced concrete floors; the ground floor piers were built "sufficiently large in blue brick to carry the external wall as well as the load from the floors" [88]. The "external wall" actually amounted to masonry strips supporting the pillars on the building's facade. (Figs 3 and 6 show the correlation between the engineering and architectural plans of the building). Bylander contributed a 13 page, fully illustrated account of the Selfridge store's construction to the March 1909 issue of *Concrete and Constructional Engineering* in which he explained that:

> All the interior walls, except the west party wall, are carried on steel framing, and the floors are built independent of the walls. The exterior wall to Oxford

34 *Steel Frame Architecture*

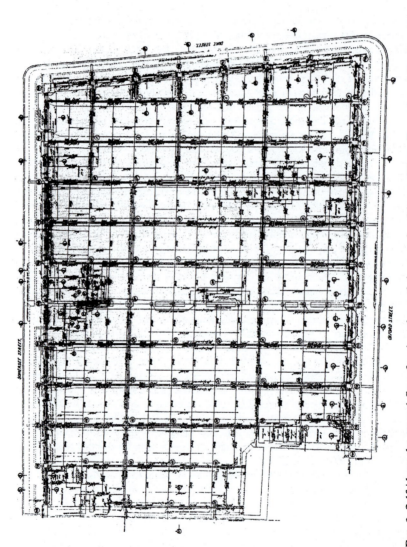

FIG. 3. Selfridges: the ground floor framing plan and the completed layout (from *Concrete and Construction Engineering*, March 1909).

J. C. Lawrence 35

FIG. 4. The constructional steelwork of Selfridges (from *Concrete and Constructional Engineering*, March 1909).

36   *Steel Frame Architecture*

Fig. 5. Selfridges: the steelwork erected to the third floor except on the last bay (from *Concrete and Constructional Engineering*, March 1909).

Street and Duke Street is faced with Portland Stone and the backing is blue brick for piers. The frontage to Somerset Street is brick. One of the most noticeable features of the building is the great distance between the columns, and the omission of brick or stone mullions. The window area, therefore, is very large, and good lighting has thus been obtained, also the weight of the exterior walls has been materially reduced. The window frames and mullions are of cast iron. [89]

Importantly, the internal division walls were carried on steel and not self-supporting, so they could be removed at a later date if and when the LCC would permit more than 450,000 cubic ft in each section of the building. Placed at approximately 40 ft intervals, many of these walls were taken down 20 years later, when legislation allowed a greater cube for divisions within buildings [90].

The open interior spaces, combined with the great degree of window area, created "an impression of lightness and brightness" throughout the floors of the store [91]. Shop fixtures such as counters were purposely built lower than the usual height so that, Bylander claimed, one could "see from end to end of the building" [92]. (Fig. 7 affords an interior view of the newly-opened premises). These wide internal spaces were allowed under the 1908 LCC (General Powers) Act which, in effect, the Selfridge venture had helped to enact. As noted in the editor's introduction to the article on Selfridges which Bylander contributed to *Concrete and Constructional Engineering*:

> ... The building is one of the first, if not the first, in the Metropolis to which the recent amendments to the London Building Act have been applied, and which thus comprises a number of compartments of 450,000 cubic feet each, separated from one another by divisional walls, in which the door openings are also of larger area than was allowable before the passing of the new Act—12 ft by 12 ft. [93]

The journal's editor also praised Selfridge, who "by his perseverance did much, not only to obtain a building of very high qualities, but also to improve the legislative conditions under which it was executed" [94].

The Steel Frame Act

The efforts of H. G. Selfridge, his architect R. Frank Atkinson, his engineer Sven Bylander, and the Concrete Institute were instrumental, also, in the enactment of the LCC (General Powers) Act of 1909. Known as the Steel Frame Act, this was the legislation which finally gave the Council the power to regulate the construction of reinforced-concrete structures, and decreed that:

> ... it shall be lawful to erect subject to the provisions of this Section buildings wherein the loads and stresses are transmitted through each storey to the foundations by a skeleton framework of metal, or partly by a skeleton framework of metal, and partly by a party wall or party walls ... [95]

The Act provided guidelines for the encasement of steelwork with fire-resistant material, and laid out required wall thicknesses of 8.5 in. for the topmost 20 ft of a building and 13 in. for the remainder of its height, but allowed for this regulation to be modified or waived [96].

Yet in some ways the passage of the Steel Frame Act complicated, rather than

38 *Steel Frame Architecture*

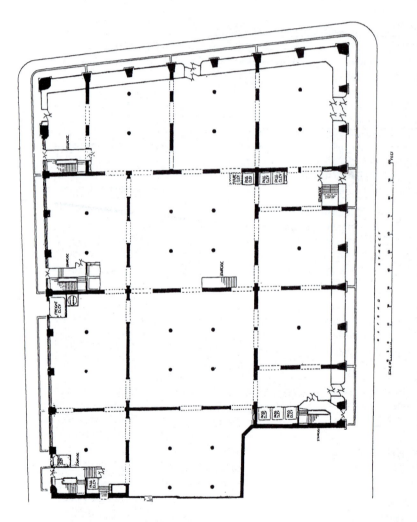

FIG. 6. Selfridges' ground floor plan (from the *Architectural Review*, June 1909).

FIG. 7. A showroom in the completed Selfridges (from the *Architectural Review*, June 1909).

40 Steel Frame Architecture

simplified, the problems faced by structural engineers. There was no consensus on how to interpret the legislation, for it contained insufficient details. "When the Act first came out, engineers had to consult the district surveyor in each particular district in order to find out what was his reading of it, because it would probably be opposite from that of his neighbour" [97]. The new Act did not apply to buildings designed under the old regulations. And difficulties also stemmed from the fact that the legislation was in the form of an Act of Parliament rather than a local bye-law. As evidenced by the time taken to pass the General Powers Acts of 1908 and 1909, innovations in building technology could not quickly be introduced, and the process of amendment was slow [98]. Finally, 450,000 cubic ft remained the maximum space allowed for divisions within commercial buildings.

Conclusion

Selfridges department store opened its doors to the public on 15 March 1909. The building occupied the whole of its 250 by 175 ft site. There were nine passenger lifts, two service lifts, and six staircases. The store's eight floors (five above ground and three below) averaged 15 ft in height, and housed over 100 departments as well as a vast range of amenities, including an Information Bureau; First Aid Room with trained nurse; French, German, American and Colonial retiring-rooms "typically furnished"; restaurant, luncheon-hall, tea-room and roof garden. Some 1400 employees had been hired to ensure the smooth running of Oxford Street's new commercial palace [99].

In *The British Building Industry*, Marian Bowley suggests that "the need for new buildings for new purposes" may stimulate innovation in construction methods [100]. Selfridges provides an example of such an enterprise and demonstrates, indeed, that modern construction techniques were critical to the success of the venture. However, in order to construct the store H. G. Selfridge envisioned, the obstacle of the London building regulations had to be overcome. The highly publicised raising of the Ritz steel frame in 1904-5, followed by the much promoted Selfridge undertaking in 1906-9, were important events in the transformation of the building regulations to permit recognition of steel-frame and reinforced-concrete methods of construction. Both projects drew attention to modern American methods of structural engineering, and introduced British engineers to standardisation techniques in the production of drawings and specifications, as well as in the actual steelwork. The Ritz, constructed under the old Building Act of 1894, was covered in masonry of the required thickness, and its steel-frame construction was therefore not apparent. But Selfridges, with its wide plate glass windows and near-absence of external walls, was clearly a different sort of building, achieved only after much negotiation with the LCC. The Building Act reforms of 1908 dealing with cubic footage, and the steel-frame and reinforced-concrete sections in the 1909 (General Powers) Act were, at least in part, due to H. G. Selfridge's determination to build a Chicago-style department store in London.

Selfridge's novel approach to building, that of planning in anticipation of legislative changes, and then pushing for the necessary reforms, surfaced again in 1919. At that time he determined to construct a massive 300 ft tower on top his emporium, as part of the western extension designed by Sir John Burnet and Thomas Tait in association with Burnham & Co.'s Chicago successor firm, Graham, Anderson, Probst & White [101]. Building work, including the laying of foundations for the tower, was begun in 1919 and completed in 1924 [102]. In this instance, however, the LCC Building Act Committee could not be persuaded to waive their regulations. The Committee

J. C. Lawrence 41

remained unconvinced that Selfridge's should be allowed a monumental tower which would vie with the dome of St Paul's; permission to exceed the 80 ft height regulation was not granted and the tower was never constructed.

In effect, the construction techniques introduced to London through the 1909 Selfridges building had a significant impact upon the urban landscape. The steel frame allowed wide interior spaces and permitted the installation of very large plate glass windows which provided the store with considerable natural light, whilst also creating grander window shopping possibilities for passers-by. As stated in *The Architects' Journal* in 1920, "The building gave a new scale to Oxford Street and has exercised a strong influence over the design of many big structures that have since been erected in the metropolis" [103]. These features were already becoming standard architectural design for retail premises elsewhere; to the extent allowed by the revised but still restrictive Building Acts, H. G. Selfridge's monument to commerce brought modern American department store design to London.

Acknowledgements

This paper derives from my master's thesis, 'THE 'AMERICAN INVASION' OF LONDON: MODERN AMERICAN METHODS OF CONSTRUCTION CROSS THE ATLANTIC IN H. GORDON SELFRIDGE'S OXFORD STREET DEPARTMENT STORE OF 1909' (University of London, 1986). I would like to thank Maxine Copeland, Ellen Miles and Robert Thorne. Special thanks are due to Adrian Forty and Nicholas J. Morgan, who provided much appreciated comments and suggestions and to the Selfridge's Archivist, Fred Redding.

Correspondence: J. C. Lawrence, American Studies Program, Yale University, 1504A Yale Station, New Haven, Connecticut 06520–7425, USA.

References

[1] *Draper*, 13 March 1909, p. 256.

[2] *Drapery Times*, 20 Feb. 1909, pp. 359–60. The phrase "American Invasion" held potent meaning for British tradesmen at the turn of the century; see William T. Stead, *The Americanization of the World* (1902; reprinted New York, 1972), pp. 132–9.

[3] *Draper*, 13 March 1909, p. 256.

[4] *Drapery Times*, 13 March 1909, p. 523. Selfridge argued for the validity of commerce as a worthy profession in *The Romance of Commerce* (1918), particularly pp. 377–85.

[5] Quoted in C. C. Knowles and P. H. Pitt, *The History of Building Regulations in London 1189–1972* (1972), p. 93. For the Act itself, see W. R. Griffiths & F. W. Pember, *The London Building Act, 1894* (1895).

[6] Bernard C. Molloy, *London Building Acts (Amendment) Act, 1905* (1905).

[7] Horace R. Chanter, *London Building Law* (1946), p. 302.

[8] H. D. Searles-Wood & Henry Adams, *Modern Building* (1921), p. 157.

[9] For biographical information on Selfridge see: Richard Kenin, 'The Captains of Commerce and Journalism', *Return to Albion: Americans in England 1760–1940* (Washington, D.C., 1979); Lloyd Wendt & Herman Kogan, *Give the Lady What She Wants!* (Chicago, 1952); Reginald Pound, *Selfridge: A Biography* (1960); A. H. Williams and W. H. Allen, *No Name on the Door* (1957); Gordon

42 *Steel Frame Architecture*

Honeycombe, *Selfridges, Seventy-Five Years: the Story of the Store* (1984); and Robert W. Twyman, *History of Marshall Field & Co., 1852–1906* (Philadelphia, 1954).

[10] Wendt & Kogan, *Give the Lady*, pp. 201–41.

[11] Joseph Siry, *Carson-Pirie-Scott: Louis Sullivan and the Chicago Department Store* (Chicago, 1988), p. 112; Siry provides an excellent account of this building, and the development of the department store as an urban building type, in the context of turn of the century Chicago.

[12] Siry, *Carson-Pirie-Scott*, p. 112.

[13] Wendt & Kogan, *Give the Lady*, p. 241; for description of what such a modern store entailed, see Wendt & Kogan, pp. 201–41, and Neil Harris, 'Shopping—Chicago Style', in John Zukowsky (ed.), *Chicago Architecture 1872–1922: Birth of a Metropolis* (Munich, 1987), pp. 145–7.

[14] F. H. W. Sheppard (ed.), *Survey of London XLI, Southern Kensington: Brompton* (1983), pp. 17–23; see also 'Shops' in H. D. Searles-Wood & Henry Adams, *Modern Building* V (1922) p. 24.

[15] For the meeting of Waring and Selfridge see Pound, *Selfridge*, p. 33.

[16] PRO BT31/11562/89184. For particulars of Waring's shareholding involvement with both Selfridge and Waring Ltd and Selfridge & Co. Ltd see *Drapery Times*, 12 June 1909, p. 1262, and Pound, *Selfridge*, pp. 33, 40–1.

[17] Waring & Gillow Ltd Administration Chart, in Selfridge's 1906–8 Scrapbook, Selfridges' Archives, 400 Oxford St., London W1A 1AB.

[18] Letter, S. J. Waring to H. G. Selfridge, 24 March 1909, Selfridges' Archives.

[19] Lease Catalogue and Company Books, Selfridges' Archives; *Draper's Record*, 10 April 1909, p. 105.

[20] Obituary, *Trans. of the American Soc. of Civil Engineers* 109 (1944), p. 1548–9.

[21] Designed by R. Frank Atkinson, Waring and Gillow's new furniture and furnishings emporium, complete with art galleries, furnished rooms, restaurant, and reading rooms, was described in detail in *The Times*, 11 June 1906, p. 4; 13 June 1906, p. 13.

[22] PRO. BT31/10695/81048 & BT31/11783/91435.

[23] Obituaries in *Structural Engineer*, Nov. 1943, pp. 475–6, and *Junior Inst. of Engineers Journ. and Record of Trans.* LIV (1943–4), p. 118; for Bylander's American experience see *Concrete Inst. Trans. and Notes* IV (July 1912), p. 88 & *Structural Engineer*, XVII (March 1939), pp. 471–2; for his move to London see *Concrete Inst. Trans. and Notes* (Oct. 1913), p. 57.

[24] See S. Bylander, 'The Architectural and Engineering Features of the Royal Automobile Club Building,' *Junior Inst. of Engineers Journ. and Record of Trans.* XXI (1910–11), pp. 243–70. The Carnegie hand-book is mentioned by S. Bylander, 'Steelwork in Buildings—Thirty Years' Progress', *Structural Engineer* (Jan. 1937), p. 3. Bylander also was engineer (with Waring & White) or consultant (after 1912) on the 'Morning Post' building; Australia House; the Waldorf Hotel; London Opera House (Palladium); Imperial House, Kingsway, London; and several Calico Printers Assoc. Buildings in Manchester, among others. Work in N. America included the Parliament Buildings, Winnipeg; other foreign work ranged from a Yokohama hotel to a Costa Rica hospital. For a more complete list see 'The Consulting Engineer and the Great Value of His Services' in *Industrial World* 27 (Sept. 1933); construction details are in Bylander, 'Steelwork in Buildings—Thirty Years' Progress'.

[25] Thomas S. Hines, *Burnham of Chicago: Architect and Planner* (New York, 1974), pp. 378–82. The Marshall Field Wholesale Store by H. H. Richardson (1885–7) was an exception.

[26] e.g. see the description of Burnham's Philadelphia Wanamaker Building in 'Technical Department: A Modern Department Store,' *Architectural Record* 29 (April 1911), p. 277–88.

[27] Other Burnham department stores include Filene's, Boston and the May Company, Cleveland (both 1912). See Ira J. Bach (ed.), *Chicago's Famous Buildings* (Chicago, 3rd edn., 1980). For illustrations, see *The Architectural Work of Graham, Anderson, Probst and White, Chicago and Their Predecessors D. H. Burnham and Co. and Graham, Burnham and Co.* (1933), Vol. 1, plates 121–70.

[28] Drawings not located. D. H. Burnham & Co. plans dated 21 Feb. 1907 are noted in *LCC Minutes* (April–June 1907), Appendix A, 'Applications under Building Acts', no. 1023.

[29] For Burnham's diary entries on this meeting see Charles Moore, *Daniel H. Burnham, Architect—Planner of Cities* (New York, 1968), pp. 32–3.

[30] *American Architect*, XCIV (28 Oct. 1908), p. 140.

[31] Francis Swales, 'The Influence of the Ecole Des Beaux-Arts Upon Recent Architecture in England', *Architectural Record* 26 (Dec. 1909), pp. 422–3.

[32] Ibid, pp. 421–3. Selfridge and Waring paid Swales £29 presumably for his sketch, in Nov. 1906: Selfridge & Waring Cash Book, p. 31, Selfridges' Archives.

[33] *American Architect*, XCIV (28 Oct. 1908), p. 140; *Builder*, 16 May 1947, p. 464.

[34] Griffiths & Pember, *London Building Act, 1894*, p. 12.

[35] Ibid, p. 86.

[36] *LCC Minutes* (April–June 1907), Appendix A, 'Applications under Building Acts', no. 1023.

[37] For encounters with the London building regulations when erecting Selfridges see Pound, *Selfridge: a biography*, pp. 34–8.

[38] *Draper's Record*, 12 March 1904, p. 717; obituary, *RIBA Journ.* XXX, 14 July 1923, p. 566.

[39] *RIBA Journ.*, 14 July 1923, p. 566. Atkinson divided his work between Liverpool and London commissions, and from 1908–12 was engaged upon his principal building, Liverpool's Adelphi Hotel.

[40] At this time Atkinson also petitioned the LCC on behalf of Waring & Gillow for a furniture warehouse in Holborn, alterations to premises on Castle-street E. Marylebone, and an advertising screen in Hammersmith: *LCC Minutes*, 'Building Act Committee Report', 24 March 1908, p. 712; 31 March 1908, p. 802; and 7 July 1908, p. 94.

[41] Griffiths & Pember, *The London Building Act, 1894*, p. 13.

[42] For details of effects of building legislation on internal planning of Harrods, see F. H. W. Sheppard (ed.), *Survey of London XLI, Southern Kensington: Brompton* (1983), pp. 17–23.

[43] LCC *Minutes of Proceedings* (April–June 1907), Appendix A, no. 1062–4; *Builder*, 28 Sept. 1907, p. 339; 18 May 1907, p. 608.

[44] The extension to D. H. Evans, "the building of which has been pushed on rapidly of late" opened simultaneously with the Selfridges' grand opening in March 1909. See *Draper*, 20 March 1909, p. 329, and *Drapery Times*, 19 June

1909, p. 1309. Though its street-level display windows and greater cubic extent indicate use of structural steel-work, the new D. H. Evans building, designed by John Murray, was heavily clad in masonry with much Beaux-Arts detailing. Also at this time, Harrods, Whiteleys, and Swan & Edgar opened new accommodation.

[45] 'A Year's Work Under the London Building Act, 1894,' *Builder*, 12 Oct. 1907, p. 393–4.

[46] *Builder*, 3 Aug. 1907, p. 145.

[47] Ibid.

[48] *Builder*, 19 Oct. 1907, p. 417.

[49] *Builder*, 26 Jan. 1907, p. 92.

[50] Whiteleys, for example, suffered five fires in 7 years during the 1880s alone, see *Draper's Record*, 13 Aug. 1887, p. 26. In a widely publicised case, five girls died in the 1913 Barkers', Kensington blaze which occurred after LCC suggestions for fire prevention were not carried out. See P. C. Hoffman, *They Also Serve* (1947), pp. 60–3, and *Shop Assistant* 12 June 1909, p. 392; 27 March 1909, p. 202–3. While Harrods did not have employees living-in, on the upper floors were luxury flats, an equally dangerous situation.

[51] Knowles & Pitt, *History of Building Regulations*, p. 97.

[52] Capt. Hemphill of the LCC Building Act Committee, quoted in *Builder*, 18 May 1907, p. 608.

[53] *LCC Minutes*, 'Building Act Committee Report', 20 Oct. 1908, p. 676. In 1905, Atkinson unsuccessfully petitioned the Council, on behalf of Waring & Gillow, for internal wall openings of 10×16 ft. see: *LCC Building Act Committee Minutes*, 20 March 1905, p. 582.

[54] Swales, 'The Influence of the Ecole Des Beaux-Arts,' p. 423.

[55] *LCC Minutes*, 'Building Act Committee Report', 24 June 1907, p. 751; 2 July 1907, p. 73; 20 Oct. 1908, p. 676.

[56] Editor's note, S. Bylander, 'Steel and Concrete at the Selfridge Stores, London', *Concrete and Constructional Engineering*, March 1909, p. 9.

[57] Horace R. Chanter, *London Building Law* (1946), p. 2; the bill is described in *Builder*, 14 Dec. 1907, p. 651.

[58] Joseph Siry describes adoption of the steel frame for Chicago's retail buildings during the 1890s in *Carson-Pirie-Scott*, pp. 39–63; see also Marian Bowley, *The British Building Industry* (1966), pp. 9–12.

[59] L. E. Kent and G. W. Kirkland, 'Construction of Steel-Framed Buildings,' *The Structural Engineer Jubilee Issue, 1908–1958*, July 1958, p. 105.

[60] Bowley, *British Building Industry*, p. 13.

[61] Ibid, p. 33–4.

[62] *Concrete Inst. Trans. and Notes* V (Oct. 1913), p. 57.

[63] W. G. Perkins, discussion of Bylander's paper, ibid, p. 107.

[64] Kent & Kirkland, 'Construction of Steel-Framed Buildings,' p. 106.

[65] E. Fiander Etchells, discussion of Bylander's paper, *Concrete Inst. Trans. and Notes* (Oct. 1913), pp. 109–10. Lack of a clear definition of 'steel frame' among early twentieth century professional engineers and architects highlights the difficulty for historians interpreting contemporary accounts of the building process, and even published handbooks, as evidence. Since not even the experts were using a uniform technical vocabulary, interpretation of their work based on contemporary sources can be problematic.

[66] Griffiths & Pember, *The London Building Act, 1894*, pp. 196–9. Outside London, such stringent impediments to steel-frame construction were not the norm., e.g. the John Walsh store, Sheffield (1899) had no internal walls—the interior consisted of six sales shops, each 25 ft wide by 200 ft long, separated only by structural columns. See *Sheffield and Rotherham Independent*, quoted in Michael Moss and Alison Turton, *House of Fraser: a legend of retailing* (1989), p. 65. Also, a number of Glasgow stores had removed all or most of their internal walls by the turn of the century.

[67] S. Bylander, 'Steelwork in Buildings—Thirty Years' Progress,' *Structural Engineer*, Jan. 1937, p. 2. Because of confusion surrounding the term 'steel frame', Bylander himself was not sure that the Ritz was the first such building in London.

[68] Bylander, *Steel Frame Buildings in London*, p. 71.

[69] 'The Ritz Hotel', *Builder's Journ.*, 30 Nov. 1904, p. 286; 22 March 1905, p. 148.

[70] Waring & White (1906) Ltd, with Bylander as chief engineer, also worked with Mewes and Davis on offices for "The Morning Post" (1906–8) and the Royal Automobile Club (1910–11).

[71] 'The Ritz Hotel,' *Builder's Journ.*, 28 Sept. 1904, p. 165.

[72] 'The Ritz Hotel,' *Builder's Journ.*, 2 Nov. 1904, pp. 235–6. Much attention was paid to the guy boom derrick used on the Ritz site, a type of crane not in general use in England until 1922. See 'The Consulting Engineer and the Great Value of His Services,' *Industrial World*, 27 Sept. 1933.

[73] S. Bylander, *Concrete Inst. Trans. and Notes* IV (July 1912), p. 88.

[74] 'The Ritz Hotel', *Builder's Journ.*, 22 March 1905, p. 148. German manufacture of steel was also noted in *Builder's Journ.*, 2 Nov. 1904, p. 235. Bylander's Ritz drawings are held by the Bylander-Waddell Partnership, Middx. I would like to thank James Robertson and Douglas Scott of Bylander-Waddell.

[75] 'The Ritz Hotel,' *Builder's Journ.*, 22 March 1905, p. 148–56; 13 Sept. 1905, p. 146–8.

[76] Tom Harley-Haddow, 'Structural Engineering 1910–1939' in A. R. Collins (ed.), *Structural Engineering—two centuries of British achievement* (Chislehurst, Kent, 1983), p. 90. The RIBA's Joint Reinforced Concrete Committee, set up for similar reasons in 1906, had been boycotted by both the Inst. of Civil Engineers and the Inst. of Mechanical Engineers. See Bowley, *British Building Industry*, pp. 23–5.

[77] See S. Bylander, 'Ferro-Concrete', *Junior Inst. of Engineers Journ. and Record of Trans.*, XVI (1905–1906), pp. 309–32; Patricia Cusack, 'Agents of Change: Hennebique, Mouchel and ferro-concrete in Britain, 1897–1908,' *Construction History* 3 (1987), pp. 61–74; Bowley, *British Building Industry*, pp. 15–27.

[78] Bowley, *British Building Industry*, p. 25.

[79] *Concrete Inst. Trans. and Notes* (Feb. 1909–Dec. 1910), p. xi.

[80] Bylander was present at Concrete Inst. meetings, contributed frequently to discussions, and presented several papers to the Institute. He also joined the Junior Inst. of Engineers in 1905.

[81] Bylander, *Steel Frame Buildings in London*, pp. 71–2.

[82] 'The Ritz Hotel,' *Builder's Journ.*, 22 March 1905, p. 148.

[83] S. Bylander, 'Steel and Concrete at the Selfridge Stores, London.' *Concrete and Constructional Engineering*, March 1909, p. 26.

[84] Bylander, *Steel Frame Buildings in London*, p. 70.

46 *Steel Frame Architecture*

[85] C. H. Reilly, *Scaffolding in the Sky: a Semi-Architectural Autobiography* (1938), p. 118.

[86] R. Frank Atkinson, 'The Selfridge Store, London', *Architectural Review* 25 (June 1909), p. 296. Cast iron work was by Walter MacFarlane & Co., Saracen Foundry, Glasgow.

[87] *LCC Minutes*, 'Building Act Committee Report', 24 June 1907, p. 751.

[88] Bylander, *Steel Frame Buildings in London*, p. 71. Bylander's drawings for Selfridges are retained by the Bylander Waddell Partnership.

[89] Bylander, *Steel and Concrete at the Selfridge Stores, London*, p. 22. Cast iron work by Walter MacFarlane & Co. See R. Frank Atkinson, 'The Selfridge Store, London', *Architectural Review* 25 (June 1909), pp. 292–301, for an account of the building by its London architect.

[90] Bylander, *Steelwork in Buildings*, p. 6; Summary, *Waring White Building Co. Estimate for Selfridge Store Oxford Street W, 8 Oct. 1908*, Selfridges Archives; A. Stuart Gray, *Edwardian Architecture: A Biographical Dictionary* (1985), p. 70.

[91] S. Bylander, 'Concrete and Steel Construction at the Selfridge Stores', *Builder's Journ.*, 31 March 1909, p. 280.

[92] Ibid.

[93] Editor's preface to Bylander, *Steel and Concrete at the Selfridge Stores, London*, p. 9. While the *LCC Minutes* record Atkinson's petitions for use of rolling iron shutters as a fire prevention measure, the quote above indicates that the shutters actually installed were steel.

[94] Ibid, p. 9.

[95] 'Steel Frame Act,' H. D. Searles-Wood & Henry Adams, *Modern Building* (1921), pp. 157–62.

[96] Ibid, pp. 158, 161.

[97] E. Lawrence Hall, discussion of Bylander's 'Steel Specifications' paper, *Structural Engineer* IV (March 1926), p. 120.

[98] 'The London County Council Regulations,' *Concrete and Constructional Engineering* III (Aug. 1913), p. 522–3; also discussed are the complications faced by architects and engineers building under the Acts of 1894, 1905, 1908 and 1909.

[99] Bylander, *Steel and Concrete at the Selfridge Stores, London*, p. 10; R. Frank Atkinson, *The Selfridge Store, London*, p. 292; *The Lady*, 18 March 1909, p. 462; *New York Times*, 18 April 1909, p. 4.

[100] Bowley, *British Building Industry*, p. 35.

[101] Drawings by Burnet and Tait for Selfridges, including studies for the tower, are held in the offices of Sir John Burnet, Tait & Partners, London. Graham, Anderson, Probst & White's London representative, Albert Millar, was engaged as Selfridges' House Architect throughout the 1920s; today the MacDonald Price Partnership, Surrey retains drawings for various Selfridges' projects c. 1919–30, signed by Millar. I would like to thank Gavin Tait and Brian MacDonald for access to these drawings

[102] For initial stages of the western extension see: 'Retaining Walls and Foundation for Selfridge's New Building', *Architects' Journ.*, 15 April 1925, pp. 221–2; 'Development of Mechanical Appliances in Building', *Builder*, 6 Feb. 1920, pp. 167–71.

[103] 'Retaining Walls and Foundation for Selfridge's New Building,' *Architects' Journ.*, 18 Feb. 1920, p. 222.

Name and Place Index

Please note: references to illustrations and tables are indicated by italic page numbers, and notes by the use of square brackets (e.g. 163 [n. 10] means page 163, note 10).

Subject Index

Please note: references to illustrations and tables are indicated by italic page numbers, and notes by the use of square brackets (e.g. 163 [n. 10] means page 163, note 10).